Planning and Administering Early Childhood Programs

Sixth Edition

CELIA A. DECKER

Northwestern State University

JOHN R. DECKER

Sabine Parish, Louisiana, School System

MERRILL

an imprint of Prentice Hall

Upper Saddle River, New Jersey
Columbus, Ohio

Library of Congress Cataloging-in-Publication Data
Decker, Celia Anita.
    Planning and administering early childhood programs / Celia A. Decker, John R. Decker.—6th ed.
      p.   cm.
    Includes bibliographical references and index.
    ISBN 0-02-327991-5 (pbk.)
    1. Early childhood education—United States. 2. Educational planning—United States. 3. Day care centers—United States—Administration. 4. Instructional systems—United States.   I. Decker, John R. II. Title.
  LB1139.25.D43   1997
  372.2180973—dc20

96-22350
CIP

Cover photo: Michael Newman/Photo Edit
Editor: Ann Castel Davis
Production Editor: Patricia S. Kelly
Copyeditor: Linda Poderski
Design Coordinator: Julia Zonneveld Van Hook
Text Designer: Kip Shaw
Cover Designer: Raymond Hummons
Production Manager: Patricia A. Tonneman
Director of Marketing: Kevin Flanagan
Advertising/Marketing Coordinator: Julie Shough
Electronic Text Management: Marilyn Wilson Phelps, Matthew Williams, Karen L. Bretz, Tracey Ward

Photo credits: pp. 1, 29, 59, 95, 131, 223, 281, 341 © John Shaw; pp. 203, 255, 313 courtesy of Step 2 Corporation.

This book was set in Zapf Book and Swiss 721 by Prentice Hall and was printed and bound by Quebecor Printing/Book Press. The cover was printed by Phoenix Color Corp.

© 1997 by Prentice-Hall, Inc.
Simon & Schuster/A Viacom Company
Upper Saddle River, New Jersey 07458

Earlier editions © 1992 by Macmillan Publishing Company and © 1988, 1984, 1980, 1976 by Merrill Publishing Company.

Printed in the United States of America

10 9 8 7 6 5 4 3 2 1

ISBN: 0-02-327991-5

Prentice-Hall International (UK) Limited, *London*
Prentice-Hall of Australia Pty. Limited, *Sydney*
Prentice-Hall of Canada, Inc., *Toronto*
Prentice-Hall Hispanoamericana, S. A., *Mexico*
Prentice-Hall of India Private Limited, *New Delhi*
Prentice-Hall of Japan, Inc., *Tokyo*
Simon & Schuster Asia Pte. Ltd., *Singapore*
Editora Prentice-Hall do Brasil, Ltda., *Rio de Janeiro*

To Kelcey and Keith, our twin sons, and Kristiana, our daughter, who have helped with the clerical and computer aspects of the writing of this book.

Preface

Planning and Administering Early Childhood Programs, Sixth Edition, is built on the conviction that thoughtful planning and administration are essential to the success of early childhood programs. Our main priority is to present the rationale for this thoughtful planning and administration. The more administrators know about factors influencing quality programs, the better equipped they will be to plan and administer programs. From our perspective each child, parent, staff member, and sponsor deserves nothing less. We know how important planning is, so we are committed to helping new and experienced administrators and students of administration make sense of what they are doing.

TEXT ORGANIZATION

The text is organized to suggest how early childhood administrators must structure their thinking as they make decisions about their local programs. Thus, following a brief overview of the current status of early childhood education, the text is divided into three parts. Part I is concerned with the framework for program planning such as choosing the program rationale and abiding by regulatory constraints. Part II focuses on the operational aspects of the program—the more purely administrative component. Staffing, housing, equipping, and financing decisions must stem from the selected program rationale.

Part III discusses the program's services. Services for children involve planning for their activities; meeting their nutritional, health, and safety needs; and assessing, recording, and reporting their progress. Services for parents include involvement through communication between staff and parents and through parent participation, and provisions for parent education and family resource and support programs. Each program service for children and parents must mirror the selected program rationale. Finally, to be truly professional, administrators must contribute to their own profession in direct ways.

NEW FEATURES

The sixth edition of the text reflects a balanced concern for all types of early childhood programs, with their varying purposes, sponsorships, and ages of children. Early childhood is becoming a more broadly based field, and this text reflects that outlook on early education and child care aspects.

The perspective of this new edition is that administrative decision making must be based on a chosen theory, perspective, and/or philosophical position. Several of these alternatives are discussed, along with the reasons for the lack of consensus in program goals and the discrepancy between beliefs and actual practices. Throughout the text there are discussions on how a chosen view affects decisions in all areas of program planning.

There are three major focuses of this new edition. The first focus is on the growing need for affordable, quality early childhood programs for children from infancy through the primary grades (levels). Thus, the new edition has an expanded emphasis on infant/toddler programs, primary grade (level) programs, and school-age child care programs. The second focus is on the professional concern over the heavy academic emphasis that led to various position statements by professional associations. The reasons for the call for "appropriate practices" are explained in Chapter 2 and are developed throughout the text. Third, there are calls for more coherence within the profession. Ramifications of incoherence are explained in various chapters.

This sixth edition also offers the following new features:

1. More comprehensive information on the regulation and litigation involved in services for children with special needs.

2. New information, including drawings, on specific learning/activity centers. Comprehensive information on purchasing computer hardware and software.

3. Recent information on the costs of early childhood programs.

4. More information on leadership in curriculum planning (especially in establishing goals for meeting individual needs and interests, in providing a multicultural/antibias focus, and in using computers and other technologies) and in translating curriculum goals into program competencies.

5. More emphasis on safety practices and education.

6. More comprehensive information on authentic assessment, performance records including the portfolio, and ideas for reporting.

7. Each chapter now has a trends and issues section.

All text and resource information has been thoroughly updated. The citations throughout the text, the "For Further Reading" section at the end of each chapter, and other bibliographies refer to the most current information.

PEDAGOGICAL FEATURES

Readers will find the three subdivisions of the book helpful because these parallel the planning processes of an administrator—deciding on the program's framework, operationalizing the program, and implementing the children's program. The trends and issues and summary sections of each chapter will also help readers focus on the main themes of the book.

We have raised issues to stimulate early childhood leaders to reexamine their own beliefs and then take another look at their programs' rationale and practices. Thus, relevant studies are included throughout. Cookbook formulas are omitted and options are given because single solutions are obviously not appropriate for everyone.

The text provides information needed by all early childhood programs. The field is diverse, but there is a great deal of overlap of the types of competencies needed in various programs. We have attempted to provide a balance among research and supported statements, applied ideas for implementation, and resources for further thought and consideration.

Like the five before it, this edition will aid in initial planning of early childhood programs and be a source of helpful information after programs are under way. The purpose of this book will be fulfilled when the reader makes wiser judgments about planning and administering early childhood programs.

ACKNOWLEDGMENTS

We thank the following reviewers of this edition for their helpful comments: Jill E. Gelormine, Hofstra University; Berta Harris, San Diego City College; Craig H. Hart, Brigham Young University.

Celia A. Decker
John R. Decker

Brief Contents

Contents

CHAPTER 9
Assessing, Recording, and Reporting Children's Progress   281

CHAPTER 10
Working With Parents   313

CHAPTER 11
Contributing to the Profession   341

APPENDIX 1
Resources for Program Planning   349

APPENDIX 2
State Licensing and Certification Agencies   360

APPENDIX 3
Accreditation Criteria Examples   367

Contents   xiii

Chapter 1

❁ ❁ ❁ ❁ ❁

Overview of Early Childhood Programs

❁ ❁ ❁ ❁ ❁

The momentum for early childhood programs has been building for the last three decades and shows no signs of abatement. Among the extensive and varied programs concerned with the total development of human potential, early childhood programs are in the forefront. Demographic data detail an ever-increasing need for high-quality early childhood programs. Professionals agree on many factors that make for effective programs, and research extols the benefits of high-quality programs and the damaging effects of poor ones. The importance of high-quality early childhood programs to families has resulted in a ripening awareness in political and economic circles although the United States has had a long history of interest in early childhood care and education especially in times of war and depression. When President Bush announced the national educational goals in his second State of the Union Address in January 1990, the stage was set for a marked departure from policy as usual. The first goal made a governmental commitment (a) to *all* young children, (b) to show concern for children's holistic development, and (c) to support parents' roles in the lives of their children.

Congress ranked early childhood care and education the third highest priority—behind the deficit and defense—and began backing its commitment by passing record amounts of legislation in the 101st Congress (Kagan, 1991b). Governmental attention matched the interests of voters. About 69% of Americans rated child care a major priority, and 55% of Americans stated that government should play a greater role in providing child care assistance (Child Care Action Campaign and Communications Consortium Media Center, 1994). Concerned with the workforce of tomorrow, key business groups, such as the Business Round Table and the Committee for Economic Development, have issued reports supporting early childhood care and education too (Kagan, 1991b).

Despite the obvious need for high-quality early childhood programs, the empirically based rationale for planning programs, the promising data confirming such programs' benefits for young children and their families, and the seeds of political and economic support, complex challenges lie ahead. As an unprecedented number of groups and individuals in both the public and private sectors set off to implement programs for our young children, the need for adequate planning and administration seems self-evident; yet, judging by the frequent absence of a rational, conceptual, and systematic approach, planning and administration are often considered irrelevant to program quality. Careful attention to planning and administration can prevent costly, frivolous, and counterproductive mistakes and can protect program growth in the face of far-outstretched resources so that program quality is maintained and enhanced.

NATURE AND EXTENT OF PROGRAMS

Effective planning and administration begin with some perspective on the nature and extent of early childhood programs. An overview of the influential factors and the status and types of programs for young children will provide a setting from which to view the nature of their planning and administration.

Factors Influencing Early Childhood Programs

Early childhood programs are the products of their exciting heritage and an expression of our society's determination to provide the best for its young. Several factors appear to influence the nature and extent of today's programs. First, literature reveals a growing conviction that a child's early years are highly important to the remainder of development. Because of evidence that early life experiences, including those of the newborn, influence later development, the quality of early childhood experiences is believed to determine, to a large extent, how effective later development can be. Consequently, programs designed to meet the needs of young children are receiving high priority.

Further, major changes have occurred in the ecology of childhood. Hernandez (1994) has traced how changes in the U.S. family, society, and economy have changed children's access to resources. Over one fourth of America's young children live in poverty (U.S. General Accounting Office [GAO], 1993). Poverty rates are 27% for children under age 3. And, child poverty rates moved higher for white, black, and Latino children (Children's Defense Fund, 1994). Families make up more than one third of all homeless people (McChesney, 1992), and 43% of all homeless families have children (Children's Defense Fund, 1994). More than 50,000 children under age 5 are homeless (National Institute of Medicine, 1988). Homeless children have poor health status, high rates of developmental delay, and emotional and behavioral problems (Molmar, Rath, & Klein, 1990). These social and demographic trends are likely to continue and even rise, partially because of popular beliefs about children and families in poverty that impede more adequate social policies (Chafel, 1990).

In the 1960s, fewer than 10% of all children under age 18 lived with one parent; now almost 25% do. This trend is primarily because of rising divorce rates and births to unmarried mothers. Almost half of all children can expect to experience a divorce during childhood and to live an average of 5 years in a single-parent family. Over one fourth of all children are born to unmarried mothers (Carnegie Corporation of New York, 1994). The majority of these unmarried mothers are teens. Half of all children are born to teen mothers, and half of these mothers are single parents (Taaffe, 1994). Zimiles (1986) calls these changes in family lifestyle (e.g., more divorce, more single-parent families, fewer extended families, more teenage parents) the **diminishing mothers** factor.

Child abuse and neglect continue to increase. More than 2.9 million children were reported abused and neglected in 1992. This figure is triple the number reported in 1980 (Children's Defense Fund, 1994). Almost 90% of children who died of abuse and neglect were under age 5, and 53% of those who died were younger than 1 year old (Taaffe, 1994). Abuse is even occurring prenatally by pregnant women who engage in activities known to harm fetuses. For example, the prevalence of fetal alcohol syndrome (FAS) is 1.3 per 1,000 live births (Hawks, 1993). No estimates are available for the babies who are stillborn or spontaneously aborted because of FAS (Black, 1993). Most of the costs of prenatal abuse are incalculable (e.g., lessened quality of life for victims, reduced contributions to society). Our nation also pays enormous calculated treatment costs. For example, in 1991 the estimated annual costs for treating FAS was $74.6 billion (Taaffe, 1994).

Because of America's vulnerable children and families, children in foster homes increased by 50% between 1987 and 1991, and infants are the fastest growing category of children in foster care (Carnegie Corporation of New York, 1994). This trend is expected to continue because of the use of crack cocaine by mothers and the death of parents from acquired immune deficiency syndrome (AIDS; Children's Defense Fund, 1994).

Basic health care for many children is lacking. Over one fourth of all women receive belated prenatal care (after the 3rd month of pregnancy) or none at all. The lack of prenatal care increases the likelihood of low birth weight—now 7 per 100 births—and infant mortality—8.9 per 1,000 births (Children's Defense Fund, 1994). The average cost of prenatal intensive care is $1,000 per day, and the total lifetime medical cost for a low birth weight infant averages $400,000 (Taaffe, 1994). About 45% of the nation's children under age 2 are not fully immunized (Children's Defense Fund, 1994).

Between 10% and 15% of all children are in special populations—children with physical or sensory impairments, motor disabilities, chronic health problems, serious neurological conditions, or behavioral disorders (Fraas, 1986). The number of young children identified as needing and eligible for intervention is growing and will continue to grow throughout the 1990s (Harkin, Gallagher, & Terry, 1991). The greater incidence is correlated with children born into poverty, maternal substance abuse, and inadequate prenatal care.

More and more children need care in productive group environments. The number of children under age 5 with mothers in the workforce has doubled since the mid-1970s (Casper, Hawkins, & O'Connell, 1991). Over 57% of women in the workforce have preschool-age children. Those parents needing infant and toddler care are almost as many (1 or 2 percentage points less) as those needing care for 3- through 5-year-olds (Perreault, 1991). Only about 12% of U.S. families are comprised of a father who is the sole breadwinner and a mother who is a full-time homemaker (Walter & Goldsmith, 1990). W. Johnston (1987), in his report *Workforce 2000*, estimated that 64% of all new entrants to the workforce will be women and that early childhood care and education demands will thus increase. One out of three parents with infants, and one out of four parents with preschool children have had difficulty securing child care and education arrangements (Friedman, Galinsky, & King, 1990). Child care and education demands are increasing among nonworking mothers as much or more than among working mothers (Perreault, 1991).

Finally, against the background of today's social problems, early childhood programs are seen as support systems for families. In some ways, these programs have come full circle. They are seen today as they were seen under the leadership of Jean Oberlin, Friedrich Froebel, Elizabeth Peabody, Susan E. Blow, Kate Wiggin, Patty S. Hill, Maria Montessori, and Rachel and Margaret McMillan as the best hope of reducing poverty of mind and body.

Even today's advantaged families often feel inadequate in trying to meet the demands of our rapidly changing society. Thus, universally available early childhood programs are now considered worthwhile to provide an essential service to families and an enriched, productive environment for young children.

Status of Early Childhood Programs

Early childhood programs come in all sizes and shapes and with differing perspectives that form the basis for each program's practice and, like most things, with various degrees of excellence. Young children and early childhood programs are big business from almost every standpoint. Early childhood programs, which came into their own about 30 years ago, are no longer the additional service of an affluent public school system, the special project of a philanthropic organization, an undertaking of a state welfare agency, or the result of a federal program. Currently, all states provide monies for universal public school kindergartens; since 1980, movement has been toward public education of economically disadvantaged 4-year-olds. More and more children from infants to school age are in child care and education programs; the federal government funds such projects as Head Start, corporations operate early childhood programs, and resource and referral centers provide needed services.

Universities are training people on all levels of the career lattice (J. Johnson & McCracken, 1994) and are bombarding the scholarly market about young children and their programs as seen in the recent development of two new journals, *Early Childhood Research Quarterly* and *Early Education and Development*. Early childhood programs have encouraged a burgeoning commercial market for educational toys, equipment, and books. Although early childhood programs have greatly expanded, the body of data for the whole field is incomplete (Willer, 1992). Figures inadequately reflect care by relatives, children in multiple care arrangements, and school-age child care. Several trends are evident, however.

On the one hand, universal education for all 5-year-olds is, for all practical purposes, a reality. On the other hand, infant/toddler and school-age child care are very scarce. Programs for children in low-income families are expanding with Head Start enrollments and public school programs for pre-kindergarten at-risk children (especially 4-year-olds). This expansion, however, lags farther and farther behind the growing numbers of poor children in the United States. About 49% of these poor children do not have access to preschool programs (U.S. GAO, 1993).

TYPES OF EARLY CHILDHOOD PROGRAMS

One of the first problems encountered in attempts to differentiate among the various types of early childhood programs is that the term **early childhood** lacks precise definition. Educators, child psychologists, and others used vague synonyms or different chronological ages or developmental milestones. The National Association for the Education of Young Children (NAEYC) defines *early childhood* as birth through age 8 (NAEYC, 1991b, p. 1). Early childhood leaders in state departments expressed that the policy that would help them the most is having the early childhood period considered "as continuing through age 8" (S. Robinson, 1993/94, p. 86).

One simple classification of early childhood programs is by their source of funding. Generally, early childhood programs are under the jurisdiction of one of the following: (a) public schools (e.g., kindergartens); (b) private control (e.g., nursery schools, parent cooperatives, business-operated programs, and programs for young children sponsored by churches, service organizations, and charities); (c) federal programs (e.g., Head Start); (d) national private agency programs (e.g., American Montessori schools); and (e) university laboratory programs (e.g., nursery, kindergarten, and primary-level schools). Closely paralleling the sources of funding are the legal forms of organization: propri-

etorships, partnerships, corporations, and public agencies. (For details on these legal forms of organizations, see Chapter 3.)

Early childhood programs may be classified as providing direct services to children, to parents (e.g., some home-visiting programs and resource and referral programs), or to both children and their parents. Finally, early childhood programs may also be described according to their origins. Early childhood care and education has a history of more than 200 years.

Knitting School

Jean Frederick Oberlin, a Lutheran pastor from Alsace, France, made one of the first attempts to "teach" young children in a group setting. Children 2 years of age and older would gather around the "teachers" as they knitted—hence, the term *knitting school*. Two teachers would give lessons in handicrafts, nature, history, and moral songs. Oral lessons were given in the dialect to younger children and in standard French to older children, but reading and writing were not stressed. Play and exercise were also part of the program. The only instructional materials were pictures of subjects from the Scriptures (Deasey, 1978; Raymont, 1937).

The knitting school began between 1767 and 1769 and expanded to several villages prior to Oberlin's death in 1826. Probably because of the French Revolution, the program never expanded beyond a few miles (Spodek & Brown, 1993).

Dame Schools

Dame schools were early childhood programs operated by widows and young, single women in Colonial America. Much like the knitting school teachers, these women did their daily tasks as they taught 4- to 7-year-old children (Woody, 1966).

The curriculum depended on the capability and enthusiasm of the dame. Rudimentary instruction in the three R's (with little emphasis on 'rithmetic), morals, and etiquette were taught. Needed fine-motor skills, such as knitting, sewing, and breadmaking, were also taught. The materials of instruction were the Bible and hornbooks or slates. Dames were paid with currency, with food or other household products, and with bartered services.

Shortly after the Constitution was signed, dames were restricted to teaching girls and very young boys. The continued emphasis on women's education was, to a great extent, due to Quaker influence. The dame schools later evolved into fashionable boarding schools (Wyman, 1995).

Common Schools

Common schools were considered the appropriate education for boys by the 1780s. Men, not women, were deemed the appropriate teachers. Children were expected to follow a classical curriculum, with memorization and recitation as the teaching/learning method. Moral education was the focus of the school. A negative view of the child, originating in church teachings of the Middle Ages and reflecting Puritan beliefs, resulted in ridicule and corporal punishment of "wrongdoers." Moral teachings coupled with punishment were thought to curb the sinful nature of children.

Perhaps because of the costs and bother of locating "private" programs, parents allowed their young children to attend the common school with elder siblings. As enrollment of young children (some even under age 4) grew, resistance emerged. Resistance was a result of the costs to the school system and of the expressed concern about the risks of early academic programs (Strickland, 1982).

Infant Schools

The Industrial Revolution saw advances in machinery, but long hours, unsafe environmental work conditions, and the overreliance on women and child labor took their toll on humans and family living. Social reformers began to express their concerns. Robert Owen, a mill owner and social reformer in Scotland, instituted changes in the lives of families through reduced hours, better wages, and the establishment of child labor reforms.

To prepare people for a new society as he envisioned it, Owen established the Institute for the Formation of Character (in New Lanark, Scotland) in 1816 (Reisner, 1930). The school was to train children of workers, and even young adult employees, in his model mills. When Owen and his followers came to Indiana in 1825, they brought the *infant school* with them. Owen's school gained the attention of reformers who saw it as a way to help poor children. Because of civic-minded women, working men, and journalists (Strickland, 1969), Owen's educational ideas flourished from New England through the Middle Atlantic states (May & Vinovskis, 1977). Unlike the dame schools and the common school, Owen's schools were to be "happy places" in which children learned by reason, not by coercion. The school was to train children in "good practical habits." The curriculum for the first level was for children ages 3 to 6. The curriculum consisted of the three R's, geography, history, sewing, dance, music, and moral principles. Unlike many other schools of the time, however, activity prevailed because of Pestalozzi's influence (Spodek, 1973b). (Pestalozzi is considered the educator who most influenced Froebel [founder of the kindergarten in Germany] and Horace Mann [founder of the free public schools in the United States]. Pestalozzi was a Swiss educator who moved away from memorization and recitation and called for activity [hands-on experiences] in the classroom. Because the kindergartens came to the United States and Mann's public school ideas caught on, Pestalozzi's principles were highly influential.) Not all infant schools followed the child-centered approach, however (S. White & Buka, 1987).

The most famous infant school in the United States was founded by Bronson Alcott (McCuskey,

1940). Because of Alcott's belief in transcendentalism, he began to study children's moral insights. His publication of *Conversations With Children on the Gospels* and the admission of a black child caused his school to fail (O. Shepard, 1937). Because of the controversy over Alcott's practices, families removed their children from infant schools. The schools thus declined because they lost their sole financial support—parents' fees (Pence, 1986; O. Shepard, 1937).

Fireside Education

The collapse of the infant school movement and the development of print media led to *fireside education*, an antebellum parent education movement. Clergy and women also saw the family as weakening. Because of this concern, the three themes that emerged were the home, the mother, and the child. The home, no longer the center of economic productivity, was seen as the upholder of morals in a materialistic society. Mothers' responsibilities were to nurture their children and to provide moral education. Emphasis on cognitive development, especially intellectual precocity, was considered evil (Kuhn, 1947; Strickland, 1982).

Fireside education did not meet the needs of the poor. Poor mothers did not have the formal education needed to educate their children. Furthermore, mothers could not be full-time homemakers unless the family was financially comfortable. Thus, poor children did not receive a fireside education. In fact, the poor were seen as a threat to child-rearing practices in proper homes (Ryan, 1975).

Kindergartens

Kindergartens are publicly or privately operated programs for 4- and 5-year-old children. More specifically, the term **kindergarten** is used to define the unit of school that enrolls 5-year-olds prior to entrance into the first grade.

Historically, the kindergarten ("children's garden") was an 1837 German institution that enrolled children 3 through 7 years old and provided teaching suggestions to mothers of infants. As the founder of the kindergarten, Friedrich Froebel's ideas focused on romanticism and transcendentalism, as had his predecessors in the infant school movement (Snyder, 1972). Froebel's farsighted contributions included (a) freedom of movement for the child; (b) a planned sequence of activities centered on the "gifts" (small blocks for building, developing mathematical concepts, and making designs), reinforced by the "occupations" (craft work) as well as other activities, and surrounded by a verbal "envelope" (poems, songs, storytelling, and discussions); (c) the emphasis on the relationship and order of ideas; (d) the education of mothers, nurses (baby-sitters), and prospective kindergarten teachers; and (e) the desire that the kindergarten become a state-supported institution. Kindergartens came to the United States in 1855 via a German immigrant, Margarethe Meyer (Mrs. Carl) Schurz. Although many kindergartens became English-speaking institutions, following the endeavors of Elizabeth Peabody, the kindergartens were philosophically a Froebelian transplant.

In the late 1800s, two influences undermined Froebel's kindergarten: the growth of public school kindergartens and the child study movement of G. Stanley Hall coupled with the progressive education movement of John Dewey (Woody, 1934). Although the first public school kindergartens were Froebelian, the trickle-down phenomenon from elementary education began with the expansion of kindergartens (Snyder, 1972). Less gifted teachers began to prescribe a rigid teaching sequence (Downs, 1978; S. White & Buka, 1987), and teachers modeled activities with the gifts rather than allow child play (Troen, 1975). When the child study movement began in the early 1900s under the direction of G. Stanley Hall, a divisive debate ensued between the Froebelian kindergarten leaders (under the direction of Susan E. Blow) and the progressive kindergarten leaders (headed by Patty S. Hill). Dewey thought the use of Froebel's gifts were contrived experiences for children. Dewey wanted children to learn from the real experiences of his day, such as carpentry and weaving. Constructive play and concepts integrated across curriculum areas were the cornerstones of Dewey's curriculum (Dewey, 1964). The role of the teacher was not only to plan the environment and guide the children but also to act as a researcher who gained insights through observations and recordings, a close tie to the ongoing child study movement (National Society for the Study of Education, 1929). Eventually, the progressives gained control of the kindergarten leadership and replaced the Froebelian curriculum.

The Depression was devastating to the growth of the public school kindergarten, which began to expand by the 1890s. Since the 1940s, however, enrollment in public school kindergartens has steadily increased. Today, every state provides financial support for its public kindergartens. Several states make attendance compulsory. Thus, more children have the opportunity to attend publicly supported kindergartens prior to first grade. In some states, however, children will attend three times as many hours as children in other states because of variations in the total number of hours per day and the number of days per week (S. Robinson & Lyon, 1994).

Concerns about the kindergarten curriculum have been voiced since the 1930s. Headley (1966) has stated that the use of the letter *K* has made the kindergarten appear to be an "integral part of the education program and yet somewhat different from grade school education" (p. 42). Kindergartens vary in the amount of emphasis on academic skills, but academic programs have increased since the 1960s. Professional associations have voiced concerns (see Chapter 2).

Montessori Schools

Maria Montessori, the first woman to graduate from an Italian medical school, became interested in children with mental disabilities as a result of her medical practice at the psychiatric clinic at the University of Rome. She worked with these children, who were institutionalized with the insane children. Montessori studied the works of two French physicians—Jean Itard and his student Edouard Séguin—who worked to educate persons with disabilities. Montessori's lectures on persons with disabilities led to the creation of an orthophrenic school in Italy, which she directed. She actually taught the children enrolled in the school, and at night she analyzed the results and prepared new curriculum ideas, methodology, and materials. Almost from the beginning, Montessori believed that children without disabilities learn in the same way. After 2 years of directing the orthophrenic school, she resigned and enrolled in philosophy and psychology courses.

In 1906, a building concern backed by the principal banks of Italy constructed some apartments in a slum area of Rome. While the parents who occupied the building were away at work, their children, too young for school, damaged the property. The property owners decided that it was more economical to provide group care for these children than to repair the damage they were doing. Montessori was asked to oversee the program, housed in a room in the apartment complex. Thus, the *Casa dei Bambini* (Children's House) was founded in Rome in 1907. Slum children between the ages of 2½ and 7 years attended the all-day program. Montessori's contributions included the following ideas:

Parents should be given training in child development and regulations for extending the principles taught to their children.

Parents collectively owned the "Children's House."

Children have "sensitive periods" in which they are ready to "absorb" certain concepts.

Children can teach themselves with minimal adult guidance, and this mode of learning carries over into adulthood when they are spontaneous learners and self-starters (Elkind, 1983).

Children develop sensory perceptions that serve as a basis for all other learnings with Montessori-designed didactic materials, learn care of self and of environment through "work" with reality-oriented, practical-life experiences, and become language and math literate through the use of manipulative and self-correcting materials.

Teachers learn through their interactions with children, prepare the environment, trust children to take the lead in their own learning, and do not force children to focus on more limited and adult-determined directions (Elkind, 1983).

Children need a child-sized and orderly environment (Kramer, 1988).

Montessori's ideas were immediately popular but met with sudden death in the 1920s. Her ideas were dissonant with the psychology of the times (Hunt, 1968). Montessori's ideas were revitalized in the 1960s for two reasons. First, new conceptions of psychological development formulated in the 1960s were more in step with Montessori's pedagogy (Hunt, 1968). Second, an Americanized version of Montessori practice was introduced with the opening of the Montessori school in Greenwich, Connecticut, (in 1958) and with Rambusch's publication *Learning How to Learn: An American Approach to Montessori* (1962). The Americanized Montessori approach included some of the content of other early childhood programs, such as creative art, dramatic play, science activities, and large-muscle play on playground equipment, as well as the traditional Montessori content. Much debate stemmed from these new practices; the dispute later led to a division of thinking within the Montessori ranks. Those who hold to the traditional Montessori method are members of the Association Montessori Internationale, and those who support innovations join the American

Montessori Society (see Appendix 4). Today, about 3,500 Montessori schools for preschool-age children exist in the United States (Cushman, 1993).

Nursery Schools

The term **nursery schools** is difficult to define because these programs are a loose array of individual facilities. It is often applied to programs for 3- and 4-year-old children although some nursery schools serve younger children.

Nursery schools developed in the 20th century. Rachel and Margaret McMillan opened a medical clinic in London. The children had repeated illnesses because of their impoverished environment. To protect the children's health, the McMillan sisters opened an early childhood program in 1911. These nursery schools, as they were named, made such an impression on the British government that it passed the Education Act of 1918. This act provided tax money for services to 2- to 5-year-old children.

The McMillan nursery schools were designed to meet the needs of poor children and to establish cooperation between home and school (Bradburn, 1989). Like Montessori, the McMillan sisters believed in providing children with sensory experiences, but unlike Montessori, they preferred real experiences, the atrium garden and everyday experiences, rather than apparatuses. The curriculum consisted of physical care of the child, perceptual-motor activities, self-expressive activities (e.g., art, block building, dramatic play), and language activities (e.g., stories, songs, discussions). The teacher's role was both teacher and nurse (Steedman, 1990).

With the advent of nursery schools came the beginning of scientific child study. Those involved in scientific child study thought that parents at all socioeconomic levels failed to provide the "best" for their children. In contrast with the English nursery schools, nursery schools in the United States were middle- and upper-class institutions. In 1923, the child study movement and nursery education received the

Lucy Spelman Rockefeller memorial funds. The trustees of these funds decided to use the monies for three purposes. The first purpose was to model exemplary educational practices. Common philosophies of these nursery schools were that (a) young children have a developmental need for group association with peers; (b) play is beneficial for investigation of environment and for alleviating emotional stress; (c) children should begin the process of social weaning—that is, becoming detached from parents; (d) the routine bodily functions of sleeping, eating, and eliminating should be managed; and (e) teachers should provide guidance and guard against emotional stress (Forest, 1927). Parent education and participation, often an admission requirement, emphasized child development and observation in home and school (Davis, 1932). Because the scientific child study movement attracted people from many different disciplines, nursery schools established in various institutions had somewhat different objectives. The second purpose was to provide resources for child study research. The third purpose was to educate parents about the implications of research. Parent education was perhaps nursery schools' strongest selling point because many parents were hesitant about early education outside the home (Eliot, 1978).

Day Nurseries and Child Care

The term **child care** generally refers to programs that operate for extended hours (often 12 hours) and offer services for children from birth through school age. Most programs for young children are of the child care type because they involve the care and education of children separated from their parents for all or part of the day. Child care programs may also be the night-care type program.

The forerunners of child care centers in the United States were the *day nurseries.* Day nurseries came into existence about the same time as infant schools flourished. Medical discoveries of the mid-1800s aroused greater concern for children's sanitation and health. In 1854, a Nursery School for Children of Poor Women was established in cooperation with the Child's Hospital of New York City. It was patterned after the 1844 French crèche, which was designed as child care for working French women and as a method of reducing infant mortality rates. Concern for physical well-being soon broadened to include concern for habits, manners, and vocational skills (Forest, 1927).

As immigrants settled in urban areas, settlement-house day nurseries opened (e.g., Hull House nursery in 1898; E. Kahn, 1989). These day nurseries were considered necessary to counter many social evils (e.g., the exploitation of women and children in the labor force) and to help alleviate immigrants' cultural assimilation problems. Education was deemed essential for true social reform. Thus, some day nurseries added kindergartens, and some were sponsored by boards of education and opened in public schools (e.g., Los Angeles). Parent education became a component of the day nursery's educational program. Parents were taught various household skills and management and care of children (Wipple, 1929).

In time, however, some social reformers began to believe that day nurseries might supplant the role of the family in child rearing. Consequently, emphasis was placed on the importance of mothering (nurturing), and mothers were encouraged to remain in the home. To help mothers "afford" to stay in the home, the Mother's Pension Act was enacted in 1911, a forerunner of Aid to Families With Dependent Children. Thus, the stigma of child care began. (It was thought essential for mothers to care for their own children. When the Pension Act provided financial help to stay-at-home mothers, mothers who still elected to put their children in child care were considered mothers who were not fulfilling their most important role.) Enthusiasm for day nurseries further declined when the National Federation of Day Nurseries drew attention to the poor quality of some programs.

Concern over the appropriateness of day nurseries stimulated the development of nursery schools in the 1920s (Forest, 1927).

Day nurseries regained their status during the Depression, when the government for the first time subsidized all-day programs to aid children and unemployed schoolteachers. Although they were called Works Progress Administration (WPA) nursery schools, they are included here because of their all-day schedule. Early childhood nursery school educators associated with the National Association of Nursery Education, the Association for Childhood Education, and the National Council on Parent Aid formed an advisory committee to assist in supervising and training teachers for WPA nursery schools and in developing guides and records (Davis, 1964). The positive effect was a "nursery school" philosophy for all children (J. Anderson, 1947); however, "nursery school" teacher training standards were undermined (Frank, 1937). The major model of the WPA nurseries was habit training. Health and nutrition services were also provided. Federal funds were withdrawn at the end of the Depression.

Federal funds for all-day child care were again provided in 1942 by Public Law (P.L.) 137 (the Lanham, or Community Facilities, Act). The stigma of enrolling in public nurseries was replaced by the spirit of patriotism because parents were now working for the war effort. The purpose of the funds was to provide for the child's physical needs, and nursery school educators again assisted. Although some centers had inadequately trained staff, outstanding examples of such centers were the two Child Service Centers established by Kaiser Shipbuilding Corporation in Portland, Oregon, and directed by Lois Meek Stolz and James L. Hymes, Jr. (Hymes, 1944). These centers also provided such support services as precooked meals for parents and children, on-site grocery stores, and clothes mending, to ease the burden of working parents. The theories of the child study movement had replaced habit training. The philosophy was

based on the work of Isaacs (1933) and Baruch (1939). Play was considered important as mental health therapy (Hartley, Frank, & Goldenson, 1957). Support ended with termination of the Lanham Act in 1946. During the Korean War, appropriation of funds under the Defense Housing and Community Facilities and Services Act (1951) was negligible (Kerr, 1973).

The Economic Opportunity Act (1964) funded Head Start, child care services for migrant workers, and child care for children whose parents were involved in the various manpower projects (e.g., Job Corp, Foster Grandparents). The Housing and Urban Development Act, Title VII (1965), the Model Cities Act (1966), and the Parent and Child Centers (funded with Head Start monies) also assisted the child care efforts.

In the 1980s, federal funds for various types of child care programs decreased. Today, governmental support for child care is seen in the Child Care and Dependent Care Tax Credit begun in 1975–76 and expanded in 1982–83, and in the Child Care and Development Block Grant (CC&DBG) Act of 1990, which provides funds to states to cover child care services. Thus, child care has shifted back to state and local control for the most part.

Basic Types of Child Care.   The two basic types of child care are **center care** and **family child care**. A **child care center** is defined as an out-of-home program and facility serving children who need care for a greater portion of the day. Usually, the schedule fits the working hours of families who use the center. Drop-in centers also provide occasional, part-time care. Child care centers are regulated by state licensing requirements and other standards and may be licensed to serve children from infancy through school age. For-profit centers are usually owned and operated by individuals or family corporations, but about 10% are operated as large chains or franchises (Neugebauer, 1989). Not-for-profit centers are sponsored by state and local governments, religious groups (which sponsor half of all group child care for 3- and 4-year-olds; B. Caldwell, 1990), women's organizations, and parent cooperatives.

Family child care is defined as nonresidential care provided in a private home other than the child's own. Usually, the group of children is small—approximately 6 children, including the caregiver's own children. About half the states also define a private home in which 7 to 12 children are cared for and additional staff are hired to meet adult-child ratios as a **group home.** Group homes are also called **large homes** or **mini-centers** under some licensing laws; these group homes are licensed as centers, rather than as family child care. Family child care may be operated as an independent business or may receive public funds. Most family child care programs operate as independent businesses, and about 60% are unregulated (Willer et al., 1991). Family child care, especially those receiving public funds, may be part of one of three systems: (a) **sponsored homes,** in which a local agency assumes administrative control of homes and organizes services (e.g., recruits caregivers, screens children, aids in licensing the home, collects fees, keeps financial records); (b) **limited affiliates,** in which a local agency provides an organizational structure for licensed, independent homes to qualify for the U.S. Department of Agriculture (USDA) Child Care Food Program; and (c) **provider networks,** in which caregivers form a network for informal exchange or support (e.g., go together when purchasing supplies). Governmental agencies would rather monitor public subsidies for child care with one system than negotiate with and monitor each individual home.

Trends in Child Care.   Child care is part of early childhood care and education, like kindergartens and nursery schools, but for much longer hours. Before entering school, a child will spend more than 2,000 hours per year in child care, in contrast to just over half that amount of time for a 7-hour daily public school program. Because of school-age child care, the time children spend in child care may equal the time spent in school from kindergarten until graduation.

Increased Demands.   Demand for child care has increased because of maternal employment and the child care desires of unemployed mothers. Statistics show that almost three fourths of all children attended child care programs or nursery schools prior to kindergarten (West, Hausken, Chandler, & Collins, 1991). The availability of child care programs is not equal across the nation. The Children's Defense Fund (1994) reported that 31 states and the District of Columbia had waiting lists with a projected waiting period of over 1 year for child care. Cadden (1994) also reported differences in the availability of child care across the United States.

Center care has grown three times faster than the overall child care market. It is estimated that, by the year 2000, about 50% of all care will be center care (Neugebauer, 1992a). The shift away from family child care to center care is the result of the decrease in relative care. Relatives are now seeking out-of-home employment and are not available to care for children (Perreault, 1991).

Different kinds of families use different kinds of care. Families with preschoolers rather than infants and toddlers use center care more than do families with very young children (U.S. Bureau of the Census, 1987). However, care of infants and toddlers in centers is growing (Whitebook, Howes, & Phillips, 1990). The U.S. Bureau of the Census (1987) report shows that African American mothers are more likely than Anglo American or Latino mothers to enroll their children in centers. The census report also shows that mothers with more formal education and who work in management or the professions use centers more than lesser educated and service-employed mothers. Mothers who work full time, as compared with mothers who work part time, use centers more often (Hayes, Palmer, & Zaslow, 1990). Figure 1-1 shows the enrollment patterns in various types of child care by the child's age and by the maternal employment status. In reviewing statistics, one

Children Under Age 3

Employed Mothers

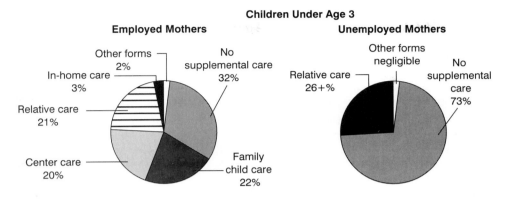

Other forms 2%
In-home care 3%
Relative care 21%
Center care 20%
Family child care 22%
No supplemental care 32%

Unemployed Mothers

Other forms negligible
Relative care 26+%
No supplemental care 73%

Children Ages 3 and 4

Employed Mothers

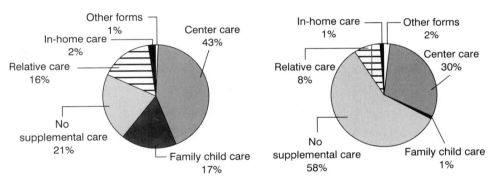

Other forms 1%
In-home care 2%
Relative care 16%
No supplemental care 21%
Family child care 17%
Center care 43%

Unemployed Mothers

In-home care 1%
Other forms 2%
Relative care 8%
Center care 30%
No supplemental care 58%
Family child care 1%

Children Ages 5 to 12
(Excluding School Attendance)

Employed Mothers

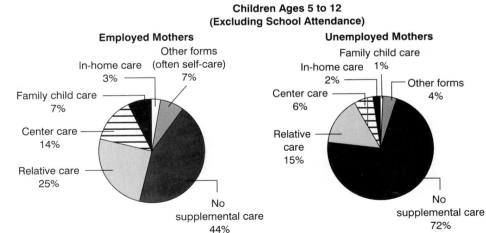

In-home care 3%
Family child care 7%
Center care 14%
Relative care 25%
Other forms (often self-care) 7%
No supplemental care 44%

Unemployed Mothers

Family child care 1%
In-home care 2%
Center care 6%
Relative care 15%
Other forms 4%
No supplemental care 72%

Figure 1-1   Child Care Enrollment Patterns

Source: Based on the statistics provided by Willer, B. (1992). An overview of the demand and supply of child care in 1990. *Young Children, 47*(2), 19-22.

must realize that many families use more than one type of care, especially if they have different ages of children and if they need supplemental care in addition to their "regular" arrangements.

Groups of Children Served. As already noted, most 5-year-olds are now in kindergarten programs. Three- and 4-year-old children form the bulk of the enrollment for all programs combined. Trends, however, are increasingly toward *extending the age range* of the children served (infants/toddlers and school-age), as well as including children who were mildly ill.

Infant/toddler child care usually refers to care given to children from birth to age 3. Although the number of infant/toddler programs is increasing, they still constitute one of the most difficult forms of child care to find. Neugebauer (1993a) reported that center care for infants and toddlers is the number one demand from employers. This is expected, given the fact that 52% of mothers return to their jobs within their child's 1st year (Galinsky, 1990b). Some concern has been expressed about infant programs. For years, infant/toddler programs were thought of as usurping family rights or breaking apart the family unit and stressing the common good of all children over individual needs. Some concern has also been expressed that the positive attachment between the mothering figure and baby would be prevented, possibly leading to problems such as depression and developmental lags reported in attachment studies beginning in the 1940s. Klimer's (1979) extensive review of research, however, led to the summary statement that few differences were found between infants and toddlers attending group child care and peers who stayed home with their mothers. Characteristics of the infant/toddler programs, especially adult-child ratio, staff turnover, and staff training, have been strongly implicated in the outcomes for infants and toddlers (Howes & Hamilton, 1993). (See Appendix 1 for program planning.)

A second trend is referred to as **school-age child care** (SACC) programs. **SACC** is a more encompassing term, defined as nonparental care of the 5- to 16-year olds during periods when school is not in session—before and after school, on holidays or vacations during the school term, and during the summer. School-age children make up the bulk of children (2 to 7 million or more) referred to as **latchkey children,** or **children in self-care,** an alternative label many think is a linguistic cop-out for such a serious problem. Being unsupervised after school is believed to contribute to childhood fear, depression, loneliness, depressed school achievement, crime, and increased sexual activity (Todd, Albrecht, & Coleman, 1990). In a national survey of public school teachers (kindergarten through Grade 12), children in self-care were ranked the number one cause of school difficulty (Harris, Kagaj, & Ross, 1987). Zigler and Lang (1991) stated that all children in Grade 6 and below are in need of SACC.

SACC is growing; 15 states now have special legislation on SACC, some with and some without funding (Seligson & Gannett, 1992). A majority of programs are affiliated with schools, child care centers, and youth-serving agencies. Seligson and Fink (1989) reported that 20% of public schools and nearly 50% of independent schools run SACC. In the majority of schools, space is provided to other sponsors of SACC, such as the YMCA, to operate these programs. (Approximately 65% of the nation's YMCAs operate SACC programs.) Other groups that operate SACC are churches, park and recreation facilities, housing authorities, military bases, and family child care programs. Quality programs are often collaborative in nature because several programs can provide more diverse activities as well as share expenses. Gannett (1990) has profiled six models of city collaboration projects. Regardless of sponsorship, the basic goals of school-age programs are (a) supervision (protection, shelter, food, and guidance); (b) recreation (supervised play to specific skill development); (c) diversion (e.g., crafts, drama, field trips); and (d) stimulation (formal lessons or practices). A new type of SACC activity is called "clubs," in which parents choose from a "menu" for their children (Howells, 1993). Many resources are now available for activities (see Appendix 1). SACC is not without problems. A survey conducted by the National School-Age Child Care Alliance and Exchange (Neugebauer, 1993c) found that the main challenges as seen by providers were (a) providing appropriate activities for older children; (b) staff who can work split shifts; (c) quality programs versus affordability to parents versus adequate wages for staff; and (d) shared space with public schools. The concerns expressed over schools entering the child care business center on the extent of school liability, charges for building use and maintenance, and costs of providing programs on an already tight budget (Seligson, 1986). A legal manual for public school administrators is available (Cohen, 1984). Because SACC has so many models and sponsors, checks on quality (as discussed in Chapter 3) are a problem.

Another trend is the growing need to find **special alternative care for mildly ill children** who attend child care centers and other programs but who are either too ill to attend their regular program or are prohibited from attending by policy. At least three types of alternative care are being used. One type includes centers specializing in the care of sick children (e.g., "Chicken Soup" in Minneapolis, Minnesota). A second type is infirmary care in pediatric wards of hospitals (e.g., Heights General in Albuquerque, New Mexico). A third type of alternative care is to send trained workers into homes to care for ill children (e.g., Sick Child Home Health Care Program, Tucson Association for Child Care, Inc., Tucson, Arizona). Work/Family Direction publishes an excellent guide, *A Little Bit Under the Weather: A Look at Care for Mildly Ill Children*, which describes prototype programs, gives criteria for programs, and provides an annotated list of currently operating programs.

Child Care and the Employer.   Business has become an important player on the early child-

hood care and education scene. Prior to World War II, business and labor involvement in child care was primarily limited to the health profession and a few industries. With mothers entering the workforce during World War II, public child care in defense plants (e.g., Kaiser Shipbuilding Corporation) served thousands of children. After the war, however, industry-sponsored child care declined sharply. Once again, businesses are concerned because employed parents have urgent child care needs (Galinsky, 1991). In one study, 25% of employed parents with children under age 13 had experienced a breakdown in their child care arrangements in the last 3 months (Neugebauer, 1993a). Businesses concerned about the viability of the future workforce, given the increasing numbers of at-risk children, now see child care as a highly important investment for 21st century productivity (Committee for Economic Development, Research, and Policy, 1987). The active role that businesses are now taking is called **employer-supported child care.**

Employer-supported child care is growing. A 1978 survey identified 9 child care centers sponsored by industries, 7 sponsored by the Amalgamated Clothing and Textile Workers Union, 14 sponsored by governmental agencies, and 75 sponsored by hospitals. A 1985 survey estimated 2,500 employer-supported child-care initiatives. In 1988, only 3,300 of the 44,000 employers with 100 or more workers provided child care assistance (Congressional Caucus for Women's Issues, 1988). In 1993, 11% of all companies with 10 or more employees provided some form of child care benefits or services (Neugebauer, 1993a). A 1992–93 survey showed that over half of the companies reported an increase in the demand for child care services and that less than 10% reported a decrease in demand (Neugebauer, 1993a).

Employer interest in child care varies by type of business. The U.S. Department of Labor (1988) reported that 26% of governmental agencies, 11% of service industries, and 6% of goods-producing industries provide some form of child care benefits. The army has the largest employer-sponsored early childhood program in the country (Council for Early Childhood Professional Recognition, 1993). Other major sponsors of child care are employers who (a) have a local labor shortage, (b) have a local culture of community involvement, (c) are located in areas where high-quality care is unavailable, (d) hire many women, (e) are in good financial health or are not in good financial health and want to recruit employees, and (f) employ one or more individuals who have taken up child care issues. Child care programs serving college campuses are growing too (Neugebauer, 1993d).

Employer-supported child care may take a variety of forms (Galinsky, 1989b):

1. **Multibusiness center or consortium,** in which several firms share responsibility and costs for a center. Small companies in an area are joining together to provide benefits. Large companies are also coming together to enhance their employees' dependent care needs. For example, IBM and 10 other corporations established the American Business Collaboration for Quality Dependent Care (Neugebauer, 1993a).

2. **Single-business center,** in which a corporation owns and operates an on-site facility. Although on-site child care has many benefits to employees and to the corporation (Waxman, 1991), it is also a burden because it costs, on the average, $100,000 per year (LaFleur & Newsom, 1988) and increases administrative burden and corporate legal liability. Companies with sales between $250 million and $500 million have the most on-site centers (Neugebauer, 1993a). Corporations are turning to outside contractors to operate their centers, such as a local or regional center, a national chain (e.g., Kinder Care Learning Centers, Children's World, Childtime, Children's Discovery Centers), or organizations dedicated solely to managing centers (e.g., Bright Horizons, Greentree, Corporate Child Care Management Services, Resources for Child Care Management; Neugebauer, 1992b).

3. **Family satellite program,** in which employers assist neighborhood families to become child care providers.

4. **Corporate reserve slots,** given to employees in local child care agencies at a rate less than the corporation paid or perhaps free.

5. Corporation use of a **voucher system,** in which the corporation reimburses the employees for all or part of their expenses.

6. Employer-provided **resource and referral services.** (See later section in this chapter.) Parent seminars are also being conducted. The content of the seminars is similar to the resource and referral services.

7. Employer-provided assistance through a **tax savings** under the firm's flexible benefit package, whereby salary reductions are used to fund child care. *Flexible spending accounts (FSAs),* as they are called, are made possible by Section 125 of the IRS Code. Employees cannot use both FSA and Dependent Care Tax Credit (under Section 129 of the IRS Code).

Figure 1-2 shows the major ways in which large companies offer child care services. In small companies, work schedules are more often adjusted for employees with children than through other means of assistance. These work schedule adjustments include **flextime** (employees have core work hours with flexible starting and stopping times); **compressed time** (work more hours per day but fewer days); **task contracting** (assigned tasks to be completed within a given time frame but need not specify time worked); **flexiplace** (location of where work performed is flexible, such as in one's home); and **job sharing** (two or more employees share one job and the salary/profits).

Head Start

In 1964, the federal government asked a panel of child-development experts to develop program guidelines to help communities overcome the handicaps borne by disadvantaged preschool

Figure 1-2   Child Care Services Offered by Large Companies
Source: Based on Congressional Caucus for Women's Issues. (1988). Results of the child-care challenge on employer-sponsored child-care services. *Young Children, 43*(6), 60-62.

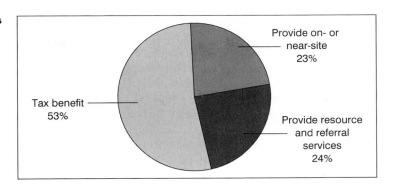

children. The report became the blueprint for Project Head Start, launched as an 8-week summer program that soon became a full-year program (Greenberg, 1990). Collins (1993), in defining Head Start, as a two-generational program, stated: "A two-generational program is one that promotes children's development within a family context. Major program goals target children together with parents and other family members" (p. 27). Head Start currently serves more than 600,000 children and their families (Collins, 1993) and has served more than 13 million children and their families since 1965 (Advisory Committee on Head Start Quality and Expansion, 1994).

Head Start is locally administered by community-based not-for-profit organizations and school systems. Grants are awarded by the Health and Human Services Regional Offices (10 regional offices, American Indian Program Branch, and the Migrant Program Branch). Head Start legislation states that the federal grant to operate a local Head Start program shall not exceed 80% of the approved costs of the program, with 20% to be contributed by the community in either cash or services. Head Start experience has shown that the needs of children vary considerably among communities and that programs should be individualized to serve local needs most effectively. Therefore, Head Start permits and encourages local sponsors to develop and implement various options (see Appendix 7).

Zigler, an architect of Head Start, stated that the overall goal of Head Start is to enhance children's social competence so that children will be "better able to perform effectively in school and beyond" (Raver & Zigler, 1991, p. 3). Head Start has four major components: (a) education, (b) health care (medical and dental, nutritional, and mental health), (c) parent involvement, and (d) social services. In 1975, performance standards were adopted to ensure that every Head Start program provides the services necessary to meet the goals of each of these components (Head Start Bureau, 1986). According to Mallory and Goldsmith (1990), Head Start has been successful because it (a) has provided comprehensive services to children and their families; (b) involved parents in parent education classes, in policy-making bodies, and as program volunteers and paid staff; (c) was designed to meet local community needs and to use the most feasible delivery system; (d) was supported by training and technical assistance; and (e) has used a collaborative approach with other organizations at the national and local levels.

Research on Head Start indicates that high-quality intervention for infants and preschool children has lasting effects (Berrueta-Clement, Schweinhart, Barnett, Epstein, & Weikart, 1984; Lazar & Darlington, 1982). Unfortunately, the documenting of Head Start's success has been and continues to be a problem because of the narrow focus on gains in children's intelligence quotients, rather than on broader measures of social competence (Raver & Zigler, 1991).

Since Head Start's 3-decade-ago inception, the face of poverty and thus the needs of children and their families have changed. Looking toward the 21st century, the bipartisan 47-member Advisory Committee on Head Start Quality and Expansion was formed in 1993. Three broad recommendations of the committee were to (a) ensure quality and strive for excellence at the local level, (b) respond flexibly to the needs of today's children and their families, and (c) forge new partnerships at the community, state, and federal levels (Advisory Committee on Head Start Quality and Expansion, 1994).

Two major advances have occurred in the last few years. The emphasis of Head Start has been on programs serving 3- and 4-year-olds. Head Start has had a history of serving some children younger than 3 since 1967, however, when Parent-Child Centers (PCCs) became a component of Head Start. The urgent need to serve these infants and toddlers was recognized through the Human Services Reauthorization Act of 1990, which included authorization for doubling the number of Head Start Parent-Child Centers. Performance standards are being written. Head Start has also launched some innovative services directed at parents and other family members. In the 1960s, Head Start called for parent involvement on policy councils and boards, as classroom volunteers, and as paid staff. In an effort to strengthen families, the Head Start of the 1970s launched Home Start, Child and Family Resource Programs (CFRPs), and Project Developmental Continuity. Today, Head Start is attempting to respond more adequately to family needs. Collins (1993) believes that Head Start must (a) continue to promote the concept that parents are the key people in the lives of their children, (b) set goals for parents and families as well as children, (c) strengthen and formalize collaboration with other federal agencies, (d) obtain technical assistance and program management support, and (e) set realistic overall

goals and assess results. If Head Start is able to implement the recommendations of the Advisory Committee on Head Start Quality and Expansion (1994) and of its own Silver Ribbon Panel (Lombardi, 1990) and if researchers can truly assess social competence, it may become **the** model for holistic early childhood care and education.

Primary Schools

Primary schools grew out of the common schools. The original purpose of primary schools in America was to instruct children in the three R's, especially in reading, as expounded in the Preamble to the Puritan School Law of 1647 (commonly referred to as the "Old Deluder Satan Law"). The methodology was rote memorization and recitation. During the 18th century, the schools were seen as a unifying force for the emerging America. State support of education and the concept of free, universal education were born during this century. Curriculum and methodology changed in the primary schools of the 19th century. The schools began to add aesthetic education, nature study, geography, and physical education to the three R's curriculum. The Pestallozzian system of an activity-oriented methodology was accepted, and the still frequently used unit-system of teaching evolved from the 19th century Herbartian method. *Normal schools* began teacher training programs as the need for trained teachers emerged. Although primary schools have continued to change with the demands of the times, many people still consider them the level at which skill subjects of reading, writing, and arithmetic must be mastered and content subjects (e.g., science, social studies) are introduced in a more structured atmosphere than is found in most preprimary programs.

Public Pre-Kindergarten Programs

Although public schools have only recently begun programs for pre-kindergarten children, these programs are rapidly expanding (Strother, 1987). Preschool funding by states doubled from 1988 to 1990 (Brady & Goodman, 1991). Today, about 60% of preschool children are enrolled in early childhood programs, but only about 14% of these children participate in public programs (S. Robinson & Lyon, 1994). Only three states have any programs for 3-year-olds, and only three states provide programs for at least 20% of their 4-year-old population. Many states do provide programs for pre-kindergarten children who qualify for special education (S. Robinson & Lyon, 1994). Besides funding programs for children with exceptionalities, states seem mainly interested in funding preschool programs for disadvantaged (now often referred to as "at risk") children. Some states are even subcontracting with private agencies (Brady & Goodman, 1991). Thus, relatively few children, except those with special needs, have experiences in publicly funded programs prior to kindergarten.

Some early childhood professionals advocate the shifting of all funding for child care and education for 3- and 4-year-olds to local systems (Zigler & Lang, 1991). Conversely, many early childhood leaders have voiced concern about public school pre-kindergarten programs. These leaders have said that the public schools had not appropriately served 5- to 8-year-old children and have expressed fears that pre-kindergartens would have inappropriate curricular content and teaching strategies and that public programs would also harm the enrollments of privately sponsored programs (G. Morgan, 1985). The Public School Early Childhood Study (Marx & Seligson, 1988), which compared public school-operated programs and community-based programs, found that (a) the range of practices in both went from very appropriate to not appropriate; (b) although public school programs were well-equipped, equipment was often not used well; (c) public school programs neglected large-muscle play; and (d) public school programs were good if the program administrators were well grounded in early

childhood education and child development and were influential with the district superintendent. The study found that public school programs competed with community-based programs for children if the community-based program served at-risk children (e.g., Head Start). Staff competition was seen during the original staffing of the public school program if the community-based programs offered low salaries. Without careful planning, however, service may be over-represented for one age-group or for high-risk children and ignored for other groups.

Resource and Referral Centers

Resource and referral centers (R & Rs) are counseling services designed to assist parents in locating and selecting child care services that are suited to their needs, preferences, and ability to pay. Most R & Rs are community funded; California and Massachusetts have state-supported R & R agencies. R & Rs must (a) collect and analyze data on community child care supply and demand, (b) recruit new child care providers and offer training opportunities and technical assistance to providers, (c) maintain a computerized database with detailed information on all licensed child care providers in the area, and (d) provide consumer education and referrals (often by telephone with a follow-up mailing). R & R centers refer parents to a range of choices, rather than to a specific program. Thus, parents' rights to select appropriate care are protected, and liability for child care choices rests with parents.

SERVICES AND PROGRAMS ADDRESSING POPULATIONS WITH SPECIAL NEEDS

Vulnerability has always been a reality for special needs children—children who are in or near the poverty level, children with disabilities, and children who are part of our linguistically and culturally diverse population. All of these children have special needs in today's early childhood care and education programs.

Children Who Are At Risk

As we have discussed, early childhood programs have always been partners in social initiatives for the poor throughout history. During the 1960s and 1970s, several hundred intervention programs were funded. Research was conducted on these programs through universities and various research centers. A descriptive compilation of many of these programs and the research results are available (M. Day & Parker, 1977; Fallon; 1973; Haith, 1972; Maccoby & Zellner, 1970; Weber, 1970).

Some of the programs were for infants and toddlers (see "Family Services" in this chapter). Most of these intervention programs were for 3- and 4-year-old children. All of the model programs designed for the disadvantaged preschooler were effective because they were well conceptualized and coherent versions of a particular knowledge base. Today, Head Start programs and public school pre-kindergartens are serving many at-risk preschoolers. Spodek and Brown (1993) stated that the most consistently popular curriculum approach from the initiatives of the 1960s is the High/Scope model. They think this may be because of the availability of written materials and of teacher training programs.

Kindergarten programs, such as Make Every Child Capable of Achieving, Project TALK, and Early Prevention of School Failure, are being used for at-risk 5-year-olds. Karweit (1993), after reviewing the research on effective kindergarten programs, concluded that the "systematic aspects" of the program were more important than the "philosophical approach." Similar to effective preschool programs, effective kindergarten approaches had teachers who followed a systematic plan and incorporated specific materials, activities, and management techniques that fit the context of the program.

Unfortunately, many programs for at-risk children are not well planned. Others that attempt to follow a model do not have the funds to keep an optimal child-staff ratio, hire well-qualified staff, and so on. Research is needed on how far a program may deviate from its model and still be effective.

Children With Disabilities

The history of serving children with disabilities in early childhood care and education programs has two roots: school programs serving school-age children with disabilities and early childhood programs serving disadvantaged (at-risk) children. Parents of children with disabilities started preschools and also advocated for governmental funding. P.L. 90-538, the Handicapped Children's Education Assistance Act, was passed in 1968. Head Start began the inclusion of children with disabilities in 1972. Thus, an early intervention focus was beginning.

Programs for children with special needs solidified with the passage of P.L. 94-142, the Education for All Handicapped Children's Act of 1975 (renamed Individuals With Disabilities Education Act in 1990). From the mid-1970s until the mid-1990s, experimentation in curricular content and program delivery occurred.

Early childhood care and education and special education became inseparable partners with the passage of P.L. 99-457, which extended the ideas of P.L. 94-142 to children from birth to age 3 and emphasized the family as the most viable supportive partner. With the passage of P.L. 99-457, a new field, early childhood special education (ECSE), was born and is rapidly growing.

Because intervention includes both young children and their families, many programs for young children with special needs use home visits as the delivery system (see "Family Services" in this chapter). The Portage Project (Bluma, Shearer, Frohman, & Hilliard, 1976; Boyd, Stauber, & Bluma, 1977; Shearer & Shearer,

1972; Sturmey & Crisp, 1986), which began in 1969, has been a long-time successful model for home-visiting programs serving children with special needs and their families. The other basic delivery system, the inclusion of children in early childhood programs to fulfill the "least restrictive environment" mandate of P.L. 94-142, has moved from mainstreaming (in which children were placed in "regular" programs for short, daily time periods but without constant supports from ECSE personnel), to integration (in which children with special needs were helped by ECSE professionals to adjust to the "regular" program), and now to inclusion (in which early childhood programs are designed to meet the needs of all children). The Jowonio School, created in 1969, is an early model of inclusion (Donovan, 1987).

In addition to the Portage Project and the Jowonio School, many other model programs for children with special needs have been attempted (Berres & Knoblock, 1987; Biklen, 1985). Research has been conducted on the various types of programs (Odom & McEvoy, 1988). Similar to the findings regarding programs for at-risk children, Odom and McEvoy (1988) stated that inclusion is not enough in itself; program quality is the critical factor.

Children From Linguistically and Culturally Diverse Backgrounds

The United States has always been a land of many peoples. Our population has become increasingly diverse. By 2020, almost half of the nation's schoolchildren will be children of color (Pallas, Natriello, & McDill, 1989). Our society has moved away from the early 1900s idea of the great "melting pot" to the idea that we are a diverse nation in which all children should have equal educational opportunities and should develop positive attitudes and behaviors toward all others. Spodek and Brown (1993) classified early childhood models concerned with diversity

as programs designed to serve specific populations and as programs for all children that foster positive attitudes and behaviors concerning diversity.

Programs designed to serve linguistically and culturally different populations were included in the program models designed for at-risk children. Some of these were bilingual efforts (Fallon, 1973; Saracho & Spodek, 1983). Today, the Tucson early education model incorporates the child's culture, including language into all classroom activities. Children are also taught in their primary language until they have oral proficiency in English (Arizona Center for Educational Research and Development, 1983). Project P.I.A.G.E.T. is a bilingual program for young children. In addition to the children's program, it also incorporates parent education by "native tongue" trainers (Yawkey, 1987).

The multicultural approach designed to aid all children in developing positive attitudes and behaviors toward others grew out of the "intergroup movement" of the 1950s. Studies of this time showed how children developed biases and how these attitudes affected their intergroup behaviors. Human relations curricula were designed to counteract biases (Guillean, 1991). Another root of multicultural education today was the "ethnic studies movement" of the 1970s. Although the curriculum developers of this movement had good intentions, it failed because of its tourist approach to non-Euro-American cultures (Derman-Sparks & the A.B.C. Task Force, 1989). Today, the trend is to integrate learning about diversity into the ongoing early childhood program. Even this idea has been criticized for not paying direct attention to social inequities (Ramsey, 1987). Derman-Sparks and the A.B.C. Task Force (1989) developed the *Anti-Bias Curriculum*. This approach is designed to teach children to not only respect diversity but also actively confront biases.

Multicultural approaches are value laden and thus subject to much criticism. Grant and

Sleeter (1989) discuss some of these issues, and Derman-Sparks and the A.B.C. Task Force (1989) address the possibility that some parents may not agree with her *Anti-Bias Curriculum.* Curriculum approaches for multiculturalism likely will remain an issue into the 21st century. However, the need for multicultural education is not debated among early childhood care and education professionals (Derman-Sparks & Ramsey, 1992).

FAMILY SERVICES

Early childhood care and education has had a long history of interest in the family as evidenced by the work of the day nursery, nursery schools, Montessori schools, kindergartens, and Head Start programs. Because research has confirmed the role of families in their children's development, programs designed for families, especially low-income families, have become increasingly popular.

Today's programs have their roots in the parent-infant classes begun in the late 1960s, such as Caldwell-Lally Children's Center (B. Caldwell, 1968), the Florida Intervention Program (I. Gordon, 1969), the Gray and Klaus project (Gray & Klaus, 1970), and the Levenstein Toy Demonstration project (Levenstein, 1970). Other projects based on the encouraging results of these pioneering programs were soon initiated. Head Start, too, had launched 36 PCCs in 1967 (Head Start Bureau, 1991); unfortunately, the Office of Economic Opportunities' longitudinal research project on the PCCs, the Parent-Child Development Center, was never completed (Dokecki, Hargrove, & Sandler, 1983).

By the mid- to late-1970s, policy makers were disenchanted with the idea of remediating family weaknesses. The new family service projects were interested in being a partner with the family. The Family Resource Coalition (FRC) was founded in 1981. Programs associated with the FRC are based on the idea that families and professionals will share ideas and support. Weiss

(1983) has outlined the "chain of defining assumptions" used by the FRC.

The more than 2,000 family resource programs differ considerably. Some of these programs are federal initiatives, such as the PCCs and Even Start Family Literacy Programs launched in 1988 (see Appendix 7). Other programs are state initiatives, such as the Minnesota Early Learning Design (Payne, 1983), and others are local programs. Information on these programs is available through the Family Resource Coalition (see Appendix 5).

Family service projects may be center based or home based. **Home-visiting programs,** as home-based programs are often called, are strategies for supporting the development of young children through professional home visits. Home-visiting programs vary in their approach. Powell (1990) has discussed three ways in which they may differ:

1. The content of the visit may focus on the child only (Levenstein, 1987) or on the child and the family (Kagan, Powell, Weissbourd, & Zigler, 1987). It is argued that unless the family's needs are met, the child's needs will be unfulfilled. Conversely, the child's needs may go unmet if the family needs are too pressing, or the general quality of services may diminish when home visitors attempt to provide a broad range of services.

2. The relations between parent and home visitor differ from program to program. Because the visitor is on the "parent's turf," the home visitor is the one who adapts. In some programs, parents are very actively involved, but in other programs, parents assume a spectator role. Programs also differ in the ways in which they attempt to get parents involved; in some programs, the professionals develop and model the activities for the parent, whereas in other programs, parents assume the planning and executing roles gradually.

3. Individualization of the home visit differs from program to program. Some professionals

individualize program services as they feel the need. Others individualize the content of the curriculum (sequencing activities in the order that seems most appropriate for a parent/child, selecting activities from a predetermined range of options, or encouraging parents to adopt the activities). (Families in early childhood programs are discussed further in Chapter 10.)

ISSUES AND NEW IDEAS IN EARLY CHILDHOOD CARE AND EDUCATION

Throughout their history, early childhood programs have been designed to meet various societal goals. Grubb (1991) traces these four goals:

1. *To extend the functions of the home.* In the kindergartens prior to their entrance into the public school setting and in the nursery schools, the teacher was a mother surrogate, and the program, similar to the home, emphasized affective development through play. Today, some unemployed women use supplemental care as a way to aid their children's learning and as an aid to socialization of their children (which is seen as more important in today's "smaller families").

2. *To provide custodial care for children while parents learn job skills or work in order to avoid public assistance.* Custodial care was seen in the day nurseries. Today, child care is provided under the Family Support Act of 1988 as part of the Job Opportunities and Basic Skills Program.

3. *To provide child care and education while parents work.* These families use various types of early childhood programs.

4. *To provide compensatory education.* These programs began with the infant school movement in America. In the 1960s, intervention programs were designed for children at high risk for developmental problems because of their environment. Head Start became the most visible example of a program designed for compen-

satory education. Intervention programs for children with special needs began major expansion after the passage of P.L. 94-142 and P.L. 99-457.

Thus, social needs resulted in early childhood programs changing directions frequently to reflect diverse goals. Although many needs have been met, the historical diversity of early childhood programs has led to issues and new thinking.

From Different Historical Perspectives to a Kaleidoscope of Program Practices

The different historical perspectives have led to a kaleidoscope of practices in the implementation of children's programs. These contrasting orientations come from program planners, administrators, and/or teachers' beliefs about what is right for children. Sometimes, these beliefs can be articulated in terms of very specific psychological theories about how children learn and philosophies about what is important for children to learn. In many other cases, staff of early childhood programs cannot articulate what they do in terms of theory and philosophy; rather, staff say, "It works for us"; "The parents like our program"; "I've always done it this way"; "Today's children need . . . "; and "It's required (e.g., in terms of state curriculum guidelines)."

On the one hand, programs designed by researchers often have a very consistent adherence to one theoretical and philosophical view. On the other hand, most programs use very eclectic approaches in which they combine differing theories and philosophies. Sometimes, these differing approaches are at opposite ends of a continuum from a narrow learning emphasis to a holistic development emphasis, and yet the staff do not see the practices as possibly contradictory. For example, in some early childhood programs, teachers use drill and structured materials to teach the three R's but allow independent exploration of science materials, blocks, and puppets. As another example, in some programs, children engage in projects with adults helping each child reflect on his or her learnings, and yet class management centers on teacher-prescribed rules reinforced through the use of objects, food treats, or stickers. Changes undoubtedly will continue to take place in early childhood programs as we enter the next century. With regard to the children's program, it is difficult to see a clear trend. Certainly, developmentally appropriate practice (DAP), which is discussed in Chapter 2, is part of almost everyone's professional vocabulary. Although substantial movement has occurred in the direction of DAP and many seek specifics on its implementation, a significant number of other professionals choose other foci for program planning. Even if DAP were adopted, program differences would need to occur to make the curriculum *age* and *individually* appropriate.

From Focus on the Child to a Family-Centered Vision

The historical roots of early childhood programs focused on the child. Parent education programs, however, also have a rich heritage. Until recently, parents were primarily passive recipients of what early childhood educators thought was in their best interests as parents.

A shift toward a family-centered approach has begun. The trend was stimulated by the research that looked at the child's development within the context of the family (Bronfenbrenner, 1979) and by the research on model early childhood programs that found the program to be more effective when the focus was on the parent rather than only on the child (Lally, Mangione, & Honig, 1987). In addition to the research, the family support movement, begun in the 1970s and 1980s, took the ecological perspective that the child was not separate from the family and that the family was not distinct from the local community and even larger society. This new thinking led to the family-centered approach, a "community center in which parents and teachers learn from one another and in

which parents' adult needs are met" (Galinsky & Weissbourd, 1992, p. 47).

From Care Versus Education to Comprehensive Services

Various early childhood programs have served different societal needs, and thus many see care and education as two different entities. This misunderstanding perhaps emanates from the fact that the development of kindergartens and nursery schools was separate from the development of child care. Some writers indicate that, in the 1930s, child care was an essential part of child welfare programs. Efforts were made to differentiate between child care as a philanthropic activity and nursery school as an educational activity, as noted in the following statement: "This purpose (care and protection), the reasons for which a family and child may need it, and the responsibilities shared with parents distinguish a child care service from educational programs" (Child Welfare League of America, 1960). Conversely, others believe that nursery school thinking was assimilated by workers prior to World War II, in that child care programs, in keeping with nursery school philosophy, see the teacher as assisting the child in each developmental stage, use play as the core of their curriculum, and seem to rank language and intellectual development slightly behind children's physical and affective well-being (Read, 1976). B. Caldwell (1990) believes that, through these artificial distinctions between *care* and *education* and our devotion to labels, we exclude rather than include. Similarly, Kagan (1988) states that such a differentiation leads to "undervaluing our profession" and to inappropriate practices by those who are trying to prove they *teach*. Thus, B. Caldwell has proposed the term **educare** as a way to enhance the field conceptually (to embrace the many services provided). Hymes (1987) has proposed the term **publicdaycareandschooling,** "all mixed up in one." Kagan (1989) has pointed out that three forces have mandated an interdependence between care and education: (a) the mandates of equal educational opportunities (e.g., *Brown v. Board of Education* decisions [1954, 1955], Title I of the Elementary and Secondary Education Act of 1965, and P.L. 94-142); (b) research that underscores the interdependence of parent, child, and community; and (c) policy makers' concern about the state of our children and the ineffectiveness of delivering public services in uncoordinated ways.

This new thinking naturally leads to a holistic approach to meeting the needs of the child within the ecological context (interdependence of parent, child, and community). Comprehensive services are needed to meet these needs. Lombardi (1992) sees comprehensive services as including (a) developmentally and culturally appropriate services for all children, (b) parent involvement and family support, and (c) attention to the health needs of both children and parents.

From Program Deficiencies and Inequities to Quality Programs for All

Programs designed for services to a particular group of children often resulted in excluding other children. For example, the early U.S. private kindergartens excluded the poor, causing Elizabeth Peabody and Susan Blow to work on behalf of all children via public school kindergartens. Today, the poor still face glaring inequities. Conversely, government-funded programs such as Head Start excluded children whose families were not poor. Many families whose modest incomes made them ineligible for these programs were not able to afford the tuition to quality private early childhood programs. In other cases, quality programs do not exist in a given area, making availability rather than affordability the problem.

In 1990, President Bush and the 50 state governors established six national educational goals. The first goal addressed early childhood care and education. The goal read that "by the year 2000 all children in the United States will start school ready to learn." The three objectives for this goal were concerned with (a) high-

quality and developmentally appropriate programs, (b) parents' roles as their children's first teachers and their right to the training and support they need for this endeavor, and (c) nutrition and health care beginning at the prenatal stage (National Education Goals Panel, 1993). This is the first time that the needs of *all* children have been the focus of concern.

From "Salad Bowl" Services to Program Linkages/New Systems

The diversity of early childhood programs has led to "salad bowl" services. B. Caldwell (1991) describes the current situation as the "diversity of settings in which early childhood programs operate and the cacophony of labels applied to them" (p. 72). The lack of coordination among services has led to many programs (e.g., services "stacked" in high-need areas and not available in other areas; programs pitted against each other for staff, space, and children; many other problems discussed throughout this book; I. Goodman & Brady, 1988; Kagan, 1991a). In fact, in this nonsystem of programs, the National Academy of Sciences (1990) could not determine the exact number of federal programs that support early childhood care and education.

At the 1993 National Institute for Early Childhood Professional Development (Galinsky, Shubilla, Willer, Levine, & Daniel, 1994), eight critical components for systemic reform were identified. One of these components was "linkages" across all programs serving families and children. The panel recommends that, instead of providing services in isolation, professionals go beyond collaboration and "create new systems" (p. 54).

NATURE OF PLANNING AND ADMINISTERING EARLY CHILDHOOD PROGRAMS

The board's or the administrator's responsibility begins with the determination of legitimate goals for children and their families to be served by the local program. Once these goals are chosen, decisions regarding policies; personnel; housing and equipping children's activities; assessing, recording, and reporting children's progress; and the parent program should be consistent with the chosen view. Thus, once the goals are chosen, the next step in planning is to articulate these goals clearly to all those involved in the planning and implementation process. Administrators must then determine the process by which these goals will be met, operationalize the means for their achievement, and provide feedback and evaluation. A few responsibilities in administration are only indirectly related to goals but are critical to the planning, such as meeting regulations and planning for nutrition and safety.

Because the first step in planning is to develop the goals, which we call **program base,** for the local program, this is discussed in Chapter 2. From this point, there is no linear progression in planning an early childhood program. In fact, all other aspects of planning should be considered simultaneously because all facets influence each other. In short, congruity should exist between the program base and each of the other aspects of the local program. The remaining chapters of this book consider each step in the process.

SUMMARY

Early childhood programs have experienced growth unlike any other U.S. enterprise except the computer industry. The increased demand for child care and education in a society whose workforce involves and will continue to involve more women and greater ethnic/racial diversity has fostered this growth, as has the desire to help children in poverty with a better start in life, and the expanding body of research that shows the benefits of quality programs.

Early childhood programs, taken collectively, constitute a diverse, rather uncoordinated

system contributed to by various individuals and by public and private organizations with differing historical roots. Some of the trends include very diverse program practices, more emphasis on the child within the family setting and meeting the family's needs, greater realization of the need for comprehensive services, a vision of quality programs for all children, and linkages across the various auspices funding early childhood programs.

In an effort to meet the needs of the whole child within an ecological context, it becomes crucial for administrators to select an appropriate program base. The administrator must then plan and implement all of the program components in keeping with the chosen program base.

FOR FURTHER READING

Baum, S. J., & Edwards, E. P. (1972). *History and theory of early childhood education*. Belmont, CA: Wadsworth.

Bradburn, E. (1989). *Margaret McMillan: Portrait of a pioneer*. London: Routledge.

Cahan, E. D. (1989). *Past caring: A history of U.S. preschool care and education for the poor, 1820-1965*. New York: Columbia University, National Center for Children in Poverty.

Elkind, D. (1983). Montessori education: Abiding contributions and contemporary challenges. *Young Children, 38*(2), 3-10.

Greenberg, P. (1990). Before the beginning: A participant's view. *Young Children, 45*(6), 41-52.

Hernandez, D. J. (1993). *America's children: Resources from family, government, and the economy*. New York: Russell Sage Foundation.

Hymes, J. L., Jr. (1991). *Twenty years in review: A look at 1971–1990*. Washington, DC: National Association for the Education of Young Children.

Weber, E. (1969). *The kindergarten: Its encounter with educational thought in America*. New York: Teachers College Press.

Zigler, E., & Muenchow, S. (1992). *Head Start: The inside story of America's most successful education experiment*. New York: Basic Books.

Part One

═══════════════ ❈ ❈ ❈ ❈ ❈ ═══════════════

Constructing the Early Childhood Program's Framework

❈ ❈ ❈ ❈ ❈

Chapter 2

Planning, Implementing, and Evaluating the Program

Directing program planning, implementation, and evaluation is the major task of the early childhood administrator. Every aspect of a program must be designed to contribute to children's development and family needs.

For more than three decades, a concentrated effort to improve program planning, implementation, and evaluation has occurred, in part, because more people are concerned about the care and education of young children. Certain standards have been met by high-quality early childhood programs. All effective programs have staff who are concerned for the children in their care and for their families. All meet the health and safety needs of children in their care. All have housing and equipment that are more or less designed with children in mind. And all provide activities for children.

Beyond these basic features, however, high-quality programs vary enormously. There is no consensus as to what goals are the "best" for children (what type of intellect, skills, knowledge, and values should be fostered); how educators should achieve these goals (the type of pedagogical method to be used); where to conduct the program (the home or group setting, the public- or privately-operated program); when to time the experiences (age at which children will be involved); or how to evaluate the results. Therefore, implicit or explicit individual perspectives form the basis for each program's practice. Such a viewpoint that is well-constructed may be referred to as a **program base.** Simply defined, a program base is a statement about the experiences of learning and teaching and the choices that educators make to control these experiences.

Administrators must determine or select a program base and use this base to develop program rationale. Administrators are responsible for making implementation decisions consistent with the rationale. Figure 2–1 depicts the role of the administrator in planning, implementing, and evaluating the program.

FACTORS DETERMINING THE PROGRAM BASE

Few early childhood educators have a systematic program base from which they determine practice. Without such a base, problems and confusions arise. And all too often, the reverse happens; namely, theories and value statements are used to justify current practices.

Proper Sources

The two most relevant sources for determining program base are theoretical and philosophical positions. The theoretical position comes from (a) psychological theories that help in answering questions about "what children can learn" and (b) the ecological perspective of the child (the sociocultural context) that examines the impact of the socialization processes on the child's development. The philosophical position comes from values for children individually and collectively, both now and in the future, and thus is concerned with "what children ought to know."

Psychological Theories. Three major psychological theories have influenced early childhood education. The first school of thought is the **maturational** view, in which development is seen as the result of the maturation of structures within the individual. According to this view, the dominant aspect of development is genetic construction. Maturationists maintain that humans are alike in many ways because they are members of the same species; differences can also be accounted for by genetic makeup. Although the genes guide the process of maturation, teaching or nurturing determines the specific content of what an individual learns (e.g., naming colors, riding a bicycle, using proper table manners) and influences to some degree the rate and extent of learning. The maturational view holds that teachers should provide educative experiences when the child shows interest or should provide instruction when the child is ready. This theory,

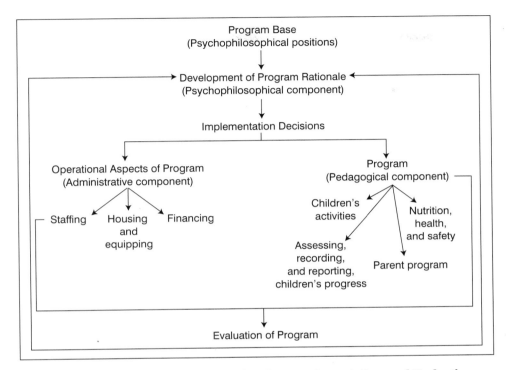

Figure 2-1   Framework for Program Planning, Implementation, and Evaluation

formulated by Gesell (1931), permeates the literature from the 1930s through the 1950s. Through the use of norms, the maturationists have developed "expectations" for children at different ages that prevent a child from being hurried by poorly timed experiences. In the 1950s, the integration of assumptions from the psychoanalytic theories with the maturational theory brought about the child development approach (Jersild, 1946).

The second school of thought, which was initially implemented in a laboratory setting, is the **behavioral-environmental** view (Skinner, 1938). In this approach, development is viewed as environmental inputs and behavioral outputs. In short, the environment, rather than genetic construction, has the dominant role in development. The focus is not on mental processes, but on eliciting and reinforcing verbal, perceptual, and

motor behaviors. Two teaching approaches are based on this view. One approach is to wait for desired behaviors to occur and then to reinforce them with praise or object-type rewards. The second approach is to communicate the desired behavior verbally or to physically model the behavior and reinforce the child for making the appropriate response following the cue. Use of the behavioral-environmental view in teaching has two limitations: (a) What is reinforcing to one individual may not be so to another, and consequently adults may be rewarding (or punishing) behavior without being aware of it; and (b) because of the variety of reinforcement sources, there may be a stronger reinforcement for certain responses outside the program setting.

The third school of thought is the **constructivist** (sometimes called *interactionist*) view. It was a direct challenge to the behaviorists. Constructivist theorists see genetic makeup and environment, nature and nurture, as more or less equal in shaping development. Unlike the behaviorists, both the maturationists and the constructivists describe the child as moving from one stage to another. Unlike the maturationists, who see the progression of development generated from within the organism that emerges given time (and at more or less predictable ages), constructivists see development as the result of experience coupled with the way in which the human interprets, recognizes, or modifies experience. Five main influences shape an individual's interactions throughout his or her development: (a) maturation or mainly genetic factors, (b) experience or environmental input, (c) developmental tasks through which an individual interacts with his or her environment, (d) consultation with other people, and (e) the interaction of all the foregoing influences (Educational Products Information Exchange Institute, 1972). Piaget began developing the constructivist theory in the 1920s, but the theory was not generally received until the 1960s. Vygotsky (1978) is also a constructivist theorist.

Ecological Perspectives.   Bronfenbrenner believes that most constructivists have not spent enough time studying the dynamic impact of the environment on behavior. Bronfenbrenner (1979) suggests that an ecological perspective be applied to all behaviors—that is, consideration of the interrelationship of the organism and the setting in which a behavior is observed. The essence of an ecological system is that behaviors not only are influenced by the environment but also influence the environment. In addition, the environment closest to a person (e.g., day-to-day activities at home and school) influences his or her behaviors to a greater degree than more distant ecological systems (e.g., values, customs).

Bronfenbrenner describes the ecological context that a child experiences and that affects development as four different but overlapping systems. The *microsystem*, the immediate and powerful socializer of children, is comprised of the family, child care or school, peers, media, and community. The second system, the *mesosystem*, consists of overlapping microsystems, such as parent-teacher interaction or employer-supported child care. The third system, the *exosystem*, consists of parents' jobs, city government, school board, community services, and federal government. A child may be influenced indirectly by the exosystem. For example, if the parents' employment requires conformity, this is likely to result in an autocratic or authoritarian parenting style. The broadest system is the *macrosystem*, which consists of socioeconomic, racial/ethnic, geographic and American ideological, religious, and political cultures. In short, the macrosystem is culture and thus has a profound effect. E. Hall (1976) believes that people from different macrosystems not only view the world differently but also are not even aware of alternative ways of perceiving. Furthermore, changes in the macrosystem can result in changes in all other systems. Some of the many recent macrosystem changes in our society include high technology, a world economy, need for networking, and multiple-options on almost all products and services (Naisbitt & Auberdine, 1990).

The ecological perspective allows us to acknowledge the complexity of all our behaviors. This perspective cautions us to look carefully before making decisions or judgments. It also lets us see the interrelatedness of children's lives. The young child and his or her family are no longer isolated facets; the child brings the home to the early childhood program and the program to the home. This example is only one pattern in the kaleidoscope of overlapping systems.

Philosophical Positions.   Schools are designed to meet social purposes. This fact has been recognized since the time of Plato, who described education in *The Republic* as preparation of children to do the state's bidding. Like Plato, Dewey believed that education is the fundamental lever of social progress (Dewey, 1897). Even more recently, Hymes (as cited in Senn, 1975), who supported the child development approach, also understood the necessity of a philosophical position; he characterized himself as "trying to be something of a bridge between child development and children's experiences in school" (p. 8).

During the 1960s, the emphasis on psychological theories almost overshadowed philosophical positions. In the early 1970s, recognition was voiced that psychological theory alone cannot be the sole basis for determining program design. Egan (1983) stated that the dominance of psychological theories has led to ineffective educational practice. Other program designers thought a blend of the psychological and the philosophical views was needed. Kohlberg and Mayer (1972) stated that philosophically desirable ends must be rooted in the "facts of development." Furthermore, "philosophical principles cannot be stated as ends of education until they can be stated psychologically" (p. 485). They also saw psychological theories as having either implicit or explicit values and stated that when theories are used as the basis for program design, they become an ideology. In E. Shapiro and Biber's (1972) viewpoint, Erikson, Werner, Piaget, and Dewey are all credited with providing insights. A basic tenet of their developmental-interaction approach is that cognitive functions (e.g., acquiring and organizing information, using symbols) cannot be separated from the growth of the personal and interpersonal processes (e.g., development of self-esteem, internalization of impulse control). Educators must choose methods for fulfilling the first goal that never violate the second goal, and must find methods for fulfilling the second goal that make the first goal more realizable (Biber, 1970).

Consideration of these viewpoints led to a questioning of values. B. Caldwell (1977) pointed out that the current generation is seemingly afraid to specify what it wants for its children. According to Caldwell, Americans say they want their children to become "what they are capable of becoming"; however, we know that what they are capable of becoming depends to a great extent on experiences chosen for them by adults. Similarly, Americans say the school's purpose is "to let children find out who they are," and it is unfashionable "to say we teach them anything." Caldwell believes that this lack of specific educational goals is a result of a vague national ideology or a voiced national ideology inconsistent with what is observed (e.g., ethics in high places). She concludes that U.S. schools must be based on articulated values—values considered good for society.

The need for a philosophical position as a base for program design seems clear. Whether the lack of a philosophical basis is the result of a vague ideology (B. Caldwell, 1977), dominance of psychological theories (Egan, 1983), or other causes, the dilemma posed by this gap in value base is pinpointed by Sommerville (1982), who states, "Children are going to school for an ever-longer period, but we seem less and less sure about what they should be getting from it" (p. 16).

Synthesis of Proper Sources.   As seen in the previous section, Kohlberg and Mayer (1972) and E. Shapiro and Biber (1972) saw a need for synthesis of proper sources. Even before the 1970s, Hunt (1961) voiced a concern about considering only psychological theories in program planning. When the National Association for the Education of Young Children (NAEYC) first issued its position statements on developmentally appropriate practice (DAP; Bredekamp, 1987), the statements seemed to lean very heavily on both psychological theories and ecological perspectives in calling for age- and individually-appropriate curriculum.

Criticisms were expressed that DAP did not address (or obscured) other aspects of program planning (Kostelnik, 1992; Spodek, 1991a; Swadener & Kessler, 1991b). In an attempt to address these concerns, the NAEYC provided a second document (Bredekamp & Rosegrant, 1992). Bredekamp and Rosegrant (1992) acknowledged that curriculum must also consider the "knowledge base of various disciplines and the values of culture and community" (p. 17). Bredekamp (1987) acknowledged that the NAEYC supports John Dewey's vision of schools and society. (DAP is further discussed throughout this book.)

Spodek's (1991a) dimensions for program planning and evaluation seem to be a synthesis of psychological theories, ecological perspectives, and philosophical positions. He calls for the use of these three dimensions for judging educational programs: (a) developmental (considers what children can learn and the methodology employed in teaching); (2) cultural (acknowledges society's values—that is, what we want children to be and become); and (c) knowledge (addresses what children need to know today and in the future to function successfully). Katz (1991a) says that three interrelated a priori questions must be asked to identify appropriate program development: (a) What should be learned? (this deals with goals), (b) When should it be learned? (this deals with child development), and (c) How is it best learned? (this considers program implementation of goals).

Improper Sources

Several improper sources have been used for program design. Later school content (a top-down perspective) and narrow definitions of readiness, assessment practices, and policies of funding agencies are the most common improper sources.

Later School Content and Narrow Definitions of Readiness.   Generally speaking, on the one hand, goals of the present program should be consistent with those of the programs that children will be involved in later. For example, Follow Through was initiated to continue the work of Head Start because children who went into a traditional program from the Head Start program soon lost the advantages they had gained. Also, Miller and Dyer (1975) found that participa-

tion in one type of preschool program may interfere with learning in a later program if the programs are greatly disparate in approach. The concern for continuity in early childhood programs in all areas, such as curriculum and assessment, environment, management, and links to parents and the community, is of major concern today (Barbour & Seefeldt, 1993; Love, Logue, Trudeau, & Thayer, 1992).

On the other hand, the goals of any program should center on the child's present benefit and not merely on preparation for the future. A great deal of concern has been expressed over the accelerating downward shift of what were next-grade expectations into lower grades (L. Shepard & Smith, 1988, p. 136). This may be thought of as a top-down curricular perspective. Closely related to top-down curriculum is the narrow definition of readiness. For many years, the term **readiness** had been applied to many activities of the early childhood program (e.g., reading readiness, mathematics readiness) and even to the names of some of the assessment devices used with young children (e.g., *American School Reading Readiness Test*, *Metropolitan Readiness Tests*). These readiness skills were considered necessary to prepare children for later schooling. For example, some intervention programs, such as that of Bereiter-Englemann, were based on a philosophy of overcoming specific "readiness deficits." Concerns have surfaced over using an academically narrow definition of readiness to learn (Goal 1 Technical Planning Group, 1993; R. Hitz & Richter, 1993; S. Robinson, 1993/94). ("Readiness" for school, another definition of readiness, is discussed in this chapter under "Obstacles in Developing Program Goals.") Although some "readiness skills" may be worth learning, and continuity between present and future programs is valuable, planning a program solely on the basis of future content is faulty because (a) readiness skills are not goals in themselves, but rather are means to goals; (b) the advantages gained in "crash" preparation may be lost; (c) formal readiness training may be detrimental in itself (Stephen, 1973, p. 336); and (d) the use of later school content as a source for early childhood program design is circular reasoning that avoids assessing value.

Assessment Practices.   Assessment of children's progress in a program is essential. If the content of the assessment instruments and the techniques used in the assessment process relate closely to a program's objectives, assessment results may be used to add to or revise content or methodology to help meet stated objectives. However, one must avoid the pitfall of using assessment instruments that do not match a program's goals and of letting those instruments determine content or methodology. (The purposes of and concerns in assessment practices are elaborated on in Chapter 9.)

Policies of Funding Agencies.   Funding agencies have a great deal of control over a program. Examples of this control may be seen in established goals of federal programs (e.g., Head Start Performance Objectives), legislation and master plans developed by state task forces for public school curriculum, local boards' (school boards or boards of directors/advisors) decisions on curricular practices, and curriculum guides published by the funding agencies. Program design must be in the hands of the professional. When funding agencies alone determine program design, it is similar to test items being used for program design (the "tail wagging the dog").

OVERVIEW OF CURRICULUM MODELS

A **curriculum model** is based on the program base and contains the administrative and pedagogical components of an educational plan. The model is presumed valid for achieving certain outcomes (Spodek, 1973a).

Models Based on Psychological Theories

Fein and Schwartz (1982) contrast theories of development with theories in practice. A **theory of development** offers general statements about factors affecting children's behaviors. Such theories do not offer principles for modifying or generating those factors. In contrast, a **theory of practice** describes what a practitioner must do to encourage particular behaviors. The following section discusses how three theories of development have been applied to early childhood programs—that is, have become theories of practice.

Application of the Maturational Theory.   Until the 1960s, most early childhood programs serving middle-class populations were based on concepts stemming from the **maturational** theory. Programs following this model were referred to as "permissive-enrichment programs" (Bissell, 1973), a "child-centered curriculum" (Weikart, 1972), the "child-development model" (Mayer, 1971), and "developmental-maturationist" (D. Ellis, 1977). Table 2-1 presents a synopsis of the three components of the maturational models. Additional information on specific programs is located in Appendix 1.

Application of the Behavioral-Environmental Theory.   Programs following the **behavioral-environmental** theory aim to teach facts and skills the program designers consider necessary for future functioning in the culture but lacking in the children served. Programs applying the behavioral-environmental theory have been referred to as "structured-information" (Bissell, 1973), the "programmed approach" (Weikart, 1972), the "verbal-didactic model" (Mayer, 1971), and "behavioristic-theoretical" (D. Ellis, 1977). Table 2-2 presents a synopsis of three components of the behavioral-environmental models. Additional information on specific programs is located in Appendix 1.

Application of the Constructivist Theory.   Programs under the umbrella of **constructivist** theory usually follow an "open framework" curriculum, in which the teacher initiates ideas and responds to the child's activities (Weikart, 1972).

Table 2-1   Maturational Model

Psychophilosophical Component

Based on theories of Gesell, Freud, and Erikson.

Considers children to be born with a genetic blueprint for certain patterns of behavior. Sees behavioral changes occurring as a result of physiological maturation (readiness) and environmental situations that encourage certain behaviors (developmental tasks).

Administrative Component

Housing	Roomy environment is calculated to give maximum mobility. Learning centers are only somewhat defined.
Equipment	Rich assortment of multidimensional materials that serve many modes of expression (e.g., language, mathematics, motor, aesthetic) are chosen. Developmental levels of children served are considered.
Staff	Provide a warm, supportive environment. Do few, if any, prescribed learning activities, but "enrich" ongoing activities when children need to expand their understandings/skills.
	Set limits and redirect unacceptable social behaviors.

Pedagogical Component

Activities	Units and broad themes based on studies of children's interests are introduced; children are free to "sample" activities as they wish.
	Activities based on the theme are carried out by play with materials located in the learning centers and by field trips.
	Activities are almost completely child-selected, rather than adult-prescribed.
Motivational strategy	Verbal extrinsic motivation (e.g., praise).
Grouping	Heterogeneous grouping (family grouping) is most common. Occasional loosely defined homogeneous groups are based on age/stage.
Scheduling	Flexible schedules are designed to fit children's needs and interests.
	Large blocks of time in which a child may work on a single activity or change activities are typical.
Assessment of children	Attempts are made to observe the whole child (physical, cognitive, and affective), primarily using naturalistic observations.

Program Evaluation

A program is seen as successful if children progress according to physical, cognitive, and affective norms. Allowances are made when children are seen as having hereditary or environmental constraints placed on their development.

Table 2-2   Behavioral-Environmental Model

Psychophilosophical Component

Based on theories of Skinner, Baer, Bijou, and Bandura.

Considers children to be born with a "blank slate"; passive children's behaviors are shaped by the environment.

Sees behavioral changes occurring as a result of reinforcing planned or unplanned events.

Administrative Component

Housing	Less roomy environment is calculated to focus children's attention and to avoid distractions. Areas within the room are clearly defined—often with high dividers.
Equipment	More narrowly focused and unidimensional materials are used that meet program-selected objectives and serve one mode of expression (e.g., language).
Staff	Plan and control the environment. Almost all activities are adult-prescribed. Do much direct (expository) teaching of small units of materials that have been broken down from larger tasks and sequenced.
	Use principles of behavior modification to prevent and control deviant behavior.

Pedagogical Component

Activities	Goal-oriented activities designed to achieve specific cultural learnings, usually academic in nature, are provided; the same learnings are often expected of all children.
	Activities are conducted by direct teaching, often in a "drill" format.
	Activities are adult-prescribed, rather than child-selected.
Motivational strategy	Incentive systems with extensive sources of motivation—token-economy systems.
Grouping	Homogeneous grouping dominates.
Scheduling	Brisk-paced program is presented on a "tight" schedule ("clock-bound").
	Blocks of time are short, with all children in a group staying "on task" throughout the lesson.
Assessment of children	Instructional levels are sequenced. Initial instructional levels are diagnosed by formal evaluation. As children meet the objectives at a given level, they progress to the next "rung on the instructional ladder."

Program Evaluation

A program is seen as successful if children have achieved specific learnings, which are often academic (a preparation for later school learnings).

Some constructivist models are based on the Montessori-type program and are often referred to as the "structured-environment" or "pre-pared-environment approach" (Bissell, 1973), the "sensory-cognitive model" (Mayer, 1971), and "cognitive-interactionist" (D. Ellis, 1977). Other constructivist models follow Piagetian theory and are referred to as "structured-cognitive pro-grams" (Bissell, 1973), the "verbal-cognitive model" (Mayer, 1971), "cognitive-interactionist" (D. Ellis, 1977), and "constructivist" (DeVries & Kohlberg, 1987). Still another constructivist model bases its theory on that of Piaget, Erikson, and Werner and is referred to as the "develop-mental-interaction approach" (Biber, 1977). Table 2-3 presents a synopsis of the three com-ponents of the constructivist model. Additional information on specific programs is located in Appendix 1.

Differences Within a Theory.   Models that derive their program rationale from the same theoretical base often differ in many essential ways because some elements of theory get dis-carded and other parts are added. For example, Forman and Fosnot (1982) analyzed six Piagetian programs in relationship to four propositions that undergird Piagetian theory. Each of these six programs focused on these propositions in a different way in its pedagogical design. Under the behavioral-environmental theoretical umbrella, the Behavioral Analysis Program of Project Follow Through focuses on a set of nar-row goals (Bushell, 1973), in comparison with the goals set forth by Bijou (1976).

Within-theory differences also occur in model programs because of the ages of children served. On the one hand, Honig and Brill (1970) used the sensory motor stage theory of Piaget to enhance the development of infants during their first year of life. On the other hand, the Early Childhood Education Project (Sigel, Secrist, & Forman, 1973) in Buffalo, New York, used Piaget-ian theory on representational knowledge (not-ing real "things" can be represented in two- and three-dimensional forms) as the pedagogical component for 2- and 3-year-old children.

When more than one theoretical base is combined in a model program, the pedagogical design differs from single-base programs. For example, Biber's (M. Day, 1977) initial foundation for the Bank Street Program was the educational philosophy of John Dewey. Later, Piaget's and Erikson's psychological theories were used to give a firmer foundation for the Bank Street Pro-gram's pedagogical component. In fact, Biber (1984) questions the use of one theory as the foundation for practice. She calls for a broader theoretical base achieved by combinations of theories that have a common ideological base but differ in substantive ways.

Current Thinking.   Development of program models slowed by the 1980s because of cutbacks in federal funds. For the most part, program designers worked to keep funds for their existing programs although they continued to make pro-gram modifications based on their research. A few new program initiatives occurred in the 1980s. These newer approaches seemed con-cerned with specific populations in our diverse society, such as Hale-Benson's (1982, 1986) *African American Early Childhood Education Pro-gram,* and with promoting more caring among diverse groups, such as Carlsson-Paige and Levin's (1985) "peace education curriculum" and Derman-Sparks and A.B.C. Task Force's (1989) *Anti-Bias Curriculum.*

Summary of Programmatic Research

In the 1960s, many early childhood programs were designed to break the cycle of poverty. It was assumed that family poverty led to scholastic failure and to subsequent poverty as an adult. Many types of models were tried and compared. Some of these early programs were thought to develop the whole child, but most were designed to correct perceived language, perceptual, and conceptual deficits. Proponents of academically

Table 2-3　Constructivist Model

Psychophilosophical Component

Based primarily on the theories of Piaget and Vygotsky.

Considers children a product of heredity and environment.

Describes development as occurring when a person's self-organization (denoted by a stage that is qualitatively different from other stages) is challenged to an optimal degree by experiential events.

Administrative Component

Housing	Roomy environment is designed to give children opportunities to be actively involved. "Learning centers" are more defined than in the maturational model, but children's interaction among learning centers is encouraged.
Equipment	Multidimensional materials encourage exploration and problem solving and are arranged in a way to convey the idea of a conceptual order.
	Children's needs for concrete and representational materials are considered.
Staff	Arrange activities that challenge the current level of development. At times, the adult is active (giving new challenges); at other times, the adult is passive (waiting for the child's new learnings to be stabilized). Adults often emphasize language that accompanies children's developing concepts.
	Plan and guide children toward self-discipline.

Pedagogical Component

Activities	Emphasis is placed on the heuristics of learning (e.g., problem-solving strategies, elaboration skills, questioning techniques); academic content, often presented in units or themes, is seen as a means to an end, not an end in itself.
	Planned activities are provided, and children are encouraged to be actively involved. Adults interact in ways to help structure children's activities (e.g., ask open-ended questions).
	Activities are adult-arranged for their potential to engage and challenge; children select among the activities.
Motivational strategy	Intrinsic motivation (e.g., epistemic curiosity).
Grouping	Heterogeneous grouping dominates; much individual work.
Scheduling	Sequenced activities are thought to aid children's temporal concepts; however, there is built-in flexibility.
	Large blocks of time are provided so that children may explore.
Assessment of children	Progress is noted if thinking skills change (if a child moves to a more advanced stage of development).

Program Evaluation

A program is seen as successful if children progress to higher stages of development in terms of Piaget's theory (e.g., physical knowledge, logicomathematical knowledge, spatiotemporal knowledge, social knowledge, representation).

oriented programs argued that their programs were most important in enhancing intellectual and school achievement. Discovery, or informal method, supporters saw social skills and autonomy as areas of major importance to young children. Taking a midpoint view were those who looked to Piagetian theory as a basis of curriculum design. These programs tried to influence children's thinking and processing skills. Programs were also extended upward (e.g., Follow Through) and downward (e.g., infant and toddler programs).

Now, two decades later, researchers are seeking the link between short-, mid-, and long-term effects. The model for linking the effects is as follows:

1. Children from impoverished families who attend a quality preschool program are better prepared for school cognitively and affectively.

2. This preparedness results in greater school success (fewer grade retentions and less need for special education placements).

3. This greater success in school leads to greater life success (lower rates of delinquency, teenage pregnancy, and welfare usage, and higher rates of school completion). Table 2-4 presents a summary of the research on compensatory education models of the 1960s and 1970s.

The two themes dominating early childhood special education studies prior to the mid-1980s were the efficacy of early intervention and the use of the "mainstreamed" environment. With the passage of P.L. 99–457 in 1986, the social context, especially the family, was included in the studies of early intervention. Table 2-5 presents a summary of the findings from major studies on early childhood special education.

To summarize, examination of program effectiveness does not indicate that one program base is more effective than others. All were effective at least in the short-term on cognitive func-

tioning, and all had some lasting benefits (Karweit, 1993). Early efficacy studies on intervention seem promising. Integration programs are successful when the articulated program base emphasizes the importance of accepting diversity (C. Peck, Furman, & Helmstetter, 1993). Family-centered approaches will be fully implemented as the next step (McCollum & Maude, 1993).

Programmatic research has some problems. Research problems are a major reason for the lack of definitive answers as to the effects of different early childhood programs. The research's major shortcomings include assessment of program implementation, inadequate measuring instruments, establishment of comparable experimental and control groups, and limitations in interpretation of data. Attrition rates have minimized the effectiveness of many longitudinal studies (Cooley, 1975; Fewell & Vadasky, 1987; Guralnick, 1988; Meisels & Wasik, 1990; Powell & Sigal, 1991). Much of the research has so many shortcomings that it is virtually uninterpretable (Seitz, Apfel, & Efron, 1976).

Aside from methodological problems, perhaps even the idea of comparing early childhood models has its limitations. Outcome measures were narrow and thus favored some models over others (House, Glass, McLean, & Walker, 1978). B. Hanson (1973) argues that researchers should not be testing models by comparing them. She believes that researchers should test each model by manipulating various parameters within the model (e.g., small group vs. large group). P. Goodman (1982) suggests that drawing conclusions on positive effects of preschool programs is questionable, considering that available data primarily come from high-quality programs such as the Ypsilanti study.

More research is needed to study the relationship between process variables (e.g., teacher behavior, child behavior, classroom environment) and child outcomes, to assess curriculum areas other than reading and mathematics, to measure specific rather than global achievement, and to develop more assessment devices

Table 2-4 Summary of Research on Compensatory Education: Models of the 1960s and 1970s

Single-Project Research Results

Cognitive functioning (as measured by IQ tests) for participants was immediately sizable but diminished throughout the elementary years (Berrueta-Clement et al., 1984; Gray, Ramsey, & Klaus, 1982; Irvine, 1982; McKey et al., 1985; Westinghouse Learning Corporation, 1969).

Participants had fewer grade repetitions, fewer special education placements, and more high school completions (Berrueta-Clement et al., 1984; Gray et al., 1982; Irvine, 1982; McKey et al., 1985).

Participants were more likely to be employed as adults (Berrueta-Clement et al., 1984).

Participants had fewer arrests (Berrueta-Clement et al., 1984).

Achievement differences for participants were minimal and tended to fade out (Berrueta-Clement et al., 1984; Gray et al., 1982; Westinghouse Learning Corporation, 1969).

When Gray et al.'s (1982) data were analyzed by gender, the program benefited girls more than boys.

Curriculum Comparison Studies

Head Start Planned Variation Study (Smith, 1975).

All children who participated scored higher on IQ tests and other cognitive measures than nonparticipants.

Children in constructivists models scored better on IQ tests than children in other models.

Children in behaviorist models scored better on recognition of letters and numbers than children in other models.

Children who were called "less ready" did better in directive models, whereas "more competent" children did better in less directive models.

Louisville Experiment (Miller & Dyer, 1975).

Immediate effects on cognitive functioning were greater for the more didactic programs, but stable effects (more than 4 years) were in noncognitive areas.

Different effects were found on the different preschool models for boys (e.g., boys in the Montessori program did better on achievement tests later in the elementary school).

Curriculum Demonstration Project (Karnes, Shwedel, & Williams, 1983).

No one preschool model was superior in effects.

Positive effects of all models faded.

Three Preschool Curriculum Models (Schweinhart, Weikart, & Larner, 1986).

All models had positive academic results.

Table 2-5   Summary of Research on Early Childhood Special Education

Efficacy of Early Intervention

Intervention is powerful during the first 3 years of life (Guralnick, 1989).

Secondary handicaps may not occur if early intervention remediates a primary handicap (M. Hanson & Lynch, 1989).

Intervention services improve the developmental status of the child (Meisels, 1985; Schweinhart & Weikart, 1985)

Early intervention reduces the need for special education programs later (Barnett & Escobar, 1990).

Benefits of Mainstreaming

Social interaction between children with disabilities and children who are developing normally requires teacher planning and teaching interaction to be effective (Guralnick, 1990).

Social interactions benefit children with disabilities (Jenkins, Speltz, & Odom, 1985) and nonmainstreamed children (Strain, Hoyson, & Jamieson, 1985).

Family Involvement

Studies of intervention directed to the infant/toddler alone have not yielded clear results (Simeonsson & Bailey, 1990).

Intervention with infants/toddlers is much more likely when a family's needs are met and family members take an active role in the intervention process (Guralnick, 1989).

for the affective domain. Many question IQ and achievement as the most important child outcomes (Hauser-Cram, 1990; Raver & Zigler, 1991; Zigler & Berman, 1983). As those interested in education reflect on past and plan future research, they must also remember that statistically significant differences cannot necessarily be equated with educational or social significance. L. Shepard (1991) has voiced the age-old concern that evaluation often inappropriately drives the curriculum.

OBSTACLES IN DEVELOPING PROGRAM GOALS

Since the beginning of formal education, various conceptual frameworks have been proposed. In the 1960s, leading psychologists and educators were encouraged to apply conceptual curriculum alternatives in programs for young children. Programmatic research was generated from these diverse psychophilosophical positions. Although three major psychophilosophical positions (maturational, behavioral-environmental, and constructivist) were identified, today the diversity is, to a great extent, reduced to two program orientations: (a) to nurture the total development of the young child (primarily the constructivist position) and (b) to help the child master cultural literacy demands (primarily the behavioral-environmental position).

The constructivist and behavioral-environmental approaches are radically different in terms of their perceived aims of education and in the curriculum content and methodology deemed necessary to achieve these aims. On the one hand, the constructivists believe that the primary goal of education is to develop individuals who are "creative, inventive, and discoverers" and that the secondary goal of education is to develop critical minds that question rather than merely accept information (Ripple & Rockcastle, 1964). And, to help children "want to know" (Elkind, 1989), teachers choose curriculum materials that are real and relevant for the children's present life and with general future needs in mind, as opposed to specific future school content. These materials are also matched to the level of each child's total developmental abilities.

The behavioral-environmentalists, on the other hand, believe that the primary aim of education is to help children achieve the facts and skills possessed by culturally literate adults, such as expounded in *Nation at Risk: The Full Account* (National Commission on Excellence in Education, 1984), *The Closing of the American Mind* (A.

Bloom, 1987), and *Cultural Literacy: What Every American Needs to Know* (Hirsch, 1987). This "derived" type of knowledge (Elkind, 1989) is then analyzed to determine the level of mental ability that is required for its mastery. (Other aspects of development are at least secondary to mental development and may be totally ignored.) Children are then ability-matched to the curriculum. Learning consists of the acquisition of a set of isolated skills (often the three R's) accomplished primarily by direct teaching and reinforcement. Elkind (1989) says that, with this approach, children come to "know what we want" (p. 116).

Lack of Consensus in Program Goals

The main issue has centered on curriculum content and teaching methodology. From the 1960s until the mid-1980s, early childhood programs moved away from their conceptual heritage of the more constructivist approach toward the more behaviorist approach. The Educational Research Service survey provides data on this trend. The survey found that 22% of principals surveyed have "academics" (skills and achievement) as the primary focus of their kindergarten programs and that 63% have "preparation" (academic and social readiness) as the primary focus. Only 8% have developmental goals as their primary focus. In 85% of the kindergartens, principals reported that their program goals ignored two or more of these areas of development—physical, social, and emotional; conversely, cognitive development was not ignored in any of the programs (Cheever & Ryder, 1986). A somewhat similar trend occurred in pre-kindergarten programs. Over half of these programs had a narrow, cognitive focus (Marx & Seligson, 1987). Some Head Start programs had moved away from Zigler's conception of social competence, a holistic view of development (Raver & Zigler, 1991). All early childhood professionals have seen many privately funded early childhood programs that have an academic focus too. Even

family child care was found to use a great deal of "structured time" (Innes, Woodman, Banspach, Thompson, & Inwald, 1982).

To summarize, the traditional early childhood program, with its holistic view of the child and its play orientation, has become, at least in many places, more and more academic; that is, it has become difficult to distinguish the early childhood curriculum from that of the later elementary grades and secondary schools. The following practices illustrate this trend:

1. Curricular content is often adult-prescribed, at least 1 year more difficult (traditional first-grade curriculum presented at the kindergarten level) and divided into separate subjects, with each subject taught for a prescribed number of minutes.

2. Activities are conducted via paper-and-pencil tasks in workbooks and worksheets, referred to as "seatwork" in the elementary grades and aptly named because the tasks require a "sit still" attention span.

3. The focus is on the academic product, the achievement of prescribed objectives, as assessed by standardized tests.

Causes of Trend.   Elkind (1986) has described political, social, and economic pressures as responsible for this trend. Until the 1960s, early childhood education was out of the spotlight—and therefore insulated from outside pressures. At this time, three pressures converged, putting early childhood programs in the center arena. First, in the late 1950s, education was criticized when the Soviet Union launched *Sputnik I* and moved ahead in the space race. Achievement test results raised concerns as early as World War II and especially following *Sputnik*. Progressives became the scapegoat for all educational concerns (Goodlad, Klein, & Novotney, 1973). Second, according to Elkind, the civil rights of minorities had become an issue. Minority children were experiencing inferior-quality education in segregated schools. Some educators rationalized, however, that the schools were providing sound education and that the problem was with the minority student who was not prepared for school. Hence, Head Start and other early childhood programs were funded with the idea of young minority children "catching up" with their middle-class cohorts. Many of the curriculum initiatives of the 1960s were based on the so-called deficit model designed for quick cognitive success in the three R's (a behaviorist view) although some programs had a constructivist orientation. Third, the conception of the **competent** child was fostered by the emotions of these political and social movements. According to Elkind, no new data surfaced that suggested changes in the competence of children, but rather the "selection and interpretation" of certain theories supported notions of competence (e.g., J. Bruner's *The Process of Education*, J. McV. Hunt's *Intelligence and Experience*, and B. S. Bloom's *Stability and Change in Human Characteristics*). Furthermore, the competent-child idea was in keeping with the changing lifestyles of families (especially working mothers) who needed to believe that their children were competent to withstand the stresses and even profit from early education, including the academically oriented programs. And finally, some people thought that children's competence had grown as a result of the influence of high technology.

Associated Issues. Outgrowths of the controversy centering on the academic curriculum content and expository teaching methods are three associated issues: age of entrance, placement and retention practices, and length of the daily session. These practices were thought to be pragmatic ways of protecting some young children from a too-difficult academic program.

Age of Entrance. Some proponents of the more academic early childhood programs believe that raising entrance age is the easiest way to handle the problem of the "not ready" child. Some studies did show that older kindergarten children do

better than younger kindergarten children in initial academic achievement (Karweit, 1988; Uphoff & Gilmore, 1986). This is called the **birth date effect.** Thus, the trend is toward moving back enrollment dates. For a number of reasons, however, later entrance is not really a viable policy:

1. A more comprehensive review of the research shows that younger children's problems are not as severe as once thought. Major differences in older and younger children are seen only in those who are below the 25th percentile. Furthermore, the differences in achievement have totally disappeared by third grade (L. Shepard & Smith, 1986).

2. Holding back a child who is "ready" may result in negative consequences (Proctor, Black, & Feldhusen, 1986).

3. Raising entrance age by 3 months denies schooling for 1 year to one fourth of age-eligible children. The increased number of children in preschool services results in an additional burden to the already short supply of available spaces for pre-kindergarten children and in an additional year of child care expenses for families whose children do not attend government-sponsored programs.

4. A group with any entry age always has younger and older children. The effects of age are not due to absolute age, but rather to the relative position of a child within the group.

5. Parents are discouraged from enrolling their age-eligible children because of their anxiety over the difficulty of the program (Katz, Raths, & Torres, 1987). Unfortunately, being the oldest does not ensure success.

6. The "gift of time" (as delayed entrance is supposed to ensure) denies kindergarten to children who could benefit the most from an appropriate curriculum and the social interaction with age-mates.

Placement and Retention Practices. Again, in an effort to protect the not-ready child from the academic program, screening practices, popularized by the Gesell Institute, are used to determine placement. If a child scores low on the screening test and/or other measures, the age-eligible child is said to be at risk for failure in the regular kindergarten program. And the early childhood program provides one or both of these options:

1. The child is placed in a pre-kindergarten, usually called **developmental kindergarten** (a program with traditional kindergarten curriculum content and teaching methodology) the first year and then is promoted to kindergarten (an academic program) the second year and to the first grade at age 7 if successful. In a few cases, the at-risk child may test out of the academic kindergarten after the year in the developmental program, but this is rare because the more abstract academic skills were not taught in the developmental kindergarten.

2. If no developmental kindergartens are available, the parents are asked to keep their child out of kindergarten for another year. Because the child is expected to mature during the calendar year, this practice is referred to as the **gift of time** for the child.

These placement policies have many flaws, such as the following: (a) The tests and the testing process have many problems, as described in Chapter 9; (b) children who attended developmental kindergarten show almost no advantage over equally at-risk children who were placed in the kindergarten, and emotional costs are associated with staying back (L. Shepard & Smith, 1986); (c) children who are given the "gift of time" may have the same disadvantages as the later-entrance child, except these age-eligible at-risk children will be even older; and (d) developmental placement often implies failure to parents and to the children themselves before schooling begins.

Testing, with all its problems, is often conducted in the spring of the kindergarten year to determine whether children will be retained in

kindergarten, will enter a pre-first-grade class (often called a **transitional class,** a form of retention), or will be promoted to first grade. The academic kindergarten programs have increased the risk of kindergarten failure. The common remedy for dealing with low achievement in the elementary school is retention, and this trend now seems to be supported by kindergarten teachers. For example, M. Smith and Shepard (1988) found that teachers think student careers should be determined by "competence" (or "readiness"), not by "social promotion," and they act according to these beliefs. Other reasons for retention are children's general cognitive abilities, behavior, gender, socioeconomic status (SES), and minority status (Mantzicopoulos, Morrison, Hinshaw, & Corte, 1989). Retention policies, including placement in the transitional classes, have these problems:

1. No academic advantages seem to be gained by retention. For example, L. Shepard and Smith (1987) found no differences at the end of first grade between children who had been retained and those in matched control groups who were recommended for retention but not retained. Another study found that transitional-class children fall below, or at best perform equally to, children eligible for transitional class who were placed in a regular classroom (Gredler, 1984). In an effort to explain why retention does not work, M. Smith and Shepard's (1987) studies have led them to conclude that retention lowers expectations of parents and teachers and thus decreases the possibility that retained children will attain their potential.

2. Many teachers believe that early retention does not have the same negative effects as later retention. Contradictory evidence is found in the literature. Some educators believe that retention removes stress, but in reality it produces trauma (L. Shepard & Smith, 1987). For example, in one study over one fourth of the children interviewed would not admit to having been retained. Children rated the idea of retention most stress-

ful, next to blindness and the death of a parent (Byrnes & Yamamoto, 1985).

3. Retention is associated with misconduct. Moran (1989) believes that retention and misconduct have a synergistic effect; that is, aggressive students are more apt to be retained than nonaggressive students, and retained students are more apt to become delinquent than promoted students.

4. The drop-out rate of retained students increases significantly, as compared with that of promoted students (Schuyler & Turner, 1986/87).

5. Retention brands students as failures, and minorities, low-income children, and males are disproportionately represented among children retained (National Association of Early Childhood Specialists in State Departments of Education, 1987).

Length of the Daily Session.   Session length of kindergartens is only an associated issue when the all-day kindergarten is seen as a tool to enhance the learning time for academic subjects. Learning cannot be rushed. Certainly, one does not make an inappropriate curriculum appropriate by simply extending the length of instruction.

The "Backlash" Effect.   Raising entrance ages, placing at-risk kindergarten children in developmental kindergartens, retaining kindergarten children by having them repeat kindergarten or attend a transitional class, and increasing the length of the day and thus the length of time spent on teaching/learning academic subjects were all designed to protect the "immature," the "unready," or the "at-risk" child, but in reality, these practices exacerbate the problem of academic curriculum content and didactic teaching methods. Once these immature children (by whatever name they are called) are no longer in the kindergarten program, curriculum planners and teachers are given license to further increase the academic demands of the curriculum. As demands increase, however, even the

brightest children may be injuriously stressed. Any given group always contains some less mature children. What happens to them—even later school entrance ages imposed? more stringent placement requirements? an even longer day of academic training? These practices (the associated issues) are, at best, only short-term solutions for educators who want to match the child to the curriculum, rather than the curriculum to the child. This impermanence has left many educators asking the most serious long-term question: What price will our young children and their families pay for "miseducation"? *Miseducation* is the term by which Elkind (1987b) refers to this academic push.

Initial Professional Reactions.   Many educators have been concerned about program issues. Teachers are reporting **philosophy-reality** conflicts—that is, discrepancies between their beliefs and required instructional practices (Hatch & Freeman, 1988a). Teachers report that they have "little control over what they are being asked to do," and this reality conflicts with "their views of what is best for children" (Hills, 1987, p. 266).

The source of the problem is always identified as parents, administrators, or legislators (Seefeldt & Barbour, 1988). Today's parents are influenced by "toys" that promise early achievement, publications about raising smarter children, and other parents' claims of their children's achievements (Simmons & Brewrer, 1988). Parents may even be misled by their own child's knowledge of "bits and pieces" (e.g., ability to sing the alphabet song at age 3). Thus, parents insist that their child be taught more—especially expecting their child to learn to read before first grade. And, in their focus on cursory academic skills, they fail to see how other aspects of the curriculum (e.g., the arts, block building, dramatic play) contribute to the overall learning experience (Hills, 1987; Simmons & Brewer, 1988).

Administrators are also pressuring early childhood teachers. In some cases, this attitude is a result of their lack of knowledge about young children (Schweinhart, Koshel, & Bridgmann, 1987). Administrators are also influenced from the "outside" by public demand for more stringent educational standards (which are often measured by children's achievement on standardized tests) and from the "inside" by pressures from primary teachers who, in turn, are feeling pressures because of escalating elementary school standards.

As previously discussed, social and political critics have exerted pressures concerning the nation's educational system. During the last decade, at least two major publications have outlined new demands and reforms for education: the National Commission on Excellence in Education's *A Nation at Risk* (1983, 1984) and the Carnegie Forum on Education and the Economy's *A Nation Prepared* (1986). Demands such as these have been translated by state legislative bodies into legislation for policy statements that dictate when children may be legally enrolled in public school programs, what they should learn, and how they should be taught and assessed. Although everyone wants excellence, unfortunately most of the legislative planning is essentially a top-down experience (Evans, 1982). And this lack of attention to young children's unique learning styles, to a great extent, is the origin of program issues on the contemporary scene.

Early childhood teachers themselves are also unwittingly responsible for the academic trend. For example, teachers often *say* young children learn best by direct encounters with materials and events and then, in practice, eschew the dramatic play, music, and art materials in favor of workbooks/worksheets. Durkin (1987) reported that most teachers said reading should *not* be taught in kindergarten but considered the drill work in phonics "readiness," not "reading." As noted, teachers have been in favor of raising entrance age, screening for placement, retention, and full-day kindergarten for academic purposes because they wanted to relieve the stress placed on at-risk children and to free themselves from accountability for children's academic achievement, as measured by their groups' assessment scores.

Professional associations began to see the need to take a stand on the issues. Thus, position statements were issued on behalf of young children. Because pre-first-grade reading instruction was one early academic issue, the following was one of the first statements issued:

> Early Childhood and Literacy Development Committee of the International Reading Association. (1986). *Literacy development and pre-first grade: A joint statement of concerns about present practices in pre-first grade reading instruction and recommendations for improvement in conjunction with Association for Childhood Education International, Association for Supervision and Curriculum Development, National Association for the Education of Young Children, National Association of Elementary School Principals, National Councils of Teachers of English.* Newark, DE: Author.

In July 1984, the NAEYC's governing board created a commission for the purpose of developing a position statement on appropriate education for young children. The commission, chaired by Bernard Spodek, worked from July 1984 to July 1985. A statement was first published in 1986 and expanded in 1987 under this title:

> Bredekamp, S. (Ed.). (1987). *Developmentally appropriate practice in early childhood programs serving children from birth through age 8* (exp. ed.). Washington, DC: National Association for the Education of Young Children.

The statement was widely read, and soon the term **developmentally appropriate practice (DAP)** appeared everywhere in speeches and written materials. Other position statements include the following:

> Association for Childhood Education International. (1986). *When parents of kindergartners ask "why."* Wheaton, MD: Author.

Association for Supervision and Curriculum Development. (1988). *A resource guide to public school early childhood programs.* Alexandria, VA: Author.

National Association of Early Childhood Specialists in State Departments of Education. (1987). *Unacceptable trends in kindergarten entry and placement: A position statement of the NAECS/SDE.* Lincoln, NE: Author.

National Association of Elementary School Principals. (1990). *Standards for quality programs for young children.* Alexandria, VA: Author.

National Association of State Boards of Education. (1988). *Right from the start: A report of the NASBE task force on early childhood education.* Alexandria, VA: Author.

National Black Child Development Institute. (1987). *Safeguards: Guidelines for establishing programs for 4-year-olds in the public schools.* Washington, DC: Author.

Besides these, numerous state organizations have issued position statements.

Position statements are not only concerned with curriculum content and pedagogy. Readiness as **gatekeeping** (used for placement and retention decisions) is also of major concern (R. Hitz & Richter, 1993; Kagan, 1992; Willer & Bredekamp, 1990). Katz (1991a) has pointed out that even when goals are appropriate, between 20% and 30% of all children will "need some systematic help" (p. 65). Concern about readiness as gatekeeping prompted a position statement on this aspect of DAP (NAEYC, 1990). Other position statements have been published regarding assessment, as discussed in Chapter 9.

More Professional Reactions.   Although early childhood care and education has traditionally drawn from studies in child development and although it has been almost a decade since the position statements on DAP were issued, a lack of consensus remains. One source of the problem in consensus is that behavioral approaches have been in early childhood for almost four decades. Elkind (1988) states that behaviorist ideas are even more entrenched in elementary and secondary education. According to Elkind, the behavioral version of learning and knowledge is reflected in Hirsch's (1987) and A. Bloom's (1987) writings. As discussed earlier, a top-down perspective and standardized test content and format have influenced early childhood practice. Furthermore, many public school early childhood teachers had their elementary teaching certificates endorsed when kindergartens became universal and even mandated and when programs for even younger children became part of public education. Many of these "retrained" teachers carried their elementary practices into the early childhood programs. Some early childhood teachers were trained in college programs using the more academic approaches. These teachers are simply finding a change to DAP difficult (W. Ayers, 1992). Similarly, public school administrators, who often do not have teaching experience in early childhood programs, are not familiar with DAP or may find it "foreign" to their training.

A growing voice against DAP has been a group of early childhood educators who call themselves the **reconceptualists.** At the Bergano Curriculum Theory and Classroom Practices Conference in 1989 and at the Annual Meeting of the American Educational Research Association in 1990, these reconceptualists began to take issue with DAP. Two decades earlier, this group had begun to move away from traditional behavioral objectives, planning, and evaluation to an emphasis on a political, cultural, gender, and other social issues orientation. The reconceptualists criticize child development as a conceptual basis for early childhood care and education and, more particularly, DAP as the guiding construct for the program base for early childhood. They refer to DAP as a "well intentioned white liberal or progressive education" trend (Swadener & Kessler, 1991a, p. 88). Table 2-6 contrasts the views of the reconceptualists and the proponents of DAP.

Table 2-6   Different Views of Reconceptualists and DAP Proponents

Reconceptualists' Views	DAP Proponents' Views
Unlike elementary education, early childhood care and education relies too much on the principles of developmental psychology and child development (Bloch, 1991). Walsh (1991) thinks DAP does not take into account all the recent research on children's learning processes.	Psychological theories have long been used in early childhood care and education as a source of program base. Constructivists have used the theories of Piaget (DeVries & Kohlberg, 1987; Fosnot, 1989) and Vygotsky (1978). Other theories used in early childhood programs include Erikson's (1950, 1951) psychosocial theory, Skinner's (1953) learning theory, and Bandura's (1977) constructs.
DAP leads to a belief in fixed stages and in the individual totally separated from his or her social context (Kessler, 1991b; Walsh, 1991).	DAP is based on *both* age and individual appropriateness (Bredekamp & Rosegrant, 1992).
Reliance on child development causes educators to ignore gender, politics, culture, and historical context (Kessler, 1991a; Swadener & Kessler, 1991). Jipson (1991) thinks DAP considers only one cultural view without regard to cultural issues.	Early childhood programs have served children of lower socioeconomic status (SES) throughout their history (see Chapter 1). The relationship of DAP and culture can be noted in the use of Bronfenbrenner's (1979) ecological perspective and also in the writings of Bowman (1992).
DAP does not prepare children for life in a democracy (Kessler, 1991a).	Dewey was long associated with early childhood programs (Greenberg, 1987, 1992; Hendrick, 1992). Dewey's philosophy was overwhelmed by Thorndike's ideas (Levin, 1991).
DAP focuses on the "how" rather than the "what" of teaching (Walsh, 1991).	DAP is a framework for instruction (Bredekamp & Rosegrant, 1992). Curriculum guidelines are suggested (National Association for the Education of Young Children & the National Association of Early Childhood Specialists in State Departments of Education, 1991).
DAP does not have adult guidance. Teachers prepare the environment and then stand back (Kessler, 1991a; Swadener & Kessler, 1991). Teachers see DAP as chaotic (Jipson, 1991).	DAP includes both content and process, states that programs must develop their own goals, and uses Vygotsky's ideas of scaffolding (Bredekamp & Rosegrant, 1992). Many have refuted the idea that, in DAP, one prepares the environment and then stands back (Burts et al., 1992), never uses direct instruction (Fowell & Lawton, 1992), and ignores academics (Bredekamp & Rosegrant, 1992).

Professionals employed by the NAEYC began to recognize the misunderstandings about DAP, as well as the "thoughtful criticism" (Bredekamp & Rosegrant, 1992, p. 4). Because of these problems in interpretation of DAP, *Reaching Potentials: Appropriate Curriculum and Assessment for Young Children* (Vol. 1) was issued (Bredekamp & Rosegrant, 1992).

Research studies are also looking at DAP. Beginning in 1988, researchers at Louisiana State University studied the effects of DAP and developmentally inappropriate practices (DIP) on the behavior and achievement of young children (Charlesworth, Hart, Burts, & DeWolf, 1993). These researchers found that all kindergarten children, regardless of age, experienced more stress in DIP than in DAP classrooms. They also found that DIP appears to cause the most stress in low-SES children, African American children, and males. All children, those in both DAP and DIP classrooms, experienced stress when administered standardized achievement tests. Using "teach-to-the-test" instruction in DIP classrooms resulted in depressed achievement for low-SES students, as indicated by scores on California Achievement Tests and by grades on report cards as compared with achievement of low-SES students in DAP classrooms. Similarly, Marcon (1992) found that 4-year-olds in DAP classrooms demonstrated the greatest mastery of basic skills when compared with children in DIP programs and programs that were "in-between" on the DIP and DAP continuum. Reutzel (1992) found that children learn the alphabetic principle through reading and writing in authentic situations and thus did not need to learn the alphabetic principle by the traditional letter-a-week format. Schweinhart, Weikart, and Larner's (1986) earlier research also supports DAP practices with low-SES children.

Finally, some professionals believe that the DAP issue could be resolvable if extended. As previously discussed, Spodek (1991a) believes that program planning must include the developmental component but also must go beyond to the cultural and knowledge dimensions in order to be educationally worthwhile. Katz (1991a) calls for a curriculum that is intellectually oriented (but not academically oriented) and that uses informal methods—a curriculum known as *open education* in the 1960s. Fowell and Lawton (1992) also express their concern about the narrow definition of DAP. They believe that the Early Childhood Program at the University of Wisconsin-Madison is really appropriate because it is based on the theories of Ausubel, Bruner, and Piaget. All their components are DAP (by the criteria of the NAEYC), except that the program uses "formal instruction" conducted in a way different from that of traditional academic instruction and for a relatively short block of time. Thus, they believe that the narrow definition of DAP is dangerous because "we may box our discipline into a position from which it may take years, or even decades, to advance to a less circumspect view of the organization of early learning" (p. 71).

Lack of Quality in Early Childhood Programs

Quality is directly related to the development and fulfillment of program goals. When quality is lacking, automatic constraints are placed on program goals for services to children and their families. Administrators and teachers who are not well trained in early childhood programs cannot develop, implement, and evaluate program goals. Lack of appropriate housing and equipment directly hampers the implementation of goals too. The bottom line, however, seems to be an increase in funding. Adequate funding goes hand in hand with upgrading the qualifications and preventing undue turnover rates of early childhood care and education staff and is directly related to quality in housing and equipping. (These topics are discussed in detail in later chapters.)

IMPLEMENTING THE PROGRAM

After carefully considering all the factors that determine a program base, the person or board must develop a preference for a particular view. How a program base is chosen and implemented depends on the program's organization. In small, privately owned programs, the director (who is often the owner as well) usually makes the decision about the program goals and implements the program. In larger programs, the director may present his or her views to the board of directors for approval, or the director may work with a board of advisors in planning goals; in either case, the director implements the program. Boards of large corporations that either provide services to a large center or to centers at several sites or that provide management services only (e.g., Bright Horizons) make all major program decisions, and the directors are then answerable to their boards for implementation.

The "ideal" program base is the one that best suits the needs of the children and families they serve. Personal beliefs, whether articulated or maintained as a preconscious set of values, influence decision making. Spodek (1988) has discussed how **implicit theories** affect teachers' professional behaviors. For starters, administrators need to think through questions pertaining to the pedagogical component of their own programs. They should ask themselves questions such as the following:

1. What are the goals and objectives of my early childhood program—to provide an environment conducive to the development of the whole child? to teach young children academic skills? to provide intensive instruction in areas of academic deficits and thinking skills? to develop creativity? to build a healthy self-concept? to spur self-direction in learning?

2. What provisions for children's individual differences are consistent with my program's goals? Should I expect the same or varying levels of achievement? Are individual differences acceptable in some or in all academic areas? in some or in all developmental areas (psychomotor, affective, cognitive)? Are activities child-chosen and appropriate to his or her own interest and developmental level, or staff-tailored to meet individual differences? Are activities presented for one or several learning styles?

3. What grouping strategy is in accord with my program's rationale—homogeneous (chronological age, mental age, achievement, interest) or heterogeneous groups? fixed or flexible? staff-determined or child-interest? large or small?

4. What schedule format is needed to facilitate my program's objectives—a full- or a half-day schedule? same session length for all children, or length of session tailored to each child's and/or parent's needs? a predetermined or flexible daily schedule based on children's interests?

Administrators must also consider questions pertaining to the operational components of the program, such as:

1. What staff roles are necessary to implement the learning environment as set forth in my program base—persons who dispense knowledge, resource persons, or persons who prepare the environment? persons who use positive or negative reinforcement? group leaders or individual counselors? academic content specialists or social engineers? persons who work almost exclusively with young children or who provide parent education?

2. What staff positions (director, teachers, volunteers) are needed to execute my program? What academic or experiential qualifications are required or desired? What type of orientation or in-service training is needed? What child-staff ratio is required?

3. What equipment and materials are required—equipment and materials that are self-correcting or that encourage creativeness? that are designed to stress one concept (color paddles) or many concepts (blocks)? that require substantial or minimal adult guidance? that are designed for group or individual use? that provide for concrete experiences or abstract thinking?

4. What physical arrangement is compatible with the goals of my program—differentiated or nondifferentiated areas for specific activities? fixed or flexible areas? outside area used primarily for learning or for recess? equipment and materials arranged for self-service by the child or for teacher distribution?

And then the crucial question must be answered: Do the answers have a supportable rationale? Relevant and irrelevant beliefs, appropriate and inappropriate values, and timely and outdated information can be recognized as one considers the alternatives. Bowman (1986) has stated that the tremendous increase of knowledge from interdisciplinary sources provides us with a rich base to plan for children, but it also encourages us to "tolerate faddism, quackism, and just plain foolishness" (p. 6).

EVALUATING THE PROGRAM

Administrators are held accountable for the programs under their leadership and direction. With a constant demand for excellence, evaluation has become one of the administrator's most significant responsibilities. Funding and legal sources require evaluation reports. Accreditation (self-evaluation) is based on standards set by the accrediting agencies, such as professional groups. Furthermore, the staff objectively and subjectively make judgments as they work in the program. Parents question program quality, and public interest in program value is heightened, especially on the part of taxpayers. Administrators must answer to each of these groups.

A discussion of evaluation leads to classification of the types of evaluation. Dopyera and Lay-Dopyera (1990) identified two types of evaluation: intuitive and formal. And they subdivided *formal* into objectives-based evaluation, standards-based evaluation, and evaluation research.

Intuitive Evaluation

Intuitive evaluation might be called a **personal construct** by a researcher or **practical knowledge** by others. **Intuitive evaluation** is an unexamined, internal map, or a notion about what constitutes the right way to achieve something. Unlike formal evaluation, which is planned, implemented, and analyzed, intuitive evaluation concerns how people survive on a minute-by-minute basis. Intuitive evaluation is used when a person chooses to take an umbrella to work because "it looks as if it may rain" or when a person seasons food because "it tastes as though it needs . . . "

Similarly, early childhood teachers and administrators have notions about their professional practice. Although these notions guide their day-to-day practice, they are difficult to articulate. These notions come to light when a clash occurs between one's own ideas or actions and those of another who is respected or when the outcomes of what one expects and what ensues differ.

Studies of intuitive evaluation are rather recent (Clark & Peterson, 1986; Katz, 1984; Spodek, 1987). Two points, however, seem to be established:

1. Early childhood educators take their book-learned knowledge and guided observations and integrate these with their values and practical knowledge. For example, Spodek (1987) states that **values** are (a) what we desire for children now and in the future and (b) practices that we believe are professionally ethical; and Elbaz (1983) identifies **practical knowledge** as knowledge integrated by each individual teacher from his or her theory-based knowledge, accumulated experience, and understanding of milieu and self.

2. Intuitive evaluation is important because educators must often make judgment calls so quickly that they do not have time to reflect on theory and empirical findings; thus, intuitive evaluation guides practice.

Formal Evaluation

Formal evaluation had its roots in concern over accountability to the funding agencies. With an increasing number of mandates for evaluation, the evaluation profession grew, and activities involving formal evaluation increased. Many educational endeavors required formal evaluation, such as the needs and demands for certain services (**needs assessment**); analysis of the components of a program, such as staff, curriculum, and materials (**program analysis**); and the effectiveness of a program as it relates to cost per child (**cost effectiveness**) or to positive changes in the child or family that affect society (**program impact**).

Administrators must determine the appropriate type of evaluation to serve their needs. Objectives-based and standards-based evaluation are both concerned with accountability. Evaluation research is concerned with the interplay of various aspects of a given program related to outcomes.

Objectives-Based Evaluation. **Objectives-based evaluation** is the most common form of formal evaluation. It focuses on what children achieve as a result of participation in a specific program. Thus, the criteria used for evaluation are program specific (developed by examining the program's goals/objectives). The analyses of evaluation data provide information on the degree to which program goals/objectives are met.

Evaluation may be conducted at two points in the program. **Formative evaluation** is used to determine the effectiveness of various aspects of the program (e.g., grouping practices) while program changes are still being made. **Summative evaluation** determines the effectiveness of the overall program at some ending point.

Standards-Based Evaluation. **Standards-based evaluation** is an appraisal of a program based on a set of standards (criteria) developed outside any specific program. These standards may be deemed worthwhile by a professional association (e.g., National Academy of Early Childhood Programs' Accreditation), the monitoring agency (e.g., Head Start Performance Objectives, licensing regulations for child care), or a researcher (e.g., *The Early Childhood Environment Rating Scale*).

Following are several standards-based evaluations:

1. *Day-Care Environmental Inventory.* The inventory was developed by E. Prescott (1975) and her associates. Prescott references the developmental stages defined by Erikson (1950)

and Cumming and Cumming (1967). Prescott's inventory includes an observational recording system for collecting information about children's behavior and physical space. The behavior schedule provides a description of the child's experiences within the larger setting of the center; each activity is described in terms of (a) whether it was within a free-choice or teacher-directed structure, (b) the physical setting in which the activity took place, (c) the equipment and props used, (d) the degree of mobility, (e) the people with whom the activity occurred, and (f) the teacher influence. The inventory provides a description of the center and its effects on children. The administrator/staff can then determine whether what they saw happening was what they wanted for the children. To use the inventory, trained evaluators are needed, several children must be observed for various periods of time under different situations, and computer analysis of data is required.

2. *Naturalistic Evaluation for Program Improvement.* The evaluation is built on the ecological perspective of Bronfenbrenner (1979) that one must examine not only the effects of program and staff on children but also the effects of children on program and staff (D. Day, Phyfe-Perkins, & Weinhaler, 1979). The evaluation is also based on the research of D. Day and Sheehan (1974). Day and Sheehan concluded that children's behavior in an early childhood program was a function of their interactions with three environmental factors: (a) the extent to which the staff had considered the importance of the physical environment and how it was arranged, (b) the use of materials, and (c) the amount and kind of teacher-child interactions. Children's natural behaviors during their day in the program are observed. Observations are made on 34 behaviors in seven areas: task involvement, cooperation, autonomy, verbal interaction, materials, maintenance, and consideration.

3. *The Early Childhood Environment Rating Scale (ECERS).* The scale was developed by

Harms and Clifford (1980), who see an early childhood program as an ecological system with more parts than just the individual within the program. ECERS is used to examine 37 attributes that cover seven areas of quality: personal care routines, furnishings and display, language/reasoning experiences, fine and gross motor activities, creative activities, social development, and adult needs. Ratings are given for each area, and a total rating can be calculated for each group. Scores on all the groups within a center may be compiled to get a quality score for a center. Kontos and Stevens (1985) field-tested ECERS. They noted that (a) directors saw ECERS useful for improvement of the center and for providing the focus of staff training, (b) staff began making changes, (c) staff resistance to change was minimized, and (d) staff liked the idea that "adult needs" must be met in quality programs.

4. *The Family Day-Care Rating Scale (FDCRS)*. The FDCRS was developed by Harms and Clifford (1989) and follows the same pattern as their ECERS. FDCRS is used to examine 32 attributes that cover six areas of quality: space and furnishings for care and learning, basic care, language and reasoning, learning activities, social development, and adult needs. Each item is described in four levels of quality: inadequate, minimal, good, and excellent. Eight "supplementary items" are provided when a child with special needs is included in the child care home.

5. *Infant/Toddler Environment Rating Scale (ITERS)*. The ITERS was developed by Harms, Cryer, and Clifford (1990) and follows the same pattern as their ECERS and FDCRS. The ITERS consists of 35 items for the assessment of the quality of center-based child care for children up to 30 months of age. These items are organized under seven categories: furnishings and display for children, personal care routines, listening, talking, learning activities, interaction programs structure, and adult needs. Each item is presented on a 7-point scale, with descriptors for 1 (inadequate), 3 (minimal), 5 (good), and 7

(excellent). ITERS items correspond with the Child Development Associate competency goals.

6. *The Instrument-Based Program Monitoring Information System (IPM) and Indicator Checklist for Child Care (IC)*. In most states, licensing workers make an on-site visit and prepare a summary of observations along with interpretive and evaluative comments. This is not only a laborious task for the licensing agency, but centers are also expected to be in total compliance for licensing. The IPM and IC were designed by Fiene (1985). The IPM is a system of assigning weights to items in the state's child care regulations so that scores reflect the relative importance of the regulations. The IC is a questionnaire or checklist that contains selected, predictive items (e.g, director qualifications, health appraisal of staff, adult-child ratios, hazard-free environment, nutrition, emergency contact information, medication, safety carrier, supervision of children, program observation) from the comprehensive instrument that a state uses in licensing. Not only does the IC increase the licensing agency's efficiency in checking centers, but the state's policy also may be made even more effective from a regulatory point of view (identifying the better quality programs as opposed to low-quality programs; Fiene, 1986a, 1986b).

Researchers have begun working on instruments needed for empirical studies of DAP. Different types of instruments have been developed to fit the researchers' investigations. For example, M. Hitz and Wright (1988) developed an instrument to note the degree of change in academic emphasis of early childhood programs (from DIP to DAP). Bryant, Clifford, and Peisner (1991) developed an instrument to determine teachers' knowledge and attitudes about DAP. Similarly, P. Oakes and Caruso (1990) measured teachers' attitudes about authority in the classroom. These researchers also developed observation instruments to confirm the "self-reports." Charlesworth, Hart, Burts, Thomasson, et al. (1993) thought of DIP and DAP on a continuum.

They used a Leikert-type scale and measured *Teachers Belief Statements* and a self-report of classroom practices called the *Instructional Activities Scale.* Their observation scale, *Checklist for Rating Developmentally Appropriate Practice in Kindergarten Classrooms,* rated practices in curriculum goals, teaching strategies, integrated curriculum, guidance of social-emotional development, motivation, evaluation, and transitions on a continuum from most DAP to most DIP. (Other standards-based assessments, such as licensing, certification, and accreditation, are discussed in Chapter 3.)

Evaluation Research.   Evaluation research examines how various aspects of a program impinge on outcomes for children or families. The purpose of such research is to better understand the interplay of variables. Researchers are concerned about all effects generated by program components; thus, they go beyond specific program goals/objectives and standards that have been deemed worthwhile. Evaluation research studies are often longitudinal, and all are rigorous in their research methodologies. Evaluation research studies on early childhood programs were discussed under "Summary of Programmatic Research" in this chapter.

An Important Consideration

Evaluation generates program changes mandated by external commands (e.g., regulatory agencies) and/or stimulated by internal visions or problems. The most meaningful evaluations are most often those stimulated by internal factors, rather than those resulting from external mandate. Flaherty (1980) found that evaluations mandated by external sources were perceived as useful only when data were also used for internal center purposes. Changes affect programs in different ways, such as (a) change is more difficult if program restructuring rather than program enriching is required; (b) change is more difficult when all staff are involved, rather than just a few employees; (c) fast change is as difficult as slow change with staff turnover; and (d) change is difficult under staff resistance. To overcome the negative effects of evaluation, staff must acknowledge the interdependent effects of all program components, and evaluation must include all components, be ongoing, and include all those involved in a program.

Pressures for answers from within and without the program will not seem so unbearable, or the difficulties involved in overcoming content and methodological problems so insurmountable, if one keeps in mind the major purpose of program evaluation. If evaluation is seen as a means for program improvement, it becomes a continuous process, and its results become starting points for future planning.

TRENDS AND ISSUES

DAP has certainly become part of every early childhood care and education professional's vocabulary. Although DAP is talked about, it is not being implemented rapidly. Perhaps, it will not be long before the constantly expanding knowledge of children is considered in program planning. The ecological perspective is highly important as early childhood programs become more inclusive of children from diverse groups and of children with special needs. Without this perspective, programs cannot provide a smooth transition from the home setting.

Undoubtedly, more discussion of DAP will and should take place. Many professionals see the need for a broader program base in which other concerns are addressed. Although the consensus on the *process* aspects of DAP as discussed by Fowell and Lawton (1992) is not complete, the need for *content* guidelines seems to be the weakest aspect of DAP. Spodek (1991a) and Katz (1991a), as well as the reconceptualists (Swadener & Kessler, 1991b), have addressed this need.

Well-conceived and coherent program models, especially those for compensatory education and early childhood special education, have been more or less successful. Other questions, however, need to be answered, such as, Under what conditions does the model work? (Guralnick, 1988; Meisels, 1985). Many have tried to transport models to new sites. Kagan (1991a) believes that this will not work; thus, program developers should launch site-specific models. Furthermore, even if a model were adopted at another site, it is not known how far a program can deviate from its model (e.g., in child-staff ratio, in group size, in staff training, in expenditures per child) before the positive effects disappear.

Another issue in implementation is the discrepancy between professed beliefs and actual practices. This has long been recognized and recently reported in studies of DAP. Researchers need to determine the reasons for discrepancy if teachers are to implement the program base.

Diversity of early childhood programs has heightened the complexity of program evaluation. Efforts to find accurate and efficient methods of program evaluation are needed for both formative and summative purposes. Katz (1994) suggests evaluation from these five perspectives: (a) evaluation from the *top down perspective* (determining the quality of a program through the eyes of program administrators and assessors from regulatory agencies), (b) evaluation from the *bottom up perspective* (determining how a program is experienced by children), (c) evaluation from the *outside-inside perspective* (assessing a program through the eyes of the family), (d) evaluation from the *inside perspective* (determining how a program is experienced by staff), and (e) evaluation from the *ultimate perspective* (determining how the local community and even larger society are served).

SUMMARY

The administrator's main task is providing leadership in program planning, implementation, and evaluation. The administrator, as a first step, must understand various program bases and curriculum models. The factors that should determine a program base are a synthesis of psychological theories, ecological perspectives, and philosophical positions. A curriculum model consists of the psychophilosophical base and the administrative and pedagogical components emanating from the base (Figure 2–1). Since the 1960s, the constructivist and the behavioral-environmental models are the most commonly used. Because these two approaches are diametrically opposed, much controversy has arisen over curriculum practices and the associated policies of admission, placement, retention, and length of the daily session. This controversy has led to the position statements of professional associations that favored the constructivist point of view. The reconceptualist has expressed negative reactions to these position statements. Others within the early childhood profession basically agree with DAP but believe that additional concerns must be addressed in constructing a program base. Thus, the issue of appropriate program base is far from resolved.

After considering the curriculum models and understanding the controversy, the board or administrator must choose a curriculum model as a second step. Every aspect of implementation of the program should be in keeping with the curriculum model.

The final step is making program evaluation plans. Evaluation may be of two types: intuitive and formal. Unplanned, intuitive evaluation is constantly functioning; thus, attempts should be made to understand the criteria being used by all involved in the local program. Formal or planned evaluation may be objectives-based, standards-based, or research evaluation. The administrator and the staff should jointly determine the reasons for evaluation (e.g., needs assessment, program analysis), the appropriate type of evaluation, the specific instrument to be used, and the timing of the implementation for both formative and summative evaluations. And as shown in Figure 2–1, evaluation results should provide feedback into future program planning.

FOR FURTHER READING

Bredekamp, S., & Rosegrant, T. (Eds.). (1992). *Reaching potentials: Appropriate curriculum and assessment for young children* (Vol. 1). Washington, DC: National Association for the Education of Young Children.

Elkind, D. (1991). Developmentally appropriate practice: A case study of educational inertia. In S. L. Kagan (Ed.), *The care and education of America's young children: Obstacles and opportunities* (pp. 1-16). Chicago: University of Chicago Press.

Evans, E. D. (1982). Curriculum models and early childhood education. In B. Spodek (Ed.), *Handbook of research on early childhood education* (pp. 107-134). New York: Free Press.

Goldbaber, D. (1979). Does a changing view of early experience imply a changing view of early development? In L. G. Katz (Ed.), *Current topics in early childhood education* (Vol. 2; pp. 117-140). Norwood, NJ: Ablex.

Kagan, S. L., & Zigler, E. F. (Eds.). (1987). *Early schooling: The national debate.* New Haven, CT: Yale University Press.

Schweinhart, L. J., & Weikart, D. P. (1991). Success by empowerment: The High/Scope Perry Preschool Study through age 27. *Young Children, 49*(1), 54-58.

Spodek, B. (1986). Using the knowledge base. In B. Spodek (Ed.), *Today's kindergarten: Exploring the knowledge base, expanding the curriculum* (pp. 137-143). New York: Teachers College Press.

Swadener, B. B., & Kessler, S. (Eds.). (1991). Reconceptualizing early childhood education [Special issue]. *Early Education and Development, 2*(2).

Weber, E. (1984). *Ideas influencing early childhood education: A theoretical analysis.* New York: Teachers College Press.

Chapter 3

❀ ❀ ❀ ❀ ❀

Considering Regulations
and Establishing Policies

❀ ❀ ❀ ❀ ❀

The continuing growth of early childhood programs has required greater emphasis on regulations designed to ensure not only that minimum standards are met but also that existing quality standards for care and instruction are raised. Today, researchers are making distinctions between **structural quality,** which refers to readily regulatable qualities (e.g., housing size, group size, staff education, adult-child ratio, safety measures), and **process quality,** which refers to variables that are more proximal to children's development (e.g., sensitive caregiving, appropriate activities; Howes, 1992). Unfortunately, process quality is not as assessable to regulation as structural quality. Yet, process quality is associated with positive cognitive outcomes, such as higher levels of play (Howes & Stewart, 1987) and higher intelligence and language scores (McCartney, Scarr, Phillips, & Grajek, 1985), and with positive social outcomes, such as attachment to staff (C. Anderson, Nagle, Roberts, & Smith, 1981) and consideration for other children and for staff (D. Phillips, McCartney, & Scarr, 1987).

Some people consider maintaining affordability more important than maintaining quality. On the one hand, these people argue that regulating high standards further limits program availability and that program quality will improve as a result of the free enterprise system. On the other hand, early childhood professionals note that families may not understand the implications of lack of quality, may not have the expertise or time to monitor programs carefully, and may not have the income to pay for high-quality programs (Willer, 1987). Thus, parents should have a right to expect that the government will assure them that their children will receive a minimum level of protection, just as it assures the population of a minimum level of safety in other areas (e.g., foods and drugs, water supply, police protection). Furthermore, high-quality programs benefit all segments of society—the children whose lives are enhanced, the parents who are assured of quality and who are thus bet-

ter employees, and the populace at large, which profits from its self-sufficient members.

Regulations are the rules, directives, statutes, and standards that prescribe, direct, limit, and govern early childhood programs. The following characteristics are generally representative:

1. Regulations cover all aspects of a program—administration organization, facilities, personnel, funding, and services.

2. Various regulations apply to different types of early childhood programs. Some regulations govern private programs—for example, licensing and incorporation; others may affect federal and state programs—for example, direct administration and Head Start performance objectives. Many regulations must be met by virtually all programs, such as those concerning building codes, fire safety, sanitation, zoning, transportation, staff qualifications, the Civil Rights Act, local board regulations, and laws for special needs populations.

3. Regulations vary in comprehensiveness—for example, licensing regulations cover the total program—but certification requirements affect only the educational preparation of the staff.

4. Most regulations are mandatory. Two exceptions are accreditation, which is self-regulation, and model standards.

5. Regulations come from various sources. Federal agencies regulate some early childhood programs because they provide funds through various grants and subsidies. In the 1960s, federal programs often dealt directly with community agencies; today, most federal programs do not bypass state administration. Thus, more control occurs at the state level. State agencies regulate some early childhood programs they fund because public education is a state responsibility. Local governments regulate other programs through community ordinances and health and safety codes. The judiciary system even regulates some aspects of early childhood programs through decisions affecting civil rights

and the responsibilities of agencies and schools. It is not always easy to determine which of several agencies has jurisdiction over programs.

The various regulatory agencies assume protective roles by assuring parents that the early childhood program meets at least minimum standards. Although this protective role is essential, the regulations have at least five problems:

1. Regulations can keep early childhood programs at minimum levels. The overriding question should not be whether harm or risk has been prevented, but whether a child's development is enhanced.

2. Regulations may deter innovation. Regulations are often too concerned with uniformity.

3. Most states do not have a single agency or legislative committee responsible for early childhood programs. Often, gaps appear in regulations or regulation jurisdictions collide. Establishing state offices of child development may help remedy this situation.

4. Some regulations are simply "on record," with little or no enforcement, such as registration of family child care homes.

5. Continuous consultation is often omitted. Continuous in-service training opportunities are necessary for providing and maintaining high-quality in programs.

In an effort to ensure that children will be served in high-quality programs, many administrators are assuming an active role in influencing social policy on regulations. (Advocacy is discussed in detail in Chapter 11.)

The remainder of the chapter is a discussion of the regulations governing all programs (private *and* public), private programs, public programs, accreditation, and model standards. In some cases, these regulations do not perfectly fit the category in which they are placed; for example, P.L. 94–142 is financed with public monies, but the law affects children with disabilities in private as well as public programs.

REGULATIONS GOVERNING ALL EARLY CHILDHOOD PROGRAMS

Various types of minimum regulations are common to all programs. These regulations include health and safety, fiscal concerns, children's rights, staff regulations, and services for children with special needs. Some overlap occurs in regulations imposed by various agencies of the federal, state, and local governments. When regulations of a similar nature are under more than one jurisdiction, an early childhood program must be in compliance with each. For example, a private early childhood program is subject to the fire safety standards of the local city code and the state licensing law. Furthermore, to help ensure that both standards are met, most state licensing agencies require an application for licensure of an early childhood program to include proof of compliance with all applicable city ordinances.

Health and Safety Regulations

Health and safety regulations are among the most stringent affecting all early childhood programs. These include zoning, building codes, fire safety and sanitation, and transportation. (Other health regulations are discussed in Chapter 8, and housing regulations for meeting the needs of children and adults with disabilities are discussed in Chapter 5.)

Zoning Regulations

Zoning regulations restrict the use of land. Each city and town is enabled by a state zoning law to divide its land into districts. Within those districts, it can regulate the use of the land itself and the erection and use of buildings. Regulations are stated in the form of local zoning ordinances, bylaws, and zoning codes. Generally, zoning regulations become more stringent as population density increases.

Zoning regulates the location of early childhood facilities. Child care facilities, unlike elementary schools, are often not included as a permitted use within a zoning plan. They are treated as "problem use" (excluded from residential sections because of noise and from commercial sections because such areas are not considered good places for children). States are now working to prevent local zoning from outlawing child care.

Building Codes and Requirements for Fire Safety and Sanitation

The statutory basis for building codes and requirements for fire safety and sanitation rests in public safety and health laws. These may be municipal ordinances or state regulations with local enforcement. The Life Safety Code of the National Fire Protection Association provides guidelines for appropriate fire codes for centers, group homes, and family child care.

Transportation Requirements

In each state, the agency that regulates matters pertaining to motor vehicles has the legal mandate to protect children transported in buses and private vehicles. Some states have devised special regulations for child care transportation in addition to those required for licensure.

Federal Occupational Safety and Health Act of 1970

The Federal Occupational Safety and Health Act of 1970 requires all employers to provide a work environment free from any recognizable hazards that could cause death or serious harm. Records must be kept in programs employing seven or more staff members.

Fiscal Regulations

Many fiscal regulations are specific to given programs. Most contracts and Internal Revenue Service (IRS) regulations, however, must be complied with by all early childhood programs. (IRS regulations applying to certain legal program categories are discussed in later sections of this chapter, and mandatory state unemployment insurance and the Federal Insurance Contributions Act [Social Security] is described in Chapter 4.) Fraud or failure to comply with fiscal regulations results in serious consequences.

Contracts. Contracts are legally enforceable agreements that may be oral or written (e.g., insurance policies; employment contracts; contracts with parents for fees; contracts for food, supplies, and services; contracts with funding sources; leases). A contract has three elements: (a) the **offer**—the buyer's proposal to the seller or the seller's invitation to the buyer to purchase a given object or service at a stated price (money or service); (b) **acceptance**—the buyer's acceptance of an offer or the seller's acknowledgment of the buyer's willingness to accept an offer; and (c) **consideration**—the legal term for the price or value of what each party exchanges (e.g., a subscription to a professional journal for $40 per year). Breaking a contract is called a **breach,** and the potential penalty is referred to as **damages.**

IRS Regulations. Many IRS regulations apply to all early childhood programs:

1. *Employer identification number.* Each organization employing people on a regular salaried basis is required to obtain a federal employer identification number. A program cannot file for a tax-exempt status without first having obtained this number, using IRS Form SS-4.

2. *Tax returns.* Employers file quarterly tax returns, IRS Form 941. This form is filed with the regional IRS service center. A penalty is assessed for late filing. Salaried employers of public early childhood programs file the appropriate schedule on IRS Form 1040. All private programs must file tax returns. Sole proprietors and partnerships with other incomes file the appropriate schedule on Form 1040; partnerships without other incomes file IRS Form 1065; for-profit corporations file Form 1120; and not-for-profit corporations file Form 990.

3. *Withholding Exemption Certificates and IRS Form 1099.* A Withholding Exemption Certificate, IRS Form W-4, is required for each employee. The certificates are used for determining the amount to withhold for federal, state, and city income taxes. The form indicates marital status and number of dependents and must be completed before the first paycheck is issued. Employees must sign new forms if marital status or number of dependents changes or if the employees want more of their wages to be withheld. An annual statement of taxes withheld from an employee's earnings (Form W-2) is sent to each employee no later than January 31 of the year following the year in which the employee was paid. Occasionally, early childhood programs hire someone to do a temporary job, such as plumbing or electrical work. Because withholding taxes would not have been deducted from the wages, all centers paying $600 or more to any individual who is not a regular employee must file IRS Form 1099.

Children's Rights and Protection Regulations

Historically, children's rights were viewed in moral and ethical terms, rather than in legal terms. Several groups have formulated children's rights. For example, the United Nations Convention on the Rights of the Child, a 1990 international treaty, defines minimum standards for economic, social, cultural, and political rights of children (NAEYC, 1993). In 1991, the National Education Association (NEA) also developed "A Bill of Rights for Children" (NEA, 1992).

Promoting General Rights. Children's legal rights are primarily in the form of "protection," rather than rights concerning freedom of choice. Protection rights for children are primarily assumed by parents who have rights of guardianship (e.g., determine level of financial support, provide religious and moral teachings, make choices regarding services such as educa-tion and health care). In some cases, society, through the law, protects children from the results of their own lack of judgment (e.g., children are not held responsible for their contracts), develops laws on behalf of children (e.g., school attendance and child labor laws), and intervenes between parents and children when the courts find that the children need more protection—the concept of *parens patriae* (e.g., foster care and the administration of health services in life-threatening situations). Children have recently been given some direct legal rights (e.g., due process and fair treatment in schools and juvenile courts). Protection rights of children implies responsibilities on the part of all those involved—parents, society, and even children themselves. B. Caldwell (1989) has developed a triadic model of these rights and responsibilities. Early childhood administrators are responsible for providing high-quality programs (meeting standards of licensing codes, fiscal monitoring, accreditation, or model standards), as discussed in later sections of this chapter, and for protecting children who are involved in custody disputes or who are victims of child abuse.

Handling Custody Issues. Custody issues arise when two adults have a right to some degree of legal or physical custody of a child. **Legal custody** is the right and responsibility of a person or agency to make a decision on behalf of a child; **physical custody** is the right and responsibility of a person to provide immediate care. Custody issues arise frequently when children are from single-parent families or under the legal custody of the state and in the physical custody of foster parents.

All early childhood programs need to protect children involved in custody disputes. Children can be protected if administrators follow this procedure:

1. Clarify custody of all children at or prior to time of enrollment. (Information must be in writing, dated, signed, and kept current.)

2. Name(s) and address(es) of those authorized to pick up the child must be given in writing.

3. Administrators should provide a statement to each person enrolling a child that the child will be released only to those persons named on the forms as being authorized to receive the child.

4. If an unauthorized party attempts to receive a child, follow these steps: (a) tell the person he or she is unauthorized, regardless of the-oretical rights; (b) show him or her a copy of the authorization; (c) notify the authorized person of the problem; and (d) if the unau-thorized person does not leave, call the police.

Reporting Suspected Child Abuse.   State laws govern reports of suspected child abuse. Early childhood educators certainly want protection for children, and these professionals may incur criminal or civil penalties, loss of a job, or loss of a license for not reporting. All programs should establish written policies regarding the report-ing requirements and internal processes. Poli-cies may include responsibilities for reporting, definitions of reportable cases, descriptions of the internal processes (e.g., who will make the report), and statements about liability. (Preven-tion of child abuse in centers is discussed later in this chapter.)

Staff Regulations

Staff regulations are designed to protect the employee (e.g., prevention of discrimination) and the program (staff qualifications). Staff regu-lations involve prevention of discrimination, wage-law compliance, board regulations, staff qualifications, potential vulnerability to legal actions, and civil rights of staff with disabilities.

Title VII of the Civil Rights Acts of 1964 and as Amended by the Equal Opportunity Act of 1972.   Fair employment practices are manda-tory for organizations, companies, and people having contracts with the federal government. The practices are also mandatory for any entity employing or composed of 15 or more people. Employees subject to this act and its amendment must not discriminate against any individual on the grounds of race, creed, color, gender, national origin, or age. Employment practices must be based on relevant measures of merit and competence. The employer must also base job qualifications on bona fide occupational qualifications (BFOQ); thus, job descriptions must clearly specify the tasks to be performed. (More specific information on recruiting and employing staff is given in Chapter 4.)

Americans With Disabilities Act.   The Ameri-cans With Disabilities Act (ADA), P.L. 101–336, was signed into law on July 26, 1990. ADA estab-lished civil rights for people with disabilities. The part of the law concerning employment states that employers with 15 or more employees must avoid job-related discrimination based on the employee's disability. To be protected under the law, the employee must satisfy bona fide busi-ness qualifications that are job related and be able to perform those tasks that are essential to the job *with reasonable accommodations* (e.g., making the facility accessible, modifying equip-ment, modifying work schedule, providing read-ers or interpreters) if necessary. Furthermore, the employer is legally liable if other employees discriminate or do not make adjustments to employees with disabilities (Surr, 1992). (Other aspects of ADA are discussed in this and other chapters.)

Fair Labor Standards Act.   The Fair Labor Standards Act of 1938 as amended applies equally to men and women. Employers subject to this act and its amendments must pay employees the current minimum wage; over-time (hours worked over the 40-hour week) at the rate of 1½ times the employee's regular rate of pay; regular wages and overtime pay for atten-dance at training sessions, whether the sessions are conducted at the place of work or at another site; and equal wages for equal work. The act does not apply to members of one's immediate family.

Regulations Concerning Administrator Qualifications.   Administrators of public school early childhood programs must hold a state administrator's certificate that grants legitimate authorization to administer a school program. The state education agency issues various types of administrator certificates (e.g., an elementary principal's certificate). All public school administrators hold teaching certificates, have had teaching experience, and have taken graduate courses in administration. Although they are well educated and experienced in "school matters," only seven states require administrators to receive specialized early childhood training, and in these states training varies from "limited exposure" to 60 clock hours.

Nationwide, with few exceptions, public school administrators are not prepared for young children and their programs (S. Robinson & Lyon, 1994). Directors of early childhood programs not under the state educational agency must meet the educational and experience requirements of their state's licensing law. In some states, the minimum educational requirement for a director is a high school diploma, but other states require 2 or more years of college work. Preservice training for center directors is not required in 22 states (G. Morgan et al., 1993). Minimum experience requirements range from no experience to 2 years of successful experience in an early childhood program. Administrative in-service training is rarely required.

Regulations Concerning Teacher Qualifications.   A teacher of young children performs many roles every day, including those of language model, arouser of artistic sensitivity and creativity, relater of knowledge, questioner, stimulator of curiosity, learning diagnostician, guidance counselor and mediator of conflicts, diplo-

mat with parents, and classroom administrator. Because the teacher also has total responsibility for all that happens to children in the program setting and for the quality of education, regulations help in ensuring that qualified teachers are placed with young children.

Certification of Teachers in Public School Early Childhood Programs.   **Certification** is the function of granting authorization to teach. Certificates may be standard or provisional and are limited to special fields and levels of instruction. In most states, the legislature delegates certification responsibilities to the state department of education (see Appendix 2). These responsibilities usually include the power to issue, renew, or revoke a certificate; the task of writing minimum requirements for each type of certificate; and the task of developing guidelines for colleges and universities to follow in planning a program for prospective teachers. Although the bases for certification are left to each state, most certification standards specify U.S. citizenship, age and health requirements, earned college degree with special course requirements, and possibly a recommendation from the college or university. Many states also require additional tests of competency (e.g., National Teacher Exam [NTE]).

Education of early childhood teachers has a long history. When American kindergartens were first established, prospective kindergarten teachers received their training in Germany and other European countries. The growing kindergarten movement, however, necessitated establishing kindergarten training schools in the United States. The first training institution was founded in Boston in 1868. These schools offered instruction in Froebelian theory and methods and on-the-job training in kindergarten classrooms. "The training given emphasized the kindergarten as a unique form of education apart from and having nothing in common with the school" (Holmes, 1937, p. 270). In the decade from 1890 to 1900, many public schools adopted kindergartens. The kindergarten training schools were continued as private, self-supporting institutions because the normal schools were not able to supply the increasing demand for trained teachers.

Many educators realized the desirability of employing state-certified kindergarten teachers, rather than having the kindergarten work "carried on by people who play a piano and love dear little children" ("Marked Kindergarten Progress," 1925, p. 303). Consequently, many colleges and universities reorganized their curriculum to meet the needs of students preparing to teach kindergartens. By 1925, in the 40 states that had kindergarten legislation, all but 5 had teacher certification laws for kindergarten. Most of the certificates were based on a high school diploma and a 2-year professional program and were special-subject certificates valid only for teaching in the kindergarten. In 4 states, a kindergarten-primary certificate, based on a 2-year professional program, was issued (Vandewalker, 1925). Gradually, almost all states developed certification requirements for teachers of young children (often kindergarten-level only) that required a bachelor's degree and that were patterned after elementary certification requirements.

McCarthy's (1988) analysis of state certification of early childhood teachers revealed that 32 states and the District of Columbia have specific certification for teachers of young children. This certificate is called "early childhood education" by 23 states and the District of Columbia although these certificates rarely encompass the entire age range (birth to age 8). Eleven certification departments issue level/age-specific certificates or both "early childhood education" and level/age certificates. Thirteen departments endorse the elementary certificate for kindergarten, and 2 of the 13 departments also endorse for nursery school. (Endorsement requirements range from two courses to six courses and student teaching; 1 department endorses if candidates are successful on the "General Knowledge" part of the NTE.) Nineteen departments include kindergartens in their elementary certificates, with only 6 of these 19 departments having special kindergarten

requirements. Seven departments now have Early Childhood Special Education certificates. McCarthy concluded that states more or less following the National Association for the Education of Young Children (NAEYC, 1982) guidelines mainly accommodate only two units (preprimary and primary—ages 3 through 8). Only 3 departments certify teachers for the full age-span. No certification requires teachers to teach at two of the three levels (birth to age 3; age 3 through kindergarten; primary grades/levels 1 through 3) although teacher training institutions may meet this requirement. McCarthy stated, "Discussions with many of the certifications officials gave the impression that they have no vision of the future or awareness that early childhood education is a rapidly changing field" (p. 5).

Since McCarthy's analysis, little has changed. Today, 16 state departments have no early childhood training certificate or endorsement. These teachers teach without any specific preparation for work with young children. Only 21 of the 35 states that have special certificates or endorsements require experience (e.g., fieldwork) with children under kindergarten age (G. Morgan et al., 1993)

In an effort to meet the ever-increasing demand for teachers in the 1980s while ensuring standards of quality for teaching (decreasing or eliminating "emergency certificates"), almost half of the states developed "alternative certification" programs (Feistritzer, 1986). **Alternative certification programs** generally enroll individuals with a bachelor's degree, usually in the arts and sciences, and offer a curricular shortcut to teaching. In 1988, only one state allowed this route for prospective early childhood teachers (McKibben, 1988).

In the Public School Early Childhood Study, A. Mitchell (1988) found that teachers trained in early childhood education and child development were more likely to carry out appropriate practices than teachers with no early childhood background whose previous teaching experience was with older children. The early childhood profession has looked at many issues in the preparation of early childhood teachers, including the following:

1. *What general education coursework should be required?* In 1986, two reports (Carnegie Forum on Education and the Economy, 1986; Holmes Group, 1986) called for abolishing the undergraduate degree in education. Under these plans, the prospective teacher would receive a liberal arts undergraduate degree and a professional education graduate degree. Several states have moved in this direction (e.g., Texas, Virginia, New Jersey) by abolishing the undergraduate education major. Although an individual may receive a certificate after completion of a bachelor's degree, "education hours" are limited, and a major is required in the arts and sciences. Other states have elected to increase the general education requirements in an effort to provide a broader liberal arts base for prospective teachers. Additional courses are often in economics, computers, English, and music (Spodek, Davis, & Saracho, 1983). Shulman (1986) states that it is highly important to restore subject matter knowledge as an integral component if teachers are to help children make connections among the disciplines.

2. *What professional education coursework should be required?* McCarthy (1990) has described pedagogical knowledge currently considered important as (a) the philosophical, psychological, and historical foundations of early childhood education; (b) home, school, and community relations; (c) curriculum; (d) organization and management of the learning environment; (e) mainstreaming children with disabilities; (f) infant and toddler programs; (g) health, nutrition, and safety; (h) assessment and evaluation; (i) legal rights and responsibilities; and (j) professionalism. (These are discussed in appropriate chapters in this book.)

3. *Is one philosophical orientation better than another?* Barbour (1990) describes the following three models of teacher education:

   a. **Competency-based teacher education** focuses on the technical aspect (a body of professional content to be learned and specific teaching skills to be mastered) of teacher education. In these programs, the predetermined objectives are stated in behavioral terms and are sequenced. Prospective teachers are pretested for level of competency and then follow standardized procedures for accomplishing the program's goals.

   b. **Humanistic teacher education** is based on perceptual and developmental psychologies. While developing psychological maturity, prospective teachers are encouraged to try out a number of approaches and techniques and to discover the method of teaching that best suits their unique personalities.

   c. **Inquiry-oriented teacher education** prepares teachers as critical thinkers. The teacher is challenged to relate the theory of the college classroom to the reality of early childhood programs. Prospective teachers are encouraged to examine issues and to determine the consequences of their own and others' actions. Most teacher training programs are eclectic in nature (Zeichner & Tabachnick, 1982).

4. *How important are field experiences?* The trend is toward increasing both the number and length of these experiences (Spodek et al., 1983). This trend has both positive and negative aspects: Positively, prospective teachers connect university knowledge with the reality of the classroom; negatively, the experience can encourage teachers simply to become technicians who support the status quo (Zeichner, 1983). Prospective teachers use field experiences to learn the technical aspects of teaching, rather than to develop reflective attitudes about their experiences. J. Henderson (1988) states that students should engage in reflective interplay between their values and beliefs and the professional knowledge base.

5. *What should performance testing measure?* The most popular paper-and-pencil test is

the NTE. On-the-job performance tests are required, in addition to the paper-and-pencil tests in about two fifths of the states (McCarthy, 1990).

The NAEYC addressed the problem of professional content at the associate, bachelor's, and advanced degrees in the early 1980s. Guidelines for the bachelor's degree were approved in 1981 and were approved by the National Council for the Accreditation of Teacher Education (NCATE) in 1982. By the mid-1980s, the NAEYC developed guidelines for associate degrees in early childhood education. In 1986, the NAEYC and the National Association of Early Childhood Teacher Educators (NAECTE) worked cooperatively on developing graduate degree guidelines. These were approved by the NCATE in 1988.

On the basis of a review of state standards for teacher certification (G. Morgan et al., 1993) that showed serious weaknesses in early childhood education certification, the NAEYC and the Association of Teacher Educators (ATE) published a joint statement on early childhood teacher certification or licensure (NAEYC, 1991b). In July 1994, the NAEYC's governing board approved revised guidelines for the associate, bachelor's, and graduate degrees. The NCATE has also approved the bachelor's and advanced degree guidelines. (NCATE does not accredit the associate degree programs.) The new guidelines (NAEYC, 1995b) contain more emphasis and specificity on cultural and linguistic diversity, individualization of curriculum and instructional practices, and knowledge of the central concepts and tools of inquiry in various curriculum disciplines. More emphasis is placed on technology, the protection of physical and psychological health, use of a family-centered approach in working with families, and performance-based assessment.

Similarly, the Division for Early Childhood (DEC) for the Council for Exceptional Children (CEC) developed a position paper on guidelines for the preparation of early childhood special educators. The DEC for the CEC's guidelines were endorsed by the NAEYC in the same way as the NAEYC's guidelines had been previously endorsed by DEC for the CEC.

Teacher Qualifications in Head Start and Child Care Programs.   The Head Start Act mandates that, by 1994, every Head Start classroom will have a teacher with a Child Development Associate (CDA) credential or other appropriate qualification, such as an associate degree in early childhood education/child development. The CDA Consortium grew out of efforts by Head Start to recognize competent performance of staff. (The CDA Award system is described later in this section.)

Personnel employed in child care programs are determined by each state's licensing regulations. (Programs included under licensing agencies are discussed in this chapter.) D. Phillips, Lande, and Goldberg (1990) found that only 9 states required both pre- and in-service preparation for center-based child care staff. An additional 29 states and the District of Columbia require either preservice or in-service training, and 16 states do not require any training. Eight states allow experience to be substituted for preservice training. Often, in-service training is meager; for example, in 15 states in-service training requirements are 10 or fewer clock hours per year. In 40 states, no training is required of family child care workers, and only 3 states require both pre- and in-service training. G. Morgan and her co-researchers (1993) found only some improvements since the study by D. Phillips et al. (1990). Preservice training for child care center teachers is not required in 36 states and is rarely required of family child care providers. In-service training for center staff is usually required and averages about 12 clock hours annually. In the few states that require in-service training of family child care providers, 6 clock hours annually is a typical requirement (G. Morgan et al., 1993). Eleven states identify two levels of roles for center teachers, with more training required of "lead" teachers; this career lattice allows for mobility. No state has developed a similar policy for family child care providers (G. Morgan et al., 1993). In some states, staff working in pre-kindergarten programs under the auspices of public schools must have training closely tied to teachers certification (P. Bloom, 1992). Less than half of the states require specialized training for those who work with infants and toddlers, school-age children in SACC programs, or children with special needs (G. Morgan et al., 1993).

Because of the meager requirements for Head Start and child care teachers, these teachers have far less formal training than teachers in public school programs. The National Child Care Staffing Study (Whitebook, Phillips, & Howes, 1993) found that only 12% of center staff had bachelor's or graduate degrees in a field related to early childhood education and that 38% had no education related to early childhood education at all. Other staff members were in-between. Although child care is still seen by many as an unskilled occupation, states are beginning to strengthen regulations. Different guidelines are used for minimal staff qualifications and for training. These guidelines include *Federal Model Child Care Standards* (U.S. Department of Health and Human Services, 1985), *Accreditation Criteria and Procedures for the National Academy of Early Childhood Programs* (NAEYC, 1984), and the *Family Day Care Accreditation Profile* (National Association for Family Day Care, 1988).

The CDA credential is used by teachers in a variety of child care settings, including Head Start. The CDA program has had an interesting history. Launched in 1972, the consortium's goals were to establish competencies needed for working in early childhood education, to develop methodologies for assessing such competencies, and to issue appropriate credentials. On March 25, 1975, the board of directors formally adopted the Credential Award System and authorized the awarding of the CDA credential

to anyone who could demonstrate competence by completing the requirements of the consortium. Because of federal funding cutbacks, the consortium disbanded in 1979, and credentialing was shuffled around. In 1985, the NAEYC took responsibility for credentialing, establishing a separate, not-for-profit corporation—the Council for Early Childhood Professional Recognition. From 1985 to 1988, through a cooperative agreement between the federal government (represented by the Administration for Children, Youth, and Families) and the early childhood profession (represented by the NAEYC), the council worked to develop a new training program leading to a CDA credential and to revise procedures for direct assessment of candidates who received their CDA training by other means. Once the training program and the direct assessment plans were approved, the council became an independent entity in 1989. The Professional Preparation Program consists of these three phases: (a) fieldwork guided by an early childhood adviser who uses council-designed manuals; (b) seminars, conducted in higher education settings, that cover the knowledge base of early childhood education; and (c) integration of field experiences and coursework, with candidates completing a series of exercises and performance-based assessments and a council representative conducting a series of interviews and receiving documentation. Direct assessment includes a competency-based evaluation and a written assessment of the candidate's knowledge. For more information contact:

> Council for Early Childhood Professional
>   Recognition
> 1341 G Street, NW, Suite 400
> Washington, DC 20005-3105
> 1-800-424-4310

In addition to pursuing advancements through the CDA program, some child care staff pursue college degrees.

Teacher Qualifications in American Montessori Schools.   Because the American Montessori

Society is a national private agency, the instructional staff of a Montessori school would have to meet the licensing code requirements of the state or, in some states, the requirements of the state board of education. In addition to the state's regulations, the American Montessori Society has its own certification requirements:

1. A degree from an accredited 4-year college or equivalent foreign credential is required, but no specific field of study is stipulated.

2. About 300 clock hours of academic work are required. This may include workshops or seminars in the historical and philosophical foundations of American education and the relationship of Montessori education to current knowledge of child development; knowledge of Montessori theory, philosophy, and materials for instruction as presented in seminars and as seen in observation of laboratory classes; and training in language arts, mathematics, science, art, music, social studies, and motor perception.

3. An internship of 9 months is required. This must be on a site approved by the course director under the approved American Montessori Society supervisor during which the intern is observed by a training program representative (American Montessori Society, 1973).

Criminal History Background Checks. The National Child Protection Act of 1993 (H.R. 1237) establishes procedures for national criminal background checks for child care providers. The act requires states to report child abuse crime information to the national criminal history background, maintained by the FBI. The act also allows states to conduct background checks on child care providers.

Local Board Regulations. Public school programs and private centers (except family child care and small child care centers owned by one or two persons or perhaps a family) often operate under the auspices of a board. Each faculty and staff member employed by an early childhood program is governed by the regulations of its governing board, which must be in keeping with the restrictions and authorizations of federal, state, and local laws, directives, and guidelines. The governing board's regulations may cover such items as the following:

Staff qualifications in addition to certification or licensing requirements

Salary and related benefits

Absences and leaves granted

Promotions

Evaluations of staff

Grievance policies

Housing of the program

Equipment used in the program

Curricular assistance given to teachers, in the way of resource materials, in-service training, resource personnel, or no curricular assistance

Plan of staffing for instruction (e.g., self-contained classroom or team teaching)

Teaching and nonteaching duties

Nature of communication with the public, through publicity, citizens' visits, or participation in schools

Administrative, instructional, and discipline requirements to be employed in working with children (e.g., attendance regulations, methods of determining and reporting children's progress, discipline)

Each administrative and supervisory employee's responsibility in giving direction to faculty and staff

Potential Vulnerability to Legal Actions. Three legal principles often apply in legal actions involving any business:

1. An employee is hired to perform certain types of duties, with certain expectations as to how these duties will be performed. When an

employee's actions are consistent with those expectations, an employee is said to be "acting within the scope of authority." An employee is not liable when acting within the scope of authority, but is liable when acting beyond it.

2. Except for "negligence" of employees, employers are responsible for all torts (civil wrongs) committed by employees. The legal phrase used for this principle is *respondent superior*—the boss is responsible. This principle does not apply to independent contractors, who are responsible for their own torts.

3. Principals (e.g., boards of directors) are responsible for torts committed by their agents (e.g., directors) acting on the business of the principal and within the scope of employment.

Liabilities vary, depending on the form of organization. Programs fully liable are sole proprietorships, partnerships, and for-profit corporations. Liability is limited in some states by the "charitable immunity doctrine" for programs operated as not-for-profit corporations. Public agency programs, such as public school early childhood programs and Head Start, have generally been immune from full liability as provided by Section 1983 of the Civil Rights Act (Mancke, 1972). Under the Civil Rights Act, immunity was not extended to the following three types of suits: (a) intentional injury (e.g., corporal punishment resulting in lasting injury to body or health; restraint of a person, such as physically enforcing the time-out technique; defamation, such as implying a student's lack of ability in nonprofessional communication); (b) negligence (e.g., failure to give adequate instruction, failure to take into account a child's abilities, improper supervision, inadequate inspection of equipment); and (c) educational negligence (careless or incompetent teaching practices; Scott, 1983).

Several implications can be drawn concerning the potential vulnerability to legal action. First, all employees should have job descriptions spelling out their scope of authority. Second,

adequate staffing, safe housing and equipment, administrative diligence, staff awareness and training in care of children, and documentation will do much to reduce the risk of torts. Finally, all involved in programs should realize that situations leading to liability are ever-present concerns and that all employees are vulnerable to legal actions.

Services for Children With Special Needs: Regulation and Litigation

Services for children with special needs has had a long and varied history. The history of special education involves identification of individuals needing special assistance, techniques and equipment/materials used in assisting individuals, and special schools and programs that serve as models for the delivery of services. Today, the inclusion of individuals with disabilities in the mainstream of society has been a growing concern and trend. **Inclusion** is not a legal term; rather, *inclusion* is a state-of-the-art term for placing individuals with disabilities in integrated settings of all kinds—educational, employment, living arrangements, and others. The history of services for children with special needs is filled with laws that have mandated and encouraged specific services and with litigation.

Early History.   Jean-Marc Itard, one of the first to attempt to understand and help children with disabilities, studied deaf-mutes during the French Revolution. Itard's pupil, Edouard Séguin, in the mid-1860s brought pioneering work to the United States, where he is credited with founding the American Association on Mental Deficiency. Montessori began with the ideas of Itard and Seguin in her work as a medical doctor serving children with mental deficiencies. Later, Montessori carried the ideas she had developed through her readings and practice to her program for children who were not mentally deficient but who had environmental disadvantages.

In 1904, Alfred Binet, a French psychologist, was asked to develop a test to determine which children could succeed in public schools. Reformers in France developed special schools for children identified by Binet's intelligence test as those in need of special education.

Educators in the United States also developed special programs for individuals with disabilities. Thomas Hopkins Gallaudet opened an asylum for the deaf and dumb in 1817. Samuel Howe founded an asylum for the blind in the 1830s, now the Perkins Institution. Other residential schools followed. The federal government became involved in special education in 1864, with the establishment of Gallaudet College for the Deaf in Washington, D.C., named after the younger son of T. H. Gallaudet, Edward Miner Gallaudet. In 1896, the first special education class for the mentally disabled was opened in the public schools of Providence, Rhode Island.

More Recent History.   The federal government established a Section on Exceptional Children and Youth in the Office of Education in 1930. Title V of the Social Security Act of 1935 established three programs for children with special needs: (a) maternal and child care health services, (b) crippled children's services, and (c) child welfare services. In 1939, Title V provided grant funding for innovative programs, called Special Projects of Regional and National Significance.

Because parents saw the need to educate their children with disabilities and because the federal government has provided matching funds to state and local agencies and has supported special education with monies for research, dissemination of information, and consultative services, the number of special education classes in public schools has greatly increased since World War II. Special education received much federal support beginning in the mid-1960s. Funds for University Affiliated Programs, formerly called University Affiliated Facilities, for training and service for "mental retar-

dation" were provided under P.L. 98-164 in 1963. In 1965, Medical Provisions of the Social Security Act provided early medical and health prevention and intervention programs for poor children, including the screening of children for potential causes of mental retardation. Similarly, in 1967, P.L. 20-248 established the Early and Periodic Screening, Diagnosis, and Treatment (EPSDT) Act. This law called for early health screening and case finding for children in poverty, referral, and treatment.

P.L. 90-538, the Handicapped Children's Early Assistance Act (HCEEAA) of 1968, established the Handicapped Children's Early Education Program (HCEEP) within the Bureau of Education for the Handicapped. Funds were authorized for experimental and demonstration preschools and were referred to as the "First Chance Network" or "HCEEP." P.L. 92-424 in 1972 and P.L. 93-644 in 1974, both amendments to the Economic Opportunity Act, mandated that Head Start make 10% of its total enrollment available to children with special needs and provide services to these children. P.L. 93-112, the Rehabilitation Act of 1973, mandated that states offering public school services to preschoolers without disabilities must also offer services to preschoolers with disabilities.

Litigation of the 1950s through the 1970s. Litigation has also been an important part of the history of publicly supported education for children with disabilities. The constitutional right of extending equal educational opportunities to all children, including those with disabilities, was settled by the United States Supreme Court in the case of *Brown v. Board of Education* (1954, 1955). More recent litigation has been concerned with methods of extending "equal educational opportunity." In *Madera v. Board of Education, City of New York* (1967), parents were to participate (with legal counsel) in and be informed of placement decisions. As a result of various court cases, children must be tested in their primary language and in English and be reevaluated within a specified length of time, and additional services must be provided to those students returning to the regular class following special class placement (Nuttall, DeLeon, & Valle, 1990).

Two precedent-setting cases were decided in the early 1970s. In a federal district court action, *Pennsylvania Association for Retarded Children (PARC) v. Commonwealth of Pennsylvania* (1972), parents invoked the equal protection clause of the Fourteenth Amendment. The clause requires that if the state provides a publicly supported program of education, it must be made available on an equal basis. PARC showed that inappropriate assessment instruments and labels led to incorrect placement or exclusion of children from school and that it was more economical to educate children with mental disabilities in the public schools than to provide special institutions or welfare assistance. As a result of this case, the Pennsylvania State Board of Education agreed to provide students with disabilities equal educational opportunities and to implement due process hearings concerning children's placements. The outcome of the second especially significant judicial decision, *Mills v. Board of Education* (1972), was similar to that of the *Pennsylvania* case. In this case, however, the plaintiffs included not only children with mental disabilities but all children with special needs.

Individuals With Disabilities Education Act (IDEA).

The Individuals With Disabilities Education Act (P.L. 101-476) is the 1990 reauthorization of P.L. 94-142 of 1975 and its amendment, P.L. 98-199 of 1983. P.L. 94-142, the Education for the Handicapped Act (EHA), is considered the most significant piece of legislation on behalf of children with special needs. This law provides funds to state education agencies, and through them to local education agencies, for the education of children and young adults (ages 3 to 21) with disabilities. It is based on six principles: (a) nonrejection education, (b) free and appropriate public education, (c) nondiscriminatory classification, (d) least restrictive placement, (e) due process

(based on P.L. 93-380), and (f) parent participation through consent, procedural due process, and parent training (Decker & Decker, 1992). Soon after its enactment came a growing awareness that P.L. 94-142 did not address the unique needs of the youngest children. Services were uncertain, and those that were available lacked interagency collaboration (Shonkoff & Meisels, 1990). It was also thought that parents should be more involved in decision making (Turnbull & Turnbull, 1986). Furthermore, under P.L. 94-142, services for children ages 3 through 5 and for young adults ages 18 through 21 were permissive. States could make the decisions whether to include programs for these age-groups. Although Part B of this law offered states incentive monies for offering programs for children ages 3 through 5, many states did not take advantage of the opportunity (Carran, 1984). Finally, many professionals thought the categorical labels required by the law were difficult and even inaccurate for young children (Meisels & Wasik, 1990).

The 1990 reauthorization of P.L. 94-142 as P.L. 101-476, IDEA, reflected a change in philosophy of labeling children as *handicapped*. These children are now referred to as *children with disabilities*.

The Education for All Handicapped Children Act Amendment of 1983.

P.L. 98-199, the Education for All Handicapped Children Act Amendment of 1983, provided financial incentives for states to extend services to children younger than those designated in the original P.L. 94-142. More specifically, this law provided funds for young children from birth through age 5 and their families.

Public Law 99-457.

P.L. 99-457, the Education of the Handicapped Act Amendment of 1986, addressed many of the concerns about P.L. 94-142. **Part B** of P.L. 99-457, the Preschool Grant Program, amends Title II of P.L. 94-142. Part B states that each state must provide free and appropriate education for all 3- through 5-year-old children or lose other portions of federal funding relating to this population. Part B makes all provisions of P.L. 94-142 applicable to preschoolers, and implementation is the responsibility of each state's department of education. Some changes were made in P.L. 94-142. The narrow categorical classifications of Part B are no longer required for preschool children because each state may add a new category called "developmental delay" and may define the term but within certain limitations. Part B also provides that the individualized education program (IEP) include "parent counseling and training" as a related service if desired by the parents. Variations in service delivery are also options.

Part H of P.L. 99-457, the Handicapped Infants and Toddlers' Program, does not amend P.L. 94-142, but adds a new section to Title I of P.L. 94-142. Part H establishes a new state program for children with disabilities from birth through age 2. Unlike Part B, Part H is permissive in nature. If a state chooses to participate, its governor puts the administrative structure in place (National Center for Clinical Infant Programs, 1989). Because the intent is for collaborative efforts between public and private services, any state agency may be designated the lead agency. The lead agency, in turn, establishes a State Interagency Coordinating Council (ICC) to facilitate collaboration. Part H does not define "education plus related services," but provides for an array of services. Services are not multidisciplinary but are interdisciplinary because all information and recommendations are brought into a single service plan (Harbin & McNulty, 1990). Family roles are strengthened. Families are involved from policy development to individual service delivery. Services must meet all family needs that are related to the child's development through the Individualized Family Service Plan (IFSP; Meisels, 1989b). P.L. 99-457 was reauthorized by passage of P.L. 102-199 in 1991.

Americans With Disabilities Act.   P.L. 101-336, known as the Americans With Disabilities Act

(ADA), is civil rights legislation. As it pertains to children with special needs, this act is concerned with physical access, discrimination, and appropriate program practices. First, ADA requires full physical access to facilities for children or family members with disabilities. Thus, older housing facilities must be changed unless structural changes cause an "undue burden," and new structures (beginning in 1993) must meet ADA accessibility guidelines. Vans or buses must also meet ADA accessibility guidelines. Second, this act prohibits enrollment discrimination based on a child's disability. A program may reject only if it can prove that the training of staff or the purchase and use of equipment necessary to accommodate a child result in an "undue burden." Third, children with disabilities must be provided integrated settings in the least restrictive environment (LRE), and staff must follow P.L. 99-457 (now P.L. 102-199) in implementing the IEP or the IFSP according to the child's age.

Head Start Amendment of 1993.   The Head Start Amendment of 1993 gives eligibility criteria for enrollment of children with disabilities. The amendment also provides guidance in providing comprehensive services to children and their families, in screening children, in using evaluative criteria to determine eligibility for special education services, in developing IEPs, and in designating a coordinator of services for children with disabilities.

Litigation Concerning Inclusion.   Before 1990, court cases such as *Briggs v. Board of Education of Connecticut* (1989) and *Barnett v. Fairfax County School Board* (1991) often favored the assertions of school districts that, for specific children, the more appropriate settings were segregated programs. More recently, the courts are more assertive in rendering decisions favoring inclusion, such as *Greer v. Rome City School District* (1991, 1992) and *Oberti v. Board of Education of the Borough of Clementon School District* (1993). Courts still review specific circumstances, and inclusion may be denied, as in *Clyde K. and Sheila K. v. Puyallup School District* (1994).

Other Laws.   Laws have been passed (e.g., the Bilingual Education Act of 1965, reissued in 1974) that help meet the needs of students with limited English by providing English as a second language (ESL) programs. In 1974, transitional bilingual programs expanded to help children function in more than one language/culture. The Gifted and Talented Children's Education Act was passed in 1978 and terminated in the 1980s. In 1988, the Jacob K. Javits Gifted and Talented Student Education Act was funded to create a National Center for the Education of the Gifted, to train teachers of the gifted, and to identify and serve gifted and talented students.

REGULATIONS GOVERNING PRIVATE EARLY CHILDHOOD PROGRAMS

Many types of private programs are available for young children. A private early childhood program may be a single class conducted by one teacher or a multiclass school staffed by a large faculty. The private program may be not-for-profit or for-profit, with all varieties or combinations of financial support possible. And as described in Chapter 1, private early childhood programs have many typologies, each with its own historical origins and present goals. Certain regulatory procedures are unique to private programs. Some create the legal existence of a private program (sole proprietorships, partnerships, and corporations). Others pertain to the level of quality of a private program (licensing and registration). Each state determines what is meant by a private early childhood program/facility and establishes the regulations by which the program is operated as a sole proprietorship, a partnership, or a for-profit or not-for-profit corporation. Each state also provides the means, through licensing and registration regu-

lations, for meeting the minimum standards for programs not funded or regulated by governmental agencies.

Proprietorships, Partnerships, and Corporation Regulations

Proprietorship, partnership, and corporation are legal categories for three types of private ownership. Legal requirements for operating an early childhood program under any of these categories vary from state to state; this discussion focuses on common features of the laws. Legal assistance should be sought before establishing a private early childhood program.

Proprietorship.   Under a **proprietorship,** a program is owned by one person. This person has no partners and is not incorporated. Sole proprietorships may have a one-person owner and operator, or a larger staff with one person as owner. The legal requirements are simple: To create a proprietorship, the owner must file with the city clerk a True Name Certificate or, if the owner is not going to use his or her real name, a Fictitious Name Registration, such as "Jack and Jill Center."

The Assumed Name Law informs clients and creditors of true ownership of the business. In a sole proprietorship, the owner has full decision-making authority as long as decisions are consistent with governmental regulations (e.g., owner must file a personal tax form). The owner may sell, give away, or go out of the business with no restrictions except the payment of outstanding debts and the completion of contractual obligations. The owner assumes full personal liability, however, for debts, breaches of contract, torts, taxes, and regulatory fees; the liability is not limited in amount and may even exceed the owner's personal funds.

Partnership.   In a **partnership,** two or more people usually join together for purposes of ownership. However, a partnership may involve minor children, a sole proprietorship, or a corporation as a partner. (The sole proprietor and the corporation would be involved in their own business, as well as the business owned by the partnership.) A partnership has limited transferability. A partner may sell or give away his or her interest in the partnership only if all other partners consent. If one partner dies, the partnership is dissolved. The law recognizes two types of partnerships:

1. **General partnership.** In this partnership, each partner is a legal coequal. Each partner has the right to make equal contributions, but not necessarily the same kinds of contributions, to the program. Because contribution is a right and not an obligation, it may be worked out in reality on an equal or unequal basis. A general partnership can be risky because each partner has full authority to make binding decisions independently of other partners, sharing equally in any financial obligations including full personal liability. As with a proprietorship, the partners must file a True Name Certificate. Although partners have individual tax obligations, they also file an information return IRS Form 1065.

2. **Limited partnership.** This partnership must consist of one or more general partners and one or more limited partners. Each general partner faces risks identical to those of a general partnership. Each limited partner is responsible and liable to the extent of his or her financial or service contribution calculated on a monetary basis at the time the center was created. Partners must file a True Name Certificate and a Limited Partnership Certificate that spells out the limitations of responsibility and liability. The limited partnership document is written and filed with the secretary of state or is publicized according to the state's laws. Many partnerships find it desirable, though not mandatory, to prepare a partnership agreement, a document containing facts about how a program is to be operated and terminated. Because of limited liability, a limited partner participates only in decisions involving finances.

Corporation.   A **corporation** is a legal entity established on a for-profit or not-for-profit basis. Corporations exist as legal entities forever unless dissolved by the board of directors or a court. Most private early childhood programs legally organized as corporations are independent (not part of other businesses). Work-site child care programs may be organized as a division of the parent corporation, a subsidiary corporation, or an independent not-for-profit corporation.

The corporation protects individuals from certain liabilities by creating a decision-making and accountable board of directors. Although the board may delegate decision-making power to a director, it is still responsible. Individual board members can be held personally liable in certain areas, such as fraud and failure of the corporation to pay withholding taxes on employees' salaries. In short, personal financial liability is greatly diminished in a corporation, as compared with the proprietorship or partnership.

In addition to diminished personal financial liability, regulations governing taxation may provide incentive to operate a program as a corporation. There is often a monetary advantage in paying corporate taxes rather than paying all the taxes on the program's profits as personal income. Furthermore, not-for-profit centers must be incorporated to be eligible for tax-exempt status; proprietorships and partnerships are not eligible for tax-exempt status.

Because the corporation is a legal entity, several documents are required. The forms are usually somewhat different for for-profit and not-for-profit corporations. Three documents are required in the process of incorporating:

1. **Articles of incorporation** or **certificate of incorporation.** The organization's legal creators, or incorporators, give information about the corporation, such as the name and address of the agency; its purposes; whether it is a for-profit or not-for-profit corporation; its powers—for example, to purchase property and make loans; membership, if the state requires mem-

bers; names and addresses of the initial board of directors; initial officers; and the date of the annual meeting.

2. **Bylaws.** The IRS requires bylaws if the corporation is seeking tax-exempt status. Bylaws simply explain how the corporation will conduct its business, its power structure, and how the power may be transferred.

3. **Minutes of the incorporator's meeting.** After the incorporators prepare the aforementioned documents, an incorporator's meeting is held. The name of the corporation is approved, and the articles of incorporation and bylaws are signed. The incorporators elect officers and the board of directors, who will serve until the first meeting of the members. In for-profit corporations, the incorporators vote to authorize the issuance of stock. Formal minutes of the incorporators' meeting, including votes taken, are written and signed by each incorporator.

These documents, along with payment of a fee, are filed with the secretary of state or are publicized according to state laws. Once the state approves the proposed corporation, a corporate charter is issued. The incorporators no longer have power. Board members carry out the purposes of the organization, and the members own the organization. When corporations dissolve, they must follow state law if they are for-profit corporations and must follow federal regulations if they are not-for-profit corporations.

Early childhood programs may operate either as **for-profit** or **not-for-profit** corporations. Although the titles are somewhat descriptive, they are often misleading, particularly when incorrectly called profit-making and nonprofit corporations, respectively.

For-profit corporations are organized for purposes of making a profit. Early childhood programs in this category, as well as proprietorships and partnerships, are businesses. A for-profit corporation may be a closed corporation, in which members of a family or perhaps a few friends own stock, or an open corporation, in which stock is traded on exchanges. If the corporation makes a profit, it pays taxes on the profits; individual stockholders file personal income tax forms listing such items as salaries and dividends received from the corporation. In a closed corporation with a subchapter "S" status, granted by the IRS, the corporation may distribute its profits or losses in accordance with the proportion of stock held by each individual, who in turn pays taxes or files a depreciation schedule.

The main purpose of *not-for-profit* corporations is other than to make a profit, but they are permitted to make a profit. Any surplus, or profit, however, must be used to promote the purposes of the organization as set forth in the articles of incorporation. In other words, the profit may be used for housing, equipping, or merit raises in the present or future. Proprietory operators have also organized not-for-profit corporations; such organization gives them certain advantages, such as rent money for the facility, a salary for directing the program, and free surplus food for children in the program. Child care has two types of not-for-profit corporations: (a) those organized for charitable, educational, literary, religious, or scientific purposes under section 501(c)(3) of the Internal Revenue Code and (b) those organized for social welfare purposes under section 501(c)(4) of the Internal Revenue Code. Tax-exempt status is not automatic. The not-for-profit corporation must file for and be granted tax-exempt status at both federal and state levels.

Besides incorporation regulations, several additional regulations should be noted. Separate bank accounts should be obtained for any early childhood program. Corporations are required to have separate accounts, and some governmental agencies will not send funds to a program that does not have a separate account. Also, a banking resolution, stating the name of the person authorized to withdraw funds, is required of corporations (and in some states, of partnerships). Not-for-profit corporations with a certain income level, and other programs receiving monies from certain funding sources, are required to have an audit. In most states, not-for-profit corporations are required to file an annual financial report following the audit.

Franchises and chains may fall under any of the three legal categories of private organizations but are most often corporations. Franchises and chains are differentiated as follows:

1. A **franchise** is an organization that allows an individual or an entity to use its name, follows its standardized program and administrative procedures, and receives assistance (e.g., in selecting a site, building and equipping a facility, and training staff) for an agreed-on sum of money and/or royalty.

2. A **chain** is ownership of several facilities by the same proprietorship, partnership, or corporation. These facilities are administered by a central organization. Kinder Care Learning Centers is an example of a chain.

Licensing: Minimal Quality Regulations

Licensing is the procedure by which a person, association, or corporation obtains from its state licensing agency a license to operate or continue operating a private child care facility. A state-specified, licensed facility is recognized by the state agency as having met only minimum standards of child care; that is, licensing is a regulation reflecting the criterion of preventing harm to children, rather than of providing exemplary care.

Licensing does not concern some child care facilities. Most states have dropped the definition of licensing as covering only programs that do not define themselves as "primarily educational" (G. Morgan, 1991). (Using the "primarily educational" definition allowed many programs to escape coverage by any regulatory agency.) Non-licensed facilities may include the following:

1. *Programs operated under public auspices*, such as public school programs and Head

Start. Public agencies are expected to implement their own standards and to exercise supervision of their own facilities. Sometimes, programs that have their own standards are licensed too. For example, Head Start is covered by its own performance standards; Head Start is also licensed if operated by a private agency (e.g., community action association) but not if operated by a public school.

2. *Early childhood programs*, especially preschools and kindergartens, in organized private school systems.

3. *Day camps* as defined by the various state codes.

4. *Nurseries or other programs in places of worship during religious services.* In a few states, other types of religion-related child care services are exempt from licensing.

5. *School-age child care (SACC) programs operated by private schools and other agencies,* such as the Young Men's Christian Association (YMCA). Only seven states do not exempt SACC programs operated by public schools (Marx, 1990).

6. *Baby-sitting services* as defined by the various state codes. (The minimum number of children not related to the provider and the place of operation are used to make a distinction between child care and baby-sitting services.)

Licensing originated in New England when a board of charities was created in 1863 to inspect and report on various child care facilities. In 1873, the National Conference of Charities and Correction was created. The conference urged state regulation of private agencies, including those concerned with child care (Class, 1972). The first licensing law was passed in Pennsylvania in 1884; however, general interest in licensing did not begin until the early 1900s, when public scandals arose over the abuse of children in some child care facilities. This concern led to regulations for minimum standards of care and supervision of the publicly subsidized agencies. The first White House conference on the care of dependent children (1909) recommended that each state regularly inspect all agencies dealing with minor children and regulate the incorporation of new agencies (Children's Bureau, 1966.) Three years later, the U.S. Children's Bureau was created. The bureau urged the establishment of standards for child care agencies. The Child Welfare League of America, established in 1920, developed such a set of standards (Class, 1972). By then, most states had some regulation of child care. As a result of the federal grant-in-aid funds of 1935, state child welfare departments were able to procure better qualified personnel; child care facilities were brought under child care licensing statutes; social workers took an active interest in protective services; and licensing was identified as a state child welfare function (Class, 1968).

The Licensing Agency.   The state regulates child care from its constitutional authority to protect the welfare of the child. Licensing of child care facilities falls under the auspices of the Department of Public Welfare or the state's equivalent to the Department of Child and Family Social Services (see Appendix 2). According to Class (1968), the licensing agency is a regulatory agency with both quasi-legislative and quasi-judicial authority. The quasi-legislative powers include responsibility for establishing standards; the quasi-judicial powers include responsibility for making decisions to issue or deny a license application and for conducting hearings in grievance cases. The major tasks of the licensing agency are (a) interpreting the fact that child care is an activity affecting public interests and is therefore recognized by the state as an area of regulation, (b) formulating and reformulating licensing standards that will reduce the risk of improper care, (c) evaluating each applicant's situation to decide whether to issue the license, and (d) supervising to maintain conformity to standards and, usually, consulting to upgrade care.

Features of Child Care Licensing Laws.   The different types of child care facilities may be covered by a general or differential licensing law. Differential licensing laws have varying standards for these types of programs: child care (family child care homes, group child care homes, and child care centers); educational facilities (private kindergartens and programs that carry the term *school* in their title); foster care (foster homes and group foster homes); child-placing institutions; residential facilities; children's camps; and centers for children with disabilities. (This section is concerned only with the licensing of child care centers; regulation of family child care is discussed later.)

The content of licensing regulations originates with an advisory group comprising interested persons, child development and early childhood education experts, politicians, and consumers. Those with concerns regarding licensing laws look to this task force for action. Public hearings are held on the draft. The agency then issues a legal statement, which becomes the law.

Regulatory laws governing child care centers differ widely from state to state. To learn specific regulations of a state, contact the state's licensing agency and request a copy of the regulations (see Appendix 2). Areas covered in most licensing codes include the following:

1. *Licensing laws and procedures.* For purposes of licensing, the state says it is illegal to care for another person's child. Then, the state says a person may care for other people's children if he or she applies for and is given permission (a license) by the authorized agency of the government. This section of the code covers terms such as *child care,* programs that must be licensed, policies for obtaining and submitting an application for a license, fees, application approval, duration of license, criteria for revoking a license, policy for posting of license, and conditions requiring notification of the licensing agency.

2. *Organization and administration.* State licensing laws require an applicant to indicate purposes and sponsorship of the organization, whether the program is for-profit or not-for-profit, ways in which administrative authority is placed (e.g., boards, director), policies concerning children (e.g., admission, termination, nondiscrimination provision, fees), child-staff ratio, and financial solvency for immediate and continuous operation.

3. *Staffing.* Regulations concerning staffing usually include categories of personnel (director, primary program personnel, and support program personnel); age, education, health, character, and temperament characteristics of staff members; personnel records to be kept; and child-staff ratio.

4. *Plant and equipment.* Licensing codes require applicants to meet local zoning, health, and fire standards and state health department standards before applying. The majority of states have regulations concerning the indoor housing (e.g., size, type, and number of rooms needed), environmental control, drinking water sources, sanitary facilities, kitchen facilities, and outdoor space needed. Some equipment regulations are common, such as equipment for naps. Specific regulations on other equipment may not be given but may be listed as "suggested" equipment.

5. *Health and safety.* Health and safety requirements concerning physical facilities, health forms, and nutrition are very specific. Two areas receiving serious attention are (a) sexual abuse as previously discussed and (b) concern over infectious diseases in all child care and especially infant programs (G. Morgan, 1986). (See Chapter 8 for a discussion of infectious diseases and early childhood programs.)

6. *Program.* Some states have detailed program specifications. Because child care is not considered educational but a public welfare service in some states, program regulations tend to be more lax than most other licensing regulations. Other state licensing departments desire

minimum regulation or believe that parents and staff should have a great deal of autonomy and control over program content and scheduling.

7. *Discipline.* Many states stipulate "no harsh discipline" and give suggestions for guidance of children. The outlawing of corporal punishment in state codes is the issue behind much effort by certain religious groups to exempt their child care from licensing.

8. *Parent involvement.* Most states require that parents be involved in the child care program. Suggested means include serving on boards of advisors, visiting the facility during hours of operation, having parent-staff conferences, and being given materials on the program's goals and policies.

Improving Licensing Laws.   G. Morgan, Curry, Endsley, Bradford, and Rashid (1985) state that licensing laws can be judged in terms of whether (a) standards are high or low; (b) the state code covers all forms of child care—infant/toddler programs, family child care homes, and group child care homes; (c) the standards are implemented fully; (d) the licensing system has a broad base of support in the state; and (e) the state has adequate numbers of trained workers in the licensing agency. During the 1960s and 1970s, when federal funding of early childhood programs was plentiful, the Federal Interagency Day-Care Requirements (FIDCR) were instituted to ensure a high quality of standards for programs receiving federal funds. Many states patterned their licensing codes after the FIDCR. These requirements were replaced in 1980 with the more stringent Department of Health and Human Services Day-Care Requirements (DHHS-DCR), which were eliminated in 1981. Licensing codes in many states eroded following the elimination of all federal standards; this erosion resulted in non-enforcement and/or movement to exempt certain programs.

Professionals see a need for strong licensing laws. According to G. Morgan et al. (1985), providers must be willing to meet standards, parents must be willing to pay for high quality, and the general public must support enforcement. These authors also note that the history, values, and cultures of a state influence what can be done in regulatory policy, and in some states, deregulation (e.g., voluntary licensing and registration) is most attractive to policy makers. Licensing standards should reflect current research in developing standards (Bredekamp, 1990; D. Phillips, 1987). The following suggestions have been made for the improvement of licensing: (a) enforce compliance; (b) regulate all types of programs serving children; (c) set standards that are appropriate for various types of settings and the number of children served; (d) make the licensing agencies highly visible (agencies are known about and accessible to parents and providers); (e) write standards in clear and reasonable terms; (f) fund at levels necessary for full implementation of the regulatory and service aspects of the agency; and (g) develop a regulatory system that is responsive to the needs of both providers and parents ("Public Policy Report," 1987).

Registration and Other Forms of Regulation

More than 5 million children are cared for in family child care homes. Twice as many families use family child care or use center-based care for infants and toddlers (U.S. Bureau of the Census, 1989). Only 10% to 40% of family child care providers are regulated (A. Kahn & Kamerman, 1987). Others either choose not to comply, are unaware of regulations, or are aware but know they serve too many children. In the study by Galinsky, Howes, Kontos, and Shinn (1994), only 9% of family child care homes were rated "good" and 35% were rated "inadequate" ("growth harming"). B. Caldwell (1990) states that the lack of regulation of the family child care system "is one of the factors responsible for the field's slow climb to legitimacy" (p. 4). The main problems in regulating family child care programs are the

increasing numbers of these programs—more than 2 million providers, according to Hofferth and Phillips (1987)—and the high turnover rate of the homes serving children. It is even questionable whether center-based regulations should apply to family child care programs (D. Phillips et al., 1990).

Several options are available for regulating family child care homes. In addition to traditional licensing, registration is becoming a popular approach. **Registration** is a process by which a state's licensing agent publishes regulations, requires providers to certify that they have complied with the regulations, and maintains records on all family child care homes. For registration to be effective, it must be mandatory and about one fifth of the homes must have a routine inspection each year (G. Morgan et al., 1985). Another regulatory model is the **supervisor model,** in which an early childhood professional participates in the licensing of a home and in enforcement by frequent visits (e.g., twice a month). **Accreditation** (discussed later in this chapter) may also be used when other forms of regulation are nonexistent or are insufficiently provided by state government (Corsini, Wisensale, Caruso, 1988).

REGULATIONS GOVERNING PUBLIC EARLY CHILDHOOD PROGRAMS

A public agency is an organization that is part of the federal, state, or local government. Three major funded systems that provide child care and education are (a) Head Start, (b) public school early childhood programs, and (c) state social service programs that purchase care and education by contract with privately licensed facilities. (Examples of state-subsidized funding are federal Social Services Block Grant funds, state tax dollars, and welfare reform dollars.) Although states may develop their own separate programs, they usually "buy in" to the private network of early childhood programs, used also by nonsubsidized parents and called *purchase-*

of-service network (G. Morgan, 1991). Publicly funded early childhood programs are not subject to licensing. Instead, all publicly funded programs, such as public school and federally supported early childhood programs, are regulated by a state or federal agency, respectively. A specified state or federal agency is required by law to prepare regulations. Some of these regulations are deemed inadequate by many professionals. For example, public school pre-kindergarten programs are exempt from child care regulations in nearly every state; state codes, written with school-age children in mind, rarely include specific provisions for young children. Furthermore, because publicly funded programs are self-monitoring or answerable only to elected officials, program quality depends on citizen involvement.

Public School Regulations

Legally, public schools are public agencies. Public school education in the United States is a state function. The organizational structure is similar in each state. In most states, the chief state school officer is the superintendent of public instruction or the commissioner of education, who is either elected or appointed. Early childhood education programs in the public schools fall under this officer's jurisdiction. The chief state school officer and the state board of education, composed of elected or appointed board members, comprise the policy-making group for public education in the state. With the state board's approval, the chief state school officer selects the personnel and operates the department of public instruction or state education agency. Within the department of public instruction is a bureau concerned with early childhood education programs. Duties of the bureau may include approving requests for state aid, evaluating teacher certification applications, responding to requests for information or assistance, supervising programs in the local school districts, appraising legislative proposals that affect early childhood programs, and publishing information on regulations or trends in early childhood education.

The local school district may be, according to each state's law, a large urban district, a small community district, a cooperative arrangement among several communities, or a county district. The board of education or trustees, an elected group that represents the district's interests, is the policy-making group. As authorized by state laws, the board approves all school expenditures, plans for building projects, makes personnel appointments, and determines the services offered to students and parents. The superintendent, appointed by the school board, is the administrative officer for the school district. The superintendent's function is to execute, within limits of state law, the board's actions.

Directly superior to the early childhood education teacher is the building principal, who is the instructional leader and administrator of the school physical plant, records, and personnel. Supervisors or supervisor-administrators may be assigned by the superintendent's office to supervise and assist early childhood education teachers. The early childhood education teacher is responsible for caregiving and instruction of the children, for the management of the classroom, and for any assistant teachers or aides placed in the early childhood classroom.

Fiscal Monitoring

Fiscal monitoring refers to standards associated with funding. When the government buys or creates a service through a grant or contract, it establishes specifications for quality. Based on contract law, the relationship of the government to the provider is that of purchaser or contractor. *Funding standards* are the conditions or standards for receiving a grant or contract. If the agency runs its own program, then the relationship is even more direct. *Operating standards* are the conditions or standards under which a governmental agency operates ("runs") a program.

In short, in publicly funded programs, specifications for quality are simply administrative accountability via fiscal monitoring. Some states require the public program to meet the standard used in licensing; others require a level of quality higher than licensing. One example of fiscal monitoring is the Head Start Performance Standards, which local Head Start programs must meet for future funding. Another example of fiscal monitoring is the now defunct Federal Interagency Day-Care Requirements (Decker & Decker, 1984). (One reason for its failure was public confusion between fiscal and licensing standards.) Some states (e.g., North Carolina, Massachusetts) have their own funding standards; however, few states have provided funds necessary to cover the costs of meeting fiscal standards. (G. Morgan, 1991).

ACCREDITATION

Accreditation is a process of self-regulation; thus, regulations governing programs (e.g., certification of staff, licensing, registration) differ from accreditation in several ways. Regulations are mandatory minimum standards requiring 100% compliance, are determined or set by governmental or funding agencies, and often are imposed at the local and state levels although some regulations have federal scope (e.g., IRS regulations, civil rights acts, P.L. 101-476, P.L. 102-199). Conversely, accreditation standards are voluntary high-quality standards requiring substantial compliance, are sponsored by professional organizations, and are operated at the national level. Failure to meet regulation standards means legal sanctions, but failure to become accredited signifies failure to gain professional status. Early childhood programs accredited by a particular association or agency are not necessarily superior to other programs although they are often superior because staff members have voluntarily pursued a degree of excellence.

Accreditation, as a process of self-regulation, involves three major steps. The first step involves an application and fee payment to the accrediting association, followed by a **self-study** in which the program attempts to meet the accreditation standards as delineated by interpretive statements, usually called *criteria* (see Appendix 3). The self-study is submitted in a specified written format to the sponsoring association. Traditionally, associations have used, and most still use, a rather voluminous description of the program's compliance with each criterion. The National Academy of Early Childhood Programs, however, uses a 3-point rating scale (criterion fully met, criterion partially met, criterion not met) for its "Program Description." The second step involves on-site **validation,** which is a visit to the program by a team of validators (highly qualified professionals with association training to interpret the accreditation standards and procedures). As their title suggests, these validators verify that the written information is an accurate reflection of daily program operations. The validators then report their findings to the accrediting agency. The third step is the **decision-making process** by the accrediting agency. Programs are informed in writing concerning their accreditation status, along with their strengths and weaknesses. Accredited programs have a term of accreditation; to stay accredited, program officials must reapply and successfully complete the entire process before the term expires. Furthermore, most associations now require annual reports from their accredited programs regarding each program's current status and maintain the right to revoke accreditation if the program does not maintain quality standards or fails to comply with any procedures. For deferred programs, appeal procedures and also association assistance plans are available for helping these programs meet the standards and become accredited.

Several accreditation agencies are involved in early childhood programs. In 1982, the National Association for the Education of Young Children (NAEYC) began developing an accreditation system for early childhood programs serving a minimum of 10 children within the age-group of birth through age 5 in part- or full-day group programs, and age 5 through age 8 in before- and after-school programs. No family child care programs are included at this time. To accomplish the goals of accreditation, the NAEYC established a new organization—the National Academy of Early Childhood Programs (the Academy). Programs working toward accreditation join the Academy as "candidate programs" and become members when accredited. The self-study consists of four parts: (a) an *Early Childhood Classroom Observation, (b)* an *Administrative Report,* (c) a *Staff Questionnaire,* and (d) a *Parent Questionnaire.* The criteria are centered on the following 10 components of group programs for children: interactions among staff and children, curriculum, staff-parent interaction, staff qualifications and development, administration, staffing, physical environment, health and safety, nutrition and food service, and evaluation (NAEYC, 1991a). Recently, the Academy completed two follow-up studies. Analysis of data from the annual report submitted on programs 1 year after their accreditation revealed that the high standards not only were maintained but also were being improved (Bredekamp & Berby, 1987). Data from a survey of reaccredited programs completed 3 years after their original accreditation suggest that because of changes in programs, a complete self-study/validation leading to reaccreditation every 3 years is appropriate (Mulrooney, 1990). An even more recent study of directors' perceptions of the benefits of accreditation found that 55% of directors of accredited programs thought their programs were more visible and 38% reported accreditation made marketing easier. Over 90% of directors reported improvement in their programs, especially in curriculum, administration, health and safety, and the physical environment components but not in staffing and food and nutrition components. The directors also stated that children benefited by better staff morale, improved knowledge and understanding of

developmentally appropriate practices, and parent understanding of the components and standards necessary for high-quality care (Herr, Johnson, & Zimmerman, 1993).

In an effort to give family child care programs an opportunity to gain professional recognition, the National Association for Family Day Care developed an accreditation program in 1988. Family day care providers rate their programs by using the Assessment Profile for Family Day Care to measure 186 criteria, which fall into seven categories: indoor safety, health, nutrition, interaction, indoor play environment, outdoor play environment, and professional responsibility. Parent questionnaires, parent observation, and validator observation are also used.

The Child Welfare League of America provides accreditation to child welfare agencies such as Child Day-Care-Center Based, Child Day-Care-Family Based, and Child Protective Services through its Council of Accreditation of Services for Families and Children. The accreditation process begins with the completion of a checklist. If no major questions are raised, the agency may begin the accreditation process.

Public schools are necessarily accredited by the state education agency. Because early childhood programs in public schools are considered part of the elementary school, these programs are accredited with the elementary schools in a local school district. In addition to the various state education agencies, early childhood programs that are part of elementary schools may be accredited by the Southern Association of Colleges and Schools. (Among the six regional accrediting associations, only the Southern Association of Colleges and Schools has an arrangement for accrediting elementary schools.)

Teacher preparation institutions may be accredited by the National Council for the Accreditation of Teacher Education (NCATE). As has been discussed, the guidelines prepared by the NAEYC are the standards used by the NCATE for accreditation of early childhood teacher education programs (a 4- or 5-year teacher preparation curriculum for those who want to be teachers of children from birth through age 8; NAEYC, 1995b). A teacher preparation program can become accredited in several ways. Recently, about 60% of states have entered into state/ NCATE partnerships. Accreditation within the partnership may be accomplished under several basic frameworks (Interstate New Teacher Assessment and Support Consortium [INTASC], 1992; McCarthy, 1994). The NCATE is also moving away from competency-based to performance-based teacher education programs (McCarthy, 1994). In 1993, the NCATE commissioned a national opinion poll on teacher education. The poll revealed that 82% of respondents favored requiring teachers to graduate from nationally accredited professional schools, and 78% favored national accreditation standards for schools of education ("For Your Information," 1993).

MODEL STANDARDS

Model standards, developed by experts, are standards of practice based on the most recent knowledge available and the highest standards for the profession. Model standards are not new. For example, the Children's Bureau, established in 1911, described what children's programs could be like as a contrast to the then current conditions (Oettinger, 1964). The U.S. Department of Health, Education, and Welfare (1972) adopted *Guides for Day Care Licensing* as a model licensing standard. More recently, the American Public Health Association and the American Academy of Pediatrics (1992) developed national health and safety performance standards.

ESTABLISHING POLICIES

After local program planners have considered regulations, accreditation, and model standards that affect their program, they should establish policies. **Policies** are judgments that express a program's intentions for achieving certain pur-

poses (e.g., in-service education of staff, budgetary priorities, program evaluation). Although practices exist in any early childhood program regardless of whether written policies exist, policies establish the bases for authoritative action. The phrase "rules, regulations, and procedures" describes a specific course of action based on policies.

Reasons for Policy Establishment

A policy may be established for several reasons:

1. In many states, the state licensing agency and the state board of education require that programs under their respective jurisdictions have written policies covering certain aspects of the local program; these policies must be in keeping with the restrictions and authorizations of state law.

2. Policies provide guidelines for achieving the program's goals. Inadequate policies or their absence result in (a) hesitancy on the part of the director because of an inability to judge whether a decision will result in endorsement or admonishment, (b) running from emergency to emergency, and (c) inconsistency in making decisions.

3. If policies are constant and apply equally to all, they ensure fair treatment. Policies thus protect the program, staff, children, and parents.

4. Policies provide a basis for evaluating existing plans and for determining the merit of proposed plans and are usually required by various funding agencies.

5. Policies may be requested by auditors.

Formulation, Interpretation, and Implementation of Policy

The responsibility for policy is in the hands of the director and/or board of directors. Regardless of the program's organization, policy is the administration's responsibility.

In small centers, especially those owned and operated as proprietorships, partnerships, or "family-owned" corporations, policy formulation is often done by the director-owner who frequently serves as a teacher too. Many of these small programs would find board-made policies intimidating, even threatening. Thus, policy is formulated, interpreted, and implemented in a pattern similar to that of a democratic family organization but with the lead taken and the final decisions made by the director.

Medium-sized centers operated by a local sponsor such as a church may have a board of directors or advisors that works with the director in policy development. The relationship between the director and the board is often more of a give-and-take relationship than a chain of command or management system.

In these medium-sized centers, the director is the "expert" on children's matters and the spokesperson for the staff, whereas the board addresses the sponsor's concerns, such as use of space and utilities, days and hours of operation, and overall program goals that reflect the sponsor's intent in operating the early childhood program.

The chain of command or line of management is the administrative structure used for most large, corporate child care programs, chain- and franchise-type child care programs, Head Start, and public school programs. In these programs, policy formulation, interpretation, and implementation are formally structured, with the responsibilities of the director and board clearly delineated. In large management types of organizations, the director again serves as an "expert" and spokesperson for the early childhood program but usually through other levels of staff. For example, a superintendent in a public school works with the school board on policy and sees that adopted policy is implemented, but only through other staff levels—that is, assistant superintendents and/or principals. Unlike small and even middle-sized programs, informal policy administration in large programs would be chaotic.

By examining policy formulation, interpretation, and implementation of policy in manage-

ment types of organizations, it is easy to grasp the nature of this administrative function in all programs. The board of directors is the policy-making and governing body of an early childhood program. More specifically, the board of directors, usually comprised of 10 to 12 members who change periodically as new members are elected or appointed, usually performs the following policy functions with the director under the program's bylaws:

1. *Formulates major policies for achieving overall goals of the program.* The board must develop or adopt the program base and provide an outline of services.

2. *Adopts all proposed policies planned by the director.* Usually, the director formulates policies, but the board must adopt all policies prior to execution.

3. *Supports the annual budget.* Usually, the director formulates the budget, and the board approves it before implementation. The board can also authorize expenditures exceeding the specified limits of the budget.

4. *Approves all personnel hired.* The director selects staff within the guidelines set by the board, and the board acts on the director's recommendations and issues the contracts.

5. *Develops criteria for evaluating the program.* The director is expected to inform the board of various evaluation instruments. Once the board selects the instrument, the director implements the evaluation.

6. *Participates in community relations.* The board represents the program in the community.

If the program is especially large and requires a great deal of policy development, the board, which always has a chairperson, may work on policies through chair-appointed committees. The suggestions of each committee are presented for total board action.

The execution of policy is the responsibility of the program's director (the local superintendent of schools in the public school system is equivalent to a director in administrative responsibility). The director is selected and hired by the board. The director, who has specialized knowledge in early childhood programs and administration, is charged with furnishing necessary information to the board, relating and interpreting information and policies back to the staff through the management process, and serving as the administrator of the staff. The board determines the degree of decision-making power delegated to the director and, in turn, the director can be empowered by the board to further delegate responsibility.

A great deal of interchange occurs between the board and the director. For example, the director should inform the board of needs for additional policies or changes in existing policies, of inconsistencies in policies, and of the community's attitudes and values; the board should provide adequate written and verbal reasons for and explanations of policies to facilitate execution and should suggest methods of executing policy.

Characteristics of Viable Policies

Developing viable policies requires that directors or boards examine their potential to achieve a program's goals, overcome the tradition of operating a program by expediency, understand the technique of policy making, and devote the time required for planning and evaluating policy. The following are some characteristics of viable policies:

1. Local program policies must conform to state law, to the policies of the funding agency, and to the policies of any other regulatory agency. The autonomy of local programs in providing care for an education of young children (developing local policy) has given way, in varying degrees, to policy and regulations of federal and state agencies. Some of these regulations may provide a needed protective role, but they also place serious constraints on the local pro-

gram. For example, assessing children's progress with a specified assessment device shapes the program accordingly, or limiting funds for staff and equipment makes it impossible to operate "the best" program. (Additional discussion of how programs are affected by the policies of funding agencies is included in Chapter 6; some ways in which early childhood leaders can affect public policy are discussed in Chapter 11.)

2. Policies should cover all aspects of the local program or, at minimum, those situations which occur frequently.

3. Internally consistent (noncontradictory) policies should be developed for the various aspects of the program. The likelihood of consistency among policies is greater if the program base and goals have been previously determined.

4. Generally speaking, policies should be followed consistently. When exceptions are necessary, they should be stated or allowed for in the policy. Frequent requests for exceptions often indicate a need for policy review.

5. Policies should not be highly specific, as they are guidelines for establishing administrative consideration and action. The administrator should be allowed discretion in solving the day-to-day problems. Furthermore, if policies are specific, they must be changed frequently. The "specifics" should be stated in the rules, regulations, and procedures developed from the policies. For example, the fee policy should indicate criteria for assessing fees, and the fee regulation should state the specific amount charged.

6. Policies should be written and made readily available so that they can be interpreted with consistency by those concerned. A written policy minimizes the probability of sudden changes. Because the board formulates policy, it can make changes at its discretion; however, the board feels the necessity for explanations more frequently when policies are written than when they are not.

7. Policies should be relatively constant. Policy should not change with changes in the membership of the board. As has been noted, the specifics (rules, regulations, and procedures) can change without resulting in a change of policy.

8. Local program policies should be subject to review and change because their validity rests on current state laws and regulations of other agencies. Because of the necessity of having adequate and current policies, a procedure requiring periodic review of all policies may be written, or certain policies may be written containing a stipulation that they be reviewed by the director or the board 1 year from the date they go into effect.

Policy Categories

As mentioned, policies should cover all aspects of the local early childhood program. Because of variations in programs, the categories of policies and especially the specific areas included in each category differ from program to program. Most early childhood programs have policies in the following categories:

1. *Program service policy.* This states the primary program services to be provided (e.g., care, education), along with other services (e.g., food, transportation, social services, parent involvement).

2. *Administrative policy.* Some specific areas included are the makeup of and procedures for selecting or electing members to the board of directors, advisory group, parent council, or other councils or committees; the appointment and functions of the director and supervisory personnel; and the administrative operations, such as the "chain of command" and membership and functions of various administrative councils and committees.

3. *Staff-personnel policy.* Areas covered often involve qualifications; recruitment, selection, and appointment; job assignment; staff training/development; supervision (e.g., state-

ment of purpose of supervision and use of data, steps in supervision sequence, copy of observation and/or rating forms, guidelines for corrective actions); tenure; promotion; termination process (e.g., circumstances for, procedures, and documentation involving firings, along with fair hearings); salary schedules and fringe benefits; payroll dates; absences and leaves; personal and professional activities; and records policies.

4. *Child-personnel policy.* This category may comprise requirements for service eligibility, including governmental and agency rules for the determination and documentation of family needs, maximum group (class) size, child-staff ratio, attendance, program services and provisions for child welfare (e.g., accidents, insurance), assessment and reporting of children's progress, and termination of program services.

5. *Health and safety policy.* This category may cover evaluation of children before admission, daily admission, care or exclusion of ill children, medication administration, health services (e.g., screening, immunizations), management of injuries and emergencies, nutrition and food handling, provision for rest/sleep, health and safety education, staff training in health and safety, and surveillance of environmental problems.

6. *Business policy.* Some areas included are sources of funding, nature of the budget (e.g., preparation, adoption, publication), procedures for obtaining funds (e.g., fees), guidelines and procedures for purchasing goods and services, persons responsible for financial management and fiscal record keeping, persons involved in disbursement of money, and a system of accounts and auditing procedures.

7. *Records policy.* Some areas included are types of records to be kept, designation of "official" records versus "staff members" notes, place where records are kept, which official will be responsible for records, and basic procedures for handling provisions of P.L. 93–380, Family Educational Rights and Privacy Act of 1974.

8. *Parents policy.* This category may comprise ways of meeting parents' needs, parent involvement in program, and basic procedures for parents to follow in making contact with the director or staff for various purposes (e.g., children's admission or withdrawal, obtaining children's progress reports, involvement in the program, services for parents).

9. *Public relations policy.* This category relates to participation by the public (e.g., citizens' advisory committees, volunteers), use of program facilities, relations with various agencies and associations, and communication with the public.

TRENDS AND ISSUES

Throughout the history of regulation, trends can be traced in both forward and backward steps. The need for regulating early childhood programs is evident when one considers the health and safety needs of children and the structural quality required before process quality can occur. Negligence has occurred, however, in protecting our defenseless clients—our children—as seen in the gaps in regulation, the two-tiered system of teacher regulation, the mistaken belief that minimum standards equal quality, and the inability to provide the training and financing needed to support higher standards.

Gaps in Regulation

When it comes to child care and the education of young children, the social norm has always been that parents make the decisions. Governmental regulations are often seen as intrusive on the rights of families (McCartney & Phillips, 1988). Various religious groups also oppose outside intervention on decisions concerning what they deem appropriate for the training of children in their programs (Sanger, 1985). Thus, regulations foment resistance by some who see the standards as intrusive.

This resistance has led to early childhood programs under certain auspices being exempt from licensing (e.g., religion-operated progra... in some states). A few regulations are simply not meaningful for early childhood programs (e.g., general school codes; A. Mitchell, Seligson, & Marx, 1989). Some programs "fall between the cracks" of two regulatory agencies and end up being not regulated. Finally, most of family child care either is not regulated or regulation is not enforced. Although some standards are higher (accreditation and model standards), these standards are met by relatively few programs.

Two-Tiered System of Teacher Regulation

Historically, two separate agencies have regulated teaching credentials: (a) child care licensing departments and (b) teacher certification offices within state departments of education. Thus, licensing has its roots in social welfare, and certification has its roots in education. Licensing accepts experience in place of formal academic preparation (college degrees) and thus encourages employment at the expense of formal education. Conversely, certification places emphasis on formal preparation with some supervised field and clinical experiences at the expense of "real" daily employment experiences. G. Morgan (1994) sees the need for a bridge to span the two tiers—a way to transform the working experiences and pre- and in-service training into some college credit. Grubb (1991) suggests creating a system that allocates different administrative functions to different existing state agencies and then coordinating all of these agencies through an existing state office (e.g., Massachusetts uses the Governor's Office of Human Resources as the coordinating agency). Such a coordinated system could help reduce the two-tiered system.

Mistaken Belief That Regulations Equal Quality

Unlike accreditation and model standards, regulations represent minimum acceptable standards. For example, all states and the District of Columbia regulate staff-child ratios. For infant programs, licensing codes in 20 states are out of compliance with the NAEYC's 1:4 recommendation. Of the 20 states, 8 use the 1:5 military standards (D. Phillips & Zigler, 1987). Only 3 states meet the Health, Education, and Welfare Day Care Regulations (HEWDCR) of 1:3. (Although the 1980 standards were never enforced, HEWDCR has become "model standards.") Furthermore, variability is even greater for older children in staff-child ratios (D. Phillips et al., 1990).

Many states have weak certification requirements for college students preparing to work with young children. Broad certification (certification for a wide age/grade span) weakens the education and training of students for work with young children. Narrow certification makes the potential employee less attractive to the employer because of fewer placement possibilities. Furthermore, college students may also find their chances of employment limited with a narrow certification simply because they must compete for fewer openings. For example, a school that employs 3 full-day kindergarten teachers will employ 9 teachers in Grades 1 through 3 and 18 teachers in Grades 1 through 6, and many schools employ teachers for half-day kindergarten programs in which one teacher has two different classes per day. (The most available positions in early childhood care and education do not require certification and thus have the least monetary compensation.) Furthermore, broad certification standards make it difficult to build quality programs at the university level. Students simply cannot get adequate training and experience with children from birth to age 8 without extending the length of the baccalaureate training. Without quality programs, excellent students are often reluctant to enter a program, and this situation further damages the early childhood program at the university level (McCarthy, 1988).

Inability to Provide Training and Financing

Training for child care is often not available, and financial support to pursue training is often insufficient. G. Morgan and her associates (1993) reported (a) scarcity of training for teachers working with infants and toddlers and with school-age child care, (b) scarcity of materials for training those working with families and children from diverse ethnic and linguistic groups, and (c) scarcity of training for administrators. Funds are often not available to support training although some funds are available for early childhood training through the Child Care Development Block Grant, CDA Scholarship, and Head Start (see Appendix 7). Schuster, Finn-Stevenson, and Ward (1990) state that an infrastructure of support for family child care is emerging. Support services are available through provider associations, child care resource and referral agencies, corporations, educational agencies, and child care agencies.

Trained personnel must be compensated. Higher salaries and a good staff-child ratio will make it harder for parents to meet child care and education costs. G. Morgan (1991) suggests that differentiated roles be identified in programs under licensing regulations (e.g., assistant teachers, teachers, lead teachers) and that these roles be linked to training. Lead teachers would have salaries comparable to public school teachers, with less compensation for teachers and still less for assistant teachers. Without governmental subsidies or large private grants, however, the problem of quality and affordability seems to be omnipresent and worsening.

SUMMARY

Regulations are the rules, directives, statutes, and standards that prescribe, direct, limit, and govern early childhood programs. Regulations, which are mandatory, come from governmental and funding agencies. For the most part, regulations represent minimum standards. Regulations covering health and safety, fiscal matters, protection of children's rights, staff qualifications, and matters concerning individuals with special needs govern all early childhood programs. Because early childhood programs differ in various ways (e.g., have different purposes, are private or public, are private not-for-profit or private for-profit), different regulations apply. On the one hand, private early childhood programs are seen as having a legal existence and thus are governed by each state's laws regarding proprietorships, partnerships, and corporations. Because these private programs are in a child care business, they are also subject to minimum standards, such as the state's licensing codes or registration requirements. On the other hand, public early childhood programs, such as those operated as part of the public school system, receive their governance directly from the state. Head Start, which is federally supported, must conform to federal guidelines and also to either licensing or school codes, depending on the agency under which it operates.

Unlike mandatory regulations, accreditation is a nonmandatory form of self-regulation, which simply means that programs that underwent self-study/validation and that received accreditation have achieved a high level of quality. Programs adhering to model standards are also of high quality.

Many issues pertain to regulations. Gaps in regulations are common—such as religion-related early childhood programs that are exempt from licensing in some states, and the family child care systems that have regulations but whose regulations are often not enforced. Another issue involves the two-tiered system of teacher preparation, with some teachers, especially public school teachers, receiving formal education and with the majority of teachers in child care centers and family child care homes often learning through only modest amounts of pre- and in-service staff development and day-to-day experiences. Also of concern is the mistaken idea that regulation equals quality. From this belief comes issues concerning the feasibility of getting the public to support licensing codes closer to professional recommendations (but that will drive up program costs) and of

convincing public school personnel to desire teachers with in-depth learning in early childhood care and education (but whose narrow certification limits their placement possibilities). The final issue addressed is the inability to provide the needed preparation for child care positions because of insufficient pre- and in-service training and materials and/or insufficient funds. Training is a vital part of raising standards and thus is linked to compensation and the dilemma of program affordability.

In addition to regulations, accreditation, and model standards, local early childhood programs need to develop policies that are the guidelines for achieving local program goals effectively and efficiently. Local policy formulation, implementation, and evaluation are the responsibilities of the director and/or board of directors.

FOR FURTHER READING

Allen, K. (1984). Federal legislation and young handicapped children. *Topics in Early Childhood Special Education, 4*(1), 9-18.

Early childhood teacher certification: A position statement of the Association of Teacher Educators and the National Association for the Education of Young Children. (1991). *Young Children, 47*(1), 16-21.

Hofferth, S., & Phillips, I. (1987). Child care in the United States: 1970-1995. *Journal of Marriage and the Family, 47*, 93-116.

Isenberg, J. P. (1990). Teachers' thinking and beliefs and classroom practice. *Childhood Education, 66*, 322, 324-327.

Kahan, E. D. (1989). *Past caring: A history of U.S. preschool care and education for the poor, 1820-1865.* New York: Columbia University, School of Public Health, National Center for Children in Poverty.

Mitchell, A., Seligson, M., & Marx, F. (1989). *Early childhood programs and the public schools: Between promise and practice.* Dover, MA: Auburn House.

Morgan, G. (1991). Regulating early childhood programs: Five policy issues. In S. L. Kagan (Ed.), *The care and education of America's young children:*

Obstacles and opportunities (pp. 173–198). Chicago: University of Chicago Press.

National Association for the Education of Young Children (NAEYC). (1987). Public policy report: NAEYC position statement on licensing and other forms of regulation of early childhood programs in centers and family day care homes. *Young Children, 42*(5), 64-68.

National Association for the Education of Young Children (NAEYC). (1991). *Accreditation criteria and procedures of the National Academy of Early Childhood Programs* (Rev. ed.). Washington, DC: Author.

Phillips, D. (Ed.). (1987). *Quality child care: What does research tell us?* Washington, DC: National Association for the Education of Young Children.

Shonkoff, J. P., & Meisels, S. J. (1990). Early childhood intervention: The evolution of a concept. In S. J. Meisels & J. P. Shonkoff (Eds.), *Handbook of early childhood intervention* (pp. 3-32). New York: Cambridge University Press.

Spodek, B., & Saracho, O. N. (Eds.). (1990). *Yearbook in early childhood education: Vol. 1. Early childhood teacher preparation.* New York: Teachers College Press.

Whitebook, M., Howes, C., & Phillips, D. (1989). *Who cares? Child care teachers and the quality of care in America.* Oakland, CA: Child-Care Employee Project.

Part Two

❀ ❀ ❀ ❀ ❀

Operationalizing the
Early Childhood Program

❀ ❀ ❀ ❀ ❀

Chapter 4

❀ ❀ ❀ ❀ ❀

Leading and Managing Personnel

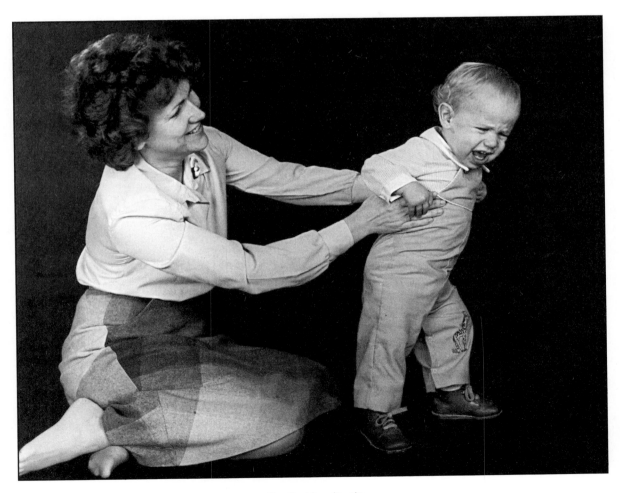

❀ ❀ ❀ ❀ ❀

The staff is the single most important determinant of the quality of early childhood programs (Arnett, 1989). To most people, a job is more than a means of earning money, it is a work situation in which an individual feels secure and accomplished. To ensure job satisfaction for staff as well as program quality, three criteria must be met in staffing: (a) The personnel must meet at least minimal qualifications for their specific duties although an employer hopes to select employees who seem to have the most potential; (b) those selected must be willing to work within the program base; and (c) personnel must believe in the program's rationale in order to work together effectively and harmoniously.

TRENDS IN STAFFING

Advocacy efforts have resulted in an increased recognition of the importance of early childhood education. In addition to the acceptance of kindergartens and primary programs as an integral part of public education, the growing consensus is that enough high-quality infant/toddler and preschool programs should exist to meet the developmental needs of these children, as well as the needs of young children's families, all at a cost that families and society can afford.

All the characteristics of high-quality programs depend on adequate numbers of well-trained staff members. Early childhood programs need increasingly larger staffs for several reasons. First, more early childhood programs are becoming comprehensive in nature; this change necessitates additional staff to provide expanded program services to children and their families and to evaluate programmatic results. Second, an adequate staff-child ratio based on the ages and needs of children served and a small group size are major factors in program quality. Unfortunately, as a result of today's economic problems, the tendency is toward fewer staff and larger groups. Third, with the inclusion of children with special needs in the program, support staff are needed for screening

and identifying such children and for helping integrate them into regular classrooms.

The demographic data on early childhood program staff are not encouraging. However, more complete data are needed. Problems include (a) an inaccurate count of the number of early childhood program personnel—especially those employed in private centers and family child care homes; (b) job titles that no longer reflect the field; (c) inaccurate salary data because of the failure to classify 12-month versus 9-month positions; (d) the need for job categories that reflect differences in education and experience; and (e) data on enrollment in training programs and final job choices for students (D. Phillips & Whitebook, 1986). Despite these inconsistencies, demographics do give a somewhat appropriate view of several trends in staffing.

Staff Shortage: A Deep-Rooted Problem

A staffing crisis is at hand. The greatest problem is not in public school early childhood programs; rather, the problem is primarily in child care programs and Head Start. Public school programs, however, cannot afford to stay unconcerned for these three reasons: (a) Pre-kindergarten children are headed for the public schools; (b) the pressure for public schools to offer pre-kindergarten programs is growing; and (c) college students have a decreasing interest in education careers, at a time when half of U.S. teachers are approaching retirement age (Whitebook, 1986).

Child care and Head Start programs are facing a staffing crisis that is now identified as "the most difficult problem" facing the nation's early childhood programs (Galinsky, 1989a). With a labor shortage, recruiting is a problem. Six out of 10 early childhood child care and Head Start employees are between the ages of 18 and 24. The number of people in this age range decreased by approximately 5 million between 1980 and 1990 (Galinsky, 1989a). Expected teacher shortages in the elementary grades will lure some of these teachers to Grades 1 through 3.

Retention of staff especially affects program quality. Staff are leaving child care and Head Start programs at alarming rates, as shown in the following retention data (as measured by turnover, separation, and tenure).

1. The **turnover rate** (number of teachers who leave a program during the year) has been extremely high. Whitebook and Granger (1989) reported an annual turnover rate between 40% and 60%. The high rates were confirmed by the National Child Care Staffing Study, which reported that staff turnover in centers rose from 15% in 1977 to 41% in 1988 (Whitebook et al., 1990). More recent documentation shows an annual teacher turnover rate of 25%. The statistics do not include turnover of assistants or aides. Turnover is concentrated in specific programs. Half of the centers experienced no turnover, and half experienced 50% turnover. Public schools had the lowest turnover rates (Kisker, Hofferth, Phillips, & Farquhar, 1991). The turnover rate in family child care is 37% to 58% annually (Nelson, 1990).

2. The **separation rate** (percentage of workers who leave an occupation during a year) is also high. Bureau of Labor Statistics (1987) data show separation rates are 35.2% for the category Child Care Worker, Except Private Household. This rate is lower than the turnover rate because it measures individuals who have changed job categories, rather than those who have simply changed employers. Thus, separation rates are highly critical to the staffing crisis because these rates represent a total loss of individuals to the profession.

3. The **tenure rate** (amount of time individuals are in a given position or in a given field) is not good. Bureau of Labor Statistics (1987) data on tenure show 2.7 years for the job category Child Care Worker, Except Private Household versus 6.6 years for the average of all jobs.

Tenure rates may be improving, however. The National Child Care Staffing Study found that two thirds of staff members viewed child care as a career, rather than as a temporary job. This view showed in the tenure. Although 29% of teachers and 58% of assistants had been employed in early childhood programs for less than 3 years, 19% had been involved for 10 years or more (as compared with the 5% involved 10 years or longer in 1977) (Whitebook et al., 1990). The U.S. General Accounting Office (GAO; 1990) reported that assistant teachers had been in their present position for 1½ years, that teachers had been in their present position for 3½ years, and that directors had held their current position for 5 years.

The staffing crisis is not caused by job dissatisfaction. The National Child Care Staffing Study found that teachers expressed very high levels of satisfaction with their work (Whitebook et al., 1990). The most important predictor of staff turnover was wages. Almost three quarters of those who left for better paying jobs in early childhood or other fields left because of inadequate compensation (Whitebook et al., 1990). Other causes included (a) lack of benefits (e.g., health, retirement), with many staff members hired on a less than full-time basis at minimum wage so that employers can avoid the costs of benefits; (b) lack of a career ladder; (c) low social status; (d) stressful working conditions (Whitebook, Howes, Phillips, & Pemberton, 1991); and (e) lack of training (Shirah, Hewitt, & McNair, 1993). (Needed benefits, career ladders, stressful working conditions, and lack of training are discussed in later sections of this chapter; compensation is discussed in Chapter 6; and the social status of the profession is reviewed in Chapter 11.)

The staffing crisis is detrimental to all those involved. Children are affected by the change in rituals and by the loss of people associated with the rituals. These less-secure children spend less time involved with peers and more time in "aimless wandering" and show drops in cognitive activities (Whitebook et al., 1990). Changes in staff are especially detrimental to infants and toddlers who do not score as well on cognitive tests (Clarke-Stewart & Gruber, 1984) and who develop less secure attachments (Howes & Hamilton, 1992), as compared with infants and toddlers experiencing no turnovers in care. It also takes time for parents to feel comfortable with new staff. And, of course, staff are affected too. For example, directors try to teach and still handle administrative responsibilities. Some centers violate licensing regulations by using unqualified personnel. The National Child Care Staffing Study reported that 55% of infant/toddler rooms and 57% of preschool rooms had only one teacher available for the bulk of the day—an impossible situation if young children's lives are to be enriched (Whitebook et al., 1990).

Staff Diversity: An Urgent Need

Early childhood staff are predominantly female (96% to 98%), under 40 years of age (80%), and members of the majority (95%) (Jorde-Bloom, 1992b; Whitehurst, Witty, & Wiggin, 1988). The need for more diversity in staff is indisputable.

The presence of men is advocated more in theory than in practice (B. Robinson, 1981). During the 1940s and 1950s, men rarely taught in early childhood programs because people believed that a man was out of his element in the kindergarten and the lower grades (Tubbs, 1946). In the 1960s and 1970s, men were recruited for early childhood staff positions to ameliorate some effects of father absence in the home for both boys and girls and to prevent children from viewing the school as a feminine environment. Scant research justifies these expectations (Seifert, 1988). Then, in the late 1970s and early 1980s, much research was conducted on the development of gender roles and androgyny (the blending of both conventional masculine and feminine traits into one personality). Men were encouraged to take positions in early childhood programs for the balance they would provide, rather than for the more "macho" image. Research sup-

ports the idea that men in early childhood programs downplay their conventional masculine behaviors and that no gender-specific differences exist in how men and women work with young children (B. Robinson, 1988). However important men may be to children's development, relatively few enter and stay in early childhood programs. This exodus may be a result of poor salaries and of a general prejudice against them by female administrators and teachers.

Older people can make major contributions to early childhood programs. Older adults help children build positive attitudes toward older people (Kocarnik & Ponzetti, 1986), help prosocial behavior (Lambert, Dellman-Jenkins, & Fruit, 1990), and help form attachment to older adults (T. Smith & Newman, 1993). Employment helps older adults by preventing feelings of isolation, by supplementing incomes, and by using their talents and lifetime experiences (Newman, Vander Ven, & Ward, 1992). Older people are also effective with parents because young parents see older people as surrogate parents (T. Smith & Newman, 1993).

Many professionals believe that the quality of programs can be improved when the staff as a whole reflect the cultural and racial diversity of the United States. This diversity provides opportunities for all children to see representatives of their own and other groups in various staff roles. Since the 1960s, the number of minority staff has waxed and waned. Today, the pool of minority teachers is getting smaller in relation to the population in public school programs. Minorities have grown to 30% of the child population, and the percentage of teachers has shrunk to 5% (Whitehurst et al., 1988). Fewer minority students are entering teacher education programs because of failure on college qualifying examinations and on state teacher competency tests (Fields, 1988).

STAFFING AN EARLY CHILDHOOD PROGRAM

After developing a program base and goals on paper, an administrator is faced with the task of determining the staff needed and of matching job requirements with staff members. This task is a continual one; staffing patterns change as a program expands or vacancies occur.

Roles and Qualifications of Personnel

Although all staff members must be in good physical and psychological health and have the personal qualities necessary to work with young children, a person's needed qualifications depend on his or her specific roles. And even roles with the same title may vary from program to program.

Personnel may be classified as either primary program personnel or support program personnel. **Primary program personnel** have direct, continuous contact with children; these include teachers, associate teachers, and assistant teachers. **Support program personnel** provide services that support or facilitate caregiving and instructional program. Although a staff member is classified by the major role, he or she may occasionally function in another capacity. For example, a teacher may occasionally clean the room or serve food, or a dietitian might discuss good eating habits with children or console a child who drops a carton of milk.

Director. A **director** is someone who may or may not be in charge of the total program. Directors of early childhood education programs in public schools are often supervisors, helpers, or resource personnel. In Montessori programs, teachers are traditionally given the title of director or directress. The title of director is frequently given to the person legally responsible for the total program and services, be it the operation of a public or private child care center, a private nursery school or kindergarten, a university or college laboratory nursery school or kindergarten, or a Head Start program. Caruso (1991) defines directors as those who supervise staff.

Role. Caruso (1991) uses the following terms to define the roles of directors: *executive director* (one who administers a large child care agency that may comprise several social service programs), *program director* (one who runs the day-to-day operations of a program), *educational coordinator* (one who is responsible for the educational component, including staff development and curriculum development, of an agency or a single program), *head teacher* (one who oversees one or more classrooms), and *supervisor* (one who oversees teachers and support personnel). The director's responsibilities may include (a) providing professional assistance to the board of directors or advisory board by supplying needed information, by recommending changes in policy, and by assisting in program evaluation; (b) developing program base and goals and providing leadership for program planning; (c) planning school policies that concern children and parents; (d) demonstrating awareness of current laws and regulations that affect children, families, and education, and ensuring that regulatory standards are maintained; (e) recruiting, employing, supervising, and training staff; (f) delegating responsibility to and terminating employment of staff; (g) supervising building maintenance and managing the program and auxiliary services; (h) representing the institution in the community; (i) establishing and maintaining school records; and (j) preparing an annual budget for the board's consideration, keeping the board informed of financial needs, and operating within the budget. In short, the role of the director is to manage the decision-making process.

Professional Qualifications. The professional qualifications of directors vary, depending on the program's organizational pattern. As you read in Chapter 3, the lowest requirements are for directors of private child care centers. Whitebook et al. (1990) found that less than half (41%) hold a bachelor's degree. Caruso (1991), in a 1989 sample, found that only 13% of those with a bachelor's degree had their major work in early childhood education/child development. At the other end of the formal education preparation are public school administrators who hold graduate degrees but who may never have taught younger children. Directors must also know how to conduct their specific early childhood programs. This knowledge may include understanding and communicating the program base, along with implementing the program and the procedures supporting it (e.g., community contacts).

Personal Characteristics.   Regardless of the program, personal characteristics of effective directors are similar. These characteristics include physical and mental stamina, openness to new ideas, flexibility of expression and thought, ability to learn from mistakes, cheerfulness, warmth and sensitivity to both children and adults, personal sense of security, desire to succeed, and honesty.

Primary Program Personnel.   As discussed in Chapter 1, distinctions between *care* and *education* should not be made. Similarly, distinctions between *child care workers* and *teachers* are no longer useful. The Governing Board of the National Association for the Education of Young Children (NAEYC) approved the following titles and descriptions:

1. **Early childhood teacher assistant** is a preprofessional with no specialized early childhood preparation who implements program activities under direct supervision.

2. **Early childhood associate teacher** is a professional with minimal early childhood preparation (holds a CDA credential or an associate degree in early childhood education/child development) who independently implements activities and may be responsible for a group of children.

3. **Early childhood teacher** is a professional with an undergraduate degree in early childhood education/child development and is responsible for a group of children ("NAEYC Position Statement on Nomenclature," 1984).

Role.   Very little distinction can be made between the tasks performed by teachers in the various early childhood programs. The role of professional teachers should vary, depending on education and experience. The role may include the following responsibilities: (a) serve in a leadership capacity with other staff members, (b) implement the program base by observing and determining children's needs in relation to program goals and by planning activities, (c) communicate verbally and sympathetically with children, (d) respond effectively to children's behavior, and (e) model and articulate to parents and other staff members practices in keeping with the program's rationale. Teachers must also be acquainted with, accept, and use children's differences due to special needs and culture.

Professional Qualifications.   Professional qualifications of early childhood teachers in various programs were discussed in Chapter 3. Although the formal education and the compensation may vary, except in programs with team teaching, the duties performed by teachers, teacher associates, and teacher assistants are essentially the same (Whitebook, Howes, Darrah, & Friedman, 1982). In public school programs, inexperienced certified teachers and teachers on "emergency-type certificates" are immediately given total responsibility for a group of children.

Personal Characteristics.   Personal characteristics associated with an effective teacher are difficult to define. Opinion varies as to what constitutes a good teacher of young children. In addition, teaching styles (personality traits, attitudes) are interwoven with teaching techniques (methodology). Characteristics and skills often associated with effective early childhood teachers include warmth, flexibility, integrity, sense of humor, physical and mental stamina, vitality, emotional stability and confidence, naturalness, and ability to support development without being overprotective (Read & Patterson, 1980). Feeney and Christensen (1979) wrote that the most important characteristic of a good teacher is the ability *to be with* young children, rather than what one *does to* or *for* young children.

Balaban (1992) described 12 ways in which teachers are with young children; among these ways are as anticipators and planners, listeners and watchers, protectors, providers of interesting environments, elicitors of language, and smoothers of jangled feelings.

Rosen (1975) found that the content of what college students recalled about their relations with their parents can predict their ability to relate to children and their effectiveness in working with children of different ages. For example, the most effective teachers of the youngest children described their own joy and sense of security during those years. Those judged most effective with 5- to 8-year-olds recalled their desire for independence and the early need to achieve basic skills. The college students judged most effective with older children remembered adults and older siblings who had stimulated a love of learning in them. Another study suggests that the majority of college students entering early childhood education are people-oriented, rather than idea-oriented (McCauley & Natter, 1980). In addition to the foregoing characteristics, teachers who work with infants should be able to develop very close bonds with infants, "read" behavioral cues (e.g., distinguish among cries), and make long-term commitments to programs so that infants are provided continuity. Because teaching is so complex and multifaceted, more research needs to be conducted on personal characteristics and effectiveness.

Support Program Personnel. The major role of support program personnel is to furnish services that support or facilitate the program, such as dietitians and food-service personnel, medical staff, psychologists, caseworkers, maintenance staff, general office staff, transportation staff, and volunteers. A new category of support program personnel are **case managers,** a position created through the Individualized Family Service Plan (IFSP) requirements of Part H of P.L. 99-457. Similar in role to caseworkers, case managers are child and family advocates who serve as a linking agent between families and needed service agencies. Unlike caseworkers, who are traditionally from the social work profession, IFSP case managers are chosen because of expertise in relation to a given child's primary problem and thus may be, for example, a nutritionist, a physical therapist, or a speech pathologist. Some categories of support personnel are found mainly in public school and government-funded early childhood programs. In very small proprietorships, food service, maintenance, and office work are done by the director, teachers, and/or parent volunteers. Support program personnel must have the qualifications of their respective professions (Decker & Decker, 1992). They must also be knowledgeable about age-level expectations of young children. Personal qualifications include the ability to communicate with children and to work with all adults involved in the program.

Substitute personnel should have the same professional qualifications and personal characteristics as the regularly employed personnel whom they replace. To ensure program continuity, careful plans should be made. Such plans are most essential where substitute personnel will be working alone (e.g., in a self-contained classroom), rather than in a team approach, especially kindergartens and primary grades/levels. Because substitute teachers are the most often hired substitute personnel, the following is a discussion of how plans for these teachers can be made. Planning for any substitute, however, would use some of the same methods.

Directors of early childhood programs must develop a list of potential substitute teachers who meet the same qualifications as the teachers for whom they will be working. Each program must establish a procedure for obtaining substitute personnel; usually, the absent teacher contacts the director who, in turn, secures the substitute.

The teacher has an important responsibility in planning for substitute personnel. Because impending illness or emergency gives few advance warnings, plans must be made soon after the teacher begins employment; the plans must be kept current. Some suggestions for planning for substitute personnel follow:

1. As soon as the children are secure in the early childhood program, prepare them for the possibility of a substitute. Young children are often frightened unless they are prepared in advance. One way to do this is to have prospective substitutes visit (or even employ them for work) before they are needed. The visitation can also serve as an orientation of the prospective substitute to the program or as a check to determine whether this person seems to fit into the program.

2. In as much detail as possible, have the procedures for the following in writing: for greeting the children, such as where to meet them and the greeting ritual; for meals, snacks, and toileting; for types of activities planned in each major block of time on the schedule; for moving the children from one activity to another within the room, such as a verbal, light-blinking, or musical signal; for moving children outdoors and to other parts of the building; for emergencies, such as evacuation of the building and illness of a child; for conducting the administrative functions, such as attendance or meal counts or sending notes home to parents; and for departure of children, such as the method of getting home, to the exit door, and onto the correct bus.

3. Write plans for a minimum of 2 or 3 days. Plans should be ideas appropriate any time of the year and should not burden substitute personnel by requiring extremely careful supervision or extensive preparation or cleanup time.

4. Provide a shelf or cabinet for the specific equipment and materials needed for the plans, such as a storybook and record/tape for rhythmic activities. Large pieces of equipment, such as record/cassette players and playground balls, may be left in their usual places. Because substitute personnel do not know the children's names, name tags should be placed with the equipment and materials.

5. Keep an up-to-date list of the children and note those with special problems—physical, intellectual, or emotional—and procedures to follow with these problems.

6. Keep a note taped to your desk or in some other obvious place, telling where to find the information and materials for substitute personnel.

7. Leave on the desk the schedule of semi-regular activities, such as library time, special duty, or times for special-subject teachers or other personnel to work with children.

8. If the substitute did a good job, call and express appreciation. The substitute should relate any special problems that occurred. Inform the director or building principal of the quality of the substitute's work so that a decision can be made about rehiring the substitute.

Assessing Needs and Recruiting Staff

The director may seek a diverse staff through an informal needs assessment or a rigorous affirmative action plan. Because the budget is usually limited, the director must also determine priorities. Other considerations may include the potential staff available, the amount of space needed for staff offices and other facilities, and the amount of training and supervision to be conducted. The necessary positions must then be translated into job descriptions.

The director or personnel administrator is responsible for advertising the positions. Programs must follow affirmative action guidelines in recruiting and hiring. **Affirmative action** entails identifying and changing discriminatory employment practices and taking positive steps to recruit and provide an accepting working environment for minorities and women. Manuals on affirmative action programs are available. The Americans With Disabilities Act (ADA) outlaws employment discrimination due to disability. The Economic Employment Opportunity

Commission will consider the job description and whether reasonable accommodations can be made. The NAEYC adopted a general (comprehensive) antidiscriminatory policy in 1988 stating that employment decisions must be based solely on the competence and qualifications of persons to perform "designated duties" ("NAEYC Business," 1988). Possible steps in recruiting staff include developing/gathering recruitment materials, advertising, having applicants complete job applications, obtaining documentation of credentials, interviewing, and hiring for a probationary period.

Developing/Gathering Recruitment Materials. Recruitment materials must include job descriptions that list duties in terms of "essential functions" and how frequently each must be performed, responsibilities, and authority and give qualifications and skills required. Public relations brochures and policy manuals are also good recruitment materials. (Job descriptions, contracts, and other personnel records are discussed later in this chapter.)

Advertising.   The director should first notify persons already involved in the program of an opening and then make the advertisement public. The advertisement should be in keeping with the job description and state all nonnegotiable items, such as required education and experience, so that unqualified applicants can be quickly eliminated. It should also include the method of applying and the deadline for application. Figure 4-1 is an example of a newspaper advertisement.

The method of applying and the acceptance of applications will depend on the abilities and experiences of applicants and the director's time. Thus, the method of application may vary from a telephone call or completion of a simple to a lengthy application form, a resume, and a letter requesting transcripts and credentials. A simple application form is given in Figure 4–2 as an example.

After the deadline for application, the director or other staff member in charge of hiring will screen applications to eliminate unqualified applicants. The administrator is required by affirmative action guidelines to list reasons for rejection and to notify applicants.

Obtaining Documentation of Credentials and Interviewing.   The director can legally contact all references given on the application and all former employers concerning work history and character. These references are aids in seeing how the applicant performed in the eyes of others. A sample application letter and accompanying reference form are shown in Figure 4–3.

Figure 4-1   Job Advertisement

Early childhood teachers wanted for a college-sponsored child development center. Responsibilities include planning and implementing developmentally appropriate activities for a group of twelve 3-year-old children. A.A. degree in child development/early childhood education or a C.D.A. certificate required; teaching experience preferred. Essential functions include constantly maintaining visual supervision of children to ensure safety and occasionally lifting, carrying, and holding children. Write for an application to Mrs. A. Jones, Director, Johnson County Community College Child Development Center, (*address*) or call (*telephone/fax*) Monday through Thursday between 2:00 and 4:00 p.m. Deadline for applications, August 1. We are an Equal Opportunity Employer.

Application For Teacher Position

JOHNSON COUNTY COMMUNITY COLLEGE CHILD DEVELOPMENT CENTER

Name of applicant _____ _____ _____
                        Last   First   Middle or maiden

Address _____ _____ Zip _____

Telephone number (___) _____

RECORD OF EDUCATION

High school(s) attended

Name of school	School address	Years attended	Years completed (check)
1. _____	_____	From _____	Fr. _____ Soph. _____ Jr. _____
	_____	to _____	Sr. _____ Graduated _____
2. _____	_____	From _____	Fr. _____ Soph. _____ Jr. _____
	_____	to _____	Sr. _____ Graduated _____

College(s) attended

Name of college	Address	Years attended	Level completed (check)
1. _____	_____	From _____	No degree: _____
	_____	to _____	Degree received: _____
			Major: _____
2. _____	_____	From _____	No degree: _____
	_____	to _____	Degree received: _____
			Major: _____

Figure 4–2 Simple Application for Teacher Position

Teaching certificates: _____

(Name of certificate)

RECORD OF WORK EXPERIENCE

Name and address of employer(s)	Date(s) of employment	Nature of work (Describe)
1. _____	From ____ to ____	_____
2. _____	From ____ to ____	_____
3. _____	From ____ to ____	_____

List names and addresses of three references who are familiar with your educational progress and/or work experiences.

1. _____

2. _____

3. _____

I understand that my signature on this application legally permits authorized administrators of the Johnson County Community College Child Development Center to contact all former employers concerning my work history and character as it pertains to the position for which I have applied.

_____   _____

(Signature)   (Date)

Figure 4–2 *continued*

Johnson County Community College Child Development Center

TO: _____

FROM: _____

RE: _____
(Name of applicant)

The applicant has given your name as a person who can provide a reference on his or her qualifications. We want to select teachers whose professional preparation, experience, and personality can be expected to produce the best results at our Child Development Center. Please give your full and frank evaluation. Your reply will be kept in strict confidence. Please assist both us and the applicant by replying promptly.

Teaching Position Reference

How would you describe the applicant's ability in each of the following areas?

1. Knowledge of young children's development:

2. Ability to plan developmentally appropriate activities to enrich and extend children's development:

3. Ability to implement planned activities to enrich and extend children's development:

4. Ability to use positive guidance including disciplining techniques with children:

5. Ability to assess children's progress:

6. Ability to organize a physical setting:

7. Ability to work with parents:

8. Ability to work with other staff members as a team:

9. Capacity for professional and personal growth:

On the basis of your present knowledge, would you employ this applicant in a program for which you were responsible? _____

Please explain: _____

What opportunity have you had to form your judgment of this applicant? _____

_____

Additional remarks: _____

_____   _____   _____
(Date)   (Signature)   (Title)

Figure 4-3   Sample Application Letter and Reference Form

Since 1985, many states have passed laws requiring national criminal records checks for child care center employees. These laws were implemented to comply with federal legislation, P.L. 98-473. Criminal history records checks are the only way to defend against a claim of negligent hire (employer is held responsible for injuries to a third party if the injury was foreseeable or if the employer did not investigate before hiring). Following the screening of applications, reference checks, and criminal history records checks, all promising applicants should be interviewed. These steps should be followed in the interview process:

1. The director must follow established board policies concerning the nature, setting, and person conducting the interview, along with determining who will make the final decision regarding selection of the candidate.

2. The director must be careful to follow Title VII of the 1964 Civil Rights Act prohibiting discriminatory hiring practices. The rule of thumb is that any question asked of the applicant must have a "business necessity." Some questions to avoid are date of birth or age, marital status, spouse's occupation, pregnancy issues and number of children, child care arrangements, religious affiliation (although inquiry may be made whether the scheduled work days are suitable), membership in organization (except those pertaining to the position), race or national origin (except for affirmative action information), arrest record, type of discharge from the military, union memberships, and disabilities (only ask whether the person can perform job specific functions). Inquiring about citizenship is not considered discriminatory; the administrator may ask to see a 1-151 Alien Registration Card or a 1-94 Arrival-Departure Card.

3. The interview should reveal the applicant's ideas and attitudes toward children. The interview questions should match the type of candidate (e.g., with older candidates, focus on experiences, rather than on career paths; Newman et al., 1992).

4. The interviewer should also discuss and answer questions about the program, such as the program base, the ages of enrolled children, the guidance and discipline practices, how children are evaluated, the degree of parent involvement, salary, the length of school day and year, a complete description of job, opportunities for promotion, fringe benefits, sick leave and retirement plans, consulting and supervisory services, and the nature and use of evaluation to determine job performance and advancement. (For future reference, a staff handbook containing such information should be made available to those hired.)

Hiring. The applicants are informed about the selection at a given date and in a specified manner. The person who is hired must usually sign a contract and other required personnel papers. If no applicant is hired, the recruitment process is repeated.

Many programs give the "hired" applicant a trial work period in which the director or hiring committee tries to see how compatible the person is with program practices. The conditions of the probationary period must be clearly communicated to the new employee before hiring. The trial period should last 6 months or less, and pay should be slightly less than full salary.

WORKING WITH STAFF MEMBERS

The function of administration is to mobilize and coordinate ideas, resources (material things), and people to achieve the program's goals with effectiveness and efficiency. Working with staff requires both leadership and management skills. **Leadership** involves making decisions that mold future goals of the program. All programs must function smoothly on a day-to-day basis. **Management** involves providing continuity for program functioning.

Kagan (1994) has pointed out that leadership theory has evolved through three waves of ideas: (a) styles and behaviors in which leaders approach various tasks, (b) how the organization's history and culture influence and are influenced by leadership, and (c) the characteristics of leaders and how these characteristics affect their interactions. Although Kagan acknowledges the applicability of some of the ideas from traditional literature, she believes it is not a perfect fit for early childhood care and education. Early childhood leadership is often shared rather than sole leadership; involves small, informal programs more than large organizations; and is collaborative rather than competitive. Kagan believes that total quality management (TQM) is a better fit for early childhood care and education. TQM focuses on shared problem solving, empowerment of frontline employees, and involvement through participatory groups (e.g., quality circles; Lawler, Mohrman, & Ledford, 1992).

In working with staff, several principles are appropriate, including (a) keeping the program base in the forefront, (b) making decisions through a team approach, (c) stating plans in terms of objectives, and (d) developing a plan for action.

Keep the Program Base in the Forefront

In T. Peters and Waterman's research (1982), three of the eight attributes characterizing excellent, innovative companies dealt with the organization's program base. For example, one attribute was that companies *stick to knitting;* that is, companies do best when they stay close to the business they know. Thus, careful selection of an early childhood program base is important, and once it is chosen, all components of the program must fit the base. Another quality attribute was that companies have *tight properties.* These companies have core values that administrators use for all decision making and for evaluation criteria. These values are the focal

point for operations; thus, the third attribute—that companies are *value driven.* Early childhood programs would do well to look at the research of major quality indicators such as that of Fiene (1986a, 1986b). Fiene, in examining compliance on licensing standards, found that quality early childhood programs had a high level of compliance on certain major standards but did not necessarily show compliance on less important standards.

Make Decisions Through a Team Approach

The early childhood field has had a long history of shared leadership. Parents and professionals shared leadership in parent cooperatives and Head Start. Today, the emerging effort is toward networking and collaboration. However, the team approach is not always carried out in the real world. Data from a San Francisco study of early childhood programs revealed that only 18% of teaching staff were included in major decision making. Most staff members found themselves in a hierarchial decision-making structure, and over half said they were dissatisfied with the arrangement (Whitebook, 1981).

Kagan (1994) has developed a continuum of leadership that moves from sole leadership to supported leadership (the leader seeks input) to dual leadership (two leaders share responsibility) to shared leadership (leadership shared by all through collaboration). In an early childhood program, staff members working together can generate novel ideas, innovative proposals, and new strategies. Many of these ideas may come during informal exchanges. Gaps may occur in the sharing of ideas, however, unless a more formal method of communication is established. Staff meetings are thus essential for planning. Effective staff meetings must be carefully planned and executed and the following tips kept in mind:

1. Have a purpose for calling a staff meeting. Do not call meetings unless discussion is

needed. Routine announcements may be made in other ways.

2. If decisions to be made pertain only to a few staff members, do not call a general staff meeting.

3. Schedule meetings at times suitable to the staff. Generally, a regular time should be set aside during work hours.

4. Prepare and distribute an agenda a few days before the scheduled meeting. Certain materials to be discussed should be available prior to the meeting. The agenda should indicate the name of the person presenting an item and the amount of time allocated for the presentation. Additional time for discussion and voting should be included.

5. Stay within time limits. (Agenda items may be omitted or added and time allocations changed with group consensus.)

6. Listen to each staff member's ideas during a discussion.

7. Start and stop the meeting on time.

8. Distribute minutes of the meeting to staff. Minutes should be read and approved before sending them to the board of directors and/or filing them.

State Plans in Terms of Objectives and Develop a Plan of Action

Once plans are made, they need to be stated in terms of objectives. From management science comes a strategy called *management by objective and results (MBO/R)*, based on the assumption that people perform better and are more productive if they know what is expected and if the expectations are considered realistic and achievable. MBO/R begins with defining the program's goals, then establishing objectives in keeping with the goals, identifying performance indicators, and setting standards for individuals. Thus, MBO/R places emphasis on a sense of achievement based on knowing one's contribution to an

organization. A plan for each objective to be accomplished must be determined. Complex projects must be broken into simple components. Many organizations find time schedules useful to stimulate action.

IMPROVING QUALITY OF PERSONNEL

Although the importance of competent staff to quality programs is not debatable, it is difficult to define competence in terms of the exact background needed. Ruopp, Travers, Glantz, and Coelen (1979) found specialized education and training the chief predictor of competence; conversely, authors of the National Child Care Staffing Study concluded that formal education, as opposed to specialized training, was the strongest predictor (Whitebook et al., 1991). Both studies agreed that experience was not a reliable predictor of competence. Vander Ven (1986) believes that early childhood professionals, especially those who work directly with children, must meld craftsmanship with specialized knowledge. Katz and Raths (1986) also believe that, in addition to background, a certain teacher "disposition" is necessary to be effective.

Regardless of whether professional development occurs as preservice or in-service or whether it is primarily formal education or workshop-type training, the NAEYC (1994) has released a position statement concerning the core content of childhood professionals' knowledge base. All professionals must be able to (a) demonstrate and apply knowledge of child development, (b) observe and assess children for purposes of planning an individualized and appropriate curriculum, (c) establish and maintain a healthy and safe environment, (d) employ appropriate techniques of individual guidance and group management, (e) establish positive and productive relationships with families, and (f) make a commitment to professionalism. Bredekamp and Willer (1992) have developed diagrams of the core knowledge that show how core knowledge is a recursive cycle, revisited in greater depth and breadth at higher levels of preparation when professional development is comprehensive and articulated.

Analyses of a program's strengths and weaknesses provide a basis for improving the quality of personnel. All personnel need to refresh current skills and learn new ones. Because early childhood programs and personnel differ in many ways, methods of improvement also differ. Five methods for improving the quality of personnel are (a) formal education, (b) staff development, (c) membership in professional organizations, (d) performance supervision and (e) evaluation, and alleviation of job stress.

Early childhood is a diverse field, with people working in various roles and entering the profession at various levels of competence in both experience and education. Professional growth needs to be rewarded. Career ladders (and now a lattice) have been proposed, but there is no consensus on whether this concept is in the best interest of the professional or even practical. This issue is discussed later in this chapter.

Formal Education

The founder and early leaders of the kindergarten movement required a course of study for prospective teachers. As kindergartens and other early childhood programs became part of the public schools, teachers were required to obtain teaching certificates. Local boards of education also required refresher courses or work toward an advanced degree for renewal of a contract and/or pay raises. Katz (1972) indicates that teachers in the stages of renewal and maturity (after 3 to 5 years of experience) are in need of college work. Unlike public school teachers, teachers working in programs that must meet state licensing requirements (e.g., child care centers) and public programs (e.g., Head Start) take college courses after being employed. Com-

pared with the civilian labor force, more child care and Head Start teachers have attended college; however, fewer of the teaching staff had received a college degree in 1988 than in 1977 (Whitebook et al., 1990).

Formal education programs today consist of (a) general education; (b) educational foundations made up of knowledge about education and children; (c) instructional knowledge, such as courses related to the roles of teachers—curriculum designer, diagnostician, organizer of instruction, manager of learning, counselor, and adviser as identified by Saracho (1993), and (d) field experiences in which students relate what they have been learning to working directly with children. Cooper and Eisenhart (1990) have discussed some reforms in teaching education, such as abolishing undergraduate teacher education programs, creating extended teacher education programs, putting a cap on education hours, extending field experiences, creating internships and alternative approaches for certification, and establishing more specific (narrow, rather than broad) forms of teacher education. Another trend is a move away from competency-based to performance-based (also called *outcome-based*) teacher education as seen in the standards being developed by the National Board for Professional Teaching Standards (Willer & Bredekamp, 1993). The features of outcome-based programs can be examined in McCarthy's (1994) discussion of professional standards.

Staff Development

Another method for improving the quality of personnel is staff development. Most professionals see staff development as a major catalyst to the development of high-quality programs for young children. As has been discussed, even teachers who hold teaching certificates need renewal. Concern that adults in child care and Head Start programs often begin working before receiving adequate training and that staff in all settings often work in isolation without the benefits of sharing ideas and problems with others has led to an awareness of the need for staff development programs (Logue, Eheart, & Leavitt, 1986; Rosenholtz & Kyle, 1984). The need for staff development is so great that professional associations are most concerned. Furthermore, early childhood leaders in state departments of education have been pushing for more funding for staff development (S. Robinson, 1993/94).

The value of staff development appears to be obvious. Unfortunately, staff development needs are rarely met. Jorde-Bloom (1989) showed that less than two thirds of the approximately 1,000 centers involved in the study provided any staff development within the previous year. Similarly, Whitebook et al. (1990) found that only 25% of teaching staff had 15 hours or more of in-service training within the previous year. Directors play critical roles in the quality of their programs because the directors must guide the professional development of their staffs (Bredekamp, 1990; Jorde-Bloom & Sheerer, 1991).

Content of Staff Development.   Content for staff development must help with the changes that are occurring in teaching and with the discarding of inappropriate practices and the rebuilding of appropriate practices. Because such wide variations exist in the training backgrounds of child care staff, staff development can provide the core knowledge needed by all early childhood professionals and the specific knowledge needed due to role. For example, family child care providers have special needs (Trawick-Smith & Lambert, 1995). Thus, to be effective, staff development activities must meet the collective needs of the staff and the individual needs of staff members for improving the quality of the program.

Collective Needs.   Orientation to a specific program is needed by all staff members. Orientation should always cover the program base. Staff members cannot work as a team if they do not

understand and accept the rationale of the program base and the objectives stemming from the rationale. Other items that orientation should cover include the clientele served, the services of the program, the physical facility, and regulations and local program policies.

Development should continue throughout a staff member's tenure. To be effective, professional development must be seen as an active process of growing and learning, and not a product (e.g., a workshop presented by someone else). For staff development to be effective, group needs must be identified. Abbott-Shim (1990) recommends the use of data from individual evaluations, needs assessment surveys, and program evaluations. Data can be collected in the following ways:

1. **Staff evaluations** show the strengths and weaknesses of individual staff members. A summary of strengths and weaknesses of staff members can be used to determine potential training areas.

2. **Needs assessment surveys** are surveys in which staff check topics of perceived needs. The administrator summarizes the responses and identifies training needs. A simple needs assessment survey is given in Figure 4–4.

3. **Program evaluation measures** provide comprehensive evaluation. Several program evaluation measures were described in Chapter 2. Benham, Miller, and Kontos (1988) developed a way of identifying training needs by using the Early Childhood Environment Rating Scale (ECERS). Quantitative data can be obtained by using subarea profiles of the ECERS.

Other areas needed by all include the following:

1. *Teachers need training in child development.* Research indicates that training in child development is the best predictor of teaching quality. Teachers must learn to integrate what they learn about curriculum, assessment, and

Needs Assessment Survey of
Johnson County Community College Child Development Center

We need some information regarding your specific needs for training. After reading the entire list below, check 6 topics (from the 48 listed) that you would like to have covered in in-service training. After checking, rank the topics in order of importance, with "1" being the most important to you.

Child care

_____ Regulations/Legal issues

_____ Evaluation of children

_____ Mainstreaming exceptional children

_____ Health and safety

Child development

_____ Physical development (general)

_____ Social development

_____ Cognitive development

_____ Emotional development

_____ Morals/Values development

_____ Language development

_____ Motor skill development

Curriculum (Preschool through primary)

_____ Art

_____ Oral language

_____ Writing

_____ Literature

_____ Prereading skills

_____ Mathematics

_____ Social studies

_____ Science

_____ Music

_____ Gross-motor play

_____ Fine-motor play

_____ Incorporating computers

_____ Incorporating multicultural/multilingual learnings

_____ Cooking experiences

_____ Sand/Water/Mud play

_____ Woodworking experiences

_____ Block-building experiences

_____ Dramatic play experiences

Organization and management

_____ Arranging physical environments

_____ Use of indoor equipment/materials

_____ Use of outdoor equipment/materials

_____ Scheduling problems

_____ Transitions

_____ Grouping

_____ Encouraging effective child-child interactions

_____ Encouraging effective child-adult interactions

_____ Encouraging effective child-material interactions

_____ Guiding children's behavior (discipline)

Staff needs

_____ Credentials/Training requirements

_____ Communication skills

_____ Team teaching

_____ Evaluation

_____ Policy development

Families

_____ Parent education

_____ Parent involvement

_____ Parent support

_____ Meeting needs of special families
(e.g., single parents)

Figure 4-4   Needs Assessment Survey

group management with what they know about children (Elkind, 1991).

2. *Teachers need training in inclusion of children with special needs.* Special education personnel can help regular teachers with concepts and practices concerning holistic development, meeting individual needs, and using a family focus. Regular teachers can share their backgrounds in child development (Rose & Smith, 1993). Regular teachers need help in learning use of equipment, warning signs for pending crises, and universal precautions/infection control. Staff development opens the doors for ongoing interdisciplinary support of children with special needs and often changes the cautious and even negative attitudes frequently noted when regular teachers first face inclusion. Many regular teachers have reported becoming even more aware of the needs of all children following inclusion (Giangreco, Dennis, Coninger, Edelman, & Schattman, 1993; Kontos, 1988). D. Fink (1988) points out that staff development for inclusion is really a needed area in school-age child care (SACC) because children with special needs are often excluded.

3. *Teachers need training in multicultural/ antibias concepts and practices.* Teachers need to examine their own biases first. Jorde-Bloom (1992a) examines the ways in which teachers can assess their beliefs and attitudes.

4. *Research on other centers can be used for identifying training needs if the research pinpoints needs that are representative of needs in the local program.* For example, Benham et al. (1988), in their study of 21 centers, noted these four weak areas: (a) providing for privacy, comfort, and relaxation for children and adults in the physical facility; (b) developing a sensitivity to and planning for individual differences, differences in needs for group participation and quiet times, and needs of exceptional children; (c) promoting children's experimentation with and exploration of materials; and (d) translating developmental knowledge into goals/objectives and translating objectives into activities.

Individual Needs.   In the area of individual needs of staff members and the type of support each needs, two excellent resources are available. First, Katz (1972) has identified four stages of development and the training needs of in-service teachers at each stage:

1. *Survival.* The 1st year of teaching is filled with self-doubt. Teachers need on-site support and technical assistance.

2. *Consolidation.* During the 2nd and perhaps 3rd year, teachers consolidate the gains they have made and focus on specific skills. They need on-site assistance, access to specialists, and advice from colleagues.

3. *Renewal.* During the 3rd and 4th year, job stress is eliminated by assistance in analysis of teaching and by participation in professional associations.

4. *Maturity.* After the 5th year, teachers benefit more by additional formal education, by professional conferences, and through contributions to the profession (e.g., journal writing).

Second, instead of using experience stages, Arin-Krump (1981) has identified staff needs and training needs for seven age stages. She has based her ideas on the work of Erik Erikson, Robert Havighurst, Roger Gould, and Gail Sheehy. For example, Arin-Krump states that teachers in their 20s are in the stages of *identity* and *intimacy.* Marriage and parents are key concerns, and family life creates much stress. At this age, teachers also want to demonstrate job competence. Thus, staff development for this age-group is most successful if it (a) creates a climate that permits discussion of life stresses and (b) defines the parameters of the job and discusses means for effecting change in areas of deficit.

A self-evaluation form is also helpful as a starting point for discussions of individual needs. One example of such a form is a simple open-ended questionnaire covering achievements, challenges, and disappointments ("Staff Self-Evaluation Form," 1992).

Techniques Used for Staff Development. Techniques used in staff development should fit staff members' abilities, skills, and interests, as well as possess appropriate training content. For example, Latimer (1994) gives some pointers on training older adults. The method of presentation should be varied to hold interest. And, most important, staff must be involved and able to see direct application to their professional responsibilities.

Many techniques for staff development are used. Examples include the following:

1. *Teaching observations.* Modeling can be helpful if the person learning is free to observe and if the trainer sees him- or herself in a teaching role (e.g., giving background information concerning classroom practices) and follows up with discussions of the practices observed. Discussions must focus on the strengths, rather than call into question people's inappropriate current practices.

2. *Discussions.* Staff can learn through discussing and solving problems. Teachers can gain much from reflection on their own work. They can also gain from the sharing of personal narratives. Change in teaching occurs through the process of listening and responding (Cinnamond & Zimpher, 1990). Narratives are not new in early childhood (Ashton-Warner, 1963; C. Pratt, 1948). Recently published narratives (listed at the end of the chapter) are good for staff development. Because of staff diversity, beliefs and values about program goals and policies should be explored through discussions (Carter, 1992).

3. *Child observations.* Observing children and discussing observations with the trainer can provide insight into age-appropriate behaviors of children and/or specific behaviors (e.g., temper tantrums, altruistic behaviors).

4. *Individual conferences.* The director provides feedback to the staff member following an observation and discusses ways in which the staff member may grow and the director can be supportive.

5. *Workshops.* Workshops are the most common form of training (Kisker et al., 1991). Workshops may be provided through outside sources (e.g., professional organizations) or developed by staff themselves. Workshops often center on one topic. Carter (1993) has developed some ideas for examining cultural perspectives through a workshop approach.

6. *Consultation.* Consultants must be viewed as resource people and not as "experts" hired to solve problems if consultation is to yield lasting results (Louchs, 1983). There are at least three consultation models. In the **traditional model,** the consultant is helped to understand the nature and cause of the problem and finds possible solutions (Keister, 1969). In the **enabler approach,** the consultant is referred to as an "enabler" who comes to know the program and people and helps staff find their own solutions (Holt, 1977). In the **Yale psychoeducational clinic approach,** the consultant goes beyond the problem presented by applying knowledge, skills, and/or resources not available to the program in an effort to improve the total program (Sarason, 1966). If consultant work is to be secured, the administrator must identify potential resource people, describe (in writing) training needs, and provide a format to be completed by potential resource people. Figure 4–5 is an example of a proposal format. An evaluation of both proposed presentations and the selected presentation is essential. Figure 4–6 is an example of an evaluation format.

7. *Accreditation process.* The accreditation process is a major avenue for staff development. Buck (1987) has given pointers on how to sell accreditation to the staff.

Figure 4–5   Example of a Proposal Format

Workshop Proposal

The following information must be submitted for consideration as a resource person for the Johnson County Community College Child Development Center.

   Name, address, day and evening phone numbers of individuals submitting request.

   Main presenter resume (title, academic and professional background).

   Names and addresses and resumes of other presenters.

   Objectives of presentation.

   Outline of presentation.

      Concept:

      Delivery strategy:

      Time required:

   Method to be used to evaluate workshop effectiveness.

   Resource materials provided by consultant.

   Special requests (e.g., observation in center before presentation, audiovisual equipment).

---

8. *Professional resources.* All programs can benefit from use of professional journals, books, and audiovisual materials. Handbooks can be used for understanding the program goals and expectations for parents, children, and employees (Greenberg, 1975). A unique method was the use of viewing *Mister Rogers' Neighborhood* to increase staff warmth (Marazon, 1994). These resources lend themselves to both group and individual development.

Membership in Professional Organizations

Membership in professional organizations offers various opportunities for personnel to improve their qualifications. Unfortunately, the National Child Care Staffing Study found that only 14% of teaching staff belonged to a child-related professional group and that the ones who belonged to the professional organizations were the most educated (Whitebook et al., 1990).

Professional organizations publish literature such as journals, position papers, and other materials to aid members in professional growth and competence. Almost all professional organizations have regular national, regional, and state meetings that provide a means for hearing and seeing the "latest" and for sharing ideas with others. Professional organizations serve as public representation—advocacy—of members' views to local, state, and national governing bodies. Some organizations offer opportunities for travel and study, research assistance, and consultation. Others provide personal services to members, such as insurance policies and loans. Finally, membership in a professional association says to parents and the community in general, "I am joining with others in an effort to provide the best for our children." See Appendixes 4 and 5 for listings of many professional organizations concerned with the development of young children.

Evaluation of _____

Johnson County Community College Child Development Center

Rank each item on a 3-point scale: 1 (Excellent), 2 (Satisfactory), and 3 (Poor).

	Proposal	*Presentation*
Objectives related to training needs	_____	_____
Content related to training needs	_____	_____
Content applicable to work with children	_____	_____
Content organized	_____	_____
Content clearly presented	_____	_____
Delivery strategies held interests of participants	_____	_____
Delivery strategies encouraged give-and-take among staff members and between staff and resource person(s)	_____	_____
Evaluation seemed effective	_____	_____
Resource materials seemed practical	_____	_____

Comments: _____

_____

_____

_____

Figure 4–6   Example of an Evaluation Format

Performance Supervision and Evaluation

Educational supervision was traditionally seen as an adjunct of administration, the primary purpose of which was the inspection of the schools. Improvement of instruction was recognized as an additional objective of supervision in the 1920s. In a differing theory under the democratic supervision of the progressive movement, supervisors and teachers were viewed as equal partners in policy formulation. In just over half a century, supervision of education has progressed from an inspection role to a highly sophisticated leadership role.

Today, supervision and evaluation are generally viewed as a component of administration and, thus, are executed by administrators. Because supervisors have been called on to do many jobs—provide leadership in program planning and implementation; work with teachers, including beginning and student teachers; and evaluate teachers—supervision has been defined in various ways, such as program leadership and personnel development.

Functions of Supervision. Ambiguities and voids exist in professionals' knowledge of supervisory functions. Supervisory functions are not restrictive in nature. Because supervisors are educational leaders, their leadership role may be exercised in many ways and with many people, such as officials of state and federal regulatory and funding agencies, board members of the local program, the director, specialists involved in the program, support personnel, and other supervisors. Relating to the dynamic role of supervision, current literature suggests that supervision is composed of three functions: (a) improvement of the quality of instruction, (b) mutual growth of supervisor and teacher, and (c) evaluation.

Improvement of the Quality of Instruction. Improving the quality of instruction is the most important function of supervision because the only purpose of any program is to help children and their parents. Supervision should become the pivotal activity around which to manage program and staff development. Thus, supervisors must be involved in program and staff development to change the quality of programs for the better.

1. *Program development.* The close relationship between supervision and program development is implied in the title of one of the major professional organizations for supervisors, the Association of Supervision and Curriculum Development. Supervisors are needed to help establish the direction of an early childhood program. Supervisors may keep abreast of new ideas, try some of these ideas as pilot projects with a few teachers or in demonstration centers, and serve on committees that choose from among alternatives that seem best for the local program. After program decisions are made, supervisors must provide professional assistance while staff develop knowledge and skills for implementing the new program. More important, supervisors must help staff develop a commitment to a particular action.

2. *Staff development.* Programs are not and should not be "teacher proof." When new pro-grams are developed, all staff must have assistance and support in the implementation process. Continuous supervisory assistance is needed even when new program development is not being undertaken.

Mutual Growth of Supervisor and Teacher. Developing and implementing programs should be an experimental process for both supervisor and teacher. This process will result in improving not only the quality of the program but also the supervisor's and teacher's mutual growth. Supervisors are not all-knowing authorities, nor are teachers "blank slates" to be written on. Both must be committed to a relationship that fosters growth, learning, and exchange of ideas. Caruso and Fawcett (1986) have addressed the growth of the supervisor and those supervised. Jorde-Bloom (1993) has given some excellent techniques for effective communication.

Evaluation.   Professionals disagree about whether supervision and evaluation can be successfully accomplished by the same person. Some believe that a person cannot be both a helping hand and a judgmental figure; that is, the evaluative function breaks the lines of communication between supervisor and teacher. Others argue that if the supervisor evaluates, the teacher will most likely perform to his or her maximum ability. Regardless of the pros and cons of the supervisor's evaluative function, supervisors are usually called on to evaluate. One hopes the process engaged in during supervision will be continued by the teacher. Both creativity and self-reliance are facilitated when self-evaluation is primary and evaluation by others is secondary. Thus, supervisors should help teachers become self-supervising by serving as role models for the evaluative process.

One question in considering a personnel evaluation program is, What is the ultimate goal of evaluating personnel? Evaluation may be formative or summative. **Formative evaluation** is focused on the diagnostic (reflects the strengths and weaknesses of a staff member) and is thus used to promote growth. Formative evaluation is usually focused on one problem or a group of related problems at one time (e.g., planning or arranging the physical facility). **Summative evaluation** lets persons know how they perform against certain predetermined criteria. Summative evaluation "sums up" performance in that it looks at overall performance. Thus, summative evaluation is used for such decisions as continuing employment, offering tenure, and advancing merit pay. For the present purposes, only formative evaluation is considered. Performance evaluation for improvement is the most important because all other purposes of evaluation, such as tenure and merit pay, should be based on performance.

The administrator must follow several steps in initiating a program of evaluation. The first question is, Should all personnel be evaluated by the same criteria? Criteria should reflect the specific responsibilities of a staff member and be appropriate for the professional level of that person. Generally, personnel who provide similar services should be evaluated according to the same criteria, but personnel serving in dissimilar roles should be evaluated according to different criteria although some evaluation items might be the same.

Another question is, What criteria should be used? Characteristics frequently evaluated are (a) physical characteristics—the physical health and vitality conducive to the effective performance of the position; (b) mental ability—the ability to conceptualize the program base, the needs of the children and adults involved, and the employee's role and the roles of others as they relate to the position; (c) professional qualifications—knowledge of methods and materials used in performing one's role; and (d) personal attributes—enthusiasm, poise, ability to adjust to frustrations, ability to cooperate with colleagues, and ability to accept constructive criticism.

In addition to using criteria based on teacher characteristics, sometimes the appraisal of teacher performance is linked to the growth and development of children in a program. Several problems arise when a program uses the assessment of children as a means of appraising teacher effectiveness. First, some aspects of growth and development may occur during a given period but are not the result of effective teaching. Rather, these changes could be the result of other factors (e.g., age). Second, as Spodek and Saracho (1982) point out, many of the goals of early childhood education—especially those in the psychomotor and affective domains—are too problematic to assess in young children. Third, teachers may be more apt to base their curriculum directly on the chosen children's assessment instrument in order to get a high accountability rating.

Certain items from program evaluation (discussed in Chapter 2) are appropriate for evaluating staff. A very helpful publication is *The What, Why, and How of High-Quality Early Childhood Education: A Guide for On-Site Supervision* (Koraleck, Colker, & Dodge, 1993). Each chapter contains specifics on environment, equipment and materials, schedules, activities, and supportive interactions. The format is table-like, with information on "what you should see" and "why" if the program is of high quality. Information is also presented on "warning signs," "why this might be happening," and "how you can help" when inappropriate practices exist. The chapters are divided into centers serving various age-groups and a chapter on family child care centers.

Still another question is, What instrument will be used? After criteria for evaluating personnel performance have been determined, they must be incorporated into an appraisal instrument. Locally devised evaluation procedures may include narratives, portfolios, interview procedures, check sheets, and rating scales.

Narratives are based on observations. These observations may be open-ended or may focus on specific areas, such as guidance of children or planning. During observations, the evaluator observes the staff member and notes specific strengths and weaknesses of the performance on the basis of the criteria selected for that particular job category. Sometimes, a staff member is asked to make a self-evaluation based on personal recollections. Videotapes are also becoming a popular means of affirming the evaluator's observations and/or the staff member's self-evaluation. Videotapes can also identify facial expressions and body movements.

Portfolios are also being used in some programs. A portfolio is a collection of materials (e.g., written work, tapes, photographs) that teachers collect and assemble to represent their performance. Thus, portfolios are an extension of narratives. Portfolios allow evaluators to see what teachers value in terms of both content and pedagogy, and they are becoming very popular.

Interview procedures may be developed as evaluation instruments. On the one hand, an interview may take the form of an open-ended discussion concerning strengths, performance areas needing improvement, and discussions on how to make needed improvements. On the other hand, some interview forms may, in actuality, be verbal rating scales.

Check sheets and **rating scales** usually list evaluation criteria in categories of characteristics, such as physical characteristics and professional qualifications. Many check sheets and rating scales also include an overall evaluation for

each category of characteristics and/or for total performance evaluation. Although check sheets and rating scales are written evaluation instruments, each instrument has a distinctive style, as shown in the following examples:

1. The check sheet is used to indicate those behaviors satisfactorily completed by a staff member. The evaluator may check "yes," "no," or "not applicable" (see Figure 4-7).

2. A rating scale, a qualitative evaluation of performance, represents successive levels of quality along an inferior-superior continuum.
   a. Levels of quality may be described in words as shown in Figures 4–8 and 4–9.
   b. Levels of quality may be indicated with numerals (see Figure 4–10). Directions given on the rating scale must indicate whether numeral 1 is the most inferior or the most superior evaluation.
   c. Levels of quality may be described in words and numerals (see Figure 4–11). Cohen and Brawer (1969) discuss problems in using rating scales for measuring staff performance.

Although standardized approaches to performance assessment have not been developed

Figure 4-7   Check Sheet

	Yes	No	Not Applicable
Was prepared for lesson	———	———	———
Used a variety of teaching materials	———	———	———

Figure 4-8   Example 1: Rating Scale With Quality Described in Words

Use of step-by-step presentation

| Excellent | Good | Fair | Poor |

Figure 4-9   Example 2: Rating Scale With Quality Described in Words

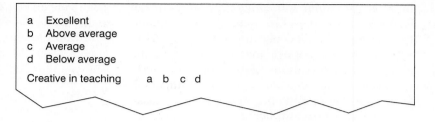

Figure 4-10   Rating Scale With Quality Described in Numerals

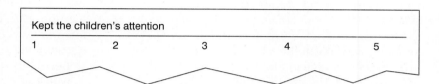

Figure 4-11   Rating Scale With Quality Described in Words and Numerals

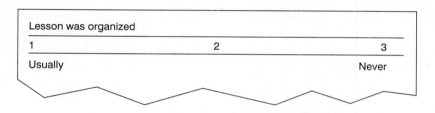

for teachers of very young children and may not be appropriate, they are worth examining for ideas. Some of these approaches involve classroom observations, semistructured interviews, and portfolios (Long & Stansbury, 1994).

Another question is, How frequently should evaluation be conducted? Informal evaluation, especially self-evaluation, should be conducted continuously; however, the policy-making body should plan, determine the frequency of, and schedule formal evaluation. Formative evaluation should be conducted several times per year.

Inexperienced teachers often need more formative evaluations than do experienced teachers. Summative evaluations are most often conducted annually.

A final question is, Who should evaluate? In most early childhood programs, the director, supervisor, or building principal evaluates all personnel although in some large programs a personnel director is charged with the responsibility. The trend toward self-evaluation is growing. If individuals were able to evaluate themselves objectively and decide on target areas for improvement, self-evaluation might be the most effective means of improving performance. Self-evaluation, however, has not been successful (Solomon & McDonald, 1970). Gathering data from multiple sources seems to be ideal. Sources include self-evaluation, peer input, child growth and development, organization of classroom, parent input, and administrative evaluations (J. Johnston, 1988; Vartuli & Fyfe, 1993).

Methods of Supervision. Supervisors may work with teachers as part of a training session or as an analysis of teachers' on-the-job performance. Both of these methods can be effective, depending on the teacher's needs and on the purposes of the evaluation.

Supervision in a Training Session. If the purpose of supervision is to provide training, the supervision may follow this format:

1. The supervisor and the teacher should discuss, demonstrate, and practice ways to reinforce and extend the children's learning experiences in a training session.

2. The supervisor should observe the teacher's performance to compare it with the training session.

3. In the supervisory conference, the teacher and the supervisor should discuss the teacher's perceptions of his or her interactions with the children. If the interactions were successful, the teacher should be praised; if not, a plan of action should be developed.

Supervisors also work with teachers in groups. Orientation and in-service are examples of group supervision. Group supervisory conferences are identical to the individual supervisory conferences, except the teacher usually discusses his or her own teaching first, followed by analyses from other teachers and the supervisor, all of whom have observed the teaching. Group supervision permits multiple perspectives to be introduced and is especially effective when sup-

port professionals, such as physicians or psychologists, are included.

Supervision as an On-the-Job Analysis. For an on-the-job analysis, the most common method of supervision involves observation of the teacher, followed by an individual conference. Certainly, the way in which the conference is conducted depends on the teaching situation and the level of functioning for both supervisor and teacher. Nonetheless, certain pointers can make a supervisory conference worthwhile:

1. The supervisor and the teacher should plan together prior to the teaching. Planning should include:
   a. Rethinking objectives, activities, and methodology. (It is assumed that the teacher has preplanned.)
   b. Proposing other strategies (by both supervisor and teacher) and predicting how children will respond.
   c. Making a decision among strategies.

2. The supervisor should observe the teacher and record in detail the interactions.

3. Children's responses should be studied by both supervisor and teacher prior to the conference. Questions may include:
   a. How did the children respond?
   b. What was the affective relationship between teacher and children?
   c. Was group management smooth or disorganized?

4. The conference should not be held immediately after observation. Teacher and supervisor need time to think about what went on in the classroom.

5. The conference should focus on patterns that tend to recur during the teaching period. Two prerequisites are essential:
   a. The supervisor should have extensive evidence to document a problem.
   b. The supervisor should be able to summarize the problem in language devoid of vague emotional jargon.

6. Most of the conference time should be spent with supervisor and teacher presenting alternative ideas for solving each problem, keeping in mind that:
   a. The supervisor should elicit and accept the teacher's ideas and feelings and positively reinforce the teacher.
   b. The teacher should be allowed to make the final decision among the alternatives discussed.
7. The next on-the-job performance evaluation should be planned on the basis of the conference.
8. The following practices should be observed:
   a. Only four or five topics should be discussed in a conference, beginning and ending with the teacher's strong points.
   b. A teaching technique should not be referred to as "bad" or "good," but rather as "appropriate" or "inappropriate" for the children and the content of the activities.
   c. Successful teaching techniques should be reinforced with praise. Praise not only makes the teacher feel more adequate but also will cause him or her to repeat the successful techniques. (The absence of criticism is not praise!)

Alleviation of Job Stress

More and more teachers are becoming victims of job stress. **Burnout** can be defined as "a syndrome of emotional exhaustion and cynicism that can occur in individuals who spend much of their time working closely with other people" (Pines & Maslach, 1980, p. 6). Stress comes from several conditions: (a) The unexpected is common because of the age of children and the fact that the curriculum designs in many programs are not highly structured; (b) undesirable working conditions, such as unpaid overtime, inability to take scheduled breaks due to staff shortage, and the lack of fringe benefits, including medical coverage, often plague teachers; (c) early childhood positions are not considered high-status jobs by some persons who see play activities as less than real teaching; (d) early childhood teachers are so indoctrinated in the importance of the early years of a child's life that they often feel let down when they do not achieve their lofty goals regardless of the underlying cause (e.g., the teacher, the child, the parents' lack of follow-through, the physical environment, problems in scheduling); and (e) teachers are unable to maintain a detached concern (they see themselves as surrogate parents; Needle, 1980). Early childhood professionals are also subjected to health hazards, such as strain of lifting children, risks of disease, and injuries from biting or kicking children (Townley, Thornburg, & Crompton, 1991).

Most susceptible to burnout are teachers in child care and Head Start programs. For the most part, these teachers are in the lowest status jobs in the early childhood field, and they receive the least compensation for their work. Stress may come from these teachers' personal lives. On the one hand, research from the National Day Care Study found that 30% of caregivers were the sole support of their families and that 69% provided more than half of their family's income (Ruopp et al., 1979). On the other hand, the National Child Care Staffing Study found high job satisfaction (Whitebook et al., 1990). Kindergarten through Grade 3 teachers reported that the following factors contributed to job dissatisfactions: problems with administrators, too much paperwork, low salaries, problems with parents, large class size, not enough time to teach, problems with colleagues, too many meetings, differences in philosophical beliefs about the education of young children, and abuse and misuse of tests (Greathouse, Moyer, & Rhodes-Offutt, 1992). Unlike other occupations in early childhood care and education, as level of education increases, disparity is often greater between perceived expectations of job rewards and actual rewards; thus, job satisfaction often decreases (Kontos & Stremmel, 1988).

As a way to help alleviate some stress, Jorde-Bloom (1988) has defined 10 dimensions of **organizational climate** (the global perception of quality attributes of a program, based on the subjective perceptions of all people working in a program). When these dimensions are positive within a program, much stress is avoided. These dimensions are (a) collegiality (supportive, cohesive staff); (b) professional growth (emphasis placed on growth); (c) supervisor support (facilitative leadership); (d) clarity (clear policies and job descriptions); (e) reward system (fairness in pay and fringe benefits); (f) decision making (staff involved in decisions); (g) goal consensus (staff agreement on goals/objectives); (h) task orientation (emphasis placed on good planning and efficiency in job performance); (i) physical setting (spatial arrangement helps staff); and (j) innovativeness (organization finds creative ways to solve problems). Some stress conditions may be stimulating unless the "unexpected" approaches chaos. Realizing that some stress is all right, even helpful, may assure some teachers. Other things may help: (a) being informed about the developmental stages of young children and the specific characteristics of the children served in the local program; (b) being prepared with flexible plans; (c) using a schedule although some adaptation of the schedule may be occasionally needed; (d) keeping records of children's development so that one can see progress in all areas; (e) detaching one's emotions from situations that cannot be changed; (f) staying in good physical and mental health with proper diet, exercise, rest, leisure activities, and medical attention; and (g) finding others who may help by providing the "shoulder to cry on."

In an effort to help early childhood programs reduce staff turnover rates and alleviate job stress, the Early Childhood Professional Development Project (with Jorde-Bloom as director) produced two instruments to assess organizational climates of early childhood programs. The informal instrument may be given to staff without permission of the project; the more in-depth instrument is sold and analyzed through the project, with ways to improve the program's organizational climate given (Jorde-Bloom, 1988). Data from staff exit interviews, such as Olsen's (1993) interview questions, can also help a program look at its organizational climate.

PERSONNEL SERVICES AND RECORDS

State boards of education and licensing agencies require that certain personnel services be provided and records kept by early childhood programs under their respective jurisdictions. In addition to those mandated personnel services and records, local boards of education or boards of directors may provide additional services and require other records permitted by state law.

For the most part, public school early childhood programs have more complete services and records than do child care centers. The National Child Care Staffing Study reported that 70% of teaching staff in child care centers worked without a written contract, 40% had no written job description, and 96% had no collective bargaining agreement. Furthermore, only 40% had health coverage and 20% had a retirement plan (Whitebook et al., 1990). These working conditions should be changed because they affect job satisfaction.

All early childhood programs should write an employee handbook that contains information on personnel services and records. Perreault and Neugebauer (1988) suggest that handbooks should include such information as (a) history of the program, (b) program base, (c) organization structure, (d) terms of employment, and (e) expectations of employees.

Contract and Terms of Employment

A **contract** is an agreement between two or more parties. In early childhood programs, a contract is an agreement between each staff member and the director or board, specifying the services a staff member must provide and the specific sum of money to be paid for services rendered. Contracts may differ, depending on job description (e.g., teacher and assistant teacher or senior citizen and younger person). All contracts should conform to the following guidelines:

A written agreement as opposed to an oral one

Specific designation of the parties to the contract

Statement of the legal capacity of the parties represented

Provision for signatures by the authorized agent(s) of and by the teacher

Clear stipulation of salary to be paid

Designation of date and duration of contract, and the date when service is to begin

Definition of assignment (Elsbree & Reutter, 1954)

In signing a contract, an employee indirectly consents to obey all rules and regulations in force at the time of employment or adopted during the period of employment. Policies that most directly affect employees may include hours per day and days per week; vacation; specific requirements, such as a uniform or driver's license; sick, emergency, and maternity leaves; substitutes; insurance; salary increases and fringe benefits; and retirement plan. Each potential and present employee should have a written copy of all current policies.

The employee may receive a contract for some specified period of time, perhaps an annual or a continuing contract. Contracts for a specified period of time must be renewed at the end of such time period. The two types of continuing contracts are **notification** and **tenure.** An individual having a *notification* continuing contract must be notified on or before a given date if the contract is not to be renewed. A tenure contract guarantees that an employee

cannot be dismissed except for certain specific conditions, such as lack of funds to pay salaries, neglect of duty, incompetency, failure to observe regulations, and immorality; furthermore, a dismissed, tenured employee has the right to a hearing in which the board must prove "just cause" for the dismissal. Programs offering tenure require that an employee serve a probationary period of a given number of years (usually 3 or 5) before receiving a tenure contract.

Special service contracts must also be written when a limited service is to be performed by a temporary employee, such as a consultant for a workshop. This type of contract must clearly specify the services to be rendered; the date(s) services are to be performed, including any follow-up services; any special arrangements, such as materials to be supplied by a temporary employee (or by the employer); and the fee. The signatures of the temporary employee and the requester should be affixed to the contract, and the transaction should be dated.

Job Description

A job description for each personnel category should be written and kept current and should include the following: (a) job title, (b) minimum qualifications, (c) primary duties and responsibilities, (d) working conditions, (e) additional duties, (f) reporting relationships and limits of authority, and (g) benefits. The Economic Employment Opportunity Commission (EEOC) will examine job descriptions for a section called *essential functions* (a part of the primary duties and responsibilities). This section must also indicate how frequently the function occurs (*occasionally*—33% or less; *frequently*—34% to 66%; and *continually*—67% and over). If someone is not employed because of a disability, then the director or board must be prepared to show that the function is essential to the job and cannot reasonably be performed by another staff member. (Essential functions must be in each job description prior to advertising.) Job descriptions should be specific to the particular early childhood program and position, rather than adopted from another program. A potential employee should review the job description before signing a contract; all employees should keep their job descriptions in their files. A sample job description is shown in Figure 4–12.

Insurance and Retirement Plans

Various kinds of insurance and retirement plans protect employees and organizations. Adequate coverage is expensive but essential. Some types of insurance and retirement plans may be mandated by state or federal laws, whereas other types may be voluntary.

Federal Insurance Contributions Act (FICA). Most centers are required to pay the FICA, or Social Security, tax. The FICA tax is generally used for retirement purposes. Tax rates are set at a percentage of the employee's salary. The employer deposits quarterly the amount of the

---

Johnson County Community College Child Development Center

Title: Teacher

Qualifications: A teacher shall have at least an A.A. degree in child development/early childhood education or hold a child development associate certificate. A teacher must also meet licensing regulations concerning minimum age and health status. The essential functions include constantly maintaining visual supervision of children to ensure safety and occasionally lifting, carrying, and holding children.

Primary duties and responsibilities: A teacher shall (1) plan and execute developmentally appropriate activities; (2) observe and evaluate children's progress; (3) provide a written report (on the forms provided) to the director and parents at least two times per year; (4) be available for informal parent-teacher contacts at the beginning and end of each session; and (5) perform other duties particular to the program.

Working conditions: A teacher is paid for an 8-hour working day. Reporting time is 7:15 a.m. Monday through Friday. A teacher should be prepared to receive children at 7:30 a.m. A teacher will eat at the noon meal with the children and will have two 15-minute breaks during the 6-hour day. The teacher's planning period is from 1:30 until 3:15 p.m. daily.

The director must be notified in the event of illness or emergencies. Paid vacation periods must be planned 3 months in advance and approved by the director. Other optional benefits include a group health insurance plan, employee retirement fund, and others particular to the program.

Additional duties: A teacher is expected to attend staff development activities on the first Tuesday of each month from 3:30 until 5:30 p.m. and a monthly parent function usually held in the evenings from 7:00 until 9:00 p.m. on the third Thursday of each month.

Reporting relationships and limits of authority: A teacher reports directly to the director of the program. *Prior commitment from the director must be obtained* for purchasing any item, approving additional or terminating any services for children, and releasing information on center activities to the media. A teacher *may take action but must inform* when releasing a child to an authorized adult during normal attendance hours, administering authorized medications, and informing a parent about a child's nonsevere illness. A teacher *may take action without informing* when developing new activities in keeping with the program's philosophy, changing sequence of daily activities except for snack and mealtimes, and talking with parents about children's development.

Benefits: Sick and emergency leave without loss of pay is 12 days for a 12-month period of employment. A 2-week paid vacation plus Thanksgiving and other national holidays are observed.

Figure 4-12   Sample Job Description

employee's contributions collected as payroll deductions, plus an equal amount from the employer. (This money is deposited in a separate account because commingling of federal funds is prohibited by law.) A quarterly report on FICA taxes is also required. Even tax-exempt corporations should keep in close contact with their district office of the IRS. Laws change, and all organizations are responsible for keeping up with current tax laws.

Workers' Compensation.   Workers' compensation is liability insurance compensating an employee injured by an accident in the course of and arising out of employment. (Independent contractors are not covered. Directors should insist that any contractors doing work for a program certify they are adequately insured so that they cannot later claim to have been acting as an employee.) Workers' compensation is required in most states, but many states have exceptions for certain classes of employers, such as organizations with few employees or organizations wishing to self-insure. The insurance company pays 100% of all workers' compensation benefits required by state law. Injured employees and, in the case of death, their dependents are eligible for one half to two thirds of their weekly wages, plus hospital and medical benefits. Employees, in turn, give up their right to sue employers for damages covered by the law, except in the rare states where such actions are permitted.

State Unemployment Insurance.   State unemployment insurance is required in most states and varies considerably from state to state. A questionnaire must be completed about the employees' activities and the tax status of the early childhood program. The insurance rates are figured as a percentage of total wages and are different for for-profit and not-for-profit corporations.

Liability Insurance.   Liability insurance protects the organization or employee from loss when persons have been injured or property damaged as a result of negligence (rather than accident) on the part of the institution or its employees; however, almost any "accident" that occurs is usually considered the result of negligence. The extent to which an institution or its employees can be held liable varies from state to state, and a liability policy should cover everything for which an institution is liable.

In the past, the insurance industry has benefited from high interest rates that produced high returns on their investment. Because of some large lawsuits, insurance companies are now canceling or not renewing policies or are renewing policies with less coverage and premium hikes. Steps to lower rates and find insurance companies willing to provide coverage are being taken by such groups as Committee on Children, Youth, and Families and the NAEYC ("NAEYC Position Statement on the Liability Insurance Crises," 1986). In most states, programs providing transportation services are required to have vehicle insurance, including liability insurance.

Health Insurance and Hospital-Medical Insurance.   Health insurance, whether fully or partially paid for by the employer or taken on a voluntary basis and paid for by the employee, may assume any of three forms: (a) medical reimbursement insurance, (b) medical service or prepaid medical care, and (c) disability income benefits. Hospital-medical plans fall into three groups: (a) basic hospitalization and medical coverage, (b) major medical insurance, and (c) closed-panel operation (service available from a limited number of physicians, clinics, or hospitals).

Crime Coverages.   Protection against loss resulting from dishonesty of employees or others is available under four forms of coverage: (a) fidelity bonds, (b) board-form money and securities policy, (c) "3-D policy" (dishonesty, disappearance, and destruction), and (d) all-risk insurance.

Retirement Programs.   Federal Social Security coverage, FICA tax, is usually mandatory. Generally, the tax is used as a federal "retirement program." Most public school program personnel are also under state retirement programs, paid on a matching fund basis by employer and employee. Private institutions may have retirement programs in addition to federal Social Security coverage.

Personnel Records

Personnel administration involves keeping records and making reports in accordance with state laws, the program's governing body requirements, and federal legislation concerning privacy of personal information. Public and private schools must keep personnel records on each regulation pertaining to employees—both program and support personnel. In most cases, personnel records are kept by the local programs, and reports are submitted to their respective state governing boards (licensing agency or state board of education); however, the governing board may inspect locally kept records.

Personnel records is a collective term for all records containing information about employees. Although these records vary from program to program, they usually embody these details:

1. *Personal information records* are kept by all early childhood programs. Most of the personal information is given by a potential employee on the application form, and the information is kept current. Personal information includes name, age, gender, address, telephone number, citizenship, Social Security number, and names and addresses of those who will give references.

2. *Personal health records* signed by an appropriate medical professional are required by all early childhood programs. These records may be detailed, requiring specific medical results of a physical examination, or may be a general statement that the employee is free from any mental or physical illness that might adversely affect the health of children or other adults. In addition to records on general health, an annual tuberculosis test is required by most programs.

3. *Emergency information* is required by many programs. This information includes names, addresses, and telephone numbers of one or more persons to be contacted in an emergency; name of physician and hospital; and any medical information deemed necessary in an emergency situation, such as allergies to drugs or other conditions.

4. *Records of education and other qualifications* are required by all programs. They must include the names of schools attended, diplomas or degrees obtained, transcripts of academic work, and the registration number and type of teacher's or administrator's certificate or any other credential needed by an employee (e.g., a chauffeur's license).

5. *Professional or occupational information records* are kept by all programs, including the places and dates of employment, names of employers, and job descriptions.

6. *Professional or occupational skill and character references* are included in the personnel records. In most cases, these references are for confidential use by the employer.

7. *Service records* are kept by some programs. These records contain information concerning date of current employment, level or age of children cared for/taught or program directed, absences incurred or leaves taken, inservice education received and conferences attended, committees served on, salary received, and date and reason for termination of service.

8. *Insurance records* are kept by all programs involved in any group insurance.

9. *Evaluation records* are placed on file in many programs. However, they should not be kept after they have fulfilled the purposes for which they were intended.

Personnel of many early childhood programs, especially Head Start and others receiving federal funding, are covered under the Privacy Act of 1974. Because a person's legal right to privacy must be guarded, administrators must keep abreast of the laws pertaining to record keeping and record security. For example, the Privacy Act of 1974 (P.L. 93–579) requires federal agencies to take certain steps to safeguard the accuracy, currentness, and security of records concerning individuals and to limit record keeping to necessary and lawful purposes. Individuals also have a right to examine federal records containing such information and to challenge the accuracy of data with which they disagree (*Title V. Section 522a*, 1977).

TRENDS AND ISSUES

The major trends and issues seem to be centered on qualifications of staff and improving quality through education and training. The early childhood profession continues to a two-tiered system in terms of qualifications of personnel and compensation. Most studies indicate that the levels of education and training for staff in center and family child care have decreased over the last two decades (Spodek & Saracho, 1992). The situation may worsen because the market for people with entry-level skills and wages are not realistic choices for college-educated people. Furthermore, as noted in Chapter 3, family child care providers are rarely licensed, and many states are also exempting certain categories of child care centers from licensing codes. Personnel in SACC often do not see themselves as "teachers." As in the past, great demands for care and education undermine standards (Frank, 1937). Conversely, teacher education programs leading to certification have become increasingly selective because of the increase in admission standards and calls for reforms (e.g., extended 5-year programs, exit tests; Hilliard, 1991).

Unless the quality of personnel and stability in the workforce improve, the early childhood profession will not be able to provide quality programs for all young children. Thus, in 1991, NAEYC announced the establishment of a new division—the National Institute for Early Childhood Professional Development. The major goal was to assist in the planning and implementation of an effective, coordinated system of professional development ("NAEYC to Launch," 1991). The NAEYC believes that such a system provides meaningful opportunities for career advancement (NAEYC, 1994).

One idea coming from the National Institute for Early Childhood Professional Development is a career lattice. The symbol of a lattice was chosen over a ladder in order to incorporate the following three ideas: (a) "Vertical lines" would represent diverse settings/roles; (b) "horizontal lines" would depict six levels of preparation, with each ascending level representing greater role responsibility and compensation; and (c) "diagonal lines" would represent movement across roles. The NAEYC believes that implementation of such a lattice would recognize diversity of roles, differing levels of preparation for each role, and the importance of ongoing professional development (J. Johnson & McCracken, 1994).

The consensus is that each person should have the opportunity for professional development and advancement. However, many see difficulties with ladders and lattices. Spodek (1991b) likens the early childhood profession to the health profession, a discontinuous field in which training at one level does not prepare the person for the next level (e.g., additional training of a registered nurse does not prepare the nurse to become a physician). Difficulties in considering a continuous field include the following: (a) People employed at one level may not qualify for admission to train at another level; (b) many people are turned off by formal education and prefer informal training (e.g., workshops); (c) individuals with specialty work at the associate degree level may be less willing to enroll in general education courses for a bachelor's degree; (d) transfer of experience or informal training to college courses work is most difficult because of lack of standards for content and lack of coordination among training sessions; and (e) even transfer of coursework from one institution to another is difficult because of course configurations and the differences in the scope and depth of coverage. Thus, the issue of professional development and career advancement remains unresolved, along with the catch-22 issues—adequate compensation/benefits and affordability of programs.

SUMMARY

The factors that influence the effectiveness of early childhood programs are incredibly multifaceted and, hence, complex. All research studies support the contention that the behavior of adults in early childhood programs does have an important impact on children.

Qualities of effective staff members have been studied. Although no simple, single response answers the question concerning what professional qualifications (knowledge and skills) and personal characteristics (personality traits and values) people need to work effectively with young children, some consensus does exist.

The consensus of personnel competencies should serve three functions. First, competencies should guide the staffing of early childhood programs as boards assess their needs and then recruit and hire directors, primary program personnel, and support program personnel who can, in turn, perform certain roles based on their professional qualifications and personal characteristics. Second, these competencies should be used as a director mobilizes the staff into providing the program's services. Third, competencies should be used as criteria for improving staff performance via formal education, staff development, membership in professional organizations, performance supervision and evaluation, and alleviation of job stress. Various regulatory agencies require certain personnel services and records. Personnel services and records also serve to make working conditions better for staff, and these better conditions aid job satisfaction.

Trends and issues seem to focus on a two-tiered system of staff in terms of qualifications and compensation. Although many attempts have been made at improving the quality of all personnel, such as the work of the National Institute for Early Childhood Professional Development, the issue of professional development linked with career advancement/compensation is far from resolved.

FOR FURTHER READING

Johnson, J., & McCracken, J. B. (Eds.). (1994). *The early childhood career lattice: Perspectives on professional development.* Washington, DC: National Association for the Education of Young Children.

Jones, E. (1986). *Teaching adults: An active learning approach.* Washington, DC: National Association for the Education of Young Children.

Kelley, R. (1991). *The power of fellowship: How to create leaders people want to follow and followers who lead themselves.* Garden City, NY: Doubleday.

Klein, N., & Sheehan, R. (1987). Staff development: A key issue in meeting the needs of young handicapped children in day care settings. *Topics in Early Childhood Special Education, 7*(1), 13-27.

Modigliana, K. (1991). *Training programs for family child care providers: An analysis of ten curricula.* Boston: Wheelock College Family Child Care Project. (ERIC Document Reproduction Service No. ED 354 104)

Nelson, B. G., & Sheppard, B. (Eds.). (1992). *Men in child care and early education: A handbook for administrators and educators.* Minneapolis, MN: Men in Child Care Project.

Newman, S., Vander Ven, K., & Ward, C. (1992). *Practitioner's manual for the productive employment of older adults in child care.* Pittsburgh: University of Pittsburgh, Generations Together.

Powell, D., & Stremmel, A. (1989). The relation of early childhood training and experience to the professional development of child care workers. *Early Childhood Research Quarterly, 4*(3), 339-356.

Snider, M. H., & Fu, V. R. (1990). The effects of specialized education and job experience on early childhood teachers' knowledge of developmentally appropriate practice. *Early Childhood Research Quarterly, 5*(1), 69-78.

Spodek, B., & Saracho, O. N. (Eds.). (1990). *Yearbook in early childhood education: Vol. 1. Early childhood teacher preparation.* New York: Teachers College Press.

Spodek, B., Saracho, O. N., & Peters, D. L. (Eds.). (1989). *Professionalism and the early childhood practitioner.* New York: Teachers College Press.

READINGS ON TECHNIQUES FOR STAFF DEVELOPMENT

Practical Ideas

Developing staff skills. (1990). Redmond, WA: Exchange Press.

Enhancing your professional growth. (1987). Redmond, WA: Exchange Press.

Fostering improved staff performance. (1991). Redmond, WA: Exchange Press.

Jorde-Bloom, P., Sheerer, M., & Britz, J. (1991). *Blueprint for action: Achieving center-based change through staff development.* Mt. Rainer, MD: Gryphon Press.

On being a leader. (1990). Redmond, WA: Exchange Press.

Narratives

Ayers, W. (1989). *The good preschool teacher: Six teachers reflect on their lives.* New York: Teachers College Press.

Bullough, R. (1989). *First-year teacher.* New York: Teachers College Press.

Jones, E. (Ed.). (1993). *Growing teachers: Partnerships in staff development.* Washington, DC: National Association for the Education of Young Children.

Newman, J. (1990). *Finding our own way: Teachers exploring their assumptions.* Portsmouth, NH: Heinemann.

Witherell, C., & Noddings, N. (1991). *Stories lives tell.* New York: Teachers College Press.

Yonemura, M. V. (1986). *A teacher at work: Professional development and the early childhood educator.* New York: Teachers College Press.

Chapter 5

Planning the Physical Facility

Many adults may have a fixed image of a school facility—long corridors lined with doors leading to classrooms; desks facing the teacher's desk with a chalkboard behind; high windows; a gritty, asphalt playground almost surrounding the building, with swings, slides, climbing equipment, and ball areas; and a high fence enclosing the sea of asphalt and its island building. Others think of the small child care center—a postage-stamp-size building, often elevated and portable; two small, metal doors; a tin roof; vinyl siding in tan or grey or occasionally crayon-bright colors; at each end are high windows with print curtains; in front of the building, scattered over well-trodden ground, are a few pieces of backyard-type play equipment, a sand patch, and a few deserted tricycles; a chain-link fence with a few sprigs of grass standing along the fence-line encloses the play yard, giving a squirrel-cage effect to the whole scene.

Fortunately, in some facilities for today's young children, neither of these atmospheres exists. The facilities, physically and psychologically more comfortable, are the result of a more profound understanding of how children develop and more accurate interpretations of child-child, child-material, and child-adult interactions. Olds (1987) believes that children's centers should have an ambience that is both soothing and stimulating. Such a pleasing and friendly ambience has a positive impact on children's feelings of content (Mintz, 1956) and even persistence (Santrock, 1976).

Before contemplating the specifics of housing, one must remember the following:

1. Location of the building is an important aspect of planning because local zoning regulations may include restrictions.

2. Regardless of the type of program, most of the occupants will be young children, so the facility should be child oriented and also comfortable for the adults.

3. Safety of children and staff is of maximum importance (and is discussed later in this chapter).

4. Housing is an important consideration in planning for the those with disabilities. Programs receiving direct or indirect federal assistance of any kind must be accessible to children and employees with disabilities. Zoning laws in many areas also require that buildings accommodate those with disabilities. Special architectural plans and room arrangements are needed for those with physical disabilities and visual impairment. Also, noise and activity levels must be controlled when children with learning disabilities and hyperactivity are integrated into the program. (Meeting standards for children with special needs is discussed in a later section.)

5. Variations in arrangements of space and materials contribute to the effectiveness of housing. There should be differences in the placements of objects in space (e.g., high, eye-level, low); sizes of areas (e.g., large areas for running, small areas for squeezing through); sound levels (e.g., noisy places, quiet areas); and light and color (e.g., cheerful, busy color schemes; quiet, relaxing hues). In short, design should be aesthetically pleasing.

6. Flexibility is essential. Housing should be planned to accommodate children's changing interests and individual and group pursuits both inside and outside. In some programs, flexibility is achieved by very open spaces.

7. Costs must be considered. The building or physical facilities require a large initial investment; however, when good facilities are amortized over 40 years, the investment represents approximately 10% of the total dollars spent on the program (Ruopp et al., 1979).

Determining the specifics of housing begins with the program base. Objectives must be defined in terms of environmental features that make the program possible. Barker (1968) refers to the "essential fittingness" between environment and behavior of its inhabitants. This is extensively elaborated on by D. Day's (1983) discussion of an ecological approach to early education. Facilities designed for behavioral-environmental programs and those designed for constructivist programs are very different, especially in the amount of enclosure, as discussed later in this chapter.

Planning a facility takes several steps. A large center or a multi-site program often begins with the appointment of a committee to conduct preliminary plans. In smaller programs, the director does the planning. Regardless of who does the planning, the following steps should be taken:

1. Specific needs of the program must be outlined, including maximum enrollment, ages of children, special needs of children, and program objectives.

2. Input should be sought through reading or be obtained from individuals and organizations specializing in housing programs, and trips should be planned to facilities housing similar programs.

3. Plans should be compared with regulations, accreditation, or model standards (as given in Chapter 3). Programs requiring board action must submit their plans to the board for approval.

Not every early childhood program will be so fortunate as to have a new building. Many will be housed in old structures or in new additions to older buildings. Renovated buildings are fine if they meet the needs of the program and are not just hand-me-downs or castoffs. The foregoing steps for planning new buildings often apply when planning an addition to an existing building. Some early childhood programs must share their children's activity room or building with other groups, such as a religious or civic group. A major problems in a shared facility is cleaning the room or building, storing equipment, and then setting up again. Vergeront (1987) gives many ideas for managing housing in programs that must share facilities.

ENTRY-EXIT AREA

Because the entry-exit area serves as the first and last picture of the facility that children and parents see every day, the area may be a major factor in communicating the attitude "It's nice here!" or "This is a good place for my child!" The entry-exit area is also the view most often seen by the public, and the public's opinion of a program may be based on what it sees—even from street distance.

An entry-exit area should be a bright, welcoming area because blind corners and dimly lit places are frightening to the young child. The entry-exit area could be a mall, with views of indoor and outdoor activity areas, a porch, a courtyard, or a gaily decorated interior room. This area should provide a view of the activity room and have a transition space (a place to say good-bye to parents and to watch from) so that young children can gradually join the activities of the program. Such a view also enables parents, returning for their children, to make a quick scan of the activity room in order to locate their children.

Because the acclimatized child will want to enter on his or her own, the entry door should operate easily. Near the entry-exit area should be a parking lot for parents who drive and a shelter from which parents can watch until their children enter the building or outdoor activity area. To accommodate young children with disabilities, a ramp into the building should be provided. The ramp should be located near the parking lot. (The curb must be cut to enter the parking lot, or the ramp should lead directly from the street.) Other specifications for the ramp include a slope of no less than 12 ft for each 1 ft of drop, a 36-in. minimum width for wheelchairs, and handrails. Thresholds to entrances should be no higher than 3 in. Doors should open readily and have 32-in. clearings.

INDOOR SPACE

The amount and types of indoor space vary from program to program. Most public school kindergartens are housed in a single activity room with an emergency-use rest room. The kindergarten shares the cafeteria, main rest rooms, isolation area, and other facilities with elementary-age children also housed in the building. A child care center is usually housed in a separate building, so some of the following suggestions are not equally applicable to all early childhood programs.

Arranging and Furnishing the Activity Room

The children's activity room is perhaps the single most important area of the building because, in this room, children work and play for most of their day. Space affects the quality of living and learning within a center:

The higher the quality of space in a center, the more likely teachers were to be sensitive and friendly in their manner toward children, to encourage children in their self-chosen activities, and to teach consideration for the rights and feelings of self and others. Where spatial quality was low, children were less likely to be involved and interested, and teachers more likely to be neutral and insensitive in their manner, to use large amounts of guidance and restriction, and to teach arbitrary rules of social living. *(Kritchevsky & Prescott, 1969, p. 5)*

Room-Directional Orientation. Room-directional orientation is important because of light and temperature. Generally, a southern or eastern exposure is better than a western exposure. Of course, programs housed in renovated buildings will not have a choice as to directional orientation; however, if the orientation is incorrect, the resulting light-reflection problems can be partially overcome by use of certain color schemes.

Room Size. Room size can be considered in three ways: (a) the number of square feet per child, (b) the total dimensions of the room, and (c) the spatial density, which is related not only to square feet per child but also to the availability of toys and equipment. Many states use 35 sq ft per child as the minimum square footage in licensing regulations (NAEYC Information Service, 1989). For infants and toddlers, 35 sq ft is adequate (Lally, Provence, Szanton, & Weissbourd, 1986). For older children, especially those in programs that require extra "activity places," 40 to 60 sq ft per child would be more adequate (NAEYC Information Service, 1989). Generally speaking, if the group of children is small, the space per child should be increased (use 60 sq ft or a little less per child). If the group of children is large, the space per child should be less (40 sq ft or a little more). One can readily see that using 60 sq ft per child with a large group would result in a very large room. (Too much space can cause problems!) If a nap period is planned for an all-day program, as much as 30 sq ft per child may be needed in addition to the suggested 40 to 60 sq ft.

Regardless of the number of children or the length of session, the children's activity room should be a minimum of 900 sq ft of clear floor space, exclusive of rest rooms, dining area, and separate napping area. Limited indoor space may be offset by sheltered outdoor space where climate permits. When floor space is small and ceilings are high, space can be stretched vertically. Balconies with railings or cargo nets can be built over cot storage or other storage; they can be the second floors of two-story houses; or housekeeping centers can be arranged on balconies with block centers below. On the one hand, a balcony built against a wall, particularly corner walls, is most stable and economical. On the other hand, a free-standing platform gives more freedom of placement. Various apparatuses, such as stairs, ladders, and ramps, can be installed for ascending and descending. For safety purposes, a railing should be provided for stairs greater than three steps. Stationary ladders are safer than rope ladders, and ladder rungs should extend above a platform for easy mounting and dismounting. Ramps covered with friction material and with railings are safer than stairs or ladders, but ramps can be used only with platforms less than 4 ft high.

In contrast with small play areas, very large play areas present problems. Children interact more and dramatize fantasy themes more in smaller than larger rooms (Howes, 1983; P. Smith & Connolly, 1980). Large play spaces result in more running and chasing and less cooperative behaviors (Clarke-Stewart & Gruber, 1984; P. Smith & Connolly, 1980). Adult-child interactions are lower in large compared with small classrooms (Howes, 1983). S. Shapiro (1975) found that some low-density centers (over 50 sq ft per child) had poor arrangements. On the one hand, negative and idle behavior was common in situations with a high density of children and few resources or equipment. On the other hand, positive and constructive behavior was prevalent in child care centers with low density (of at least 48 sq ft per child) of children and plentiful resources. The quality and quantity of resources should be increased if high density is unavoidable (E. Prescott & David, 1977). E. Prescott (1987) recommends presenting enough materials (four or five possible activities per child in each separate play space).

In short, the activity room should be small enough to be intimate. The square footage, however, should allow for uncrowded play. Enough toys should be available to prevent crowding and competition (Kontos & Fiene, 1987).

Room Arrangement. The room arrangement can affect comfort, security, autonomy, style of learning, and self-discipline. Several criteria must be considered. First, the room arrangement should have no hidden areas because these cannot be supervised. Children still have privacy and staff can supervise as long as dividers and storage cabinets are not over 4 ft high. When two rooms are joined by a wall or when a small room opens off the main room, Plexiglas panels or openings in the wall at adult height facilitate supervision.

Second, a well-organized room is somewhat closed. The height and placement of partitions affect the appearance of openness. If partitions are over 4 ft and if they almost surround an instructional area or learning center, the room appears to be closed. In addition to partitioning, room shape and dimensions affect the appearance of openness. An activity room slightly longer than it is wide is less formal looking and easier to arrange. Long, narrow activity rooms encourage running and sliding. The tunnel-like appearance can be minimized by (a) placing learning centers at each end, (b) conducting activities in the center of the room, and (c) using equipment (e.g., tables, shelves) to break straight pathways. Square rooms often have "dead space" in the center because activity areas are placed along walls instead of toward the center of the room. Somewhat closed areas, as opposed to completely open areas, seem to be more effective for three reasons:

1. Negative social behaviors, such as aggression, withdrawal, and a tendency to wander about the room (Neill & Denham, 1982; Sheehan & Abott, 1979), are seen more often in open than closed room designs.

2. Children's rooms need partitions to spatially define expected program behaviors. Facilities designed for programs adhering to the behavioral-environmental view have smaller, more enclosed (e.g., with high dividers) areas in which teacher-directed activities take place. Because the areas are enclosed and seem small, children focus their attention on "large" adults and on teacher-prescribed activities. Some less enclosed centers may be available for children's use during "free" times (see Figure 5-1).

Programs that adhere to the constructivist point of view need a roomy environment—calculated to give much more mobility. The room is often divided with low partitions into learning centers, with the size of each work space compatible with the number of children in the area at one time and the space required for both use

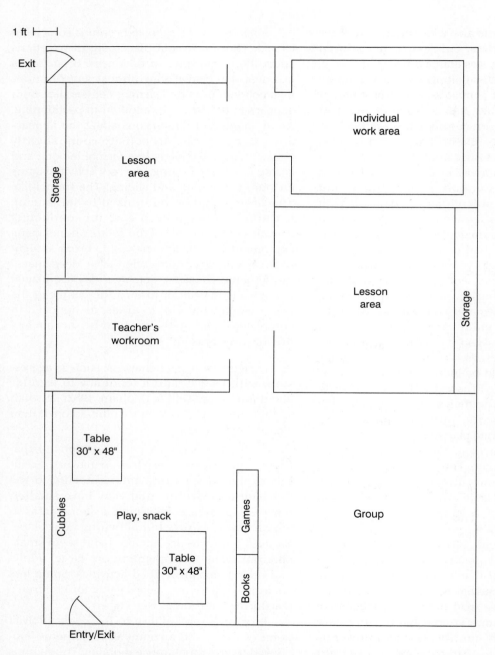

1 ft ⊢——⊣

Exit

Storage

Lesson area

Individual work area

Lesson area

Storage

Teacher's workroom

Table 30" x 48"

Cubbies

Play, snack

Games

Books

Table 30" x 48"

Group

Entry/Exit

Figure 5-1   Typical Floor Plan for a Behavioral-Environmental Program

and storage of equipment/materials. The enclosures suggest the nature of the activities (e.g., block building, art, dramatic play) and the space in which the activity is to take place. Low and less enclosing partitions (open shelves or tables instead of high walls) allow adults to observe from a greater distance and suggest to children that they are free to engage in self-initiated activities. (See Figures 5-4 through 5-17 in later sections of this chapter.)

3. Children also need privacy, and completely open spaces do not permit the need to be fulfilled. Young children need privacy to construct a sense of self (Laufer & Wolfe, 1977), to "cocoon" when the noise and other stimuli overwhelm them (Greenman, 1988; E. Prescott & Jones, 1972), to focus on their special endeavors (Meltz, 1990; P. Minuchin & Shapiro, 1983; Rubin, Maioni, & Hornung, 1976), and to gradually move into the group (Olds, 1987). D. Day and Sheehan (1974) observed chaotic and frantic child behaviors associated with centers not having privacy areas.

Window seats, special corners, alcoves, platforms, small closet with the door removed, and a few learning centers or work stations for one child all help meet indoor privacy needs (Greenman, 1988; L. Johnson, 1987; Kennedy, 1991; Olds, 1987; E. Prescott, 1978). E. Prescott, Jones, and Kritchevsky (1972) measured privacy in programs by using a continuum of seclusion-intrusion features (insulated units—protected areas for small groups; "hiding" areas—places that cozily house one or two children; and softness measures—rugs, cushions, and pillows).

Third, how much of the floor space is covered with furniture and materials affects room arrangement. In a study in which young children arranged their own environment, they opted for openness (Pluger & Zola, 1969). Most professionals, however, believe that good space organization is found where the surface is between one half and two thirds covered (Kritchevsky & Prescott, 1969).

The needs of children with disabilities should be considered when a room is being arranged. The child with a physical disability requires more space for movement. Wheelchairs require an aisle of 36 in. and corners of 42 in. minimum.

Floors, Ceilings, and Walls.   Floors, ceilings, and walls must be both functional and durable. The materials used on their surfaces should be coordinated so that they are aesthetically pleasing and comfortable.

Young children are accident-prone; they get floors wet from play activities, spilling, and bathroom accidents. When choosing floor covering, keep in mind that floors must be kept dry, sanitary, and warm for children's play. Flooring materials should be easy to clean, suited to hard wear, and noise absorbing. Because children enjoy working on the floor, good floor coverings can reduce the number of tables and chairs needed. In fact, floors should be viewed as part of the furniture.

Resilient flooring and carpet are the most prevalent materials used. Resilient flooring includes various types of vinyl floors and linoleum. Vinyl tile is the best resilient flooring. Carpet is superior to resilient flooring in softness, noise absorption, and minimizing injuries and breakage. Carpet presents problems, however—for example, difficulty of spill cleanup, retention of germs, buildup of static electricity, difficulty in moving cabinets or bins equipped with casters or in using toys with wheels, and children's possible allergic reactions to carpet fibers. High pile, shag, or even thickly padded carpet causes problems for children in wheelchairs. Of the soft floor coverings, wall-to-wall carpet is probably the most desirable, but large carpets, area rugs, throw rugs, and carpet remnants joined together with tape may be suitable. Two things must be kept in mind when choosing whether to use carpet or vinyl tile:

1. For most programs, the best choice is to use both. Carpet is best for infant/toddler rooms.

Carpet with large pillows offers a safe floor environment for nonwalkers and toddlers. Toddlers may need a bit of play space on resilient flooring for block building and for play with wheel toys. Resilient flooring is preferred under feeding and diapering areas. Similarly, programs for older children use resilient flooring for areas that get stained or that have rugged use and carpet for areas that have passive (cozy book corners) or noisy activities. Indoor/outdoor carpet is best used for preventing slipping on floors where water or sand may be spilled. (Floor covering for various areas of the room is discussed in later sections of this chapter).

2. When one cannot choose *both* carpet and vinyl tile or when one does not know which is best for a certain area of the room, vinyl tile is the better choice. Carpet can always be laid over resilient flooring. The carpet must not cause slipping, and the edges must not cause tripping. Carpet can be covered temporarily, but it is more difficult. To cover, lay down plastic sheeting and then inexpensive boards such as 1 x 12 in. boards or 4 x 8 ft plywood sheets. Boards should be free of splinters.

Many programs use platforms or wells to facilitate the floor as a place to work and play. Some infant/toddler rooms use a few-inch raised area with a low fence and a gate, both of Plexiglas or wooden bars (similar to a baby's playpen). These protect nonwalkers from the more active toddlers. Older children enjoy learning centers created by raised and sunken areas, but such areas are less flexible in use. Platforms or wells can be built into the activity room during its construction; less permanent structures can be built with wooden boxes attached to a plywood base and carpeted, or a platform can have casters. If platforms or wells are used, consider the following recommendations: (a) Raised or lowered areas should be out of the main flow of traffic; (b) changes in floor levels should not exceed 2 or 3 ft, and the steps should not be steep—five or six steps for a well 2-ft deep; (c) a

railing needs to partially surround the well; and (d) electrical outlets should be provided near the wells or platforms if electrical teaching equipment will be used.

A final problem is keeping floors warm and free from drafts. Radiantly heated floors have been used, but this kind of heat does not solve draft problems. A perimeter wall system as a supplementary heating source provides floor warmth and freedom from drafts.

Ceilings should be of differing heights to accommodate equipment of various heights. Variation in ceiling height helps with noise control and is aesthetically pleasing. A 7-ft ceiling is too low unless the space is for children only. Low ceilings make staff members appear excessively large because of the nearness of the adult to the ceiling. Such an illusion makes children feel dominated by the adult and may cause more aggression by the children (Millar, 1968). The recommended ceiling height is 10 to 11 ft. In order that the adult provide supervision yet also further minimize his or her presence during free play times, some play areas should have low-ceilinged spaces, approximately 4 ft, that exclude the adult. Low-ceilinged areas may be created by building a two-story playhouse, by using a balcony along an entire wall with learning centers on and under the balcony, or by hanging a canopy. Skylights and beams are interesting to young children.

Although permanent walls provide acoustic privacy, fewer interior walls give greater flexibility in room arrangement. Supervision becomes less of a problem when dividers and storage units, rather than floor-to-ceiling walls, delineate space. Just as low ceilings make an adult appear excessively large, so do nearby walls. If program planners desire to minimize the adult's presence, they should include fewer walls.

Color choice depends on several criteria:

1. *The amount of light in a room.* For example, soft pastels may be chosen for a southern or western exposure, but a northern exposure

may need a strong, light-reflecting color such as yellow.

2. *The size and shape of the room.* Bright colors make walls look closer and thus are more appropriate in large rooms. Mirrors and light colors on walls make rooms look larger. If slightly different shades of the same color are used on opposite walls, narrow rooms appear wider.

3. *The perception of clutter.* Bright colors and/or permanent murals or graphics may look fine in empty rooms. Once these rooms are occupied, however, they often look cluttered because equipment, artwork, and children themselves add to the room's brightness.

4. *The influence of color on academic achievement.* A limited amount of research has been reported on this topic. Research does indicate, however, that red is a good choice for areas planned for gross-motor activities and concept development activities; yellow is good for music and art activities; and, green, blue, and purple are effective in reading areas. The use of various colors may be most important in infant and toddler programs because children have a perception of color over form until 4 years of age (*Environmental Criteria*, 1971).

Walls may be covered with various types of materials. Washable wallpaper or high-quality latex paint are the overall best choices. Paneling in block areas or areas with rugged use may be a good choice. Wall finishes of soft, porous materials can deaden sound, tackboard finishes can permit the use of walls for display, and various wall treatments can be aesthetically pleasing.

Storage and Display Facilities. Every early childhood program facility must have storage. E. Prescott (1984) noted that the amount of storage was positively associated with the richness of the program. Some items, such as cleaning supplies, medicines, professional library items, teaching aids, personal records on children and staff, business records, and personal items of staff, always need to be in closed and/or secure storage.

A balance needs to be achieved between open and closed storage areas for children's items. Open storage gives children some choices, and closed storage allows staff to regulate choices. Generally speaking, programs housing older children and those following the constructivist program base have more open storage. Programs housing infants and toddlers and those following the behavioral-environmental view have more closed storage. It is interesting to note that, in programs for preschool children, if children were allowed to get things out of closed storage, even with a key, they were less destructive as compared with situations in which only teachers could get closed-storage items (E. Prescott, 1984).

For infant programs, storage shelves 4-ft high can hold items safe from the reach of infants and toddlers. Unless doors and drawers are secured with a standard lock or a child-proof device, however, items may be within the reach of a climbing toddler. Two-foot high shelves are appropriate for open storage, but they must be very sturdy because babies pull themselves up on them.

For preschool and primary programs, shelf height should be approximately 3 ft for open storage items. Shelves with or without removable doors are excellent, but bins are unsuitable except for moving heavy materials. To aid the flow of traffic and eliminate unnecessary additional steps, shelves or racks should be placed near the area where they will be used. The design and materials used in storage units should be compatible with their purpose, such as slanted shelves for books, resting-cot cupboards with louvered doors to allow air circulation, and shelf materials resistant to water damage in water play centers. Different storage designs (slanted vertically and horizontally partitioned cabinets, drawers and shelves of varying depths) help in arranging, finding, and protecting materials and equipment; they are also aesthetically pleasing.

Equipment and materials should be displayed like wares in a market so that children can "window shop" or "buy." How materials are arranged and their accessibility are almost as important as the materials themselves. For infants, items should be placed on the walls, near the floor. These items include low bulletin boards covered with simple pictures or even household objects that contrast between object and field, unbreakable mirrors, and texture/color boards. For older children, too, an abundance of "pinning space" near eye level is desirable. Backs of storage units may be covered with corkboard or Peg-Board for displaying children's work. Chalkboards should be on a level that children can reach. For children with disabilities, the lower edge of chalkboards, bulletin boards, and mirrors should be 6 in. from the floor. Portable chalkboards are more functional than permanent ones.

Furniture and Other Essentials.   Furniture used in early childhood programs should be comfortable for both children and staff and should be aesthetically pleasing. Furniture should also fit the objectives of the program. For example, programs for infants and toddlers and for older children following the constructivist view use fewer pieces of traditional school furniture and more soft pieces (e.g., pillows, hammocks, couches, beanbag chairs, even carpeted floors). Programs for older children, especially those programs following the behavioral-environmental view, are more apt to be equipped with traditional school furniture (tables and chairs, or desks).

Infants and toddlers have some special needs. These include the following:

Feeding
   car seats with trays
   feeding chairs (high chairs, low chairs)

   feeding implements (bibs, bottles, cups, plates, spoons)
   storage units
   tables (about 15 in. high) and non-tip chairs
   wastebasket (covered)

Changing and Toileting
   changing table or counter
   sink with spray nozzle
   stools (11 in. for toddlers)
   storage units
   toilet training chairs
   wastebasket (covered)

Napping
   bed linens (brightly colored patterned sheets, blankets, stuffed toys; no stuffed toys for very young infants)
   cots (24" × 42" for toddlers)
   cradles
   cribs (30" × 54" for children under 18 months)

Other Furniture and Essentials
   barrels (carpeted)
   chairs (infant seats, soft stuffed chairs, reclining baby chairs, rockers)
   couches
   cubbies (hooks at child's shoulder level, not eye level)
   evacuation crib and mattress (or 3' × 4' canvas wheeled-cart used in hotels and hospitals for collecting linen)
   pillows (large, throw)
   playpen or play yard (some are portable; some may be elevated for less floor draft problems and for easier adult accessibility)
   mattresses (including air)
   storage cabinets (approximately 11½" × 15" × 24"; open and closed)

strollers

tables (for infants, 12 in. high with raised edges; for toddlers, 14 to 15 in. high) and chairs (8-in. seat height)

toddler wagons (for transporting toddlers on "walking excursions")

Furniture for preschool (ages 3 years through 5 years) and primary-grade children (ages 6 years through 8 years) should be of the proper height and proportions, durable and lightweight, and have rounded corners. If space is at a premium, furniture, especially children's chairs, should be stackable. Tables accommodating from four to six children are advisable. Although tables are designed in many geometric shapes, rectangular tables accommodate large pieces of paper for art and craft work, and round tables are attractive in the library center. Trapezoidal tables are quite versatile because they can be arranged in many configurations. All table surfaces should be "forgiving surfaces" (easy to clean and repair) because of children's intensive use (Vergeront, 1987). Portable drawing and writing surfaces, such as clipboards and Formica-covered boards, can also be used. Formica countertops are excellent for artwork (e.g., finger painting, Play-Doh experiences) and cooking. Children's chairs should have a broad base to prevent tipping and a full saddle seat with a back support approximately 8 in. above the seat. So that children can safety carry the chairs, chair weight should not exceed 8 to 10 lbs. The distance between the seat height of the chairs and the table surface should be approximately 7½ in. In addition to regular school chairs, soft furniture (e.g., couches, easy chairs, beanbag chairs, hammocks) and stools and benches should be provided. Storage units and display facilities are also a necessity.

Specific furniture includes the following:

chairs (10- to 12-in. seat height)

children's rocking chairs, easy chairs, stools, and benches

dividers (bulletin boards, flannel boards, screens)

storage units (approximately $15'' \times 28'' \times 48''$; portable and/or built-in and open and/or closed) and cubbies

tables (16 to 20 in. high)

Furniture for school-age child care must accommodate varying sizes of children. All types of furniture are needed for the many types of activities (e.g., arts and crafts, cooking, table games, homework, watching videos). Most programs prefer that the emphasis be placed on soft, homelike furniture because many children have been at desks in hard chairs all day. Much storage space is needed for children's personal items and for program materials during nonprogram hours.

Staff and visiting adults need adult furniture for comfort. Children can also use some of the adult furniture. This furniture includes the following:

chairs (soft and wood)

closet and low cabinets with locks (for personal possessions)

desk and/or work tables

filing cabinets

General Criteria for Learning/ Activity Centers

Certainly, the age of children served and the program objectives determine whether learning/ activity centers are to be used. Most early childhood programs use some centers. Programs housing infants and toddlers and primary-grade children do not use centers as frequently as do programs housing 3- through 5-year-old children. Programs following the constructivist view often use learning/activity centers as the basis for room arrangements. Conversely, programs following the behavioral-environmental view use centers to a lesser degree.

Learning/activity centers are a series of working areas that have a degree of privacy but are related to the whole activity room. Their distinctiveness and integrity can be maintained by using the suggestions described below.

Defining Space. S. Shapiro (1975) notes the importance of organizing space and making clear boundaries between activity areas. The space should remain flexible, but there should be enough definition to provide a feeling of place. This definition of space may be accomplished by placing dividers or storage units in various configurations or by using dividers or storage units in conjunction with corners and walls to create two or more areas as shown in Figure 5-2.

Such configurations permit traffic flow but also provide containment. Space can also be defined by differences in colors or shades of wall

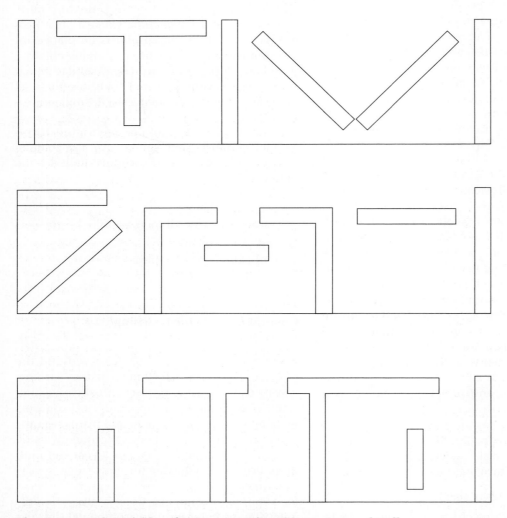

Figure 5-2   Using Dividers for Storage Units With Corners and Walls

paint or carpet in adjoining centers, by differences in light intensity in adjacent centers, and by manipulation of the floor planes with wells, pits, or platforms. Adjoining centers can also be visually separated with dividers. (A 4-ft-high divider will provide enclosure to a standing or sitting child, and a 2-ft-high divider will provide enclosure to a sitting child.)

Before deciding how to define space for a learning/activity center, one must decide whether the space is to be permanent. Differences in colors or shades of wall paint, carpet colors, and manipulation of floor planes are somewhat permanent, but placement of movable dividers or storage units and light intensity are not. Being able to change centers has advantages. A center may be infrequently used and should be eliminated or made more attractive to children. The teacher may wish to create a center to fit a new curriculum topic, a popular center may need to be enlarged, or a similar center may be created to accommodate additional children. Problems with traffic flow or storage may occur, or the activity room may be too small to house all activities at one time and may need to be rearranged during the day.

Allowing Sufficient Space.   Sufficient space should be allowed for the type of activity that a particular center is intended to accommodate. More space is required in centers with group play, large items of equipment or materials to spread out, or materials or equipment tending to cause aggressive acts among children.

Providing Acoustic Isolation.   The noise level from one center should not interfere with activities in another. Seclusion may be achieved by using adequate acoustic materials on the floors, walls, or ceilings; by providing headsets; by locating centers with similar noise levels (e.g., library and concept centers) adjacent to each other; and by placing extremely noisy centers (e.g., workshop) outside. Most of the literature suggests separating noisy and quiet areas. Nilsen (1977), however, recommends mixing areas to more accurately resemble a real-life situation and to help prevent areas of the activity room from appearing to be more "for boys" or "for girls."

The types and arrangement of centers must be in keeping with the local program's objectives. Although a professional may think in many ways about centers in relation to program objectives, one way is through Jones and Prescott's (1978) seven dimensions of activity settings, as shown in Table 5-1.

Arranging Equipment and Materials.   Equipment and materials for daily use should be so arranged. Portable objects should be placed on low shelves or in cabinets so that children can get them out and put them back. Open shelves encourage children to return their items. Heavy or nonportable objects should be placed on tables or shelves where they can be used without being moved; otherwise, children can hurt themselves or damage the items. Heavy but portable items (e.g., quadruple unit blocks) should be placed on lower shelves of cabinets.

Many early childhood facilities lack enough shelf space. According to Osmon (1971), economy of shelf use can be achieved by creating distinctiveness in the items placed on the shelves. Distinctiveness is increased by using various types of shelving (inclined, slotted, stepped, drawers) in one storage unit and by placing items with contrasting properties (color, size, shape, texture) next to each other. Extensive use of contrasting properties as a criterion for placement of materials may be confusing to children. Finding the "homes" of various materials, both a self-help skill and a visual discrimination skill, is aided by such cues as same-color labels on matching materials and shape labels provided on the storage unit.

Equipment and materials for regular but not daily use should be readily available and stored

Table 5-1   Dimensions of Activity Settings

Dimension	Explanation	Example
Dimension 1: Open/Closed	Open activity involves the use of materials with no correct outcome and no set stopping point, encourages creative experimentations, and supports interaction.	Sand play and art activities
	Closed activity involves the use of materials with "correct" outcomes and involves right-wrong feedback with a possible sense of accomplishment.	Puzzles and lotto
Dimension 2: Simple/Complex	Simple activity involves the use of usually one material with only one possible use.	Swings
	Complex activity involves the use of two or more play materials with the potential for active manipulations and alteration by children.	Sand table with digging equipment, sifters, sand molds, and water
Dimension 3: High/Low mobility	High-mobility activity requires large-muscle mobility.	Climbing equipment
	Low-mobility activity requires little to no mobility.	Puzzles
	Intermediate-mobility activity requires moderate mobility using both large and small muscles.	Blocks
Dimension 4: Social structure	Individual activity Small-group activity Intermediate-group activity Whole-class activity	Looking at a book Blocks Music activity Listening to a story
Dimension 5: Soft/Hard	Softness is based on the presence of soft textures.	Malleable materials: sand lap to sit on single sling swings grass rug/carpet water messy activities (finger paints) cozy furniture dirt to dig in animals to be held
	Hardness is based on the presence of hard textures.	Lack of the above
Dimension 6: Intrusion/Seclusion	Intrusion is "interruption" by other children.	On a climbing apparatus, a child may show off skills to another child by saying, "See me," or, "Watch."
	Seclusion is the lack of intrusion by others.	"Reading" a book while sitting in a chair off the "beaten path" does not invite intrusion.
Dimension 7: Risk/Safety	Risk activity tests the child's skills; the child sees apparent risks.	Climbing activity
	Safe activity involves no risks.	Finger painting

to prevent deterioration and damage. If space permits, they should be stored in or near the center where they will be used. Labeling also helps staff locate equipment and materials quickly. Special care must be exercised in storing consumable items, such as food, paper, paste, and paints; audiovisual equipment; science materials; musical instruments; recordings; and any breakable objects.

In addition to the objectives of the program, other factors enter into the arrangement of learning/activity centers in the room and equipment and materials within each center, such as type of floor covering required; size and quantity of equipment and materials; special requirements (e.g., a water source, an electrical outlet, a specific intensity of light, a certain type of storage); the level of noise; and the maximum number of children working in each center at one time. To prevent problems of overcrowding, popular centers may be widely separated to distribute children throughout the room. Furthermore, pathways throughout the activity room should be clear and wide enough to prevent congestion. The edges of pathways can be defined by furniture or changes in floor covering. Generally, each center should have one entrance.

The following comments are not intended as specific solutions on the arrangement of centers (or even a comprehensive list of all centers). Rather, the statements are a mixture of pertinent factors to consider in arranging centers.

Activity Centers for Infants and Toddlers

The infant/toddler activity center must be an interesting place, full of beautiful sights, sounds, and textures, that capture these babies' attentions and lead them to explore and problem-solve in their sensory and motor world. The room needs to be arranged and equipped to provide a safe and virtually restriction-free environment for babies and to promote effective and comfortable functioning of adults.

Infant/Toddler Rooms. Infants and toddlers need a room organized into distinct areas that reflect a range of activities. Several principles need to be kept in mind:

1. *Bins and toy boxes are inappropriate.* Not only is safety a factor, but the amount of play time also decreases and the amount of toy-selecting time increases when toy boxes and bins rather than shelves are used (Montes & Risley, 1975). Movable shelves aid staff response to developmental changes in children and correspond with new program demands. Children also enjoy new arrangements.

2. *Smaller activity centers for one or two children are more appropriate than the larger centers typical of programs for older children.*

3. *Activity centers can surround a large play area that becomes the center of action.* It is developmentally inappropriate to expect infants and toddlers to play exclusively in the activity areas. By 2 or 3 years of age, children recognize differences in space and know what types of behaviors are expected in certain areas. Toddlers who are ready to play in centers must have spatial areas sharply defined if order is to be maintained.

4. *Activity centers need to house items in multiple quantities.* Children at this age rarely share and spend most of their time playing alone but in the presence of others.

5. *Infants and toddlers need many secluded places.* An elevated and fenced area may protect infants from active toddlers for short periods of time. Toddlers need couches, low sturdy shelves, barrels, and other secluded places.

6. *Infants and toddlers especially need an activity room that permits high mobility, has mainly open activities, and provides materials for complex activities* (as defined in Table 5-1).

7. *Infants and toddlers need an aesthetically pleasing environment of beautiful colors,*

sounds, forms, textures (especially softness), and patterns.

8. *Adults need comfortable places to sit while playing or holding infants and toddlers.* Thus, adult-sized couches, upholstered chairs, and rocking chairs should be placed throughout the activity room.

Cataldo (1982) lists these centers for infants and toddlers: block and vehicle, small manipulative toy area, quiet area, and art. P. Adams and Taylor (1985) suggest these activity areas: listening, seeing, touch, fantasy, water and sand, quiet, gross motor, creativity, and construction. Stewart (1982) adds a music area.

Figure 5-3, a floor plan of an infant/toddler activity room, illustrates some of the principles discussed. Napping, feeding, and changing/toileting areas are discussed later in this chapter.

Figure 5-3 is only an example; administrators need to fit their plan to their own program.

Materials for Infants and Toddlers. Very young, nonwalking infants explore with their senses. Stimulation with materials is important. Items needed may include the following:

bells (to firmly attach to wrist or shoes)

faces (pictures and the live human face)

objects (attached to cribs, playpens, including mobiles facing downward for infants to see)

pictures and designs (e.g., on walls, crib linens)

rattles

recordings (of lullabies)

rings and other objects (for grasping and mouthing)

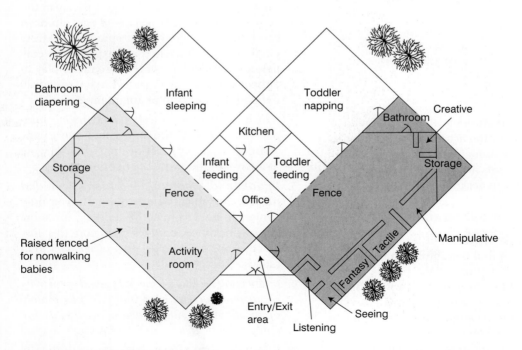

Figure 5-3A   Infant/Toddler Center. (The lightly shaded area is detailed in Figure 5–3B. The darkly shaded area is detailed in Figure 5–3C.)

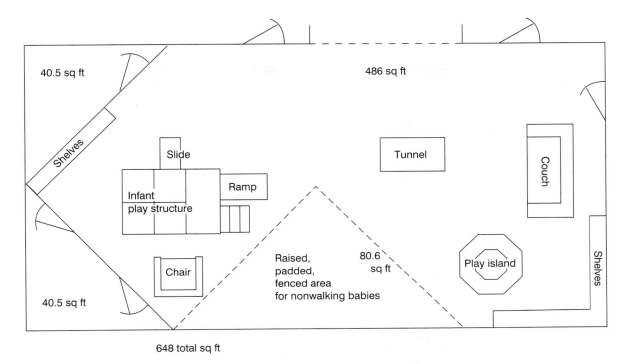

Figure 5-3B

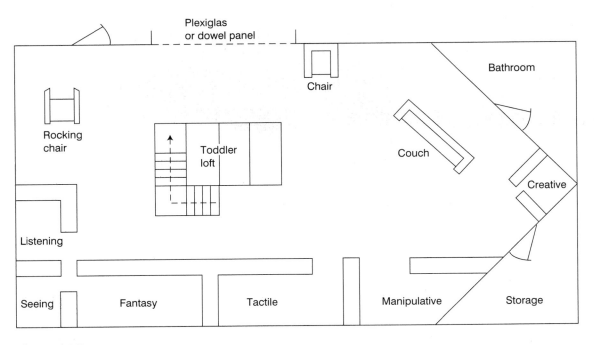

Figure 5-3C

squeak toys

squeeze toys

A wide variety of materials are used in infant/toddler centers. Many of the items listed below can be used in various centers. Because of the differences in the types of centers provided in various infant and toddler programs and the wide variety of equipment and materials, it would be impossible to list all items available for learning/activity centers. The materials may include the following:

Listening

musical toys

rattles

record or cassette players

recordings (records or tapes of books, rhymes, music, and animal sounds)

rhythm instruments (e.g., drums, bells, wooden blocks, sticks, tambourines, xylophones)

wind chimes

Seeing

aquariums

banners or streamers (especially for outside)

books (picture books of cloth, vinyl, and cardboard)

flannel boards with rather large pieces for placing on board

mirrors (unbreakable; hand-held and hung on wall)

mobiles (on eye level or with objects/pictures hung facing downward)

pictures and wall hangings

puzzles

sponges (cut into different shapes)

terrariums

Tactile

books (with "feely" pictures)

cuddly toys

"feely" balls/boxes

teething toys

textured cards and wall hangings

Manipulatives

activity boards (manipulative boards and latch-and-lock boards)

beads (wooden beads, wooden spools, and snap beads)

blocks (lightweight plastic or vinyl for stacking and large interlocking blocks, such as Lego)

block props (animals, people, small vehicles)

containers (pails, margarine tubs with lids, shoe boxes with lids, muffin pans with items to fit into cups)

cradle gyms

dressing boards (button and zipper)

hole punch

kitchen items (pots, pans, spoons, cups, egg beaters)

Peg-Boards with large pegs

push/pull toys

puzzles (simple with knobs)

rattles

sand and sand toys (pail, sieves and sifters, measuring cups and spoons, funnels, sand wheels)

sewing/lacing cards, with yarn and laces

shape sorters

stacking/nesting toys

water and water play toys (for pouring, straining, floating)

Fantasy

bags (e.g., tote)

blankets

blocks (lightweight)

cars/trucks/trains/planes

dolls (washable) with easy-to-dress clothes

dress-up clothes, especially hats

housekeeping furniture and other items—refrigerator, sink, stove, table and chairs, buggy, high chair, play food, empty (and clean) food containers, pots/pans, plastic dishes, housekeeping tools (mop and broom)

miniature settings (dollhouse, farm, airport)

mirrors

pillows

puppets

purses (including bags and suitcases)

scarves (to wave around)

shopping cart

stuffed animals

telephones

Creative

crayons (large-size and nontoxic)

easel

glue

magazines (for cutting)

markers (water color and nontoxic)

paints (watercolors, finger paints, tempera)

paintbrushes

paper (construction, manila and white drawing paper, newsprint, and finger paint)

sand and sand toys

scissors (blunt-ended and soft-handled)

sponges (for painting)

Gross Motor

balls (large rubber, soft beach, or balls designed for infants and toddlers)

bean bags and target

boxes, cardboard (to carry and crawl in)

bowling ball and pins (plastic)

bubble-making materials

climbers (low)

exercise mats

platform with railings (raised about 15 in. off the ground to make a bridge)

pounding bench

push/pull toys

ramps

riding toys (steerable, pedal, scoot)

ring toss

rocking toys (rocking boat and rocking horse)

sand and sand toys (especially outside)

slide (low or placed on slightly inclined terrain)

steering wheels (attached to platforms with sides or other stable structures for pretend play)

steps (2 or 3; not steep; with railings)

swings (special swing with straps for infants; sling-type seat for toddlers)

troughs with moving water and floating objects

truck inner tube (only partially inflated)

tunnels

wagons

walking rails (attached 15 in. off floor)

wheelbarrows

Toys, wall hangings, mirrors, and other interesting items should be available in the napping, feeding and dining, and changing and toileting areas. (Items must be not only at eye level for infants and toddlers' when creeping, crawling, and walking but also at eye level when being carried or elevated, such as in a crib.)

Learning/Activity Centers for Older Children

As previously discussed, learning/activity centers are common in preschool programs and in kindergarten and primary-level (or grade) programs using the constructivist approach. Several common learning/activity centers for preschool and kindergarten children are listed below, along with a few statements about planning the center and locating it within the activity room. The comments are not intended as specific solutions on the arrangement of centers (or even a comprehensive list of all centers); rather, the statements are simply some pertinent factors associated with each center.

Block Center/Area.   A **block center/area** is the space that is used for building with unit, hollow, or both types of blocks and for playing with the created structures and accessories (e.g., transportation toys, people/animal figures). Construction with smaller building materials takes place in the manipulative/constructive center. Block centers/areas may be housed inside and outside, on a terrace, or other firm, flat surface. Block centers/areas are often located in noisy areas of the classroom because of the noise created by handling blocks and the accompanying dramatic play. In block play, the tendency is toward expansive aggression and solitary retreat; therefore, the block center should accommodate a child who wants to work alone, with another child, or with several children. Various group sizes may be accommodated in several ways, including the following:

1. A small block center, about 75 sq ft, can accommodate two children. Small block centers, if protected by storage units or if spatially defined by using a low platform (but never a loft) or a pit, may be placed near the entrance. (For a timid child, such placement may serve as a transition area to a larger group area.) Sometimes, these centers use reduced-sized unit blocks (replicas of unit blocks whose dimensions are about two thirds of the dimensions of standard unit blocks). These blocks may be built on a table as well as the floor. Usually, about 100 to 150 blocks and a few accessories are shelved in the small block center.

2. A large block center, about 260 sq ft, can accommodate up to seven children. Because blocks require such a large area, the space may be referred to as a *block area* instead of *block center*. From 700 to 1000 standard unit blocks or 80 or more hollow blocks are recommended for a large block area. Because block constructions are easily knocked over by fast-moving traffic, the large block area should be located in the area of the room where traffic moves at a slower pace and where structures can be left up. Shelves are usually at the back and the left and right sides of the area; a movable divider (screen) can provide protection from the front and can be adjusted to the fluid nature of block construction. The large block area should be adjacent to the dramatic play center. Occasionally, large block areas can be subdivided for multiple construction sites.

3. A small set of hollow blocks (e.g., 10 long, 10 square, 10 boards), used in conjunction with dramatic play, are often housed in dramatic play centers, especially those that change themes throughout the year (e.g., store, post office, farm/ranch).

4. Large outside block areas, for building with a full set of hollow blocks or unit blocks, are usually temporary in nature. Because wooden blocks must stay dry, blocks are transported in block carts/bins and even children's wagons to and from the block building area.

Acoustic materials, such as a dense, low-pile carpet, should cover the floor and block shelves. Even outside, indoor/outdoor carpet protects children from either rough cement or possible splinters. Storage shelves are open. A well-equipped block center takes three or four storage shelves (4' × 3' × 1'), with three horizontal divisions creating shelves 1 ft apart. Vertical subdivisions create cubicles. Small cubicles (about 13 in. wide) are for half units, pillars, cylinders, ramps, and floorboards. Medium cubicles (about 18 in. wide) are for triangles, switches, curves, arches, and small accessories. Large cubicles (about 24 in. to 37 in. wide) are for units, double units, quad units, roof boards, and accessories. The arrangement of blocks and accessories should be attractive and well thought-out: for example, (a) store blocks lengthwise for quick identification (blocks cannot be identified by their ends—narrow faces); (b) label each section of the shelves with a picture or drawing for easy return of materials; (c) emphasize size of blocks by shelving blocks seriated by length, with larger blocks on the bottom shelf; (d) do not pack shelves too tightly; (e) arrange a set of same-size blocks in widely separated shelves to facilitate traffic movement to and from the shelves; and (f) rearrange shelves from time to time to attract attention.

In block centers/areas in which the floor is used for building, approximately 18 in. to 24 in. in front of all storage shelves must be defined as a "no building zone" so that the shelves remain accessible. (The no-building zone can be defined by a change in floor covering or color or by "marking" with colored tape.) On the walls, pictures of buildings, bridges, and other constructions (e.g., cut from magazines, photographs of field trip sites, photographs of children's constructions) can be displayed. Figure 5-4 is an example of an indoor block center/area.

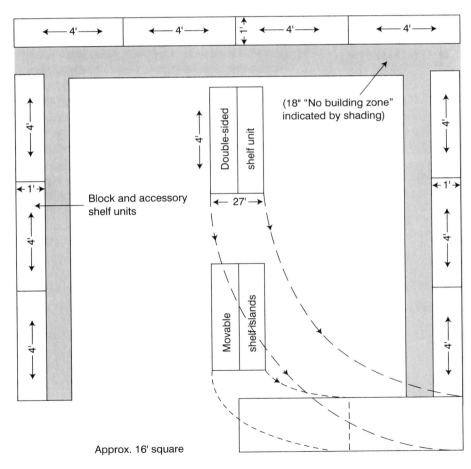

Figure 5-4   Large Indoor Block Area

The main materials for indoor block areas are unit blocks, so named because each block is the size of the unit (1⅜″ × 2¾″ × 5½″ for standard-size unit blocks) or a multiple or fraction of that unit, and hollow blocks are the main materials for outdoor block areas. Factory-made accessories designed specifically as accessories for block play are better than those not so designed because they are in correct proportion to the blocks. Figures of people and other accessories, if appropriate, should be multicultural. Materials to include in the block center/areas are as follows:

"blueprints/house plans" and "construction hats" (play props)

books related to building

accessories (art materials for making accessories or for decorative purposes; figures of people/animals; farm products; mini-furniture; traffic signs; transportation items; miscellaneous materials—colored cubes, empty wooden thread spools, small sticks, pretty stones and shells)

block shelves (for inside) and bins/carts (for outdoors)

unit blocks (see Table 5-2)

outdoor hollow blocks (see Table 5-3) or polyethylene or corrugated cardboard blocks

pictures of buildings

pencils, paper, and so on for drawing or writing about building

steering wheel (attached to a stable structure for pretend play)

Dramatic Play Center.   The **dramatic play center** is an area of the room designed specifically for children's spontaneous pretend play. In dramatic play, children act out the roles of family members and community workers, reenact school activities and story plots, and learn such social amenities as table manners and telephone courtesy. Dramatic play may occur in almost any learning/activity center; however, one or more

Table 5-2   Unit Blocks

100 units	1⅜″	×	2¾″	×	5½″
180 double units	1⅜″	×	2¾″	×	11″
200 quadruple units	1⅜″	×	2¾″	×	22″
36 ramps	1⅜″	×	2¾″	×	5½″
25 roof boards	⅜″	×	2¾″	×	11″
10 curves (elliptical)	1⅜″	×	2¾″	×	13¾″
10 curves (circular)	1⅜″	×	2¾″	×	7¾″
10 Y-switches	1⅜″	×	8¼″	×	11″
20 cylinders	2¾″	diam.		×	5½″
20 pillars	1⅜″	×	1⅜″	×	5½″
25 half-units	1⅜″	×	2¾″	×	2¾″
20 pairs triangles	1⅜″	×	2¾″	×	2¾″

Source: Starks, E. B. (1960). *Blockbuilding.* Washington, DC: National Education Association, Department of Kindergarten-Primary Education.

Table 5-3   Hollow Blocks

A	
36 units	12″ × 12″ × 6″
36 double units	12″ × 24″ × 6″

B	
1 Set: 80 blocks cut in —	
squares:	11″ × 11″ × 5½″
rectangles:	22″ × 11″ × 5½″
rectangles:	5½″ × 11″ × 5½″

C	
1 dozen	24″ × 12″ × 6″
3 dozen	12″ × 12″ × 6″
1 dozen	24″ × 6″ × 6″ with some triangles

Sources: (A) Starks, E. B. (1960). *Blockbuilding.* Washington, DC: National Education Association, Department of Kindergarten-Primary Education; (B) Berson, M. P. (1959). *Kindergarten: Your child's first big step.* New York: E. P. Dutton; (C) Leeper, S. H., Dales, R. J., Skipper, D. S., & Witherspoon, R. L. (1974). *Good schools for young children* (3rd ed.). New York: Macmillan.

centers are usually arranged specifically for dramatic play.

Unlike other learning centers that provide floor and/or table space for children's activities and cabinets for display or storage of equipment/materials, dramatic play centers are more like "stage settings" (Beaty, 1992). The most common stage setting is housekeeping, with the "house" divided into one to three "rooms." The almost universal room is the kitchen, followed by a bedroom, and then a den or living area. These rooms within the housekeeping center should look distinctive, with enclosures to give a homelike atmosphere. (Openings between the rooms must be wide enough to accommodate doll buggies, however.) A loft bedroom above the downstairs kitchen and/or living room is very effective. Because of the size of the furniture and the mobility of children during play, suggested room sizes are 80 sq ft for the kitchen; 40 sq ft for the bedroom, and more space if dress-up is included in this room; and 40 sq ft for the living room (see Figure 5-5).

In programs housing older preschoolers and primary-level children, often dramatic play is expanded beyond the prestructured housekeeping area. Because housekeeping play is still valuable, the center is retained but often as a one-room house (e.g., mainly kitchen and perhaps a doll bed or couch). Additional dramatic play space (approximately 60 sq ft) is provided for multipurpose use. In this space, children dramatize different themes (e.g., farms, stores, parks) throughout the year. This multipurpose dramatic play center is primarily floor space and storage until children create their own stage settings through the use of such materials as hollow blocks, boxes, gadgets, and theme-specific materials found in prop boxes (see Figure 5-6).

Examples of floor plans for specific themes can be seen in this reference:

Warner, L., & Craycraft, K. (1991). *Language in centers: Kids communicating*. Carthage, IL: Good Apple.

This open center can also be a place for children to play with miniature dollhouses, farms, and other replicas. (As has been stated, miniature replicas can also be housed in the *small* block center.)

Besides adequate floor space, all dramatic play centers need adequate storage for the many pieces of equipment/materials. Carpet is not required. Carpet does aid acoustic control, however, and gives warmth/softness to the housekeeping center.

Many early childhood programs also have a puppet theater housed near the dramatic play center or the language center. Usually, storage/display shelves and a puppet theater, a free-standing structure, are all that is needed.

The needed dramatic play equipment/materials depends on themes introduced. Dolls, puppets, books, and pictures should fulfill multicultural/antibias criteria. Categories of equipment/materials to consider include the following:

cameras (toy, and an instant with film)

costumes, especially hats and tools of the trade of community workers (e.g., doctor's bag and stethoscope) and costumes for reenacting stories

doll items (table and two to four chairs; doll furniture—high chair, bed or cradle, carriage, chest of drawers, refrigerator, stove, sink, cabinet for dishes, washer-dryer; doll wardrobes and linens; pots, pans, dishes, flatware—all items should be unbreakable; ironing board and iron; housekeeping articles—broom, dust mop, dustpan, and dust rag; artificial food; clothesline and clothespins; dishpan; pictures and other home-decorating items)

dolls (baby and teenage dolls)

dress-up clothes for men and women (long skirts, blouses, dresses, shirts, pants, shoes, caps, hats, boots, small suitcase, scarves and ribbons, flowers, jewelry, purses, neckties)

fabric (several strips 2 or 3 yds in length, which can be used imaginatively)

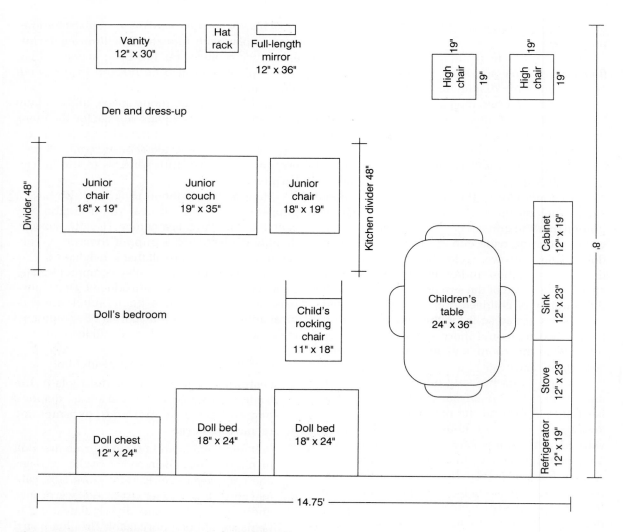

Figure 5-5   Dramatic Play Center: Housekeeping

gadgets (rubber hose, steering wheels, PVC pipe, old faucets, door locks, springs, keys, pulleys, bells, scales, alarm clocks, cash registers and play money, cartons and cans, paintbrushes, paper bags, light switches, paper punch for tickets)

miniature dollhouse, community, farm, service station, and so on

mirrors (full-length and hand-held)

pictures of community workers

play screens, cardboard houses, and so on

puppets and puppet theater

reading/writing materials (appropriate for theme)

rocking chair

stuffed animals

telephone

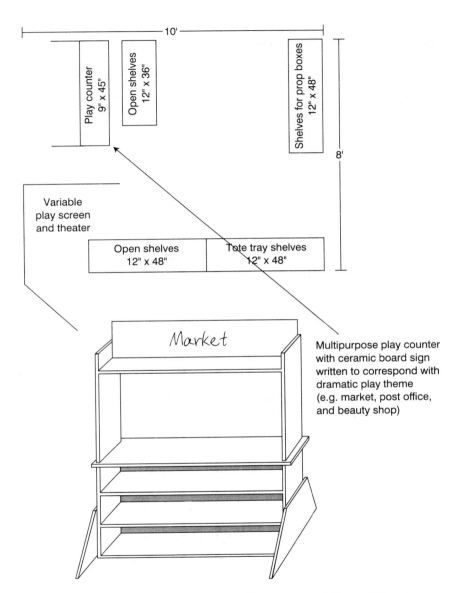

Figure 5-6   Dramatic Play Center: Multipurpose and Puppet Theater

Specific prop equipment/materials are suggested in these references:

Bender, J. (1971). Have you ever thought of a prop box? *Young Children, 26*(3), 164-169.

Myhre, S. (1993). Enhancing your dramatic play area through the use of prop boxes. *Young Children, 48*(5), 6-11.

Suskind, D., & Kittel, J. (1989). Clocks, cameras, and chatter, chatter, chatter: Activity boxes as curriculum. *Young Children, 44*(2), 46-50.

In addition to these suggestions, make prop boxes based on the occupations of the program's parent clientele.

Art Center.   The **art center** is the section of the room devoted to the making and displaying of the visual representations of children. Through paints, paper, crayons, markers, clay, and the "bits and pieces" of collage materials, young children develop their sensory/perceptual concepts of color, form, size, texture, and light/dark and their aesthetic sensitivities; represent their mental thoughts in visual products, rather than in words; display their creativity; express their emotions; and refine their small-motor skills with the tools of artists.

The art center must be a little studio that beckons children's interests through a comfortable place to work without unrealistic constraints (e.g., "Don't get a drop of paint on the floor because it will stain the carpet!"); through storage, drying, and display furnishings designed for much self-directed activities; and through the provision of a wide variety and quantity of media to explore. Specific criteria include the following:

1. The art center should look like a cheerful studio. The center is appropriately located where ample light is available from lighting fixtures or windows that provide sun-free directional light. A center near the door to the playground allows art activities to expand to outdoor areas. Cheerfulness is further enhanced by the display of children's products on walls or display boards that are painted (or covered) in one of the "rainbow" pastel colors.

2. The art center should have places for individual and group work. Work surfaces include the wall (chalkboards and murals), tilted surfaces (easels), and flat surfaces (tables). Movable stand-up tables should be approximately 20 in. high and sit-down/stand-up tables about 18 in. high. Built-in work surfaces should be 20 in. high and between 2 and 3 ft deep. The art center needs many storage shelves for supplies. To protect paper from light and dust, these storage shelves should have doors although other storage shelves may be open. Drying art products will require lines or racks for paintings and mobiles, and shelves for three-dimensional products.

3. Surfaces in the art area should be impervious to water, paint, paste, and clay and be easy to clean. Floors should not be slippery when wet, and all surfaces should dry quickly. Linoleum, Formica, or a vinyl cloth should cover the tables; ceramic tile, vinyl-coated wallpaper, or waterproof paint should cover the walls; and the floor should have a vinyl tile covering.

4. A sink in the art center or in an adjacent rest room with plenty of counter space on both sides is essential for mixing paints and cleanup. The sink should have a faucet 23 in. above the floor and should be equipped with a disposal drain for catching clay and paste. The sink counter and the wall behind the sink should be covered with an easily cleaned surface.

5. The "studio" may be rather open or cozy; however, cozy centers must be roomy enough to accommodate space-consuming tables and floor easels and children moving about with wet paintings. Thus, the art center will need to be approximately 190 sq ft. (See Figure 5-7 for a layout of an art center.)

Art equipment and materials include the following:

apron (snaps or Velcro are preferred because ties can knot)

chalk (various colors, ½- to 1-in. diameter)

chalkboards

clay (powdered and/or Play-Doh or Plasticine)

clay boards

color paddles (three paddles—red, yellow, blue)

cookie cutters

crayons

design block sets

display boards and tables

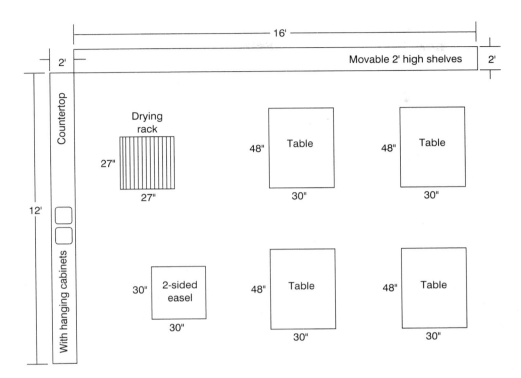

Figure 5-7   Art Center

drying rack

easels (two or three working sides with a tray for holding paint containers on each side)

food coloring

geometric shapes (e.g., insets)

gummed paper in assorted shapes for making designs and pictures

junk materials for collage work (beads, buttons, cellophane, cloth, flat corks, sewing trims, wallpaper scraps, wrapping paper scraps, yarn)

magazines for collage

markers (felt-tip, various colors)

mosaics

mounting board (approximately 22″ × 28″)

pails (plastic with covers for storing clay)

paint (fluorescent paint, finger paint, powdered or premixed tempera paint, watercolor sets)

paint jars (some that do not spill are now made)

paintbrushes (camel hair or bristle, ½-in. and 1-in. thick with long handles)

paper (cellophane; construction paper—18″ × 24″; corrugated paper; crepe paper; drawing paper—18″ × 24″, white and manila; finger paint paper or glazed shelf paper; metallic paper—10″ × 13″; newsprint—18″ × 24″; poster board; tissue paper; tag board)

paper bags

paper cutter

parquetry blocks and cards

paste brushes and sticks

paste and glue

pencils (colored)

pictures of children engaging in art activities, and reproductions of famous paintings, and pictures of sculpture and architecture

pipe cleaners

plastic canvas

printing blocks or stamps

recipes for finger paints, modeling materials, and so on

rulers

scissors (adult shears and right- and left-handed scissors for children)

scissors rack

sorting boxes for sorting colors and shapes

sponges

staff supplies (art gum erasers; felt erasers; fixative; glue; hole punch; correction fluid; masking, mystic, and transparent tapes; paper cutter; pins for bulletin boards; rubber cement; shears; stapler)

stories and poems with themes of color, shape, size, beauty of nature, and so on

textured materials (for tactile experiences)

weaving materials

yarn (various colors) and yarn needles

Music Center.   The **music center** is the area of the room devoted to children's explorations of tone and rhythm. Some activities are rather passive, such as listening to music and looking at books and pictures associated with music and dance. Other activities are more active and involve music expression, such as singing, playing instruments, and creating dances. Besides the music center, additional space is devoted to whole-group musical activities; this area is usually the same area as used for other whole-group activities. It is definitely advantageous to locate the music center adjacent to the whole-group area in order that materials such as rhythm instruments are easily accessible for whole-group music activities. However, music carts are available for easy transport of such items. Furthermore, if space permits, it is fun to open the music center (e.g., move a portable screen) to expand space for marching or dancing.

The music center is often rather small (e.g., 180 sq ft may be adequate), especially if the activities can easily expand into the whole-group area. Because singing, playing instruments, and dancing are noisy, the center should be somewhat enclosed and acoustically treated to contain sound. Carpet helps in acoustic control and minimizes the danger of falls when dancing; resilient flooring, however, permits more freedom of movement. The piano and autoharp should not be placed near windows, doors, or heating/cooling units. Tapes must be kept away from anything with a magnetic field and stored within areas having moderate temperature (50°F to 77°F) and humidity (40% to 60%) ranges.

The arrangement of the music center can be quite simple. One side of the center should have a table or counter equipped with listening stations. Space between each station is helpful for looking at books or drawing while listening. Space for stools or chairs must be included. A place to store tapes, CDs, and/or records and book display and storage should be nearby. Another side needs tables or counter area for holding xylophones, autoharps, tape players, and other "sound makers." The other side needs to be equipped with a Peg-Board or shelving for other rhythm instruments and hooks for scarves, capes, and other dress-up clothes for dancing/marching. A portable screen can be used to enclose low-mobility activities and can be pulled back to allow for more room to dance. The screen can also double as a Peg-Board for holding rhythm instruments (with outlines of instruments aiding children in "putting away") or as pinning space for pictures or drawings (see Figure 5-8).

Equipment and materials for music may include the following:

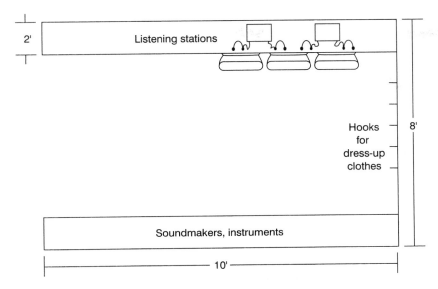

Figure 5-8   Music Center

autoharp

books—picture books about music, sound, and dancing/marching (for children) and singing, rhythm, and music appreciation books (for teacher use)

capes, full skirts, scarves (3′ × 5′), band uniforms for marching/dancing

listening stations (tape recorders and headsets)

melodic instruments (chromatic bells, electronic keyboard, xylophones)

music cart

piano (and piano bench)

pictures (musicians, musical instruments, dancers, bands, orchestras)

record player

record, cassette, and/or CD rack or cabinet

records, cassettes, and/or CDs

rhythm instruments (drums, claves, triangles, tambourines, cymbals, tom-toms, hand bells, jingle sticks, wrist bells, ankle bells, shakers, maracas, rhythm sticks, tone blocks, castanets, sand blocks, sounder, finger cymbals, gong bell)

tape recorder

Water and Sand Center.   The **water and sand center** is the area of the room in which children explore two of nature's raw materials—water and sand. Besides the properties of water and sand, the type of water and sand materials will lead to other concepts (e.g., containers lead to concepts of empty and full, heavy and light, more and less, shallow and deep, and measurement).

The water and sand area is relatively small (approximately 60 sq ft is sufficient), enclosed, and simple in arrangement. The center is often located in the noisy section of the room because children often interact in excited ways in this area. Because a water source is needed for both water and sand tables, the center is often close to the art and/or science center. If the center is near an outdoor terrace, the tables may be pushed outdoors on some days.

Because of the water and sand, floors will be slippery. Sand also tracks and can remove floor finishes. Thus, the best floor covering is an indoor/outdoor carpet that can be vacuumed with a wet/dry vacuum. If resilient flooring is used, rubber mats with tapered edges will prevent slipping. Some teachers simply keep their resilient floors dry and clean with sponge mops, sponges, and brooms/dust pans. (Preschoolers can help with cleaning if brooms and mops have short handles.) If this area is expanded to a terrace, planners must remember that concrete and outside flooring materials will also be very slippery; thus, terrace floor coverings must be carefully considered.

Shelving for water and sand play must be unaffected by water. Large items need open shelves. However, many water and sand play enhancers are small; thus, some shelving that is designed to hold tote boxes is excellent. Tote boxes can be picture/word labeled (e.g., *floating*, *measuring*). These boxes also allow for the needed rotation of items for this center (see Figure 5-9 as a center plan example).

Water and sand items include the following:

    aprons/smocks (plastic)

    detergent (dishwashing)/soap bars

    food coloring

    gloves (rubber for water play)

    mops, brooms, sponges (for cleanup)

    sand (white and brown)

    sand table

    sand toys (blocks, small; cans; cartons; cookie cutters; cups; dishes; figures, plastic animals, and people; funnels; gelatin or sand molds; ladles; marbles; pans; pitchers; planks, short; rocks, small; sand combs; sand dolls; sand pails; screens, plastic; shells; shovels; sieves; sifters; spoons; strainers; vehicles—trucks, bulldozers, tractors; watering cans)

    water play table

    water play toys (aquarium nets; balls—golf, Ping-Pong, plastic and rubber; bath toys; bowls, plastic; bulb baster; cooking whisk; corks; detergent squeeze bottles; dolls, washable; fishing bobbers; funnels; hose; marbles; medicine droppers; measuring cups, plastic; pitchers, small plastic; rocks, small; shaving brushes; shells; sponges; strainers; Styrofoam trays; watering cans, plastic)

    water pump for indoor water play table

Carpentry or Woodworking Center.   The **carpentry or woodworking center** is an area of the room in which older preschool and primary-level children enjoy sensory stimulation (from handling wood and tools, from the sound of cutting and hammering, and from the smell of sawdust), derive physical exercise, develop logico-mathematical understandings (as they measure, cut, and fit the "bits and pieces"), and represent the real world through their constructions.

The carpentry or woodworking center requires ample space (approximately 60 sq ft) and must be convenient for constant adult

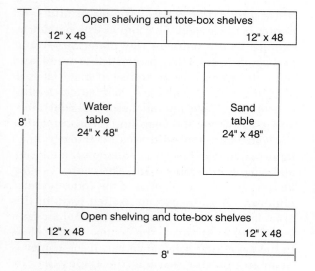

Figure 5-9   Water and Sand Play Center

supervision. It must be enclosed or at least out of the way of traffic flow. Because the center is so noisy and because children working in the center do not need distractions, many programs place the center in an empty room or hallway or on an outside terrace. If located in the room, the center is often placed near the block area. Plenty of light is needed for the center.

The area must be equipped with a sturdy workbench. Some centers also have a sawing bench. Tools are stored in a tool rack because toolboxes are dangerous for children. Tool racks should have an outline of the tools on the backboard to enable children to put away tools independently. The tool rack must either be portable in order to store tools when not in use or be a locking wall-mounted type, such as one of the styles shown by Skeen, Garner, and Cartwright (1984). Wood scraps are stored in boxes, baskets, and wooden bins. Figure 5-10 is an example floor plan for this center.

Young children cannot handle and do not need a rasp, screwdriver and screws, a plane, a brace and bits, a file, an ax or hatchet, metal sheets, tin snips, or power tools. Equipment and materials needed for carpentry or woodworking are as follows:

C-clamps (variety of)

cloth, leather, Styrofoam, cardboard, cork, bottle caps, and other scraps to nail on wood

glue

hammers (claw) of differing weights and sizes

hand drill

magnet (tied to a string for picking up dropped nails)

nails (thin nails with good-sized heads because thick nails tend to split wood)

paints (water-base)

pencils (heavy, soft-leaded)

pliers

ruler and yardstick used as a straightedge more than for measuring

safety goggles

sandpaper of various grades (wrapped around and tacked to blocks)

sawhorses

sawing bench, design shown in Skeen et al. (1984)

saws (crosscut and coping)

scraps of wood (soft wood, such as white pine, poplar, fir, basswood with no knots), doweling, wood slats, wooden spools

soap (rubbed across the sides of a saw to make it slide more easily)

tacks

tri-square

vises (attached to workbench)

wire (hand-pliable)

worktable or workbench (drawers for sandpaper and nails are desirable)

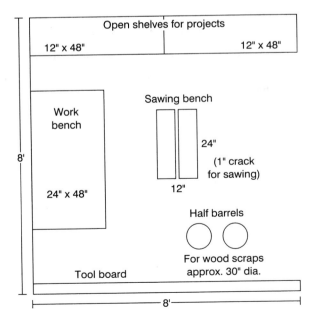

Figure 5-10   Carpentry or Woodworking Center

Science/Mathematics Center.   The **science/mathematics center** is the area of the room in which children wonder, reflect, and problem-solve in their scientific and mathematical world, see how science and mathematics are part of their everyday lives, learn to respect and appreciate their beautiful world, and develop physical and logicomathematical concepts. Unfortunately, in many early childhood programs, the "science/mathematics" center often consists of a window ledge with a plant and a small table often called the "discovery table."

Because of the diversity of science/mathematics learnings and the many different materials, some "science/mathematics" materials are housed out of the center. For example, plants are often housed throughout the room. If the center has too much sunlight, the aquarium may be located elsewhere to avoid algal buildup. Many science/mathematics learnings take place in the cooking, block, water and sand, and manipulative centers, as well as outdoors.

Generally speaking, science/mathematics centers should be moderate in size (approximately 60 sq ft) and enclosed. Because the care of animals and plants as well as other activities may be messy, the floor covering should be resilient. A sink should be in the center, or the center needs to be adjacent to the art center or another area with water. (Check state licensing standards concerning food preparation areas and the proximity of animals in cages.) Electrical outlets are a must for aquariums and incubators.

Some science/mathematics materials are left out throughout the year but other materials are changed very regularly. Thus, the following criteria must be considered in planning:

1. Display and working areas should be plentiful. Counter space and tables encourage children to observe and interact with their environment. A counter at children's sitting or standing height can hold an aquarium, terrarium, plants, animal homes, and mathematics manipulatives. Tables or counter space can also hold materials that are not out all the time—magnets, prisms, seeds, rocks, sound makers, and various models (e.g., spaceships, dinosaurs). A centrally located table draws children's attention to the current interest (e.g., getting seeds from a pumpkin). A book display rack is also effective, with a small area rug or floor cushions making for a nice reading area. Plenty of pinning space is needed for beautiful science pictures and posters.

2. Closed storage space is also needed. For example, a built-in closet can have open shelves at the top and built-in drawers to store the many science/mathematics items. Units with tote bins can also be used for storage.

See Figure 5-11 as an example of a science/mathematics center layout.

Equipment and materials needed for the science/mathematics center include the following:

abacus (or counting frame)

animal cages (for animals such as small mammals, insects, amphibians)

animals (e.g., mammals, insects, fish)

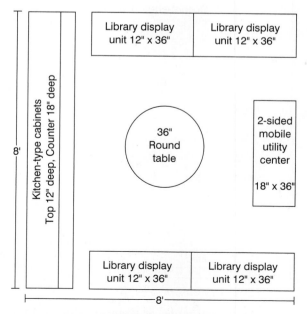

Figure 5-11   Science/Mathematics Center

aquarium (equipped with air pump and hose, filter, gravel, light, thermometer; fish net; aquarium guide)

beads (for pattern work and for developing an understanding of geometric concepts)

bird feeder

books and pictures (with science/mathematics themes)

"Broad Stair" for developing size concepts (Montessori)

bubble-making materials

chick incubator

collections (e.g., rocks, bird nests, insects, seashells)

color paddles (plastic paddles in primary colors) and prisms

compass (directional)

counting discs

Cuisenaire rods

cylinders graduated in diameter, height, and both diameter and height (Montessori)

design cubes and cards

dominoes (number)

dowel rods in graduated lengths

fabric, wallpaper, and cabinet- and floor-covering samples for pattern work

flannel board objects (for science/mathematics concepts)

gardening tools (child-sized)

geometric shape insets and solids

"Golden Beads" (for number concepts) (Montessori)

kaleidoscope

lotto (for science/mathematics concepts)

magnets (bar, horseshoe, bridge)

magnifying lenses (hand-held and tripod)

measuring equipment (linear measuring—rulers, yardsticks, tapes; measuring cups and spoons; scales—balance, bathroom,

postal or food; time instruments—sun dial, egg timer, clocks; weather gauges—rain gauge, thermometer)

models (e.g., animals, space equipment, simple machines)

number cards (sets)

numerals (e.g., cards, insets, kinesthetic, puzzles, numerals to step on)

objects to count

parquetry blocks and cards

Peg-Boards and pegs (for developing number and geometric concepts such as Cuisenaire's Geoboards)

pictures (with science themes)

"Pink Tower" for developing size concepts (Montessori)

plants, seeds, and bulbs (with planting pots, soil, fertilizer, and watering cans)

puzzles (with science/mathematics themes)

seed box (a transparent container for viewing root growth)

simple machines

sorting box

sound-producing objects

stacking/nesting materials (for size concepts)

terrariums (woodland and desert)

vases

weather vane

Miscellaneous materials are also needed (string, tape, bottles of assorted sizes, buckets, sponges, and hardware gadgets).

Cooking Center.   The **cooking center** is an area of the room in which children make and eat their products. Cooking activities are not designed to teach children how to cook; rather, the activities are designed to promote the learning of many concepts (nutrition, health, safety, language, mathematics, science, multicultural) and skills (social interaction, fine motor, decision making, problem solving) through enjoyable firsthand experiences. Cooking is a real activity and not a pretend one, too!

Many early childhood programs do not have space for a separate cooking center. With the advent of many small appliances, most teachers provide for cooking activities. Because the cooking area requires constant supervision, is noisy, needs water, and should have resilient flooring, it is often combined with the art center. If the art center is enlarged, storage units can semi-divide the art and the cooking centers. The area in which snack/meal preparation takes place can also make an excellent cooking center, especially if one counter is built at child height.

An ideal cooking center, whether a shared area or a separate area, would require approximately 30 sq ft, be enclosed, and look like a small kitchen (see Figure 5-12).

The center needs a stove with a see-through glass door, a refrigerator, a sink, and storage cabinets. Some storage cabinets need to be closed and even locked if they house potentially dangerous items (e.g., knives, electrical appliances, cleaning agents). Carts may be used to remove these items if lockable storage is not available. Pantry items need to be stored carefully to prevent bacterial growth and insect and rodent infestations.

Equipment and materials for the cooking center include the following:

air freshener
aluminum foil
apron
baking pans (various sizes)
biscuit cutter
blender
can opener
cookie cutters (wide variety)
cookie sheet
cooling racks
counter saver
cutting board
dish cloths and towels
dish drainer
dish pan
dishwashing detergent
egg separator
electric griddle
electric mixer
electric skillet
flatware, plastic (knives, forks, spoons)
garbage bags
gelatin molds
grater
ice-cream maker
kitchen scissors
knives
measuring cups (liquid and dry)
microwave oven
mixing bowls (metal and plastic)
mixing spoons
muffin pans
napkins
pantry items (foodstuffs)
paper dishes (plates, bowls, cups)

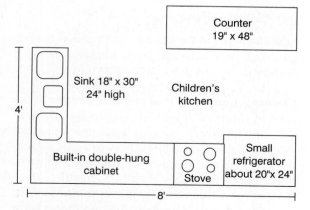

Figure 5-12   Cooking Center

paper towels

peelers (vegetable and apple)

pitchers

plastic bags (resealable)

popcorn popper

Popsicle sticks

pot holders

pot scrubbers

recipe cards (individual cards, group poster)

refrigerator with freezer

rolling pin

rotary egg beater

rubber scraper

sauce pans (various sizes)

serving trays

sifter

skillet

spatulas

sponges

storage containers (canisters, microwave dishes, refrigerator dishes)

stove (hot plate and electric oven may substitute)

strainer

straws

thermometer

timer

toothpicks (round)

warming tray

wax paper

wet wipes

whisk

Manipulative and Small Constructive Toy Center.   The **manipulative and small constructive toy center** is the area of the room in which children handle small objects. This center serves to develop fine-motor skills, eye-hand coordina-

tion, and spatial concepts (e.g., noting how to turn a puzzle piece to get it to "fit"), as well as many other concepts.

The center is not very large (approximately 100 sq ft) because of the size of materials and the low mobility of children as compared with the larger equipment and high mobility of children in the block and dramatic play areas. The center is usually very enclosed and is located in the quieter part of the room. The floor may be resilient flooring or low-pile carpet.

The center needs some open floor space for building with Tinkertoys, Junior Erector sets, or miniature unit blocks; for playing with a marble chute; or even for working a jigsaw puzzle. Tables are needed for using interlocking blocks, parquetry, design cubes, and perhaps lacing a sewing card or working a puzzle. One table should have a "plain" surface; some of these tables, especially designed for this center, have "wells" in the center, in which a recessed tote tray holds manipulatives such as beads. If Legos are used, a second type of table should also be considered that has Lego-compatible base place mats built into it. Storage cabinets with open shelves and with cubicles for clear plastic tote trays that keep materials in view are needed.

Because of the need for both open floor space and tables, the center could be subdivided by a double-sided storage peninsula. Open shelves of this unit could face the open floor side, and cubicles for tote bins could face the tables. Additional storage could be located at the back or sides of the center too (see Figure 5-13 for a layout of this center).

Equipment and materials for the manipulative and construction center include the following:

beads (for stringing)

bolt boards

construction toys (interlocking blocks, Junior Erector set, miniature unit blocks, Tinkertoys)

design materials (design cubes and cards, parquetry blocks and cards, plastic mosaics)

Figure 5-13   Manipulative and Small Constructive Toy Center

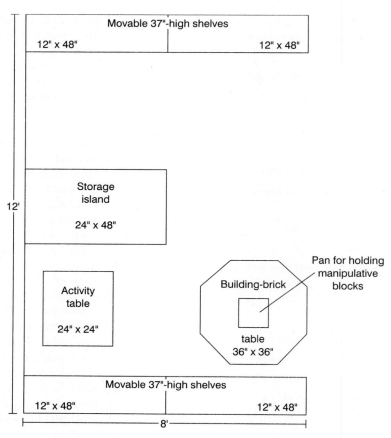

dressing materials (e.g., dolls, frames, shoes)

insets

latch frames or lock boxes

pegs and Peg-Boards

puzzles

sewing cards and/or plastic canvas

Emerging Literacy and Book Center. The **emerging literacy and book center** is an area of the room designed to focus on looking and listening activities and to have hands-on experiences with communication-developing materials.

The ideal center would be large (approximately 150 sq ft) but should be subdivided to give a more cozy atmosphere. The center should be enclosed and located in the quiet section of the room. The language center could be divided into the following three subsections as shown in Figure 5-14.

1. A loft could provide space for two book nooks. The loft itself could be equipped with a small book rack, puppet storage, and a small puppet theater. Beneath the loft, cozy floor pillows could serve as a book nook for one or two children.

2. Adjacent to the loft could be an area equipped as a communication center, with computers, listening stations, language mas-

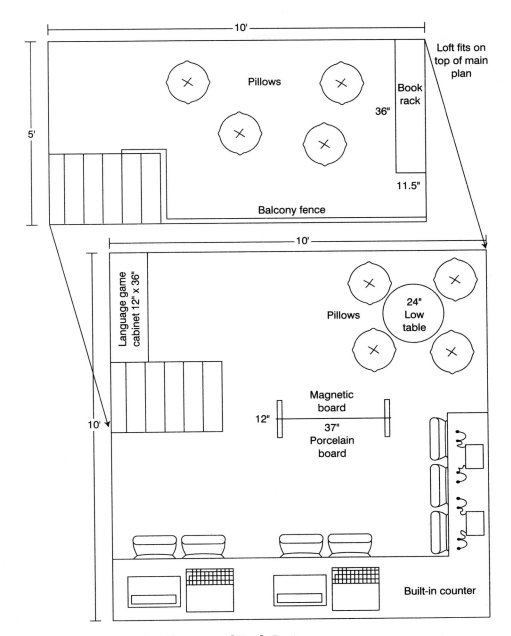

Figure 5-14   Emerging Literacy and Book Center

167

ters, projectors, and a place for writing by hand.

3. The third area could be equipped as a reading room with a book/storage display, a flannel board, a wall pocket chart, and places to sit at a table, on a couch, or on the floor. The back of the reading room could serve as a language game area with storage cabinets, a low table with floor cushions, a chalkboard room divider, and a magnetic board.

Items needed for emerging learning and book center include the following:

alphabet letters (e.g., alphabet insets, kinesthetic letters, letters to step on)

books and recordings of stories (see Appendix 6)

computers and software

filmstrips and/or slides of children's stories

flannel boards

globes (primary) and maps (simple)

lotto (covering many subjects)

magazines (children's; see Appendix 6)

perceptual and conceptual development games (absurdities, missing parts, sequencing, opposites, classification)

picture dominoes

pictures and graphic representations of finger plays, poems, and stories

puppets and a puppet theater

puzzles (e.g., jigsaw, sequencing) and puzzle rack

recordings of sounds (e.g., animal, city, and home sounds)

signs and labels

typewriter

Other Areas.   In addition to learning activity centers, a children's room should have private areas (NAEYC, 1991a). Private areas serve as places to "tune out," to enjoy being by oneself for a few minutes, or to reduce excitement. Cozy areas with soft textures are needed in facilities for young children (E. Prescott, 1987) and may be critical to the development of children with disabilities (A. Ayers, 1973). Private areas also serve as places to watch from, such as a small block center, a rocking horse, a window seat, a playhouse, or a riding toy. A place to watch from should be close to ongoing activities while providing the child with a sense of enclosure. Children also enjoy special-interest areas, such as an aquarium or terrarium; a rock, mineral, or shell collection; a garden seen from a window; a hanging basket; an arboretum; egg incubator; books; and displays connected with specific curriculum themes.

Learning Centers for Primary-Level Children. Primary-level children (ages 6 through 8) need learning centers too. Their learning centers, however, do not have to be as sharply defined (separated in appearance) as centers for younger children. Areas may include different combinations of centers used at the preschool-kindergarten level. For example, one primary program has these learning centers: cooking/science/art, dramatic play/music, reading, and mathematics/block construction. Another program uses these clusters of centers: art/cooking, construction, mathematics/computer, and language/reading. Regardless of specific centers, the rooms resemble workshops. Similar to preschool/kindergarten room design, messy and noisy areas are separated from less messy and quieter areas. The requirements for each center (e.g., floor coverings, furniture) are the same as those for centers previously described.

School-Age Child Care Activity Centers. School-age child care (SACC) activity centers are unique for three reasons. First, SACC programs must accommodate a wide age range (often ages 5 through 10 or 12). Second, programs are for shorter periods of daily time (average of 2 to 3 hours) during the school session and sometimes all-day care during holidays and summer vacation periods. Third, SACC programs are often shared-space areas (space shared with regular school programs, religious programs, or preschool child care). It is too costly to set up a permanent, nonshared center for the fewer hours of the SACC program, as compared with other early childhood programs.

Activity centers for SACC programs are often created by mobile shelves and dividers. A large storage closet or storage-workroom combination is most helpful. SACC programs are often designed with activities that are similar to quality home life for school-age children. The centers can include (a) quiet areas for reading, doing homework, listening to music with headphones, creative writing, or just resting; (b) creative area(s) for art/craft work, possibly including woodworking; (c) table games and manipulative area(s); (d) cooking and/or eating a snack area; and (e) high-technology areas, such as computers and software, VCRs, and audiocassettes. Other fun areas are block construction, science centers, and larger table games such as Ping-Pong.

School-age child care programs need a variety of materials, such as the following, to accommodate various ages and interests and needs.

Quiet

books (reference books for doing homework and a selection of trade books for leisure reading)

listening station (with headphones)

magazines (children's)

mazes

newspapers

recordings (music and stories)

word puzzles (e.g., crossword puzzles)

Games and Manipulatives

board games (e.g., Monopoly, Scrabble, chess, checkers, Chinese checkers, Life, Clue, bingo, and tick-tack-toe)

card games (e.g., cards for Fish)

interlocking blocks (e.g., Lego)

jacks

magnetic building sets

parquetry, design blocks, and design cards

puzzles (jigsaw with 100 to 500 pieces)

Woodworking

See list given for older children on page 161.

Arts and Crafts

See list given for older children on pages 156–158.

Materials for Hobbies

Items needed would depend on specific hobbies.

Writing Supplies

chalk

chalkboards or dry-erase boards

marking pens

paper (various types)

pencils with pencil sharpeners

typewriter

High Tech

calculators

computers with selected software

filmstrips and projectors

typewriters

VCRs with television and selected cassettes

Outside

ball game equipment (e.g., basketball, soft ball, dodge ball, kick ball, volley ball, soccer)

marbles

riding equipment (e.g., bicycles, skates, skateboards)

sand/water/mud (see list for older children on p. 160)

Developing a Room Layout Plan

Before drawing a floor plan, these three steps may need to be taken:

1. Decide on the centers that best fit program goals and then calculate the number of center activity places needed. To calculate the number of center activity places needed, multiply the number of children by 1.5; for example, 20 children require 30 activity places. Having more choices than children lessens waiting time and gives a reasonable number of options.
2. List the centers and give the maximum activity places (maximum number of children who can be in a center at the same time) for each center, as shown in Table 5-4.
3. Develop a matrix of centers and the requirements for each center. Requirements would need to be developed. (We used the Jones and Prescott (1978) dimensions and a few additional criteria as an example; see Table 5-5). Cluster centers that share compatible criteria are shown in Figure 5–15. These centers may be housed near each other.

Figure 5-16 is a floor plan for preschool and/or kindergarten (especially for ages 3 through 5) children's activity room. Figure 5-17 is a floor plan for primary-level (especially ages 6 through 8) children's activity room. Figure 5-18 is a floor plan for a SACC activity center. Because floor arrangements must fit the needs of the local program, the floor plans are intended for illustration of some of the principles just discussed.

Additional Areas for Children

Learning is going on all the time in an early childhood program: in the shared activity area, the rest rooms, the dining area, the napping area, and the isolation area, as well as the children's activity room. Children use many additional areas to take care of their physical needs, and staff emphasize the necessity for children's

Table 5-4   Determining Maximum Activity Places

Center	Maximum Activity Places
Cooking	3
Dramatic play	4
etc.	etc.
	Total of 30 places

Table 5-5   Center Criteria

Criteria	Centers		
	Block	Art	Library
Open	X		
Closed			
Simple			
Complex	X		
High mobility			
Intermediate mobility	X		
Low mobility			
Individual			
Small group	X		
Intermediate group			
Whole class			
Soft	X (carpeted)		
Hard			
Intrusion			
Seclusion	X		
Risk			
Safety	X		
Electricity			
Water			
Quiet			
Noisy	X		
Open storage	X		
Closed storage			
Display			

Figure 5–15   Clustering Centers With Compatible Criteria

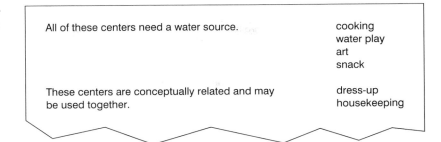

All of these centers need a water source.

cooking
water play
art
snack

These centers are conceptually related and may be used together.

dress-up
housekeeping

becoming self-reliant in taking care of these needs. Thus, designing additional areas must be done with as much care as planning the children's activity room.

Shared Activity Areas.   In some early childhood programs, several rooms open into a shared activity area, usually a large room, an exceptionally long and wide hallway, or a covered patio. Shared activity areas are often used for gross-motor activities, music, rhythmic activities, and drama.

Children's Lockers or Cubbies.   Children should have their own individual cubbies for storing personal belongings because this emphasizes personal possessions, helps children learn proper habits for caring for their belongings, and reduces the danger of spreading contagious disease. The locker or cubbie area should not be part of the entry-exit area, but should be close to this area and the outdoor space. The children's locker area should be large enough to facilitate easy circulation of staff when they help children with wraps. The floor covering in the locker area should be easily cleaned because it will get quite dirty during inclement weather.

Various combinations of storage are possible for children's possessions. Outdoor garments, extra clothing and aprons, blankets or rest mats, and personal possessions, such as crayons, show-and-tell treasures, and artwork to take home, may be stored together or separately.

Lockers usually provide places to hang garments, and overshoes are placed on the floors of the lockers. The overall dimensions of such a locker is approximately 56″ × 12″ × 15″. Lockers seldom include doors because these catch little fingers, are always in the way, and are never closed. Such a locker may be modified by adding one or two top shelves to accommodate a tote tray (usually 7″ × 8″ × 15″) for personal possessions. Another shelf about 10 in. from the bottom of the locker provides a place for the child to sit while putting on overshoes or changing clothes. Garment hooks (never use racks) are attached to the bottom of the lower top shelf or to the sides or back of the locker.

Infants' Changing Areas and Children's Rest Rooms.   The diapering area for infants should be spatially separated from the kitchen and feeding areas. The diapering table or counter should be adjacent to (a) a sink with running hot and cold water for immediate staff hand-washing and (b) closed-closet storage for soap, washcloths, diapers, and counter disinfectants. Diapers and other trash must be disposed of in containers inaccessible to both infants and older children. (See Chapter 8 for further health standards.) The area should be interesting to infants, with a mirror on the wall above the table and other displays on the wall or suspended from the ceiling. Washable toys may also be provided for infants to hold. (The main interaction should be between adult and child, however.)

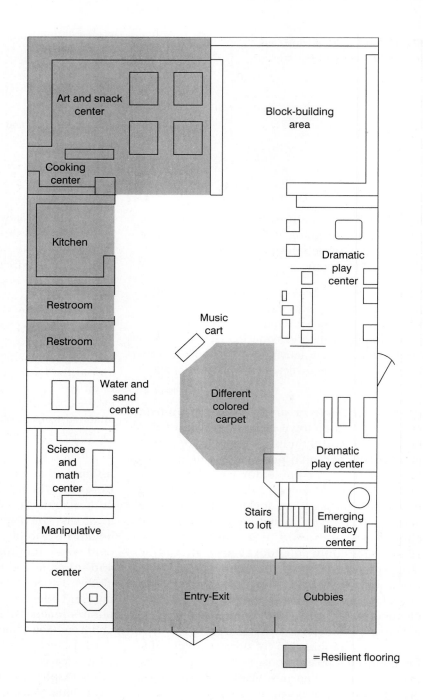

Figure 5-16   Preschool/ Kindergarten Children's Activity Room

Art and snack center

Cooking center

Kitchen

Restroom

Restroom

Water and sand center

Science and math center

Manipulative

center

Block-building area

Dramatic play center

Music cart

Different colored carpet

Dramatic play center

Stairs to loft

Emerging literacy center

Entry-Exit

Cubbies

☐ =Resilient flooring

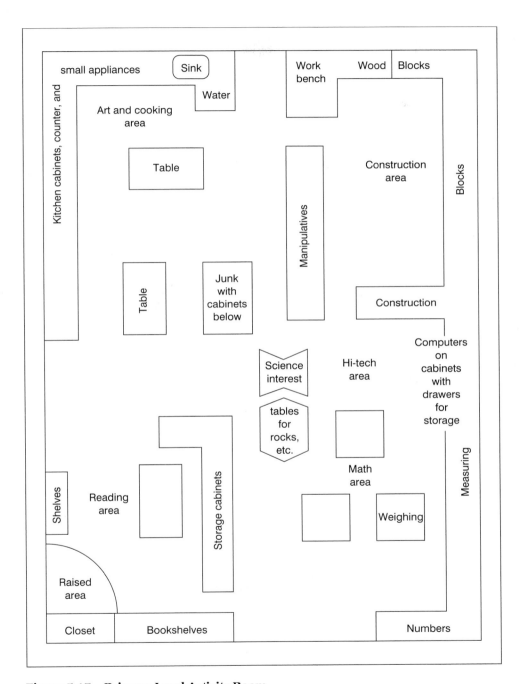

Figure 5-17 Primary-Level Activity Room

173

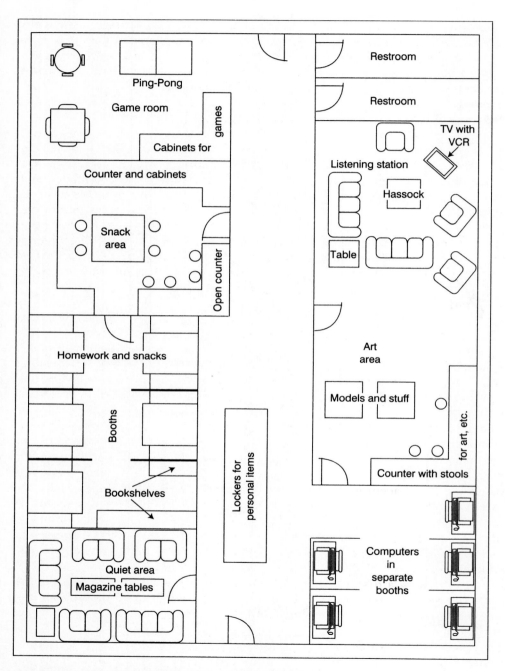

Figure 5-18   School-Age Child Care (SACC) Activity Center

Children's rest rooms should have two doors, one off the activity room and one into the outdoor area. Each rest room should be approximately 5 sq ft per child when in maximum use. When a large building houses more than 35 children, rest rooms should be in different areas. Early childhood programs for children under school age do not generally provide separate rest rooms for boys and girls. Some children like privacy; unlocked, low partitions between and in front of toilets provide this feature and permit easy supervision. Partitions rather than doors are especially helpful for children with a physical disability. The rest room should be cheerful, with windows for sunlight and ventilation, bright wall colors, and potted plants. The ratio of the number of toilets to the number of children should be approximately 1:8. Toilet seats should be between 10 and 13 in. from the floor. These toilet seat heights may be too high for the toddler or very young child; thus, the rest room may need portable "potties," a step installed to the child-sized toilets, or toilets set into the floor. For children with a disability, toilet seat height must be appropriate for wheelchair users, and toilet tissue should be not more than 6 in. from the front of the toilet bowl. Handrails should be mounted on the wall for additional safety. Urinals, especially trough rather than floor-mounted types, keep the toilet seats and floors clean.

Lavatory bowls should be adjacent to, but outside, the toilet areas and near the door. The ratio of the number of bowls to the number of children should be 1:10 or 1:8. Bowl heights should vary between 18 in. and 2 ft. A blade or lever, rather than a knob, water control should be used to help the child with a disability become independent. The water heater should be set to provide lukewarm water, thus preventing scalded hands. (Because the thermostatic control must be set higher for the dishwasher, another water heater must be installed for kitchen water.) Bowls must be equipped with disposal drains to catch clay, sand, and so forth; mirrors, preferably of safety glass or metal,

should be placed at child's height over them. Paper towels are more sanitary than cloth towels. To accommodate children with disabilities, the bottom edge of the paper towel dispenser should be mounted less than 2 ft from the floor. Bathtubs are necessary in all-day programs or ones serving younger children.

Drinking fountains should be located near the rest rooms and out of the path of fast-moving traffic. They should be made of stainless steel and be between 20 and 23 in. high. Fountains must be selected to accommodate the needs of children with disabilities. Water-bubbling level should be controlled. It takes time for young children to learn to get enough water from a fountain to quench their thirst; thus, paper cups should be available for children learning to drink from a fountain.

Feeding and Dining Areas.   The feeding area for infants and toddlers should be equipped with feeding chairs and some toddler-sized tables and chairs for family-style eating. The feeding area should be near the kitchen, which can be equipped with a half-door ("Dutch" door) to provide visual supervision when staff prepare or secure food or feeding items. Young children enjoy the contact between food preparation and eating too. Pictures on the walls and soft music add to the pleasantness of the feeding area.

Kitchen facilities need not be extensive for programs in which only snacks are served. A kitchen needs a few heating elements, a refrigerator with a small freezer compartment, a sink with hot and cold water, a dishwasher, counter space, and storage units. The Department of Agriculture publishes guides for the selection of food service equipment for programs serving main meals. Serving counters for children should be 2 ft or less in height and as close as possible to dining tables.

The dining area should be bright, cheerful, and airy, with screens on the windows. All surfaces should be made of materials that are soap-and-water scrubbable and resistant to water damage. In planning the dining area, allow plenty of space per child for accommodating wheelchairs, manipulating trays, sliding chairs back, and so forth.

Napping Areas.   Infant/toddler napping areas should be spacious, with a separate crib for each child. The napping area should be adjacent to the playroom, with an observation window in the sleeping room. The room should appear cozy, with carpet, shaded windows, and rocking chairs. A ceiling fan increases air circulation and masks outside noises. Soft music is also desirable.

For older children, a napping area should be considered for all-day programs. Sleeping areas should be isolated from noise in adjacent areas, and lighting should be controlled. If a separate napping room is used, efficient use of space can be achieved by placing cots end-to-end in rows, with an aisle approximately 4 ft wide between the rows. Small screens may be used to separate cots.

Programs that do not have separate napping areas must provide for resting in the children's activity room. The disadvantages of locating cots throughout the activity room are that more space is required, in comparison with placing cots head-to-toe; supervision is difficult; and cots must be moved at the beginning and end of each session. Cots must be stored in a well-ventilated storage unit because stacked cots in the corner of the room make an attractive but dangerous climbing apparatus.

Isolation Area.   An isolation area is necessary for caring for ill or hurt children until parents arrive. It should be cheerfully decorated, contain a bed or cot, and be equipped with a few toys and books. A small bathroom adjacent to the isolation area is helpful.

Adult Areas

Working as a staff member in an early childhood program is demanding both physically and psychologically. The quality of work life directly affects an adult's abilities to deliver effective early childhood programs. Yet, it is ironic that many programs fail to provide a comfortable place for staff, parents, or visiting adults even though some of these same programs provide a wonderful physical environment for children. Consequently, housing planners must be concerned about adult areas.

General Criteria for Adult Areas.   Although the early childhood facility is planned primarily for young children, housing must also meet the requirements of staff and parents. The two major criteria to meet in planning adult areas is that they be scaled to adult size and that the type and specific design of each area fit the needs of the program.

Parent Reception Area.   A parent reception area should make parents feel welcome and encourage exchange of information between parents and staff. A separate area adjacent to the children's activity room has the following advantages: (a) Parents have a place to sit and wait until their children complete an activity or put on wraps; (b) parents do not have the feeling of being stranded in the middle of the children's room while waiting; (c) interruptions of children's activities are minimized; and (d) parents can speak confidentially with staff members. The parent reception area should be well-defined, comfortable, and invite the parents to view the materials arranged on the bulletin board, browse through the materials placed on various tables, or visit. In laboratory schools, observation rooms may be adjacent to the reception area.

Staff/Parent Lounge.   A staff/parent lounge should be provided for resting and visiting. Comfortable chairs and a place for preparing and eating a snack should be considered in designing a staff/parent lounge. For greater privacy, adult rest rooms should not be part of the lounge, but located nearby. The staff lounge may be combined with the parents' lounge; however, in all-day programs, in which the staff may need a period of relaxation, separate lounges should be considered.

Office and Workroom.   When early childhood programs are housed with other programs under the same administrative control, office and workroom areas are usually shared. Conversely, early childhood programs housed in separate buildings or in buildings with other programs not under the same administrative control usually have office and workroom areas designed especially for their programs.

The design of the office and workroom area should fit the needs of the local program. For most early childhood programs, space will be needed for desks or tables and chairs, cabinets for filing professional materials and records, office machines, large work tables, high stools, a sink, and storage units for office supplies and other work materials.

Professional Library.   An early childhood program should have a professional library to keep staff informed and to help them in planning. The library should contain the following:

journals, newsletters, and special publications of professional organizations concerned with young children as listed in Appendix 4

instructional manuals in addition to those regularly used

curriculum guides printed by the state board of education, state department of health and human resources, local school system, and other early childhood programs that have similar objectives

professional books and audiovisuals concerned with various aspects of early childhood—child development, curriculum, guidance, and administration

catalogs and brochures from distributors of equipment and materials

newsletters or information on current legislation pertaining to child care and education

(obtained by being on your representative's or senator's mailing list)

information from local community resources (e.g., health department, dental association, and from agencies listed in Appendix 5)

bibliographies of pertinent topics in child development, care and education, and parenting skills

Environmental Control

An important consideration in constructing any early childhood facility is environmental control, including lighting, heating, cooling, ventilating, and acoustics. Lack of adequate environmental control results in a number of problems, such as eyestrain from glare or discomfort from heat or cold. It can also contribute to poor behavioral patterns, not only in children but also in adults. Adequate environmental control can also save money. Become familiar with good energy-saving practices by reading some of the many pamphlets on this topic.

Lighting.   Olds (1987) believes that lighting is extremely important to the health and development of young children. Much time is spent on visual tasks. Also, approximately one fifth of the enrolled children will have below-normal vision. Not only does lighting affect physical well-being, but it also has a psychological and aesthetic impact (Olds, 1989; Wurtman, 1982). Changing natural light patterns helps children develop concepts of passing time.

Natural light from large windows, balconies, and porches is preferred over artificial light. Full-spectrum is the most preferred artificial lighting (P. Hughs, 1980). Fluorescent lights can work if certain conditions are met, and they are less expensive to operate, though more expensive to install, than incandescent lighting. Diffused light, such as fluorescent bulbs above plastic diffusing panels, should be considered for use with young children because it provides nonglare lighting with very little heat. "Cool" shades of fluorescent lights should not be used; the best shades are the warm ones—"deluxe warm white," similar to light emitted by incandescent; or "vita lite," similar to light emitted by the sun. Because incandescent light is a concentrated source, it can spotlight learning/activity areas. Regulatory agencies frequently specify the minimum amount of light intensity for various parts of the facility. Usually 50 to 60 foot-candles of glare-free illumination are recommended. (Stein, 1975). After 50 foot-candles, the amount of light must be doubled or redoubled to increase visual efficiency; thus, task lighting is more efficient than general illumination when more than 50 foot-candles of illumination is needed.

Because lighting should be tailored to the needs of children working in each center, variable light controls should be provided in each area. For example, "the art area could have sun-free directional light from skylights or windows, the reading area could have soft incandescent light and a view of the window, and the plant area could be a small greenhouse" (Osmon, 1971, p. 97). Local lighting in a learning/activity center should not be so bright as to make other centers appear dim and hence unattractive.

Window areas should be approximately one fifth of the floor area (Headley, 1966). Approximately 50% of the required window area should be openable, and those windows that open should be screened. A windowsill 18 to 24 in. high permits children to see out. Windows, when properly placed, help soften shadows cast by overhead lighting, provide a distant visual release, and allow for a link with the outside world (Osmon, 1971).

Reflective surfaces in the room determine the efficiency of illumination. Light-colored shades on walls and ceilings are important reflecting factors. Walls should be light enough to reflect 50% of the light, and ceilings should be light enough to reflect 70% (Wills & Lindberg, 1967). There should be as little contrast as possible between ceiling and light source. Tables and countertops should reflect 35% to 50% of the light (Educational Facilities Laboratories, 1965). Even light-colored floors increase the efficiency of illumination. Louvers, blinds, and overhangs control excessive light from windows and help prevent glare. Glare is also reduced by covering work surfaces with a matte finish. Peripheral lighting keeps the level of illumination uniform and thus prevents glare (Sampson, 1970).

Heating, Cooling, and Ventilating.   The temperature of the room should be between 68° and 72°F (20° to 22°C) within 2 ft of the floor (Wills & Lindberg, 1967). Thermostats should be at the eye level of seated children. Many early childhood facilities are finding it necessary to have central air conditioning. Because it costs more to cool than to heat air, "there is a tendency to close in the space, make it more compact, increase the insulation, reduce the perimeter, and reduce the amount of window area (D. Gardner, 1968, p. 6). The circulation of of air should be 10 to 30 cu ft of air per child per minute. For comfort, the humidity should be from 50% to 65% (Wills & Lindberg, 1967). If a humidifying system is not installed, an open aquarium or water left in the pans at the water table will add humidity to the room.

Acoustics.   A moderate amount of noise is not harmful (Weinstein & Weinstein, 1979) and, in fact, may be beneficial (Olds, 1987). Conversely, extreme noise impedes cognitive development (Nober & Nober, 1975; Wachs, 1979). Private, quiet spaces are especially helpful to children with learning disabilities and to those who come from homes that are crowded and noisy (Wachs, 1979).

A nearly square room has better acoustic control than a long, narrow room (Jefferson, 1968). Acoustic absorption underfoot is more effective, and thus more economical, than overhead. Learning/activity centers that generate the greatest amount of noise should be designed and decorated for maximum acoustic absorption. Sand and grit on the floor increase noise as well as destroy the floor covering. Using table-cloths on luncheon tables, area rugs, padding on furniture legs, removable pads on tabletops when hammering, and doors to keep out kitchen noises all aid acoustics (Leeper, Wither-spoon, & Day, 1984).

OUTDOOR SPACE

Outdoor play has been an integral part of early childhood programs and hence housing facili-ties. Early childhood educators need to spend as much time planning outdoor space as indoor space. Outdoor play is important to children. In fact, when adults were asked about their favorite play experiences, over 70% reported outdoor play experiences (Henniger, 1994).

Brief History of Playground Design

Concepts about the values of certain types of play have changed over the years. Along with these changing concepts has come an evolution in playgrounds. Ideas about how to design play-grounds stem from theories of play. E. Mitchell and Mason (1948) described very early theories of play. When play was conceived of as using up surplus energy or for relaxation, children engaged in free play. When play was seen as helping children develop the skills needed for adulthood, gardening and other activities were included in the outdoor program.

Early childhood educators were especially interested in play. Froebel's playgrounds for kindergarten children were more than sites for "physical fitness." To Froebel, children's play-grounds "were nature itself." Children tended gardens, built stream dams, cared for animals, and played running games. Froebel's ideas came to the United States with the German emigrants. Also coming from Europe was Zakerzewska's "sandgarten," which influenced G. Hall to write a book called *The Story of the Sand-Pile* (1897). By the 1900s, the progressives (headed by Dewey)

and the Froebelians were at odds over many issues; however, outdoor play was not an issue. Play was most important in the progressive kindergartens, and training in play was part of teacher education (S. Parker & Temple, 1925). Nursery schools placed a major emphasis on play (H. Johnson, 1924; Palmer, 1916).

The establishment of the Playground Associ-ation of America in 1907 could have been a posi-tive influence on children's play. Unfortunately, as the focus of the organization became less and less on playgrounds (as shown by its name changes—Playground and Recreational Associa-tion of America, National Recreation Association, and National Recreation and Parks Association), the equipment became more unsafe and of little play value (Frost & Klein, 1983; Frost & Wortham, 1988).

Theorists such as Piaget (1962), M. Ellis (1973), and Smilansky (1968) recognized play as impor-tant for holistic development. Many activities, such as block play and dramatic play, were done outdoors as well as indoors (Henniger, 1985).

Types of Playgrounds

Frost and Klein (1983) have identified four con-temporary types of playgrounds:

1. *Traditional playgrounds* are located primar-ily in public parks and public schools. The equipment is selected for exercise purposes. Metal and wood structures, chosen for their durability and ease of maintenance, are the main pieces of equipment.

2. *Contemporary playgrounds* are designer-made and are primarily located in public parks. Like traditional playgrounds, they are mainly for climbing, swinging, and sliding, but the equipment is more aesthetically pleasing.

3. *Adventure playgrounds* have raw materials and tools for children to build their own structures with adult guidance (Pederson, 1985).

4. *Creative playgrounds* have structures built from discarded materials. Many complex units can be used for climbing, swinging, and fantasy play. Many loose materials (e.g., blocks, sand, props) are available. Creative playgrounds are popular in preschools.

General Criteria and Specifications for Outdoor Space

Regardless of the type of program, outdoor space should meet the following criteria:

1. Outdoor space should meet safety guidelines (as discussed in later sections of this chapter).

2. Outdoor space should preserve and enhance natural features (as described in later sections of this chapter).

3. The design should be based on the needs of children. Most early childhood professionals agree that play can enhance various aspects of development (physical, cognitive, social, and emotional) although the stress placed on various aspects of development will vary, depending on the local program goals. Frost and Wortham (1988) summarize how each aspect of development is enhanced through play and list the types of materials suited for each developmental outcome. Research studies have been designed to examine children's play on various types of playgrounds. Some of the findings are as follows:

a. Physical exercise and games with rules occurs over 75% of the time on traditional playgrounds. Dramatic play occurred almost 40% of the time on creative playgrounds, with boys engaging in dramatic play twice as frequently as did girls (although the opposite trend occurs indoors). Constructive play is also popular on creative playgrounds (Frost, 1992a).

b. On traditional playgrounds, children like action-oriented swings and seesaws more than climbers and slides. Movable props and materials were popular on cre-

ative playgrounds and enabled children's play to spread out over a wide range of equipment as they adapted the materials to the play situation (Frost, 1992a). Children like adventure playgrounds the most and traditional playgrounds the least. Complex social and cognitive behaviors occur on creative more than traditional playgrounds (Hartle & Johnson, 1993).

c. Differences in playgrounds may only be cosmetic. Thus, research studies have been designed to look at desirable features. Desirable features include equipment that can be rearranged and linked into different patterns; encapsulated spaces; multifunctional play structures; equipment for dramatic play; loose parts; action-oriented equipment, especially swings (for primary-level children); wheeled toys (especially for kindergartners); moderately structured, as opposed to highly structured, materials to allow for creativity; equipment that accommodates to diverse skill/ability levels; and places for solitary, parallel, and group play (Hartle & Johnson, 1993). Similarly, J. Johnson, Christie, and Yawkey (1987) found that two playground design features associated with high levels of play are flexible materials (materials that children can manipulate, change, and combine) and materials providing a wide variety of experiences. Interestingly, children preferred the inexpensive play environments to the more expensive varieties (Frost, 1992a). (Specifics for various age-groups are discussed in "Outdoor Space Arrangement.")

d. Playgrounds must also meet the needs of children with disabilities, as discussed later in this chapter.

4. Outdoor space should be aesthetically pleasing and appeal to all the senses. Talbot and Frost (1989) have proposed some design qualities (e.g., sensuality, brilliance, "placeness," juxtaposition of opposites) that should be considered in

designing playscapes that address the child's sense of wonder and awareness.

Specifications for the outdoor space should be sufficiently flexible to meet local needs and requirements and should include such considerations as location, size, enclosure, terrain, surface, shelter, and storage

Location.   Outdoor activity areas should not surround the building because supervision would be almost impossible. The area is best located on the south side of the building, which will have sun and light throughout the day. The outdoor space should be easily accessible from the indoor area. To minimize the chance of accidents as children go in and out or vice versa, a facility should have (a) a door threshold flush with the indoor/outdoor surfaces, or a ramp if an abrupt change in surface levels is present; (b) adjoining surfaces covered with material that provides maximum traction; (c) a sliding door or a door prop; and (d) a small glass panel in the door to prevent collisions.

Indoor rest rooms and lockers should be adjacent to the outdoor area. If this arrangement is impossible, one rest room should open off the playground. The sometimes difficult problem of managing clothing makes speedy access to a rest room important. A drinking fountain should also be easily accessible to children during outdoor play.

Size.   Most licensing regulations require a minimum of 75 sq ft per child for outdoor activity areas (NAEYC Information Service, 1989). The Child Welfare League of America (1984) recommends 200 sq ft per child. For example, an area 50' × 60' (300 sq ft) would be needed for 15 children. The amount of space varies by age of children, with infants/toddlers requiring much less space than older children. The average optimal space is 75 to 100 sq ft per each actual child user per day. A minimum of 15 sq ft per child should be added for a sheltered area or terrace. Approx-

imately one third of the square footage of the outdoor area should be used for passive outdoor play, as in a sand pit or outdoor art center, and the remainder for active outdoor play, such as climbing and running. "Adventure" or junk playgrounds may be ½ to 2½ acres in size (F. Thompson & Rittenhouse, 1974).

Enclosure.   Enclosure of the outdoor area relieves the staff of a heavy burden of responsibility, gives children a sense of freedom without worry, and prevents stray animals from wandering in. Nonclimbable barriers approximately 4 ft high are adequate as boundaries that adjoin dangerous areas (parking lots, streets, ponds), but minimal barriers such as large stones or shrubbery are adequate in areas where the outdoors has no potential dangers. Besides safety, consider what children will hear and see on the other side of the "fence" in choosing enclosures. Beauty may be enhanced by flowers/plants along "fence" line.

In addition to the entry from the building, the outdoor area should have a gate opening wide enough to permit trucks to deliver sand or large items of play equipment. If children are allowed to use the outdoor area for after-program hours, a small gate should be installed and benches placed on the periphery to give adults a place to relax while watching and supervising.

Terrain.   Flat terrain with hard surfacing is dangerous because it provides no curb for random movement. A rolling terrain has several advantages. Mounds are ideal for active games of leaping and running and are a natural shelter for such passive games as sand or water play. Mounds can be used in conjunction with equipment; for example, slides without ladders can be mounted to a slope so that children can climb the mound and slide down the slide. Ladders and boards can connect the mounds. Tricycle paths can wind on a rolling terrain. Hills should be relatively small (no more than 3 ft measured vertically, with no more than 10° slope).

Surface.   Surfaces for infants and toddlers should be mainly grass, wood, sand, and dirt. Outdoor activity areas for older children should also have a variety of surfaces and be well-drained, with the fastest drying areas nearest the building. Low areas should be filled in with topsoil; however, if permanent equipment is placed over these areas, feet will re-create the basin. It is desirable to have one half to two thirds of the total square footage covered with grass, and about 1000 sq ft covered in hard surfaces for activities such as wheeled-toy riding and block building (Foster & Rogers, 1970). Some areas should be left as dirt for gardening and for realizing "a satisfaction common to every child—digging a big hole!" (Baker, 1968, p. 61). Areas underneath equipment need special resilient materials (as discussed in "Safety").

Shelter.   The building, trees and shrubs, or a rolling terrain should protect children from excessive sun and wind. Knowledge of snow patterns and prevailing winds may lead to the use of snow fences or other structures to provide snowy hills and valleys. A covered play area should be planned as an extension of the indoor area. The shelter's purpose is for passive play during good weather and for all play during inclement weather. It should be designed to permit a maximum amount of air and sunshine.

Storage.   Outdoor storage can be attached to the main building, perhaps next to a terrace where the storage can provide shelter. If detached from the building, outdoor storage should be of a design and material to fit and not detract from the main building. If a separate building is used, it should serve as a windbreak to the outdoor activity area.

Storage structures can be single units or smaller "bins." A single storage unit 12 ft long, 10 ft wide, and 7 to 8 ft high is sufficient for most early childhood programs. The doorway should be 6 ft wide and should be a tilt- or roll-a-door garage-type. Hooks or pegs for hanging can be installed 4½ ft above the floor along one side of the storage shed, and shelves for storing equipment in daily use can be built 2 or 3 ft above the floor along the back of the shed. A high shelf can be used for storing seasonal items or items for staff use. Outdoor storage areas should have slightly raised flooring to prevent flooding after a substantial rainfall. A ramp would facilitate moving equipment into and out of the storage shed and minimize tripping over different levels. This type of storage unit can also serve as a prop for dramatic play. The roof might be fenced to serve as an additional play area, and the inside could serve as a playhouse during inclement weather and for some daily play activities that require a firm surface.

Smaller storage "bins" located near certain centers, such as sand, block building, and dramatic play, are preferable for some materials. These storage areas are usually closed/locked storage cabinet structures, at child height, and made of materials that can withstand moisture, such as cedar. These bins also require a firm surface, preferably concrete, to allow for stability and to prevent flooding.

Outdoor Space Arrangement

The outdoor space needs to be appropriate for the age-group for which it is designed. The outdoor area should be planned to further the purposes of the early childhood program. The indoor space should be extended outdoors, and the outdoor space should be extended indoors. Dempsey, Strickland, and Frost (1993) have developed an excellent evaluation tool to use in planning or redesigning playgrounds for infants/toddlers and preschoolers.

Outdoor Area for Infants and Toddlers.
Many people think of playgrounds as areas for rough-and-tumble play. Thus, when one says an "infant and toddler playground," it almost sounds oxymoronic. Infants and toddlers need fresh air and sunlight, however, and delight in

exploring their outside environment. Perhaps it would seem less strange to call the planned outdoor environment an *outdoor place* or *park*.

Although general specifications for outdoor space have already been discussed, three criteria are extremely important in planning an outdoor place for the infant and toddler. First, it must be scaled to the size of these very young children to be safe, comfortable, and rich for exploring. Second, it must be safe—that is, a gentle terrain for crawling, walking, running, and stepping up and down; no high play structures; and no harmful materials if eaten (e.g., no gravel, only sand protected from animals, plant life safe in all stages of growth; Decker, 1995); and free from foreign objects. Third, the outdoor place must meet the sensory motor explorations of the very young. Differences in hardness, textures, light, and temperatures (sun and shade) are needed, as well as contrasts in colors, in open and breezy areas and encapsulated and still areas, and high areas and low areas.

According to Frost (1992a), four design principles should be used in planning a play environment: (a) Allow for a wide range of child-initiated movement via pathways, hills, ramps, and tunnels; (b) stimulate the senses; (c) provide for novelty, variety, and challenge; and (d) make the area safe and comfortable. Wortham and Wortham (1992) think of three cells of possibilities in the design of infant/toddler playgrounds: (a) structures that lead to specific types of play, such as a slide; (b) natural environment experiences, such as examining living things and weather; and (c) areas for open-ended activities that promote creativity, such as sand and water areas, and that use construction-type toys and dramatic play props.

For noncrawling infants, an enclosed area should have a surface that encourages reaching, grasping, and kicking. These infants also enjoy baby "sit-up swings" and "swinging cradles." The area should stimulate visual and auditory senses with colorful streamers, soft wind chimes, prisms and mirrors, and natural sounds (e.g.,

breeze in the trees, bird songs). A stroller path would also be appropriate.

Unlike older preschool and primary grade children, toddlers either ignore or do not comprehend the function of separate play centers; thus, they will attempt to push a trike up a climber or pour sand on a crawling baby. A creative use of barriers will restrict children to developmentally appropriate areas by requiring certain skills in order to reach an area and will serve to help keep certain activities within an area. For example, two or three steps can lead to a 15-in. high platform, half-buried tires can form mini-tunnels around the sand area, a small gate can lead to the garden, and shrubs can curb the push-pull toy path.

Crawling and walking pathways in an infant/toddler outdoor place not only assist traffic flow but also can serve as a means for exploring. The surfaces of these paths should be a mosaic—changing from dirt to grass with "cobblestones" of slatted plank squares, patterned rocks, colored bricks, and half logs buried along the way. Raised (15 in. maximum) walkways with railings are also exciting.

Various structures are effective in an infant/toddler outdoor place, such as the following:

set-in-the-ground ladders

slides inset in a hill

swings with baby seats, porch swings, and swinging platforms for looking at the "moving ground" or the clouds

14- or 15-in. raised platforms with rope or metal railings on one side and a boarded side with "shape holes" (e.g., squares, circles, octagons) large enough to stick one's head and shoulders through to "survey one's world"

mini-tunnels (half-buried tires) and longer tunnels to crawl through

logs or low, anchored benches to straddle or climb over

wobbly structures, such as a board with springs or a low swinging bridge

roofs for playhouses

block-building areas

pathways for push-pull and ride-on toys

sand areas—the favorite material

elevated trough with moving water

garden

dirt-digging areas

objects that react with movement and sound to wind or touch, such as colorful banners, canopies, tree branches, wind chimes, and pans for hitting

The safe, natural environment—trees, shrubs, flowers, pine cones, and tree stumps—should be left. As much as possible, play areas for toddlers need to integrate sensory, exploratory, and action-oriented devices. For example, a structure can have panels to look at and feel, objects to manipulate (e.g., pulleys, drums, steering wheels), and structures that promote action (e.g., climbers, slides). Infants and toddlers need loose materials too. Finally, the outdoor place must have many benches for adult sitting and supervision and holding infants and toddlers.

Figure 5-19 is a plan for an infant/toddler outdoor place. It illustrates some of the principles discussed and is only one example of an outdoor activity area.

Outdoor Area for Older Children.   Older children need playgrounds that fit their developing motor skills, their advancing cognitive skills, and their growing peer interactions. They need a smooth transition in playgrounds from infancy to preschoolers. For example, preschoolers still need structures that integrate sensory, exploratory, and action-oriented activities, but the structures should be more complex than those seen on toddler playgrounds. Like toddlers, they need dramatic play materials, but for preschoolers, props need to encourage more

advanced symbolism and more cooperative play, as compared with props for toddlers. Likewise, a smooth transition in playground design must occur in programs serving preschool and primary-level children. Primary-level children need more open, grassy areas, more gymnastic-type apparatuses, and more pretend toys than do preschool children (Elder & Pederson, 1978; Fein, 1975; Frost, 1992a).

For challenging older children's total development, J. Johnson et al. (1987) list four types of play experiences: (a) functional play or exercise that involves practice and repetition of gross-motor activities, (b) constructive play that involves using such materials as paints or sand to create, (c) dramatic play or pretend play that is often conducted in enclosed places, and (d) group play or play that involves more than one child (e.g., seesaws, rule games, often dramatic play). Various playground designers suggest different centers or play zones, but all meet the play needs of older children. For example, Howard (1975) discusses the following nine centers on playgrounds: (a) digging, (b) water play, (c) dramatic play, (d) climbing, (e) pushing/ pulling or riding, (f) construction, (g) open running, (h) gardening, and (i) quiet. Esbenstein (1987) suggests these seven areas: (a) transition, (b) manipulative/creative, (c) projective/fantasy, (d) focal/social, (e) social/dramatic, (f) physical, and (g) natural element. The five play zones given by Guddemi and Eriksen (1992) are (a) a nature zone with plants, animals, and rocks housed in an active or quiet area; (b) an adventure zone for construction and digging that requires close and continuous adult supervision and is fenced in (because it is unsightly); (c) an active play zone for chase and ball games on open grassy areas for preschoolers and on both grassy and hard-surface areas for primary-level children, for sand/water play, and for play on play structures; (d) a quiet learning zone with easels, water/sand tables, book area, and snack area; and (e) a quiet play zone for dramatic play. Centers can integrate more than one type of

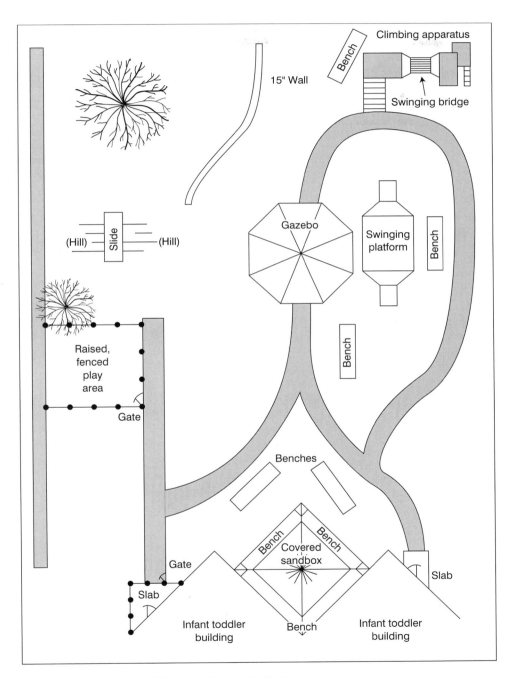

Figure 5-19   Infant/Toddler Outdoor Activity Area

play. For example, digging can be both constructive and dramatic (Howard, 1975).

Basically, the indoors is extended outdoors. Outdoor centers, however, are different from indoor centers. Outdoor centers are often less structured; the divisions between centers are less clear (e.g., a "car wash" involves water play, dramatic play, and push-pull and riding toys); centers may be located in several areas (e.g., dramatic play may be in a playhouse under a play structure, in tents under the trees, or in the garden); children have more freedom to move; there are fewer restrictions on the number of children allowed per center; and more seasonal changes are obvious in outdoor centers (e.g., water play in warm weather), as compared with indoor centers (Vaughn, 1990).

Because the outdoor space is an extension of the indoor area, areas must be provided for active and passive play. No clear-cut distinction is made between the two types of play. Large-muscle play is usually active, but walking on a balance beam may be passive; water play is usually passive, but running from a squirting hose is active.

Passive and active play areas must be separated, and space must be left around each activity area for safety reasons (as discussed in the section "Safety"). In passive play, children need protection from excessive wind or heat and from other fast-moving children. Passive play areas should be enclosed and protected from more active play areas. Enclosure may be accomplished with shrubbery or large stones, with small openings between these areas, by changing the terrain, or by providing a sheltered area. Additional protection may be obtained by building a slightly winding path or by separating the two types of play areas. Often, a great deal of physical inactivity occurs in outdoor areas; thus, children need places to cluster and sit. Boulders or logs are perhaps more enjoyable than park or picnic benches. Active play areas require more space because of the vigorous, whole-body movement. The following suggestions should be considered in planning these play zones:

1. *Open area.* The open area needs to be large for playing with balls, Frisbees, and Hula Hoops, as well as just running.

2. *Road for vehicles.* A hard-surfaced area can form a tricycle, wagon, or doll buggy road extending through the outdoor space and returning to its starting point. The road should be wide enough to permit passing. A curving road is more interesting, but right-angle turns should be avoided because these cause accidents (Baker, 1968).

3. *Sand pit.* Because the outdoor sand pit involves the child's whole body, a sand pit for 20 children must be approximately 250 sq ft. To prevent overlap of the sand area (and hence child aggression), the sand pit should be narrow. A winding river of sand is more aesthetically pleasing than an oblong-shaped box. Children should have flat working surfaces, such as wooden boards or flat boulders, beside or in the sand. An outdoor sand pit should have a boundary element that "should provide a 'sense' of enclosure for the playing children, keep out unwanted traffic, protect the area against water draining from adjacent areas, and help keep the sand within the sand play areas (Osmon, 1971). Boundaries can be built or created by a rolling terrain. The sand pit should be partially shaded but with exposure to the purifying and drying rays of the sun. Water should be available so that the sand is not bone dry, and the water source should be at the periphery of the sand pit, with the runoff flowing away from the sand.

4. *Water areas.* Outdoor water play activities should allow for more energetic play than indoor water activities. Water places can include bird baths, fountains, elevated streams, water tables, sprinklers, and splash and wading pools. Concrete wading pools must have slip-proof walking surfaces and a water depth of 6 in. Water temperature should be between 60° and 80°F (16° and 27°C). In colder weather, a drained wading pool makes an excellent flat, hard surface for passive play. For programs on a meager

budget, an inflatable pool can be used, and a garden hose with a spray nozzle or water sprinkler attached can serve as a water spray.

5. *Garden.* Gardens can have almost any kind of living plant life—flowers, herbs, vines, shrubs, trees, and even weeds! An outdoor garden should be fenced to protect it from animals or from being accidentally trampled. The garden should be narrow, perhaps 2 ft wide, to minimize the need for the child gardener to step into the garden (especially important when the plot is muddy). A narrow garden can take on an aesthetically pleasing shape as it parallels straight fences or encircles large trees.

6. *Play structures.* Complex play structures that are discussed in detail by Vergeront (1988) have almost totally replaced the separate, large-muscle pieces of equipment (e.g., climbing frame, slides, gliders) seen on "traditional playgrounds." Children use these structures not only for developing gross-motor skills but also for engaging in dramatic play.

Figure 5-20, a plan for an outdoor activity area for older children, illustrates some of the principles discussed and is only one example of an outdoor area. For more open space for primary-level children or SACC programs, the dirt mound and the sand pit could be designed as "rivers." If the storage unit were relocated, much more open space would be available.

Equipment and materials must be carefully planned for the outdoor area. Some items include the following:

art materials

assorted toys for open area play (e.g., balls, hoops)

construction materials (e.g., blocks, woodworking equipment)

dramatic play props

musical game recordings

nature materials (e.g., animals, binoculars, cages for animals, feeders, gardening bulbs,

plants, seeds and tools, magnifying lenses, weather instruments)

play structures (for criteria, see Vergeront, 1988)

sand/water toys (for types of sand and water tables, see Morris, 1990)

wheeled toys

THE EARLY CHILDHOOD FACILITY

As part of the planning process, the spatial relationship between the indoor and outdoor space must be carefully planned. Other areas, such as the office, workroom, parents' receiving room, isolation room, and perhaps an observation room, must be included in the plan. Figure 5-21 illustrates the arrangement of the children's activity room, the outdoor activity area, and the other children's and adults' areas of an early childhood facility. The illustration of the physical plant layout shows only one possible arrangement of the various areas. Figure 5-21 is not intended as a model layout, but is presented to graphically depict some of the ideas discussed in the chapter.

OTHER CONSIDERATIONS

There is more to planning housing than designing the indoor and outdoor space and selecting equipment. Early childhood administrators must always be mindful of whether their facility meets safety standards and accommodates the needs of children and adults with disabilities. Early childhood administrators should make wise decisions in purchasing and caring for equipment and materials and in securing insurance coverage for the facility and its contents.

Safety

Safety of children, staff, parents, and others is of maximum importance. A safe environment encourages children to work and play without

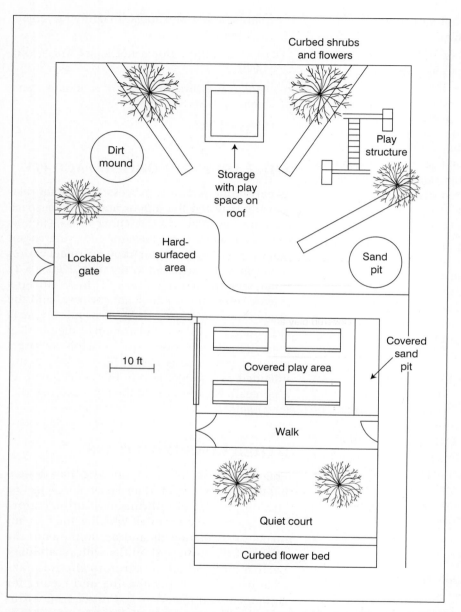

Curbed shrubs
and flowers

Dirt
mound

Storage
with play
space on
roof

Play
structure

Hard-
surfaced
area

Lockable
gate

Sand
pit

10 ft

Covered
sand
pit

Covered play area

Walk

Quiet court

Curbed flower bed

Figure 5-20   Preschool, Kindergarten, and Primary-Level Outdoor Activity Area

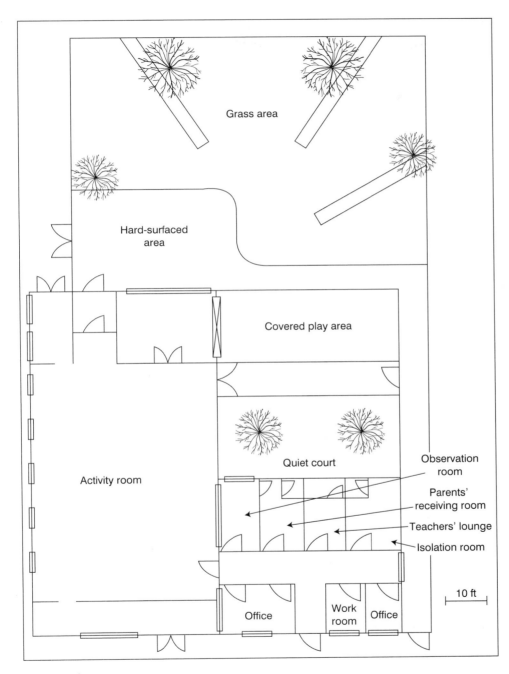

Grass area

Hard-surfaced
area

Covered play area

Quiet court

Activity room

Observation
room

Parents'
receiving room

Teachers' lounge

Isolation room

10 ft

Office

Work
room

Office

Figure 5-21   Early Childhood Facility

heavy restrictions that wear on both children and adults and that prevent maximum program benefit. The outdoor play area is the most hazardous area in most facilities. Problems come from many sources.

Regulations.   Wallach and Afthinos (1990) found that licensing regulations for outdoor areas lag behind those for indoor areas. Similarly, Wallach and Edelstein (1991) found public school outdoor play areas virtually unregulated. Accreditation standards do not give as much attention to outdoor housing as they do to indoor areas. Many model safety criteria are not included in state licensing regulations (Runyan, Gray, Kotch, & Kreuter, 1991). Furthermore, the regulations are not consistent although the Consumer Product Safety Commission (CPSC) and the American Society for Testing Materials (ASTM) are working toward consistent standards.

Supervision.   Playground safety programs for staff rarely exist even in public schools. A few child care agencies with many center sites, such as the U.S. Air Force and Kinder Care Learning Centers (Frost, 1992b), are now developing safety programs.

Teachers need to be aware of the potential seriousness of playground injuries. Playground fatalities are more likely to occur in the early childhood years than in middle childhood years and beyond (half of the fatalities occur to children under age 6, and two thirds occur to children under age 9; CPSC, 1989). Teachers also need to know where these potential dangers lie. Deaths are primarily due to head injuries from falls and strangulation/asphyxiation because of loose items of clothing (e.g., hoods on coats, cords, and frayed materials), to improperly used equipment (e.g., ropes, hoops), or to equipment that entraps (spaces between 3½ and 9 in.). Equipment involved in injuries, in descending order, are swings, climbing equipment, slides, and seesaws (CPSC, 1989).

Adequate supervision also requires that teachers see the entire play area. Playground arrangement, especially storage units, fences, shrubs/trees, and large play structures, must not block vision. Passive play zones must not be hidden between two active play zones.

Playground supervision requires the same adult to child ratio as do indoor activities, and even more adult help is preferred. Although staff need breaks, outdoor play time is highly inappropriate as a break time or even an adult visitation time. Beyond the safety concern, outdoor areas are learning areas too; in quality programs, teachers are interacting with children, including teaching them safe play practices.

Separating Play Areas.   Play areas must be separated for safety reasons. Space around each piece of equipment must be equal to the child's potential action outward or the maximum distance children can jump, slide, or swing forward from any position on the equipment. Children also need space to bypass a piece of equipment. Paths should be 3 to 5 ft. wide, adjoin safety areas, and be slightly curving. If paths are too curvy, children tend to cut through one play area to reach another play area; and supervising staff may not be able to adequately supervise all play areas.

Equipment Hazards.   Safety includes proper design for the age of children and for children with disabilities, proper spacing and installation, and adequate maintenance of equipment. Equipment must also be of high-grade construction, nontoxic, and appropriate for climate conditions. A complete discussion of safe equipment is beyond the scope of this book, but a few recommendations are given in Table 5-6 for the more potentially dangerous pieces of equipment. A listing at the end of the section "Safety" also provides sources for further information. The CSPI 1991 guidelines give detailed information on safe equipment.

Surfacing Under Fall Zones.   A major safety problem is hard-packed surfaces under and around outdoor equipment (Tinsworth &

Table 5-6 Safety Specifications for Selected Playground Equipment

Swings

Tire or shrub barrier around swings

24" between swings; 36" between swings and support posts; greater distance for tire swings

Swing seats fitted to child and lightweight (e.g., canvas)

Infant swings with safety straps and special swing seats, exergliders, and wheelchair swings for children with disabilities

No animal-type swings

S-hooks completely closed

8" to 10" of loose soil underneath

Slides

Slope—no more than 30°

Side height—minimum of 2.5", safest at 7.5"

Platform deck—10" wide at top

Exit surfaces—16" long, parallel to ground, exit height of 8" to 12", 24" of loose soil underneath

Climbing equipment

Maximum height 24" (toddler) to 54" (primary level)

Vertical barriers 30" to 38" high on walkways and decks that are over 30" high

Access to decks and climbers (use all three)—(a) ladders with rungs at 75° to 90° angles; (b) ladder steps with rungs at 50° to 75° angles; (c) stairway with steps at 35° angles or less

Protective caps over bolts

4" to 6" of loose soil underneath for 24" structures, and 12" of loose soil underneath for 54" structures

Kramer, 1989). Changes in types of surfacing should be level to prevent children from tripping. Special surfacing is needed under any equipment from which a child might fall. When a child falls, either the surface gives to absorb the impact or the child gives with a resulting bruise, broken bone, spinal injury, head injury, or even death. The following are three types of surfaces, each with its disadvantages, used under equipment:

1. *Organic loose material* (e.g., pine bark, mulch) maintained at a depth of 8 to 12 in.

Organic materials must be kept fluffed up and at the maximum depth to be effective. Unfortunately, the material scatters and decomposes.

2. *Inorganic loose material* (e.g., sand, pea gravel, shredded tires) maintained at a depth of 8 to 12 in. Animals may use sand as a litter box, and it loses its resiliency in wet, freezing weather. Gravel is hard to walk on, and shredded tires stick to clothing. Pea gravel surfaces are unsuitable for children under 5 years of age and dangerous for children

under 3 years of age because it gets into their eyes, ears, and nose (Frost, 1992a).

3. *Compact materials* (e.g., rubber and foam mats). These materials require a flat surface and professional installation. These costly items are also subject to vandalism.

A 6-ft zone with protective in all directions as well as underneath stable equipment and a 7-ft. zone with protective surface around and under equipment with moving parts, such as swings (Vergeront, 1988) should be provided. The latest guidelines on surfacing safety were published by the CPSC in 1991 (see the section "Safety").

Other Safety Considerations.   Safety can be provided by the following:

1. *Fencing the play area* (4 ft. high around most hazards and 6 ft. high around water hazards) *and making all electric equipment inaccessible to children.* One third of family child care homes had no enclosure around the outside play area (Wasserman, Dameron, Brozicevic, & Aronson, 1989). Electrical equipment (boxes, transformers, outlets, connections for underground utilities, heat pumps/air conditioners) must be located outside the outdoor playground.

2. *Providing physical supports* such as railings on platforms, decks, and walkways *and color-coding complex features* (e.g., rungs of ladders that require spatial judgments).

3. *Removing toys and playing children from obstructing landing or fall zones around equipment.*

4. *Keeping sand boxes covered and following Aronson's (1993) cleaning and disinfecting procedures.*

5. *Correcting and removing all hazards.* (*Hazards* are accident-causing problems that a child cannot identify or cannot evaluate the seriousness of. *Risks* are challenges that are not "hidden" and can be evaluated by the child. Chil-

dren develop because of managed risks but suffer most of their injuries because of hazards!) Resilient fall-zone surfacing must be maintained. Protrusions and sharp edges must be repaired. Broken or rusting equipment or equipment with potential pinch or crush areas must be removed. Frost (1992b) recommends a thorough inspection weekly. He suggests using a checklist, making repairs immediately, and documenting inspection and repairs.

6. *Following all safety regulations and using additional guidelines* such as the following:

Consumer Product Safety Commission (CPSC). (1990). *Playground surfacing: Technical information guide.* Washington, DC: Author.

Consumer Product Safety Commission (CPSC). (1991). *Handbook for public playground safety.* Washington, DC: Author.

Frost, J. L. (1990, Summer). Playground equipment catalogs: Can they be trusted? *Texas Child Care,* pp. 3-12.

Frost, J. L., & Wortham, S. C. (1988). The evolution of American playgrounds. *Young Children, 43*(5), 19-28.

Hogan, P. (1990). *The playground safety checker.* Phoenixville, PA: Playground Press.

Jambor, T., & Palmer, S. D. (1991). *Playground safety manual.* Birmingham: University of Alabama, Injury Control and Research Center.

Planning Facilities for Accommodating Children and Adults With Special Needs

The need for early childhood programs to accommodate children and adults with special needs comes from a body of literature supporting the benefits of inclusive settings and from legal mandates (see Chapter 3). Unresolved professional issues and legal interpretations exist because of the recent convergence of early childhood and special education (Bredekamp,

1993). Many questions arise concerning what are "reasonable steps" (as required by the Americans With Disabilities Act) and whether all disabilities must be addressed in a given program. Substantial amounts of research are lacking for planning and evaluating facilities, as well as defining "best practices," for inclusion. Finally, other questions arise concerning the training of staff to provide appropriate experiences and to monitor safety (Finn-Stevenson & Stevenson, 1990; Stayton & Miller, 1993).

The indoor and outdoor facilities and the various areas within the facility (e.g., learning centers/play zones, rest rooms, eating areas) must be accessible for all children and adults. Accessibility is often achieved by more open space, doors and paths that accommodate wheelchairs, ramps with appropriate slopes, grab bars and hand rails, raised tables with wheelchair indentions, and lower shelves, water fountains, and doorknobs. Accessibility to facilities is a priority because, without accessibility, inclusion cannot occur and because students with physical disabilities are the fastest growing population of children receiving services (T. Caldwell, Sirvis, Todaro, & Accouloumre, 1991).

Housing and equipment must also allow those with disabilities to safely take part in activities and to make choices from a range of activities as provided for those without disabilities. Fully integrating the program is much more difficult than merely providing basic accessibility. Furthermore, integrated outdoor environments are more difficult to achieve than indoor environments (Aronson, 1991). Permanent structures, most of which are located outdoors, require the most expensive adaptations; however, these adaptations are being incorporated into the designs for lofts and small play structures used indoors and in play structures and other equipment used outdoors. Loose materials are easy and appropriate ways to provide a more integrated setting, but these materials are mainly used in indoor activities and are only recently being incorporated into quality, creative-type playgrounds.

Specific environmental design features for integrated settings are beyond the scope of this book. The following sources provide most of the basics for planning.

Children's Playgrounds, Inc. (1990). *Catalog supplement: Accessible structures.* Holliston, MA: Author.

Dempsey, J. D., & Frost, J. L. (1993). Play environments in early childhood education. In B. Spodek (Ed.), *Handbook of research on the education of young children* (pp. 306-321). New York: Macmillan.

Eichinger, J., & Woltman, S. (1993). Integration strategies for learners with severe multiple disabilities. *Teaching Exceptional Children, 26*(1), 18-21.

File, N., & Kontos, S. (1993). The relationship of program quality to children's play in integrated early intervention settings. *Topics in Early Childhood Special Education, 13*(1), 1-18.

Keller, M. J., & Hudson, S. (1991). Theory to practice: Creating play environments for therapeutic recreation experiences. *Journal of Physical Education, Recreation, and Dance, 62*(4), 42-44.

Moore, R. C., Goltsman, S. M., & Iacofano, D. S. (Eds.). (1987). *Play for all guidelines: Planning, design, and management of outdoor play settings for all children.* Berkeley, CA: MIG Communications (with contributions by J. Beckwith & L. Scheneekloth & illustrations by Y. Asanoumi).

Raschke, D. B., Dedrick, C., & Hanus, K. (1991). Adaptive playgrounds for all children. *Teaching Exceptional Children, 24*(1), 25-28.

Ross, H. W. (1992). Integrating infants with disabilities? Can "ordinary" caregivers do it? *Young Children, 47*(3), 65-71.

Purchasing Equipment and Materials

The purchasing of equipment and materials is of immeasurable significance. Items not meeting the needs of the program or insufficient in quantity for activities planned hamper rather than facilitate the program. Moreover, careful purchasing of equipment and materials helps ensure that quality items that last longer are chosen. In today's inflationary world, careful planning is essential if the items are to be secured within budgetary limitations.

Purchasing Guidelines. Many considerations must be given to purchasing equipment and materials. The following suggestions are only minimal guidelines:

1. The buyer should purchase equipment and materials that will facilitate program goals. For example, programs following the behavioral-environmental approach will use materials that are task-directed, autotelic (self-rewarding), and self-correcting in the skill areas of reading readiness and mathematics (see also Table 2-2). Conversely, constructivists use materials that encourage creativity, experimentation, and peer social interaction. For example, constructivists use more raw or primitive materials (any materials that do not duplicate reality—e.g., a lump of clay, a scrap of cloth, a bead). Children with various degrees of competence and differing interests can work with such materials. Raw materials also permit children to use various symbols to stand for a real object (see also Table 2-3). Materials must meet the needs of children with disabilities and be usable to teach multicultural, nonsexist concepts. These items include dolls and hand puppets with a range of skin tones or characteristic features and books, puzzles, and pictures depicting various ethnic and racial groups and nontraditional sex-role behaviors. The buyer should consider equipment and materials that can be used in a variety of situations, that are suitable for individual differences, and that need to be stored infrequently.

2. The buyer should check on the amount of money available and the procedures for purchasing. Material and equipment needs are determined by the director in small programs or through staff input in larger programs. Needs should be determined prior to developing a budget. Once the budget is written by the director (in small programs) or written by the administrator and approved by the board (in large corporate programs and in public school or federally funded programs), purchasing can begin. Restrictions are placed on the purchasing authorizations in the large and tax-supported programs. For example, specifications may have to be prepared to determine whether bidding will be used. In cases in which purchases do not involve substantial amounts or in cases with no prospect of competition in the bidding, purchases are negotiated. If small centers in close geographic proximity would purchase as a group, they could probably obtain better prices and reduced shipping costs and would have more clout in dealing with companies that sell inferior equipment.

3. The buyer should keep a perpetual inventory and list of items needed. The inventory record is an essential aspect of the purchasing procedure. This record should list and identify all equipment and materials that have been purchased and delivered. The inventory record should indicate date of acquisition, current cost of replacement (often more than the initial cost), and maintenance provided. The inventory serves as a record of the quantity of materials purchased and of the location of items; it becomes the basis for preventing duplication, determining what equipment and materials need to be replaced, deciding insurance needs, calculating loss or theft of items, and assisting in budget planning with yearly readjustments.

4. The buyer should be economical by negotiating prices or requesting bids. In comparing costs, the bottom line is total delivered costs. Differences in prices may be offset by freight charges. Service is as important as low prices. The buyer should also be economical by determining whether the item can be adapted

from a previously purchased item or staff-made and whether a nonconsumable, expensive item can be shared.

5. The buyer should not overbuy consumable items. As a general rule, consumables are more susceptible to deterioration than permanent pieces of equipment and materials.

6. A buyer should purchase only from reputable companies (see Appendix 6).

7. The buyer should consider building space for using and storing equipment and any additional building specifications for use of any item (e.g., electrical outlet, water source).

8. The buyer should select only safe, durable, relatively maintenance-free, and aesthetically pleasing equipment and materials.

Purchasing Kits and Sets.   The available kits and sets of early learning materials cover a range of psychomotor, affective, and cognitive-developmental tasks and embody the contents of various curricular areas. Kits and sets differ from singly packaged items in several ways: (a) The materials are collected and arranged to provide for a range of individual and group activities; (b) various learning methods are employed while working with materials (listening to records and stories; manipulating objects; viewing books, pictures, and filmstrips; and talking); (c) a manual or teacher's guide provides guidance in using the kit; (d) components of the kit or set are sold as a unit although components may be sold separately in kits that divide materials into distinct instructional units or that have consumable materials; (e) kits are rather expensive; and (f) the materials are encased in a drawer-, cabinet-, or luggage-type storage container. Some kits are published with staff-training materials, supplementary materials for children's activities, and assessment materials.

As is true of all instructional materials, however, the user should carefully evaluate kits or sets. Before purchasing a kit or set, a person should ask the following questions:

1. Do *all* the materials match the goals of the program and the developmental level of children both in its content and format?

2. How does having the kit benefit teachers (e.g., Does it save time in collecting or making materials? Do teachers need the kit/set as a guide in presenting concepts or skills?)?

3. What is the total cost (e.g., Can several teachers in the program use the same kit/set with their groups of children? Are special services needed, and are they covered in the cost, such as training of staff and installation/maintenance? What is the cost of replacement or consumable parts? Is other equipment needed for using the kit/set, such as audiovisual equipment? What is the cost of shipping?)?

4. Are the materials and storage case durable, easily maintained, and safe?

5. How much space is needed to use and store the kit/set?

Purchasing Children's Books and Magazines.
Children's books are used extensively in most early childhood programs. Selection of books is important for two reasons: (a) Because of the varying quality of published books, it is possible for children to have a steady diet of poor to mediocre books, and (b) books should enhance the specific goals of the local early childhood program. Books are usually selected by using one or more of the following criteria:

1. The book has a theme considered interesting to most young children (e.g., nature, machines, holidays).

2. The book has a theme that can help young children overcome some general concerns (e.g., common fears, making friends, cooperative play) or can help specific children cope with their particular problems (e.g., divorce, working mothers, minority-group membership, a disability, mobility). Using books from the viewpoint of children's needs is referred to as **bibliotherapy.**

3. The book has a theme that correlates with thematic unit or project. Books are available to extend and enrich almost every concept.

4. The book has a theme that can teach a value (e.g., sharing, fair play).

5. The book is considered high-quality literature (received awards).

Early childhood educators may use several sources in finding titles of quality books, as given in Appendix 6.

Purchasing Computer Hardware and Software.

In providing microcomputer technology for both administrative and curricular use, careful purchasing is important. The potential of computer technology in educational settings is increasing. Furthermore, from the cost perspective, technology represents a major investment, and from the standpoint of advances in technology, technology that is "in" today may be obsolete tomorrow. Thus, purchasing decisions should match the needs of the administrator and the goals of the children's program and should be on the cutting edge of the technology market. Care must be taken in purchasing both *hardware* (physical components of a computer system, such as a central processing unit [CPU], the monitor, and the keyboard) and *software* (computer program packaged as one program or as two or more related programs).

Hardware. An early childhood program needs one computer for administrative purposes and a minimum of one computer for every 10 children enrolled. Buckleitner (1993) sees the choices as Macintosh (Apple Computer, Inc.) and IBM-compatible. Computers made by Apple have been the choice of schools for years because of their ease of use, as compared with IBM-compatibles. Today, over 88% of all schools use Apple products (Haugland & Shade, 1994). As for "ease of use," Buckleitner believes that the Macintosh and the IBM-compatibles are getting more difficult to distinguish. Most of the recently released software has been for IBM-compatibles (Haugland & Shade, 1994) although both Macintosh-compatible and IBM-compatible versions of the same software program are often available and many newer Macintosh models (Power-Macs) are capable of running both Macintosh and IBM-compatible software.

Peripheral devices (input/output devices that are not part of and hence peripheral to the CPU) must be carefully chosen too. A color monitor, one or more input devices (e.g., keyboard, mouse or trackball, switch, touch window screen, touch tablet, Muppet Learning Keys), and a printer (preferably a laser printer, rather than the slower, noisier dot-matrix) are not optional. Some optional peripherals are *modems* (devices that allow computers to communicate or network via telephone lines), stereo speakers, graphics tablet, and a CD-ROM (compact disc read-only memory—a device that stores large amounts of computer programs or data). Specific features to look for in hardware are given in Table 5-7.

Hardware needs to be adapted for children with special needs. Many organizations (see Appendix 6) provide information on available hardware and training in its use.

Table 5-7   Desirable Hardware Features

14″ color monitor with 256+ colors

One or more 3.5 floppy disk drive(s)

100 MB (megabytes) hard disk drive

Minimum 8 to 12 MBs of RAM (*random access memory*, the memory used to store programs and data while a given program is running; graphics and sound, often used in children's software, require large amounts of RAM)

Upgradable computer as measured by MHz (*megahertz*, or 1 million machine cycles per minute) and expansion features (e.g., slots for CD-ROM, soundboards, or more MBs of RAM)

Software.   In selecting software, it is imperative that the computer's hardware components (called the *configuration*) and the software match in terms of (a) size of the hard disk drive and amount of space available, (b) type of disk drive, (c) amount of RAM, (d) version of the operating system, (e) type of graphics display and speech/sound enhancement, (f) type of input device (e.g., touch window, keyboard, mouse), and (g) need for/type of printer. If the buyer knows the computer configuration, the software producer can determine the match.

Many large early childhood programs purchase a *database management system*—software that allows the user to create, maintain, and access data on a database for administrative functions. Common database applications are children's records; accounts receivable/payable; payroll; meal planning (USDA); personnel management; general ledger; scheduling children/staff; on-line check-in/out; and report, letter, and label writing. Many producers sell these applications in individual modules, but an entire package can cost approximately $3,000. Small programs often use word processing and/or spreadsheet programs to do their administrative record keeping. They may even share the "family computer" or "church computer" and simply keep their program records on separate disks.

Software for the children's program must be chosen with just as much care as other materials for three reasons:

1. Software is expensive and is rapidly increasing (Software Publishers Association, 1993). The average price for a one-title program is $45, but some super software packages can cost thousands of dollars. Administrators can save money by making careful choices, by checking software specialty stores or mail-order companies, or by using shareware (freeware). Teachers may exchange titles or borrow titles from libraries (but it is illegal to copy software except shareware, just as it is illegal to copy copyrighted print materials).

2. The software should meet quality criteria, such as (a) makes effective use of computer capacity, (b) is easy to install, (c) is childproof, (d) is easy to use (simple to operate with few commands that allow children to work independently of adults), (e) has correct content, (f) has quality design features, and (g) provides for differences in children's interests and abilities.

3. Software must match the goals of the program. The two types of available software are (a) open-ended, discovery software programs—*simulations* (programs that model real-life situations so that children can use their skills and concepts in lifelike settings that are close to the "real thing") and *microworlds* (programs in which children act on software to make something happen, rather than respond to close-ended questions or situations); and (b) drill-and-practice programs in which the child is rewarded for selecting the correct answers to the problems. Microworlds and simulations are used by constructivists, and drill-and-practice programs are used by the behavioral-environmentalists. Microworlds and simulations are becoming increasingly popular, but 75% of software releases is still of the drill-and-practice type (Shade & Haugland, 1993). Most of the awards for quality of sound and graphics have gone to drill and practice (Shade, 1992). Thus, constructivists have fewer choices in the software market. Haugland and Shade (1994) asked early childhood teachers what they wanted software publishers to know. Teachers indicated that they wanted to have software in many content areas so that they as teachers may infuse technology into the curriculum, rather than have complete programs (super software packages). These teachers also wanted to see less drill-and-practice software and more microworlds and simulations software (see publishers of software in Appendix 6).

Software must be carefully evaluated. The hype on software makes descriptions different from actuality. Fite (1993) says that software evaluation systems use different criteria for their evaluations; thus, the evaluation system's philosophy must be consistent with the chosen program base (see Appendix 6). Software evaluations for children with disabilities are provided by the same organizations that provide information on adaptive hardware products.

Teachers need to go beyond considering software descriptive and numerical evaluations. They need to take a comprehensive look at the program itself. Teachers need to view themselves as test pilots who push the software to its limits and who see the software through the eyes, hands, and minds of children in the program.

Caring for Equipment and Materials

Caring for equipment and materials teaches children good habits and helps prevent expensive repairs and replacements. Teachers should keep the following suggestions in mind:

1. The room and shelves should be arranged to minimize the chance of accidents and to maximize housekeeping efficiency. Equipment and materials should be shelved close to the working space; objects susceptible to damage should be used in areas out of the main flow of traffic; breakable items or those likely to spill should be placed on shelves within easy reach (if frequent accidents involving the same item occur, try setting it in a different place). Enough open space should prevent accidents.

2. Children should be taught how to care for equipment and materials. Staff should establish a routine for obtaining and returning equipment and materials and for using facilities. To establish a routine, every item must have a place, and time must be allowed for returning all items there.

3. Spilled materials should be cleaned up. In some cases, a teacher can create a science lesson on "how to clean it up."

4. Staff should set good examples in caring for equipment and materials.

5. Staff should station themselves properly for adequate supervision.

6. Children should be removed from an area when they deliberately destroy or damage equipment or materials.

7. Equipment and materials should be repaired as soon as possible. Items should not be used until they are repaired.

8. Equipment should be cleaned regularly. Toys for infants and toddlers should be cleaned daily with a disinfectant, and equipment for preschoolers should be cleaned weekly.

9. Staff should periodically check equipment and materials. They should tighten loose nuts, bolts, clamps, and other hardware; replace or sand rusted parts; repaint rusted tubing; oil metal parts; sand wooden equipment where splinters are found; paint or use clear protective coatings on wooden equipment and remove loose paint; repair torn fabric and secure fasteners on doll or dress-up clothes; and replace broken-off or sharp plastic equipment. To report a product one believes to be unsafe, write to

Standards Development Service Section
National Bureau of Standards
Washington, DC 20234

or

Consumer Product Safety Commission
Washington, DC 20207
(toll free, 800-638-2772; or Maryland residents only, call 800-492-2937)

10. Staff should consider what heat, light, moisture, and storage methods may do to the equipment and materials.

11. Plenty of equipment and materials should be available so that each child has something to do and does not have to wait too long for a turn. Tempers flare and damage occurs when children are not constructively involved.

12. Poisonous or dangerous items should be stored where children cannot get to them. To request information about a product, call the

Consumer Product Safety Hot Line 800-638-2666 (Maryland residents only, call 800-492-2937). The telephone number of the local poison control center should be posted too.

Purchasing Insurance

Adequate insurance for a facility, as well as equipment and materials, is of utmost importance. Coverage is required for mortgaged buildings and is recommended for all owned buildings and for the contents of rented buildings. Basically, fire insurance covers fire and lightning. Most policies can have an extended-coverage endorsement attached that covers such things as losses from wind, hail, explosion (except from steam boilers), civil commotion, aircraft, vehicles, smoke, vandalism, and malicious mischief. If the program moves equipment and materials to various buildings, the insurance should include a floater policy to protect against loss resulting from such transportation. To have adequate fire insurance (basic or extended coverage endorsement), the administrator must maintain up-to-date property records that reflect current values. Other types of insurance may also be necessary. If the program owns vehicles, insurance should be secured to protect against losses from material damage or the destruction of the vehicle and its material contents (liability insurance is usually required by law). Theft insurance may be needed in some areas but is usually expensive.

TRENDS AND ISSUES

The body of literature on designing children's play environments is growing. Dempsey and Frost (1993) refer to the environment as the "interface between the teacher and the child" (p. 306). They cite evidence of the growing interest in play environments, such as the safety standards developed by the ASTM, the formation of the Association of Child Care Consultants Inter-national (an association of consulting firms on the professional design of child care environments), and the publication of a new journal, *Children's Environments Quarterly.*

In the body of literature on play environments, one area that lags is the design of environments for the safe and educationally profitable inclusion of children and adults with special needs. Several professional designers, including some members of the American Association of Children's Right to Play, are currently planning play environments that integrate individuals with and without disabilities. Quality indicators in the environmental designs for integrated programs have not been fully developed. File and Kontos (1993), however, have done some work toward this end but had to use a combination of safety measures. Although federal assistance with the costs of ADA compliance (Surr, 1992) is available, the cost factor may slow the erection of play environments appropriate for full inclusion.

Safety regulations also lag behind knowledge and recommendations in the design of outdoor environments. Falls account for the majority of accidents in both family child care and center settings, and over 80% of severe injuries are from these falls (Kotch, Loda, McMurray, Harms, & Clifford, 1991; Revara, DiGuiseppi, Thompson, & Calonge, 1989). The greatest injury-causing factor in outdoor play areas is the combined effect of the height of equipment and the surfacing below the equipment. A survey of state licensing regulations showed that no state specified maximum height of equipment and that 96% of the states' regulations failed to even mention surfacing (Runyan et al., 1991). Costs, especially of surfacing, may slow the adoption of regulations on playground surfacing. Hendricks (1993) reports that the installation of a fall zone under a single slide costs between $350 and $1,000, depending on materials.

The appearance of the microcomputer in the early childhood environment is the major trend in equipping the play environment. Some serious hurdles in technology need to be overcome, such as the high cost, the provision for teacher training, and the creation of hardware and software products designed with young children in mind (e.g., products that are not simply electronic ditto sheets). As described by Char and Forman (1994), the future of interactive technologies can offer powerful tools for young children's development.

SUMMARY

Careful planning is required for housing an early childhood program. The program base and objectives of the local program should determine the housing facilities. To a great extent, housing determines the quality of an early childhood program. Housing can be thought of as the stage upon which all interactions take place—child-child, child-adult, and child-material. Housing involves (a) the entry-exit area in which the child makes the transitions from home to program and from program to home and the area from which parents most frequently view the program; (b) the children's activity room, with its planned arrangement designed to meet the child's needs as defined by the program objectives; (c) the additional areas for children (shared activity areas, lockers, changing areas/rest rooms, feeding/dining areas, napping area, isolation area); (d) adult areas (parent reception area, lounge, office/work-room); and (e) the outdoor space—an extension of the activity room. Because of the wide variety of equipment and materials available for use in early childhood programs, many people may believe that the early childhood curriculum is entirely contained in such materials. Certainly, the uses of equipment and materials are powerful regulators of children's experiences. Thus, selection of the types of equipment and materials purchased and the ways in which they will be used must be carefully determined by the local program.

Once housing facilities are constructed or selected and materials and equipment chosen, they determine the staff members' abilities to work with and supervise children, the types and convenience of activities, the accessibility of equipment and materials and of places to work and to play, and the safety of children. In short, one should never have to adapt the program to the physical setting; rather, the physical setting should always serve the purposes of the program.

FOR FURTHER READING

Christie, J. F., & Johnsen, E. P. (1989). The constraints of settings on children's play. *Play and Culture, 2,* 317-327.

Eskensen, J. B. (1987). *The early childhood playground: An outdoor classroom.* Ypsilanti, MI: High/Scope Press.

Frost, J. L. (1989). Play environments for young children in the USA: 1800-1990. *Children's Environments Quarterly, 6*(4) 17-24.

Frost, J. L., & Sunderlin, S. (Eds.). *When children play.* Wheaton, MD: Association for Childhood Education International.

Greenman, J. (1988). *Caring spaces, learning places: Children's environments that work.* Redmond, WA: Exchange Press.

Hart, C. H. (Ed.). (1993). *Children on playgrounds.* Albany: State University of New York Press.

Jones, E., & Prescott, E. (1978). *Dimensions of teaching-learning environments II: Focus on day care.* Pasadena, CA: Pacific Oaks College.

Kaden, M. (1990). Issues on computers and early childhood education. In C. Seefeldt (Ed.), *Continuing issues in early childhood education* (pp. 261-275). New York: Merrill/Macmillan.

Krantz, P., & Risley, T. (1972). *The organization of group care environments: Behavioral ecology in the classroom.* (ERIC Document Reproduction Service No. ED 078 915)

Lanser, S., & McDonnell, L. (1991). Creating quality curriculum yet not buying out the store. *Young Children, 47*(1), 4-9.

Peck, N., & Shores, E. F. (1994). *Checklist for diversity in early childhood education and care.* Little Rock, AR: Southern Early Childhood Association.

Picciano, A. G. (1994). *Computing in the schools: A guide to planning and administration.* New York: Macmillan.

Sanoff, H., & Sanoff, J. (1988). *Learning environments for children: A developmental approach to shaping activity areas.* Atlanta, GA: Humanics Press.

Sutton-Smith, B. (1986). *Toys are culture.* New York: Gardner.

Weinstein, C. S., & David, T. G. (Eds.). (1987). *Spaces for children: The built environment and child development.* New York: Plenum.

Chapter 6

❦ ❦ ❦ ❦ ❦

Financing and Budgeting

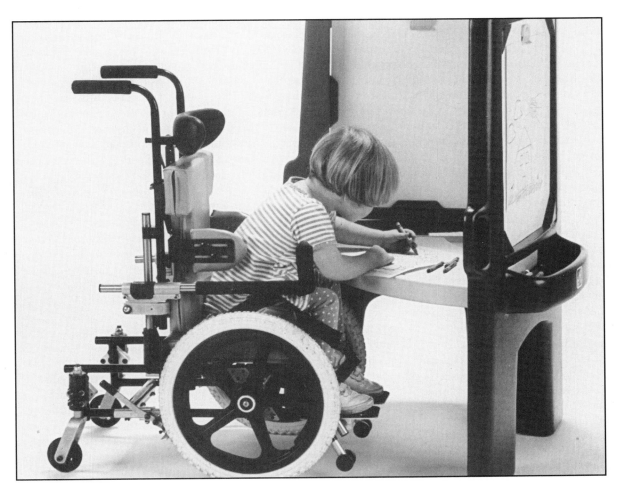

❦ ❦ ❦ ❦ ❦

Early childhood programs are expensive. In 1986, child care in the United States was a $12 billion industry. By 1991, child care had grown to a $15.3 billion industry, and it is expected to rise to $48 billion before the turn of the century (Perreault, 1991). The National Association for the Education of Young Children (NAEYC) has stated that the crisis facing early childhood programs is rooted in this nation's failure to recognize the antinomy of three basic needs: (a) children's need for services, (b) staff's need for adequate compensation, and (c) parents' need for affordable programs. These needs are very difficult to fulfill simultaneously. In 1987, the NAEYC Governing Board adopted a position statement that all children and their families should have access to high-quality programs and that staff should be offered salaries/benefits commensurate with their qualifications (NAEYC, 1987).

Both the scope and the quality of services are related to the financial status of a program although programs with similar hourly costs range in quality from poor to excellent. Even with careful budgeting, however, good programs cannot operate effectively for long depending on donations and volunteers without weakening the quality and quantity of their services and without damaging the morale of those involved. Although total budget may not be directly related to program quality, Olenick (1986) did find a positive relationship between program quality and budget allocations for teacher salaries and benefits (programs that spent approximately two thirds of their budgets on salaries and staff benefits tended to be of high quality, and quality diminished considerably in programs spending less than one half of their budgets on salaries and staff benefits). Similarly, Whitebook et al. (1990) stated that the single best predictor of teacher effectiveness was salary.

Few early childhood administrators receive adequate training in fiscal management. Such training is important because parents, funding agencies, and taxpayers who believe that their early childhood programs are properly managed are more likely to subsidize the program. As is true of all other aspects of planning and administration, fiscal planning begins with the goals of the local program. Unless the proposed services and the requirements for meeting those services, in the way of staff, housing, or equipment, are taken into account, how can a budget be planned? And although program objectives should be considered first, probably no early childhood program is entirely free of financial limitations.

Fiscal planning affects all aspects of a program; consequently, it should involve input from all those concerned with the local program (e.g., board of directors or advisory board, director, primary program and support program personnel, parents). By considering everyone's ideas, a more accurate conception of budgeting priorities, expenditure level, and revenue sources can be derived. Furthermore, planning and administering the fiscal aspects of an early childhood program should be a continuous process. Successful financing and budgeting will only come from evaluating current revenue sources and expenditures and from advance planning for existing and future priorities.

Fiscal affairs are probably the most surveyed aspect of an early childhood program. A central criterion used to evaluate the worth of a program is often economic—that is, using funds efficiently and showing benefits that exceed costs. As described in Chapter 2, many federally financed early childhood programs that began in the 1960s and 1970s conducted longitudinal studies that showed these programs' economic worth to society.

Not-for-profit programs are responsible to their funding agencies, for-profit programs are accountable to their owners and stockholders, and all programs are accountable to the Internal Revenue Service. Even if the average citizen doesn't understand the problems of fund management, any hint of fund misuse will cause criticism. Administrators must budget, secure revenue, manage, account for, and substantiate expenditures in keeping with the policies of the early childhood program in a professional and businesslike manner.

COSTS OF EARLY CHILDHOOD PROGRAMS

Reported costs of early childhood programs show extensive variation. Costs may vary with the type of program, the level of training and size of the staff, sponsorship (a federal program, public school, or parent cooperative), the delivery system (center based, home visitor, or television), and with the children enrolled (age and with or without a disability). Another factor contributing to variations in costs is whether the program is new or is offering new, additional services and thus has "start-up costs"—such as salaries of planning personnel and initial expenditures for housing, equipping, and advertising—or whether the program is already underway and has continuing costs. Geographic location, the amount of competition, and the general economy also contribute to the varying costs.

Estimates of Program Costs

Quality child care is labor intensive and expensive. When adjusted for inflation, program costs have not risen much since the mid-1970s (Willer, 1992). The Cost, Quality, and Outcomes Study Team (1995) found that **cash costs** (the amount charged/paid for services) for centers meeting minimal standards (but not those with good to excellent ratings) was $2.11 per child hour ($95 per child week, or $4,940 per child year). Geographic differences in cash costs ranged from $1.50 per child hour in North Carolina to $2.88 per child hour in Connecticut.

Cash cost and the **full cost** (amount it would require to operate a program if all costs were included) are different. Administrators lower their cash costs by hiring teachers at or near minimum wages and/or by increasing the number of children per adult, both of which reduce

quality. Administrators also rely on volunteer help and other donations. The Cost, Quality, and Outcomes Study Team (1995) found that full cost for child care services was $2.83 per child hour ($127 per child week, or $6,604 per child year). The 72¢ per child hour difference between cash cost and full cost was absorbed in foregone wages and benefits of child care employees (who absorbed 19% of full cost, or 54¢ per child hour), occupancy donations (that absorbed 6% of full cost, or 14¢ per child hour), and donated goods and volunteer services (that absorbed 2% of full cost, or 6¢ per child hour). Willer (1992) also reported how employees' foregone wages have subsidized the provision of early childhood care and education services. She found that teacher salaries (excluding salaries of aides and assistants) have declined nearly 25%, adjusted for inflation, since the mid-1970s. In 1991, the average salary for center teachers, employed for a 30-hour week and a 50-week year, was $11,500. The average yearly salaries for regulated family child care teachers and nonregulated family child care teachers was $10,000 and $2,000, respectively.

The Cost, Quality, and Outcomes Study Team (1995) estimated that the difference in today's cash (not full) costs of going from minimal-quality services was 10% (from $4,940 to $5,434 per child year). This percentage assumes that 10% is spent on items related to quality enhancement. The U.S. General Accounting Office (1990) estimated the full cost for preschoolers in a center was $5,000 per child year. Willer (1990) estimated the full cost of high-quality center care was $8,000 per child year for children under age 5.

Different types of programs vary in their costs. Neugebauer (1993b) conducted a national survey of fees charged to parents. He used as the baseline the fees charged for 3- and 4-year-olds attending centers full time (all day for 5 days per week). For full-time care, the fees for toddlers were 15% higher, and the fees for infants were 28% higher, than the baseline. The percentages were rather consistent from center to center. School-Age Child Care (SACC) fees for before- and after-school care were 26% less than the baseline, and fees for after-school care were 55% less than the baseline. SACC fees, however, were reported to vary "dramatically" from center to center; thus, the percentages are less meaningful. Facilities in continuous use (e.g., preschool child care) are cost-effective in comparison with facilities with "downtime" (e.g., half-day nursery schools, SACC programs). Meeting the needs of children with disabilities is also expensive. Costs are functions of the type and degree of exceptionality—with intellectually gifted the least expensive and those with physical disability the most expensive—and of the type of services offered (e.g., transportation for children with physical disabilities is often more expensive than tutors for children identified as having a learning disability). Program sponsorship, however, has little bearing on costs. For example, the Cost, Quality, and Outcomes Study Team (1995) found that for-profit and not-for-profit centers charge similar fees per child hour and receive similar (3.7%) profit (in for-profit programs) or surplus (in not-for-profit programs).

Cash costs of programs seem to remain low at the expense of employees' salaries/benefits and program quality for children because of at least three reasons:

1. The government contributes to low-quality care when its agencies impose low payments for child care services or fail to provide higher reimbursement for higher quality. Generally speaking, governmental agencies use estimated cash costs to determine what they will pay for services, and thus, to some degree, circularity results. In other words, because agencies pay a certain number of dollars, program designers plan their programs on the basis of expected amounts of money. If funded the first year, program designers write a similar program the next year in hopes of being refunded. Thus, the agency pays approximately the same amount again, and the cycle is continued. So, the program is designed around a specific dollar value, whether or not it makes for the "best" program.

2. Labor is the most expensive aspect of early childhood programs. In the highest quality programs, about 70% of the budget is in salaries/benefits. The easiest way to make a program more affordable and to ensure profit/surplus is to decrease wages and increase the number of children per staff member. Low wages result in less qualified employees at the point of entry, less incentive for employees to increase skills because of the lack of significant monetary reward, and greater employee turnover rates. The trade-off for low salaries/benefits is a low-quality program.

3. Inadequate consumer knowledge on the part of parents reduces incentives for centers to provide high-quality programs. The Cost, Quality, and Outcomes Study Team (1995) found that 90% of parents rated centers "very good" but that trained observers rated these same programs "poor to mediocre." The team concluded that perhaps parents rate the programs too high because they cannot monitor the programs' services, they may value a given service of the program so much that this leads to bias about other services (leads to overlooking other, less than quality services), and/or they have no basis for program comparisons (the parent may not have seen good-quality care). Hayes et al. (1990) noted that parents report difficulty in finding high-quality care but that once care is found, these parents report satisfaction with the arrangements. The satisfaction seemed to be based on parents' needs for convenient and low-cost care, and not on their children's needs for quality services.

Costs to Families

Child care represents the fourth largest expense for the working family after housing, food, and taxes (LaFleur & Newsom, 1988). Many families cannot afford to pay for the current delivery systems, let alone pay for high-quality child care.

The Cost, Quality, and Outcomes Study Team (1995) found that dual-earner households paid 8% of the 1993 median before-tax income on child care and that full-time employed single parents paid 23% of the average before-tax income.

Costs to families differ. Friedman (1986) reported that child care costs a family from $1,500 to $15,000 per year; the average cost is $3,000. Costs to families differ for the following reasons:

1. Programs differ in costs because of quality of services, geographic location, age of children served, and ability of the program to take advantage of scale economics (serve more children and/or provide more hours of service than competing programs).

2. Even in programs that charge similar fees per child hour, the costs per family may vary because of various types of subsidies. The subsidies include the following:

a. *Multi-child discounts.* About half of for-profit centers offer multi-child discounts; however, the fee discount varied greatly (Neugebauer, 1993b).

b. *Fees subsidized by public funds.* About 33% of all programs (outside of public schools) provide care for children whose fees are subsidized by public funds. If public schools are included, the proportion is 40% (Willer, 1992). The Cost, Quality, and Outcomes Study Team (1995) looked at program costs to families. Among all the families in the sample (those who pay full tuition and those who are subsidized), the costs to families are $1.55 per child hour ($70 per child week, or $3,640 per child year) or 73% of center revenue (at $2.11 per child hour) and 55% of full center cost (at $2.83 per child hour). Among families who pay full tuition (excluding families who receive subsidies via public funds), the average payment is $1.92 per child hour or 92% of center revenue and 68% of full center cost.

c. *Tax credits.* Federal income tax deduction is allowed for child care services (IRS Form 2241 filed with 1040 and IRS Schedule 2 filed with 1040A). The Child and Dependent Care Credit covers a percentage of a family's annual child care expenses for one or more dependent children under age 13. The higher the child care expenses and the lower the amount of family income, the larger the amount of credit (to the maximum of $1,440). The Cost, Quality, and Outcomes Study Team (1995) found that if families took the federal child care tax credit available to them, their estimated full tuition would be $1.72 per child hour or 82% of center revenue and 61% of full center cost. Interestingly, Willer (1992) found that only 25% to 33% of families whose incomes were above $25,000 reported that they claimed federal tax credit for child care. Families who claimed the credit did not perceive this as a direct subsidy although tax credit is the single largest subsidy for early childhood programs. Families are also eligible for Earned Income Credit of up to $2,211 if they earn up to $25,296 a year and have one or more qualifying children. Because few eligible families claimed their tax credits, the National Woman's Law Center launched the Child Care Tax Credits Outreach Campaign. This direct subsidy has three problems. First, tax credit does not address the quality of early childhood programs. Second, poor families may not earn sufficient income to take advantage of this bill. Third, dependent care tax credit is not reimbursable; thus, poor families with little or no tax liability are unable to recoup any of their expenditures for child care.

The amount of foregone income when a family member provides child care services rather than obtains outside employment is another expense that varies from family to family. The income is considered foregone when a family member provides child care services either without payment or on an intrafamilial income transfer. In either case, the amount of foregone income depends on the caregiver's employable skills and availability of employment, or on the caregiver's potential income. (Of course, one should consider costs of outside employment, such as transportation, clothing, organization or union dues, and higher taxes, in calculating foregone income.)

Although child care costs have not risen substantially since the mid-1970s, costs to parents have increased from 70% to 76% to compensate programs for their loses in subsidies over the same time span (Willer, 1992). Thus, child care has become less affordable to most families. Families do not have equitable financing either. Because families living in poverty (with incomes of $15,000 or less) can have their child care fees subsidized, their children are as likely to be enrolled in early childhood programs as those children coming from high-socioeconomic families (with incomes of at least $50,000). The majority of lower socioeconomic families are not having their child care needs met through subsidized fees, however; about 60% of these families use unpaid relatives for child care (Mayore, 1989). And, the least likely to have adequate child care assistance are families just above the poverty level (those with incomes between $15,000 and $25,000; Willer, 1992).

Cost Analysis of Programs

The decision to fund an early childhood program and the kind of investment to make depends on "answers" based on cost analyses. Given today's economic situation, programs applying for public monies are reviewed in terms of costs versus savings (social benefits to the individuals involved and to society in general). Social benefits quantified in economic terms are always difficult to calculate and, especially in the case of early childhood programs, are made almost impossible because many of

the benefits cannot be measured until young children reach adulthood.

Cost analyses are of several types. The reason for doing a cost analysis determines the type of analysis employed. **Cost-effectiveness analysis** compares the costs of two or more programs that have the same or similar goals to find the least-cost method of reaching a particular goal. Programs that offer a low-cost approach compared with other approaches to achieve certain objectives are referred to as cost-effective programs.

Cost-efficiency analysis usually follows cost-effectiveness analysis. Cost-effective programs can further reduce costs by developing a least-cost, within-program management plan. Cost efficiency is achieved when all program components are optimally used (e.g., staffing patterns, curriculum, scheduling). When the management of a single program is providing optimal desired outcomes, it is considered a cost-efficient program.

Cost-benefit analysis, the most difficult analysis, measures the value of the program to the child and his or her family and to society minus the costs of the program. As has been stated earlier in this chapter, it is difficult to put a dollar value on benefits, and it is impossible to project benefits for 15 or 20 years hence or for generations to come. However, a program is referred to as a cost-beneficial program when the monetarily calculated benefits exceed the monetarily calculated costs. For example, a cost-benefit analysis in the 1980s showed that 1 year of a good preschool program yielded seven times the cost of that year in lifetime earnings and welfare savings (Berrueta-Clement et al., 1984).

The cost analysis of a program varies greatly with the elements included in the analysis. For example, the following distinctions must be made in an analysis:

1. **Fixed and variable costs.** Fixed costs (e.g., program planning) do not vary with the number of children served, but variable costs

(e.g., building, teacher salaries, equipment) vary with the number of children served.

2. **Marginal costs.** Marginal costs are the increased cost "per unit" (total program costs divided by the number of recipients) of expanding a program beyond a given size. Marginal costs may decrease to a given point and then increase when additional staff or housing are required.

3. **Capital versus operating costs.** Capital costs (e.g., building) are basically one-time costs, whereas operating costs (e.g., salaries, consumable materials) are recurrent.

4. **Hidden costs.** Hidden costs are costs free to a program but paid by someone else (e.g., religious organizations that permit "free" use of their facilities). **Joint costs** are somewhat "hidden" too because they are shared costs (e.g., two separately funded programs that share a staff workroom or audiovisual equipment). **Foregone income costs** (e.g., income foregone because of services or goods provided a program) are difficult to calculate.

Comparisons of costs must be made on the same basis, and cost analyses must include all of these costs to be accurate.

FINANCING EARLY CHILDHOOD PROGRAMS

Early childhood programs receive funds from local, state, and federal sources, as well as from foundations, fees and tuition, and miscellaneous sources. Various regulations govern (a) a program's eligibility to receive revenue from a source, such as the federal government; (b) procedures for obtaining revenue; (c) use made of the revenue; and (d) which personnel are accountable for the expenditure. Because of the many types of programs and the intricacies and variations involved in funding, only a brief description of the sources of financing are given here.

Public School Financing of Kindergartens and Primary Programs

Public school programs are supported by local, state, and federal monies. Ninety percent of funding comes from state and local sources (Schweinhart & Weikart, 1985). Taxation is the major source of monies available for funding; consequently, revenues for public school programs are closely tied to the general economy of the local area, state, and nation.

Local Support. Tax funds, usually from real and personal property taxes, are used to maintain and operate the schools, and the sale of bonds is used for capital improvements and new construction expenses. The local school board's authority to set tax rates and to issue bonds for school revenue purposes is granted by the state; that is, authority is *not* implied. When granted the power to tax, state laws concerning tax rates and procedural matters must be followed by the local school board in an exacting manner. In this way, the state protects the public from misuse and mismanagement of public monies (for more information, see Decker & Decker, 1992).

State Support. The amount of state support for public schools varies widely from state to state. Almost every state has some form of foundation program designed to equalize the tax burden and educational opportunities among school districts. Generally, the foundation program begins with a definition of minimum standards of educational service that must be offered throughout the state. The cost of maintaining the standards is calculated, and the rate of taxation prescribed. The tax rate may be uniform or based on an economic index ability— the ability of a local school district to pay. If local taxes do not cover the cost of maintaining minimum standards, the balance of the costs is provided via state monies. States vary considerably in the machinery they use for channeling state monies to local school districts, the most common plans being flat and equalization grants (for more information, see Decker & Decker, 1992). Recently, the issue of equalizing funding among school districts within a state has resulted in a rash of school finance litigation (Verstegen, 1994).

Federal Support.   Since the 1940s, the federal government has become the chief tax collector. Until recently, the trend has been toward unprecedented expenditures for education. Consequently, public schools (as well as other institutions, agencies, and organizations) relied more and more on federal assistance programs to supplement their local and state resources. Federal funding of public schools is used for two purposes: (a) to improve the quality of education (e.g., research, experimentation, training, housing, equipping) and (b) to encourage greater effort by state and local districts to improve the quality of education by providing initial or matching funds for a program. In the past few years, federal expenditures in education have declined because of reduction of types of programs funded or the amount of funds available in retained programs. The two major programs receiving federal support are Chapter 1 (a compensatory education program formerly called Title 1) and services for children with special needs as required by P.L. 101-476 and P.L. 102-199.

State Financing of Early Childhood Programs

States are increasing their financing of programs for pre-kindergarten children. Most of the programs financed are center-based settings, including the public schools although some include home-based components. None of the 50 states offer universal early childhood education, but the majority of states target their programs to 3- and 4-year-olds who have been identified as "at risk" (economically disadvantaged, deficient in English, and/or identified as having academic difficulties that will lead to school failure).

The amount spent by the states varies considerably. States also use various methods for dispersing early childhood funds. For example, some states allocate money to school districts on the basis of school finance formulas (as previously discussed). Some states use a categorical aid system to allocate early childhood funds to school districts. The most common method of state funding of early childhood education, however, is through grants or contracts awarded by a state administrative agency, usually the department of education. Most of the grants are awarded through a competitive process. For example, grants may go to school districts or private agencies whose programs are approved by the state board of education or by other regulatory guidelines. In some states, grants are used for pilot programs only. A few states use noncompetitive ways of awarding grants, such as school districts that have high concentrations of low-income students or elementary students with low standardized achievement test scores. Several states require that state money be matched with local, federal (e.g., Chapter 1), or in-kind services. This matching is necessary in some states because of statutory restrictions on state spending for these programs. Jordan, Lyons, and McDonough (1992) conducted a research review of the funding and financing of programs serving kindergarten through third-grade at-risk children. They found competitive discretionary grants (grants awarded on the basis of the merits of the competing project proposals) to be the weakest funding method and the index of need allocation strategy (the index is a proxy for the magnitude of the need, rather than numbers of students) to be the strongest funding method. Their findings on the evaluation of funding options should apply to pre-kindergarten children.

Legislative support for early childhood programs is expected to grow. Legislative concerns about expenditures will result in closer scrutiny of early childhood program expenditures. Future initiatives will undoubtedly address increased funding and methods of reducing costs by coordinating efforts with similar local programs (e.g., local child care, Head Start; Warger, 1988).

Federal Financing and Foundation Support

In addition to programs receiving some federal fiscal support, such as the public schools, the federal government remains the primary source of support for some comprehensive early childhood programs. The modern era of federal support for early childhood care and education began with Head Start in 1965. Other programs soon followed, such as Title IV-A of the Social Security Act, which provided funds for child care beginning in 1967. The Comprehensive Child Development Act of 1971, passed by Congress but vetoed by the president, called for the placing of all major child care and development efforts under a single National Center for Child Development in order that standards for early childhood programs would be uniform (Zigler & Lang, 1991).

Federal funding, targeted primarily for low-income families and including programs for young children, continued to grow until 1977. While federal support for social programs declined from 1977 to 1988, federal support for early childhood programs (e.g., Head Start) remained rather constant in dollar amounts; in actuality, federal support declined because the number of children living in poverty increased (Einbinder & Bond, 1992) and inflation took its toll on the value of the dollar. After 1988, federal support once again increased. Head Start was to be expanded through the Human Services Reauthorization Act of 1990. Also in 1990, for the first time in 20 years, comprehensive child care legislation was passed by the 101st Congress and was signed into law. The new program, called the **Child Care and Development Block Grant,** gave states money to provide families assistance with their child care expenses and to improve the availability and quality of early childhood programs. Tax credit (an increase in the Earned Income Tax Credit) and health credit were also included in the federal package. Recently, child care and early education programs are once again facing spending cuts.

Throughout the modern era of federal financing, the purpose of most federal assistance programs is to accomplish particular educational objectives or to meet the needs of specific groups. Most federal assistance programs have these characteristics: (a) require early childhood programs to meet specified standards, (b) give priority or restrict services to certain client groups, (c) require state and/or local support in varying amounts, and (d) specify funds to be used for certain purposes (e.g., food, program supplies), which in turn curtail a program's flexibility.

Concerns.   Several concerns are ongoing. One concern is the bewildering array of funding agencies and assistance programs. Because, at present, no federal centralized program of child care exists, the extent of federal involvement in early childhood programs is not easily determined. The National Academy of Sciences (1990) showed that the exact number of federal programs that support early childhood is not known. Along with the problem of dealing with the number of federal sources, a jumble of rulings from agencies results in many different standards. Assistance programs are constantly being deleted and added, and appropriations may fall below congressional authorization. (Problems that result from this lack of centralization were seen by those who proposed the Comprehensive Child Development Act of 1971).

Another concern is the nature of services the federal government should provide. Zigler (1988) believes that the government should fund programs, but Osborne and Gaebler (1992) believe that the government should guide delivery through policy decisions but not provide direct services. The trend has been toward federal "deregulation." **Block grants** are considered a middle ground between the federal control of **categorical grants** (grants used for specified, narrowly defined purposes) and **gen-**

eral revenue sharing (funds provided on a formula basis to state and/or local governments, with few or perhaps no limits to how money is spent). In a block grant, federal aid is provided for more broadly defined activities so that state or local groups can have greater discretion in designating programs to meet local needs. Recipients must comply with some federal regulations (e.g., fiscal reporting and nondiscrimination requirements).

Funding Sources.   Federal funding sources are in a state of constant change. The latest edition of the *Catalog of Federal Domestic Assistance* (available from the Government Printing Office) describes the federal agencies administering various assistance programs and the projects and services funded under these agencies. (Some specific federal programs that provide funds for early childhood programs are listed in Appendix 7.)

Obtaining Federal Funds.   Most federal funds are obtained by writing and submitting a grant proposal and having the proposal approved and funded. One person on the early childhood staff can best oversee the entire writing of the proposal although input should be obtained from all those involved in the program. In fact, early childhood programs that plan to seek regular federal assistance may find it advantageous to hire a staff member with expertise in the area of obtaining federal as well as other funds, such as foundation grants, that require proposal writing. Proposal writing can vary according to an assistance program's particular requirements, but most use a similar format.

A certain terminology is used in obtaining federal funds and must be understood by those involved in locating appropriate grants and writing proposals. The following terms are frequently used:

1. **Assets.** The amount of money, stocks, bonds, real estate, or other holdings of an individual or organization.

2. **Endowment.** Funds intended to be kept permanently and invested to provide income for support of a program.

3. **Financial report.** A report detailing how funds were used (e.g., listing of income and expenses).

4. **Grant.** A monetary award given a program. Grants are of several types:
   a. **Bricks and Mortar Act.** An informal term for grants for building or construction projects.
   b. **Capital support.** Funds for buildings (construction or renovation) and equipment.
   c. **Declining grant.** A multiyear grant that grows smaller each year in the expectation that the recipient can raise other funds to compensate the difference.
   d. **General-purpose grant.** A grant made to further the total work of the program, as opposed to assist a specific purpose.
   e. **Matching grant.** A grant with matching funds provided by another donor.
   f. **Operating-support grant.** A grant to cover day-to-day expenses (e.g., personnel salaries).
   g. **Seed grant** or **seed money.** A grant or contribution used to start a new project.

5. **Grassroots fund-raising.** An effort to raise money on a local basis (e.g., raffles, bake sales, auctions.)

6. **In-kind contribution.** A contribution of time, space, equipment, or materials in lieu of a monetary contribution.

7. **Proposal.** A written application for a grant.

Preproposal Planning.   Preproposal planning is, in essence, research. And, as is true with any research, problem identification is the first step. What is needed? If the assistance program sends out a "Request for a Proposal" (RFP), the need is already defined in broad or general terms.

The second step is gathering documented evidence in the population or potential population served by the early childhood program.

Also, assessment must be made as to how critical or extensive the need is. Most proposals require that needs and the degree of these needs be described in terms of demographic, geographic, and socioeconomic distribution, as well as racial/ethnic makeup. Because proposals often have to be written quickly (perhaps in 2 to 4 weeks), an up-to-date notebook should be kept with these data available. Data may be secured from the following and other sources:

community action associations (local)

Department of Health and Human Resources (local and state)

federal publications (found in the *Monthly Catalog of U.S. Government Publications)*

U.S. Department of Commerce, Bureau of the Census

U.S. Department of Labor, Bureau of Labor Statistics

U.S. Department of Labor, Employment and Training Administration

The literature must be reviewed to see whether others have handled the problem and with what results. To prevent duplication of services in a local area, the administrator must also present evidence as to whether the same or similar needs are being met by other local programs. The duplication check needs to be made with local social service organizations, which can be identified through the telephone directory, the department of public welfare, and agencies served by the United Fund or Community Chest.

The final step is the writing of a two- or three-page preproposal prospectus. The prospectus should contain a statement of the proposed problem, what will be done about the problem, the target group to be served, the number of people to be served, and whether the proposed early childhood program is needed. The prospectus is helpful in clarifying thinking and in getting the opinions of others, including reviewers of funding agencies. (Some federal agencies require a prospectus before accepting a complete proposal.)

Funding sources must also be identified. Federal assistance sources may be found in the *Catalog of Federal Domestic Assistance Programs,* the *Code of Federal Regulations,* the *Commercial Business Daily,* and the *Federal Register.*

Writing the Proposal.   Federal agencies have their own guidelines for writing a proposal; they differ from agency to agency, but the guidelines should be followed exactly. Most guidelines want the following points to be covered in the body of the proposal:

1. *Title page.* Title of project, name of agency submitting application, name of funding agency, dates of project, and names, addresses, and signatures of the project director and others involved in fiscal management.

2. *Statement of problem.* General and specific objectives, documentation of needs and degree of needs, review of literature of programs that have tried to meet the specified needs, and description of any local programs currently involved in meeting specified needs.

3. *Program goals and objectives.* Description of broad program goals and specific, measurable outcomes expected as a result of the program.

4. *Population to be served.* What qualifications will children and/or parents need for inclusion in the program? Will all who qualify be accepted? If not, how will the participants be chosen from those who qualify?

5. *Plan of procedure.* Were several alternative approaches available for solving the problem? If so, why was a particular alternative selected? How will each objective be accomplished?

6. *Administration of project.* What staffing requirements are being proposed? Indicate how the program will be managed by includ-

ing an organization chart and writing brief job descriptions. Include a short vita of the program director. What is the program's capability to conduct the proposed project? Does it have community support? Show a time schedule of activities that will occur from the day of funding until project termination.

7. *Program evaluation.* What assessment devices will be used? Who will conduct the assessment? How and in what format will the evaluation be submitted?

8. *Future funding.* How will the operation of the program be continued at the conclusion of federal assistance?

9. *Budget.* Must show sound fiscal management.

10. *Appendixes.* Job descriptions, director's vita, organizational structure of the early childhood program.

Some agencies also require completion of an application form that usually asks for information about the general subject; to whom the proposal is being submitted; the legal authorization; the project title; the name of the person submitting the proposal; the program director's name, address, and telephone number; the probable budget; the amount of funds requested; and the date the application is transmitted. Some agencies have a form for a proposal abstract, and usually agencies require that this summary be no longer than 200 words. Forms assuring protection of human subjects and nondiscrimination may be required.

Foundation Support.   Many fields, including education, have benefited from foundation giving. Foundations are one of several kinds of nongovernmental, not-for-profit organizations that promote public welfare, including that of young children, through the use of private wealth. Other similar organizations are trusts and endowments. Foundation aid is typically given to support research. Because of increased federal support of education, foundation grants to edu-

cation have decreased in the past few years. Nevertheless, administrators of early childhood programs should investigate foundations as potential sources of funds (see Appendix 7).

Similar to the process of obtaining federal funds, foundation funds are also obtained through submission and approval of a proposal. The foundation's board of directors determines the guidelines for submitting proposals, sets a deadline for application, reviews proposals, and selects recipients.

Fees, Tuition, and Miscellaneous Sources of Funds

For-profit programs operate almost exclusively on tuition and fees and are usually the most expensive. Although some parents pay up to 25% of their incomes for full-day child care for one or more children, a more reasonable and manageable figure is 10% of the family's gross income. Child care is costly; however, for-profit centers do not make huge profits. For example, Stephens (1991) found that for-profit independent centers yielded a net profit after taxes of $11,288 in 1989 and $13,249 in 1990.

Fees and tuition for early childhood programs may be determined in several ways. One method is to determine costs and the amount of profit (or surplus) needed. The cost is distributed among the children on a fixed fee, a sliding scale fee, or two fixed fees for different income brackets. Because children are not in attendance all the time, the tendency is to underestimate income from fees. The administrator may compensate by adding about 15% (Rowe & Husby, 1973) or by using G. Morgan's (1982) method of calculating last year's **utilization rate** (take last year's actual income and divide by maximum income from fees; the utilization rate is a good estimate to use even if fees are increased). Another method was developed by Stephens (1991). He advocates regularly using a break-even analysis (managerial tool that identifies the point at which a program generates enough revenue to cover expenses). He then uses the break-even point to evaluate the impact of various changes, such as raising or lowering tuition.

In addition to carefully calculating fees and tuition, an early childhood program must have definite policies on fee payment. Loss of income may occur as a result of absenteeism or child turnover. The following suggestions might be considered in establishing a fee policy:

1. Set a deposit fee at time of enrollment, to be returned at time of withdrawal if all monetary policies have been met—2 or 3 weeks' tuition or fees is reasonable.

2. Several weeks' notice should be given to withdraw a child. (The fee deposit covers this if notice is not given in advance.)

3. Children on the waiting list must be enrolled within a stated period of time after notification or else their place on the waiting list will be forfeited.

4. Payments may be no more in arrears than the amount of the initial deposit.

5. Payments must be made when a child misses a few days, or a withdrawal notice should be given for an extended absence.

Neugebauer's (1993c, 1993d) reports on his national study gives specific examples of fee policies in for-profit centers.

Funds for early childhood programs have several miscellaneous sources.

1. Public support via a community campaign can help balance the difference between the program's anticipated income and its expenses. For example, some programs qualify for United Way funds (which may be called by some other name). Specific eligibility requirements must be met to qualify for such local funds.

2. In-kind contributions (noncash contributions) are often available through some community resource, such as a charitable orga-

nization. In-kind contributions include program and support program volunteer services, free rent, and payment of utility bills.

3. Endowments may be given in someone's memory, or scholarships may be awarded.

4. The early childhood program may engage in fund-raising projects to supplement income from other sources. A cash-benefit analysis should be done before mounting a fund-raiser. Yields from $10 to $25 per hour, after expenses, are of marginal value; raising funds above $25 per hour is worthwhile. Scallan (1988) provides information on how to conduct a well-orchestrated fund-raising campaign.

BUDGETING

A **budget** is a list of all goods and services for which payment may be made. Budgets are important because no matter how good a program is, it cannot continue to operate if it is not on a sound fiscal foundation. Limited funds require making decisions about priorities, and funding and regulatory agencies require information about monetary functions. No attempt is made to project the expenditure level of a particular program because costs vary with types and quality of services, with the extent of a program, and with the geographic area, but features of budgeting that apply to most programs are described here.

Regulations Governing Budget Making and Adoption

Budgets of small, privately owned programs are developed by their owners/directors and are not subject to regulations unless the program receives some subsidies from public funds, such as food programs. Budgets of larger private and publicly funded programs are subject to many budgetary regulations. Generally speaking, the budgets for these early childhood programs are developed by local program directors or the superintendents of schools for public school programs. Efforts are usually made to include the opinions of various personnel in the first draft of the proposed budget. The budgets are presented to their respective boards of directors or advisors for approval. In addition to the board's approval, regulations may require that the budget be presented to licensing and/or funding agency personnel before approval. In publicly funded programs, funds and thus fiscal control may come from several governmental agencies that will be involved before the adoption process ends.

Developing a Budget

Budgets usually have three components: (a) a synopsis of the program; (b) specifically itemized expenditures for operating the program, including direct costs (items attributed to a particular aspect of the program, such as personnel salaries) and indirect costs (overhead items not attributed to a particular aspect of the program, such as interest on bank loans, utility costs, and advertising); and (c) anticipated revenues and their sources, including in-kind contributions. Before writing the budget, the administrators should list the program's objectives and needs. The program's goals and needs and the fiscal plan should be carefully related and reflected in the written budget. Although data may be presented in many ways, an effective way is to present it under the same headings as the proposed expenditures.

The proposed expenditures are careful estimates of monies required to operate the local program and should be organized under headings that fit the local program. Frequently, publicly funded programs use a specific system designated by their funding agencies. These headings are referred to as the **budget format.** Two types of format are as follows:

1. **Functional classification.** This format assembles data in terms of categories for which money will be used, such as administration, child instruction, parent education, food and health services, and transportation. The advantage of the functional classification format is that one can readily link expenditure categories to program purposes. One disadvantage to this approach is that functional categories tend to be somewhat broad and thus raise questions as to expenditures within a classification. Another disadvantage is the lack of distinct classifications for some items; for example, health services may be listed under several classifications.

2. **Line-item classification.** This format lists the sums allocated to specifics of the program (e.g., salaries of designated personnel, gas, electricity, water, telephone, postage). The major advantage of this approach is that it shows specific accountability for expenditures. A disadvantage occurs if the categories are very fine because the director has little power to exercise changes in expenditures.

Many computer-assisted finance programs are available for use in preparing budgets and in performing and recording financial transactions.

Costs to operate the various components of early childhood programs vary from program to program. The estimated costs are as follows: personnel—69% to 73%; housing, space, and utilities—10% to 12%; equipment—2% to 3%; supplies, excluding food—2% to 3.5%; food—11% to 15.5%; and miscellaneous—the remainder (Abt Associates, 1980; Keener & Sebestyen, 1981; Seaver & Cartwright, 1986; Willer, 1990). As shown, salaries account for the major part of the budget. For-profit centers making the most profits spend a lower percentage of their revenues on salaries (53.7%) than do centers making the least profits (62.4%; Stephens, 1991). Yet, as previously discussed, quality of programs and salaries are highly correlated. Income must increase dramatically to provide the recommended level of compensation for early childhood professionals ("NAEYC Position Statement on Guidelines for Compensation of Early Childhood Professionals," 1990). This correlation brings on the trilemma; that is, quality, staff compensation, and affordability are so interrelated that working on one problem makes it more difficult to solve the other two. Examples of budgets are available for a family child care system (Lauritzen, 1988) and for an infant-care system (Schrag, Khokha, & Weeks, 1988).

After the expenditure section, the administrators should furnish actual figures for the current fiscal year. Any significant difference between current services and expenditures and those proposed should be explained. In planning the expenditure section, administrators should keep the following points in mind:

1. Wages or salaries must be paid on time.
2. A desirable inventory level is one that will carry a program through 2 months of operation.
3. A program may have cash-flow problems. Federal funds do not pay ahead of time for expenses; receipts and proof of money spent are required for reimbursement, and even reimbursement checks may come irregularly.

To prevent cash-flow problems, an administrator should follow these practices:

1. Initial enrollment should not be overestimated.
2. All equipment should not be purchased at the beginning. Equipment estimates should be calculated on cost per use, rather than on the purchase price. For example, it is more expensive to spend $100 on equipment and then not use it than to spend $500 on equipment that will be in constant use.
3. The number of staff hired should correspond to initial enrollment.
4. Enrollment variations—for example, a summer lull—should be expected.
5. The administrator should check with the governmental agency for its reimbursement

schedule, which may be 6 months or longer. He or she should determine whether the local bank will give credit or a short-term loan to state or federally funded centers that receive governmental reimbursements.

The third part of the budget is an estimate of income or receipts. This section should clearly indicate monies from specified sources, such as tuition fees, contributions, and fund-raising projects. An excellent source of useful budgeting information is:

Morgan, G. G. (1982). *Managing the day-care dollars: A financial handbook.* Cambridge, MA: Steam Press (Gryphon).

A budget may be written in many ways with only one absolute rule of budget formulation: Planned expenditures cannot exceed projected income.

TRENDS AND ISSUES

Although most people agree that early childhood care and education yield direct benefits to young children and their families and public benefits as well, a crisis is emerging that centers on financing. The problem has two facets: (a) quality of programs and (b) affordability to parents and/or funding agencies. The problem is simply defined: If quality goes up in terms of wages, child/staff ratios, and program services, programs become less affordable and vice versa. All professionals agree that no trade-off should exist between quality and affordability; however, the reality is that trade-offs are occurring and that quality is, more often than not, the loser. As more and more programs fail to meet even minimum standards, this new question arises: Will the money not spent today, along with major interest, be used to pay the Pied Piper in a not-so-distant future?

A second issue is the problem of funding diversity. The lack of coherence begins at the federal level, where the government cannot decide on one funding mechanism (e.g., tax credit or expansion of direct funding to early childhood programs) and thus has compromised by doing a little bit of everything. This lack of coherence in funding is perpetuated by the literally countless federal agencies that administer federal funds and by the two major state divisions (Department of Health and Human Resources and the Department of Education) that administer some of the federal funds and handle state supplementary revenues. By the time the paltry funds reach the local level, often there is no longer a good match between local needs and goals of programs and no connection (transition) between programs. In all likelihood, there will be duplication of many program services, confusion for parents who will find either too many program options or no viable program for their children, and children who will be placed in programs with inappropriate practices. A tri-partnership among the federal, state, and local levels is needed to create a coherent funding policy that can make the most out of these "bits and pieces."

SUMMARY

Programs for young children are expensive. A quality program will cost $5,000 or more per child per year. Although families seldom pay the absolute costs, early childhood programs can be a large expenditure of the family budget, especially for middle- and low-income families. And, for many families, quality early childhood programs are simply not affordable.

Public early childhood programs are financed through local, state, and federal funding sources. For-profit early childhood programs are supported primarily through tuition and fees.

Budgets must be carefully made in keeping with program goals; that is, expenditures should reflect the goals of the program. Fiscal planning

is important for several reasons. First, the quality of a program is determined to a great extent by expenditures, especially staff compensation. Unfortunately, inadequate staff compensation has resulted in a staffing crisis in child care programs. Second, the central criterion for evaluating a program is often economic (benefits should exceed costs). Third, administrators must show fiscal responsibility.

A major crisis centers on financing. Decisions about funding are decisions about program quality. Any trade-off between affordability and quality will result in a loss of benefits to young children, their families, and all segments of society. Funding diversity outside some framework of coherence further erodes the judicious use of funds for the creation and maintenance of high-quality programs for all children.

FOR FURTHER READING

Barnett, W. S. (1993). New wine in old bottles: Increasing the coherence of early childhood care and education policy. *Early Childhood Research Quarterly, 8,* 519-558.

Guide to successful fund-raising. (1989). Redmond, WA: Exchange Press.

Kamara, B. (1994). Moving forward toward financing a collaborative, comprehensive early childhood professional development system. In J. Johnson & J. B. McCracken (Eds.), *The early childhood career lattice: Perspectives on professional development* (pp. 176-185). Washington, DC: National Association for the Education of Young Children.

Marketing your child care program. (1987). Redmond, WA: Exchange Press.

Morgan, G. G. (1982). *Managing the day-care dollars: A financial handbook.* Cambridge, MA: Steam Press (Gryphon).

O'Donnell, N. S. (1994). Financing an optimal early childhood education and care system: One state's efforts. In J. Johnson & J. B. McCracken (Eds.), *The early childhood career lattice: Perspectives on professional development* (pp. 170-175). Washington, DC: National Association for the Education of Young Children.

Stephens, K. (1991). *Confronting your bottom line: Financial guide for child care centers.* Redmond, WA: Exchange Press.

Stoney, L. (1994). *Promoting access to quality child care: Critical steps in conducting market rate surveys and establishing rate policies.* Washington, DC: Children's Defense Fund.

Tools for managing your center's money. (1987). Redmond, WA: Exchange Press.

Willer, B. (1987). Quality or affordability: Trade-offs for early childhood programs? *Young Children, 42*(6), 41-43.

Willer, B. (Ed.). (1990). *Reaching the full cost of quality in early childhood programs.* Washington, DC: National Association for the Education of Young Children.

Part Three

ꕤ ꕤ ꕤ ꕤ ꕤ

Implementing the Children's Program

ꕤ ꕤ ꕤ ꕤ ꕤ

Chapter 7

❀ ❀ ❀ ❀ ❀

Planning the Children's Program

❀ ❀ ❀ ❀ ❀

✿ ✿ ✿ ✿ ✿

The focus of planning and administering an early childhood program is on planning and implementing children's activities. All other administrative tasks—meeting regulations, establishing policies, leading personnel, planning the physical facilities, and financing—are performed in reference to planning and implementing the children's program. The role of the administrator is to serve as the local program leader in defining the program base (combining knowledge of children and the concerns of parents and staff members), in defending the pedagogy (being knowledgeable and sensitive to program implementation), and in working in collaborative efforts with those agencies in the community that provide support services (e.g., health care, family support, social services).

If a program base has been carefully considered and chosen, it should be implemented in the children's program. Otherwise, the program base is simply meaningless "words." More specifically, the program base of the local program should determine grouping practices and curricular plans—determining curricular goals, translating goals into written competencies, and implementing the curriculum. Regardless of the program base of the local program, careful planning is essential. When programs take on a laissez-faire posture, goals are not met, stress occurs in children and staff, and chaos is inevitable.

CURRICULUM PLANNING

Curriculum is a way of helping teachers think about children and organize children's experiences in the program setting. The long-range goals contained in a program's rationale are explicitly defined in terms of curriculum planning. These plans, including the activities, teaching-learning approaches, and materials used in implementation, become the tools in realizing these goals. Because young children learn from every experience, curriculum for young children includes such things as "discipline" tech-

niques, recess, individual and group activities, routines such as snack time, and all other aspects of a child's day at school, as well as the activities teachers think of as educational (J. Peck, McCaig, & Sapp, 1988). In short, the curriculum that professionals select is the "actual membrane between the world and the child" (Weikart, 1989, p. 28). This chapter looks at different ideas concerning curriculum goals, program competencies, and implementation. Looking at different conceptions of what constitutes the "best programs" for young children should help readers identify these types of programs in their communities and focus on differences in order to understand the program issues. Because of the professional position statements as discussed in Chapter 2, however, this chapter focuses on curriculum more from the constructivist viewpoint than from the academic (behaviorist) viewpoint.

Establishing Goals

Many considerations need to enter into establishing goals. A major decision must be made about the program's psychological and philosophical orientation. Decisions must also be made about goals for meeting individual needs and interests, for exposing children to cultural diversity, and for using computers and related technologies.

Considering Program Orientation. As explained in Chapter 2, early childhood programs of recent years have had one of two orientations. One orientation was to focus on specific academic skills and knowledge needed to succeed in language, reading, and mathematics and in attitudes deemed necessary for success in school and in the world of work (e.g., persistence, delay of gratification). Because these school subject skills were tied to the accountability movement, only the cognitive domain was emphasized. The second orientation was to support children in their efforts to think critically, solve problems, represent ideas, become confident as learners, develop positive self-images, and see from the perspectives of others. This orientation was supported by educators who thought the more academic approach was developmentally inappropriate and by others who saw the need for preparing children for increased complexities and future uncertainties (Hartman, 1977). All domains were considered equally important.

Psychological orientations themselves do not directly prescribe goals of early childhood programs; however, these two orientations tended to embrace different theories (see Appendix 1). The designers of early childhood programs found their program goals and the tenets of a given theory compatible. Many program models having the academic skills and knowledge orientation (e.g., Bereiter and Englemann's Academically Oriented Preschool) embraced the behavioral-environmental view. Creators of the behaviorist preschools thought their disadvantaged (at-risk) children could not risk further delays. Thus, they wanted the children to focus on learning the identified academic content and skills (rather than work to reach their potential in all domains) and to learn at a fast rate to catch up with their advantaged peers. The designers thought their children could miss needed concepts and skills in early childhood programs in which discovery and play were the major teaching-learning methods. Certainly, the practices advocated by the behaviorists placed teachers in charge of their learning environments.

In the meantime, Piaget's and Vygotsky's works were stirring the thinking of others. *Constructivists* was the name used by followers of these developmental theories. These constructivists were soon noting that similar principles had been used by John Dewey in the progressive education movement. Desiring to make application of Piaget's and Vygotsky's works, these constructivists quickly went beyond psychology and epistemology and entered education, including early childhood education, as seen in several major works (L. Berk & Winsler, 1995; DeVries & Kohlberg, 1987; Forman & Hill, 1984; Fosnot, 1989). Although these and other constructivists (e.g., Kamii, Malaguzzi, Lavatelli, and Weikart) made somewhat different applications to early childhood programs, they all held a view in direct opposition to behaviorists. They saw the digesting of adult knowledge and skills and the learning of meaningless symbols (especially "signs") as superficial learning at best. Dewey, too, had criticized the irrelevancy of the education of his day. DeVries and Kohlberg (1987) contrasted the two orientations in this way: Constructivists believe in "forming," not "furnishing," the mind (p. 17).

As discussed in Chapter 2, philosophical orientation refers to the ways in which educational programs are designed to meet social purposes. The philosophical orientation of academic programs seems to center on preparing children to be literate in the so-called basics. Such literacy is deemed necessary for school and work success. Although constructivists advocate literacy, they use a broader value. They believe that children's programs should be consistent with democratic values; that is, schools must be little democratic communities—a practice that has its roots in John Dewey's ideas of school and society (Bredekamp, 1987). Constructivists believe that the rationale for a child-centered, experiential learning, and cooperative endeavors program approach are all consistent with democratic values and are also appropriate for children now and for their future roles as contributing citizens of a free society.

Meeting Individual Needs and Interests. All educators realize that children have individual needs and interests, and these differences must be considered in planning. Administrators of many academic early childhood programs believe that they meet the problem of differences through testing and placement. Some of the early behaviorist models used one teacher for every four or five children who had been ability-tested and placed in a homogeneous group. Constructivists, though, advocate a curriculum that is developmentally appropriate by age/stage and by individual needs and interests (Bredekamp & Rosegrant, 1992). Primarily on the basis of knowledge of child development and on continual observations of each child, teachers plan (and implement) the curriculum to fit each child's needs. Constructivists also use the interests of children to determine theme topics or projects.

In addition, the education of young children with special needs must be considered. Services to these children are required under several laws, as discussed in Chapter 3. Although these children are a diverse group, Bailey and Wolery (1992) have identified seven goals. Other goals of the integrated classroom must include an emphasis on the importance of accepting diversity. The goals on each child's individualized education program (IEP) constitute the goals of his or her program. According to Wolery, Strain, and Bailey (1992), these goals must be very specific and will usually require adult assistance for children to attain them. Services focusing on measurable, specified outcomes are highly compatible with the behaviorist view. Intervention can also be implemented in constructivist classrooms, however, by evaluating the goals and objectives for children with special needs within the context of the goals for other children. Implementing the specialized intervention is not disruptive and is easy in constructivist programs because the curriculum is already so individualized. (Readings on "Inclusion of Children With Special Needs" are found in Appendix 1.)

Establishing a Multicultural/Antibias Focus.

The United States is becoming a more diverse nation, or less of a "melting pot" and more of a "salad bowl" (Bowman & Brady, 1982). Estimates are that, by the year 2020, one in three Americans will be black, Hispanic, or Asian (Kirst, 1986). Moreover, during the last two decades, the gap between the wealthy and the poor widened (McLoyd, 1990). These statistics take on added

significance as concern mounts over the challenges that early childhood programs will face in caring for and educating young children. Thus, teachers need to be aware of potential cultural differences as found in the writings of Bowman and Brady (1982), Hadley (1987), and Hale-Benson (1982). Teachers must also analyze the strengths and needs of families in the local programs, however, because diversity has many dimensions (e.g., race, nationality, socioeconomic status, religion, family composition). More specifically, Longstreet (1978) identified five aspects of ethnicity: (a) language and conventions about when and how language is used; (b) nonverbal language—gestures and body language; (c) orientation mode—behaviors that are not intended to communicate, such as a sitting mode; (d) social values—roles and priorities of a particular group; and (e) intellectual modes, such as learning styles. In short, broad generalizations do not work.

Just as diversity has many dimensions, multicultural/antibias education takes on many approaches. Local programs are often uncertain about which goals to pursue (Derman-Sparks & A.B.C. Task Force, 1989). Sleeter and Grant (1988) have identified and critiqued the following five approaches: (a) programs that help children fit into the educational mainstream, (b) programs that help children identify their biases and develop skills in getting along with many types of people, (c) programs that teach about specific groups of people, (d) programs that infuse ideas about human differences and similarities in a context of respect, and (e) programs that teach children how to fight discrimination. Derman-Sparks (1992) sees the following four goals for a multicultural/antibias curriculum for young children: (a) developing personal and group identity; (b) seeing similarities as well as differences; (c) identifying unfair or untrue images, speech, or behaviors and realizing that such things hurt; and (d) confronting bias by "speaking up." C. Phillips (1994) looks at three distinct ways to plan: (a) Programs can focus on changing negative responses to cultural diversity, (b) programs can begin with the culture of the home and build transitions to mainstream lifestyle, and (c) programs can embrace biculturalism by asking parent assistance in maintaining home cultural values and lifestyles.

The goals of the local program should reflect the needs and strengths of families and the views of the staff. Goals may also fit the cultural composition of the program (see Derman-Sparks, 1992). (The many readings on "Multicultural/Antibias Understandings" listed in Appendix 1 should help local programs in identifying their goals.)

Using Computers and Other Technologies.

Young children now have computers. Clements and Nastasi (1993) reported that the ratio of computers to preschool children in 1984 was 1:125 and that almost a decade later it is 1:12. Undoubtedly, the inclusion of the computer and other technologies in early childhood programs will affect children's learnings by extending and enriching many concepts being offered in the classroom.

Regardless of the program orientation, computers and other technologies will provide several benefits. First, children will learn about technology (e.g., people control technology by making up rules that, in turn, control how technology works; different programs work by using different rules; technology is part of the everyday world). Second, new hardware and software features are permitting children with disabilities to use these technologies (Behrmann & Lahm, 1994). Third, some "manipulatives" are easier to use on the computer than similar concrete objects (Char, 1989; P. Thompson, 1992). Finally, Van Dyk (1994) sees these technologies as allowing teachers to meet the diverse needs of children. For example, Emihovich and Miller (1988) found the visual nature of Logo well suited to African American children's thinking style.

The curricular values of these technologies, however, are dependent on the selected software

and on the degree of technology integration into the curriculum. Thus, program orientation must be considered in all decisions. Programs with academic orientations have primarily used **drill-and-practice software,** a form of software that resembles a ditto sheet or workbook page and is sometimes referred to as an "electronic ditto sheet." Some drill-and-practice software programs are small, separate programs, but others are drill-oriented **integrated learning systems (ILSs),** a super-software package that provides a complete curriculum in a subject, especially reading or mathematics, through an extensive sequence of lessons. Much research has been conducted on the effects of using drill-and-practice software. Children who used these programs increased their reading skills (Hess & McGarvey, 1987) and showed even greater gains in mathematics (Clements & Nastasi, 1992). On the negative side, drill-and-practice use may diminish children's feelings that they control technology (Elkind, 1987a), may cause a loss of creativity (Haugland, 1992), and will not improve children's conceptual skills (Clements & Nastasi, 1993). In the affective domain, drill-and-practice software encourages turn taking (*not* collaboration) and competition (Clements & Nastasi, 1992).

Constructivists prefer **open-ended software,** software in which children are free to do many different things (e.g., drawing but *not* "coloring in" predrawn pictures, word processing, and programming in Logo). Furthermore, because children do not accomplish much when asked to "freely explore" (Lemerise, 1993), distinctions must be made between open-ended projects and "freely exploring" the computer. Research has shown that open-ended software results in gains in intelligence quotients, nonverbal skills, structural knowledge, long-term memory, manual dexterity, and self-esteem (Haugland, 1992). Haugland (1992) also found the gains were greater when children used supplemental activities (activities beyond the computer). For example, when compared with a drill-and-practice group of children, the "off-and-on" group showed gains of more than 50% over the drill-and-practice group in verbal, problem-solving, and conceptual skills although the drill-and-practice group had worked on the computer three times longer. Research has also shown that open-ended software aids critical thinking (Clements & Nastasi, 1992; Kromhout & Butzin, 1993; Nastasi, Clements, & Battista, 1990) and allows for connection of ideas from different areas (Bontá & Silverman, 1993; Winer & Trudel, 1991). Unlike drill-and-practice software, open-ended programs encourage collaboration (Clements, 1991, 1994; Clements & Nastasi, 1992).

Other high-tech opportunities can be provided through digital videos, electronic mats (Char, 1990), computer-controlled robots called "Roamers" (Valiant Technology LTD, Elmhurst, IL), and objects that communicate with computers (Forman & Pufall, 1988). These new technologies may significantly enhance young children's learning in the 21st century.

Translating Goals Into Program Competencies

The goals selected for a local program will be rather broad and general. Only a few statements (often less than 18) will constitute the goals of a program. An example of a **goal statement,** the collection of written goals, is provided by the National Association for the Education of Young Children and the National Association of Early Childhood Specialists in State Departments of Education (1991). Local programs need to further delineate goal statements by identifying competencies and what actions might be taken by teachers to assist children. Curriculum is always planned with specific children in mind. Generally speaking, the competencies identified by academic programs come from the three R's. For example, competencies may include physical knowledge concepts, visual and auditory skills, language development, number concepts, and small-motor coordination skills. Competencies may also be written concerning attitudes,

such as persistence and delay of gratification. Because these concepts are adult prescribed and direct instruction is often used, the competencies are even further defined. For example, specific physical knowledge concepts may be listed as color, shape, size, texture, temperature, taste and odor, volume, weight, position, and motion concepts. Table 7-1 is an example of one of these concepts written in a competency format.

Competencies in the constructivist curriculum are broad in comparison with academic programs. Competencies cover all domains. Broad competencies permit the offering of a wide range of activities. Varying levels of skills and interests are accommodated, and a variety of performance criteria are valued. Tables 7-2, 7-3, and 7-4 show examples of some of the competencies that might be used in constructivist programs.

Implementing the Curriculum

Once program goals and competencies are written, plans for implementing the curriculum must be made. The steps include (a) making the plans, (b) deciding on the delivery system, (c) grouping, (d) scheduling, and (e) determining the responsibilities of staff. All aspects of implementation should be considered simultaneously, rather than linearly, because all facets influence each other. The program base (academic or constructivist) has a major influence on implementation.

Making Plans.   Daily planning includes designing teaching-learning activities and providing for routines. Planning for special times is also important.

Teaching-Learning Activities.   In academic programs, competencies are adult-prescribed. These competencies are carefully sequenced. For example, teaching number concepts may begin with rote counting; this activity is followed by one-to-one correspondence, rational counting, recognition of written numerals, and number combinations (adding) using objects, objects and symbols, and symbols only. Instructional

	Needed Competencies	Sample Curriculum for Preschoolers
Table 7-1 Sample Competency Writing for Academic Programs Age-Group: Preschoolers	Preschoolers need to:	For preschoolers, adults need to:
	Identify eight basic colors (red, orange, yellow, green, blue, purple, black, and brown) by:	
	(1) matching	Provide materials for matching like colors.
	(2) pointing to (3) naming	Using colored paper, (a) name colors and ask child to point to color; and (b) point to colors and ask child to name.
	(4) making secondary colors	Ask child to name primary colors and then secondary colors. Provide paints, color paddles, or crayons and paper and ask child to make secondary colors.
	(5) coloring/painting with colors as directed	Provide a color sheet with directions for child to follow (e.g., color the ball "red").
	(6) sorting color "families"	Provide materials showing various shades/tints of each of the eight basic colors. Ask child to group these into color families or to seriate shades/tints into color families.

plans are usually in the form of lesson plans that have the following components:

1. *Goal statement.* Often a written competency

2. *Performance objective(s).* Statements of what the child(ren) will be able to *do* (given in specific, observable, and measurable terms) at the end of instruction

3. *Procedure.* Teacher inputs and children's actions that help children accomplish the objective

4. *Assessment.* Either a performance of the expected behavior or a product that can be used to measure whether the objective was accomplished

5. *Materials.* A listing of needed equipment/ materials to conduct the lesson

In academic programs, lesson plans are commonly written for language/reading and mathematics. Lesson plans may be written for *all* "subject matter" areas. Many academic programs use a unit approach in which teachers predetermine the activities and write the activities as lesson plans on particular topics. The unit topics are often broad and may even be so general that *theme* would be a better term; in fact, many programs call their units *thematic units*. These units often last 1 week. Information on the topic is given by the teacher to the whole group in a daily unit lesson. Usually, art, music, cook-

Table 7-2 Sample Competency Writing for Constructivist Programs
Age-Group: Infants/Toddlers

Needed Competencies	Sample Curriculum for Infants/Toddlers	
Infants and toddlers need to:	For *infants* adults need to:	For *toddlers* adults need to:
Develop a sense of trust and a loving relationship.	Read infant cues and meet their physical and psychological needs quickly and warmly.	Support attempts to accomplish tasks, comfort when tasks are frustrating, and express joy at successes.
		Respect security objects, such as a favorite toy.
Develop a sense of self.	Call infant by name.	Name body parts.
	Place mirrors on eye level, including near the floor.	Respect children's preferences (e.g., toys and food).
		Support attempts at self-care.
Have social contact.	Engage in face-to-face contacts, use physical contact, and have vocal interactions.	Help children control negative impulses and comfort when they fail.
		Help children become aware of others' feelings.
		Model interactions for children to imitate.
Explore their world.	Take children to their world of experience or bring objects and activities to them.	Provide support for active exploration (be near but refrain from too many adult suggestions for play).
Sample sensory experiences.	Provide pictures and objects to touch, taste, and smell.	Place books and objects on shelves.
		Decorate room with pictures and objects.
Undertake motor experiences.	Provide safe places for movement.	Provide safe places and equipment and materials that aid large-muscle development (e.g., stairs, ramps, large balls, push/pull toys).
	Encourage movement (e.g., place objects slightly beyond reach).	
	Express joy at successes.	Express joy at successes.

ing, and literature, as well as other activities, will more or less reflect the unit theme. (Because teachers design these activities, children may not see the connection.) Often, prereading and mathematics desired competencies are presented as contrived thematic activities. For example, children may match capital and lower-case letters written on laminated paper pumpkin shells and on "detached" laminated paper pumpkin stems, respectively. The child places the correct stem on each pumpkin. Matching is seldom learned in 1 week or even in one semester; thus, the matching will continue but the patterns will change to correspond with the unit themes.

Table 7-3   Sample Competency Writing for Constructivist Programs
Age-Group: Preschoolers and Kindergartners

Needed Competencies	Sample Curriculum for Preschoolers and Kindergartners
Preschoolers and kindergartners need to:	**For *preschoolers and kindergartners* adults need to:**
Feel reassured when fearful or frustrated.	Use positive statements.
	Provide comfort when frustrated and demonstrate needed rules repeatedly.
Become more independent.	Provide opportunities for practicing self-help skills, such as having dressing dolls and providing time and just the needed assistance in toileting and eating.
Make friends.	Permit children to form their own play groups.
	Encourage onlookers to join a play group by suggesting roles for them (e.g., a grandmother in housekeeping center in which the other roles are already taken).
	Model positive social interactions for them to imitate.
Explore their world.	Provide many materials that children can manipulate (e.g., water, sand, blocks, latches) in order to discover relationships.
	Provide dramatic play props for children to use in trying on roles.
Exercise their large muscles and control their small muscles.	Provide equipment to climb on, "vehicles" to ride on, and balls to throw and catch.
	Provide materials to manipulate (e.g., art tools, puzzles, pegs and pegboards, beads to string).
Engage in language experiences.	Talk to, read to, sing to, tell and dramatize stories, and play singing games (e.g., Farmer in the Dell).
	Write children's dictated stories.
	Have classroom charts and other print in view.
	Provide materials (e.g., paper and writing tools) for children to draw, scribble, write, copy signs, etc.
Express themselves creatively.	Provide a variety of art media and various forms of music for creative expression.
Develop concepts of themselves and the world around them.	Provide opportunities to learn skills (e.g., mathematics) and content areas (e.g., social studies, science) in integrated ways (while working on projects instead of times set aside to concentrate on each area).*
Become familiar with symbols.	Provide props for dramatic play.
	Provide books for "reading."
	Write children's dictated stories.
	Provide art and writing materials.
Make choices and implement their ideas.	Permit children to select many of their own activities.
	Provide a physical setting that encourages individual or small, informal groups most of the time.

*Key readings on the content of and teaching strategies for skill and content curricular areas are listed under the heading "Readings on Curriculum Planning" at the end of this chapter.

Table 7-4   Sample Competency Writing for Constructivist Programs
Age-Group: Primary Grades/Levels

Needed Competencies	Sample Curriculum for Children in Primary Grades (Levels)
Children in primary grades (levels) need to:	For children in *primary grades (levels)* adults need to:
Show more self-control.	Prevent overstimulation when possible and help children deal with fears and excitements (e.g., talking about them).
	Set clear limits in a positive way and involve children in rule making.
	Use problem solving to manage discipline problems.
Gain more independence.	Permit children to identify areas needing improvement.
	Support children in their work toward mutually established goals.
Work with other children.	Provide opportunities through small groups for children to cooperate with and help other children.
Explore their world.	Provide materials that are concrete and relative to ongoing projects.
	Plan for field trips and resource people to enhance classroom projects.
Use large and small muscles.	Provide appropriate materials.
Use language as a way of both communicating and thinking.	Provide materials for both reading and writing that will enhance ongoing projects.
	Provide quality literature.
	Read aloud stories and poems each day and ask child readers to share in the oral reading.
	Plan projects, such as preparing a class newspaper or making books.
Express themselves creatively.	Plan ways to integrate art, music, dance, and drama throughout the day.*
Develop concepts.	Integrate curriculum (skill and content areas) in such a way that learnings occur through activities such as projects, rather than in an isolated format.*
Use symbol systems.	Provide manipulatives.
	Assist children in developing skills in reading, writing, and mathematics when these are needed to explore or solve meaningful problems.*
Make choices.	Provide opportunities to work individually and in small groups with self-selected projects and materials for a greater part of the time.
	Involve children in their own self-management (e.g., setting their own goals, budgeting their time, evaluating their own efforts, cooperating with others).

*Key readings on the content of and teaching strategies for skill and content curricular areas are listed under the heading "Readings on Curriculum Planning" at the end of this chapter.

Once topics are chosen and activities are planned, they are repeated year after year. In some schools, all the teachers on a given level (e.g., kindergarten) are using many of the same materials.

Constructivist programs use broader goals. Constructivists do not think of curriculum as specific skills and content to be "covered" by teachers and "absorbed" by children. Rather, constructivists would say that curriculum must be based on the needs and interests of children in the group and thus would not look the same from year to year or from one classroom to the next. Instead of using the teacher-determined thematic units, constructivists use **projects,** extended investigations of real topics. The project approach had its roots in progressive education (Dewey, 1916; Kilpatrick, 1918). New (1990) states that project ideas can result from children's natural encounters with the real environment, mutual interests of children and teacher, and the teacher's response to an observed need in children. In this way, the curriculum is said to *emerge*, rather than be preplanned. The topic of the project is written as a "narrative line" used to convey the direction of children's investigation (e.g., instead of using the broad thematic unit topic of "Water," a project topic might be "How We Use Water" or "The River in Our Town"; Katz & Chard, 1989). Also, unlike the academic programs, competencies in all domains are applied as needed. Criteria used for determining project topics include the following: (a) They must be related to children's own everyday experiences; (b) the study must involve real objects; and (c) opportunities must exist for collaboration, problem-solving, and representation (e.g., artwork, block building, dramatic play).

According to Katz and Chard (1989), projects go through three phases. In Phase 1, teachers begin thinking about a project topic and may even "web" to see the possibilities (see Workman and Anziano's article listed under "Curriculum Planning: General" at the end of this chapter). The teacher checks for children's knowledge

and interests by having the children verbally share their experiences about a topic and express them through representation. Phase 1 lasts about 1 week and forms the basis for modifying plans. During the 2nd and 3rd weeks, Phase 2 occurs. Children gain new information. They get firsthand, real-world experiences and are led to recall and represent details. Children have many opportunities to reflect on their expanding and refining knowledge through multiple representations. A unit grows from the input of children, teachers, and parents and through the introduction of materials (Cassidy & Lancaster, 1993). Phase 3, the concluding project, allows children time to further assimilate their ideas through play or share their understandings. Often, Phase 3 leads to new ideas and new projects. Although teachers may do some formal, teacher-directed activities in the constructivist approach (Katz & Chard, 1989), the teaching activities are very different in the academic and constructivist approaches, as summarized in Table 7-5.

Regardless of the program rationale, several other points need to be considered in planning:

1. *Staff.* Does each staff member understand and accept the program's basic rationale? Does each staff member recognize the rationale of each activity as a step in realizing long-range goals? Is the program adequately staffed in terms of the number and needs of children, the physical layout of the building and grounds, and the nature of the activities?

2. *Amount and arrangement of indoor and outdoor space.* Is it adequate for the planned activities? Is supervision of children difficult because of the vastness of space or its arrangement? Is much time spent in moving equipment and materials between one activity and the next? Do accidents occur frequently because of the amount or arrangement of space?

3. *Availability of resources.* Are appropriate equipment and materials available in sufficient

Table 7-5   Teaching-Learning Activities in Academic and Constructivist Programs

Academic	Constructivist
Content is covered in a "one-shot" weekly thematic unit.	Projects are extended studies (several weeks in length), with concepts revisited many times.
Curriculum is compartmentalized (taught as separate subjects).	Curriculum is integrated.
Content or skills presented in teacher-prescribed lessons are often foreign to children.	Understandings are built as children recall past events in order to understand new ideas (Forman & Hill, 1980).
Skills often do not meet individual needs because the same competencies are deemed necessary for all children and the lessons are teacher-prescribed without child input or choice.	Projects are collaboratively planned. Children choose among the activities.
Competencies learned through separate subject lessons may seem useless beyond the classroom doors.	Competencies gained through projects are learned in the "real" world setting and thus seem more relevant now and in the future.

quantity for the activities? Are community resources available?

4. *Time.* Are too many or too few activities planned? How much time is involved in getting out and putting away, in going to the rest room or to lunch, and in conducting administrative duties such as attendance and lunch counts? Are the blocks of time suitable for the various types of activities?

5. *Backup or alternative activities.* What kinds of activities can be used to forestall problems that result from a lack of interest, inclement weather conditions, unforeseen scheduling changes, or breakage of materials or equipment? What other activities can be used to help children achieve the planned goals and objectives? Can other personnel or material resources be used if needed? Can the same topic be approached by using a different learning modality? Does the planner know where the activity fits within the sequence of skills in case

the "match" is not appropriate—the activity is too easy or too difficult?

6. *Modification of activities for children with disabilities.* Does the desired outcome of the activity need to be modified? Does the child need different materials/different directions? Will the child need special assistance? Will the alternative activity arrangements interfere with the ordinary routines? (Special arrangements should *not* interfere with other children's involvement or call undue attention to the child with special needs.) McCormick and Feeney (1995) provide an example of a checklist form for "activity customization."

Providing for Routines. The academic approach helps children follow set procedures in physical care activities (e.g., children gather for snacks at a given time; children are seated; snacks are distributed in a predetermined way; cleanup procedures are followed). In the constructivist view, physical care activities are used for socialization (e.g., table manners are emphasized during eating) and cognitive enrichment also takes place (e.g., children discuss nutrition and properties of foods—color, size, texture, and shape of foods).

Planning for Special Times.   Special plans must be suitable to children's needs and must be as carefully developed as daily plans. Although daily plans should be changeable, special plans require even more flexibility. Certain routines—especially eating, toileting, and resting—should always be followed as closely as possible. Planning for first days, field trips, and class celebrations are discussed in this chapter because of the almost universal need for making special plans for these situations.

Whether the first days represent children's first experiences in early childhood programs or denote their entry into different programs, children view the first days with mixed feelings of anticipation and anxiety. The first days should be happy ones because they may determine children's feelings of security and attitudes toward programs. Initiation of children into an early childhood program is often done gradually. Preliminary orientation of children to the staff and routine may be handled in several ways:

1. If the group is small, all children may attend for half the normal session.

2. If it is a large group, two plans could be used: (a) The daily session could be divided into two sections, with half the children coming to each; or (b) two evenly divided groups could attend alternate-day sessions, full or half time.

3. A few children may come the first day for the full session or for half the session. Each day, additional children are added. This plan works well with multiage groups. Children who know the routine assist the staff in helping new children make initial adjustments.

4. If all children enter on the same day, additional adult assistance should be secured for the first days.

Generally speaking, planning for first days requires that more time and individual attention be given to greeting children and their parents, to establishing regular routines, and to familiarizing children with teachers and with the physical plant. The following suggestions will facilitate children's orientation to an early childhood program:

1. Name tags help staff become acquainted with the children.

2. For the first days, use equipment and materials and have activities that most children of that age are familiar with and enjoy and that require minimum preparation and cleanup time.

3. Begin to make mental notes (if not written) on strong and weak points in your plans. Also, begin to note the children's strengths and problems, but be careful not to pass judgment too fast or to compare a fall group to last year's spring group.

4. Plan what to do about children who will not leave their parents or who cry after their parents leave.

A field trip is a planned journey to somewhere outside the school building or grounds. Since the early 1900s, early childhood programs have used community resources. Field trips and resource people are used extensively in projects. Thoughtful planning of field trips and for resource people is important both because of benefits to children's learning and because of the added dangers of taking children beyond the building and grounds. Field trips require a great deal of planning and supervision. The teacher must do the following:

1. Help children achieve the goals of the program.

2. Make arrangements with those in charge at the point of destination. Staff should keep a perpetual inventory of local places to visit and of resource people suitable to their program's needs. In compiling such an inventory, list name

of place, telephone number, person at location in charge of hosting visitors, age limitations, time of day visitors are welcome, number of children the place can accommodate, how long a tour takes, and additional comments. Preferable apparel, whether advance notice is required, what children can see or do and what the host provides for children, and number of adults requested to accompany the group should also be stated. Refer to this inventory in making plans. Make arrangements for the visit, and if the host is to give explanations, make sure he or she can communicate with young children. Make arrangements for care of the physical needs of children, staff, and other adults assisting with the field trip, such as locations of places to eat and rest rooms. One staff member should visit the destination before final plans are made.

3. Provide enough qualified supervisors. Good judgment and experience in working with young children are qualities to look for in supervisors. The ratio should be one adult for every four or five children. Supervisors should have a list of the names of children under their care; when they do not know the children, name tags should be worn for easier identification.

4. Obtain written parent consent for each field trip and keep the signed statement on file. Notice the example of a field trip form in Figure 7-1. The signed form is essential because the signature serves as evidence that the parent has considered the dangers of his or her child's participating in the field trip experience. No statement on the form should relieve the teacher and director of any possible liability for accidents. Such a statement is worthless because a parent cannot legally sign away the right to sue (in the child's name) for damages, nor can staff escape the penalty for their own negligence as shown in judicial decisions (*Fedor v. Mauwehu Council of Boy Scouts*, 1958; *Wagenblast v. Odessa School Dist.*, 1988).

5. Obtain permission for the children to participate in the field trip from the director or building principal. Policies of early childhood programs often require that teachers complete forms giving the specifics of the field trip.

6. Become familiar with the procedures to follow in case of accident or illness. Take children's medical records and emergency information records along in case an accident or illness requiring emergency treatment occurs during the field trip.

7. Make all necessary arrangements for transportation and determine whether all regulations concerning vehicles and operators are met.

8. Prepare children by helping them understand the purposes of the field trip and the safety rules to be observed.

9. Evaluate all aspects of planning the field trip and the field trip itself.

Class celebrations of birthdays and holidays are traditional in early childhood programs and require special planning. Celebrations should relate to the program's objectives because "tacked on" celebrations may be counterproductive. A policy should be written to cover the following points:

1. The specific celebrations the children will observe should be determined. Which celebrations are most appropriate to the program's objectives and learning activities? Will children's birthdays be celebrated? Which holidays will be celebrated?

2. If birthdays are observed, the following decisions should be made: (a) the nature of and responsibility for birthday celebrations; (b) whether a parent is responsible or can help; (c) the policy on treats, favors, decorations, and entertainment; (d) the type and quality (homemade or purchased) of food; (e) advance notice needed by the staff; and (f) the use and cleanup of kitchen and dishes. If staff have full or part responsibility, the foregoing decisions, plus the amount of money to be spent, also need to be noted.

Figure 7-1   Field Trip Form

Dear Mom and Dad,

Our class will be making a field trip to the _____ bakery on May 13. A baker will take us on a tour of the bakery. We hope to learn how bread and rolls are made. We will be leaving school at 9:00 a.m. and will be returning in time for lunch. We will ride on a bus to the bakery and back to our school. We all think it will be fun to ride on the bus with our teacher, Mrs. Smith, and three mothers. Please sign the form below to give your permission for me to take the trip.

Jody

- -

I, _____ , give my permission for
              (Name of parent)

_____ to attend a field trip to
              (Name of child)

_____.
              (Destination)

My child has permission to travel _____.
                                        (In a parent's car, on a school bus)

I understand that all safety precautions will be observed.

Date _____ Signature _____

3. If holidays are to be observed, all policy decisions mentioned for birthday celebrations need to be considered.

4. The places where celebrations can take place should be regulated. Are certain areas of the building more suitable for celebrations than others? Can the outdoor space be used, or can children be taken to places beyond the organization's property for celebrations?

Deciding on the Delivery System.   In addition to planning the teaching-learning, the staff must plan the delivery system. The program base will determine not only goals but also the delivery system. The academic approach places heavy emphasis on learning episodes. The constructivist approach often uses both learning centers and learning episodes, but the emphasis is on learning centers.

Designing a Learning Episode.   A **learning episode** is any form of direct teaching involving one child, a small group, or the entire class. Episodes usually focus on rather narrow competencies. With learning episodes, teachers do not wait to take advantage of children's spontaneous activities. Learning episodes make "coverage" of a concept quicker than it would be learned through spontaneous play. Learning episodes can be used to introduce something new to the children and to evaluate their progress.

Prearranging Activities in Learning Centers.   A **learning center** is a place where equipment and materials are arranged, as explained in Chapter 5. The materials and equipment are selected and arranged by the teachers although children also have input into the environment. The environment is designed to inform and stimulate children's understandings and interests in the thematic unit or project. In a learning center, the **unit of instruction** is the **activity.** "Activity" differs from a "lesson" in that it (a) does not have a formal beginning, middle, and end; (b) is often open-ended; and (c) is not teacher-prescribed. Children carry an activity forward and determine its content (Spodek, 1985). In short, learning centers allow children to (a) choose among alternative centers and/or materials; (b) explore ideas in depth, in their own way, and at their own pace; and (c) work with peers and adults. The teacher's role in learning centers is as an observer of each child's needs, interests, and progress and as a facilitator of children's explorations.

Grouping.   U.S. society acknowledges the importance of the individual by encouraging and recognizing individual achievement and by granting and protecting the individual right to think, speak, and act in accordance with personal beliefs; yet, a chaos-free society must have some conformity—some group-mindedness. From birth until a child enters an early childhood program, his or her individuality is fostered, tempered only to some extent by the "group needs" of his or her family. In contrast, because of the number of children involved and the time limits imposed, the program is forced to put some emphasis on group needs except in infant/toddler programs. (Infants and toddlers function totally as individuals in quality programs.) Although the individual is most important throughout the early childhood years, group needs become more important as children advance in age. In fact, it is often said that a child enrolling in an early childhood program is entering a "group setting."

Size of Group.   The term *group* can mean many things, such as the number of children in a room or in a learning center or the number of children assigned to a teacher. The National Association for the Education of Young Children (NAEYC, 1991a) defines **group** as the number of children assigned to a staff member or to a team of staff members occupying an individual classroom or a well-defined physical space within a larger room.

Although group size is not directly related to program base (both those with academic and constructivist orientations have had large and small groups). The literature is replete, however, with the benefits of small group sizes. Children in smaller groups are less noisy and express more positive affect (Cummings & Beagles-Ross, 1983), engage in more fantasy and pretend play (Howes & Rubenstein, 1985), are more creative (Ruopp et al., 1979), rate high in social cognitive measures (Clarke-Stewart & Gruber, 1984), and show increases in cognitive achievement (Glass & Smith, 1979). Small group size is critical to children needing more individual attention—infants and toddlers, children with special needs, and children who are experiencing a lack of continuity in their lives. Appropriate group size influences teachers positively too. Teachers who have small groups use less restrictive management techniques (Howes, 1983), socialize more with the children (Ruopp et al., 1979; P. Smith & Connolly, 1981), and try different teaching strategies (Leitner & Tracy, 1984). The National Academy of Early Childhood Programs recommends a maximum group size of 8 for infants; 12 for toddlers up to 30 months; 14 for toddlers between 30 and 36 months; 20 for 3-, 4-, and 5-year-olds; 24 for 6- to 8-year-olds; and 28 for 9- to 12-year-olds in SACC programs (NAEYC, 1991a).

Adult-Child Ratios.   **Adult-child ratio** is the number of children cared for by each adult. Data from Howes, Phillips, and Whitebook (1992) showed that children in programs that met NAEYC-recommended adult-child ratios experienced more developmentally appropriate activities, as compared with children in programs not meeting NAEYC recommendations. Other advantages of good adult-child ratios over less favorable ones are that (a) infants and toddlers exhibit more competent play behavior (Lamb, Stern-berg, Hwang, & Broberg, 1992) and vocalize more (Francis & Self, 1982; Howes & Rubenstein, 1985); (b) preschool children played more with peers and played in more elaborate ways (J. Bruner, 1980; Field, 1980; Howes & Stewart, 1987) and were more persistent, compliant, and better able to self-regulate (Howes & Olenick, 1986); and (c) teachers were more sensitive to children's needs (Howes, 1983).

The NAEYC (1991a) has concluded that smaller group sizes and lower adult-child ratios are strong predictors of program compliance with indicators of quality, especially appropriate curriculum and positive adult-child interactions. The recommended adult-child ratio within group size is detailed in Table 7-6.

Grouping Patterns.   **Grouping,** or organizing children for learning, is an attempt to aid individual development in a group setting. Grouping has been devised to make caring for and teaching children more manageable and effective. Once curricular plans are formulated and the basic delivery system is chosen, decisions about grouping patterns follow.

1. *Moving children from program to program.* Either a **graded** or **nongraded** approach is used to move children from program to program. The graded approach began at the turn of the century when a uniform age of entry was established for 1st grade and progress through the grades on the basis of age became a regular practice (D. Pratt, 1983).

Table 7-6   Recommended Group Sizes and Adult-Child Ratios

Age of children	\multicolumn{11}{c}{Group size}										
	6	8	10	12	14	16	18	20	22	24	28
Infants & Toddlers											
Infants (birth to 12 mos.)	1:3	1:4									
Toddlers (12 to 24 mos.)	1:3	1:4	1:5	1:4							
2-year-olds (24 to 30 mos.)		1:4	1:5	1:6							
2½-year-olds (30 to 36 mos.)			1:5	1:6	1:7						
Preschoolers & Kindergartners											
3-year-olds					1:7	1:8	1:9	1:10			
4-year-olds						1:8	1:9	1:10			
5-year-olds						1:8	1:9	1:10			
Primary-Level Children											
6- to 8-year-olds								1:10	1:11	1:12	
SACC Children (older than 8 years)											
9- to 12-year-olds										1:12	1:14

Source: From *Accreditation Criteria and Procedures of the National Academy of Early Childhood Programs* (Rev. ed.). by National Association for the Education of Young Children, 1991, Washington, DC: National Academy of Early Childhood Programs. Copyright 1991 by the National Academy of Early Childhood Programs. Reprinted with permission.

The graded system is based on the concept that children of similar ages are homogeneous in ability. Thus, a child enters the graded system at a specified age (usually 6 years for 1st grade) and, at the end of a year's instruction, moves to the next level. The graded system is the most typical practice of elementary schools today. Early childhood programs adhering to the behavioral-environmental approach, as well as other programs, such as "traditional" nursery schools, whose grouping practices are based on the assumption that children should be grouped according to their stage and that age is the best predictor of stage, use this "lock-step" method of moving children.

Recognizing that children of similar ages are not necessarily homogeneous in achievement, constructivists are apt to use a nongraded approach. Goodlad and Anderson (1963) define the **nongraded approach** as a plan that enables children to advance in the sequenced curriculum at their own rates. Early childhood programs that have used nongraded approaches (self-pacing) include Froebelian kindergartens, Montessori schools, and the more recent "open education" models (e.g., British Infant Schools, the New Zealand schools).

2. *Grouping within the classroom.* **Ability grouping** is really achievement-level grouping. It is based on the assumption that both children and teachers profit from a homogeneous-achievement group. Ability grouping is common in programs adhering to the behavioral-environmental position. Thus, it is widely practiced in elementary schools and particularly during reading and mathematics instruction. Ability or achievement-level grouping is also practiced in early childhood programs with academic, "top-down" orientations. As discussed in Chapter 2, these early childhood programs often make placement decisions based on scores from a standardized instrument. Once the children are "placed" (grouped) in separate classes, teachers use their prescribed objectives and activities

with groups of children thought to be similar in abilities. In an attempt to get their instructional groups even more alike, many teachers place children in three or four intraclass groups for prereading, reading, and/or mathematics instruction.

Although there is a movement toward removing heterogeneity in early childhood programs by screening and tracking, there has also been a resurgence of interests in multiage grouping. Lodish (1992) reported that several states mandate multiage groups and that other states are considering such legislation. **Multiage grouping** is also called "family" grouping and is defined as placing children who are at least 1 year apart in age in the same classroom group. Multiage grouping is highly associated with a nongraded approach. Multiage grouping of elementary-age children began with the one-room schoolhouse (Webb, 1992) and was more recently seen in "open" education models. Froebel and Montessori used multiage classrooms, and today family grouping is often seen in programs based on the constructivist approach. Developmentally appropriate practices are based on the concept that curriculum is matched not only to the child's stage but also to the child's individual needs. Katz (1991b) believes that early childhood programs must be responsive to a wide range of developmental levels and the individual backgrounds and experiences of children. Individual needs can be more readily met in family groups.

A great deal of research has been conducted on family-versus-ability grouping. The advantages of family grouping over ability grouping are as follows:

1. Teachers accept a wider range of behaviors and plan activities and schedules for individuals and small groups (Gallagher & Coche, 1987).

2. Children who lag behind children of the same age find it less stressful because the inter-

actions with younger children enhance self-confidence (Mobley, 1976).

3. Social advantages can be noted. Friendships transcend age-mates (Brody, Stoneman, & MacKinnon, 1982); older children use facilitative leadership tactics (e.g., use organizing statements and solicit opinions in play; French, 1984); older children take more responsibility for task completion (Grazinano, French, Brownell, & Hartup, 1976); older children become more self-regulated when put in the role of rule enforcer (Lougee, Grueneich, & Hartup, 1977); older children who are behind developmentally become leaders in groups of younger children, rather than become isolated (Furman, Rahe, & Hartup, 1979); children use classroom learnings in working out sibling relationships (Freedman, 1982); and children are more cooperative (Katz et al., 1990).

4. Some cognitive advantages are also noted. Older children create complex play for younger children and structure play roles for themselves and the younger children (Howes & Farver, 1987). In learning tasks, older children often become the "experts" who assist their "novices" (Slavin, 1987). Older children refine the skills they have learned when they play with younger children (Mounts & Roopnairne, 1987).

Family grouping does have some difficulties that must be worked out. Family grouping requires more teacher skill as a diagnostician of what children need to enhance their development, more planning in terms of managing schedules and equipment/materials, and a greater ability to operate in a team-teaching situation. Family grouping also requires parent education because many parents think their older children are not being stimulated because of the presence of younger children in the group. Several excellent readings on strategies for programs implementing mixed-age groups are available (Katz et al., 1990; Nachbar, 1989).

Scheduling.   Scheduling and planning are equally important because decisions about sched-

uling greatly influence children's feelings of security, the accomplishment of program goals, and the staff's effectiveness. **Scheduling** involves planning the length of the session and timing and arranging activities during the session.

Length of Session.   Early childhood programs traditionally have been half-day sessions. Exceptions have been full-day sessions in child care programs that are becoming increasingly popular because more mothers have jobs outside the home and because of the awareness of the needs of disadvantaged children.

A great deal of controversy surrounds the length of the session. Advocates of half-day sessions cite these advantages: (a) Children do not get as tired; (b) staff have more time for planning, assessing, and working with parents (unless teachers are employed for two half-day sessions), and half-day sessions help prevent staff "burnout"; and (c) young children have an opportunity to be with their parents for part of the day. Supporters of full-day sessions enumerate these advantages: (a) fewer transportation problems, (b) longer blocks of time for lengthy activities, (c) care for children whose parents work, (d) time for staff to get to know the children better, and (e) more time for academic experiences or more time for emphasis on play, depending on the program approach. Some evidence suggests advantages for children in full-day sessions, as compared with those in half-day sessions (Nieman & Gastright, 1981). It is obvious, however, that the quantity of time spent in school is not as significant as the quality of the experience (Jalongo, 1986). Other educators, rather than advocate a half-day or a full-day session for all children, support an individualized schedule to meet the needs of each child. Berson (1968) states, "Kindergartens and their timetables are not sacred; children are" (p. 29).

Timing and Arranging Activities.   Regardless of whether the session is half- or full-day, good schedules for early childhood programs have certain characteristics:

1. A good session begins with a friendly, informal greeting of the children. Staff should make an effort to speak to each child individually during the first few minutes of each session. A group activity, such as a greeting song, also helps children feel welcome. This is also a good time to help children learn to plan their activities. Casey and Lippman (1991) provide some specific strategies on helping children plan.

2. Children's physical needs, such as toileting and eating, should be cared for at regular intervals in the schedule. Special times should be set aside for toileting early in the session, before and after each meal or snack, and before and after resting. Meals should be served every 4 or 5 hours, and snacks should be served midway between each mealtime; however, each child's individual needs must be considered. This aspect of the schedule must remain very flexible.

3. The schedule must provide a balance between physical activity and rest. Young children are prone to become overtired without realizing their need for relaxation.

4. The schedule should fit the goals of the program and the needs of the children as individuals and as a group. A balance should be maintained between indoor and outdoor activities, group and individual times, and child-selected and staff-determined activities.

5. The schedule must be flexible under unexpected circumstances, such as inclement weather, children's interests not originally planned for, and emergencies.

6. A good schedule should be readily understandable to the children so that they will have a feeling of security and will not waste time trying to figure out what to do next.

7. A good session ends with a general evaluation of activities, straightening of indoor and outdoor areas, a hint about the next session, and a farewell. Children need to end a session with the feeling they have achieved something and with a desire to return. These feelings are important to staff too!

Schedules must fit the length of the program day, week, and year. However, *scheduling* usually refers to the timing of daily activities. Every program should devise its own schedule. Programs that serve children of different age-groups must prepare more than one schedule so that each group's needs will be met.

In general, schedules are often referred to as fixed or flexible. Programs place more emphasis on group conformity by having **fixed schedules,** by expecting children to work and play with others at specified times, and by taking care of even the most basic human differences—appetites and bodily functions—at prescribed times except for "emergencies." Often, programs for primary-grade (level) children have fixed schedules. (State departments of education/instruction often specify the total length of a school day and the number of minutes of instruction in each of the basic subjects). Open education primary-level programs are an exception. Academic preprimary programs are very time oriented too. An excellent example of a fixed schedule is that used in Bereiter and Englemann's (1966) program.

Conversely, **flexible schedules** allow for individual children to make some choices as to how to spend their time and require children to conform to the group for only a few routine procedures (e.g., the morning greeting) and for short periods of group "instruction" (e.g., music, listening to stories). Infant programs have perhaps the most flexible schedules of all early childhood programs because infants stay on their own schedules. Child care programs often have flexible schedules because of their longer hours of operation, children's staggered arrivals and departures, and the varying ages of children the center serves. Programs adhering to the constructivist approach also have long, flexible time periods. For an excellent example of a flexible schedule, see the schedule used in Nimnicht, McAfee, and Meier's (1969) program. The NAEYC states that flexible schedules are developmentally appropriate (Bredekamp, 1987). Constructivists believe that the clock should not put constraints on the teaching-learning process.

The following schedule examples for different age-groups are only suggestions; they are not prescriptive. Examples are not given for infants who follow their own schedules or for public school programs adhering to state regulations regarding scheduling.

1. *Toddler schedules.* Toddler schedules usually revolve around the children's feeding and sleeping periods but should include some manipulative activities, outside play, creative activities, and storytime. An example of a schedule for a full-day session is described in Figure 7-2.

2. *Nursery school schedules.* Nursery schools serve children of pre-kindergarten age (usually exclusive of infants) and are frequently operated for half-day sessions. Children arrive and depart at approximately the same times. Generally, nursery school schedules have short group times and longer blocks of time for active work and play periods. An outline of a nursery school schedule is shown in Figure 7-3.

3. *Child care center schedules.* Child care centers have perhaps the most flexible schedules of all early childhood programs because of their longer hours of operation, children's staggered arrivals and departures, and the varying ages of children the center serves. An example of a child care center schedule is shown in Figure 7-4.

4. *Kindergarten schedules.* Kindergartens are usually half-day programs with children arriving and departing at approximately the same times. Kindergartens usually schedule longer group times than nursery schools because public school kindergartens often have more structured activities. An example of a half-day kindergarten schedule is shown in Figure 7-5. Some kindergartens have full-day sessions. An example of a schedule for a full-day session is shown in Figure 7-6.

5. *School-age child care program schedules.* School-age child care (SACC) programs usually follow very flexible schedules. An outline of a SACC program is shown in Figure 7-7.

Figure 7-2   Toddler Schedule

7:00–8:30 a.m.	Arrival, changing or toileting, and dressing babies who are awake, and individual activities
8:30–9:00 a.m.	Breakfast snack, songs, stories, and finger plays
9:00–10:00 a.m.	Manipulative toy activities conducted by staff, and changing or toileting
10:00–11:00 a.m.	Naps for those who take morning naps and outside play for others. (Children go outside as they awaken.)
11:00–11:45 a.m.	Lunch and changing or toileting
11:45–1:00 p.m.	Naps
1:00–2:00 p.m.	Changing or toileting as children awaken and manipulative toy activities
2:00–2:30 p.m.	Snack, songs, stories, and finger plays
2:30 p.m.until departure	Individual activities

Figure 7-3 Nursery School Schedule

9:00–9:15 a.m.	Arrival, group time activities, such as attendance count, greeting song, and brief exchange of experiences
9:15–10:15 a.m.	Active work and play period with child-selected activities in the activity centers
10:15–10:30 a.m.	Toileting and snack
10:30–10:45 a.m.	Group time for story, finger play, music, or rhythmic activities
10:45–11:15 a.m.	Outdoor activities
11:15–11:30 a.m.	Rest
11:30–11:45 a.m.	Cleaning up and discussing the next session; "What we will do tomorrow . . ."
11:45–12:00 noon	Quiet activities and farewells as children depart

Figure 7-4 Child Care Center Schedule

7:00–9:00 a.m.	Arrival, breakfast for children who have not eaten or who want additional food, sleep for children who want more rest, and child-initiated play (which should be relatively quiet) in the activity centers
9:00–9:30 a.m.	Toileting and morning snack
9:30–11:45 a.m.	Active work and play period, both indoor and outdoor. Field trips and class celebrations may be conducted in this time block
11:45–12:00 noon	Preparation for lunch, such as toileting, washing, and moving to dining area
12:00 noon–1:00 p.m.	Lunch and quiet play activities
1:00–3:00 p.m.	Story, rest, and quiet play activities or short excursions with assistants or volunteers as children awaken from naps
3:00–3:30 p.m.	Toileting and afternoon snack
3:30 p.m. until departure	Active work and play periods, both indoor and outdoor, and farewells as children depart with parents
5:00 p.m.	Evening meal for those remaining in center, and quiet play activities until departure

Figure 7-5 Half-Day Kindergarten Schedule

8:15–8:30 a.m.	Arrival and greeting of individual children
8:30–9:00 a.m.	Greeting of group, opening exercises, such as good morning song and flag salute, sharing of experiences, and planning for the day
9:00–10:00 a.m.	Active work and play in the activity centers (with small-group learning episodes in some kindergarten programs) and cleanup
10:00–10:30 a.m.	Music and rhythmic activities
10:30–10:45 a.m.	Toileting and snack
10:45–11:15 a.m.	Group time for stories and other quiet activities (with full-class learning episodes in some kindergarten programs)
11:15–11:45 a.m.	Outdoor activities
11:45 a.m.–12:00 noon	Evaluation of the day, preparing for next session, straightening of room, and farewells

Figure 7-6 Full-Day Kindergarten Schedule

8:15–8:30 a.m.	Arrival, greeting of individual children, and toileting
8:30–8:45 a.m.	Greeting of group, opening exercises, sharing of experiences, and planning for the day
8:45–9:45 a.m.	Active work and play in activity centers (with small-group learning episodes in some kindergarten programs) and cleanup. Field trips and class celebrations may be conducted during this time block.
9:45–10:15 a.m.	Outdoor activities
10:15–10:45 a.m.	Music and rhythmic activities
10:45–11:00 a.m.	Toileting and preparing for lunch
11:00–11:45 a.m.	Lunch
11:45 a.m.–12:45 p.m.	Rest and toileting
12:45–1:30 p.m.	Outdoor or indoor activities
1:30–2:15 p.m.	Active work and play in activity centers and cleanup
2:15–2:45 p.m.	Toileting and snack
2:45–3:00 p.m.	Evaluation of day, preparing for next session, cleanup of room, and farewells

Figure 7-7   SACC Schedule

6:30–7:00 a.m.	Arrival, and activities such as quiet games or reading
7:00 a.m. until departure from school	Breakfast, grooming, and activities such as quiet games or reading
3:00–3:15 p.m.	Arrival from school
3:15 p.m. until departure	Snack, and activities such as homework, tutorials, outdoor play, craft projects, table games, and reading

As mentioned in the characteristics of good schedules, feeding, toileting, and resting were placed on all the foregoing schedules. These health needs should be provided on an "as needed" basis but also should be offered at regularly scheduled times. Flexibility is a must for children with special needs too. McCormick and Feeney (1995) provide excellent suggestions for helping these children prepare for program transitions and follow transition directions. Furthermore, the health care services provided for children with special needs (e.g., ventilating, breathing treatments, tube feeding) should be planned to meet the individual needs of these children and when it causes least disruption to peers.

Determining the Responsibilities of Staff.   In making daily plans, coordination of the responsibilities of staff is essential. Without careful planning, the program will have duplication of tasks, omissions in services, and a general lack of staff efficiency. Criteria to consider in planning the responsibilities of the staff are (a) the goals of the program as they reflect the needs of children; (b) specific organizational policies (the way in which children are grouped for care or instruction); (c) the number of staff involved and the qualifications and skills of each individual; (d) the layout of the building and grounds and the nature of equipment and materials; and (e) the specific plans for the day.

The responsibilities of staff must be in keeping with legal authorizations (e.g., certification)

and with the policies of the board of education or board of directors. The director usually determines the responsibilities of staff; however, in some cases, teachers may assign duties to assistant teachers and to volunteers. Specific responsibilities may be delegated by the director or "lead" teacher, but mutually agreed-on responsibilities in keeping with the basic job descriptions are usually more satisfactory. A periodic exchange of some duties lessens the likelihood of staff "burnout" and the frustration of always having less popular responsibilities, such as straightening the room. Staff morale will be higher and the program will function more coherently and smoothly when all staff members are involved in the program from planning to execution.

TRENDS AND ISSUES

Three major trends and issues seem to be occurring in program planning. One concern is the definition of what constitutes program quality and, more especially, curriculum quality. A second concern is how to implement quality curriculum. The third concern is how to provide children with smooth transitions from home to program and from program to program.

Defining Quality Curriculum

As discussed in Chapters 1 and 2, concern about quality programs, including quality curriculum

(Galinsky, 1990a; Zigler & Lang, 1991), has been growing. Early childhood professionals desire quality programs for all young children. Research supports that quality programs for infants and toddlers result in higher levels of play (Howes & Stewart, 1987) and stronger attachments (C. Anderson et al., 1981). Preschoolers in quality programs have higher intellectual and language test scores (McCartney, 1984) and higher levels of self-esteem (Vandell, Henderson, & Wilson, 1989).

Although every professional agrees on "quality," curricular issues are far from resolved. The emphasis on academic programs has resulted in calls from professional associations to provide young children with "developmentally appropriate practices" (DAP). Research has begun on DAP. The "LSU Studies" (Charlesworth, Hart, Burts, & DeWolf, 1993) found that DAP is a measurable construct. From this research has come the following conclusions about DAP versus "developmentally inappropriate practices" (DIP): (a) Children in preschool and kindergarten DIP classrooms experience more stress than children in DAP classrooms; and (b) very vulnerable for stress in DIP classrooms are children from low socioeconomic families, African American children, and males and particularly those children who fit two or three of these categories. Standardized testing compounds the stress in both DAP and DIP classes. Low socioeconomic status (SES) children who receive "teach-to-the-test" instruction seem to do more poorly on standardized achievement tests and report card grades than low-SES children in DAP classrooms. Finally, attendance in a DAP kindergarten results in positive effects on achievement in the primary grades. Although professional position statements and the research favor developmentally appropriate programs for young children, some professionals are cautioning that DAP alone is not enough. The professionals point out that the curriculum needs to be educationally worthwhile; that is, curriculum for young children must consider the values and knowledge systems of society. (See Chapter 2 for a more extensive review of this issue.)

Implementing Quality Curriculum

In addition to the interests over the content of programs is the concern about whether the quality perspective will remain a goal or become a reality. The status of quality programs is far from clear. In a study conducted in North Carolina, researchers found that about 60% of observed classrooms fell well below the researchers' criterion of quality, 20% near it, and only 20% met it (Bryant, Clifford, & Peisner, 1989). Raver and Zigler (1991) believe that the curriculum and program evaluation measures now being advocated by the Head Start's central administration are narrowly cognitive in orientation. Over 67% of teachers questioned in one study thought that what they did each day was in conflict with their personal beliefs favoring DAP (Hatch & Freeman, 1988b). Results of a national survey show mixed DIP and DAP classroom characteristics. For example, 93% of surveyed teachers indicated that curricular activities were teacher-prescribed, and 80% of teachers reported a separate subject rather than an integrated curriculum (Love et al., 1992).

The cause for lack of implementation of DAP may be pressure by parents for achievement. Such pressure may be caused by the worry of many parents and by the push of fast-track parents. Parent pressure is verified in surveys. For example, Love et al. (1992) reported parent pressure for academic programs. Another survey reported that 60% of 3- to 5-year-old children had parents who taught them letters, words, and numerals, 39% had parents who read to them or taught them songs, 35% had parents who visited a library with them, and 34% had parents who engaged in arts and crafts with them ("Status Report on Childhood in America," 1992). Other causes for the lack of implementation of DAP may include (a) the national mania for accountability, (b) inexperienced staff whose feelings of insecurity lead to dependence on prescribed activities, and (c) the cost of quality programs.

Conversely, we see signs of movement toward DAP. In a survey of early childhood leaders in state departments of education (S. Robinson, 1993/94), 20 leaders said their state's primary focus was a movement toward DAP. For example, fewer placements of kindergartners took place on the basis of test results. These leaders noted, however, that in the absence of state mandates, philosophies and practices vary not only among local school districts but also among teachers serving the same age-groups. One state leader reported that the state curriculum guides promote DAP but that local curriculum guides are primarily skill-and-ability focused. Other leaders reported test-driven curricula. When asked what assistance they needed to help them in their jobs as state leaders, one state department early childhood leader said that the most pressing need was to know "how to truly initiate DAP in public schools" (p. 85).

Providing Smooth Transitions

Transitions represent a period of adjustment. Transitions from home to group programs and transitions from program to program can have a long-term effect on young children. S. Ramey and Ramey (1994) note that transitions are both developmental (children's needs for support differ by age and experience) and transactional (the social interactions of peers, families, programs, and communities that make the program experiences supportive for children) processes.

Concern over transitions has had a long history. Pestalozzi called for teachers to provide continuity with the mother-love relationship (Heafford, 1967). Similarly, Froebel's *Mother Plays* were written to extend the link between home and school. So too, Froebel's *occupations* (e.g., weaving) and other activities (e.g., gardening) were curricular attempts to provide continuity between domestic and school activities (Froebel, 1895). Dewey saw the school as an extension of the home. He wanted the school to help children become aware of their link to the community as citizens in a democratic society (Dewey, 1900). Discontinuities in early childhood programs appeared early, however. Arguments about whether early childhood programs should have a child-centered play approach or should become more structured and incorporate behaviorist ideas surfaced long before the 1960s (National Society for the Study of Education, 1929; Schlossman, 1976). Concern over the lack of smooth transitions led Patty S. Hill to call a meeting of nursery educators to discuss differences in programs (Finkelstein, 1988).

Unfortunately, the problem of transitions is still unresolved. Love et al. (1992) found that transition activities are not widespread. For example, only 10% of schools report systematic communication between kindergarten teachers and children's previous teachers, and only 12% of schools have kindergarten curricula designed to build on the curricula of preschool programs. Transitional activities are a part of formal policy in only 13% of schools. The best transitions occur when pre-kindergarten programs (e.g., state-funded preschools, Head Start programs, special education programs) are housed within the school buildings. B. Caldwell (1991) summarizes five barriers to continuity in early childhood programs of today: (a) differences in curriculum and pedagogy as children change programs, (b) disjunction in program sponsorship, (c) peer turnover, (d) confusion for parents who are told that early learning is important but then are told that some things should not be taught early, and (e) a lack of a coherent early childhood system. Many attempts have been made to improve the effectiveness of continuity. Some of these attempts have been successful. For example, Follow Through was planned to build upon Head Start, and children in Follow Through programs did sustain Head Start benefits better than non-Follow Through children (Copple, Cline, & Smith, 1978). Other projects that received good results from smooth transitions were Ramey's Abecedarian Project (C. Ramey, 1977) and Caldwell's Kramer Project (Elardo & Caldwell, 1974). Many suggestions are now available to help implement smooth transitions. References with suggestions for transitions include the following:

Bredekamp, S. (1987). *Easing the transitions from preschool to kindergarten.* Washington, DC: U.S. Department of Health and Human Services.

Hains, A. H., Fowler, S. A., Schwartz, I. S., Kottwitz, E., & Rosenkoetter, S. (1989). A comparison of preschool and kindergarten teacher expectations for school readiness. *Early Childhood Research Quarterly, 4,* 75-88.

Hubbell, R. (1987). *Final report: The transition of Head Start children into public schools* (Vol. 1). Washington, DC: U.S. Department of Health and Human Services, CSR, Inc.

Love, J. M., Logue, M. E., Trudeau, J. V., & Thayer, K. (1992). *Transitions to kindergarten in American schools: Final report of the National Transition Study.* Washington, DC: U.S. Department of Education, Office of Policy and Planning.

Mangione, P. L. (Ed.). (1992). *Links to success: New thinking on the connections between preschool, school, and community. A readings symposium. Proceedings paper.* Washington, DC: Office of Educational Research and Improvement. (ERIC Document Reproduction Service No. ED 342 499)

Ramey, S. L., & Ramey, C. T. (1994). The transition to school: Why the first few years matter for a lifetime. *Phi Delta Kappan, 76*(3), 194-198.

SUMMARY

Curriculum is a way of helping teachers think about children and organize the child's experience in the program setting. The first step in curriculum planning is to establish goals based on the program orientation. Other considerations include children's individual needs and interests, the need for a multicultural/antibias focus, and the employment of technology. From these sources, goal statements must be generated.

Goal statements are then translated into written program competencies that further refine the broad goal statements. The final step is to plan for implementation of the curriculum. Teaching-learning activities, routines, and special plans must be carefully developed, along with a delivery system that further aids children in reaching program goals. Grouping and scheduling children aid in the implementation of the curriculum. Finally, equitable staff responsibilities must be determined.

Three trends and issues seem to be occurring in program planning. These trends and issues are concerned with exactly what constitutes quality curriculum, how to implement a quality program, and how to make young children's transitions "seamless" as they move from home to program and from one early childhood program to another. Attempts are being made to resolve all of these issues, but many barriers are still to be removed.

FOR FURTHER READING

Caruso, D. A. (1988). Play and learning in infancy: Research and implications. *Young Children, 43*(6), 63-70.

Cassidy, D. J., Kimes, B., & Benion, P. E. (1987). Early childhood planning: A developmental perspective. *Childhood Education, 64*(1), 2-8.

Greenberg, P. (1990). Why not academic preschool? *Young Children, 45*(2), 70-80.

Greenberg, P. (1992). Why not academic preschool? Part 2. Autocracy or democracy in the classroom? *Young Children, 47*(3), 54-64.

Kagan, S. L. (1990). Readiness 2000: Rethinking rhetoric and responsibility. *Phi Delta Kappan, 72*(4), 272-279.

Katz, L. G., & Chard, S. C. (1989). *Engaging children's minds: The project approach.* Norwood, NJ: Ablex.

Kenney, M. T. (1991). Long-term projects. In B. Spodek (Ed.), *Educationally appropriate kindergarten practices* (pp. 41-51). Washington, DC: National Education Association.

National Association of State Boards of Education. (1988). *Right from the start: A report of the NASBE Task Force on Early Childhood Education.* Alexandria, VA: Author.

Peck, J. T., McCaig, G., & Sapp, M. E. (1988). *Kindergarten policies: What is best for young children?* Washington, DC: National Association for the Education of Young Children.

Spodek, B., & Saracho, O. N. (Eds.). (1991). *Issues in early childhood curriculum: Yearbook in early childhood education* (Vol. 2). New York: Teachers College Press.

READINGS ON CURRICULUM PLANNING

General

Adcock, D., & Segal, M. (1983). *Play together, grow together: A cooperative curriculum for teachers of young children.* White Plains, NY: Mailman Press.

Berk, L. E., & Winsler, A. (1995). *Scaffolding children's learning: Vygotsky and early childhood education.* Washington, DC: National Association for the Education of Young Children.

Bredekamp, S., & Rosegrant, T. (Eds.). (1992). *Reaching potentials: Appropriate curriculum and assessment for young children* (Vol. 1). Washington, DC: National Association for the Education of Young Children.

Campbell, P., & Fein, G. (Eds.). (1986). *Young children and microcomputers.* Englewood Cliffs, NJ: Prentice Hall.

Cartwright, S. (1993). Cooperative learning can occur in any kind of program. *Young Children, 48*(2), 12-14.

Cartwright, S. (1987). Group endeavor in nursery school can be valuable learning. *Young Children, 42*(5), 8-11.

Clements, D. H. (1985). *Computers in early and primary education.* Englewood Cliffs, NJ: Prentice Hall.

Crary, E. (1984). *Kids can cooperate: A practical guide to teaching problem solving.* New York: Parenting Press.

Dodge, D. T., Koralek, D. G., & Pizzolongo, P. J. (1991). *Caring for preschool children* (Vols. 1 & 2). Washington, DC: Teaching Strategies.

Education Testing Service. (n.d.). *Strategies for teaching critical thinking across the curriculum.* Princeton, NJ: Author. (Request adaptation for elementary school educators, ETS, School Service, Mailstop 88D, Princeton, NJ 08541-0001)

Fluegelman, A. (Ed.). (1989). *The new games book.* Garden City, NY: Doubleday.

Frick, T. W. (1991). *Restructuring education through technology.* Bloomington, IN: Phi Delta Kappa Foundation.

Greenwald, N. L. (1991). A user-friendly model to teach thinking. *Teaching Pre-K-8, 21*(5), 63-67.

Haiman, P. E. (1991). Viewpoint. Developing a sense of wonder in young children: There is more to early childhood education than cognitive development. *Young Children, 46*(6), 52-53.

Hendrick, J. (1992). When does it all begin? Teaching the principles of democracy in the early years. *Young Children, 47*(3), 51-53.

Jones, E., & Nimmo, J. (1994). *Emergent curriculum.* Washington, DC: National Association for the Education of Young Children.

Kamii, C., & DeVries, R. (1980). *Group games in early education: Implications of Piaget's theory.* Washington, DC: National Association for the Education of Young Children.

Katz, L. G., & Chard, S. C. (1989). *Engaging children's minds: The project approach.* Norwood, NJ: Ablex.

Kelman, A. (1990). Choices for children. *Young Children, 45*(3), 42-45.

Kohn, A. (1991). Group grade grubbing versus cooperative learning. *Educational Leadership, 48*(5), 83-87.

Kotloff, L. J. (1993). Fostering cooperative group spirit and individuality: Examples from a Japanese preschool. *Young Children, 48*(3), 17-23.

Murphy, D. G., & Goffin, S. G. (1992). *Project Construct: A curriculum guide.* Jefferson City: Missouri Department of Elementary and Secondary Education.

National Association for the Education of Young Children & National Association of Early Childhood Specialists in State Departments of Education. (1991). Guidelines for appropriate curriculum content and assessment in programs serving children ages 3 through 8. *Young Children, 46*(3), 21-38.

Nourot, P. M., & Van Hoorn, J. L. (1991). Research in review: Symbolic play in preschool and primary settings. *Young Children, 46*(6), 40-50.

Onosko, J. (1992). Exploring the thinking of thoughtful teachers. *Educational Leadership, 49*(7), 34-38.

Read, K. H. (1992). The nursery school: A human relations laboratory. *Young Children, 47*(3), 4-5.

Resnick, L. B. (1987). *Education and learning to think.* Washington, DC: National Academy Press.

Schmuck, R. A., & Schmuck, P. A. (1988). *Group processes in the classroom* (4th ed.). Dubuque, IA: Wm. C. Brown.

Seefeldt, C. (1989). How good is your kindergarten curriculum? *Principal, 68*(5), 11-15.

Slavin, R. E. (1991). Synthesis of research on cooperative learning. *Educational Leadership, 48*(5), 71-82.

Smith, C. A. (1979). Puppetry and problem-solving skills. *Young Children, 34*(3), 4-11.

Sobel, J. (1983). *Everybody wins: 393 non-competitive games for young children.* New York: Walker.

Tudge, J., & Caruso, D. (1988). Cooperative problem solving in the classroom: Enhancing children's cognitive development. *Young Children, 44*(1), 46-52.

Workman, S., & Anziano, M. C. (1993). Curriculum webs: Weaving connections from children to teachers. *Young Children, 48*(2), 4-9.

Language

Dailey, K. A. (1991). *Writing in kindergarten: Helping parents understand the process.* Wheaton, MD: Association for Childhood Education International.

Dyson, A. H. (1988). Appreciate the drawing and dictating of young children. *Young Children, 43*(3), 25-32.

Enriching classroom diversity with books for children, in-depth discussion of them, and story-extension activities. *Young Children, 48*(3), 10-12.

Goodman, K. S., Goodman, Y. M., & Hood, W. (1989). *The whole language evaluation book.* Portsmouth, NH: Heinemann.

Jalongo, M. R. (1988). *Young children and picture books: Literature from infancy to six.* Washington, DC: National Association for the Education of Young Children.

Kamii, C., Manning, M., & Manning, G. (Eds.). (1991). *Early literacy: A constructivist foundation for whole language.* Washington, DC: National Education Association.

Lamme, L. L. (1979). Handwriting in an early childhood curriculum. *Young Children, 35*(1), 22-27.

Lamme, L. L., & McKinley, L. (1992). Creating a caring classroom with children's literature. *Young Children, 48*(1), 65-71.

Mavrogenes, N. A. (1990). Helping parents help their children become literate. *Young Children, 45*(4), 4-9.

Miller, J. (1990). Three-year-olds in their reading corner. *Young Children, 46*(1), 51-54.

Mills, H., & Clyde, J. A. (1991). Children's success as readers and writers: It's the teacher's beliefs that make the difference. *Young Children, 46*(2), 54-59.

Raines, S. C., & Canady, R. J. (1989). *Story s-t-r-e-t-c-h-e-r-s: Activities to expand children's favorite books.* Mt. Rainier, MD: Gryphon House.

Raines, S. C., & Canady, R. J. (1991). *More story s-t-r-e-t-c-h-e-r-s.* Mt. Rainier, MD: Gryphon House.

Schickedanz, J. A. (1986). *More than the ABCs: The early stages of reading and writing.* Washington, DC: National Association for the Education of Young Children.

Walton, S. (1989). Katy learns to read and write. *Young Children, 44*(5), 52-57.

Wolter, D. L. (1992). Whole group story reading? *Young Children, 48*(1), 72-75.

Mathematics and Science

Baker, D., Semple, C., & Stead, T. (1990). *How big is the moon? Whole math in action.* Portsmouth, NH: Heinemann.

Baroody, A. J. (1989). *A guide to teaching mathematics in the primary grades.* Needham Heights, MA: Allyn & Bacon.

Charlesworth, R., & Lind, K. K. (1995). *Math and science for young children* (2nd ed.). Albany, NY: Delmar.

Dighe, J. (1993). Children and the earth. *Young Children, 48*(3), 58-63.

EQUALS Staff, Assessment Committee of the California Mathematics Council Campaign for Mathematics, & Stenmark, J. K. (1989). *Assessment alternatives in mathematics: An overview of assessment techniques that promote learning.* Berkeley: University of California Regents.

Forman, G., & Kaden, M. (1987). Research on science education for young children. In C. Seefeldt (Ed.), *Early childhood curriculum: A review of current research* (pp. 141-164). New York: Teachers College Press.

Goldhaber, J. (1992). Sticky to dry; red to purple: Exploring transformation with play dough. *Young Children, 48*(1), 26-28.

Greenberg, P. (1993). Ideas that work with young children. How and why to teach all aspects of preschool and kindergarten math naturally, democratically, and effectively (for teachers who don't believe in academic programs, who do believe in educational excellence, and who find math boring to the max)—Part 1. *Young Children, 48*(4), 75-84.

Hein, G. E. (Ed.). (1990). *The assessment of hands-on elementary science programs.* Grand Forks: North Dakota Study Group on Evaluation.

Holt, B-G. (1989). *Science with young children* (Rev. ed.). Washington, DC: National Association for the Education of Young Children.

Kamii, C. (1982). *Number in preschool and kindergarten.* Washington, DC: National Association for the Education of Young Children.

Kamii, C. (1983). *Young children reinvent arithmetic.* New York: Teachers College Press.

Kamii, C. (1989). *Young children continue to invent arithmetic: Second grade.* New York: Teachers College Press.

Kamii, C., & DeVries, R. (1978). *Physical knowledge in preschool education: Implications of Piaget's theory.* Englewood Cliffs, NJ: Prentice Hall.

Leeb-Lundberg, K. (1985). *Mathematics is more than counting.* Wheaton, MD: Association for Childhood Education International.

McCracken, J. B. (1987). *More than 1, 2, 3: The real basics of mathematics.* Washington, DC: National Association for the Education of Young Children.

McIntyre, M. (1984). *Early childhood and science.* Washington, DC: National Science Teachers Association.

National Association of State Boards of Education. (1991). *It all adds up: Science and mathematics education policies for the future.* Alexandria, VA: Author.

National Council of Teachers of Mathematics. (1989). *Curriculum and evaluation: Standards for school mathematics.* Reston, VA: Author.

Payne, J. N. (Ed.). (1990). *Mathematics for the young child.* Reston, VA: National Council of Teachers of Mathematics.

Perry, G., & Rivkin, M. (1992). Teachers and science. *Young Children, 47*(4), 9-16.

Raizen, S., Baron, J. B., Champagne, A. B., Haertel, E., Mullis, I. N. V., & Oakes, J. (1989). *Assessment in elementary school science education.* Washington, DC: National Center for Improving Science Education.

Rivkin, M. (1991). "Feeling is first" in early childhood science. *Teaching Education, 3*(2), 171-176.

Rivkin, M. (Ed.). (1992). Science is a way of life. *Young Children, 47*(4), 4-8.

Social Studies

Beane, J. A. (1990). *Affect in the curriculum: Toward democracy, dignity, and diversity.* New York: Teachers College Press.

Brophy, J. (1990). Teaching social studies for understanding and higher-order applications. *Elementary School Journal, 90,* 351-417.

Carlsson-Paige, N., & Levin, D. E. (1992). Making peace in violent times: A constructivist approach to conflict resolution. *Young Children, 48*(1), 4-13.

Curry, N. E., & Johnson, C. N. (1990). *Beyond self-esteem: Developing a genuine sense of human value.* Washington, DC: National Association for the Education of Young Children.

Dimidjian, V. J. (1989). Holidays, holy days, and wholly dazed. *Young Children, 44*(6), 70-75.

Lickona, T. (1989). *Educating for character: How our schools can teach respect and responsibility.* New York: Bantam.

National Commission on Social Studies in the Schools. (1989). *Charting a course: Social studies for the twenty-first century.* Washington, DC: Author.

Purpel, D. E. (1989). *The moral and spiritual crisis in education.* New York: Bergin & Garvey.

Richards, B. (1976). Mapping: An introduction to symbols. *Young Children, 31*(2), 145-156.

Riley, S. S. (1984). *How to generate values in young children: Integrity, honesty, individuality, self-confidence, and wisdom.* Washington, DC: National Association for the Education of Young Children.

Seefeldt, C. (1989). *Social studies for the preschool-primary child* (3rd ed.). New York: Merrill/Macmillan.

The Arts

Barclay, K. D., & Walwer, L. (1992). Linking lyrics and literacy through song picture books. *Young Children, 47*(4), 76-85.

Bos, B. (1984). *Please don't move the muffin tins: A hands-off guide to art for the young child.* Roseville, CA: Turn-the-Page Press.

Clemens, S. (1991). Art in the classroom: Making every day special. *Young Children, 46*(2), 4-11.

Dean, J., & Cross, I. L. (1992). Teaching basic skills through art and music. *Phi Delta Kappan, 73,* 613-618.

Dixon, G. T., & Chalmers, F. G. (1990). The expressive arts in education. *Childhood Education, 67,* 12-17.

Feeney, S., & Moravcik, E. (1987). A thing of beauty: Aesthetic development in young children. *Young Children, 42*(6), 6-15.

Hoffman, S., & Lamme, L. (Eds.). (1989). *Learning from the inside out: A guide to the expressive arts.* Wheaton, MD: Association for Childhood Education International.

Jalongo, M. R., & Collins, M. (1985). Singing with young children! Folk singing for nonmusicians. *Young Children, 40*(2), 17-22.

Lasky, L., & Mukerji, R. (1980). *Art: Basics for young children.* Washington, DC: National Association for the Education of Young Children.

National Dance Association. (1991). *Early childhood creative arts.* Reston, VA: American Alliance for Health, Physical Education, Recreation and Dance.

Schirrmacher, R. (1986). Talking with young children about their art. *Young Children, 41*(5), 3-7.

Wolf, J. (1992). Let's sing it again: Creating music with young children. *Young Children, 47*(2), 56-61.

Blockbuilding, Dramatic Play, and Mud, Sand, Water Play

Barbour, N., Webster, T. D., & Drosdeck, S. (1987). Sand: A resource for the language arts. *Young Children, 42*(2), 20-25.

Bender, J. (1978). Large hollow blocks: Relationship of quantity to block building behaviors. *Young Children, 33*(6), 17-23.

Betz, C. (1992). The happy medium. *Young Children, 47*(3), 34-35.

Cartwright, S. (1990). Learning with large blocks. *Young Children, 45*(3), 38-41.

Griffing, P. (1983). Encouraging dramatic play in early childhood. *Young Children, 38*(2), 13-22.

Hill, D. M. (1977). *Mud, sand, and water.* Washington, DC: National Association for the Education of Young Children.

Hirsch, E. S. (Ed.). (1984). *The block book.* Washington, DC: National Association for the Education of Young Children.

Kinsman, C. A., & Berk, L. E. (1979). Joining the block and housekeeping areas: Changes in play and social behavior. *Young Children, 35*(1), 66-75.

Segal, M., & Adcock, D. (1981). *Just pretending: Ways to help children grow through imaginative play.* Englewood Cliffs, NJ: Prentice Hall.

Play

Bergen, D. (1987). *Play as a medium for learning and development.* Portsmouth, NH: Heinemann.

Christie, J. F., & Wardle, F. (1992). How much time is needed for play? *Young Children, 47*(3), 28-32.

Engstrom, G. (1971). *The significance of the young child's motor development.* Washington, DC: National Association for the Education of Young Children.

Fein, G., & Rivkin, M. (Eds.). (1986). *The young child at play: Reviews of research* (Vol. 4). Washington, DC: National Association for the Education of Young Children.

Frost, J., & Sunderlin, S. (1985). *When children play.* Wheaton, MD: Association for Childhood Education International.

Miller, K. (1989). *The outside play and learning book.* Mt. Rainier, MD: Gryphon House.

Monighan-Nourot, P., Scales, B., Van Hoorn, J., & Almy, M. (1987). *Looking at children's play.* New York: Teachers College Press.

Poest, C. A., Williams, J. R., Witt, D. D., & Atwood, M. E. (1990). Challenge me to move: Large muscle development in young children. *Young Children, 45*(5), 4-10.

Rogers, C., & Sawyers, J. (1988). *Play in the lives of children.* Washington, DC: National Association for the Education of Young Children.

Sinclair, C. B. (1973). *Movement of the young child.* New York: Merrill/Macmillan.

Sullivan, M. (1982). *Feeling strong, feeling free: Movement exploration for young children.* Washington, DC: National Association for the Education of Young Children.

Wardle, F. (1995). Alternatives . . . Bruderhof education: Outdoor school. *Young Children, 50*(3), 68-73.

Chapter 8

❀ ❀ ❀ ❀

Providing Nutrition, Health, and Safety Services

❀ ❀ ❀ ❀

❀ ❀ ❀ ❀ ❀

Increasing emphasis on nutrition, health, and safety in society has resulted in expanded programs for young children. Nutrition, health, and safety are highly interrelated. For example, long-time inadequate nutrition affects health status, and inadequate nutrition for a short period of time can affect a child's alertness and thus safety. A comprehensive approach to nutrition, health, and safety services in early childhood programs requires the provision of services to children, a healthy and safe environment, and education to children, staff, and parents. This comprehensive approach is supported by the third objective of Goal 1 of *America 2000* (1991), which states, "Children will receive nutrition and health care needed to arrive at school with healthy minds and bodies, and the number of low birthweight babies will be significantly reduced through enhanced prenatal health systems" (p. 61). Thus, today's emphasis is on total health and safety, rather than on only control of contagion.

NUTRITION

Because of the effects of hunger and malnutrition on young children, early childhood programs are becoming more concerned about nutrition. Adequate nutrition is essential for the fulfillment of one's potential for physical or biological growth and development and for maintenance of the body. During periods of rapid growth, a child is especially unprotected against malnutrition. The permanent effects of malnutrition on brain size and composition would most likely occur before 4½ years of age and especially before 1 year of age (Winnick, 1976). The effects of malnutrition depend not only on the point at which deprivation occurs but also on its severity and the nutrients involved. Because malnutrition interferes with development of the central nervous system, it also affects mental functioning; it can impair learning during critical periods and can change motivation and other aspects of behavior (Norwood

1984; Pertz & Putnam, 1982). And nutrition habits, like many others, are formed early in life.

Current nutrition programs are broadly based, encompassing more than food preparation, serving, and cleanup. The comprehensive approach is evidenced in the Nutrition Education and Training Act of 1966 (Section 19, as amended, 42 U.S.C. 1988), which provides funds to states and local programs that encourage the dissemination of nutrition information to children participating, or eligible to participate, in school lunch and related child nutrition programs. Four broad objectives seem to be an integral part of the early childhood nutrition programs: (a) planning food service, (b) identifying children's nutrition problems, (c) implementing nutrition education for children, and (d) assisting parents in meeting children's nutrition needs.

Planning Food Service

Planning food service for an early childhood program is comprehensive. It involves providing and serving nutritious meals and snacks, hiring staff, providing facilities and equipment, purchasing food, and meeting sanitation requirements.

Providing and Serving Nutritious Meals and Snacks. A program must provide for a nutritionally adequate diet. Specific nutrition requirements depend on the total number of hours a child spends in a program, the licensing laws of the state, whether the program is following the United States Department of Agriculture (USDA) Child and Adult Care Food Program, or whether the program is a Head Start program and must follow its guidelines. Although licensing regulations contain minimum nutrition requirements, a 1969 White House Conference on Food, Nutrition, and Health recommended that child care programs provide 80% of the child's total nutrition requirements. Snacks are important because they make up 22% of all foods young children consume daily (Beyer & Morris, 1974). Appetites vary among young children too.

A nutrition program should expose children to a wide variety of foods so that they will develop a taste for many foods (Birch, Johnson, & Fisher, 1995), should provide for direct dietary consultation to meet the needs of children, and should provide menus to parents to aid in food selection for the remaining part of the child's diet. Not only do providing and serving nutritious meals and snacks feed the child's body and mind, but meals and snacks also provide an opportunity for the child to learn about new foods, new ways foods can be served, and social amenities.

Planners of food services for young children in early childhood programs need to consider age of the children and any special needs. Although it is imperative to check all regulations, some general guidelines follow.

Infants.   Because infants are so vulnerable nutritionally, program administrators should seek medical advice for each infant. The USDA Infant Meal Pattern is given in Table 8-1. When infants are ready to begin solid foods, offer only one new food at a time and continue for 3 or 4 days before you introduce another food. Start with 1 to 2 tsps and gradually work up to the recommended amounts. Introduce cereals first, then strained fruits and vegetables, and finally strained meats. Fruit juices must also be offered one at a time. Dried bread or a teething biscuit helps teething babies. Mashed and finely chopped foods are introduced once babies can chew.

Practices to follow in feeding infants include the following:

1. Wash your hands before getting formula, food, or items used in feeding.

2. Change the infant's diaper. Then, wash your hands again.

3. Before feeding, place a bib or similar article under the infant's chin.

4. Hold infants under 6 months of age comfortably in a semi-sitting position. Eye contact and cuddling are essential to affective development. Never prop bottles. Babies taking bottles in a reclining position are more prone to choking and developing ear infections and dental caries than infants who take their bottles in a semi-sitting position. Older infants may be fed in low chairs or feeding tables. Adults must supervise at all times.

5. If solid foods are to be offered, present them before the major portion of the formula or breast milk is given.

6. Discard opened or leftover formula.

7. Keep infants upright for 15 minutes after feeding to help avoid regurgitation of formula, breast milk, or food.

8. When returning young infants to bed, place them on their right sides to prevent aspirating formula or breast milk.

9. Allow older infants to explore and handle food and try to feed themselves.

10. Use great patience in beginning spoon feeding. Babies push food from their mouths as a reflexive action of the tongue.

11. Clean the infants' hands, faces, and necks after feeding.

Young Children.   Meal and snack patterns are based on the USDA's 1992 Food Guide Pyramid, which replaced the 1956 Basic Four Food Group Plan as a guide for making daily food choices. Young children must learn to eat a variety of nutritious foods. Table 8-2 is a meal and snack plan developed by the USDA.

The following are some other practices for planning enjoyable meals and snacks:

1. Large portions of food are overwhelming to children; serve food in small portions and permit second helpings.

2. When serving a new or unpopular food, try the following: (a) Serve a tiny portion with a more generous portion of a popular food, (b) introduce only one new food at a time, (c) intro-

Table 8-1   Child Care Infant Meal Pattern

Birth–3 Months	4–7 Months	8–11 Months
Breakfast		
4–6 fl oz formula* or breast milk	4–8 fl oz formula* or breast milk	6–8 fl oz formula*, breast milk, or whole milk
	0–3 tbsp infant cereal[+] (optional)	2–4 tbsp infant cereal[+]
		1–4 tbsp fruit and/or vegetable
Lunch or Supper		
4–6 fl oz formula* or breast milk	4–8 fl oz formula* or breast milk	6–8 fl oz formula*, breast milk, or whole milk
	0–3 tbsp infant cereal[+] (optional)	2–4 tbsp infant cereal[+]
		and/or
	0–3 tbsp fruit and/or vegetable (optional)	1–4 tbsp meat, fish, poultry, egg yolk, or cooked dry beans or peas, or ½–2 oz cheese
		or
		1–4 oz cottage cheese, cheese food, or cheese spread
		¼ tbsp fruit and/or vegetable
Supplement		
4–6 fl oz formula* or breast milk	4–6 fl oz formula* or breast milk	2–4 fl oz formula*, breast milk, whole milk, or juice[#]
		0–½ bread slice or
		0–2 crackers (optional)[§]

* Iron-fortified infant formula
[+] Iron-fortified dry infant cereal
[#] Full-strength fruit juice.
[§] From whole-grain or enriched meal or flour.

Source: Data from *Federal Register,* 53(129),25309, July 6, 1988.

duce new food when children are hungry, (d) eat the food yourself, (e) have children prepare the food, and/or (f) keep offering the food because the more often children are offered a food, the more they are inclined to try it (Birch, Marlow, & Rotter, 1984).

3. Plan special menus for holidays and birthdays but avoid junk foods (Wardle, 1990).

4. Do not serve the same food, or virtually the same food, such as meatballs and hamburgers, on consecutive days.

5. Consider children's ethnic backgrounds and plan meals to include familiar foods.

6. Take advantage of children's likes and dislikes as to how foods are prepared and served. Young children generally like a variety of

foods (different sizes, shapes, colors, textures, and temperatures); foods prepared in different ways; foods served in bite-sized pieces or as finger foods; vegetables with mild flavors; strong-flavored vegetables served only occasionally and in small portions; fruit (but not vegetable) combinations; good texture (fluffy, not gooey, mashed potatoes); and foods that are not too hot or cold.

7. Provide a good physical and emotional climate by having adults set a good example of eating; by having an attractive room setting with furniture, dishes, silverware, and serving utensils suited to young children; by either avoiding serving delays or using activities such as singing and simple games while waiting; by providing a quiet time before meals; by making mealtime pleasant; by permitting the child to have choices and recognizing that young children occasionally go on food sprees (wanting the same food every day or even several times a day); and by understanding that young children do not have an adult's sense of time and are not prone to hurry to finish.

Children With Special Needs.   In providing and serving nutritious meals and snacks, the program must meet the special needs of a child with a disability. For example, children with delayed feeding skills may need special help, and children with metabolic problems and food allergies will need a carefully planned diet. Excellent information on nutrition and feeding of children with special needs is provided by Pipes and Glass (1989).

Hiring Staff.   Foods may be prepared at either an early childhood facility that complies with health standards or at another approved facility and transported safely to the program by using appropriate sanitary containers and temperatures. Programs with a large enrollment that serve a main meal should have a staff dietitian registered with the American Dietetic Association. If a full-time dietitian is not available, one

should be hired as a consultant. Enough personnel should be employed so that meals and snacks can be prepared in the time allowed. Each state's licensing standards for private programs or state and federal regulations for public programs indicate the qualifications necessary for food service personnel. Anytime personnel have infected cuts or sores or any communicable diseases, they should not prepare or serve foods.

Providing Facilities and Equipment.   Meals and snacks must be prepared and served with the available facilities and equipment. A registered dietitian can help plan the equipment and kitchen layout. An excellent publication concerning food service equipment is the booklet *Food Service Equipment Guide for Child Care Institutions* (USDA—PA 1264) and available from your state agency or USDA/FNS Regional Office. Some equipment, such as the automatic dishwasher, must meet local and state health agency regulations.

Purchasing Food.   Planning food purchases helps control costs and reduces waste. The following suggestions should be considered when purchasing food:

1. Check several food companies or stores in the area for quality food at reasonable prices and for such services as credit or delivery.

2. Know food products. Purchase government inspected meats, fish, and poultry; pasteurized, Grade A milk and milk products; properly sealed breads and pastries; and frozen foods that are kept hard-frozen and perishable foods that are kept under refrigeration. Notice which brand names prove most satisfactory.

3. Carefully calculate quantities of food needed. Use standardized recipes that always yield a specific quantity. One source is the USDA's publication *Quantity Recipes for Child Care Centers* (USDA—FNS-86). A

Table 8-2   Meal Pattern for Children in the Child Care Food Program

	Children 1 and 2 years	Children 3–5 years	Children 6–12 years
Breakfast			
Milk, fluid	½ cup	¾ cup	1 cup
Juice or fruit or vegetable	¼ cup	½ cup	½ cup
Bread and/or cereal, enriched or whole grain			
bread or	½ slice	½ slice	1 slice
cereal: cold dry or	¼ cup[1]	⅓ cup[2]	¾ cup[3]
hot cooked	¼ cup	¼ cup	½ cup
Midmorning or Midafternoon Snack (Supplement) (Select two of these four components)			
Milk, fluid	½ cup	½ cup	1 cup
Meat or meat alternative[4]	½ ounce	½ ounce	1 ounce
Juice or fruit or vegetable	½ cup	½ cup	¾ cup
Bread and/or cereal, enriched or whole grain			
bread or	½ slice	½ slice	1 slice
cereal: cold dry or	¼ cup[1]	⅓ cup[2]	¾ cup[3]
hot cooked	¼ cup	¼ cup	½ cup

standardized recipe can be adjusted to provide the number of servings needed for a meal or snack.

4. The types of food (perishable or nonperishable) and the amount of storage space must be carefully considered in determining when to purchase food.

5. Keep accurate records of type and quality of food purchased, when and how food was used in the program, cost, and any other notes useful for other purchases.

6. Study the USDA's *Food Buying Guide for Nutrition Programs* (USDA—PA 1331).

Meeting Sanitation Requirements.   All sanitation requirements must be rigidly enforced to avert disease. Sanitation must be considered in all aspects of food service.

1. All food service employees must meet state and local health requirements, must be free of infections on the skin and contagious diseases, and must be clean.

	Children 1 and 2 years	Children 3–5 years	Children 6–12 years
Lunch or Supper			
Milk, fluid	½ cup	¾ cup	1 cup
Meat or meat alternative			
Meat, poultry, or fish, cooked (lean meat without bone)	1 ounce	1½ ounces	2 ounces
Cheese	1 ounce	1½ ounces	2 ounces
Egg	1	1	1
Cooked dry beans and peas	¼ cup	⅜ cup	½ cup
Peanut butter or other nut or seed butters	2 tablespoons	3 tablespoons	4 tablespoons
Nuts and/or seeds	½ ounce[5]	¾ ounce[5]	1 ounce[5]
Vegetable and/or fruit (two or more)	¼ cup	½ cup	¾ cup
Bread or bread alternative, enriched or whole grain	½ slice	½ slice	1 slice

[1] ¼ cup (volume) or ⅓ ounce (weight), whichever is less.
[2] ⅓ cup (volume) or ½ ounce (weight), whichever is less.
[3] ¾ cup (volume) or 1 ounce (weight), whichever is less.
[4] Yogurt may be used as a meat/meat alternative in the snack only. You may serve 4 ounces (weight) or ½ cup (volume) of plain, or sweetened and flavored yogurt to fulfill the equivalent of 1 ounce of the meat/meat alternative component. For younger children, 2 ounces (weight) or ¼ cup (volume) may fulfill the equivalent of ½ ounce of the meat/meat alternative requirement.
[5] This portion can meet only one half of the total serving of the meat/meat alternative requirement for lunch or supper. Nuts or seeds must be combined with another meat/meat alternative to fulfill the requirement. For determining combinations, 1 ounce of nuts or seeds is equal to 1 ounce of cooked lean meat, poultry, or fish.
CAUTION: Children under age 5 are at the highest risk of choking. USDA recommends that any nuts and/or seeds be served to them in a prepared food and be ground or finely chopped.

2. Preparation and serving utensils and dishes must be thoroughly washed, sterilized, and properly handled. A dishwasher should be set for a water temperature of 160-165°F (66-74°C), using 0.25% detergent concentration or 1 oz of detergent per 3 gal of water.

Follow these four steps if washing by hand:
   a. Wash with soap or detergent in hot water (110-120°F or 43-49°C).
   b. Rinse in warm water.
   c. Sanitize by immersing for at least 1 minute in clean, hot water (at least 170°F or 76°C) or by immersing for at least 3 minutes in a sanitizing solution of 1 tbsp household bleach per 2 gal of water.
   d. Air—do not wipe—dry.

3. Foods should be checked on delivery, protected in storage, used within the specified time, and kept at appropriate serving temperatures: hot foods at 140°F (60°C) or above and cold foods at 45°F (7°C) or below.

4. Wash raw foods carefully and cook other foods properly.

5. Dispose of all foods served and not eaten.

6. Help children develop habits of cleanliness.

Identifying Children's Nutrition Problems

Much concern has been raised about the role of nutritional problems in physical health (Committee on Nutrition Education, 1986; Lebow, 1984; C. Rogers & Morris, 1986) and in learning disabilities and behavioral disorders (Norwood, 1984). Nutrition assessment is part of the final regulations of the Department of Health and Human Services' Early and Periodic Screening, Diagnosis, and Treatment (EPSDT) Program for people under 21 years of age (*Federal Register,* 1979). Referral for medical and dental examinations and laboratory tests reveals nutrition conditions, such as overweight, underweight, iron deficiency anemia, food allergies, and faulty food habits, that need remediation. If treatment is necessary, staff should follow the recommendations while the child is in the program; if necessary, they should assist the family in carrying out the care plan and ascertaining whether the child has received follow-up assessment. Staff should have in-service training in awareness of specific nutrition problems.

Implementing Nutrition Education for Children

Early childhood programs should include nutrition education for young children. In the past, nutrition has been a part of the health component of the curriculum or has centered on specific food activities, rather than being an integral part of the total curriculum. Children should talk about foods and good diets and learn about food origins, storage, and preparation. Cooking experiences will help them learn to measure, follow directions, cooperate with others, coordinate eye-hand movements, use language as a means of expression, recognize differences in food preferences of the various ethnic groups, and eat foods prepared in different ways. Chil-

dren also need to develop socially acceptable eating behavior and adaptability to various meal settings—at home, in restaurants, or on picnics. Herr and Morse (1982) provide a good example of how to integrate one nutrition concept throughout the early childhood curriculum. The following is a list of other available resources.

Association for Childhood Education International. (1976). *Cooking and eating with children: A way to learn.* Washington, DC: Author.

Center for Action-Based Leadership Experiences Publications. (1978). *Good times with good foods: Classroom activities for young children.* Greensboro, NC: Author.

Church, M. (1979). Nutrition: A vital part of the curriculum. *Young Children, 35*(1), 61-65.

Cosgrove, M. S. (1991). Cooking in the classroom: The doorway to nutrition. *Young Children, 46*(3), 43-46.

Endres, J. B., & Rockwell, R. E. (1994). *Food, nutrition, and the young child* (4th ed.). New York: Merrill/Macmillan.

Ferreira, N. (1973). Teachers' guide to educational cooking in the nursery school: An everyday affair. *Young Children, 29*(1), 23-32.

Margerey, A., Worsley, A., & Boulton, J. (1986). Children's thinking about food: 1. Knowledge of nutrients. *Journal of Nutrition, 43*(1), 2-8.

Margerey, A., Worsley, A., & Boulton, J. (1986). Children's thinking about food: 2. Concept development and beliefs. *Journal of Nutrition, 43*(1), 9-16.

Marotz, L., Rush, J., & Cross, M. (1993). *Health, safety, and nutrition for the young child* (3rd ed.). Albany, NY: Delmar.

McAfee, O. (1974). *Cooking and eating with children: A way to learn.* Washington, DC: Association for Childhood Education International.

McWilliams, M. (1986). *The parents' nutrition book.* New York: Wiley.

Oliver, S. D., & Musgrave, K. O. (1984). *Nutrition: A sourcebook of integrated activities.* Needham Heights, MA: Allyn & Bacon.

Randell, J., Olson, C., Jones, S., & Morris, L. (1980). *Early childhood nutrition program.* Ithaca, NY: Cornell University.

Rothlein, L. (1989). Nutrition tips revisited: On a daily basis, do we implement what we know? *Young Children, 44*(6), 30-36.

Wanamaker, N., Hern, K., & Richarz, S. (1979). *More than graham crackers: Nutrition education and food preparation with young children.* Washington, DC: National Association for the Education of Young Children.

Many cookbooks are available for children. Some contain recipes children prefer; others are designed to teach children how to cook:

Ackerman, D. (1981). *Cooking with kids.* Mt. Rainier, MD: Gryphon House.

Baxter, K. M. (1981). *Come and get it: A natural foods cookbook for children* (3rd ed.). Ann Arbor, MI: Children First.

Bruno, J., & Dakam, P. (1974). *Cooking in the classroom.* Belmont, CA: Lear/Siegler/Fearon.

Catron, C. E., & Parks, B. C. (1986). *Cooking up a story.* Minneapolis, MN: T. S. Denison.

Cristenberry, M. A., & Stevens, B. (1984). *Can Piaget cook?* Atlanta, GA: Humanics.

Edge, N. (1975). *Kids in the kitchen.* Port Angeles, WA: Peninsula.

Fagella, K. (1985). *Concept cookery.* Weston, MA: First Teacher Press.

Harms, T. (1983). *Learning from cooking experiences.* Menlo Park, CA: Addison-Wesley.

Jenkins, K. S. (1982). *Kinder-krunchies.* Pleasant Hill, CA: Discovery Toys.

Johnson, B., & Plemons, B. (1990). *Cup cooking: Individual child portion picture recipes.* Lake Alfred, FL: Early Educator's Press.

McClenahan, P., & Jaqua, I. (1976). *Cool cooking for kids: Recipes and nutrition for kids.* Belmont, CA: Fearon Pitman.

Ontario Science Center. (1987). *Foodworks.* Reading, MA: Addison-Wesley.

Palmer, M., & Edmonds, A. (1981). *Vegetable magic.* Storrs: Connecticut State Board of Education.

Veitch, B., & Harms, T. (1981). *Cook and learn.* Menlo Park, CA: Addison-Wesley.

Warren, J. (1982). *Super snacks/sugarless.* Everett, WA: Warren.

Zubrowski, B. (1981). *Baking chemistry.* Boston: Little, Brown.

Serving Parents' Needs

Parents as well as early childhood educators have an impact on children's nutrition habits. Although children decide on *how much* (or even *whether*) to eat, adults are responsible for *the foods* children are offered. Parents can help their children develop appropriate nutrition concepts and attitudes. Parents need to be informed on various topics concerning nutrition for children, including (a) foods needed for a healthy child; (b) planning, buying, storing, and preparing varieties of foods; (c) common eating problems of children; (d) children who need special diets; and (e) money savers.

Staff need to know the social realities of the families with whom they work, or else they may make nutrition demands that families cannot meet. Parents can be reached in parents' meetings, demonstration classes, home visits, and through newsletters. Some specific suggestions follow:

1. Staff can aid parents in planning nutritious meals by using the Food Guide Pyramid. A list of foods in each section of the pyramid may help parents in planning adequate meals or may help those who are already

planning adequate meals see how they can vary their food choices.

2. Newsletters can contain information about food planning and preparation and recipes as a way of developing the young child's interest in foods and snacks.

3. Menus should be posted for parents.

4. Other information on nutrition should be made available, such as the nutrient content of foods in relation to cost, the nutrient content of food after storage and preparation, and the relationship between nutrition and the health of infants and young children.

5. Using volunteers in food education may be helpful in informing parents.

HEALTH

Attention to health issues in programs for young children dates back to 1945 (Child Welfare League of America, 1945). Research concerning health has been sporadic until recently. Today, the concern is about children's health status in early childhood programs, practices aiding children's health, and staff members' health. Early childhood leaders in state departments of education report that their states are giving increased attention to the relationship of health and well-being to learning (S. Robinson, 1993/94). Administrators of early childhood programs must develop health policies for children and staff in keeping with current information. (Some health policy categories were suggested in Chapter 3.)

Children's Health Status

Concern about the problems of disease spread in early childhood programs is increasing. Children in child care are highly vulnerable because of (a) close physical contacts among children and adults—feeding, diapering and toileting, sharing objects including moist art media and water tables, and affection giving and receiving; (b) children's lack of immunity; (c) children's small body structures, such as the distance between the nose and throat and the middle ear; (d) children's bumps and scrapes on the skin that afford entry of infectious agents into the body; and (e) children's lack of understanding of how to protect themselves from infectious agents.

Clarke-Stewart (1985) states that attendance in early childhood programs is not detrimental to the physical growth of children but that children in early childhood programs may "catch" more diseases than those raised at home. Children in programs, however, are not at a substantially increased risk of developing an infectious disease, compared with others kept at home (Howell, 1985). When young children spend time with peers or have older siblings who themselves are with nonhousehold children in groups, preschool illness patterns are more like those of children who attend early childhood programs. Evidence indicates that, except for infants under 1 year of age and a greater incidence of runny noses in large centers (those with more than 50 children), children reared at home have the same type and number of respiratory infections as those in early childhood programs (Aronson, 1991).

Health concerns are great for infants and toddlers in group programs. These very young children do show an increased incidence of respiratory illnesses and diarrhea, as compared with infants and toddlers not in group settings (Harms, 1992). The incidence of infectious disease can be substantially reduced, however, when an education program for staff involves both personal hygiene and environmental sanitation (Kotch, 1990).

Practices Aiding Children's Health

Early childhood program staff can play important roles in aiding children's health. Staff serve in liaison roles as they work with parents in maintaining children's complete and up-to-date health records and aid parents in securing health services. They also work directly with children to maintain good health.

Health Records.   Licensing and other regulations usually require that each child has a recent medical examination and an up-to-date immunization record before admission to a program. Because immunizations are required by law, 97% of all children receive needed vaccinations prior to school entry ("Preschool Immunizations," 1991). Most regulations require that the medical examination be given within the last 6 months before entry; however, an examination 1 month prior to entry provides maximum protection for all children. Health records should contain (a) a record of immunizations, (b) pertinent health history, and (c) a signed physician's statement concerning the child's ability to participate in the program's activities and any special health needs, such as food allergies or restrictions of physical activities (see Appendix 8). The American Academy of Pediatrics has published *Recommendations for Preventive Pediatric Health Care;* it describes the type of routine medical assessment that should be made at various ages (Early Childhood Education Linkage System Staff, 1993). Parents may want to add information on health habits, such as dental hygiene and foods preferred.

Because children are being cared for more and more frequently in early childhood programs, staff need to work with children's physicians. A staff member may have important information to convey to a child's physician or may wish to obtain the physician's advice on handling a particular health problem in the center. Dixon (1990) provides some guidelines that make communication easier.

Health Services.   All children need to receive high-quality health services. Early childhood programs are required by various regulatory agencies to provide some health services (e.g., employ health consultants). In addition, early childhood administrators need to locate available resources and to obtain their criteria for assistance for the children and families served by the early childhood program. For starters, administrators need to check health departments; clinics operated by hospitals and medical schools; voluntary groups such as United Fund, American Red Cross, civic clubs, religious groups, and family service associations; medical assistance under Medicaid (Title XIX); armed forces medical services; and insurance and other prepayment plans.

Basic Health Practices.   Safe environments for both children and adults can be achieved by following certain health practices. Some of the basics are listed below:

1. Safe environments are programs with fewer than 50 children, with small groups of non-toilet-trained infants and toddlers (Hadler, 1982), and that separate children in diapers (Pickering & Woodward, 1982).

2. As discussed in this chapter, food service must meet health standards.

3. The diapering area in an infant center is the most dangerous for the growth of illness-causing microorganisms. These practices reduce risks in diapering:

   a. Change a child on a table with a plastic-covered pad that has no cracks and that has a restraint device.

   b. Place paper bags, computer paper, or wax paper squares under each child before changing. Special paper is now available on rolls that can be attached to some changing tables (like that used in physician's examination rooms). Also use paper to pick up the diaper.

   c. Use disposable gloves to augment hand-washing procedures.

   d. Wash the diapering surface twice daily and after any diaper leaks. Scrub with detergent and water. Rinse with clean water treated with a disinfectant (1/4 c chlorine bleach to 1 gal water) kept in a spray bottle. The disinfectant must be made fresh daily and stored away from children.

e. Wash your hands after diapering, using running water. If a sink with elbow controls, which is desirable in this area, is unavailable, use a paper towel to turn off the faucet.

f. Post procedures for diapering in area.

4. Require consistent attention to hand washing. Children and adults should wash their hands before serving or eating food, after each diaper change or use of rest rooms, and after wiping a nose. Proper hand washing requires the following:

a. Use soap in soft-water areas and detergent in hard-water areas. Liquid soap is more sanitary than bar soap. Liquid soap dispensers should be cleaned and refilled on a regular basis. If bar soaps are used, the bar should be rinsed before and after use and kept dry. An antiseptic form made from alcohol and lanolin (e.g., "Alcare," manufactured by Vestal Labs) is effective in place of soap.

b. Work the soap in the hands for 2 to 3 minutes; rinse with running water; clean under nails; keep elbows higher than hands; turn off faucet with a paper towel; and dry hands with a disposable paper towel.

c. For hand washing of infants and young toddlers, wipe the hands with damp towels moistened with a liquid soap solution, wipe with towels moistened with clean water, and then dry with paper towels. For older children, squirt drops of liquid soap on their hands from a squeeze bottle; children rinse their hands under running water and dry them with a paper towel.

5. Wear disposable gloves when cleaning wounds and augment with thorough hand washing.

6. The facility and equipment must be cleaned regularly. The following are suggestions for cleaning:

a. General cleaning of the building should be done daily when children are gone.

b. Clean cribs, strollers, and tables daily, using the same procedure and cleaning materials as described for cleaning the diapering table. This should also be done with wooden toys and laminated books.

c. Wash high chair trays in a dishwasher.

d. Daily, wash toys that are put in the mouth. This can be done more quickly if toys are placed in nylon mesh bags (used for hosiery), washed, rinsed, and hung to dry.

e. Rinse rattles and other dishwasher-safe mouth toys before placing in the dishwasher. (Saliva forms a film when heated, aiding in the growth of microorganisms.).

f. Use bedding with one child only; wash weekly or after soiling.

g. Clean and disinfect bath fixtures daily or after soiling.

h. Remove trash daily.

i. Soiled diapers should be disposed of or held for laundry in a closed container.

j. Never place dishes or bottles on the floor.

k. Clean floors and other surfaces after feeding.

7. Use a sanitation checklist where health practices are checked off by date and time and initialed by the person fulfilling the requirement. (See *Sanitation Checklist*, prepared by K. Albrecht and staff at the Department of Home Economics, Child and Family Development Center, Southwest Texas State University, San Marcos, Texas 78666, or use the Soap and Detergent Association's *The ABC's of Clean Teachers' Guide*.)

Child Care for Infectious Diseases.   Until recently, most regulations required children with any communicable disease be removed from the group setting. Such regulations and policies have been debated on the basis of the following questions:

1. *Does removing an ill child reduce the spread of infection?* Programs with stringent policies for excluding ill children, compared with less strict programs, showed no difference in the amounts or kinds of illnesses. For many illnesses, it is difficult to diagnose the risk of spread of infectious diseases for these reasons: (a) Children with no symptoms may spread infection; (b) children often spread infection several days before and after symptoms; and (c) the presence or absence of certain symptoms, including fever, is not correlated with the amount of infectious disease a child is spreading.

2. *Can family members afford to stay home with a mildly ill child?* Parents may feel unable to lose work time and thus leave an ill child at home alone, under the care of an older sibling, or under the care of a neighbor who is to "check" on the child. Parents may try to cover the illness by trying to cover the symptoms. Parents may also feel guilty about not providing total care of their child and supposedly exposing the child to an illness spread in the program.

3. *What is best for ill children?* Ill children do not need to feel guilty about the inconvenience their illness causes their parents or their caregivers. Ill children may need more comfort, but often not much more care, than well children. If the child is to be kept in the program, staff need to (a) maintain information on the onset of and current symptoms, possible contributing factors (e.g., vaccinations), complicating illnesses (e.g., chronic illnesses), intake (food and drink) and output (times urinated and number of bowel movements), and care given; (b) follow basic health practices, especially hand washing; (c) follow approved practices for caring for children with fever, vomiting, or diarrhea; and (d) provide place and play materials suited to an ill child.

4. *Can parents pay for short-term special care when their children are ill?* Program

administrators have special care options: (a) hiring additional staff for ill children; (b) providing a "get well room" with a familiar caregiver; and/or (c) forming a linkage with nearby families to provide temporary family home care or with a sick child center. (See Chapter 1 on alternative care centers.) In each of these options, the parents pay for the special care.

Administrators of programs must develop policies for specifying limitations on attendance of ill children, provisions for notification of parents, and plans for the comfort and care of ill children. Parents need to be informed of program policy and any available special care options.

Today, children are usually excluded from group programs if the ill children cannot participate in routine activities; if the illness requires staff care that, in turn, compromises the care of the other children; and if the ill child poses increased risks of spreading the illness to others. For detailed information on exclusion policies, see Appendixes K and N in *Model Child Care Health Policies* (Early Childhood Education Linkage System Staff, 1993). Some communicable diseases must also be reported to the health department, which in turn will make recommendations for informing parents of children who may have been exposed.

One designated staff member must make decisions concerning care of ill children based on policy. For example:

1. *Mildly ill child admitted to program.* If a mildly ill child is admitted to a program, a symptom record (see Figure 8-1) must be kept and a copy given to the parent each day. The parent and caregiver must consult on treatment. Medication administration policies must be followed.

2. *Child becomes ill after program admission.* The teacher must complete a symptom record and notify the designated staff member to make a decision concerning the continued care of the child. If the child may stay, the parent

Child's Name: _____

Date: _____

SYMPTOMS

Major Symptoms

    Respiratory: runny nose; sore throat; difficulty in breathing; cough; other

        (Please describe) _____

        _____

    Skin: itch; rash; oozing; lesion; other

        (Please describe) _____

        _____

    Gastrointestinal: nausea; vomiting; diarrhea; trouble urinating; frequent urinating with pain; other

        (Please describe) _____

        _____

    Body movement: stiff neck; limp; other

        (Please describe) _____

        _____

When symptom began: _____

CHILD'S REACTIONS

    Food/fluid intake

        (Please describe) _____

        _____

    Urine, bowel, and/or vomiting

        (Please describe) _____

        _____

    Crying, sleeping, other behavior

        (Please describe) _____

        _____

Figure 8-1 Symptom Record

EXPOSURE

Ill children or staff

(Please describe) _____

_____

Ill parent or sibling

(Please describe) _____

_____

New foods

(Please describe) _____

_____

Ingestion of or contact with potentially harmful substance (e.g., art materials, cleaning materials, room paint, plants, animals)

(Please describe) _____

_____

CARE AND ADVICE

First aid, emergency care, or other care

(Please describe) _____

_____

Health provider advice

(Please describe) _____

_____

Parent consultation

(Please describe) _____

_____

_____
(Signature of person completing form)

is called and the same procedure is followed as given for a mildly ill child admitted to the program. If the child is too ill to stay, the parent is called and the child is carefully supervised until a parent arrives.

Child Care for Noninfectious Chronic Illnesses and Disabilities.   Many children who have a chronic illness and a disability are eligible for services under P.L. 101–476. Planning needs to be done prior to accepting these children. Some points to consider include (a) prognosis of illness or disability, (b) adaptations in program activities or in schedule, (c) special housing arrangements needed, (d) special equipment needed, (e) special dietary needs, (f) coordination of home and program administration of medication, and (g) possible special care and emergency procedures (e.g., replacement equipment should failure occur, backup power source, supplemental oxygen, resuscitator bag, and suctioning catheter). Although some children require intensive services beyond the usual early childhood program, most children with a chronic illness and a disability will require only minor adaptations.

Medication Administration.   Legally, the administration of medication is an act by an adult that can alter the metabolism of a child in a way not always susceptible to immediate control. Before making a policy, the program administrator should check licensing or other regulations. In writing a policy, these points should be considered: (a) A parent provides the written order of a physician authorizing the use of the medication for a specified length of time for a particular child; (b) the parent provides a written request that a staff member administer the medication (see Appendix 8); (c) the medication is labeled with the child's name, name of drug, and directions for its administration; (d) staff maintain a written record of the date and time of each administration and the name of the staff member administering the medication (spills and refusals to take medication should be noted

on a log; see Figure 8-2); and (e) safe and appropriate (e.g., refrigerated) storage places for medications are designated.

Children's and Adults' Mental Health

Health has many dimensions, and perhaps the most important is mental health. Thus, striving for mental health in group programs and in the homes of children must be a top priority. Regulations governing group programs address positive guidance in general terms and state that staff must help children learn to be fair and respect people and property. Regulations also prohibit corporal punishment; humiliation; withdrawal (including the threat of) of bathroom, food, or rest opportunities; and any other form of abuse. As important as these statements are, they do not give enough attention to mental health strategies and rarely even address adult needs.

The emotional domain is perhaps the most compelling aspect of development in young children. Honig (1993) states that the most serious problems for infants and toddlers "lie in the domain of social/emotional functioning" (p. 69). During these early years, children must build secure relations and also develop independence. Honig sees parent and staff education, professional resources, and environmental changes aimed at reducing stress as all important in ensuring these young children's mental health. Even for preschoolers, group programs can be sources of great tension. These children often feel "one among many" for very long hours and lonely and separated from their families. Primary-age children are coping with the stress of "school" and often with the daily transition of school to child care programs or school to "home alone."

Adults feel stress too. Parents feel the anxiety of separating from their babies and young children and of meeting the dual and often conflicting demands of employment and parenting. Staff often feel frustrated with distressed infants, the defiant toddler, and the aggressive or withdrawn preschooler, with parents whom they believe could do better jobs of parenting, and with the

Figure 8-2   Medication Administration Log

Child's name _____
Date _____

Time	Safety Check of Label and Storage	Notes	Staff Member's Initials

(Give copy to parent when child is picked up.)

human and physical qualities of the workplace. Finally, some children and adults are also experiencing less than optimal and even abusive home lives; these "from home" stresses will be played out on the stage of the group setting.

In short, the dynamics of the group setting can lead to stress and crises for both children and adults. With appropriate mental health measures, valuable lessons come from constructive coping strategies by all those involved in early childhood programs. (A list of excellent readings for developing appropriate mental health strategies is given at the end of this chapter.)

Protecting Staff Members' Health

The health of adults is a key element in the quality of an early childhood program. A staff member's illness can become a health hazard to children and other staff members, is costly to a program in which substitutes must be hired, and can cause a lack of consistent child care.

Medical examinations are an important means of protecting staff health. Programs need standard requirements and policies to include content of examination, which can differ for the various staff positions; the criteria for "passing" the examination; when examinations are indicated (e.g., prior to employment, after a severe illness); where the examination may be given; who receives the findings; and who pays for the examination.

In addition to medical examinations, adequate paid sick leave protects the health of adults. When sick leave is not available, staff might not leave when they are ill or may return before they should resume their duties.

SAFETY

Safety is no longer seen as sheltering the child. Safety includes environmental care, emergency preparedness, child protection, and safety consciousness and education. Thus, safety is an integral part of the daily early childhood program.

Environmental Safety

Environmental safety needs close attention. Environmental safety includes setting limits for children, facility safety, vehicular safety, and sanitation and hygienic practices.

Setting Limits for Children.   Children will take risks—many of which are good learning experiences. At other times, though, an adult must stop or redirect a child in a potentially harmful situation. Children must begin learning how to predict hazards and choose safe alternatives. Staff must decide on a few rules based on the population of children (e.g., younger children and children with special needs often need more precisely defined limits), facilities and equipment, activity, and the supervision available. These rules should always be stated in positive ways with the alternative behavior given (e.g., Fences are to keep us safe. Climbing is fun. If you want to climb, you must climb only on the gym. The gym is made for us to climb").

Facility Safety.   General facility safety is given in Chapter 5. Each program needs to establish environmental safety guidelines to fit its own special needs. Procedures also need to be developed for following through on the established safety guidelines. Each program should develop a safety checklist based on the local facility. The following sources may prove helpful in developing a checklist:

> American Red Cross. (1990). *The American Red Cross child care course: Health and safety units.* Washington, DC: Author.
>
> *Facility design for early childhood programs.* (1989). Washington, DC: National Association for the Education of Young Children.
>
> Frost, J. L. (1992). *Play and playscapes.* Albany, NY: Delmar.
>
> Lovell, P., & Harms, T. (1985). How can playgrounds be improved? A rating scale. *Young Children, 40*(3), 3-8.

Staff should continuously scan for safety hazards but do a thorough safety check once a month and after any program disruption or

vacation time. Different people should do the safety check. Hazards should be fixed immediately, or actions should be taken to prevent children's contact with the hazard.

Vehicular Safety.   Transporting children means taking additional safety precautions. Each driver must be a responsible person, possess a current license appropriate for the number of passengers, and have liability insurance in keeping with state law. Vehicles must have current safety inspection stickers in states requiring these inspections. The vehicle must be equipped with appropriate restraint systems for age/size/special needs of children and for adults.

For each field trip, special safety plans must be made. For example, how and where to load and unload must be preplanned. A copy of each child's emergency information form (see Appendix 8), blank accident forms, and first-aid kit must be taken on the field trip. A minimum of two adults must be with each group of children at all times.

Sanitation and Hygienic Practices.   When parents and teachers work together on the assumption that preventive measures rigorously practiced are in the best interests of all children and adults, those involved in group programs are less vulnerable to disease. A health care professional is invaluable as a resource person for advising on policies, occasionally monitoring practices, and providing in-service education to parents and staff. As discussed in previous sections of this chapter, the three most effective ways to interrupt the transmission of infectious agents are hand washing, environmental cleaning, and using group-limiting strategies (e.g., small groups, grouping by toileting status, designating toys for certain groups of children).

Emergency Preparedness

Emergencies arise even when early childhood programs take every possible measure to protect children's health and safety. To minimize the risks to children, procedures for handling them must be developed. The key elements in handling emergencies include the following:

1. Preplan necessary action for evacuating children in the event of fire or explosion and measures to take during tornadoes, flash floods, smog alerts, and civil defense emergencies. Consult with the local fire department and local Red Cross chapter or Civil Defense chapter in developing guidelines. Have the exit route and procedures posted near or on exit doors. Have flashlights, first-aid kit, completed emergency information forms, and class lists on a shelf by each exit door. Plan a designated meeting place and procedures for checking on the presence and well-being of each person at the designated area. Practice the desired plan (and alternative plan) once a month or more often if necessary.

2. Have a first-aid kit (see Figure 8-3) and current references for handling emergencies, such as:

American Red Cross first aid: Responding to emergencies. (1991). St. Louis, MO: C. V. Mosby.

Aronson, S. (1988). *First aid in child-care settings.* Washington, DC: American Red Cross.

Dworkin, G. (1987). *CPR for infants and children: A guide to cardiopulmonary resuscitation.* Edison, NJ: Child Welfare League of America.

Green, M. (1986). *A sigh of relief: The first-aid handbook for childhood emergencies.* New York: Bantam.

Pediatric basic life support. (1986). *Journal of the American Medical Association, 255*(21), 2954-2960.

Staff need to be trained and informed of their responsibilities for administering first aid. They must also recognize when an accident or illness requires immediate medical help.

3. Parents or legal guardians must be notified. They should be given the opportunity, if possible without endangering the child, to participate in making decisions and aiding in the treatment procedure.

4. The child's records should contain a consent form authorizing emergency medical treatment and transportation if parents cannot be reached. The emergency information form usually includes names, addresses, and phone numbers of parents and other persons who can accept responsibility for the child when parents cannot be contacted; name and phone number of the physician to be contacted; and name and address of the hospital to which the child may be taken (see Appendix 8). This form should be updated every 6 months and should be taken on each field trip (see Chapter 7, Figure 7-1).

5. Forms should also be available for staff to document the procedures they followed in handling an emergency or illness. Careful documentation helps prevent mistakes in caring for children and also lessens potential liability to the program (see Figure 8-4). Once a month, perhaps with the fee statement or during check-in, parents should be asked to verify information on the emergency information forms.

Child Protection

The maltreatment of children in families or in programs cannot be tolerated. Early childhood professionals need to be informed on state child abuse/neglect laws (see Chapter 3), identification of suspected abuse/neglect and program policies for reporting these cases, and ways to help, including recognizing adults in crises and helping them secure assistance before abuse occurs.

Staff must also protect children in cases of disputes over custody. Staff must remember the stress of all those involved—the child, both parents (or biological and adoptive parents), and even other family members. Staff must realize they cannot take sides in these issues but must perform their responsibilities on behalf of the child in accordance with legal decisions (see Chapter 3).

Figure 8-3   Contents of First-Aid Kit

Bandages (assorted sizes, including triangular)

Cold pack

Container for carrying insect, plant, or spider specimens
    (for medical identification)

Cotton balls (for applying pressure)

Eye dressing

Eye irrigation solution

First-aid books/charts

Gauze (pads—2″ × 2″ and 4″ × 4″; flexible roller gauze—
    1″ and 2″ widths)

Gloves (disposable and nonporous)

Insect sting preparation (if needed by anyone in program) and
    baking soda (to soothe insect stings/bites)

Note pad and pen/pencil

Safety pins

Scissors

Soap (preferably liquid)

Syrup of ipecac

Tape (adhesive—½″ and 1″ widths)

Telephone numbers for emergency aid and coins for pay phone

Thermometer

Towels (1 large and 1 small)

Tweezers

Safety Consciousness

Early childhood professionals must never become complacent about safety. Each staff member must learn to assess risks, including the activity, the setting (e.g., learning center), how a specific group of children will respond, and even teacher stress that increases risks. Even accurate assessment cannot guarantee safety, however. Every situation has risks. For example, some teachers do not understand outdoor dangers; thus, the child:staff ratio is often reduced to allow teacher breaks (as discussed in Chapter 5). Other teachers think the most serious accidents occur outdoors; thus, they become complacent

about play indoors. (Yet, in family child care settings, most accidents occur indoors.)

Professionals are expected to provide for children's safety. Thus, they are legally responsible. Failure to be responsible is considered **negligence.** Negligence has two categories:

1. Acts of *omission,* in which adults fail to take precautionary measures needed to protect children (e.g., failure to inspect facility for safety, failure to supervise or provide adequate supervision)

2. Acts of *commission,* in which adults' actions or decisions involve risks (e.g., taking a field

trip although several needed parent volunteers did not show up to accompany the children)

Administrators can protect children and themselves from liability judgments against themselves or their staff by carefully writing job descriptions, obtaining safety training for staff, maintaining appropriate records (especially accident report forms), and securing liability insurance. Although safety management is challenging because of the ages of children in early childhood programs, acting responsibly can save lives and prevent negligence from being proved by the courts. (See Chapter 3 for additional information on liability.)

HEALTH AND SAFETY EDUCATION

Parents and early childhood professionals are very aware of their responsibilities to protect children. Most adults, however, are deficient in health and safety information. Information is needed in many areas, such as (a) relationship of health to total well-being, (b) prenatal care, (c) characteristics of the child's developmental stage associated with health problems and safety hazards, (d) nutrition and exercise for the growing child, (e) injury prevention, (f) stress management in children and adults, (g) detection and management of symptoms of common childhood infectious diseases, (h) prevention of child abuse and detection and reporting of suspected child abuse/neglect, (i) agencies and resources for health and safety education and assistance, and (j) emergency preparedness. Training must be provided in these and other areas of need and interest. Staff training on various topics must be repeated so that new staff members can receive training and all other staff members can replenish their knowledge and skills.

Children also need health and safety education. Most education for young children is done through incidental learning experiences and imitation of adults. Although these teachable

moments are the most meaningful for children, they need more specific instruction on coping with emergencies, how to get help, and even first-aid basics for older preschool and primary-level children (*First Things First*, n.d.; Marchand & McDermott, 1986).

TRENDS AND ISSUES

Health concerns are still great for young children in early childhood programs. Especially vulnerable to infectious diseases are infants and toddlers and the teachers and parents who care for them. The health of some children with special needs also presents problems to staff. With the great increase of these children in group programs, professionals are calling for better education and more consistent monitoring of health and hygienic practices.

Early childhood professionals are asking regulatory agencies to write and/or enforce more comprehensive regulations. Particular needs include a focus on infants and toddlers and on children with special needs, on dangerous and/or improperly installed outdoor equipment (see Chapters 3 and 5), and on "child proofing" family child care homes (Wasserman et al., 1989).

Many see the need for greater and more consistent health and safety consciousness among early childhood professionals and parents of young children. Compared with the other years in a child's schooling, teachers' responsibilities for nutrition, health, and safety are greatest in the early childhood years. Compared with other aspects of preservice and in-service teacher preparation, however, training in these areas is much less extensive. Furthermore, a recent survey of parents shows the need for more parent education. The survey results showed that almost 44% of surveyed parents thought they cannot do anything to lessen accidents, 76% were not particularly interested in getting materials on child safety, and only 33% of these parents thought their children would heed safety information given in the schools (Mick-

Child's name: _____

Birth date: _____

Parent location information: _____

_____

Child's physician: _____

(Telephone) _____

- -

Injury

  Date: _____ Time: _____

  General description (e.g., bite, burn, cut): _____

  _____

  Where/how injury occurred: _____

  _____

  Staff supervisor (at time of injury): _____

  Other adult witnesses to the injury: _____

  _____

Action Taken

  Child's apparent symptoms and reaction: _____

  _____

First Aid (if any)

  Nature of: _____

  _____

  _____

  Administered by: _____

  Assisted by: _____

Figure 8-4   Injury Report Form

Medical Help Sought (if any)

From whom: _____

Time of contact: _____

Advice: _____

_____

_____

Parent Contact

Attempts: _____

Parent advice: _____

_____

_____

Followup Care

Description: _____

_____

_____

Condition of Child at Time of Release

Description: _____

_____

_____

_____

_____
(Signature of person completing form)

NOTE: For "quick reference" and as a time saver, always have a form with information above the
      dotted line completed on each child.

alide, 1993). Undoubtedly, these statistics indicate the need for parent education.

SUMMARY

Nutrition, health, and safety practices and education are essential ingredients of quality early childhood programs. Nutrition is highly important in programs for young children for two reasons: (a) Early childhood programs need to provide up to 80% of a young child's total nutrition requirements, and (b) children develop lifelong eating habits as a result of early eating experiences. Thus, staff of early childhood programs need to know the nutritional requirements of young children, how to provide a nutritious diet, and how to create an appropriate meal and snack environment. Health affects each area of a person's development. The health goals in early childhood programs are to provide routine health care; to prevent health problems, including mental health problems; and to coordinate health plans with parents and children's health care providers. Similar to health, safety includes environmental care, emergency preparedness, child protection, and safety consciousness and education. Thus, both health and safety are broad in scope in quality programs.

Trends and issues include concern about the control of infectious diseases in early childhood care and education programs, especially those serving infants and toddlers, and the care of children with chronic health conditions. Many also see the need for greater health and safety consciousness among those who write and enforce regulations and among those who have direct contact with young children—professionals and parents.

FOR FURTHER READING

American Academy of Pediatrics. (1991). *Right from the start*. Elk Grove Village, IL: Author.

American Public Health Association and the American Academy of Pediatrics. (1991). *Caring for our children—National health and safety performance standards; guidelines for out-of-home child care programs*. Washington, DC: American Public Health Association.

Association of Early Childhood Education. (1990). *Child abuse: A handbook for early childhood educators*. Ontario, Canada: Author.

Caughey, C. (1991). Becoming a child's ally: Observations in a classroom for children who have been abused. *Young Children, 46*(4), 22-28.

Edelstein, S. F. (1992). *Nutrition and meal planning guide in child-care programs: A practical guide*. Chicago: American Dietetic Association.

Fauvre, M. (1988). Including young children with "new" chronic illnesses in an early childhood education setting. *Young Children, 43*(6), 71-77.

Frieman, B. B., & Settel, S. (1994). What the classroom teacher needs to know about children with chronic medical problems. *Childhood Education, 70*(4), 196-201.

Kendrick, A. S., Kaufman, R., & Messenger, K. P. (1987). *Healthy young children: A manual for programs*. Washington, DC: National Association for the Education of Young Children.

NAEYC Information Service. (1994). *Child care and ill children and healthy child care practices*. Washington, DC: National Association for the Education of Young Children.

READINGS FOR DEVELOPING APPROPRIATE MENTAL HEALTH STRATEGIES

Buzzelli, C. A., & File, N. (1989). Building trust in friends. *Young Children, 44*(3), 70-75.

Cannella, G. S. (1986). Research: Praise and concrete rewards: Concerns for childhood education. *Childhood Education, 62*(4), 297-301.

Clewett, A. S. (1988). Guidance and discipline: Teaching young children appropriate behavior. *Young Children, 43*(4), 26-31.

Crosser, S. (1992). Managing the early childhood classroom. *Young Children, 47*(2), 23-29.

Fenichel, E. (1991). Learning through supervision and mentorship to support the development of infant, toddler, and their families. *Zero to Three, 12*(2), 1-9.

Gartrell, D. (1987). Assertive discipline: Unhealthy for children and other living things. *Young Children, 42*(2), 10-11.

Gottfried, A. E. (1983). Research in review: Intrinsic motivation in young children. *Young Children*, 39(1), 64-73.

Greenberg, P. (1987). Ideas that work with young children. Child choice—another way to individualize—another form of preventive discipline. *Young Children*, 43(1), 48-54.

Greenberg, P. (1987). Ideas that work with young children. Good discipline is, in large part, the result of a fantastic curriculum! *Young Children*, 42(3), 49-50.

Greenberg, P. (1988). Ideas that work with young children. Avoiding "me against you" discipline. *Young Children*, 44(1), 24-29.

Greenberg, P. (1988). Ideas that work with young children. The difficult child. *Young Children*, 43(5), 60-68.

Greenberg, P. (1988). Ideas that work with young children. Positive self-image: More than mirrors. *Young Children*, 43(4), 57-59.

Greenberg, P. (1991). *Character development: Encouraging self-esteem and discipline in infants, toddlers, and two-year-olds.* Washington, DC: National Association for the Education of Young Children.

Greenberg, P. (1992). Ideas that work with young children. How to institute some simple democratic practices pertaining to respect, rights, roots, and responsibilities in any classroom (without losing your leadership position). *Young Children*, 47(5), 10-17.

Gronlund, G. (1992). Coping with Ninja Turtle play in my kindergarten classroom. *Young Children*, 48(1), 21-25.

Hitz, R., & Driscoll, A. (1988). Praise or encouragement? New insights into praise: Implications for early childhood teachers. *Young Children*, 43(5), 6-13.

Honig, A. S. (1987). *Love and learn: Discipline for young children* (brochure). Washington, DC: National Association for the Education of Young Children.

Honig, A. S. (1991). For babies to flourish. *Montessori Life*, 3(2), 7-10.

Honig, A. S. (1992). Dancing with your baby means sometimes leading, sometimes following. *Dimensions of Early Childhood*, 20(3), 10-13.

Karnes, M. B., Johnson, L. J., & Beauchamp, K. D. F. (1988). Enhancing essential relationships: Developing a nurturing affective environment for young children. *Young Children*, 44(1), 58-65.

McCracken, J. B. (Ed.). (1986). *Reducing stress in young children's lives.* Washington, DC: National Association for the Education of Young Children.

Miller, C. S. (1984). Building self-control: Discipline for young children. *Young Children*, 40(1), 15-19.

National Association for the Education of Young Children (NAEYC). (1986). *Helping children learn self-control: A guide to discipline* (brochure). Washington, DC: Author.

Nelson, J. (1987). *Positive discipline.* New York: Ballantine.

Stone, J. G. (1987). *A guide to discipline* (Rev. ed.). Washington, DC: National Association for the Education of Young Children.

RESOURCES FOR HEALTH AND SAFETY INFORMATION

Centers for Disease Control and Prevention
1600 Clifton Road, NE
Atlanta, GA 30333

Clearinghouse on Child Abuse and Neglect
P.O. Box 1182
Washington, DC 20013

National Child Safety Council
P.O. Box 1368
Jackson, MI 49204

National Institute of Health and Human Development
Office of Research Reporting
9006 Rockville Pike, Bldg. 31
Bethesda, MD 20892

Pre-School Stress Relief Project
P.O. Box 42481
Atlanta, GA 30311

Soap and Detergent Association
475 Park Avenue South
New York, NY 10016

U.S. Consumer Product Safety Commission
Washington, DC 20207

(See also Appendix 5.)

Chapter 9

Assessing, Recording, and Reporting Children's Progress

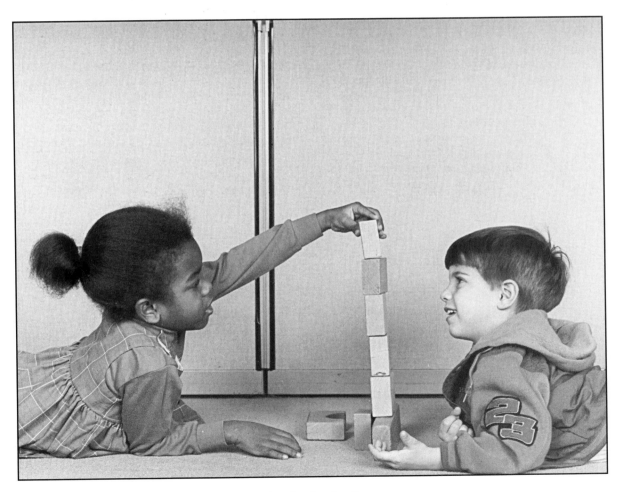

Assessing, recording, and reporting children's progress is one of the most controversial aspects of program development for young children. Among the various types of early childhood programs, greater diversity appears in the area of assessment than in almost any other aspect of the programs. The controversy centers on (a) the purposes of and the methods used in assessment; (b) the staff time spent in recording children's progress, the possibility that records will negatively stereotype children, and the indiscriminate release and use of information about children and their families; and (c) the problem of what and how to communicate assessment results to parents about their children and to the community or sponsors about the program.

ASSESSING

Assessing goes beyond measuring, grading, or classifying. **Assessment** involves four separate processes. First is determining the need and thus the purpose of assessment. Second is the gathering of qualitative and perhaps quantitative evidence by the appropriate method. Recently, many concerns have been raised about appropriate assessment instruments. Third is processing the information so as to permit the formation of judgments. Processing may be as simple as converting raw scores into local stanines or as involved as using many types of data collected over time to form an individual profile. And fourth is the making of professional judgments. At this point, assessment is simply a tool in the decision-making process. As professionals, we never remove ourselves from the assessment process because only well-trained humans can make the "call"—the value judgment.

Types of Assessment in a Historical Perspective

The history of assessment is a history of learning about children's growth and development and of various initiatives to improve educational programs. From this history, two types of assess-

ment have emerged: authentic assessment and standardized assessment. Understanding these alternative methods of assessment is needed before examining the history of early childhood assessment and today's concerns about assessment practices.

Types of Assessment. *Authentic assessment* is a relatively new term but not a new concept. Authentic assessment is sometimes called *performance assessment* because authentic assessment requires children to demonstrate what they know and what they can do. **Performance assessment** has been defined by R. Berk (1986) as the "process of gathering data by systematic observations for making decisions about an individual" (p. ix). Bergen (1993/94) makes a distinction between performance and authentic assessment. She sees **authentic assessment** as performance assessment connected to the "real world" or a simulation of that world (the performance is an application of the learning). Others define *performance assessment* by using the same criteria as Bergen uses for authentic assessment. For example, R. Berk includes as a criteria for *performance assessment* the idea of applying knowledge within the context of a real or simulated situation. Basically, the two terms seem to be used interchangeably. Authentic or performance assessment has the following characteristics:

1. Assessment areas are based on the total curriculum content that was designed to meet each child's needs in all domains of development (as opposed to testing isolated "bits and pieces" of the curriculum covering the cognitive domain almost exclusively).

2. Assessment data are gathered by observing children in their day-to-day tasks and in the familiar setting or by examining the products of children's performance (e.g., the art creation).

3. Assessment is part of the continuous teaching-learning process, rather than a separately scheduled event. (Summary records are completed periodically, however.)

4. Qualitative criteria are used in making professional judgments. If the evaluator references the child's performance to its position on a path of development, the term *developmental assessment* is frequently used.

Characteristics of authentic assessment can be further delineated. For example, Wiggins (1989) uses 27 standards to define authentic assessment.

Standardized tests can be thought of as "store bought" tests developed by people familiar with test construction and as more formal assessment devices than authentic assessments. Standardized tests have the following characteristics.

1. Specific directions for administering the test are stated in detail, usually including even the exact words to be used by the examiner in giving instructions and specifying exact time limits. By following the directions, teachers and counselors in many schools can administer the test in essentially the same way.

2. Specific directions are provided for scoring. Usually, a scoring key is supplied that reduces scoring to merely comparing answers with the key; little or nothing is left to the judgment of the scorer. Sometimes, carefully selected samples are provided with which a student's product is to be compared.

3. Quantitative data are usually supplied to aid in interpreting the part and composite scores. Generally, the test is referred to as a **criterion-referenced measure** (a measure in which a person's behavior is interpreted by comparing it with a preselected or established standard or criterion of performance) or a **norm-referenced measure** (a measure in which a person's behavior is interpreted against the behavior of others—hopefully, but not always, of similar backgrounds on the same testing instrument).

4. Information needed for judging the value of the test is provided. Before the test becomes available for purchase, research is conducted to study its reliability and validity.

5. A manual that explains the purposes and uses of the test is supplied. It describes briefly how the test was constructed; provides specific directions for administering, scoring, and interpreting results; contains tables of norms; and provides a summary of available research data on the test.

Standardized tests are often classified on the basis of content. For example, standardized tests may be classified as follows:

1. *Aptitude tests.* **Aptitude tests** measure a person's capacity for learning. These tests are designed to evaluate a person's ability to progress in cognitive activities; they may measure an aggregation of abilities or one or more discrete abilities. Items on aptitude tests are "(1) *equally unfamiliar* to all examinees (that is, novel situations) or (2) *equally familiar* (in the sense that all students have had equal opportunity to learn, regardless of their pattern of specific courses)" (G. Adams, 1965, p. 182). Aptitude tests for (a) general mental ability, (b) special aptitudes (e.g., motor performance, articulation), and (c) screening tests are available.

2. *Achievement and diagnostic tests.* **Achievement tests** measure the extent to which a person has mastered certain information or skills as a result of specific instruction or training. Readiness tests focus on current skill acquisition. Diagnostic components of achievement tests pinpoint specific areas of weakness on the basis of item analysis of achievement tests. Achievement and diagnostic tests are given most frequently in the areas of reading, language, and mathematics and may also be given in other school subjects.

3. *Personal-social adjustment tests.* **Personal-social adjustment tests** are, in reality, tests of good mental health. Generally, a person is considered to have good mental health if his or her behavior is typical of his or her own age and cultural group.

Not all tests fit into one of these categories. Tests may be classified on other bases. Classification is not as important as the description of the purpose as given by the test developer.

History of Assessing Young Children.
Observations of young children, the assessment method used in authentic assessment today, were used exclusively until standardized tests were developed near the beginning of the 20th century. The earliest recorded observations were probably the baby biographies, such as Pestalozzi's *A Father's Diary*, written in 1774, and Dietrich Tiedemann's work published in 1878. Charles Darwin also published a diary of the development of his infant son in 1877. Most baby biographers were not content to simply describe natural observations, but they also tried little experiments with their children. Teachers, too, wrote of their observations, such as Elizabeth Peabody's descriptions of children's thinking in the Alcott school (Peabody, 1835).

Since the beginning of formal education, teachers have tested schoolchildren's knowledge of subject matter by using both oral and written formats. The beginning of the science of statistics and the child study movement of the 20th century, however, resulted in the development of standardized tests. These tests for young children included the Gesell Developmental Scales, the Merrill-Palmer Scale of Mental Development, Minnesota Preschool Scales, Goodenough Draw-a-Man Test, Iowa Test for Young Children, and the Cattell Infant Intelligence Scale.

By the 1930s, most schools engaged in some standardized testing, but the amount of testing per child was very small, compared with today's testing. For example, prior to 1950, few students took more than three standardized tests before graduation from secondary school; parents were rarely informed of results; and schoolwide results were not publicized (Perrone, 1990). Standardized tests were rarely given at the primary level. Young children who took standardized tests were usually the subjects of research studies.

For the most part, programs for young children, including programs established for research purposes, used systematic observations of young children. For example, preservice teachers at the Normal School in Worcester, Massachusetts, kept observational records of children as suggested by G. Stanley Hall (Haskell, 1896). Harriet Johnson, Caroline Pratt, and Lucy Sprague Mitchell, who organized the Bank Street Bureau of Educational Experiments Nursery School in New York City, kept observational records on children in their natural settings (Greenberg, 1987). Louise Woodcock (1941) published her observations of 2-year-olds at Bank Street. Susan Isaacs (1930, 1933), the gifted teacher in Cambridge, England, published many of her insightful observations. Thus, many teachers and even researchers recognized the advantages of systematic observations even after standardized tests became available.

Because the early childhood years were considered a special time in a child's life—a time when individual growth patterns were highly respected—standardized tests had little impact on young children's lives until the 1960s. A wave of standardized tests swept early childhood programs with the launching of Head Start and the model preschool programs. More than 200 preschool tests were published between 1965 and 1980 (Paget & Bracken, 1983). Most of these tests were achievement standardized tests and were used as a measure of program effectiveness. Standardized tests were also used to identify children at risk as mandated by P.L. 94-142 and P.L. 99-457 (now P.L. 101-476 and P.L. 102-199, respectively). The level of testing soared to new heights with the publication of *A Nation at Risk* (National Commission on Excellence in Education, 1983). Because of this concern, state governments became involved in further extensions of testing programs.

Concerns About Standardized Assessment Practices.
As can be seen from the history of tests and testing, standardized tests were in

keeping with the didactic ideas of behaviorists (Skinner, 1938; Thorndike, 1906). Thus, the "academic" early childhood programs (the behavioral-environmental models) used standardized tests to measure the effectiveness of the program by quantifying children's progress. Public school early childhood programs also tended to adopt the standardized testing that had been conducted in the upper elementary levels and secondary schools.

Conversely, more child-centered approaches to assessment had long been advocated by many early childhood leaders (Dewey, 1900; Frank, 1937; G. Hall, 1907; Hymes, 1955). These child-centered approaches to the education of young children were reinforced by psychological ideas receiving serious consideration beginning in the 1960s, such as Piaget (1952, 1963), Erikson (1950), Flavell (1977), Guilford (1967), Hunt (1961), Vygotsky (1978), H. Gardner (1983), Bronfenbrenner (1979), and Bandura (1977). With the explosion of standardized tests and testing, professionals, especially those in the constructivist camp, became vocal concerning how some assessment uses and practices have the potential for doing harm. The following recent concerns should be taken seriously by early childhood program administrators:

1. The assessment instrument may not match the program's rationale. One of the greatest dangers is that assessment itself can determine a program, rather than a program determining the how and why of assessment. It is almost as though the cart is placed before the horse. For example, some program planners take the content of standardized tests and plan activities to teach these items. Teaching to a test encourages a narrow academic program. "Curriculum based on tests is narrow and fails to embed knowledge in meaningful contexts, thus making it virtually unusable for the learner" (Bowman, 1990, p. 30). The order should be reversed. A program should be rationally planned and based on current and accurate

information about children; then, tests should be selected to fit the program's goals and objectives.

2. Assessment instruments may not reflect current theory used in the program. For example, the whole language approach to reading instruction is advocated by many, but reading achievement tests focus on narrow subskills (Teal, Hiebart, & Chittenden, 1987). Likewise, achievement tests in mathematics look at subskills rather than at the construction of number concepts.

3. Tests may be used for purposes other than those for which they were designed. In many early childhood programs, readiness tests instead of developmental screening tests are used supposedly to assess the child's ability to acquire skills. (Readiness test results often lead to placement and retention decisions.) Readiness and screening tests can never be used interchangeably (Meisels, 1989a).

4. Tests may not meet the standards given in the current edition of *Standards for Educational and Psychological Testing* (e.g., acceptable levels of validity and reliability, statistics appropriate to the program's purpose, lack of inherent cultural and linguistic biases).

5. Testing may be stressful for children (Charlesworth, Hart, Burts, & DeWolf, 1993). Testing itself is always a problem with young children because young children do not have a repertoire of test-taking skills. Some of the problems these children have are inadequate motor skills for taking paper-and-pencil tests, short attention spans, problems in following directions, and the problem of being influenced by the tester and/or the physical setting. Staff need to be aware of children's feelings. Parents are also under a great deal of stress when their children are being tested. Many parents are apprehensive of decisions based on testing and on labels that may be placed on their children if "inadequacies" are noted. Commercial publishers are "feeding" on parent anxieties by selling kits on test-taking skills for pre-kindergarten,

kindergarten, and first graders (J. Robinson, 1988). Some states also offer "CAT Academies" for these young children. Staff may also be under stress. Testing drains learning time and funds. In some schools, children's achievement test scores are used as the predominant indicator of a teacher's and/or a program's accountability. Unfortunately, this situation has led to teachers' basing their curriculum on certain tests and, in some instances, teaching the test items themselves, helping children with the answers during the testing session, and even tampering with recorded responses. These pressures should be removed immediately.

6. As discussed in Chapter 2, placement and retention decisions should not be based on data from one assessment source. Stiggins (1991) referred to this use of tests as the "ultimate sorting tool."

Position Statements on Standardized Testing.

Because of these concerns in assessment practices, two professional associations have issued strong statements about standardized testing of young children: the National Association for the Education of Young Children (NAEYC, 1988) and the National Council of Teachers of English (NCTE, 1990). The goal is not to prohibit all standardized testing. The goal is for early childhood administrators to recognize the following:

1. Assessment instruments should be used only for their intended purposes.

2. Assessment instruments should meet acceptable levels of quality (e.g., validity, reliability).

3. Placement/retention decisions should be made from multiple sources of data.

4. Assessment instruments should be used only if children will benefit, and benefit does not come from reduced group variation. (Schools must be more adaptive to normal variance.)

Shepard (1994) has added two principles to the NAEYC's guiding principle of assessment—

that any assessment practice should benefit children or else it should not be conducted. Shepard adds: (a) "the contents of assessments should reflect and model progress toward important learning goals" (p. 208); and (b) the methods of assessment must be developmentally appropriate. To understand how these principles are applied, 30 questions for program administrators to affirm in making assessment decisions were included in the position statement of the NAEYC and the National Association of Early Childhood Specialists in State Departments of Education (1991).

Purposes of Assessment

In early childhood programs, assessment is being used for many purposes. The following three purposes are the most common:

1. Although much concern about the role of assessment in placement and retention factors has been expressed, assessment is being used as a factor or *the* factor in placement and retention practices.

2. Assessment is being used for curriculum planning. This form of assessment is used to determine a child's progress in attaining program goals/objectives and to serve as a tool in parent-staff communication. Assessment used to modify curriculum, to determine methodology, and to provide feedback in a mastery-learning strategy is called **formative assessment.**

3. Testing is also used in program evaluation. Program evaluation permits the planning of additions to or revisions of services and even determines changes in program rationale. Assessment used to determine the effectiveness of curriculum and methodology and to provide a product measurement is called **summative evaluation.** One example of summative evaluation is the "Early Childhood Longitudinal Study: Kindergarten Cohort" commissioned by the U.S. Department of Education. Beginning in the 1998-99 academic year, a representative sample of

23,000 kindergartners will be followed through Grade 5. The Technical Planning Subgroup identified these five dimensions that should be assessed: (a) physical well-being and motor development, (b) social and emotional development, (c) approaches toward learning, (d) language usage, and (e) cognitive and general knowledge. This assessment will not look at individual children, but rather will monitor national and state trends toward achievement of Goal 1 (National Education Goals Panel, 1991).

Authentic Assessment Methods

For purposes of this book, **authentic assessment methods** are considered performance assessment closely connected to the "real world" and having the four basic characteristics listed under "Types of Assessment." Because the definition is broad, these informal methods may range from general observation of children while they engage in activities to staff-constructed tests designed to measure specific knowledge and skills. (Although this chapter treats "Assessing" and "Recording" as separate topics, one cannot really describe authentic assessment without referring to some types of records.)

Observations.   Undoubtedly, observation is the most frequently used authentic method of assessing young children's progress. Observations are also the most rewarding method of assessing children's growth and development. The NAEYC calls for more systematic observations of student performance (Bredekamp & Shepard, 1989).

The observer must be unobtrusive. Observers should not have interactions with or reactions to children's activities. Observers must never discuss their observations casually if children can be identified or professionally if any child or any adult (except adults involved with the child in the program) is within hearing distance. Written records must also be kept secure. We know of at least 19 types of observations and a number of systems for recording and storing observations, as well as for analyzing the data (Fassnacht, 1982). The purposes of the observations determine the method of observation and the recording system. Three popular methods of observing young children and some of the recording possibilities used by teachers (and researchers) are described.

Naturalistic Observations.   **Naturalistic observations** are observations of a child engaged in regular day-to-day activities within the natural setting. These open-ended observations allow the child options that, in turn, permit the teacher (or researcher) to see the uniqueness of the child.

Naturalistic observations may be recorded as an anecdotal record or a running record. An **anecdotal record** is a record of an incident in a child's life that occurred during participation in program activities or during a home visit. Characteristics of a good anecdote are as follows:

1. It gives the date, the place, and the situation in which the action occurred. This is called the **setting.**
2. It describes the actions of the child, the reactions of other people involved, and the responses of the child to these reactions.
3. It quotes what is said to the child and by the child during the action.
4. It supplies "mood cues"—postures, gestures, voice qualities, and facial expressions that give cues to how the child felt. It does not provide interpretations of the child's feelings, but only the cues by which a reader may judge what they were.
5. The description is extensive enough to cover the episode. The action or conversation is not left incomplete and unfinished, but rather is followed through to the point where a little vignette of a behavioral moment in the life of the child is supplied (D. Prescott, 1957).

Below the narrative account, space should be left for comments. These comments may be interpretive (what the observer believes about the incident) and evaluative (what the observer believes should be done to help the child developmentally; see the example in Figure 9-1).

A **running record** is similar to an anecdotal record, except it is more detailed with a total sequence of events (see the example in Figure 9-2).

A **specimen-description** is a method in which the observer records all the events within a given situation. One records the entire "stream of behavior," which is so complete it can be dramatized. Because one cannot observe/record this very complete running record and teach at the same time, specimen-descriptions are usually written by researchers. The technique is described in detail by Wright (1960), and one example is Barker's (1951) *One Boy's Day.*

Structured Observations. **Structured observations** are structured in terms of bringing children into contrived environments (e.g., how infants react when a stranger is present, while the mother is present, or while the mother is absent) or identifying a specific, defined behavior, observing it in the natural environment, and keeping quantitative records (e.g., Sarah had 2 biting episodes on Monday and 1 biting episode on Tuesday).

Two types of structured observations are **event-sampling** and **time-sampling.** For these observations, a behavior is preselected (called a **target behavior**), defined very specifically, and then observed. To record, the observer usually knows when to expect the behavior (e.g., time of day, during a certain activity, in a certain grouping pattern, and/or with a given adult). In event sampling, the observer is trying to confirm a hypothesis about what triggers the behavior. Thus, three items are recorded: (a) the antecedent behavior (what led to the target behavior), (b) the targeted behavior (complete description of the incident), and (c) the consequent event (reactions of the child, such as crying; see the example in Figure 9-3).

In time-sampling, a target behavior is preselected, carefully defined, and then observed at specified intervals. For discrete behaviors, a simple frequency tabulation is recorded (see the example in Figure 9-4).

Figure 9-1   Anecdotal Record of Behavior

Child's name _Susie_ Date _2/12/96_

Setting: _Block center in a child care center; activity child-chosen._

Incident: _Susie was building a block tower. When the seven-block tower fell, she tried again. This time, she only succeeded in getting six blocks stacked before they fell. She kicked her blocks and walked over to John's nine-block tower and knocked it over. When the teacher approached, she cried and refused help with the tower. (John left the center after his tower was knocked over.)_

Comments: _Susie is showing more patience by rebuilding—a patience not seen last month. However, her crying and destructive responses are not as mature as they should be for a 5-year-old. She must be shown ways to cope with these common frustrations._

Child's name ___Susie___ Date ___2/12/96___

Setting: ___Block center in a child care center; activity child-chosen.___

Incident		Comments
9:25	Susie watches three or four children play with the blocks.	Susie is interested in the blocks.
9:30	She calls to John, "What are you doing?" John replies, "I'm building a tall, tall building, the biggest one ever." Susie says, "I can build a big one."	She especially likes John's tower. Susie is apparently challenged.
9:31	Susie stacks seven blocks. They fall. (She counts the blocks in John's tower.) She again starts stacking blocks—with the sixth block, they fall.	Susie knows she almost got the same height tower again. Susie is willing to try again.
9:35	She kicks at her blocks three times and then walks over to John's tower and strikes it with her hand.	Her aggression spreads to John.
9:37	Mrs. Jones approaches Susie. Susie turns her back on Mrs. Jones and cries. Mrs. Jones kneels down and talks to Susie. Then Mrs. Jones picks up a block, but Susie runs away.	She is not yet willing to be comforted or helped. Teacher's approach was calming—no more aggression.
	(John left the center earlier.)	

Figure 9-2   Running Record of Behavior

Figure 9-3   Event-Sampling Behavior Record

Child's name ___Mike___ Date ___2/1/96___

Behavior: ___Biting a child on exposed skin areas___

Time	Antecedent	Behavior	Consequent Event
8:00	Children eating breakfast as they arrive. Ann has finished breakfast but takes a piece of apple off Mike's plate	Mike tries to get it back. When unsuccessful, bites Ann's hand.	Ann cries, and Mike calls out, "I didn't bite."

NOTE: Other behaviors are recorded as they occur.

Figure 9-4   Time-Sampling Behavior Record

Child's name_____ Date _____

Time 1	Time 2	Time 3	Time 4	Time 5
9:00	9:05	9:10	9:15	9:20
V+	V+	NV–	V–	0

V = verbal interaction
NV = nonverbal interaction
0 = no interaction
+ = positive
– = negative

Because the amount of writing is reduced, the observer can record observations on several children in one session by rotating observations in a predetermined and consistent manner among the children. Using the time periods in the above example, Child A would be observed during the 1st minute of each time frame—9:00 to 9:01, 9:05 to 9:06, and so on; Child B would be observed during the 2nd minute of each time frame—9:01 to 9:02, 9:06 to 9:07, and so on; and in a similar way, three other children would be observed.

For nondiscrete behaviors (e.g., crying, clinging to adult, wandering around the room), the length of occurrence or duration is often recorded (see the example in Figure 9-5).

Both frequency and duration recordings may be summarized in graphs, which give visual representations. Even two complementary behaviors may be plotted on the same graph for a better picture of a child (e.g., daily totals of aggressive and sharing acts).

Advantages and Disadvantages of Observations. Both naturalistic and structured observations are profitable with young children for two reasons: (a) Observations are appropriate for young children, and (b) observations of children are accurate with younger children who do not hide their feelings. Other reasons for the popularity of observation may be these factors: (a) A person can simultaneously work and observe children (unfortunately, many look and do not see!); (b) observations may be conducted by teachers, as well as by researchers; (c) observations may be conducted for long or short intervals of time; (d) observations may be used in conjunction with any other assessment method; and (e) observations are suitable for use in any type of program because one child or a group of children may be observed and any aspect of development can be assessed.

Disadvantages in using observations for assessment are that (a) the validity of observation depends on the skill of the observer; (b) the observer's biases are inherent in observations; (c) the soundness of observations may depend on the behaviors observed because some aspects of development, such as motor skills, are easier to observe than others, such as thinking processes; (d) when a person is simultaneously working with children and observing them, it can be difficult to "see the forest for the trees"; and (e) one-way mirrors used in observation rooms and hidden audio- or videotapes may not be ethical.

Interviews.   Interviews with parents are now used with greater frequency in early childhood

Figure 9-5   Duration Record of Behavior

Child's name _____ Date _____

Behavior: *Wandering from center to center. (Child stays less than 2 minutes at an activity in one "stretch.")*

Days	Time	Total
1	9:04–9:08	4
	9:12–9:13	1
2		
3		
4		
5		

Average: 1.9 minutes per day

programs. The interview method permits a more comprehensive picture of the child's life at home and with peer groups. **The interview method of assessment** generally has these characteristics:

1. Questions used in an interview are usually developed by staff although interviews are available in publications such as the *Vineland Adaptive Behavior Scales—Classroom Edition* (Sparrow, Balla, & Cicchetti, 1984).

2. Parents of the child are usually interviewed; others familiar with the child are occasionally interviewed.

3. Specific questions in the interview commonly include background information about the child and sometimes the family. Interview data help in assessing needs and potential program services.

Interviews with children may be structured as in the **psychometric method,** or semistructured, as in the **exploratory method.** In the *psychometric method,* the examiner must follow a standard set of procedures specified in a manual, without any deviation. With the *exploratory method,* the examiner tests a hypothesis by following the child's train of thought in a conversational way (the examiner tries to understand and be understood by the child; Kamii & Peper, 1969).

Advantages of the interview as an assessment technique are that (a) valuable information—both verbal and emotional—may be gleaned; (b) interviews can be used in conjunction with other assessment methods; (c) they are suitable for use in any type of early childhood program; and (d) interviews can help clarify and extend information found on written forms. The interview method also has disadvantages: (a) The information obtained may not be comprehensive or accurate because the questions were unclear or not comprehensive and/or because the interviewee was unable or unwilling to answer; (b) the interviewee's and interviewer's biases are entwined in the information given and in the interpretation of the information, respectively; and (c) the interview method is very time-consuming.

Samples of Children's Work.   Samples of children's work serve as an excellent authentic method of assessment if they meet the following criteria:

1. Samples of various types of children's work should be collected: dictated or tape-recorded experiences told by children; drawings, paintings, and other two-dimensional art projects; photographs of children's projects (e.g., three-dimensional art projects, block constructions, a completed science experiment); tape recordings of singing or language activities; and videotapes of any action activities.

2. Samples are collected on a systematic and periodic basis.

3. Samples are dated, with notes on the children's comments and attitudes.

Advantages to using samples of children's work as an assessment technique are that (a) the evidence is a collection of children's real, ongoing activities or products of activities, and not a contrived experience for purposes of assessment; (b) collecting samples is not highly time-consuming; (c) collecting samples works for all aspects of all programs; (d) samples can be used as direct evidence of progress; (e) if samples are dated and adequate notes taken about them, interpretations can be made later by various people; (f) some samples can be analyzed for feelings as well as concepts; and (g) samples can be used in conjunction with other assessment methods. Disadvantages are that (a) samples may not be representative of children's work; (b) samples of ongoing activities are more difficult to obtain than two-dimensional artwork; (c) some children do not like to part with their work; (d) storage can be a problem; and (e) photographs, magnetic tapes, and videotapes are relatively expensive.

Staff-Constructed   Tests.   Many staff-constructed tests are administered to children in early childhood programs; however, most of these tests are not the conventional paper-and-pencil variety that are administered to all children at the same time. Characteristics of **staff-constructed tests** are as follows:

1. Most tests are administered to individual children although a few tests are given to small groups or to the entire class at one time.

2. Administration of the tests is usually conducted by observing the skills and concepts exhibited as children engage in the program's activities, by asking questions, and by requesting demonstrations of skills and concepts. For example, a staff member might note which children can measure during a cooking experience; point to a red ball and ask, "What color is this ball?"; or request that a child skip or count beads set out on a table.

3. In most staff-constructed tests, the content of each test covers one skill or a group of related skills and is administered for the purpose of assisting staff in planning activities. Some staff-constructed tests are inventories of many skills and concepts, with the information used for referral, placement, or retention.

4. Scoring of staff-constructed tests usually consists of checking the skills and concepts each child has mastered or rating the level of mastery achieved.

The advantages of staff-constructed tests are that (a) if the tests are carefully constructed, a match will occur between test items and program goals and between test items and developmental levels; (b) they are adaptable to the program's time schedule; (c) they lend themselves to many types of responses, such as gross-motor, manipulative, and verbal; (d) they can be used in conjunction with other assessment methods and tests; and (e) they are inexpensive and do not require the services of a psychometrist for administering, scoring, and interpreting. A disadvantage of staff-constructed tests is that the match between the program goals and test items depends on the skill of the staff member who constructs the test items.

Standardized Tests

As has been discussed, standardized tests have a shaky status among many early childhood professionals (Wolf, Bixby, Glenn, & Gardner, 1991). Although the number of tests has proliferated, the types of tests have not really expanded a great deal (see Appendix 8 in Decker & Decker, 1992). Furthermore, the psychometric quality of most standardized measures designed for young children has been and continues to be inadequate (S. Anderson & Messick, 1974; Langhorst, 1989; Lehr, Ysseldyke, & Thurlow, 1987; Meisels, 1989a). Finally, misuses of tests and abuses of children, professionals, and parents have been associated with standardized tests.

Concerns about testing young children are not new, nor are they specific to standardized tests. In fact, Bredekamp and Shepard (1989) stated that the NAEYC was not anti-standardized tests as long as:

1. The tests themselves meet the *Standards for Educational and Psychological Testing* (American Educational Research Association, American Psychological Association, & National Council on Measurement in Education, 1985). In addition to the *Standards*, the Joint Committee on Testing Practices and the Code of Fair Testing Practices in Education have extended proper test use even farther (Diamond & Fremer, 1989). Some tests that meet the technical and fair testing standards are given by Langhorst (1989) and Meisels (1989a).

2. The test use must be shown to benefit children. Many professionals see standardized tests especially beneficial for these situations:
   a. The early identification and screening of children for health and developmental problems
   b. The determination of whether planned interventions of identified children are indeed effective
   c. The use in studies in which data yielded by a specific standardized test or an adaptation of the test most accurately address the phenomenon being investigated by a researcher or policymaker.

RECORDING

Record keeping, the documentation of assessment, has always been an important aspect of a staff member's duties; today, record keeping is becoming even more important and prevalent. Most early childhood programs have a philosophy of providing for children's individual differences, and record keeping allows the program to assess and improve the services it provides. There is also greater involvement with parents and increasing mobility of both children and staff. In addition, funding agencies, citizens' groups, boards of directors or school boards, and parents often require "proof" of the early childhood program's effectiveness in meeting its goals, so the evidence is often best demonstrated by the records that have been kept. Possible disadvantages to record keeping are that (a) a staff member can spend more time keeping records than in planning and working with children; (b) a staff member can make a prejudgment based on records and become positively or negatively biased toward a child; (c) because of the requirements of P.L. 93-380, the Family Educational Rights and Privacy Act of 1974, staff need special training in developing accurate, appropriate, and relevant records and in developing record protection and handling procedures (a more comprehensive discussion of P.L. 93-380 appears later in this chapter); and (d) record keeping may become a meaningless activity because the types of data required to be kept may not be congruent with the goals of the local program or because records may be filed and forgotten or may not be used effectively.

Computers are helping programs overcome some of these problems. For example, microcomputers can store information, maintain and generate files, and ensure privacy of records (by coding the computer so that only specified people have access to certain parts of a child's file). Producers of software have noted teachers' needs for quick and accurate record keeping.

Uses of Records

Records have many effective uses. Records are especially valuable to staff as guides for planning the types of experiences each child needs. The process of recording data causes staff to think about each child more profoundly. Staff are forced to consider each child, not just categories like "children with problems," "extra-bright children," or "creative children." By studying a child's records, a staff member can find evidence of strengths and weaknesses and can better judge what actions to take or whether he or she should look further. In short, records should not be used as instruments for stereotyping children; rather, they should help staff formulate a realistic but open-ended picture of a child. Good records also permit independent assessment of a child by more than one person.

Records can help staff see each child's progress. Staff who work daily with a child may not be able to see progress except through a review of the records. Records are also beneficial to a child who changes programs frequently. Records of a recently transferred child make it easier for staff to assist the child in the new situation. Finally, the child can see his or her own progress in records—especially in collected, dated, and sequenced samples of work.

Records are used in referral conferences. If a problem exists, records can make the work of specialists (guidance counselors, physicians, caseworkers) more efficient. Through records, these specialists can determine whether a problem is transient or continuous, when a problem began, and how pervasive its effects are in the child's development. On the basis of the evidence found in the records, specialists can suggest possible solutions to the problem.

Records can be used as a basis for discussion with parents. The Task Force on Early Childhood Education of the National Association of State Boards of Education advocate a multilateral relationship in which parents and staff exchange information in a reciprocal process (National Association of State Boards of Education, 1988).

Records have other uses. The local program's regulatory agency requires various records as a basis for subsequent funding. Records also help teachers see results of new teaching techniques or services. Records can also be used as data for research.

Types of Records

Records may be classified in many ways. For purposes of this book, we classify records as background information records, performance records, referral records, and summary records.

Background Information Records. Early childhood professionals are realizing that early experiences in the home and neighborhood and previous early childhood program (or school) experiences provide important "pictures" of a child. Many programs now ask for considerable information from parents. Sometimes, these records are supplemented by additional information obtained by a caseworker or specialist or are volunteered at a later date by the parents or the child.

Basic information about a child and the child's family is always part of **background information records,** including the child's legal name, home address, and telephone number; birth date, birthplace, and birth certificate number; number of siblings; legal names of parent(s)/guardian(s), home address and telephone number, occupation(s), place(s) of business, and business telephone number(s).

Medical information is also included in the background information records, and completion of medical information records is required before a child is admitted to a program. (See the section entitled "Forms" in Appendix 8.) Usually, parents complete a health history form that asks for a general evaluation of the family's health; a history of the child's illnesses (especially communicable diseases); frequent illnesses or complaints, such as colds, headaches, or sties; and any physical or personal-social disabilities that might affect the child's participation in the program. Medical professionals must complete records of recent physical and dental examinations and immunization records. These records may call for comments on any significant medical findings concerning eyes, ears, nose, throat, glands, heart, circulation, lungs, bones, joints, reflexes, and so forth; a statement as to whether the child can participate in the regular program or needs an adjusted program; the condition of teeth and gums; and dates of immunizations.

Finally, records on the child's personal-social history are frequently included as part of the background information records. This information may be supplied by a parent or by another adult who knows the child. Parents may record the information on forms, or a staff member may record the information during an interview. The child's personal-social history is likely to include information about birth history (birth weight, problems associated with birth, and/or birth defects); self-reliance; development, especially affective development and motor skills; previous experiences that aid concept development, such as places the child has visited in the community, trips taken beyond the community, and previous group experiences; problems, such as disabilities and illnesses, fears, and accident proneness; and interests, such as television programs, computers, books, toys, pets, and games. Occasionally, questions are asked about the family situation, family relationships, and parent attitudes and may encompass family income, housing, occupations, educational level, aspirations for their children, and views of child rearing, including guidance methods parents have found to be effective.

Performance Records.   Performance records include any documentation regarding children's

development and learning. A given performance record may be used as an entity, such as a composite score on an achievement test. Conversely, a performance record may be used as a professional note, such as an anecdotal record, contributing only one piece to the child's blueprint.

As stated many times throughout the book, programs coming from a behaviorist approach tend to assess performance in the three R's. For the most part, professionals in these academic programs use various types of standardized tests. For example, screening, diagnostic, or intelligence tests may be used for placement decisions; readiness tests may be used for making instructional decisions; and often achievement tests are used for measuring each child's progress toward a criterion or for comparing the achievement of children with that of the norming group. Occasionally, observational methods, samples of children's work, and staff-constructed tests are used; even then, the focus is on the end products—the narrow, observable program objectives. Conversely, in constructivist programs, professionals want to assess knowledge, skills, dispositions, and certain affective expressions in all domains and in many contexts. Constructivists find authentic assessment techniques and the performance records generated from these techniques compatible with their beliefs.

Performance records take several forms. The chosen form depends on the nature of the observation. For example, if a teacher wants to assess whether a child can name certain colors, a check sheet makes a more appropriate record than a rating scale. Conversely, a social competence, such as "getting along with others," exists on a continuum and thus is better described by using a record that has a continuum format, such as a rating scale. Common forms of performance records include the following:

1. *Log entries.* Log entries are short, dated notes. A single entry may not be significant, but multiple entries in one area of development spanning weeks and months often provide use-

ful information. Many teachers find it easier to write logs on several children (and possibly in several domains) on pages that have been divided into eight rectangles or on pages of white, adhesive labels. (The log notes will measure approximately 1½" to 2¾" × 4".) Each note or label is then transferred to an individual child's record sheet devoted to a specific domain of development (see Figure 9-6).

2. *Anecdotal entries.* Anecdotes often give more information than logs. Similar to a series of log entries, a series of well-written anecdotes in one domain can reveal patterns of development. As previously discussed, a running record is an even more thorough account of performance. Figure 9-7 is an example of an anecdotal record.

3. *Check sheets.* A check sheet is a prepared list of behaviors based on program goals. The teacher simply indicates the presence or absence of these behaviors in a child. Dating (rather than merely checking) observed behaviors provides more information. Check sheets may be completed while actually observing children because information can be recorded rather quickly, or check sheets with more summary types of statements (e.g., "Uses physical one-to-one correspondence") can come from narrative records, such as a series of log entries. Some records, called *checklists* by some professionals, are really more like rating scales because teachers are given the behavioral descriptors and then are asked to check on a continuum (e.g., "no evidence, beginning, devel-

Figure 9-6   Individual Child's Log Entries

Domain: Mathematics   Child's name _____

10/3/96
Placed a napkin at each child's plate but returned to the napkin holder for each separate napkin.

10/27/96
Watched E.M count the number of napkins needed for her table. Then imitated E.M. at her table. In putting napkins on the table, she returned to napkin holder for each separate napkin

Figure 9-7   Anecdotal Record

Sept. 27. Tim and two other boys (Stefan and Binh) were in the sandbox using dump trucks for hauling sand. Stefan remarked that his lot needed more sand than the lot to which they had just delivered one dump-truck load. Tim looked and asked, "How much more sand?" "Twice as much," replied Stefan. "Then I'll drive my truck up once and give them a load and come back for one more load of sand," Tim commented.

oping, or very secure"). An example of a check sheet in shown in Figure 9-8.

4. *Ratings.* Behaviors that can be described according to the degree to which the competence or trait exists can be recorded on rating scales. Three popular types of rating scales are:

a. *Forced-choice.* Observers must choose among predetermined (spelled-out) behaviors on a continuum (see Figure 9-9).

b. *Semantic differential.* The observer is given descriptions of the two extremes, which are, of course, opposites on the continuum. The observer chooses any marked point between the extremes. Often, the number of points between the extremes (see Figure 9-10) is an odd number (3, 5, 7, or 9).

c. *Numerical.* Numerical scales use numerals on a continuum (often 1–3, 1–4, or 1–5). Each numeral may be verbally described, or only certain numerals may be

described (e.g., endpoints or endpoints and middle numerals; see Figure 9-11).

5. *Samples of children's work.* Samples of children's work can take many forms. Common samples are drawings/paintings and papers showing language and mathematics skills. Less common, but very important samples, are (a) pictures of three-dimensional art products, block structures, and even two-dimensional materials too large to easily keep; (b) printouts from computer work; (c) audiotapes of verbal performances; and (d) videotapes of other performances (e.g., motor skills, interactions with others in the program).

6. *Test scores and diagnostic, profile information.* These records are often raw or converted scores or other graphic or descriptive information coming from performance on staff-constructed or standardized instruments.

Figure 9-8   Check Sheet

(Child's name)

Art Concepts

Can recognize these colors: red   _____

yellow   _____

blue   _____

green   _____

orange   _____

purple   _____

black   _____

brown   _____

Can arrange four varying grades
of sandpaper from rough to smooth.   _____

Can name the colors and point to
rough and smooth fruit in a
reproduction of Cezanne's painting
Apples and Oranges.   _____

Figure 9-9   Forced-Choice Rating Scale

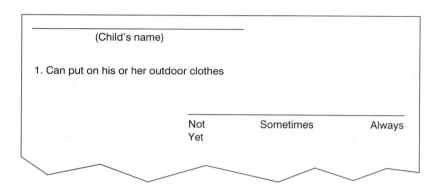

_____

(Child's name)

1. Can put on his or her outdoor clothes

Not   Sometimes   Always
Yet

Figure 9-10   Semantic Differential Scale

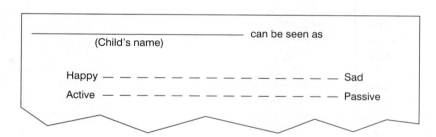

_____ can be seen as

(Child's name)

Happy — — — — — — — — — — — — — — Sad
Active — — — — — — — — — — — — — — Passive

Figure 9-11   Numerical Rating Scale

_____

(Child's name)

1. Motor skills can best be described as:

	1 = Poor skill <— — — — —> 5 = Excels in skill				
hops	1	2	3	4	5
skips	1	2	3	4	5
climbs steps (ascending)	1	2	3	4	5

Referral Records.   All early childhood programs that employ specialists for purposes of working with children who need unique assistance need **referral records.** Specialists hired as full-time staff or as part-time consultants may include medical professionals, psychometrists, counselors, speech pathologists, and physical therapists. If the program does not employ specialists for support services, it will be necessary to develop a community resource directory. In some cases, a directory may be available through the local Chamber of Commerce, the United Fund, the Community Council, or the state's Department of Social Services. Administrators who must compile their own file of community resources should include in each description the basic service; whether it is health, mental health, or recreation; name of the agency, its address and telephone number; the days and hours of operation; and a detailed explanation of the services it provides, eligibility requirements, and name of the person to contact.

The contents of referral records must be in keeping with the law. Local early childhood programs should develop a separate referral form for each type of referral (different forms for referral to medical specialists, speech pathologists, and so forth). The items on each form differ, but each type should include the signed permission for referral from parent or legal guardian; date and person or agency to which referral is being made; name of the staff member referring the child; specific reasons for referral; either a digest of or the complete reports from other referrals; comments or attitudes of parents, peers, or the child him- or herself if these are available; length of time the staff member has been aware of the problem; and what staff or parents have tried and with what success. Many referral records allow space for the specialist's report after evaluation and/or support services are provided.

Summary Records.   **Summary records** are records that summarize and interpret primary data. No new information is added, but primary data are studied and interpreted. Summary records are completed several times a year to aid teachers in better understanding each child's progress and interests for purposes of curriculum planning and communicating with parents. Summary records are used to abstract collective data (with individual children's identification removed) for aiding program administrators in their periodic reports to their funding agencies.

Historically, early childhood programs have had many degrees of quantity and quality in summary records. Most family child care programs and small child care centers have not kept any performance records. Public school programs have kept cumulative records on children from entrance to graduation. A **cumulative record,** a summary record of the entire school career, was often reduced to a card the size of a file folder. The cumulative record was limited to the child's name, birth date, and certificate number; parent's name and address; child's immunization records; and each year's attendance record, summary grades, standardized test information, and a digest of any major actions taken by the school or family (e.g., referrals). Many university-sponsored child study and teacher training programs and some government- and foundation-supported early childhood programs have kept voluminous records on young children's growth and development.

Background information records and referral records, on the one hand, are kept intact and updated but are rarely summarized. Performance records, on the other hand, written or collected by using various formats and encompassing a length of time, must be reviewed and reduced to a summary format in order to analyze them for either formative or summative purposes. Thus, summary performance records often use broad descriptors of behavior, such as "Likes to write" or "Knows that print is read left-to-right and top-to-bottom." These summary statements can be developed from the program's goals for children's development and learning in each domain. Some program administrators may prefer to look at various published summary instruments and adapt them to fit the goals of the local program. Examples of sources for summary instruments in single areas (e.g., literacy and social competence) follow:

Beaty, J. J. (1990). *Observing development of the young child.* New York: Merrill/Macmillan.

McClellan, D., & Katz, L. G. (1992). Assessing the social development of young children: A checklist of social attributes. *Dimensions of Early Childhood, 21*(1), 9-10.

Morrow, L. M., & Smith, J. K. (1990). *Assessment for instruction in early literacy.* Englewood Cliffs, NJ: Prentice Hall.

Other summary instruments, designed to assess many domains, are called *developmental assessment systems.* (These are discussed in detail in the section on "Trends and Issues.")

Portfolios, which are compatible with authentic assessment methods, are being used as both initial and summary records. A **portfolio** is a record-keeping device used to store the various records that have been discussed, as well as notes taken during communication with parents and perhaps some notes from parents. Process portfolio materials are initial records usually kept in several folders or an expandable file folder with about 12 pockets for each child. (The file folders or pockets should be labeled background information records, anecdotal records, artwork, and so forth). Archival portfolio materials include summary records and some initial records or copies of these records used to document the summary data. Archival portfolio materials are perhaps best kept in an individual three-ring binder with materials displayed in clear vinyl page-sized pockets. The archival portfolio is used for formative (and possibly summative) assessment, for parent-teacher communication, and as baseline information for the next program the child attends. Because portfolios are becoming so popular, a list of readings on portfolios is given at the end of this chapter.

Public Law 93–380

Children's records are now protected under the Family Educational Rights and Privacy Act of 1974, P.L. 93–380. This law provides that:

1. Parents of children who attend a school receiving federal assistance may see information in the school's official files. This information includes test scores, grade averages, class rank, intelligence quotient, health records, psychological reports, notes on behavioral problems, family background items, attendance records, and all other records except personal notes made by a staff member solely for his or her own use.

2. Records must be made available for review within 45 days of the request.

3. Parents may challenge information irrelevant to education, such as religious preference or unsubstantiated opinions.

4. Contents of records may be challenged in a hearing. If the school refuses to remove material challenged by parents as inaccurate, misleading, or inappropriate, the parent may insert a written rebuttal.

5. With some exceptions (e.g., other officials in the same school, officials in another school to which the student has applied for transfer, some accrediting associations, state educational officials, some financial aid organizations, the courts), written consent of parents is required before school officials may release records. Schools must keep a written record as to who has seen or requested to see the child's records.

6. Parents have the right to know where records are kept and which school officials are responsible for them.

7. Unless a divorced parent is prohibited by law from having any contact with the child, divorced parents have equal access to official records.

8. Most of the foregoing rights pass from parent to child when the child is 18 years of age.

9. School districts must notify parents (and the 18-year-olds) of their rights.

REPORTING

Reporting is becoming a more important aspect of early childhood programs as programs seek to involve parents in their children's development and as the programs become more accountable to parents, citizens' groups, and funding and regulatory agencies. As is true of all aspects of an early childhood program, reporting practices should be based on program goals. Planning reporting requires administrators to think in terms of four steps in developing a reporting practice: (a) determining the purposes of reporting, (b) facilitating reporting through assessment data, (c) determining the methods of reporting, and (d) rethinking the reporting plans. Because reporting is so tied to the assessing and recording process, it is best considered before assessment plans are completed.

Determining the Purposes of Reporting

The first step in developing a reporting practice is to determine the purposes of reporting. For most early childhood programs, the major purpose of reporting is to provide information to parents about their child's progress. Parents and staff jointly discuss the child's strengths and needs and plan the next steps in the educative process. In addition to parent-staff communication, the other major purpose of reporting is to meet the requirements of funding and regulatory agencies. (Although funding and regulatory agencies require reports on many aspects of programs, program success as measured by children's progress is a major component in the reports made to all regulating and sponsoring agencies. This chapter addresses the reporting of children's progress only.)

Facilitating Reporting through Assessment Data

Once the specific purposes of reporting have been determined, the second step is to make a connection between assessment data and purposes. Several important questions are as follows:

1. *What type of assessment meets the purposes of reporting?* More specifically: (a) What information do parents need to know about their child's progress? (Likely, much of this informa-

tion will be the same as teachers need for curriculum decisions.) and (b) What information does the regulatory or funding agency expect to know about the collective progress of children that, in turn, will demonstrate the program's value? (These data can be used in rethinking program goals too.) Basically, the desired information for both parents and agencies should be directly linked to the program goals. Programs that have the more narrow, academic goals will assess and report children's progress in those areas; programs with the more holistic developmental goals will gather and report data in many domains of children's development.

2. *In what format will assessment data be recorded?* Generally, standardized tests yield quantitative data—numerical raw scores (e.g., number correct) and numerical converted scores (e.g., percentiles, stanines, developmental ages), and authentic assessment techniques yield qualitative data (e.g., anecdotes, samples of children's work). If one considers assessment data from the standpoint of the ease of reporting *only* (not in terms of its appropriateness for program goals and the ages of children involved although these are critical criteria), quantitative data are more difficult to explain to parents who want to know what the "scores mean." Furthermore, composite scores yield no information about specific strengths and weaknesses in each child's progress; thus, reporting requires a careful interpretation of subscore data. Quantitative data, however, lend themselves to concise summary data often expected by funding and regulatory agencies; in fact, many standardized achievement tests provide class record/profile data that can be easily incorporated into agency reports. In some cases, however, quantitative scores may not be understood by those reading the agency reports. Conversely, qualitative data are much easier for parents to understand but are more difficult to summarize easily and definitely do lend themselves to tables and graphs. If both quantitative and qualitative assessment data

have been collected, the teacher must explain each type of data *and* also show how the data relate to each other.

3. *Against what criterion will assessment outcomes be measured?* For example: Is progress being compared with that of a norming group? Is progress measured against specific program goals? Is progress being compared with developmental landmarks? This information must be reported.

4. *How will data be assembled?* The ways in which data are assembled determine the ease of access and the need to summarize before reporting.

Determining the Methods of Reporting

The third step is to determine the method or methods of reporting, especially to parents. (Agencies usually have their own reporting formats.)

Reporting methods are diverse. The types of methods are both oral and written. Most parents prefer some of both types. Common methods include informal reports, report cards, check sheets, narrative report letters, and individual conferences.

Informal Reports.   **Informal reports** are perhaps the most common way of reporting—so common that staff may not even be aware they are communicating information about children's progress. This kind of report may be a casual conversation with a parent in which a staff member mentions, "Lori excels in motor skills," or, "Mark is learning the last step in tying his shoes." Parents may note their child's progress while volunteering in the program. Samples of children's work with or without teachers' comments are often sent home. Children, too, report on themselves, such as, "I learned to skip today," or, "I shared my boat with everyone at the water table."

Report Cards.   **Report cards,** written progress reports recorded on heavyweight paper or card stock, have been the traditional form for reporting children's progress. Because the items assessed supposedly represent school objectives and because the recorded data become part of the child's permanent record, report cards are seen as legal or quasi-legal documents.

Traditional Report Cards.   The traditional report card is more frequently used in early childhood programs that enroll kindergarten or primary children (programs that have an educational focus) than in programs that enroll children of pre-kindergarten age. Because the predominant marking system on report cards presents assessments of work habits, reading readiness, and mathematics readiness, report cards are used mainly in programs with the behaviorist perspective. Although rumors circulate that the report card is dead, or at least dying, it in fact survives, finding its way into homes at monthly to semiannual intervals.

Traditional report cards usually list such items as academic subjects or activities and areas of personal-social adjustment and have a blank space opposite each item for recording a symbol denoting progress. A key on the report card interprets the symbols, whether they are the traditional A, B, C, D, and F symbols (rarely used) or others. Other specifics frequently included are the child's attendance record, a space for comments, and a parent's signature line for each reporting period. Because the items selected for inclusion on the report card should fit program goals, the items vary. The following list, compiled from a nationwide sampling of kindergarten report cards, indicates the wide range of assessed achievements:

> general well-being (e.g., alertness and ability to rest)
>
> identity (e.g., writes name, knows address)
>
> social maturity (e.g., friendly, shares, controls temper)
>
> eye-hand coordination (e.g., able to use art and hand tools, able to trace shapes)

perception of direction (e.g., shows consistent handedness, knows right-left)

work habits (e.g., has adequate attention span, follows directions)

language development (e.g., speaks clearly, has adequate vocabulary, makes up stories)

reading readiness (e.g., understands sequence, shows interest in stories, recognizes likenesses and differences both visually and aurally)

mathematics (e.g., counts rationally, recognizes numerals)

science (e.g., shows curiosity, classifies)

music (e.g., enjoys listening and singing, participates in rhythmic activities)

art (e.g., enjoys arts and crafts, recognizes colors, handles tools correctly)

health, safety, and physical education (e.g., practices good health habits, obeys safety rules, participates in physical activities, shows good sportsmanship)

Traditional report cards come in various styles. One style may require the staff member to check a child's achievements. An understanding or skill the child has not developed is left unchecked. This style closely resembles the check sheet and is shown in Figure 9-12.

Another style may require staff to mark both understandings and skills the child has achieved and not achieved. A report card style that might be used for a program that serves children of bilingual families is shown in Figure 9-13.

The example shown in Figure 9-14 requires the teacher to denote each child's progress by marking one of three choices. Another style calls for the teacher to assess both effort and progress on each item, as shown in Figure 9-15. Yet another style requires the teacher to assess progress on each item on an inferior-superior

Figure 9-12   Report Card With Achievements Checked

A Message to Parents

In kindergarten, your child lives, works, and plays with other children of his or her age. He or she has learning experiences that are a foundation for all that follows in later school years. This card is a description of your child's development at this time. Each quality checked is evident in your child. You, as a parent, will help and encourage your child by your interest in his or her growth.

BEHAVIOR IN LARGE- GROUP SITUATIONS	Participates with confidence	
	Usually follows others	
	Participates in activities	
	Gets along well with others	

RESPONSE TO RULES	Cooperates when encouraged	
	Accepts group decisions	
	Follows rules of the school	

Figure 9-13   Bilingual Report Card

Name (Nombre) _____

S   Satisfactory growth at this time.
     Desarrollo satisfactorio al presente.

N   Not yet.
     Todavia no es satisfactorio el desarrollo.

Can hop Puede saltar		Puts on wraps Se pone el abrigo	
Knows age Sabe su edad		Knows address Sabe su domicilio	

Figure 9-14   Level of Progress Checked

Progress Report

Name _____

A check shows the child's performance	1st Semester			2nd Semester		
	Most of the time	Part of the time	Not at this time	Most of the time	Part of the time	Not at this time
WORK HABITS						
Takes care of materials						
Has good attention span						
Is able to work independently						
Follows group instruction						

continuum; such a style is actually a rating scale, as shown in Figure 9-16.

Newer Report Cards.   The traditional report card does not fit the needs of the constructivist-based programs that often assess children's progress by authentic methods. Good (1993) describes a report card that could be used by programs adhering to the constructivist rationale. The four major areas she includes on these report cards are (a) *the identification section* (e.g., name of school, year, grade/level, child's name, and teacher's name), which is typically included on traditional report cards too; (b) *the educa-*

Figure 9-15   Effort and Progress Checked

EDUCATIONAL GROWTH	EFFORT		PROGRESS	
	Adequate	Needs to improve	Shows development	Shows strength
PERSONAL ATTITUDES AND SKILLS				
Is interested and contributes				
Can put on outdoor clothing				
Can tie shoes				
Can wait his or her turn				
Keeps hands to himself or herself (doesn't bother others)				
STORY PERIOD				
Retells stories and rhymes				
Refrains from disturbing others				
Sits quietly				
Shows interest in story				
Listens while story is read				

tional philosophy section, in which both the general philosophy and specific features of the program are described; (c) *the progress report section,* which is tied to actual practices, rather than to "subject areas," uses checklists as shown in Figures 9-12 and 9-14, and has a place under each developmental area (e.g., fine motor, emergent literacy) for teacher comments; and (d) *the response section,* which provides space for parents to comment. A space should also be provided in which a parent-teacher conference can be requested by either the teacher or a parent.

Check Sheets.   **Check sheets** contain lists of desired behaviors. The teacher indicates that the child has developed a particular skill or has shown understanding of a particular concept by a check mark—hence, the name. Some programs use check sheets as the only method of reporting, but check sheets are more frequently used in conjunction with other methods of reporting. These sheets may be given to a parent during an individual conference or may be enclosed in the report card. Check sheets generally differ from report cards in the following ways:

1. They are usually printed on sheets of paper, rather than on cards.
2. Categories of items on check sheets are similar to those on report cards, but the items on check sheets tend to be more specific. An item on a report card might read as shown in Figure 9-17. The same category listed on a

Figure 9-16   Progress Rating Scale

Your Child's Progress

Name of child _____   Year and class _____

School _____   Teacher _____

                                                        Rarely   Constantly

GROWTH AND DEVELOPMENT

A.   Considers ideas and
      points of view of others   _____

B.   Demonstrates good
      health habits   _____

C.   Expresses ideas and
      feelings   _____

Figure 9-17   Progress Report Card

                                        Always   Sometimes

Puts on outdoor clothing   [   ]

check sheet might look like the example in Figure 9-18.

3.   Items on report cards may rate a child as to degree of accomplishment (e.g., "satisfactory," "progressing," "needs improvement"), whereas check sheets indicate whether or not the child has accomplished a specific task.

Narrative Report Letters.   Programs using **narrative report letters** usually provide forms on which staff write a few brief comments about a child's progress under each of several headings, such as psychomotor development, personal-social adjustment, cognitive development, language growth, work habits, problem-solving growth, aesthetic growth, self-reliance, and general evaluation. An example of a narrative report letter form is shown in Figure 9-19. Narrative report letters are highly appropriate for summarizing authentic assessment records. The advantage of report letters is that staff can concentrate on a child's specific strengths and needs without giving letter grades or marking "satisfactory/unsatisfactory" and without noting progress in highly specific areas, such as "knows his address" or "ties her shoes." The two disadvantages to report letters are that (a) report letters are highly time-consuming, but the use of computers lessens time spent in preparing them (the

Can button clothes . . . . _____

Can put on overshoes . . . . _____

Can zip a coat . . . . _____

Can lace and tie shoes . . . . _____

Figure 9–18   Progress Check Sheet

computer generates the report form and permits the word processing of the narrative itself); and (b) unless teachers carefully study their records on each child, they may slip into writing stereotypical comments, especially after writing the first few reports.

Individual Conferences.   Many programs schedule **individual conferences** with each child's parents. Conferences permit face-to-face communication between parents and teachers. A teacher must plan intensively for a successful conference. (General guidelines for planning the conference are given in Chapter 10.)

To effectively discuss children's progress, teachers need to plan the conference by using a written guide sheet that lists topics and main points to be discussed. The teacher should consult all records on the child and carefully transfer to the guide sheet any information to be shared with parents. A report card, check sheet, or developmental profile given to parents can be used as the guide sheet. Portfolio materials should be shared as a way to document what is

Figure 9-19   Progress Report Letter

Your Child's Progress

Name_____ Level _____

Psychomotor development (motor skills):

George can gallop, skip, run, and throw and catch a rubber ball. He enjoys all games that use movement, and his skills indicate that his attainment is high in this area of development.

Personal-social adjustment:

George does not initiate many aggressive acts; however, he still has trouble keeping his hands to himself. He responds to negative overtures from his classmates by hitting.

Language growth:

George appears to enjoy new words. He uses rhyming words and makes up words to fit the rhymes. He has not been able to express the negative feelings toward others with words, however.

General evaluation:

George is progressing nicely. More opportunities to talk with others would help him learn to express himself. He performs well in the room and on the playground as long as he is kept busy and as long as others leave him alone.

said and/or written as a summary report. Time is provided for parents to express their concerns as topics listed on the guide sheet are covered. Additional concerns of parents need to be addressed too. Conferences end on a positive note, with plans for follow-up in areas of concern at home and at school. Many program administrators are finding that if teachers give a copy of the guide sheet to each parent a few days before the conference, parents have time to think about the contents and to prepare questions and comments for the conference.

Rethinking the Reporting Plans

The final step in developing a reporting practice is to experiment with the reporting plans and revise them if necessary. Reporting practices must not only work for program personnel, but they must also open dialogue between staff and the recipients of reports, especially parents. To develop dialogue, teachers may need to experiment with reporting methods. In short, the only purpose of reporting to parents is to establish collaborative efforts on behalf of children.

TRENDS AND ISSUES

Assessment reform seems to be lagging behind the push to modify the curriculum. Many administrators and teachers agree with the concept of authentic assessment, and these professionals seem to have the support of state leaders in education departments who stated that standardized testing is one policy they would like to eliminate (S. Robinson, 1993/94). In attempts to implement authentic assessment, however, program administrators and teachers have found more questions than answers. Many have not learned the new assessment procedures. Furthermore, because most educators have relied on normative or criterion-referenced data to make decisions, they are not familiar with making professional judgments based on broader pictures of children and may even be hesitant in

taking this responsibility. In short, program professionals do not trust themselves in using authentic assessment as *the* way to assess. Thus, many early childhood programs are trying to use standardized and authentic assessment simultaneously. This use doubles the work of assessing, does not resolve any of the concerns about the use of standardized tests, and is needless because of the more accurate picture of children's progress gained through authentic assessment.

Indeed, a gap does exist between idealized portrayal of authentic assessment and its implementation. Roe (1991) found possibilities for unfairness stemming from variations in ways in which teachers implement mandates to use authentic assessment. Schweinhart (1993) believes that informal assessments offer no criteria against which to judge the value of children's activities and actions and that they do not provide evidence of reliability and validity. He believes that developmental scales with established reliability and validity are best. The more informal methods can be used to further document the developmental assessment. Examples of these developmental assessment systems follow:

1. *High/Scope Child Observation Record* (High/Scope Educational Research Foundation, 1992). The *Child Observation Record (COR)* is used to assess children ages 2½ to 6 years in developmentally appropriate programs. Using notes taken over several months describing episodes of a child's behavior in six COR categories (initiative, creative representation, social relations, music and movement, language and literacy, and logic and mathematics), the teacher rates the child's behavior on 30 5-level COR items. Teachers score the COR two or three times each year, with the initial ratings given after children have been in the program 6 to 8 weeks.

2. *Measurement and Planning System (MAPS).* MAPS assesses children's use of knowledge in a social context (e.g., use of language to communicate, such as storytelling). MAPS is

comprised of three observational instruments. The *MAPS PL (Preschool Level Scales* (Bergan et al., 1992a) and the *MAPS KL (Kindergarten Level) Scales* (Bergan et al., 1992b) assess early mathematics, nature and science, emerging literacy, and social development. *MAPS M (Motor) Scale* (Feld, Salado, Bergan, & Schwarz, 1990) assesses perceptual motor development at the preschool and kindergarten levels.

3. *Project Spectrum* (Krechevsky, 1991). Project Spectrum began in 1984 as an attempt to reconceptualize the traditional basis of intelligence tests (linguistics and logicomathematical abilities). The theoretical foundation of Project Spectrum is based on H. Gardner's (1983) theory of multiple intelligences and Feldman's (1980) theory of development in non-universal domains. Project Spectrum measures children's strengths in seven domains (numbers, science, music, language, visual arts, movement, and social) through structured tasks and less structured measures. Children's working styles (e.g., ease of engaging child in activity, child's confidence, child's focus, child's persistence) are also measured for each domain. All the information is compiled into a "Spectrum profile," a nontechnical, written description.

4. *The Work Sampling System* (Meisels, 1992). The Work Sampling System is a performance assessment system used to assess and document children's skills, knowledge, behavior, and accomplishments in seven domains (personal/social development, language and literacy, mathematical thinking, scientific thinking, social studies, art and music, and physical development) and performed on multiple occasions. The Work Sampling System is comprised of these components: (a) six checklists (accompanied by guidelines) designed to reflect common activities and expectations in a developmentally appropriate children's program; (b) a portfolio made up of "care" items (repeated work in several domains and common to all children) and "other" items (child-selected samples of their

work and thus unique to the individual portfolio); and (c) a "summary report"—a brief report completed three times per year and based on teacher observations and records of children's performance in each of the domains and judged against certain evaluative criteria.

Each of these assessment systems is authentic assessment that requires teachers' judgments of children's progress; however, these systems provide a structure for the assessment data and inform teachers of criteria that may be used in making inferences about what children can do. In addition, these systems have the qualities of strong standardized tests—that is, a strong reliability and predictive validity.

SUMMARY

Assessment, recording, and reporting are integral parts of an early childhood program. Thus, these components must be thoughtfully and carefully planned, in keeping with program goals. Providing quality assessment, recording, and reporting is not a simple matter, but requires a highly trained staff and leadership by administrators.

Similar to the professional concerns about inappropriate curriculum content and teaching strategies are concerns about standardized tests. Abuses and misuses have occurred in the way in which tests have been selected and administered; by the lack of a user-friendly format for young children; by the use of single measurements for making "high stake" decisions about children, staff competencies, and program effectiveness; and by the way in which scores have been interpreted to parents.

Professional associations have called for many changes in assessment, recording, and reporting practices. The major changes recommended include the following:

1. The *almost* exclusive use of ongoing, unobtrusive observations of children in actual

classroom situations (authentic performance assessment).

2. Documentation of authentic performance assessment done by the writing of logs and anecdotes, the checking and rating of certain specified behaviors, and the gathering of samples of children's work. Other records can include notes taken during interviews and home visits and the summaries of evaluations and services provided by specialists.

3. The development of reporting purposes and practices that mirror local program goals and that are verified by authentic performance assessment and appropriate observation records. Usually, the contents of reports are summarized performance records, with samples of actual performance used to document the summary data. The format for reporting may be written and/or oral.

Standardized tests are still being used by programs adhering to narrow academic goals. Among early childhood professionals who want to avoid the pitfalls of using standardized tests, the shift to authentic performance assessment has not been easy. Many issues and related questions have surfaced, such as the development of assessment instruments, the establishment of standards for judging performance, the use of results with parents and agencies, and the lack of appropriate staff training.

FOR FURTHER READING

Au, K. A., Schëu, J. A., Kawakami, A. S., & Herman, P. S. (1990). Assessment and accountability in a whole literacy curriculum. *Reading Teacher, 43,* 574-578.

Beaty, J. J. (1994). *Observing development of the young child* (3rd ed.). New York: Merrill/Macmillan.

Brandt, R. S. (Ed.). (1992). Using performance assessment (Special issue). *Educational Leadership, 49*(8).

Cambourne, B., & Turbill, J. (1990). Assessment in whole-language classrooms: Theory into practice. *Elementary School Journal, 90,* 137-149.

Cohen, D. H., Stern, V., & Balaban, N. (1983). *Observing and recording the behavior of young children* (3rd ed.). New York: Teachers College Press.

Gibbs, E. D., & Teti, D. M. (1990). *Interdisciplinary assessment of infants: A guide for early intervention professionals.* Baltimore: Paul H. Brookes.

Kamii, C. (Ed.). (1990). *Achievement testing in the early grades: The games grown-ups play.* Washington, DC: National Association for the Education of Young Children.

Leavitt, R. B., & Eheart, B. K. (1991). Assessment in early childhood programs. *Young Children, 46*(5), 4-9.

Meisels, S., & Provence, S. (1989). *Screening and assessment: Guidelines for identifying young disabled and developmentally vulnerable children and their families.* Washington, DC: National Center for Clinical Infant Programs.

Meisels, S. J. (1986). Testing four- and five-year-olds. *Educational Leadership, 44,* 90-92.

Morison, P. (1992). Testing in American schools: Issues for research and policy. *Social Policy Report, 6*(2), 1-24.

National Association for the Education of Young Children & National Association of Early Childhood Specialists in State Departments of Education. (1991). Position statement: Guidelines for appropriate curriculum content and assessment in programs serving children ages 3 through 8. *Young Children, 46*(3), 21-40.

Nicholson, S., & Shipstead, S. G. (1994). *Through the looking glass: Observation in the early childhood classroom.* New York: Merrill/Macmillan.

Puckett, M. B., & Black, J. K. (1994). *Authentic assessment of the young child.* New York: Merrill/Macmillan.

Stiggins, R. (1991). Assessment literacy. *Phi Delta Kappan, 72,* 534-539.

Wortham, S. C. (1990). *Tests and measurement in early childhood education.* New York: Merrill/Macmillan.

READINGS ON PORTFOLIOS

Campbell, J. (1991). Laser disk portfolios: Total child assessment. *Educational Leadership, 49*(8), 69-70.

DeFina, A. A. (1992). *Portfolio assessment: Getting started.* New York: Scholastic.

Glazer, S. M., & Brown, C. S. (1993). *Portfolios and beyond: Collaborative assessment in reading and writing.* Norwood, MA: Christopher-Gordon.

Grace, C., & Shores, E. (Eds.). (1994). *The portfolio and its use: Developmentally appropriate assessment of young children* (3rd ed.). Little Rock, AR: Southern Early Childhood Association.

Graves, D. H., & Sunstein, B. S. (Eds.). (1992). *Portfolio portraits.* Portsmouth, NH: Heinemann.

Hansen, J. (1992). Literacy portfolios: Helping students know themselves. *Educational Leadership, 49*(8), 66-68.

Herbert, E. A. (1992). Portfolios invite reflections from students and staff. *Educational Leadership, 49*(8), 58-61.

Meisels, S., & Steele, D. (1991). *The early childhood portfolio collection process.* Ann Arbor: University of Michigan, Center for Human Growth and Development.

Tierney, R. J., Carter, M. A., & Desai, L. E. (1991). *Portfolio assessment in the reading-writing classroom.* Norwood, MA: Christopher-Gordon.

Valencia, S. W. (1990). A portfolio approach to classroom reading assessment: The whys, whats, and hows. *Reading Teacher, 43,* 338-340.

Valencia, S. W., & Calfee, R. (1991). The development and use of literacy portfolios for students, classes, and teachers. *Applied Measurement in Education, 4,* 333-345.

Chapter 10

※ ※ ※ ※ ※

Working With Parents

※ ※ ※ ※ ※

Families have always been involved in the education of their children. Where no schools were available, education of the young was a family function. The public school system of the United States was founded by parents and other citizens of the community. Schools not only were established by parents and other community members but also were run by them, which resulted in local schools and school boards with a membership comprised of lay people. The Parent-Teacher Association (PTA) has had a long history in public school education (Butterworth, 1928).

Historically, many early childhood programs had parent involvement. Frederich Froebel, founder of the kindergarten, developed activities for mothers to do with their infants. From the late 1800s through the early 1900s, kindergarten teachers in the United States taught children in the mornings and spent the afternoons visiting parents in their homes (Weber, 1969). Nursery schools valued and promoted parent involvement (McMillan, 1919). Nursery schools that operated in the prestigious academic institutions of the United States involved parents. Parents were dependent on the nursery school programs under the Works Progress Administration of the Depression years and the Lanham Act Centers during World War II. Montessori highly valued the role of parents and believed that the "mission of parents" was to "save their children by uniting and working together for the improvement of society" (Montessori, 1966, p. 215). More recently, the Head Start program developed performance standards that mandate parent participation. Laws for children with disabilities require parent involvement in decisions about each child's educational placement and treatment plan.

VALUES AND PROBLEMS IN WORKING WITH PARENTS

Although families have been involved in children's programs, the nature of the involvement has changed. As schools became more organized, professionals were put in control, and parents, especially mothers, were asked to (a) get children to school regularly, on-time, clean, fed, and ready to learn; (b) oversee children's homework; and (c) help with money-raising projects (e.g., making products for bake sales and school carnivals), escorting children on field trips, and correcting papers (in the back of a classroom). Even these activities were given to parents hesitantly because many staff members have responded with alarm to parent involvement. Some professionals have seen home teaching of academics as confusing to the child, parent visits to the program as disruptive, and parents' critiques of the program's curriculum and methodology as unqualified judgments of professionals by nonprofessionals. Thus, before the 1960s, working with parents was primarily parent education—the school communicating to parents but parents not involved in major decisions. Parents began to feel as though they were "friendly intruders" (Joffe, 1977).

By the 1960s, intervention programs (e.g., Head Start) mandated parent involvement. Instead of parent involvement being defined as solely parent education in child rearing, now education was concerned more broadly as support of the family. With the inclusion of children with disabilities into early childhood programs, parents' views, abilities, and difficulties had to be considered in program decisions, and parents themselves became more vocal (Comer, 1988; Fantini, 1970). More recently, quality early childhood programs have become more family centered, and some professionals have said the parent-child relationship rather than the child is the primary client (Galinsky & Weissbourd, 1992).

Research began to look at parent involvement in terms of increased child competence and parent self-development, expanded program resources (e.g., program volunteers), and greater parent leadership role taking in institutions serving families and children. Because the parent component of early childhood programs is so important, it is assessed as a competency area for the Child Development Associate credential; staff-parent interaction is a criterion for the accreditation of centers by the National Academy of Early Childhood Programs; and family and community relationships is a standard area addressed in the preparation of early childhood professionals by the National Association for the Education of Young Children.

Benefits of Working With Parents

On the basis of Bronfenbrenner's (1986) ecological model, two of the most significant environments for the child are the home and the school. Although these two environments affect the child separately, they also overlap to form an environment in which events in one environment affect the other.

Many benefits stem from parent involvement in early childhood programs. A. Henderson (1981), in an annotated bibliography, reported on 35 studies showing that various types of parent inclusion had positive results. An update of this report summarized 18 additional studies with similar findings (A. Henderson, 1987). These benefits affect the program, the child, and the parent.

Benefits for Program.   Early childhood programs can benefit from parent involvement. Benefits for the program include the following:

1. Parent involvement frequently enables the school to comply with federal and/or state guidelines. For example, the Head Start program mandates that the local advisory boards have parent representatives and that parents serve in the classroom as paid employees, volunteers, and observers. Federal guidelines established for programs serving children with disabilities require parents to be involved in the writing of the individualized education programs (IEPs) for their children.

2. Through parent involvement, schools achieve a better adult-child ratio. Parent

assistance often enables teachers to conduct program activities that would be impossible without such assistance.

3. Parents can serve as resource people. Their special talents and interests can be useful to the program.

4. Parents have a unique empathy in explaining the program's services and problems to other parents. Some early childhood programs have had a parent educator component in which parent educators (a) trained new parents in specific activities (e.g., toy making), (b) modeled language patterns to be used with activities, (c) explained the program rationale, and (d) stressed the importance of parent involvement.

5. In addition to sharing teaching responsibilities with professionals in the classroom and in the home, parents can serve as program decision makers. Many early childhood programs have parent advisory councils (discussed in a later section of this chapter).

6. When parents are available to "explain" the child's culture to the teacher, the teacher may become more empathic.

7. Parents have a chance to see other children of the same age and gain a more realistic picture of their child's strengths and weaknesses.

Benefits for Child.   A major premise is that goals for children are best achieved if parents and teachers agree on these goals and the basic ways of achieving them. B. Caldwell (1985) has suggested that early childhood programs function as an extended family. Benefits for the child include the following:

1. More quality adult attention increases the chance for greater achievement. Parents who interact, participate in intellectually stimulating activities, foster independence, and read and discuss stories with their children have children who show cognitive gains in language, concepts, and problem-solving skills (Comer, 1986). Zigler

(1970) points out that children who do not receive enough adult attention from parents have such a high need for attention that they are not motivated to solve intellectual problems; these children put effort into attention-seeking behavior, rather than into intellectual tasks. Parent involvement in an early childhood program is motivating.

2. Children see their parents in new roles and can see that parents and staff are working together for them. This relationship affects children's affective functioning, such as a positive self-image and a productive orientation to social relations (Schaefer, 1985; Spivack & Cianci, 1987).

3. Parent assistance in the early childhood program can enhance program quality, a benefit to the child.

Benefits for Parent.   Planned parent participation in early childhood programs is viewed as a means of enhancing parents as adults and as parents. Benefits for parents include the following:

1. Participation in early childhood programs can enhance parents' feelings of self-worth and contribute to increased education and employment (Slaughter, 1983; Zigler & Berman, 1983).

2. Parent-education programs can help parents gain confidence as parents. Self-image as a parent leads to confidence in the "parent as an educator" role (Swick, 1987). B. White (1988) found that effective parents were nurturing, had clear and consistent discipline, and were skilled at designing home learning activities. Parents can profit from the educational expertise the early childhood program offers in child development and guidance by bringing it into the home. Effective parents also become more involved within the total family (Rekers, 1985).

3. As parents become more effective with their children and within their families, they become more involved in the schools (Swick,

1987). Parents learn their importance in their children's education and how to help schools maximize educational benefits.

4. Parents may be able to help other parents. For example, inclusion may be stimulated by involving parents. Powell (1989) reported that, in some programs, parents of children with and without disabilities formed informal support networks.

5. Parents may even become an early childhood program's strongest advocates.

Problems of Working With Parents

Many benefits have been stated; however, parent involvement in an early childhood program may present some problems. Jacobs (1992) stated that the greatest ethical concerns of teachers pertained to their relationships with parents. Problems in working with parents include the following:

1. Sociologists theorize an optimal social distance between home and school. The distance protects the unique characteristics of each (Litwak & Meyer, 1974). It is difficult to find the balance in early childhood education, however, because teachers must do traditional parenting-type tasks (Katz, 1980). Studies have confirmed a tension between parents and teachers (Kontos, 1987). Two examples are (a) Kontos's (1984) findings that teachers saw parents as having far poorer parenting skills than the parents felt they had and (b) Galinsky's (1990c) findings that mothers who expressed guilt about working were more likely to be seen as inadequate parents than those who worked but did not express guilt. Galinsky reported that parents and teachers felt possessive about children, and often jealousy was noted.

2. Parents and teachers may have different values, goals, and discipline techniques. These differences stem from their respective personal perspectives based on family and community

structures and other cultural influences. Greenberg (1989) states that when families feel alienated, children often believe that they must choose between home and school or "compartmentalize" their two worlds, and these children often become major discipline problems. Professionals must develop understandings about the sources of these differences and show as much acceptance for the variety of parent views as they do for differences in children. Sometimes, conflicts between professionals and parents are not caused by differences in values or goals; rather, some conflicts are caused by an incongruity in how to achieve certain goals. For example, both parents and professionals want children to succeed in school. Professionals who follow or desire to follow the constructivist approach, however, are reporting much pressure from many parents to provide a structured, academic curriculum (Stipek, Rosenblatt, & DiRocco, 1994). In these types of conflict, "education" of the parent seems to be the means of handling these differing views.

3. Some parents, particularly those from lower socioeconomic classes, feel inhibited or even inferior around staff personnel because of their limited and unsuccessful school experiences and because of the socioeconomic distance between themselves and staff. Communication with staff can be difficult or embarrassing for parents who cannot read or write English, do not have paper or pencil, or cannot get to school because of work hours, transportation, or babysitting problems. Similarly, racial minority parents may feel uneasy, especially around staff who come from the majority race. Some teachers respond negatively to lower socioeconomic class and minority parents, often discounting what they do for their children (Greenberg, 1989). Kontos and Wells (1986) concluded that the parents needing the most staff support were least likely to get it. Conversely, professionals can feel threatened by parents, especially those who are highly educated. Staff see these children coming

to programs already "knowing," having been taught by uncredentialed parent-educators (Greenberg, 1989).

4. Parents may feel helpless about their ability to contribute in a meaningful way to a program. The demographics of family structure leave little time to support program activities (Heath & McLaughlin, 1987). For example, Greenberg (1989) noted that only 50% of elementary schools now have Parent-Teacher Associations. The lack of time also translates into a general anxiety about child rearing (Galinsky & Hooks, 1977).

5. Because parents of children with disabilities have greater jurisdiction over their children's care and education than parents of children without disabilities, collaboration has some different types of impediments. Seligman (1979) reports that teachers occasionally blame parents for causing or not preventing their children's disabilities (e.g., teachers may blame parents of children who have fetal alcohol syndrome). Gargiulo (1985) found some professionals not wanting to share responsibilities with parents. Schulz (1987) stated that some professionals may even deny parents' knowledge about their own children. Similarly, parents' attitudes and actions may impede meaningful collaboration. For example, Kraft and Snell (1980) identified four types of these parents: (a) the parent who constantly calls attention to the school's shortcomings, (b) the parent who takes no initiative, (c) the parent who abuses the teacher's time, and (d) the parent who claims he or she has greater educational expertise than the professional.

6. Parents and staff bring their stress to the relationship (Galinsky, 1988). Stress often results in conflict over program policies. For example, on the one hand, parents expect staff to take into account the lack of anyone to care for sick children at home, getting to the center by bus before closing time, and their need to "pay later." On the other hand, staff members expect parents to

understand limitations of group care (e.g., caring for individual children, hours of operation, and payment of fees).

Many of these problems may be overcome. A few suggestions are given:

1. Time to work with parents must be built into staff schedules.

2. Professionals must truly listen to parents and convey the idea that the parent is the leader of the parenting team comprised of all those who support the development of the child. The roles of both the parent and the teacher must be defined. Teachers are supportive of, not substitutes for, parents. Powell (1987) has identified four teacher roles in working with parents: (a) child-rearing information and advice, (b) emotional support for parents, (c) role modeling, and (d) referrals. Parents do seem to prefer distinctions between the role of the parent and the professional; for example, Powell (1977) found that almost 85% of parents believed they should discuss center goals and expectations with staff; however, over 61% of parents did not want to share information about the family.

3. Contrary to some professionals' beliefs, most parents want to help their children. Epstein (1986) found that over 85% of parents in his study helped their children daily and were even willing to help them for longer time periods daily. Parents may not be able to participate in the traditional parent activities, but many want to be involved. Thus, programs should implement an involvement program tailored to the needs of parents. For example, Seefeldt (1985) has suggested parent participation in the curriculum of an early childhood program. She suggests sending home stories about school life dictated by children and written down by staff; booklets with lists of favorite stories, songs, and poems; and snapshots, tape recordings, and samples of children's work. Other ideas include flexible hours and baby-sitting and transportation services for school conferences.

4. Programs need to work for total support of parents, such as advocating before- and after-school child care. Seefeldt (1985) has suggested that the Foster Grandparent Program offers companionship to all members of the family rather than just to the child.

5. Professionals need to learn to work with "difficult" parents just as they work with "difficult" children. Although the literature on techniques for working with these parents is rather scarce, some effective techniques are discussed by Boutte, Keepler, Tyler, and Terry (1992). When conferring with parents whose children need special services, professionals need to consider how parents feel about having and caring for children with disabilities. Gargiulo (1985) says professionals need to know and understand the stages through which parents work (e.g., denial, anger, grief), how these stages may reappear from time to time, and how parents of one child may be in different stages of feelings.

6. Those working in early childhood programs need to be trained to work with parents. This is basically a neglected area in many teacher-training programs and in-service activities. Chavkin (1989) reported that less than 4% of early childhood professional development programs offer courses in parenting. More and more work is being done, however. For information, contact professional early childhood education associations (see Appendix 4) and the National Coalition for Parent Involvement in Education, the National Committee for Citizens in Education, and the National Congress of Parents and Teachers (see Appendix 5 for addresses).

LEGAL RIGHTS OF PARENTS

The legislative and judicial branches of government have recognized the need for parent involvement. Consequently, legislation and litigation have been a part of the history of parent involvement in schools for young children. Because of the extent of this history, only a few key examples of parents' legal rights are discussed here.

Public schools are funded and advised by the local school district. The concept of local control is fundamental to public school organization, and parents, as citizens and taxpayers, have a right to be involved in the decision-making process.

All educational agencies that receive funds under any federal program administered by the U.S. Office of Education must follow the Family Educational Rights and Privacy Act of 1974. This law allows parents access to their children's official records. Due process is also granted if parents wish to challenge the records on the grounds that they are inaccurate, misleading, or inappropriate. Parents must give written permission for the release of their children's records to a third party. Under this law, parents must be informed of their rights to access, to use the due process provision, and to determine whether records may be released.

As discussed in Chapter 3, parents of children with disabilities have specific rights, including a role in yearly diagnosis, in placement decisions, and in development of the IEPs. A due process provision is also a part of parents' rights.

Questions are not completely resolved about the status of parent rights and autonomy of the professional. In the statutes of most states, the teacher stands **in loco parentis** (in the place of the parent) to the child. This legal terminology is replaced in some state statutes by other phrases meaning the same thing. In states without such a provision, the court affirms the in loco parentis position of the teacher. To more appropriately assume this role, teachers should know what parents want for their children.

PARENT INVOLVEMENT

In a survey of early childhood leaders in state departments of education (S. Robinson, 1993/94), the change noted most frequently was increased parent involvement. The movement toward greater parent involvement in programs for young children has come about for several reasons. First, in a democracy, all citizens have the right to be involved in the operation of their social institutions, including the schools. Throughout the history of public education in the United States, citizens have professed and defended the benefits of community control over educational policy and decision making.

Second, the importance of the roles of families in children's overall development is more fully understood. The school working in isolation is likely to be impotent. Sharing goals and information can calm parent fears of educational settings and build trust in the parent-teacher relationship (J. Oakes & Lipton, 1988). Cooperation between parents and the school can give children a sense of security, knowing that both institutions are working together for their welfare. It can help both parties recognize each other's competencies and weaknesses and thus determine the best way to meet the common goal of fostering successfully functioning children.

Third, early childhood educators promote the *early* involvement of parents in programs for maximum impact. Bronfenbrenner (1979) has suggested that a setting's (e.g., home *or* school) developmental potential is improved when linkages exist between settings (e.g., homes *and* early childhood programs). Also, when parents cooperate from the beginning, there is a chance for lasting program concern and identification. Professional associations and many local parent groups work for parent involvement in the schools.

Involvement with parents includes parent-staff communication and parent participation. The National Association for the Education of Young Children (NAEYC) developed standards that called for parents to be well-informed about programs and to be welcomed as observers or participants. Subsequently, these standards were adopted as accreditation criteria for centers by the National Academy of Early Childhood Programs. Achieving optimal parent-staff communication is difficult. Research shows that communication is minimal and occurs mainly at drop-off and pick-up times (Pence & Goelman, 1987). Parent-child communication appears to be stronger in family child care than in center care (Hughes, 1985).

Bronfenbrenner (1979) believes that the best communication is individually directed and face-to-face, rather than group-directed and printed. However, parents cannot always arrange for two-way communication. Thus, maximum returns in the area of parent-staff communication require the use of various information channels: conferences, home visits, and written communication; various ways of promoting dialogue, such as individual and small-group conferences, demonstrations, and formal programs; and plans for acting on the information received— that is, methods of adjusting the services of the program to fit the needs of the child and procedures for making referrals. Parent participation should include options, too, such as parents serving in various planning and advisory capacities and parents working as volunteers, either program or support program, and as resource people.

Parent-Staff Communication

Because parents and teachers are concerned with the optimal development of the child, they are important allies. Communication centers on exchanging information about individual children and the principles of child development for the benefit of each child in the program. In addition, parents must be well informed about the program and welcome as observers and contributors.

Parent Reception Area.   The parent reception area helps parents feel welcome and encourages an exchange of information between parents and professionals. Such an area should be well defined and inviting, with adequate lighting and ventilation, comfortable chairs, a place to write,

and materials with information about child development and about the early childhood program. Suggested materials include the following:

periodicals published by organizations concerned with young children

guidelines for helping parents choose appropriate literature, toys, and other materials for young children

suggestions for good movies, television shows, local events, and any community happenings designed for children and/or parents

information about the program's services, basic schedule, names of staff members, special events, and vacation periods

directions for making things, such as finger paint, flannel boards, and bulletin boards

materials that serve as preparation for or follow-up to parents' meetings

information of concern to all parents on childhood diseases, safety in home and other play areas, warnings on products used by children, and discipline and guidance. Free or inexpensive booklets can be secured from the American Red Cross, local pediatricians, and insurance companies.

The parent reception area should invite relaxed communication among parents and between parents and professionals. Other suggestions for a parent reception area are as follows:

1. Any observation room for parents should be adjacent to or part of the parent reception area.

2. Photographs of children engaged in the program's activities and samples of children's art and other work can be displayed in this area.

3. Items for viewing, such as photographs and samples of children's work, and informational materials should be changed fre-

quently. Each child's work, rather than only "the best" work, should be displayed from time to time.

4. Refreshments may be placed in the parent reception area on special occasions (at holiday seasons and at the beginning and end of the term).

Spring or Autumn Orientation.   Many early childhood programs have an orientation meeting for parents who will be enrolling children. This is an excellent means of establishing a cooperative relationship between parents and staff. Although the orientation meeting is usually held in late spring, it can be held in early autumn. The purpose of the meeting is to orient parents to the services and requirements for admission to the program and to the techniques they can use in preparing their children for entrance.

Parents should be greeted as they arrive. An orientation meeting that begins with an informal presentation, such as songs, finger plays, and rhythmic or other typical activities by children presently enrolled gives insight into the program. If enrolled children are not available for a presentation, a slide-tape presentation is most effective. If children are invited to come with their parents, a presentation of a few activities by young children is not only entertaining but also gives the new children something to look forward to. Following the presentation, the new children should be asked to join the enrolled children and several staff members or volunteers in activities to be conducted in another room or in the outdoor area. Reluctant children may remain with their parents.

The director and other program and support program personnel should explain the program's overall goals and services in an interesting way. Through a slide presentation or a schedule on a chart, major daily activities should be explained.

Written take-home materials on entrance requirements should be provided as well as explained. If these parents have enrolled their children, admission information as well as other items can be included in a parents' handbook and distributed at this meeting. Requirements for admission usually include (a) age requirements and verification of age through presentation of a birth certificate or an acceptable alternative, (b) residence in a certain attendance area (often required by public school early childhood programs), (c) fees, (d) proof of adequate immunizations and tuberculosis test, (e) medical statement concerning the child's ability to participate in the program, (f) emergency information form completed and signed by each child's parents, and (g) parent needs for and ability to pay for the child's enrollment (sometimes required by government-subsidized programs).

In addition to admission requirements, parents should be informed about what kind of clothing children should wear and whether they are to bring a change of clothing, along with suggestions about what kinds of clothing children can most easily manage. Finally, a list of supplies to be purchased by the parents should be included. The supplies can be displayed so that parents can see exactly what to purchase. A note on the supply list can remind parents to put their children's names on all clothing, thus reducing loss of property. Some programs provide a list with children's and parents' names, addresses, and telephone numbers so that parents can get acquainted and arrange car pools if they wish.

Parents should be given opportunity to ask general questions (save individual-type questions for one-on-one communication, however). Parents often want to know how to prepare the child for an early childhood program. They should be discouraged from engaging in a "crash course" of academic preparation because young children are less likely to gain long-lasting knowledge and may develop an unfavorable attitude toward learning. Teachers, to allay parents' fears of no longer being needed in helping their children's development, should give parents a list of suggestions. These would help prepare the children for the program and include places to visit, home experiences that would be beneficial, techniques and activities for developing listening skills and oral expression, and ways to encourage independence. The teacher can indicate some materials that will be used in the early weeks of the session so that the parents can familiarize their children with them if they so desire. Separation issues should be discussed, and the parents should understand how staff want to handle the separation during the first few days of children's enrollments.

The meeting should last no longer than an hour. A social time following the meeting gives parents a chance to visit with each other and with staff. A tour of the facility is appropriate during this time.

Parent's First Individual Visit.   The first individual visit to an early childhood program is often to see the program firsthand and to register the child. The initial, individual contact between parent and staff member must go beyond the mechanics of registration, however. The parent's first visit to the program's facility is a time of direct learning and impressions for both parent and staff member.

The parent should bring the child. The conference room should contain a child-sized table and chair; books, crayons, and drawing paper; and manipulative toys. So that the parent may observe the child and the child may watch the parent, the child's table should be close to the table provided for parent and staff member. Also, the close proximity of the child allows the staff member to observe the child informally.

From the parent, a staff member should obtain (a) an impression of the relationship between parent and child, (b) an impression of how the child reacts to the new situation and how the parent feels about putting the child in the program, (c) a personal and social history of the child, (d) all necessary admission forms, and (e) tuition fees. The parent should obtain from

the staff member (a) an impression of the staff member, (b) an overview of the goals of the program, the facility and its equipment, and some ongoing activities, (c) a handbook or mimeographed information sheet (see "Handbook for Parents" below), (d) a list of items (clothing and supplies) needed before the child begins attending, and (e) receipts for tuition and fees paid.

Handbook for Parents.   The major purposes of the handbook are to help the parent become oriented to the program and to serve as a reference during the child's first year of enrollment. In planning a handbook, several points should be considered:

1. Information in the parents' handbook should be consistent with the program's goals and policies. Because goals and policies differ from program to program, the staff of each program must develop its own handbook.

2. At a minimum, the handbook should contain (a) an introduction to the goals and services of the program; (b) information about the program's policies that directly concern parents, such as hours of operation, fees, and children's celebrations; and (c) information on requirements that must be met before admission to the program. Other information the handbook might contain includes (a) developmental characteristics of young children; (b) ways in which parents can help their children's development; (c) health and safety guidelines for young children; (d) methods used to report children's progress; (e) a list of supplies; (f) ways in which parents can be involved in the center; and (g) dates of scheduled meetings, such as board and parent meetings (see Appendix 8).

3. Before writing the handbook, the frequency of revision should be determined. If annual revisions are not planned, a minimum of variable information, such as names of staff members, fees, and hours of operation, should be included. Because much of the variable information is essential, blank spaces can be left in

the handbook and completed in handwriting each year. An example is shown in Figure 10-1. For partial revision, a plastic spiral binding or a stapled handbook can be easily dismantled.

4. Information in the handbook should be arranged logically. Having a table of contents, printing each section on a different-colored paper, and cutting each section longer or wider than the preceding section for a tab effect are ways to facilitate locating specific information.

5. Information in the handbook should be concise. The handbook is a reference—not a novel!

6. The parents' level of understanding should be considered in wording the handbook. Wording should not sound condescending, nor should it be educational jargon. Bilingual handbooks should be available if the program serves children in a multicultural area.

7. The handbook should be attractive and the writing style interesting. Various colors of paper, readable printing, photographs, cartoons, or children's drawings help make it attractive. Writing style may vary (Decker & Decker, 1992.)

8. In designing a handbook, costs must be considered. Because the handbook can become expensive, various printing techniques should be explored. Several estimates should be obtained. Computer processed and printed material is cost-effective and attractive if carefully word-processed and if a laser printer is used.

Large-Group Meetings. Although individual conferences are most common, large-group meetings are worthwhile. A popular type is the "get acquainted" meeting. Unlike the spring or autumn orientation, the get-acquainted meeting is held a few weeks after the beginning of the term. It is especially important when staff do not conduct an orientation meeting. For a get-acquainted meeting, the following guidelines should be followed:

1. *Send invitations to parents.* If you include an RSVP, you can follow up on parents who do not respond, perhaps by telephone for a personal touch. A night meeting is preferable to an afternoon one because it permits more working parents to attend. Tuesdays, Wednesdays, and Thursdays are usually the best days for meetings, but check the community calendar before setting a date. Plan a meeting to last a maximum of 1 hour followed by a social period, or plan an easy "supper" followed by a conference. Child care services for the conference time almost always ensure a better turnout.

2. *Set the meeting date after you know the children* so that you can associate parents with children.

Figure 10-1   Handbook Style Written for Easy Revision

Lunch Period

A hot lunch will be served in the cafeteria every day. It costs _____ ¢ a day, or you may pay $ ____ . ____ a week. (Checks may be made payable to _____.) If your child wishes to bring his or her lunch, milk will cost _____ ¢ a day. Those who wish to know whether their children qualify for free or reduced-cost lunches may secure forms in the central office.

3. *Arrange the room to show your program to best advantage;* for example, show the program's schedule, arrange materials and equipment around the room, and display some of the children's work.

4. *Make a specific outline of your presentation;* for example:
   a. After most of the guests have arrived, greet them as a group.
   b. Introduce other staff members.
   c. Briefly describe your background and/or the program's history and express confidence in the year ahead.
   d. Outline the purpose of the meeting. Explain that individual conferences will be scheduled and that parents can call anytime about their own children.
   e. Explain the purposes of the program by using specific examples. An excellent way to communicate goals and activities is to take parents through a "typical day." A slide-tape presentation of children engaged in activities is very effective. (All children must be shown in one or more activities.)
   f. Review the policies of the program. Parents may be asked to bring their "Parents' Handbook" for reference.
   g. Suggest ways in which parents can help their children.
   h. Have a short question-and-answer period, but remind parents that particular concerns are discussed in individual conferences.
   i. Invite parents to have refreshments, to visit with each other, and to look around the room. Thank them for coming.

In addition to the get-acquainted meeting, a large-group meeting is an appropriate setting for explaining new policies and changes in previous policies, for introducing new program services, and for outlining and explaining new methods or curricular content. The large-group meeting is also an excellent medium for sampling parents' opinions about and attitudes toward the program.

Special-Topic Meetings.   Parents often have interests in certain topics. Articles, brochures, and videotapes are available from professional associations that provide quick, concise, down-to-earth messages for parents on often-requested topics. (Some of these materials are sold in multiple copies at reasonable prices.) Program directors should assess needs by contacting parents about convenient times for meetings and about topics in which they are interested. Sometimes, directors compile a list of topics for parents to consider but also encourage parents to add their own topics to the list. Small committees of parents need to be involved in planning. Delgado-Gaitin (1991) gives many ideas of how the planning phase should be conducted.

Special-topic meetings may be for all parents. If interests/needs vary considerably, however, directors should consider small-group meetings of three to six parents. The general topic is predetermined and announced. Some parents prefer to describe the situation in relation to their own children. A discussion follows among the parents, with professionals providing some additional insight as suggestions are made. Another option for a special-topic, small-group meeting is to invite an authority to lead the discussion.

Many suggestions for large-group conferences are appropriate for small-group meetings, such as a well-planned agenda with the total meeting time of 1 hour to 1 hour and 15 minutes, child care services, and refreshments. Small-group meetings have advantages over large-group meetings: (a) They are easier to schedule because fewer parents are involved; (b) they help parents who feel uneasy in an individual- or large-group meeting; and (c) they meet the special needs/interests of parents and reassure them that others have similar concerns. The major disadvantage is to the director and other professionals who have more of their own time invested, especially if the meetings are in the evenings or on weekends.

Scheduled Individual Conferences.   Individual parent-staff conferences help the parents understand the program and how their child is developing. Although the conference setting may be informal, parents can expect staff to discuss the program's goals and methodology in depth and how the child relates to the program. If questions or problems are not under the teachers' jurisdiction, teachers should direct parents to appropriate channels. Suggestions for preparing and conducting individual conferences are as follows:

1. Send out a brief newsletter explaining what individual conferences are, what parents can contribute, and what teachers hope to accomplish as a result of the conferences. (It is not necessary to send a newsletter if information about scheduled individual conferences is included in the handbook although a reminder does help.) The point of the conferences is to share with parents the ways in which teachers are helping children meet program goals and to elicit parent concerns for their children. If certain topics are to be covered, inform the parents. As noted in Chapter 9, if a child's progress is the topic of the conference, the teacher should prepare a guide sheet before the conference. Written information in a summary format is best shared with parents a few days before the conference so that they, too, may prepare for the conference.

2. Construct a schedule of appointments specifying conference times and inviting parents to choose an appointment time. Appointments are never made back-to-back. Allow a few minutes' break between each conference to jot down notes and to prepare for the next conference. Although the example schedule is designed for 20-minute conferences, many teachers find 30 minutes minimal to cover the purposes of the conference and to avoid an assembly-line appearance. If possible, it is better to schedule

only a few conferences each day—perhaps some during the hour before the program opens and some in the late afternoon and evening (Lindle, 1989; see Figure 10-2). Confirm the conference time with each responding parent.

3. Prepare your conference carefully. For example:

a. In your letter requesting parents to make appointments, explain whether they are to bring their enrolled child and other young children. If child care is provided, more parents may be able to participate in an individual conference.

b. Provide an attractive, private place for the conference. The teacher should not sit behind a desk. It might be advantageous to hold the conference in one of the parents' homes, rather than in the school. (Individual conferences with all parents in one home are not to be confused with the home visit.)

c. Provide early arriving parents with a place to wait and have another employee or parent volunteer chat with them until time for the conference. If no one can wait with them, provide professional or popular reading material.

d. Have a clear picture of the child in terms of the goals of the program. Also, list information to collect from parents; for example, you may want to obtain a developmental history of the child. Plan to elicit parent concerns for the child early in the conference. E. Morgan (1989) has helpful insights into "reading" parent concerns.

4. When conducting a conference, these suggestions may help:

a. Greet parents cordially.

b. Explain what you are doing with and for the child. In talking about the child, use your portfolio. Point out strengths or positive areas first and then areas in which greater focus is needed.

c. Never put a parent on the defensive. A teacher needs to recognize the attitudes a

Date _____

Let's get together and talk. I would like to discuss with you:

1. Developmental gains _____   5. Sharing toys _____

2. Eating habits _____   6. General adjustment _____

3. Bathroom habits _____   7. _____

4. Crying _____

Please list below some of the things you would like to talk with me about.

_____

_____

Child care will be available to your enrolled child and younger children. Please indicate the day(s) and time(s) you could come for a 30-minute conference by circling one or more of the following time periods:

Oct. 7 Mon.	Oct. 8 Tues.	Oct. 9 Wed.	Oct. 10 Thurs.	Oct. 11 Fri.
6:30–7:00 a.m.	6:30–7:00 a.m.	6:30–7:00 a.m.	6:30–7:00 a.m.	6:30–7:00 a.m.
7:15–7:45 a.m.	7:15–7:45 a.m.	7:15–7:45 a.m.	7:15–7:45 a.m.	7:15–7:45 a.m.

8:00 a.m.-5:00 p.m. Program in session

5:00–5:30 p.m.	5:00–5:30 p.m.	5:00–5:30 p.m.	5:00–5:30 p.m.	5:00–5:30 p.m.
5:45–6:15 p.m.	5:45–6:15 p.m.	5:45–6:15 p.m.	5:45–6:15 p.m.	5:45–6:15 p.m.

If these times are inconvenient, please suggest a time or times. _____

_____

I will confirm a time for your appointment.

Sincerely,

_____

Figure 10-2   Invitation to Parent-Teacher Conference

parent may take when his or her child is having problems, so the teacher does not respond argumentatively. The most frequent defensive attitudes that parents have are projection and denial. In projection, parents insist the problem must be that the teacher doesn't know how to handle the situation. In denial, parents consider the problems small or believe that their child is just active or going through stages. With either defensive attitude, parents are protecting themselves. Abbott and Gold (1991) provide some excellent suggestions for conferring with parents when the subject-matter to be discussed may be difficult because parents are unprepared to hear or accept that their child may need special services. Many of these suggestions apply equally to other difficult or potentially difficult situations.

d. Be careful about talking down to parents, using educational jargon, or giving long-winded, complicated explanations. Conduct conferences in the parents' native tongue, using a translator if necessary.

e. Do not expect to have an answer to every problem nor expect parents to solve all problems. Decisions should be reached during the discussion by listening to parents' suggestions for solving problems, by offering suggestions, by suggesting referral to special services if necessary, and by making arrangements to follow up. Follow-up is most important. If parents know they have your help, they will not feel helpless.

f. Practice professional ethics. Respect parents' confidences and do not belittle the director of the program, other staff members, other families, or other children. On a regular basis, review the *Code of Ethical Conduct and Statement of Commitment* provided as a brochure by the NAEYC (Feeney & Kipnis, 1989).

g. Do not make the parents feel rushed; however, in fairness to other waiting parents, conferences must end on schedule. If necessary, the parents can make another appointment to continue the discussion.

5. Make notes on the conference and file them in the child's folder.

A new trend in parent-teacher conferences is the "child-parent-teacher" conference. Young children are usually excluded from parent-teacher conferences. Including children in conferences in which goals for their education are being determined is helpful in securing their cooperation in meeting current goals for development, as well becoming increasingly skillful in self-evaluation and decision making. Several excellent reports address the techniques of incorporating children in conferences (e.g., Readdick, Golbeck, Klein, & Cartwright, 1984).

Nonscheduled Individual Conferences. Unlike scheduled individual conferences, which are usually staff initiated and noted on the program calendar, nonscheduled conferences may be initiated by parent or professional and held when the need arises. These conferences should be encouraged for any number of reasons: (a) learning more about the program, (b) questioning the meaning of activities observed, or (c) discussing a present or foreseeable concern.

Most communication between parent and staff occurs at the transition points when parents drop off and pick up their children. In some programs, however, the parents cannot identify a staff member with whom they have a significant relationship. If nonscheduled individual conferences are to be meaningful, one consistent person needs to reach out to parents during transition times, and professionals must receive training in parent-staff communication.

If a professional initiates the conference to discuss a concern (and certainly, many conferences have been initiated for that reason only!), the teacher should give the parent suggestions to solve the problem. In discussing a problem, the teacher should show evidence to support statements and use tact. Finally, the teacher and parent should concentrate on a few concerns, not a long list.

Home Visits.   Home visits have had a long history and are still a major part of the Head Start program, some Family Resource programs, and university laboratory schools, as well as other quality programs. Jones (1970) identified roles or combinations of roles used by professionals during the history of making home visits: (a) the *teacher-expert,* who enlists parent help by teaching the parent how to teach the child; (b) the *teacher-learner,* who seeks information from the parent about the child, such as the child's abilities and interests; (c) the *student-researcher,* who questions the parent about his or her child-rearing beliefs; and (d) the *bringer of gifts,* who, like the teacher-expert, enlists parent help in the educative process and provides instructional procedures but who also brings materials, such as games, books, and toys. Home visits have some advantages over other avenues of parent-staff communication:

1. The professional is seen as a person who cares enough about a child to visit the family; children are proud because their teacher came to see them.

2. The professional sees the child in the home environment and thus may obtain valuable information about the child that will help in meeting program goals for that child, such as alternative courses of child rearing open to the parents.

3. At home, the parent is more likely to do the talking; conversely, at the program's facility, the staff member is more likely to do the talking.

4. If a home visit is made prior to enrollment, fewer tears may be shed on the first day. A school follow-up to the home visit aids transitional anxiety. For example, in one program, a teacher takes a photograph of the child and parent(s) together and places it on a school bulletin board (and later in the portfolio), and the parent takes a photograph of the child and teacher together for the child to keep at home. In another program, the child and the teacher tell about the teacher's home visit in class the next day.

Home visits require careful planning. All visits must be prearranged for a mutually satisfactory time. (A few parents may not want to participate in home visits, and such decisions must be respected.) Teachers should call the home a day before the visit to see whether the previously scheduled time is still satisfactory. (Parents do not like to be surprised!)

Most home visits last about 1 hour. The first 5 to 10 minutes is a greeting time for parent(s)-child-teacher. The teacher and the child interact for another 20 to 30 minutes in the child's room or in a place suggested by the parent(s). A parting "ritual" is preplanned, such as a few photographs, a small school "gift" for the child, or a pleasant walk to the car. Other practical suggestions are given in many sources (e.g., Fox-Barnett & Meyer, 1992; L. Johnston & Mermin, 1994).

Parent Visitation.   Parent visitation helps make parent-staff conferences more meaningful. The parent has the opportunity to observe the program and to see the child functioning with peers and adults. The staff member has the opportunity to observe parent-child interaction in the program setting and the parent's expressed attitudes toward the program. When a parent visits the room, the staff member or a volunteer and the visitor's child should greet the parent. The parent may watch various groups of children engaging in activities or may even initiate an activity, such as reading a story. If a parent wants to see the child in action without the child's knowledge, invite the parent to use the observation room or gallery.

Parents should be encouraged to visit the program; however, many parents do not visit.

Sending a special invitation often results in more visitations and may even initiate greater involvement in the program. A sample invitation is shown in Figure 10-3.

During an Open House, parents and other family members view samples of the children's work, (e.g., artwork, stories children have written, block structures they have built), examine equipment and materials, and visit with staff and other guests. It is held at a time when the program is not in session. An example of an invitation to an Open House is shown in Figure 10-4.

Telephone Conversations.   Telephone conversations may be initiated by either a parent or the staff member. A parent may use telephone conversations to help staff better understand the child during the day. Perhaps the child was sick during the night, is worried, or is excited. Some parents may be more at ease talking over the telephone than in a face-to-face communication. Telephone conversations allow for quick, unplanned contacts.

Staff can use telephone conversations as a means of making a positive contact, which can

Figure 10-3   Invitation for Program Visitation

Dear Parents,

   Your children have been in our program for 6 weeks and have made gains in development, such as sharing with friends, handling a long-handled paintbrush, building with large floor blocks, stringing tiny beads, listening to those wonderful real and pretend stories, and so many more things. Won't you please come and enjoy being part of our day? Your children will welcome the most special people in their lives—their families.

                              Sincerely,

                              _____
                              (Teacher's signature)

Figure 10-4   Open House Invitation

Dear Parents,

   We are having Open House on Thursday, October 24, at 7:30 p.m. Examples of your child's work will be on display. We hope you will come and see some of the things your child has done in school.
   We will be looking forward to visiting with you. Refreshments will be served in the auditorium.

                              Sincerely,

                              _____
                              (Staff member's signature)

serve as a pleasant event for the child too. The following are examples of positive telephone contacts:

1. The staff member explains to the parent something interesting or successful the child did; the parent is then able to reinforce the child immediately.

2. The staff member can call to inquire about the health of family members or to congratulate a parent on the arrival of a new baby, a work promotion, or an honor.

Newsletters.   Newsletters can be sent home on a regular or irregular basis. The newsletter can be duplicated and sent to parents via the children. Newsletters help parents in communicating with their children and in developing a liaison between staff and parents. Information that might be included in newsletters are (a) announcements about the program or about daily or special activities in the program; (b) suggestions for home learning activities and methods that may be conducive to learning; (c) information on new books, play materials, and television shows for children; (d) articles to help parents; (e) announcements about community events; and (f) ideas for summer fun. An example of a newsletter to parents about television is shown in Figure 10-5. An excellent example of a newsletter format is found in the following source:

> Harms, T. O., & Cryer, D. (1978). Parent newsletter: A new format. *Young Children, 33*(5), 28-32.

Other Methods.   Several other methods aid parent-staff communication. Examples include the following:

1. *Informal Notes.* Notes are very effective and quick ways to communicate. Many varieties of notes are effective, such as:
   a. A short note praising a child's effort, a "happy note," can be sent to the parent. An example is shown in Figure 10-6.
   b. A parent needs "Thanks" too. Show your appreciation when parents support the goals of your program.

Figure 10-5   Newsletter

Dear Parents,

   Television plays a big part in your children's lives. They enjoy watching television in their spare time. Of course, it is important that they do not stay "glued" to the television. Playing outdoors in the fresh air, visiting with friends, looking at books, and getting to bed early are important.
   Because many television shows are educational and enjoyable, television can be a wise use of some leisure time. Each week, I will send home a schedule of some shows from which your child might profit. Your child might tune in these shows if they are convenient for your family.

                         Sincerely,

                         _____
                         (Teacher's signature)

_____ was a good helper. She helped a friend pick up the spilled pegs.

Figure 10-6   "Happy Note"

   c. Because parents want to share their children's days, a photograph of an activity with a note written on the back is enjoyed by any parent.

   d. Stamp and Groves (1994) suggest an "Ask Me About" badge. These badges let parents know their children have reached milestones, and parents should ask their children about these important events.

   e. Parents know you care when you send cards or notes for children's birthdays or when family members are ill.

2. *Workshops.* Workshops are great for more informal group communication among parents and staff. Two common types are:

   a. Materials workshops in which parents and staff analyze instructional materials for concepts and develop original equipment and materials for presenting these instructional concepts. It is important to find out what types of activities parents are willing to do and to provide choices in the activities parents can "make and/or take." Dodd and Brock (1994) provide many practical suggestions.

   b. Workshops may also be held in the evening for doing repair jobs on the building and grounds or on equipment and materials.

3. *Social Events.* Social meetings, such as picnics for the whole family, a coffee for parents, or a mother's or father's recognition night, stimulate good relationships between parents and staff.

Parent Participation

Involvement with parents includes parent participation in the program. Parent participation has had a long history. In parent cooperative programs, parents learned about child development through classroom involvement. Head Start called for parents to be involved as employees and volunteers and to serve on advisory councils. Like Head Start, some government-sponsored early intervention programs had parent involvement. More recently, programs serving children with disabilities require parent involvement. The National Black Child Development Institute (1987) called for parent involvement in decisions about curriculum and program policy in prekindergarten public school programs.

The early childhood program must initiate and maintain programs that enlist the worthwhile services and resources of the community. Unfortunately, just over half of all centers have parent involvement. More parents are involved in social activities and fund-raising, rather than as regular volunteers. Most of the regular participation occurs in not-for-profit centers, especially those receiving governmental support (Coelen, Glantz, & Calore, 1979) and involves parents who express feelings of life satisfaction (F. Parker, Piotrkowski, & Peay, 1987).

Parents as Members of Policy Advisory Committees and Boards of Directors.   Many early childhood programs include parents as members of planning and advisory groups; for example, parents serve as members of Head Start policy groups. Parent advisory committees (PACs) work with the director and staff of a program in generating tasks and in resolving problems. PACs are often used as "think tanks" or as sounding boards for program-parent issues. Most state licensing laws require that a not-for-profit, private early childhood organization operate under a governing board composed, at least in part, of the people it serves. Public school early childhood programs are under the jurisdiction of the local board of education or trustees, an elected, policy-making group representing the community's interests. Programs may operate under two boards—one at the program level and the other at the agency level if the program is part of a community service agency. The ultimate form of parent involvement occurs when parents serve on the board of directors.

Including parents in planning and advisory groups or on governing boards is in accordance with the democratic principles of citizens' rights and responsibilities in formulating public policy, works as a two-way public relations committee, and constitutes a partnership between professional and parents. For parents to be effective members of planning and advisory groups, these committees and councils must have the following characteristics:

1. The committee or council must be an educational group, not a pressure group. Although politically minded individuals may serve on the committee or advisory council, their input should not necessarily be considered the thinking of the majority.

2. The director must show members of the committee or council how a decision will affect the program and make sure parents have appropriate information on which to base their decisions. Parents must then have input into the decision-making process because one cannot convince parents to become involved if the most important decisions have already been made (decisions regarding goals of the program, the program's delivery system, staffing policies, fiscal matters, and program evaluation).

3. The parents and all other board members must be trained. Programs have failed because of problems at the committee or council level. Training must be given in identifying problems, investigating possible solutions, understanding regulations, learning decision-making processes, and communicating recommendations to the power structure.

4. The committee or council must be small enough to be manageable (12 or fewer members), and membership should be rotational.

Parents as Volunteers.   Parents can also participate as volunteers, on a regular, semiregular, or occasional basis. For a volunteer program to work, the director must support the volunteer program by providing general guidance in planning although parents can organize and operate the program itself. In effective programs, all parents are given a chance to participate, a choice of roles, and the freedom to determine the extent of their participation. Some parents will choose not to participate. Galen (1991) reports on how a New Jersey school used an 8-step procedure for expansion of parent involvement.

Program and Support Program Volunteers.   Parents are valuable as program volunteers because they (a) know and understand parents' working hours, transportation situations, and community mores; (b) can serve as cultural models for children; (c) help staff members understand children's likes and dislikes, strengths and weaknesses, and home successes and failures; (d) act as interpreters in bilingual programs; and (e) assist staff in program activities, such as storytelling, art, music, and gardening. Parent volunteers also (a) assist in positive control of children by understanding the values of positive guidance, by using consistent, positive reinforcement and kindness, and by solving minor concerns before they develop into major disciplinary problems; (b) accompany staff members in home-visiting programs; and (c) serve as ambassadors to the neighborhood.

Specific expectations of volunteers should be determined by the program's needs and the volunteers' abilities. Some basic considerations are as follows:

1. Volunteers should have an orientation to the program's facility and staff, to professional ethics, and to state and local laws regarding personnel qualifications and activities. Orientation could include a broad overview of the program's goals, rules and regulations, specific tasks and limits of responsibility,

classroom management (if involved with children), and a "hands on" experience with materials. Their response to the orientation will benefit future programs.

2. Professionals should be oriented toward using volunteers. After orientation, staff should be given a choice of whether or not to use volunteers.

3. A handbook is helpful for staff and volunteers, reiterating much of the information given during the orientation program.

4. Professionals should plan specific activities for volunteers. Greenberg (1989) reported that when parents are given menial jobs or are asked to perform tasks no one else wants to do, they may develop a negative attitude and become less involved. Teaching activities require careful planning; teachers should set up the activities for the volunteers so that a child or small group of children works with a parent volunteer at one time; and before demonstrating teaching techniques, a teacher should briefly explain the rationale for and the plan of the activity, the materials to be used, and the possible learnings.

5. Volunteers must be assessed by the director and should be encouraged to discuss their involvement.

Parents also can serve as support program volunteers, such as lunchroom workers, assistants to program nurses, assistants in the library-media center, assistants in distributing equipment and materials, workers in transportation services, office workers, and as resource people to gather information on services.

Occasional Volunteers.   Many parents cannot serve as volunteers on a regular or even a semi-regular basis; however, they often can and are willing to help on several occasions during the year. These parents can be very valuable as volunteers for special services. These special services can include the more traditional volunteer

areas of field-trip supervisors, contributors to fund-raising projects, and assistants during special occasions (e.g., helper during class celebrations, greeter for Open House or parent-teacher conferences). Also, parents can serve as resource persons representing various occupations and hobby groups. Staff should survey parents for their special talents and encourage them to share their talents with young children.

PARENT EDUCATION AND FAMILY RESOURCE AND SUPPORT PROGRAMS

Parent education has had a long and exciting history (Gruenberg, 1959/60). The child study movement made child rearing a science. Parent education and home visitations began early in the century as a way to help immigrants. The Children's Bureau was founded in 1913 to eradicate some child labor practices but began to publish materials on child rearing, most of it middle-class oriented.

Parent education for the middle class thrived in the 1920s with the development of the progressive education movement. Many parent and lay programs were developed during this period, such as the child study movement, the Parent-Teacher Association, mental health associations, and parent cooperative nursery schools. Nursery schools had many ways of educating parents in groups and individually. Parents were encouraged to observe children in the school setting (Committee on Preschool & Parental Education, 1929). Parent education was continued in the Works Progress Administration nursery schools. In the 1960s, the shift of emphasis was away from the middle class. Almost all early intervention programs of the 1960s and 1970s had a parent education component. For example, Head Start has had three major family support programs (Home Start, Parent Child Centers, and Child and Family Resource Programs) and two structured approaches to parent education ("Exploring Parenting" and "Getting Involved"). Similar to the early intervention programs—in fact, often directly connected with these programs—parent education programs began to focus on low-income parents. Parent education programs grew rapidly in the 1970s because data from early intervention programs showed increased effectiveness when a parent education component was included (Bronfenbrenner, 1974). Marx and Seligson (1988) stated that over 33% of the states had some form of parent education.

Today, parent programs have increased. Newer programs make use of technology (Popkin, 1990) and are designed for specific target groups, such as teen parents (Marx & Francis, 1989), fathers (McBride & McBride, 1993), and parents prone to abuse and neglect (Bavolek & Bavolek, 1985). Some programs in the 1970s were geared more for parents of elementary-age and adolescent children—namely, T. Gordon's (1970) "Parent Effectiveness Training" and Dinkmeyer and McKay's (1976) "Systematic Training for Effective Parenting." More recently, efforts have been focused on parents of babies and young children (Elkind, 1987b; Elmer & Maloni, 1988; Fox, Anderson, Fox, & Rodriguez, 1991).

Purposes of Parent Education and Family Resource and Support Programs

The basic assumption of parent education is that if the parent's role as a teacher is enhanced, the parent will be able to maximize the child's level of functioning. Several attributes seem to be critical to quality parenting, such as a positive view about the future (Sigel, 1985), a willingness to take a proactive stance in dealing with family issues (Schaefer, 1985), knowledge of child development (LaRossa, 1986), plus the use of personal experiences in guiding children's development (Bettelheim, 1987), a positive work-role attitude along with a view that work and family are harmonious (Voyanoff, 1987), and a sense of support from a spouse or friend (Galinsky, 1987). It is believed that this positive self-image as a parent

leads to confidence in the parent-educator role (Swick, 1987).

Thus, specific purposes of parent education are as follows:

1. To become more positive about oneself as a change agent within the family
2. To learn more about child growth and development
3. To develop general concepts of effective child-rearing practices
4. To acquire an understanding of the local early childhood program's rationale, program content and methodology, and support services
5. To become an important part of the educative process by expressing good attitudes about the program and staff and about education in general, by reinforcing the child's achievement, by providing continuity between activities at home and in the program, and by extending the child's knowledge and skills

A major movement toward family resource and support programs began in the 1980s. Family resource and support services differ from the more traditional education programs in that they offer a wide array of services and thus serve as a *support system* for families, rather than as a *change agent*, and they work to prevent problems, rather than repair damage in parent-child relations (Zigler & Berman, 1983).

Types of Parent Education and Family Resource and Support Programs

Parent education programs are of many types. Their nature depends on program needs, parent needs and wishes, and program goals. For example, programs that use many parent volunteers need more emphasis on parent education; Spanish-speaking parents may need bilingual education; and some early childhood programs may want to train parents to reinforce the program's concepts and language models. Techniques may vary as well. Services for parents may be either staff-directed or parent-initiated; they may have one focus or be multifaceted; and they may be direct, using organized classrooms, or indirect, with parents observing teaching and guidance techniques during program visitations. Programs may be sponsored by school systems, universities, various community agencies, or handled through a cooperative, interagency approach.

Orientation Programs.   Perhaps the most common service for parents of children enrolled in an early childhood program is orientation—through handbooks, by attending meetings, and by becoming members of parent-teacher associations. Orientation programs are designed by the staff in local programs.

Home-Visiting Programs.   Home-visiting programs were designed to help parents learn how to teach their young children, including how to prepare and collect educational materials. The exact nature of home-visiting programs depends on program objectives, the number of families to be visited, the number and frequency of visits per family, and the program's financial resources (see Chapter 1). In many home-visiting programs, a trained parent or a professional models the teaching/reinforcing style to parents in the home. The parent may later plan to teach the activities because many program planners believe that parents, not professionals, should learn to set goals for their children. In some home-visiting programs, parents are taught in groups without children present, and after group consultation parents return home and present activities to their children.

Parent Discussion Groups.   The basic goals of parent discussion groups are to clarify misconceptions of the functions of parenthood, to define the role of parents in child development, and to extend parents' knowledge and understanding of the needs of children. As has been discussed,

popular parent discussion groups emerged in the 1970s. Unstructured parent discussion groups in which parents identify an area of concern and a knowledgeable resource person leads the discussion group also became popular. Parent discussion groups can be particularly beneficial to parents of children with disabilities, with chronic or critical illness, or who are deceased or abused. Peer support helps these parents adjust and provides needed information.

Resource Centers.   A popular type of resource center for children is the toy-lending library. Such libraries help parents provide intellectual stimulation for their children and offer guidelines in using toys. Nimnicht and Brown (1972) set up a toy-lending library to develop concepts and verbal fluency in children ages 3 to 9 years. Resource centers for parents and children were established in some public libraries too (Vartuli & Rogers, 1985).

Adult resource centers have also been used for parent education. These centers provide materials that explain concepts of child development and early childhood education. For example:

1. Parents need to understand something of what children are like physically, cognitively, and affectively; what tasks the children are trying to accomplish; what experiences retard and facilitate development; and what evidence is indicative of progress.

2. Parents need knowledge about several approaches to guiding children on the basis of developmental stages.

3. Parents need to understand children's interests, what types of experiences are meaningful, and which play equipment and materials help children develop.

4. Parents need help with the specific skills children should develop, with teaching techniques (e.g., activities, language models, questioning techniques, reinforcement methods), and with teaching equipment and materials.

Parent Self-Improvement Programs. Parent self-improvement programs were designed to empower parents as individuals to improve their own lives. Services may include instruction for parent self-improvement in the areas of basic adult education, English for speakers of other languages, consumer education, nutrition, clothing, health, community resources, home repairs, and family life. Such instruction may be in the form of formal courses for high school credit or informal workshops and are usually offered by the public school system for the benefit of all adult residents of a community.

Family Resource and Support Programs. Family resource and support programs offer services for parents, such as parent education, job training, respite care, employment referral, and emotional support and services for children (health and developmental screening, home-based programs, and center care). Family resource and support programs have their roots in the research that supports the role of families in the educative process and in the parent self-improvement and parent involvement/education programs. For example, Head Start's Parent and Child Center (PCC) program was designed to provide services to low-income families with children under 3 years and to expectant mothers. Four major PCC program components were developed: (a) programs for children, including a home-visiting program, a home-care program, and a center-based program; (b) programs for parents in such areas as home economics, child development, adult education, and job counseling; (c) health and nutrition services, including medical services for children and their parents, classes in child care, safety, and nutrition; and (d) social services, such as referral, recreational, and assistance in finding adequate housing and in providing food and clothing.

Unlike the more traditional programs, parent resource and support programs are based on the following premises: (a) The validity of a variety of parenting styles and of the significance of the contexts (e.g., community and special relations) in which families are embedded should be recognized and accepted, and (b) parent behaviors do not affect children in a unilateral way (Weissbourd, 1983). Family resource and support programs are for all parents. To be effective, however, the services must be individualized to support different stages in the family life cycle and to meet other concerns (e.g., work/family issues, family crises). These programs must also stress an egalitarian relationship between parents and early childhood program staff (Kagan, 1989). A leading force in family resource and support programs is the Family Resource Coalition (see Appendix 5).

Effects of Parent Education and Family Resource and Support Programs

Vast amounts of research have emphasized the importance of parent-child relationships in the early years of a child's life. The objectives of recent parent education and family support programs are now being studied in terms of impact on child and parent, comparisons of delivery systems, and directions for future studies. The major positive research findings include the following:

1. The programs have had a short-term, positive effect on children (Andrews et al., 1982; Slaughter, 1983). A parent education component is important if the child is to benefit from compensatory education (Bronfenbrenner, 1974; Radin, 1971).
2. The programs have had a generally positive impact on parenting (Slaughter, 1983; Travers, Nauta, & Irwin, 1982).
3. One type of parent education or family support system does not seem more effective than another (Kessen, Fein, Clarke-Stewart, & Starr, 1975; Pinsker & Geoffrey, 1981).

Negative results have been found in several cases. For example:

1. "Canned" objectives and activities seem to be ineffective (Lambie, Bond, & Weikart, 1974).

Program planning must be based on the needs and knowledge of specific groups of parents.

2. Some program delivery systems work better for some parents than for others (Powell, 1985). For example, Kessen et al. (1975) found that home-based programs do not work well for families without strong emotional support systems.

3. For programs to yield maximum results, parents must be in the program for a minimum of 2 years (Lochman & Brown, 1980).

4. Powell (1984) has raised many questions about how parents deal with child-rearing information that conflicts with their own beliefs.

TRENDS AND ISSUES

Parent education was the primary way of working with families until the 1970s. The accumulation of research in parent education and the ecological views of Bronfenbrenner (1979) held that children could not be viewed separately from their families. Although many far-sighted professionals had long held this view, it became more widely accepted. Consequently, various program initiatives designed to be more responsive to families and known as *family resource and support programs* were begun. In sum, the focus moved from correcting deficits to improving the family's status.

Recently, early childhood professionals began to respond to even greater demographic changes, such as (a) society becoming more culturally diverse, in which it is estimated that about one third of all Americans will be African-, Hispanic-, or Asian-American by 2020 (Kirst, 1986), (b) a changing workforce in which mothers of infants and toddlers are the fastest growing segment, and (c) a changing family and community structure in which mutual support within and among families is often lacking. Early childhood professionals began to recognize that

both the child and the family are consumers of early childhood care and education and of various related services. Thus, programmatic attention to families' needs is now part of the field of early childhood care and education.

Collaboration among families and professionals became the watchword of the 1990s, and **family empowerment** became the term that denoted the change. S. Minuchin's (1984) family system framework provided the ideas on which family empowerment is based. Table 10-1 presents an outline of the principles and components of these collaborative efforts often called **family-centered models.** Three of these family-centered programs are the Addison County Parent/Child Center, Middlebury, Vermont; the Carole Robertson Center, Chicago, Illinois; and the Parent Services Project, Fairfax, California.

SUMMARY

Working with parents has had a long history in early childhood education. The early kindergartens and nursery schools had parent education as one of their program services. Early childhood kindergartens and primary grades (levels) housed in the public schools became more involved in communicating with parents and having parents occasionally assist in the classroom than in having parents as close allies in the educative process. By the 1960s, however, researchers involved in the intervention programs found that a parent involvement and education program component was necessary for maximum benefits to the child. Since the 1980s, the movement has been toward parent resource and support programs that serve, not as agents of family change, but rather as a support system for preventing problems while accepting family diversity.

Because of even greater demographic changes today, an empowerment paradigm has altered the more traditional views of working with parents. Programmatic attention is being given to the entire family's needs. To meet each

Table 10-1 Family-Centered Models	Principles Underlying Model	Components of Programs
	Families are viewed within their community contexts, and these contexts promote or curtail family strength.	Target the overall development of parents as individuals by acknowledging all their roles and responsibilities and by encouraging and providing empathic and supportive relationships with other adults.
	Parents are seen as individuals with many roles and responsibilities in which child rearing is only one role.	
	The parent-child relationship is influenced by parenting knowledge, but more important by parent self-esteem, family background, socioeconomic status and other cultural factors, and the community setting.	See the parent-child relationship (rather than the child) as the primary client of the program and thus work to strengthen this enduring relationship.
		Seek full collaboration with parents in planning and policy making and take a "facilitator" professional role rather than "expert" professional role in the collaborative process.
	A specific event that influences any member of the family has some effect on the family system.	Offer comprehensive services or provide community links to those needing services.

family's needs, supportive efforts and resources are shaped collaboratively (among professionals and family members) and are met through family-centered programs and other linkages to community resources.

FOR FURTHER READING

Becher, R. M. (1986). Parent involvement: A review of research and principles of successful practices. In L. G. Katz (Ed.), *Current topics in early childhood education* (Vol. 6, pp. 85-113). Norwood, NJ: Ablex.

Berger, E. H. (1991). *Parents as partners in education: The school and home working together* (3rd ed.). New York: Macmillan.

Bjorklund, G., & Burger, C. (1987). Making conferences work for parents, teachers, and children. *Young Children, 42*(2), 26-31.

Bundy, B. F. (1991). Fostering communication between parents and preschools. *Young Children, 46*(2), 12-17.

Cataldo, C. Z. (1987). *Parent education for early childhood.* New York: Teachers College Press.

Coleman, M. (1991). Planning for the changing nature of family life in schools for young children. *Young Children, 46*(4), 15-20.

Galinsky, E. (1988). Parents and teacher-caregivers: Sources of tension, sources of support. *Young Children, 43*(3), 4-12.

Galinsky, E. (1990). Why are some parent/teacher partnerships clouded with difficulties? *Young children, 45*(5), 2-3, 38-39.

Galinsky, E., & David, J. (1988). *The preschool years: Family strategies that work—from experts and parents.* New York: Times Books.

Greenberg, P. (1989). Parents as partners in young children's development and education: A new American fad? Why does it matter? *Young Children, 44*(4), 61-75.

Herrera, J. F., & Wooden, S. L. (1988). Some thoughts about effective parent-school communication. *Young Children, 43*(6), 78-80.

Knowler, K. A. (1988). Caregivers' corner. Orienting parents and volunteers to the classroom. *Young Children, 44*(1), 9.

Lynch, A. (1991). Early childhood education: The parents' perspective. In D. Elkind (Ed.), *Perspectives on early childhood education* (pp. 253–260). Washington, DC: National Education Association.

McBride, B. A. (1989). Interaction, accessibility, and responsibility: A view of father involvement and how to encourage it. *Young Children, 44*(5), 13-19.

Melaville, A. I., Blank, M. S., & Asayesh, G. (1993). *Together we can: A guide for crafting a profamily system of education and human services.* Washington, DC: Government Printing Office.

Powell, D. R. (1990). Home visiting in the early years: Policy and program design decisions. *Young Children, 45*(6), 65-73.

Rich, D. (1987). *Teachers and parents: An adult-to-adult approach.* Washington, DC: National Education Association.

Spewock, T. S. (1992). Teaching parents of young children through learning packets. *Young Children, 47*(2), 28-30.

Stipek, D., Rosenblatt, L., & DiRocco, L. (1994). Making parents your allies. *Young Children, 49*(3), 4-9.

Stone, J. G. (1987). *Teacher-parent relationships.* Washington, DC: National Association for the Education of Young Children.

Swick, K. J. (1991). *Teacher-parent partnerships to enhance school success in early childhood education.* Washington, DC: National Education Association and the Southern Early Childhood Association.

Thibault, J. P., & McKee, J. S. (1982). Practical parenting with Piaget. *Young Children, 38*(1), 18-27.

Chapter 11

⚜ ⚜ ⚜ ⚜ ⚜

Contributing to the Profession

⚜ ⚜ ⚜ ⚜ ⚜

The role of the early childhood administrator, regardless of the official title, is one of leadership. As a leader, the administrator must be concerned with the quality of early childhood care and education. The concern for quality must go beyond the local program to an interest in the overall excellence of early childhood programs. Consequently, administrators as leaders can contribute to their profession by promoting professionalization of early childhood education, attempting to influence public policy, becoming involved in research, and helping others find a place in the profession.

PROMOTING PROFESSIONALIZATION

Professionalization is defined as the dynamic process whereby an occupation can be observed to change certain crucial characteristics in the direction of a profession (Vollmer & Mills, 1966). The word **profession** is defined in terms of certain occupational characteristics, such as (a) having an existing knowledge base; (b) focusing on service; (c) performing a unique function for clients and society; (d) having a monopoly of knowledge in the field; (e) internally determining standards of education and training; (f) having professional practice recognized by some form of license or certification; (g) shaping most legislation of the profession by the profession; (h) gaining in power, prestige, and income; (i) identifying with the profession individually and as a group through a national association; and (j) seeing the profession as a lifelong occupation (D. Thompson, 1984). Houle (1981) noted these characteristics of a profession: (a) clarification of the occupation's defining functions; (b) mastery of theoretical knowledge; (c) capacity to solve problems; (d) use of practical knowledge; (e) self-enhancement; (f) formal training; (g) credentialing; (h) creation of subcultures (e.g., awareness of history of the profession and its role in the culture, staff titles reflecting current nomenclature, understanding of terminology used in the profession); (i) legal reinforcement; (j) public accep-

tance; (k) ethical practice; (l) penalties; (m) relations to other vocations; and (n) relations to users of the service. Radomski (1986) developed a series of questions that focuses on each of Houle's characteristics. A rating form is provided for local early childhood programs to assess their level of progress toward professionalization.

Early childhood care and education has many barriers that keep the field from being recognized as a profession. B. Caldwell (1990) states that the early childhood education field suffers from a lack of conceptual clarity and standard terminology. She has identified five issues critical to the professional identity of early childhood care and education: to determine "just what we do," "what we cannot (or should not) do," "how we should do that which we do," "where we should do what we do," and "how we communicate what we do." Finkelstein (1988) thinks the only barrier to professionalism in this field is that it is perceived as a woman's field. Bredekamp (1992) articulates several barriers, such as the following:

1. The field has a diverse system of regulation. With 50 teacher licensure/certification programs and 50 state child care licensing codes as well as other regulations, professional preparation is difficult to regulate.

2. Preparation programs at various institutions differ.

3. Early childhood is not a viable career option for many because of the low compensation.

4. A dilemma exists between being exclusive (keeping out unqualified persons) and being inclusive (ensuring persons access to the field although they come from diverse backgrounds). Hostetler and Klugman (1982) state that the field needs to identify commonalities among all who work with young children while simultaneously allowing for diversity.

The National Association for the Education of Young Children (NAEYC) believes that the main route to professionalism is to develop an articulated professional development system. The NAEYC formalized its quest for professionalization of the field by launching the National Institute for Early Childhood Professional Development in 1991. A career lattice was used to symbolize the roles and settings within the profession and the preparation required for persons working in each given role/setting. In developing the lattice, the NAEYC stated that the **early childhood field** includes anyone engaged in services to young children and that the **early childhood profession** includes anyone who has acquired some professional knowledge and is on a professional development path (NAEYC, 1994). Not all of us as early childhood professionals like the idea of a career ladder or lattice. Dresden and Myers (1989) discuss three myths that impede our own valuing of what we do and how we conduct our business: (a) The hierarchical model of power and working relationships is the only model for productive behavior, (b) the only way to pursue a career seriously is via a career ladder, and (c) genuine career commitment needs to exclude other commitments and connections. Spodek (1991b) sees early childhood care and education as a discontinuous field, and many difficulties are associated with ladders and lattices (as discussed in Chapter 4 under "Trends and Issues").

A **code of ethics,** a statement of professional conduct, is another sign of a mature profession. Moore (1970) calls a code of ethics "a private system of law which is characteristic of all formally constituted organizations" (p. 116). Practitioners share a code of ethics highlighting proper relations and responsibilities to each other and to clients or others outside the profession. Over a decade before a code of ethics was adopted by the early childhood profession, Katz (1977a) gave four reasons why the early childhood profession needed such a code:

1. Practitioners of education have almost unlimited power over children whose self-protective repertoire is limited. How shall children be protected?

2. The professional staff serves a multiplicity of clients—children, parents, regulatory/funding agencies, and the community. Who makes the final decisions?

3. Because of the unavailability and unreliability of empirical findings, gaps exist in the knowledge of what is best. How can educators avoid the seemingly "functional" orthodoxies or ideologies and remain open-minded?

4. Educators are responsible for the whole child, yet their expertise and power have limits. Parents, for example, are gaining more power in the decision-making process. What are the educators' limits?

The issue of professional ethics was raised with the NAEYC members. The 1985 survey was funded by NAEYC and the Wallace Alexander Gerbode Foundation. Feeney and Kipnis (1985) stated the survey showed that early childhood educators were in "ethical pain." Ninety-three percent of all respondents (and 100% of specialists) agreed or strongly agreed that attention to ethical issues and the development of a code of ethics should be an important priority in the field. Data also showed that relationships with parents and with staff and administrators are the areas of greatest concern among early childhood educators. The major ethical problems reported were unprofessional behavior, information management, child abuse and neglect, and referrals to outside agencies (Feeney & Sysco, 1986). Following workshops and another survey of the membership, a final document was approved by NAEYC's governing board in July 1989. The adopted code of ethics sets forth professional responsibilities in four areas of professional relationships: children, families, colleagues, and community and society (Feeney & Kipnis, 1989). The Ethics Commission decided that the code should be "encouraged" rather than "enforced" at this time, should be incorporated into the ongoing projects of the association, and should be reviewed at regular intervals (Feeney, 1990). As a way to better understand how to solve problems in local programs, the NAEYC has been publishing articles in *Young Children* under the title "Using NAEYC's Code of Ethics: A Tool for Real Life."

INFLUENCING PUBLIC POLICY

Advocacy is the process of maintaining, extending, or improving services to children, families, and staff. Advocacy brings together all the significant people in the child's life and tries to approach the needs of the child through interdisciplinary teamwork. Advocacy is of two types—case and class advocacy. **Case advocacy** refers to a situation in which a particular child or family is not receiving services or benefits for which it is eligible. The advocate takes the necessary steps to right the situation. **Class advocacy** involves more than an isolated incident; rather, it is advocacy on behalf of a group—migrants, people with disabilities, or minority groups—that needs help in working with the agencies established for it. Advocacy may also be viewed as an immediate action (e.g., lobbying on behalf of specific legislation or a particular regulation, building a coalition around a specific focus) or as setting goals for later initiatives (networks publicizing needs, demonstrating cost-effectiveness of specific programs, contributing to political action campaigns, and voting for candidates concerned about children).

Major advocacy efforts in early childhood began in the 1930s and 1940s when teacher educators on the President's Advisory Committee on the WPA Nursery Schools campaigned to keep the nursery schools in operation. Early childhood educators seemed less active in advocacy in the 1950s and 1960s. When the Child Development Act of 1971 was vetoed, the need for effective advocacy was noted. The federal government recognized the importance of child advocacy when the Office of Child Development established a Center for Child Advocacy in 1971. In 1980, the Center for the Study of Public Policies for Young Children, a part of the High/Scope

Educational Research Foundation, was founded by the Carnegie Corporation of New York. The goal of the center was to communicate with the federal and state policymakers about implications of research findings for policies affecting young children. Today, not only are advocacy efforts increasing, but also training for public policy and advocacy is on the rise (Lombardi, 1986).

Roles in Influencing Public Policy

Takanishi (1977) indicates three roles in public policy formulation:

1. An **expert** assesses the research literature pertinent to some issue and evaluates the likely efficacy of a proposed procedure for achieving a goal. The expert makes judgments based on consideration of alternatives and costs and benefits of alternatives and analyzes the techniques necessary to bring about and maintain policy change.

2. The **advocate** pursues or defends a program believed to be in the best interest of the child or the child's family. The advocate stays close to the database of the expert, but the advocate's main role is one of action. In a sense, professional practice itself is advocacy.

3. **Community members** must also be involved in policy making in order to prevent encroachment on local autonomy. Services should respond to the needs expressed by people of the local community. Community involvement also increases accountability; thus, administrators must devise a process for community participation.

Becoming an Effective Advocate

Becoming an effective advocate involves a number of steps:

1. *Know about the problems and the number of people in the area affected by a problem.* A child-centered approach to decisions con-

cerning public advocacy is justified on humanitarian and social equity principles (Huston, 1991) and on the children as investments in America's democratic, economic, and world leadership roles (National Commission on Children, 1991). The Child Care Information Service of the NAEYC provides demographic fact sheets, information kits, bibliographies, and directories. Other information can be obtained through the Center for the Future of Children—the David and Lucille Packard Foundation (Los Angeles, California) and through the other organizations listed in Appendixes 4 and 5.

2. *Determine the appropriate congressional committee, subcommittee, or agency responsible for correcting the problem.* Know what authority each level of government has. Those responsible may try to deny responsibility.

3. *Note legislative issues.* Examine the Association for the Advancement of Psychology's *APA Monitor.* Know the congressional representatives and how lobbies are formed.

4. *Translate ideas into concrete terms.* According to J. Fink and Sponseller (1977), child advocacy can be learned through simulation. Simulation can help in testing various alternatives and clarifying thinking.

5. *Write to members of Congress.* Use tips for contacting elected officials (E. Allen, 1983).

6. *Learn how developmental research can be brought to bear on pending legislation and the policy decisions that affect young children and their families* (McCartney & Phillips, 1993). Professionals may find that public hearings are often perfunctorily administered and thus will need some insight on how to conduct public hearings on child care (Gormley, 1992).

7. *Carefully study the work of other child development groups to avoid duplicate efforts.*

8. *Practice patience but take the offensive.* Advocacy is more than defensive in nature.

9. *Follow through on plans for correcting a situation.* Many plans have been delayed for further study or for lack of budget at the expense of child and family.

10. *Enlist more child advocates by informing others.* Many useful sources are available on how to enlist advocates (Duff & Stroman, 1979; Patton, 1993; Wingfield, 1979).

11. *Join groups that assume an advocacy role and professional organizations listed in Appendixes 4 and 5.*

BECOMING INVOLVED IN RESEARCH

Research has come to occupy a position of major importance in society. Tremendous advances have been made in business, industry, and medicine. Some businesses and industries allocate more than 50% of their budgets for research. Although advancement in education lags behind some other areas and although educational research has been conducted on a shoestring budget, research is now recognized as a major way to effect improvements in education. For example, research on Head Start changed public policy. More groups are now interested in and financially supporting research. Contributing to research and interpreting data for the benefit of children, their families, and those working on behalf of children have become recognized as part of administration.

Early childhood education is involved in both psychological and pedagogical research. Prior to the 1960s, research focused on developmental characteristics of children. By the 1960s, the cultural context of early childhood education was examined more precisely. Research centered on cognitive and linguistic "deprivation" and the effects of "compensatory" programs.

Many have denounced the distance between the researcher and the teacher (Almy, 1975; Biber, 1988; Katz, 1977b). Takanishi (1981) stated that this distance began when earlier child development researchers wanted to establish their field as more "pure" science untainted by any practical considerations. Sears (1975) called for child development research to turn back to relevancy—social problem-solving research. For research to become more relevant, differences between the practitioner's and the researcher's perspectives must be narrowed (Bolster, 1983).

Various researchers have noted the need for research in specific areas, such as:

1. The optimal settings for early childhood programs and the agencies that could best sponsor them (B. Caldwell, 1990)

2. The consequences of programs on infants and toddlers (Powell, 1989; Weikart, 1989)

3. The reasons children lose gains made in the early years (B. Caldwell, 1990)

4. Staff characteristics and staff-context variables (e.g., staff:child ratios and gender/ethnic mix of children and adults) (Grotberg, Chapman, & Lazar, 1971)

5. Teaching in early childhood settings (B. Caldwell, 1990; D. Peters, 1993)

6. Better research methodologies to assess curriculum approaches (Weikart, 1989)

7. How to help children who lack parental support (B. Caldwell, 1990)

8. Needed frequency and length of parent-staff communication (Endsley & Minish, 1991)

9. How comfortable parents and staff are with each other (Bradbard, Sinclair, & Endsley, 1987)

10. Staff competency in working with parents (Powell, 1991)

11. Nature and effects of various types of program-family interactions across the spectrum of program settings (Powell, 1991)

12. How best to communicate what we do as professionals (B. Caldwell, 1990)

All early childhood educators should become involved in research efforts. The idea of teacher as researcher has gained momentum (Duckworth, 1987; Hopkins, 1985). One effort to resolve the dilemma between formal research and functional practice is the Teachers' Research Network (Chattin-McNichols & Loeffler, 1989). Teachers might begin by volunteering or cooperating with those conducting research when requested (J. Allen & Catron, 1990; D. Rogers, Waller, & Perrin, 1987). Jalongo and McCracken (1986) have provided suggestions for writing publishable manuscripts.

HELPING OTHERS FIND A PLACE IN THE PROFESSION

Helping others find a place in the profession of early childhood care and education is a major leadership responsibility. This is certainly a form of advocacy because others are encouraged to contribute. Early childhood educators can:

1. Provide places for student teachers, interns, and others in their programs.

2. Write and verbally consult with others on careers in early childhood care and education, beginning by including childhood education as a career, along with the other careers introduced to young children in the program.

3. Share skills and knowledge with others who work with young children. Early childhood leaders in state departments expressed the need for a mechanism to share information with other states (S. Robinson, 1993/94).

4. Encourage others to continue their education through independent study, conferences, short courses, formal degrees, and participation in professional organizations and set an example by continuing their own education.

With the contributions of others, the profession grows and improves for the benefit of all young children and their families.

TRENDS AND ISSUES

Although the field of early childhood care and education has had a history of more than 150 years and many individuals have made lasting contributions, the expansion of the field and the changing social structure of society call for even greater insight and commitment. Many issues have been examined both from a broad perspective in Chapter 1 to close-up views in Chapters 2 through 10. Once again, it seems fitting to look at the broad issues. Kagan (1991a) calls for three linked strategies in "seeking excellence" in this field:

1. *Move from "programs to systems."* Professionals have had a rich history with many different roots, and the early childhood profession has come under various auspices. From the early childhood profession's many program models, professionals have learned the elements and principles that work. Most of these are now part of the standards written by various professional associations. As Greenman (1988) has said, professionals want programs in which every child can "spend a childhood." Professionals now need a commitment to institutionalize these standards more widely. Yet, local programs can be unique in meeting the special needs and desires of the families they serve.

2. *Move from a particularistic to a universal vision.* The diverse nature of our field has led to a lack of connections among programs, to confusion for policymakers, and consequently to fragmented and inefficient services. Collaboration is needed to address current and projected challenges. Collaboration is not new to early childhood programs but is even more needed today (C. Bruner, 1991; Kagan, 1991c; Kagan & Rivera, 1991).

3. *Move from short- to long-term commitments.* We need to move from thinking about early childhood programs serving limited segments of our society or fulfilling short-term needs to seeing the field as a permanent part of our social fabric. Perreault (1991) says that soci-

ety (e.g., media, government, religious and civic groups, professional associations, employers) are early child programs' "new extended family."

The hard work of making early childhood programs better must continue. Over the years, we have seen many sectors of society committed to various programs. Now, we must contribute to the profession by coming together on behalf of our children and their families.

SUMMARY

Recent years have seen many calls for professionalism in early childhood education. Professionalism is linked to many processes, such as defining early childhood education, developing a knowledge base, abiding by a code of ethics, and focusing on service and maintaining, extending, and improving that service.

The clients of early childhood educators are dependent on professionals who know their needs and who can make their needs visible to decision makers. If we as early childhood educators fail to raise our collective voice on behalf of children and their families, the problems faced by children and their families will never be solved and our commitment will be broken. Thus, advocacy is the way we actualize our professional responsibility.

As a profession, our knowledge base is created through research. Researchers in psychology and education and teachers in the field need to be working on more joint projects. Researchers need to be aware of the many concerns of daily practice, and teachers need to use the eye of the researcher as they practice.

Early childhood educators need to confirm their professionalism in helping others become involved. Encouragement and assistance are needed in helping others develop a sense of identity within the profession. We need more of the dauntless men and women who carry the banner of early care and education at every level of involvement.

The long and diverse history of early childhood care and education has filled pages with significant ideas and with the impressive accomplishments of both individuals and supportive associations, agencies, foundations, and religious, civic, and corporate groups. With the approach of the next century, professionals need to take another look at the entire field to plan the course of action. Diversity has enriched the field with ideas but also has led to problems of incoherence. At least three negative repercussions are seen as a result of this diversity. First, some ideas have stood the test of time and have worked across program settings; yet, some programs fail to incorporate these ideas. These ideas, as set forth in various standards, need to be embraced by the entire field. Second, early childhood care and education has some competing programs. These sustain incoherence. Collaboration at the national, state, and local levels is needed to give coherence to the field. Third, for young children and their families to really profit from the various efforts, a central vision and a sustained effort must be manifested.

Professionalism is dynamic. Early childhood education will continue to change in positive ways as all of us who call ourselves professionals become involved in promoting professionalization, influencing public policy, becoming involved in research, and helping others find a place in the profession. And, this profession needs administrators who take the leadership role in seizing opportunities to make a difference in the lives of young children and their families.

FOR FURTHER READING

Bredekamp, S., & Willer, S. (1993). Professionalizing the field of early childhood education: Pros and cons. *Young Children, 48*(3), 82-84.

Clapp, G. (1988). *Child study research: Current perspectives and applications.* Lexington, MA: Lexington Books.

Fennimore, B. S. (1989). *Child advocacy for early childhood educators.* New York: Teachers College Press.

Goffin, S. G., & Lombardi, J. (1988). *Speaking out: Early childhood advocacy.* Washington, DC: National Association for the Education of Young Children.

Jensen, M. A., & Chevalier, Z. W. (1990). *Issues and advocacy in early education.* Needham Heights, MA: Allyn & Bacon.

Spodek, B., Saracho, O. N., & Peters, D. L. (Eds.). (1988). *Professionalism and the early childhood practitioner.* New York: Teachers College Press.

Wilkins, A., & Blank, H. (1987). Child care strategies to move the issues forward. *Young Children, 42*(1), 68-72.

Wishon, P. M. (1994). On our watch: Connecting across generations of early childhood advocates. *Young Children, 49*(2), 42-43.

Appendix 1

※ ※ ※ ※ ※

Resources for Program Planning

INFANTS AND TODDLERS

Balaban, N. (1992). The role of the child care professional in caring for infants, toddlers, and their families. *Young Children, 47*(5), 66-71.

Belsky, J. (1988). The "effects" of infant day-care reconsidered. *Early Childhood Research Quarterly, 3,* 235-272.

Bowlby, J. (1988). *A secure base: Parent-child attachment and healthy human development.* New York: Basic Books.

Cataldo, C. Z. (1984). Infant-toddler education: Blending the best approaches. *Young Children, 39*(2), 25-32.

Cawlfield, M. E. (1992). Velcro time: The language connection. *Young Children, 47*(4), 26-30.

Couchenour, D. (1993). *Bright ideas: Learning all day.* Little Rock, AR: Southern Early Childhood Association.

Cryer, D., Harms, T., & Bourland, B. (1987). *Active learning series (for infants and ones).* Menlo Park, CA: Addison-Wesley.

Dittman, L. L. (Ed.). (1984). *The infants we care for* (Rev. ed.). Washington, DC: National Association for the Education of Young Children.

Dodge, D. T., Dombro, A. L., & Koralek, D. G. (1992). *Caring for infants and toddlers* (Vols. 1 and 2). Washington, DC: Teaching Strategies.

Dombro, A. L., & Bryan, P. (1991). *Sharing the caring.* New York: Simon & Schuster.

Dombro, A. L., & Wallach, L. (1988). *The ordinary is extraordinary: How children under three learn.* New York: Simon & Schuster.

Eddowes, E. A. (1993). *Bright ideas: Handmade toys.* Little Rock, AR: Southern Early Childhood Association.

Eheart, B. K., & Leavitt, R. L. (1985). Supporting toddler play. *Young Children, 40*(3), 18-22.

Evans, J., & Illfield, E. (1982). *Good beginnings.* Ypsilanti, MI: High/Scope.

Friedberg, J. (1989). Food for thought. Helping today's toddlers become tomorrow's readers: A pilot parent participation project offered through a Pittsburgh health agency. *Young Children, 44*(2), 13-16.

Fucigna, C., Ives, K. C., & Ives, W. (1982). Art for toddlers: A developmental approach. *Young Children, 37*(3), 45-51.

Garner, B. P. (1993). *Bright ideas: The physical environment for infants and toddlers.* Little Rock, AR: Southern Early Childhood Association.

Godwin, A., & Schrag, L. (1988). *Setting up for infant care: Guidelines for centers and family day care homes.* Washington, DC: National Association for the Education of Young Children.

Gonzalez-Mena, J. (1986). Toddlers: What to expect. *Young Children, 42*(1), 47-51.

Gonzalez-Mena, J. (1992). Taking a culturally sensitive approach to infant-toddler programs. *Young Children, 47*(2), 4-9.

Gonzalez-Mena, J., & Widmeyer, D. E. (1989). *Infants, toddlers, and caregivers.* Palo Alto, CA: Mayfield.

Gordon, I. J. (1972). *Child learning through child play: Learning activities for two and three year olds.* New York: St. Martin's Press.

※ ※ ※ ※ ※

Gordon, I. J. (1987). *Baby to parent, parent to baby: A guide to loving and learning in a child's first year.* New York: St. Martin's Press.

Gottschall, S. (1989). Understanding and accepting separation feelings. *Young Children, 44*(6), 11-16.

Greenberg, P. (1987). Ideas that work with young children: What is curriculum for infants in family day care (or elsewhere)? *Young Children, 42*(5), 58-62.

Greenberg, P. (1991). *Character development: Encouraging self-esteem and self-discipline in infants, toddlers, and two-year-olds.* Washington, DC: National Association for the Education of Young Children.

Harms, T., Cryer, D., & Clifford, R. M. (1990). *Infant/Toddler Environment Rating Scale.* New York: Teachers College Press.

Highberger, R., & Boynton, M. (1983). Preventing illness in infant/toddler day care. *Young Children, 38*(3), 3-8

Hoben, A. (1989). Caregivers' corner. Our thoughts on diapering and potty training. *Young Children, 44*(6), 28-29.

Hodge, S. (1993). *Bright ideas: Special needs.* Little Rock, AR: Southern Early Childhood Association.

Honig, A. S. (1983). Meeting the needs of infants. *Dimensions, 11*(4), 4-7.

Honig, A. S. (1985). High-quality infant/toddler care: Issues and dilemmas. *Young Children, 41*(1), 40-46.

Honig, A. S. (1987). The Eriksonian approach: Infant/toddler education. In J. Roopnarine & J. Johnson (Eds.), *Approaches to early childhood education* (2nd ed., pp. 47-70). New York: Merrill/Macmillan.

Honig, A. S. (1989). Quality infant/toddler caregiving: Are there magic recipes? *Young Children, 44*(4), 4-10.

Honig, A. S. (1993). Mental health for babies: What do theory and research teach us? *Young Children, 48*(3), 69-76.

Honig, A. S., & Lally, J. R. (1988). Behavior profiles of experienced teachers of infants and toddlers. *Early Child Development and Care, 33,* 188-199.

Howes, C., Rodnig, C., Galluzzo, D. C., & Meyers, L. (1988). Attachment and child care. *Early Childhood Research Quarterly, 3,* 403-416.

Karnes, M. B. (1982). *You and your small wonder* (Books 1 and 2). Circle Pines, MN: American Guidance Service.

Lourie, R., & Neugebauer, R. (Eds.). (1982). *Caring for infants and toddlers: What works and what doesn't* (Vol. 2). Redmond, WA: Child Care Information Exchange.

Maxim, G. W. (1990). *The sourcebook: Activities for infants and young children* (2nd ed.). New York: Merrill/Macmillan

Miller, K. (1984). *Things to do with toddlers and twos.* Marshfield, MA: Telshare.

Miller, K. (1990). *More things to do with toddlers and twos.* Marshfield, MA: Telshare.

Neugebauer, R., & Lurie, R. (Eds.). (1980). *Caring for infants and toddlers: What works, what doesn't.* Summit, NJ: Summit Care Center.

Pizzo, P. D. (1990). Family-centered Head Start for infants and toddlers: A renewed direction for Project Head Start. *Young Children, 45*(6), 30-35.

Ross, H. W. (1992). Integrating infants with disabilities? Can "ordinary" caregivers do it? *Young Children, 47*(3), 65-71.

Segal, M., & Adcock, D. (1985). *Your child at play series: Birth to one year, One to two years, (and) Two to three years.* New York: Newmarket Press.

Steinberg, M., Williams, S., & DaRos, D. (1992). Caregivers' corner. Toilet learning takes time. *Young Children, 48*(1), 56.

Stewart, I. S. (1982). The real world of teaching two-year-old children. *Young Children, 37*(5), 3-13.

Stonehouse, A. (Ed.). (1991). *Trusting toddlers: Planning for one- to three-year-olds in child care centers.* St. Paul, MN: Toys 'n Things Press.

Surbeck, E., & Kelley, M. F. (Eds.). (1990). *Personalizing care with infants, toddlers, and families.* Wheaton, MD: Association for Childhood Education International.

Tyler, B., & Dittmann, L. (1980). Meeting the toddler more than halfway: The behavior of toddlers and their caregivers. *Young Children, 35*(2), 39-46.

Vaughn, E. (1993). *Bright ideas: Books for babies.* Little Rock, AR: Southern Early Childhood Association.

Willis, A., & Ricciuti, H. (1975). *A good beginning for babies: Guidelines for group care.* Washington, DC: National Association for the Education of Young Children.

Wilson, L. C. (1990). *Infants and toddlers, curriculum and teaching* (2nd ed.). Albany, NY: Delmar.

Young Children: Constructivist View

Althouse, R. (1981). *The young child: Learning with understanding.* New York: Teachers College Press.

Ashton-Warner, S. (1986). *Teacher.* New York: Simon & Schuster.

Biber, B. (1984). *Early education and psychological development.* New Haven, CT: Yale University Press.

Biber, B., Shapiro, E., & Wickens, D. (1971). *Promoting cognitive growth: A developmental-interaction point of view.* Washington, DC: National Association for the Education of Young Children.

DeVries, R., & Kohlberg, L. (1987). *Constructivist early education: Overview and comparison with other programs.* Washington, DC: National Association for the Education of Young Children.

Educational Products Information Exchange Institute. (1972). *Early childhood education: How to select and evaluate materials.* New York: Author.

Elkind, D. (1976). *Child development and education: A Piagetian perspective.* New York: Oxford University Press.

Elkind, D. (1986). Formal education and early childhood education: An essential difference. *Phi Delta Kappan, 67,* 631-636.

Forman, G. E., & Fosnot, C. T. (1982). The use of Piaget's constructivism in early childhood education programs. In B. Spodek (Ed.), *Handbook of research in early childhood education* (pp. 185-211). New York: Free Press.

Forman, G., & Kushner, D. (1983). *The child's construction of knowledge: Piaget for teaching children.* Washington, DC: National Association for the Education of Young Children.

Fosnot, C. T. (1989). *Inquiring teachers, inquiring learners: A constructivist approach for teaching.* New York: Teachers College Press.

Fowlkes, M. A. (1991). Gifts from childhood's godmother: Patty Smith Hill. In J. Quisenberry, E. A. Eddowed, & S. Robinson (Eds.), *Readings from Childhood Education* (Vol. 2, pp. 11-16). Wheaton, MD: Association for Childhood Education International.

Greenberg, P. (1990). Ideas that work with young children. Why not academic preschool? (Part 1). *Young Children, 45*(2), 70-80.

Greenberg, P. (1992). Why not academic preschool? (Part 2). Autocracy or democracy in the classroom? *Young Children, 47*(3), 54-64.

Kamii, C. (Ed.). (1990). *(No) achievement testing in the early grades: The games grown-ups play.* Washington, DC: National Association for the Education of Young Children.

Kamii, C., & DeVries, R. (1980). *Group games in early education: Implications of Piaget's theory.* Washington, DC: National Association for the Education of Young Children.

Katz, L. G., Raths, J. D., & Torres, R. T. (1987). *A place called kindergarten.* Urbana, IL: ERIC Clearinghouse on Elementary and Early Childhood Education.

Kohlberg, L. (1968). Early education: A cognitive view. *Child Development, 39,* 1013-1062.

Lavetelli, C. S. (1973). *Piaget's theory applied to an early childhood curriculum* (2nd ed.). Boston: American Science and Engineering.

Peterson, R., & Fellon-Collins, V. (1986). *The Piaget handbook for teachers and parents: Children in the age of discovery, preschool-third grade.* New York: Teachers College Press.

Raths, J., Wasserman, S., Jonas, A., & Rothstein, A. (1986). *Teaching for thinking: Theory, strategy, and activities for the classroom.* New York: Teachers College Press.

Schweinhart, L., Weikart, D., & Larner, M. (1986). Consequences of three preschool curriculum models through age fifteen. *Early Childhood Research Quarterly, 2*(3), 15-45.

Seefeldt, C. (Ed.). (1987). *The early childhood curriculum: A review of current research.* New York: Teachers College Press.

Spodek, B. (1988). Conceptualizing today's kindergarten curriculum. *Elementary School Journal, 89,* 203-212.

Vygotsky, L. (1967). Play and its role in the mental development of the child. *Soviet Psychology, 12,* 62-76.

Wasserman, S. (1990). *Serious players in the primary classroom.* New York: Teachers College Press.

Weber, E. (1984). *Ideas influencing early childhood education: A theoretical analysis.* New York: Teachers College Press.

Weikart, D. (1989). Hard choices in early childhood care and education: A view to the future. *Young Children, 44*(3), 25-30.

Weikart, D. P., Rogers, L., Adcock, C., & McClelland, D. (1971). *The cognitively oriented curriculum.* Washington, DC: National Association for the Education of Young Children.

Young Children: Behavioral-Environmental View

Alberto, P. A., & Troutman, A. C. (1990). *Applied behavior analysis for teachers.* New York: Merrill/Macmillan.

Bijou, S. W., & Baer, D. M. (1978). *Behavior analysis of child development.* Englewood Cliffs, NJ: Prentice Hall.

Bushell, D., Jr. (1973). The behavior analysis classroom. In B. Spodek (Ed.), *Early childhood education* (pp. 163-175). Englewood Cliffs, NJ: Prentice Hall.

Engelmann, S., & Engelmann, T. (1966). *Give your child a superior mind.* New York: Simon & Schuster.

Gagne, R. (1970). *The conditions of learning.* New York: Holt, Rinehart & Winston.

Neisworth, J. T. (1985). A behaviorist approach to early childhood education. In D. L. Peters, J. T. Neisworth, & T. D. Yawkey (Eds.), *Early childhood education: From theory to practice* (pp. 83-215). Monterey, CA: Brooks/Cole.

Sherman, J. A., & Bushnell, D., Jr. (1975). Behavior modifications as an educational technique. In F. D. Horowitz (Ed.), *Review of child development research* (Vol. 4, pp. 409-462). Chicago: University of Chicago Press.

Family Child Care

Baker, A. C. (1992). A puzzle, a picnic, and a vision: Family day care at its best. *Young Children, 47*(5), 36-38.

Children's Foundation. (1991). *Helping young children love themselves and others: A professional handbook for family day care.* Washington, DC: Author.

DeBord, K. (1993). A little respect and eight more hours in the day: Family child care providers have special needs. *Young Children, 48*(4), 21-26.

Dodge, D. T., & Colker, L. J. (1991). *The creative curriculum for family child care.* Washington, DC: Teaching Strategies.

Dombro, A. L., & Bryan, P. (1991). *Sharing the caring.* New York: Simon & Schuster.

Gonzalez-Mena, J. (1991). *Tips and tidbits: A book for family day care providers.* Washington, DC: National Association for the Education of Young Children.

Manfredi/Petitt, L. A. (1991). Ten steps to organizing the flow of your family day care day. *Young Children, 46*(3), 14-16.

Modiglianai, K., Reiff, M., & Jones, S. (1987). *Opening your door to children: How to start a family day care program.* Washington, DC: National Association for the Education of Young Children.

Nash, M., & Tate, C. (1986). *Better baby care: A book for family day care providers.* Washington, DC: Children's Foundation.

Roemer, J., & Austin, B. (1989). *Two to four from 9 to 5: The adventures of a day care provider.* New York: HarperCollins.

Squibb, S. (1986). *Family day care: How to provide it in your home.* Boston: Harvard Common Press.

School-Age Child Care

Alexander, N. P. (1986). School-age child care: Concerns and challenges. *Young Children, 42*(1), 3-10.

Baden, R., Genser, A., Levine, J., & Seligson, M. (1982). *School-age child care: An action manual.* Wellesley, MA: Center for Research on Women, School-Age Child Care Project.

Blakley, B., Blau, R., Brady, E. H., Streibert, C., Zavitkovsky, A., & Zavitkovsky, D. (1989). *Activities for school-age child care: Playing and learning.* Washington, DC: National Association for the Education of Young Children.

Coleman, M., Rowland, B. H., & Robinson, B. E. (1989). School-age child care: The community leadership role of educators. *Childhood Education, 66*, 78-82.

Coolsen, P., Seligson, M., & Garbarino, J. (1985). *When school's out and nobody's home.* Chicago: National Committee for Child Abuse.

Haas, C., & Friedman, A. (1990). *My own fun: Activities for kids ages 7-12.* Chicago: Chicago Review Press.

Haas-Foletta, K., & Cogley, M. (1990). *School-age ideas and activities for after-school programs.* Nashville, TN: School-Age Notes.

Powell, D. R. (1987). Research in review. After-school child care. *Young Children, 42*(3), 62-66.

Richard, M. M. (1991). *Before- and after-school programs: A start-up and administration manual.* Nashville, TN: School-Age Notes.

Stassevitch, V., Stemmler, P., Shotwell, R., & Wirth, M. (1989). *Ready-to-use activities for before- and after-school programs.* West Nyack, NY: Center for Applied Research in Education.

SACC Resources

4-H School-Age Child Care Program
California School-Age Child Care Program
11477 E. Avenue
Auburn, CA 95603

> *Management*
> *Curriculum I*
> *Curriculum II*
> *Facilitator's Guide*

Southeastern Pennsylvania School-Age Child Care
  Project
601 Knight Rd.
Ambler, PA 19002

> *School-Age Child Care Activities and Curriculum Bibliography*
>
> *Administrative Bibliography*

School-Age NOTES
P.O. Box 40205
Nashville, TN 37204
Publisher: Richard Scofield

> (Also send for catalog of resource materials.)

Multicultural/Antibias Understandings

Abramson, S., Seda, L., & Johnson, C. (1990). Literacy development in a multilingual kindergarten classroom. *Childhood Education, 67*(2), 68-72.

Au, K. A., & Kawakami, A. J. (1991). Culture and ownership: Schooling of minority students. *Childhood Education, 67,* 280-294.

Bigelow, B., Miner, B., & Peterson, B. (Eds.). (1991). *Rethinking Columbus.* Milwaukee: Rethinking Schools.

Billman, J. (1992). The Native American curriculum: Attempting alternatives to tepees and headbands. *Young Children, 47*(6), 22-25.

Boutte, G. S., & McCormick, C. B. (1992). Authentic multicultural activities: Avoiding pseudomulticulturalism. *Childhood Education, 68*(3), 140-144.

Brady, P. (1992). Columbus and the quincentennial myths: Another side of the story. *Young Children, 47*(6), 4-14.

Brandt, R. S. (Ed.). (1991/1992). Whose culture? [Special issue]. *Educational Leadership, 49*(4).

Byrnes, D. A., & Kigger, G. (1992). *Common bonds: Antibias teaching in a diverse society.* Wheaton, MD: Association for Childhood Education International.

Caduto, M. J., & Bruchac, J. (1988). *Keepers of the earth. Teacher's guide. Native American stories and environmental activities for children.* Golden, CO: Fulcrum.

Caduto, M. J., & Bruchac, J. (1989). *Keepers of the earth: Native American stories and environmental activities for children.* Golden, CO: Fulcrum.

Carlsson-Paige, N., & Levin, D. E. (1986). The butter battle book: Uses and abuses with young children. *Young Children, 41*(3), 37-42.

Carlsson-Paige, N., & Levin, D. E. (1992). Making peace in violent times: A constructivist approach to conflict resolution. *Young Children, 48*(1), 4-13.

Christopher, G. C. (1990). *The peopling of America: A teacher's manual for the Americans All Program.* Washington, DC: Portfolio Project.

Clark, L., DeWolf, S., & Clark, C. (1992). Teaching teachers to avoid having culturally assaultive classrooms. *Young Children, 47*(5), 4-9.

Clemens, S. G. (1988). A Dr. Martin Luther King, Jr., curriculum: Playing the dream. *Young Children, 43*(2), 6-11, 59-63.

Comer, J. P. (1988). Educating poor minority children. *Scientific American, 259*(5), 42-48.

Comer, J. P. (1989). Racism and the education of young children. *Teachers College Record, 90*(3), 352-361.

Coopersmith, S. (1967). *The antecedents of self-esteem.* Los Angeles: Freeman.

Copage, E. V. (1991). *Kwanzaa: An African American celebration of culture and cooking.* New York: Morrow.

Corbett, S. (1993). A complicated bias. *Young Children, 48*(3), 29-31.

Council on Interracial Books for Children (CIBC). (n.d.). *Ten quick ways to analyze children's books for racism and sexism.* New York: Author.

Curry, N. E., & Johnson, C. N. (1990). *Beyond self-esteem: Developing a genuine sense of human value.* Washington, DC: National Association for the Education of Young Children.

Derman-Sparks, L. (1989, Fall). How well are we nurturing racial and ethnic diversity? *CAEYC Connections,* pp. 3-5.

Derman-Sparks, L. (1992). "It isn't fair!" Antibias curriculum for young children. In B. Neugebauer (Ed.), *Alike and different: Exploring our humanity with young children* (Rev. ed., pp. 2-10). Washington, DC: National Association for the Education of Young Children.

Derman-Sparks, L., & the A.B.C. Task Force. (1989). *Antibias curriculum: Tools for empowering young children.* Washington, DC: National Association for the Education of Young Children. (Also available as a videotape, *Anti-Bias Curriculum,* elaborating on these ideas. Order from Pacific Oaks College Bookstore, 5 Westmoreland Pl., Pasadena, CA 91103.)

Derman-Sparks, L., Gutierriez, M., & Phillips, C. B. (1989). *Teaching young children to resist bias:*

What parents can do [Brochure]. Washington, DC: National Association for the Education of Young Children.

Dimijian, V. J. (1989). Holidays, holy days, and wholly dazed: Approaches to special days. *Young Children, 44*(6), 70-75.

Fillmore, L. W. (1990). Now or later? Issues related to the early education of minority group children. In *Early childhood and family education: Analysis and recommendations of the Council of Chief State School Officers.* New York: Harcourt Brace Jovanovich.

Fillmore, L. W. (1991). Language and cultural issues in the early education of language minority children. In S. L. Kagan (Ed.), *The care and education of America's young children: Obstacles and opportunities. 90th yearbook, Pt. 1* (pp. 30-49). Chicago: National Society for the Study of Education.

Fillmore, L. W. (1991). Second-language learning in children: A model of language learning in social context. In E. Bialystok (Ed.), *Language processing by bilingual children* (pp. 49-69). New York: Cambridge University Press.

Foerster, L. M., & Little Soldier, D. (1978). Learning centers for young Native Americans. *Young Children, 33*(3), 53-57.

Froschl, M., Colon, L., Rubin, E., & Sprung, B. (1984). *Including all of us: An early childhood curriculum about disability.* New York: Educational Equity Concepts.

Fry-Miller, K., & Myers-Wall, J. (1988). *Young peacemakers project book.* Elgin, IL: Brethren Press.

Glover, M. K. (1990). A bag of hair. American 1st graders experience Japan. *Childhood Education, 66*(3), 155-159.

Gonzalez-Mena, J. (1992). Taking a culturally sensitive approach in infant-toddler programs. *Young Children, 47*(2), 4-9.

Grammar, R. (1986). *Teaching peace* [Cassette recording]. Toronto: Children's Group. (Distributed in the United States by Alcazar, Inc.)

Greenberg, P. (1992). Teaching about Native Americans? Or teaching about people, including Native Americans? *Young Children, 47*(6), 27-30, 79-81.

Hale, J. (1991). The transmission of cultural values to young African American children. *Young Children, 46*(6), 7-15.

Hale-Benson, J. E. (1986). *Black children: Their roots, culture, and learning styles* (Rev. ed.). Baltimore, MD: Johns Hopkins University Press.

Harris, V. J. (1991). Research in review. Multicultural curriculum: African American children's literature. *Young Children, 46*(2), 37-44.

Hatcher, B., Pape, D., & Nicosia, R. T. (1988). Group games for global awareness. *Childhood Education, 65*(1), 8-13.

Head Start Bureau. (1992). *Multicultural principles for Head Start programs.* Washington, DC: Author.

Hearst, M. R. (Ed.). (1993). *Interracial identity: Celebration, conflict, or choice?* Chicago: Biracial Family Network.

Hendrick, J. (1992). Where does it all begin? Teaching the principles of democracy in the early years. *Young Children, 47*(3), 51-53.

Hilliard, A. G., III. (1989, January). Teachers and cultural styles in a pluralistic society. *NEA Today,* pp. 65-69.

Hopkins, S., & Winters, J. (1990). *Discover the world: Empowering children to value themselves, others, and the earth.* Santa Cruz, CA: New Society.

Jones, E., & Derman-Sparks, L. (1992). Meeting the challenge of diversity. *Young Children, 47*(2), 12-18.

Jones, M., Jr. (1991, September 9). It's a not so small world: Multiculturalism is broadening the horizons of children's literature. *Newsweek,* pp. 65-64.

Katz, L. G. (Ed.). (1991). Educating linguistically and culturally diverse preschoolers [Special issue]. *Early Childhood Research Quarterly, 6*(3).

Kendall, F. E. (1983). *Diversity in the classroom: A multicultural approach to the education of young children.* New York: Teachers College Press.

Kendall, F. E. (1988, November/December). Creating a multicultural environment. *Scholastic Today,* pp. 39-51.

Koeppel, J. (with Mulrooney, M.). (1992). The Sister Schools Program: A way for children to learn about cultural diversity—When there isn't any in their school. *Young Children, 48*(1), 44-47.

Kunjufu, J. (1984). *Developing positive self-images and discipline in black children.* Chicago: African-American Images.

Lane, M. (1984). Reaffirmations: Speaking out for children. A child's right to the valuing of diversity. *Young Children, 39*(6), 76.

Lee, E. (1992). The crisis in education: Forging an antiracist response. *Rethinking Schools, 7*(1), 4-5.

Leslie, C. (1991, February 11). Classrooms of Babel: A record number of immigrant children pose(s) new problems for schools. *Newsweek,* pp. 56-57.

Little Soldier, L. M. (1989). Children as cultural anthropologists. *Childhood Education, 66*(2), 88-91.

Little Soldier, L. M. (1992). Building optimum learning environments for Navajo students. *Childhood Education, 68*(3), 145-148.

Little Soldier, L. M. (1992). Working with Native American children. *Young Children, 47*(6), 15-21.

Locust, C. (1988). Wounding the spirit: Discrimination and traditional American Indian belief systems. *Harvard Educational Review, 58*(3), 315-330.

Lynch, E. W., & Hanson, J. J. (1992). *Developing cross-cultural competence: A guide for working with young children and their families.* Baltimore: Paul H. Brookes.

McCracken, J. B. (Ed.). (1990). *Helping children love themselves and others: A professional handbook for family day care.* Washington, DC: Children's Foundation.

McCracken, J. B. (1992). *Teacher's guide to learning activities: Grades K-2.* Washington, DC: Americans All.

McCracken, J. B. (1993). *Valuing diversity: The primary years.* Washington, DC: National Association for the Education of Young Children.

McCracken, J. B. (Ed.). (in press). *Everyone counts: Applying Head Start's multicultural principles in all program components.* Washington, DC: Head Start Bureau.

McNeill, E., Schmidt, V., & Allen, J. (1991). *Cultural awareness for young children.* Reading, MA: Addison-Wesley.

Morris, L. (Ed.). (1986). *Extracting learning styles from social/cultural diversity: A study of five American minorities.* Washington, DC: U.S. Office of Education, Southwest Teacher Corps Network.

Morrow, R. D. (1989). What's in a name? In particular, a Southeast Asian name? *Young Children, 44*(6), 20-23.

National Association of State Boards of Education. (1991). *The American tapestry: Education of a nation.* Alexandria, VA: Author.

National Black Child Development Institute. (1987). *Safeguards: Guidelines for establishing programs for 4-year-olds in the public schools.* Washington, DC: Author.

National Black Child Development Institute. (1992). *African American literature for young children* [Brochure]. Washington, DC: National Association for the Education of Young Children.

National Parent-Teacher Association & the Anti-Defamation League of B'nai B'rith. (1989). *What to tell your child about prejudice and discrimination.* Chicago: Authors.

Neugebauer, B. (1990). Going one step further: No traditional holidays. *Child Care Information Exchange, 74,* 42.

Neugebauer, B. (Ed.). (1992). *Alike and different: Exploring our humanity with young children* (Rev. ed.). Washington, DC: National Association for the Education of Young Children.

Noddings, N. (1991/1992). The gender issue. *Educational Leadership, 49*(6), 65-70.

Ogbu, J. U. (1987). Opportunity structure, cultural boundaries, and literacy. In J. A. Langer (Ed.), *Language, literacy, and culture: Issues of society and schooling* (pp. 149-177), Norwood, NJ: Ablex.

Pederson, P. (1988). *A handbook for developing multicultural awareness.* Alexandria, VA: American Association for Counseling and Development.

Perry, T., & Fraser, J. W. (1993). Reconstructing schools as multicultural democracies. *Rethinking Schools, 7*(3), 16-17, 31.

Phillips, C. B. (1988). Nurturing diversity for today's children and tomorrow's leaders. *Young Children, 43*(2), 42-47.

Ramsey, P. G. (1979). Beyond "Ten Little Indians" and turkeys: Alternative approaches to Thanksgiving. *Young Children, 34*(6), 28-32, 49-52.

Ramsey, P. G. (1982). Multicultural education in early childhood. *Young Children, 37*(2), 13-24.

Ramsey, P. G. (1986). *Teaching and learning in a diverse world.* New York: Teachers College Press.

Ramsey, P. G., & Derman-Sparks, L. (1992). Viewpoint. Multicultural education reaffirmed. *Young Children, 47*(2), 10-11.

Ramsey, P. G., Void, E. B., & Williams, L. R. (1989). *Multicultural education: A sourcebook.* New York: Garland.

Rigg, P., Kazemek, F. E., & Hudelson, S. (1993). Children's books about the elderly. *Rethinking Schools, 7*(3), 25.

Root, M. P. P. (Ed.). (1992). *Racially mixed people in America.* Newbury Park, CA: Sage.

Sale, K. (1990). *The conquest of paradise: Christopher Columbus and the Columbian legacy.* New York: Penguin.

Saracho, O. N., & Spodek, B. (1983). *Understanding the multicultural experience in early childhood educa-*

tion. Washington, DC: National Association for the Education of Young Children.

Schmidt, V. E., & McNeill, E. (1978). *Cultural awareness: A resource bibliography*. Washington, DC: National Association for the Education of Young Children.

Schon, I. (1991). Recent noteworthy books in Spanish for young children. *Young Children, 46*(4), 65.

Schuman, J. M. (1981). *Art from many hands: Multicultural art projects*. Worcester, MA: Davis.

Seefeldt, C. (1984). What's in a name? Lots to learn! *Young Children, 39*(5), 24-30.

Seefeldt, C. (1993). Social studies: Learning for freedom. *Young Children, 48*(3), 4-9.

Seligmann, J. (1990). Speaking in tongues: Dios mio! Even Americans will need to know a foreign language to get along in the 21st century. *Newsweek Special Edition: Education: A Consumer's Handbook*, pp. 36-37.

Sheldon, A. (1990). "Kings are royaler than Queens"; Language and socialization. *Young Children, 45*(2), 4-9.

Shiller, P., & Bermudez, A. B. (1988). Working with non-English-speaking children. *Texas Child Care Quarterly, 12*(3), 3-8.

Sholtzs, K. C. (1989). A new language. A new life. *Young Children, 44*(3), 76-77.

Simonson, R., & Walker, S. (Eds.). (1988). *Graywolf Annual Five: Multi-cultural literacy: Opening the American mind*. St. Paul, MN: Graywolf Press.

Slapin, B. (1990). *A guide to evaluating children's literature for handicappism*. Berkeley, CA: Oyate.

Slapin, B., & Seale, D. (Eds.). (1992). *Through Indian eyes: The Native experience in books for children*. Philadelphia: New Society.

Sleeker, C. E. (Ed.). (1991). *Empowerment through multicultural education*. Albany: State University Press of New York.

Soto, L. D. (1991). Research in review. Understanding bilingual/bicultural young children. *Young Children, 46*(2), 30-36.

Southern Early Childhood Association. (1989). *Multicultural education: A position statement*. Little Rock, AR: Author.

Spann, M. B. (1992). *Literature-based multicultural activities: An integrated approach*. New York: Scholastic.

Spottswood, R. K. (1989). *Music of America's peoples: A historical perspective*. Washington, DC: Portfolio Project.

Sprung, B. (1975). *Non-sexist education for young children: A practical guide*. New York: Women's Action Alliance.

Sprung, B. (Ed.). (1978). *Perspectives on non-sexist early childhood education*. New York: Teachers College Press.

Steele, S. (1990). *The content of our character: A new vision of race in America*. New York: St. Martin's.

Trimble, S. (Ed.). (1986). *Our voices, our land*. Flagstaff, AZ: Northland.

Vold, E. B. (Ed.). (1992). *Multicultural education in early childhood classrooms*. Washington, DC: National Education Association.

Wardle, F. (1987). Are you sensitive to interracial children's special identity needs? *Young Children, 42*(2), 53-59.

Wardle, F. (1990, August). Bunny ears and cupcakes for all: Are parties developmentally appropriate? *Child Care Information Exchange, 74*, 39-42.

Wardle, F. (1990). Endorsing children's differences: Meeting the needs of adopted minority children. *Young Children, 45*(5), 44-46.

Wardle, F. (1992). *Biracial identity: An ecological development model*. Denver: Center for the Study of Biracial Children.

Wardle, F. (1992). Supporting biracial children in the school setting. *Education and Treatment of Children, 15*(2), 163-172.

West, B. (1992). Children are caught—between home and school, culture and school. In B. Neugebauer (Ed.), *Alike and different: Exploring our humanity with young children* (Rev. ed., pp. 127-139). Washington, DC: National Association for the Education Young Children.

Williams, L. R. (1989). Issues in education: Diverse gifts, multicultural education in the kindergarten. *Childhood Education, 66*(1), 2-3.

Williams, L. R., & DeGaetano, Y. (1985). *ALERTA: A multicultural, bilingual approach to teaching young children*. Menlo Park, CA: Addison-Wesley.

Women's International League for Peace and Freedom. (1989). Undoing racism. *Peace and Freedom, 49*(4), 5.

York, S. (1991). *Roots and wings: Affirming culture in early childhood programs*. St. Paul, MN: Redleaf Press.

Inclusion of Children With Special Needs

Abbott, C. F., & Gold, S. (1991). Conferring with parents when you're concerned that their child needs special services. *Young Children, 46*(4), 10-14.

Allen, K. E. (1989). *Developmental profiles: Birth to six.* Albany, NY: Delmar.

Allen, K. E. (1992). *The exceptional child: Mainstreaming in early childhood education* (2nd ed.). Albany, NY: Delmar.

Anderson, P. O., & Fenichel, E. S. (1989). *Serving culturally diverse families of infants and toddlers with disabilities.* Arlington, VA: National Center for Clinical Infant Programs.

Ayers, B., & Meyer, L. H. (1992, February). Helping teachers manage the inclusive classroom: Staff development and teaming star among management strategies. *School Administrator,* 30-37.

Bailey, D. B., Jr., & McWilliam, R. A. (1990). Normalizing early intervention. *Topics in Early Childhood Special Education, 10*(2), 33-47.

Bailey, D. B., Jr., & Wolery, M. (1992). *Teaching infants and preschoolers with disabilities* (2nd ed.). New York: Merrill/Macmillan.

Baker, A. C. (1993). New frontiers in family day care: Integrating children with ADHD. *Young Children, 48*(5), 69-73.

Benner, S. M. (1992). *Assessing young children with special needs: An ecological perspective.* White Plains, NY: Longman.

Bordner, G. A., & Tetkowski, M. (1992). Educational play: Meeting everyone's needs in mainstreamed classrooms. *Childhood Education, 69*(1), 38-40.

Bricker, D. D. (1986). *Early education of at-risk and handicapped infants, toddlers, and preschool children.* Glenview, IL: Scott, Foresman.

Brown, M. H., Althouse, R., & Anfin, C. (1993). Guided dramatization: Fostering social development in children with disabilities. *Young Children, 48*(2), 68-73.

Carta, J. J., Schwartz, I. S., Atwater, J. B., & McConnell, S. R. (1991). Developmentally appropriate practice: Appraising its usefulness for young children with disabilities. *Topics in Early Childhood Special Education, 11*(1), 1-20.

Cook, R. E., & Armbruster, V. B. (1982). *Adapting early childhood curricula: Suggestions for meeting special needs.* St. Louis, MO: C. V. Mosby.

Cook, R. E., Tessier, A., & Klein, M. D. (1992). *Adapting early childhood curricula for children with special needs* (3rd ed.). New York: Macmillan.

Davidson, D. H. (1990). Viewpoint. Child care as a support for families with special needs. *Young Children, 45*(3), 47-48.

Deiner, P. L. (1983). *Resources for teaching young children with special needs.* New York: Harcourt Brace.

Delventhol, M. (1991). This is my story—this is my song. *Young Children, 46*(6), 16-18.

Eggers, N. (1983). Influencing preschoolers' awareness and feelings regarding depicted physical disability. *Early Childhood Development and Care, 12*(2), 199-206.

Ehrlich, V. (1985). *Gifted children: A guide for parents and teachers.* New York: Trillium.

Fauvre, M. (1988). Including young children with "new" chronic illnesses in an early childhood setting. *Young Children, 43*(6), 71-77.

Fewell, R. R., & Vadasy, P. F. (1986). *Families of handicapped children: Needs and supports across the life span.* Austin, TX: PRO-ED.

Fink, D. B. (1988). *School-age children with special needs: What do they do when school is out?* Boston: Exceptional Parent Press.

Froschl, M., Colon, L., Rubin, E., & Sprung, B. (1984). *Including all of us: An early childhood curriculum about disability.* New York: Educational Equity Concepts.

Gallagher, J. J., & Vietze, P. M. (1986). *Families of handicapped persons: Research, programs, and policy issues.* Baltimore: Paul H. Brookes.

Goldstein, H. (1993). Use of peers as communication intervention agents. *Teaching Exceptional Children, 25*(2), 37-40.

Hanson, M. J., & Lynch, E. W. (1989). *Early intervention: Implementing child and family services for infants and toddlers who are at risk or disabled.* Austin, TX: PRO-ED.

Hazekamp, J., & Huebner, K. M. (1989). *Program planning and evaluation for blind and visually impaired students: National guidelines for educational excellence.* New York: American Foundation for the Blind.

Hazel, R., Barber, P. A., Roberts, S., Behr, S. K., Helmstetter, E., & Guess, D. (1988). *A community approach to an integrated service system for children with special needs.* Baltimore: Paul H. Brookes.

Heekin, S., & Mengel, P. (Eds.). (1983). *New friends.* Chapel Hill, NC: Chapel Hill Training-Outreach Project.

Heideman, S. (1989). *Caring for at-risk infants and toddlers in a family child care setting.* Minneapolis: University of Minnesota Early Childhood Studies Program.

Heitz, T. (1989). How do I help Jacob? *Young Children, 45*(1), 11-15.

Hofschield, K. A. (1991). The gift of a butterfly. *Young Children, 46*(3), 3-6.

Holder-Brown, L., & Parette, H. P., Jr. (1992). Children with disabilities who use assistive technology: Ethical considerations. *Young Children, 47*(6), 73-77.

Hrncir, E. J., & Eisenhart, C. E. (1991). Use with caution: The "at-risk" label. *Young Children, 46*(2), 23-27.

Hunt, M., Cornelius, P., Leventhal, P., Miller, P., Murray, T., & Stoner, G. (1989). *Into our lives.* Tallmadge, OH: Family Child Learning Center.

Jordan, J. B., Gallagher, J. J., Huntinger, P. L., & Karnes, M. B. (Eds.). *Early childhood special education: Birth to three.* Reston, VA: Council for Exceptional Children/Division for Early Childhood.

Karnes, M. B., & Johnson, L. J. (1989). Training for staff, parents, and volunteers working with gifted children, especially those with disabilities and from low-income homes. *Young Children, 44*(3), 49-56.

Kitano, M. K. (1989). The K-3 teacher's role in recognizing and supporting young gifted children. *Young Children, 44*(3), 57-63.

Kohler, F., & Strain, P. (1993). The early childhood social skills program: Making friends. *Teaching Exceptional Children, 25*(2), 41-42.

Landau, S., & McAninch, C. (1993). Research in review. Young children with attention deficits. *Young Children, 48*(4), 49-58.

McLean, M., & Hanline, M. F. (1990). Providing early intervention services in integrated environments: Challenges and opportunities for the future. *Topics in Early Childhood Special Education, 10*(2), 62-77.

Morris, L. R., & Schulz, L. (1989). *Creative play activities for children with disabilities: A resource book for teachers and parents.* Champaign, IL: Human Kinetics Books.

Musselwhite, C. R. (1986). *Adaptive play for special needs children: Strategies to enhance communication and learning.* Boston: College Hill Press.

Neisworth, J. T., & Bagnato, S. J. (1987). *The young exceptional child: Early development and education.* New York: Macmillan.

Odom, S. L., Bender, M. K., Stein, M. L., Doran, L. P., Houden, P. M., McInnes, M., Gilbert, M. M., Deklyn, M., Speltz, M., & Jenkins, J. R. (1989). *The integrated preschool curriculum: Procedures for socially integrating young handicapped and normally developing children.* Seattle: University of Washington Press.

Odom, S. L., & Karnes, M. B. (1988). *Early intervention for infants and children with handicaps: An empirical base.* Baltimore: Paul H. Brookes.

Odom, S. L., McConnel, S. R., & McEvoy, M. A. (1992). *Social competence of young children with disabilities: Issues and strategies for intervention.* Baltimore: Paul H. Brookes.

Odom, S. L., & McEvoy, M. A. (1988). Integration of young children with handicaps and normally developing children. In S. L. Odom & M. B. Karnes (Eds.), *Early intervention for infants and children with handicaps: An empirical base* (pp. 241-267). Baltimore: Paul H. Brookes.

Odom, S. L., & McEvoy, M. A. (1990). Mainstreaming at the preschool level: Potential barriers and tasks for the field. *Topics in Early Childhood Special Education, 10*(2), 48-61.

Paasche, C., Gorrill, L., & Strom, B. (1990). *Children with special needs in early childhood settings.* Menlo Park, CA: Addison-Wesley.

Peck, C. A., Odom, S. L., & Bricker, D. (1993). *Integrating young children with disabilities into community programs: Ecological perspectives on research and implementation.* Baltimore: Paul H. Brookes.

Peterson, N. L. (1987). *Early intervention for handicapped and at-risk children.* Denver: Love.

Powell, T. H., & Gallagher, P. A. (1993). *Brothers and sisters: A special part of exceptional families* (2nd ed.). Baltimore: Paul H. Brookes.

Project Head Start. (n.d.). *Mainstreaming preschoolers: Eight manuals.* Washington, DC: Head Start Bureau, Administration for Children, Youth, and Families.

Pueschel, S. M., Bernier, J. C., & Weidenman, L. E. (1988). *The special child: A source book for parents of children with developmental disabilities.* Baltimore: Paul H. Brookes.

Rose, D. F., & Smith, B. J. (1993). Public policy report. Preschool mainstreaming: Attitude barriers and strategies for addressing them. *Young Children, 48*(4), 59-62.

Ross, H. W. (1992). Integrating infants with disabilities? Can "ordinary" caregivers do it? *Young Children, 47*(3), 65-71.

Safford, P. L. (1989). *Integrated teaching in early childhood: Starting in the mainstream*. White Plains, NY: Longman.

Salisbury, C. L., & Vincent, L. J. (1990). Criterion of the next environment and best practices: Mainstreaming and integration 10 years later. *Topics in Early Childhood Special Education, 10*(2), 78-89.

Seligman, M., & Darling, R. B. (1989). *Ordinary families, special children: A systems approach to childhood disability*. New York: Guilford.

Souweine, J., Crimmins, S., & Mazel, C. (1981). *Mainstreaming: Ideas for teaching young children*. Washington, DC: National Association for the Education of Young Children.

Strain, P. S. (1990). LRE for preschool children with handicaps: What we know, what we should be doing. *Journal of Early Intervention, 14*, 291-296.

Templeman, T. P., Fredericks, H. D., & Udell, T. (1989). Integration of children with moderate and severe handicaps into a day care center. *Journal of Early Intervention, 13*, 315-328.

Thurman, S. K., & Wilderstrom, A. H. (1990). *Infants and young children with special needs: A developmental and ecological approach* (2nd ed.). Baltimore: Paul H. Brookes.

White, B. P. (with Phair, M. A.). (1986). "It'll be a challenge!" Managing emotional stress in teaching disabled children. *Young Children, 41*(2), 44-48.

Wolery, M., Holcombe, A., Venn, M. L., Brookfield, J., Huffman, K., Schroeder, C., Martin, C. G., & Fleming, L. A. (1993). Research report. Mainstreaming in early childhood programs: Current status and relevant issues. *Young Children, 49*(1), 79-84.

Wolfe, J. (1989). The gifted preschooler: Developmentally different, but still 3 or 4 years old. *Young Children, 44*(3), 41-48.

Appendix 2

※ ※ ※ ※ ※

State Licensing and
Certification Agencies

State	State Department Responsible For Licensing	State Department Responsible For Certification
Alabama	State of Alabama Dept. of Human Resources Office of Day-Care and Child Development S. Gordon Persons Building 50 N. Ripley St. Montgomery, AL 36130	State of Alabama Dept. of Education S. Gordon Persons Building 50 N. Ripley St. Montgomery, AL 36130
Alaska	Dept. of Health & Social Services Division of Family & Youth P.O. Box 11063 Juneau, AK 99811-0630	Dept. of Education 801 West 10th St., Suite 200 Juneau, AK 99801-1894
Arizona	Dept. of Health Services Office of Child Care Licensure 1647 East Morten Ave., Suite 230 Phoenix, AZ 85020	Dept. of Education 1535 W. Jefferson Phoenix, AZ 85007
Arkansas	Dept. of Human Services Division of Children and Family Child Care Licensing P.O. Box 1437, Slot 720 Little Rock, AR 72203	Dept. of Education 4 State Capitol Mall Little Rock, AR 72201-1071
California	Dept. of Social Services Children's Day-Care Bureau 3701 Branch Center Rd. Sacramento, CA 95812	Commission on Teacher Credentialing Licensing Branch Box 944270 1812 9th St. Sacramento, CA 94244-2700

※ ※ ※ ※ ※

State	State Department Responsible For Licensing	State Department Responsible For Certification
Colorado	Dept. of Social Services 1575 Sherman St. Denver, CO 80203-1714	Dept. of Education 201 East Colfax Ave. Denver, CO 80203
Connecticut	Dept. of Children and Families 505 Hudson St. Hartford, CT 06106	Dept. of Education P.O. Box 2219 Hartford, CT 06145
Delaware	Office of Child Care Licensing Delaware Youth and Family Center 1825 Faulkland Rd. Wilmington, DE 19805	Dept. of Public Instruction The Townsend Building P.O. Box 1402 Dover, DE 19903
Florida	Dept. of Health and Rehabilitative Services Family Support Services 1317 Winewood Blvd. Tallahassee, FL 32301	Dept. of Education The Capitol Tallahassee, FL 32399
Georgia	Office of Regulatory Services Child Care Licensing Section 2 Peachtree St., N.W., Suite 20.102 Atlanta, GA 30303-3167	Professional Standards Commission Twin Towers East Atlanta, GA 30334
Hawaii	Dept. of Human Services Public Welfare Division Program Development P.O. Box 339 Honolulu, HI 96809	Dept. of Education P.O. Box 2360 Honolulu, HI 96804
Idaho	Dept. of Health and Welfare Region IV Office State House Mail 4355 Emerald Boise, ID 83706-2099	State Dept. of Education Len B. Jordan Office Building 650 W. State St. Boise, ID 83720-3650
Illinois	Dept. of Children and Family Services 406 E. Monroe St. Springfield, IL 62701-1498	State Dept. of Education 100 N. First St. Springfield, IL 62777
Indiana	Family and Social Services Admin. Div. of Family and Children 402 W. Washington, Room 364 Indianapolis, IN 46204	Indiana Professional Standards Board 251 E. Ohio, Suite 201 Indianapolis, IN 46204

State	State Department Responsible For Licensing	State Department Responsible For Certification
Iowa	Dept. of Human Services Hoover State Office Building Des Moines, IA 50319	Dept. of Education Grimes State Office Building Des Moines, IA 50319-0146
Kansas	Dept. of Health and Environment Bureau of Adult and Child Care Landon State Office Building 900 S.W. Jackson Topeka, KS 66612	State Board of Education Kansas State Education Building 120 S.E. 10th Avenue Topeka, KS 66612-1182
Kentucky	Cabinet for Human Resources Office of Inspector General 275 E. Main St., 4E Frankfort, KY 40621-0001	Dept. of Education 500 Mero St. Frankfort, KY 40621
Louisiana	Dept. of Social Services Bureau of Licensing P.O. Box 3078 Baton Rouge, LA 70821	Dept. of Education P.O. Box 94064 Baton Rouge, LA 70804-9064
Maine	Dept. of Human Services Medicaid Policy and Program 249 Western Ave. Augusta, ME 04330	Dept. of Education Division of Certification and Placement State House, Station 23 Augusta, ME 04333
Maryland	Office of Child Care Licensing and Regulation 311 W. Saratoga St. Baltimore, MD 21201	State Dept. of Education 200 W. Baltimore St. Baltimore, MD 21201-2595
Massachusetts	Office for Children One Ashburton Pl. Boston, MA 02108	Dept. of Education 1385 Hancock St. Quincy, MA 02169
Michigan	Division of Child Care Licensing Dept. of Social Services Grand Tower Building 235 S. Grand Ave. P.O. Box 30037 Lansing, MI 48909	Office of Teacher/Administrator Preparation and Certification P.O. Box 30008 Lansing, MI 48909
Minnesota	Dept. of Human Resources Human Services Building 444 Lafayette Rd. N. St. Paul, MN 55155	Dept. of Education Personnel Licensing Section 616 Capitol Square Building 550 Cedar St. St. Paul, MN 55101

State	State Department Responsible For Licensing	State Department Responsible For Certification
Mississippi	Child Care Licensure State Dept. of Health P.O. Box 1700 Jackson, MS 39215-1700	State Dept. of Education P.O. Box 771 Jackson, MS 39205
Missouri	Child Care Bureau Dept. of Health P.O. Box 507 Jefferson City, MO 65102	Dept. of Elementary and Secondary Education P.O. Box 480 Jefferson City, MO 65102-0480
Montana	Dept. of Family Services P.O. Box 8005 Helena, MT 59604	Office of Public Instruction Certification Services P.O. Box 202501 Helena, MT 59620-2501
Nebraska	Child Care and Development Nebraska Dept. of Social Services P.O. Box 95026 Lincoln, NE 68509	Dept. of Education 301 Centennial Mall South P.O. Box 94987 Lincoln, NE 68509-4987
Nevada	Dept. of Human Resources Division of Child and Family Services Child Care Licensing 711 E. Fifth St. Carson City, NV 89710	Nevada Dept. of Education Capital Complex Carson City, NV 89710
New Hampshire	Div. of Public Health Services Bureau of Child Care Standards and Licensing Health and Welfare Building Hazen Dr. Concord, NH 03301	Dept. of Education 101 Pleasant St. Concord, NH 03301
New Jersey	Division of Youth and Family Services Mercer District Office Princess Rd., Bldg. 9-F, CN 717 Lawrenceville, NJ 08648	Dept. of Education 225 W. State St. Trenton, NJ 08625
New Mexico	Children, Youth, and Family Dept. P.O. Drawer 5160 Santa Fe, NM 87502	Dept. of Education Education Building Santa Fe, NM 87501-2786
New York	Dept. of Social Services 40 N. Pearl St. Albany, NY 12243-0001	State Education Dept. Cultural Education Center Room 5411 Albany, NY 12230

State	State Department Responsible For Licensing	State Department Responsible For Certification
North Carolina	Dept. of Human Resources Division of Child Development P.O. Box 29553 Raleigh, NC 27626-0553	Dept. of Public Instruction 301 N. Wilmington St. Raleigh, NC 27601-2825
North Dakota	Dept. of Human Services 600 E. Boulevard Ave. Bismarck, ND 58505-0450	Dept. of Public Instruction State Capitol, 9th Floor 600 E. Boulevard Ave. Bismarck, ND 58505
Ohio	Bureau of Child Care Services Dept. of Human Services 65 E. State St., 5th Floor Columbus, OH 43215	Dept. of Education 65 S. Front St. Columbus, OH 43266-0308
Oklahoma	Dept. of Human Services Sequoyah Memorial Office Building P.O. Box 25352 Oklahoma City, OK 73125	State Dept. of Education 2500 N. Lincoln Blvd. Oklahoma City, OK 73105-4599
Oregon	Employment Dept. Child Care Division 875 Union St. NE Salem, OR 97311	Teacher Standards and Practices Commission 255 Capitol St. NE Public Service Building, Suite 105 Salem, OR 97310
Pennsylvania	Dept. of Public Welfare Office of Children, Youth, and Families P.O. Box 2675 Harrisburg, PA 17105-2675	Dept. of Education 333 Market St. Harrisburg, PA 17126-0333
Rhode Island	Dept. for Children and Their Families Licensing Day Care Services 610 Mount Pleasant Ave. Providence, RI 02908	Dept. of Education 22 Hayes St. Providence, RI 02908
South Carolina	Dept. of Social Services Children and Family Services P.O. Box 1520 Columbia, SC 29202	Office of Education Professions Teacher Certification Section 1015 Rutledge Office Building 1429 Senate St. Columbia, SC 29201
South Dakota	Office of Child Care Services Dept. of Social Services 700 Governors Dr. Pierre, SD 57501-2291	Dept. of Education and Cultural Affairs 700 Governors Drive Pierre, SD 57501-2291

State	State Department Responsible For Licensing	State Department Responsible For Certification
Tennessee	Licensing Unit Dept. of Human Services Citizens Plaza 400 Deaderick St. Nashville, TN 37248-9800	Division of Teacher Licensure Dept. of Education Gateway Plaza Building, 5th Floor Nashville, TN 37243-0375
Texas	Dept. of Human Services 701 W. 51st St. P.O. Box 149030 MC 550-W Austin, TX 78714	Texas Education Agency W. B. Travis Building 1701 N. Congress Ave. Austin, TX 78701
Utah	Dept. of Social Services Office of Human Services 120 North, 200 West, Third Floor P.O. Box 45500 Salt Lake City, UT 84145-0500	State Office of Education 250 East, 500 South Salt Lake City, UT 84111
Vermont	Dept. of Social and Rehabilitation Services Children's Day-Care Unit Division of Licensing and Regulation 103 S. Main St. Waterbury, VT 05671-2401	Dept. of Education 120 State St. Montpelier, VT 05620-2501
Virginia	Dept. of Social Services Blair Building 8007 Discovery Dr. Richmond, VA 23229	Dept. of Education P.O. Box 2120 Richmond, VA 23216-2120
Washington	Office of Child Care Policy P.O. Box 45710 Olympia, WA 98504-5710	Dept. of Public Instruction Old Capitol Building P.O. Box 47200 Olympia, WA 98504-7200
West Virginia	Dept. of Health and Human Resources Office of Social Services Licensing Unit State Capitol Complex Bldg. 6, Room 850 Charleston, WV 25305	State Dept. of Education Building 6, Room 337 1900 Kanawha Blvd. E. Charleston, WV 25305-0330
Wisconsin	Office of Regulation and Licensing Bureau of Regional Operations Dept. of Health and Social Services Division of Community Services One W. Wilson St., Room 534 Madison, WI 53701	Dept. of Public Instruction 125 S. Webster St. P.O. Box 7841 Madison, WI 53707-7841

State	State Department Responsible For Licensing	State Department Responsible For Certification
Wyoming	Dept. of Family Services Hathaway Building 2300 Capitol Ave. Cheyenne, WY 82002-0490	State Dept. of Education Hathaway Building, 2nd Floor 2300 Capitol Ave. Cheyenne, WY 82002-0050

Appendix 3

❀ ❀ ❀ ❀ ❀

Accreditation Criteria Examples

ACCREDITATION BY THE NATIONAL ACADEMY OF EARLY CHILDHOOD PROGRAMS*

Each component (interactions among staff and children; curriculum; staff-parent interaction; staff qualifications and development; administration; staffing; physical environment; health and safety; nutrition and food service; and evaluation) begins with a goal statement. For example, the goal statement for the component interactions among staff and children is:

Goal

Interactions between children and staff provide opportunities for children to develop an understanding of self and others and are characterized by warmth, personal respect, individuality, positive support, and responsiveness. Staff facilitate interactions among children to provide opportunities for development of self-esteem, social competence, and intellectual growth.

The goal statement is followed by the rationale. For example:

Rationale

All areas of young children's development—social, emotional, cognitive, and physical—are integrated.

---

*National Academy of Early Childhood Programs. (1991). *Accreditation criteria and procedures of the National Academy of Early Childhood Programs.* Washington, DC: National Association for the Education of Young Children.

Optimal development in all areas derives from positive, supportive, individualized relationships with adults. Young children also develop socially, emotionally, and intellectually through peer interaction.

The criteria for the component follow. These criteria indicate whether a goal is being achieved. For example:

A–1. Staff interact frequently with children. Staff express respect for and affection toward children by smiling, touching, holding, and speaking to children at their eye level throughout the day, particularly at arrival and departure, and when diapering or feeding very young children. Staff actively seek meaningful conversations with children.

A–2. Staff are available and responsive to children; encourage them to share experiences, ideas, and feelings; and listen to them with attention and respect. Staff are aware of the activities of the entire group even when dealing with a smaller group; staff position themselves strategically and look up often from involvement.

A–3. Staff speak with children in a friendly, positive, courteous manner. Staff converse frequently with children, asking open-ended questions and speaking individually to children (as opposed to the whole group) most of the time. Staff include child in conversations; describe actions, experiences, and events; listen and respond to children's comments and suggestions.

A–4. Staff treat children of all races, religions, family backgrounds, and cultures with equal respect and

❀ ❀ ❀ ❀ ❀

consideration. Staff provide children of both sexes with equal opportunities to take part in all activities. Staff provide books, dolls, toys, wall decorations (photos and pictures), and recordings that reflect diverse images children may not likely see elsewhere. Staff make it a firm rule that a person's identity (age, race, ethnicity, or disability) is never an acceptable reason for teasing or rejecting. Staff initiate activities and discussions to build positive self-identity and teach the value of differences. Staff talk positively about each child's physical characteristics and cultural heritage.

A–5.   Staff encourage developmentally appropriate independence in children. Staff foster independence in routine activities such as picking up toys, wiping spills, personal grooming (toileting, handwashing), obtaining and caring for materials, and other self-help skills.

A–6.   Staff use positive techniques of guidance, including logical or natural consequences applied in problem situations, redirection, anticipation of and elimination of potential problems, and encouragement of appropriate behavior rather than competition, comparison, or criticism. Consistent, clear rules are developed in conjunction with children and are discussed with them to make sure they understand. Staff describe the situation to encourage children's evaluation of the problem rather than impose the solution. Staff do not force children to apologize or explain their behavior but help children recognize another child's feelings. Staff abstain from corporal punishment or humiliating or frightening discipline techniques. Food or beverage is never withheld as a discipline device.

A–7.   The sound of the environment is primarily marked by pleasant conversation, spontaneous laughter, and exclamations of excitement rather than harsh, stressful noise or enforced quiet.

A–8.   Staff assist children to be comfortable, relaxed, happy, and involved in play and other activities. Staff help children deal with anger, sadness, and frustration by comforting, identifying, and reflecting feelings, and by helping children use words to solve their problems.

A–9.   Staff recognize and encourage prosocial behaviors among children, such as cooperation, helping, taking turns, and talking to solve problems.

A–10.   Staff expectations of children's social behavior are developmentally appropriate.

A–11.   Children are encouraged to verbalize feelings and ideas. Adults intervene quickly when children's responses to each other become physical and discuss the inappropriateness of such responses.

Finally, each criterion has interpretive statements. For example, for A–6 above, the interpretive statements are:

Guidance techniques should be nonpunitive and accompanied by rational explanations of expectations. Limits are set for children but the environment is arranged so that a minimal number of *no's* are necessary, particularly for very young children.

ACCREDITATION BY THE CHILD WELFARE LEAGUE OF AMERICA*

Each standard is classified by a numbering system. For example:

D.2.06

The agency has a policy regarding access to and content of case records, whether open or terminated.

The manual states the evidence of compliance sought, which must be presented in the document of self-study and must be available for the on-site visit. For example:

Evidence of Compliance (D.2.06, D.2.07, D.2.08)

Provide policies and procedures that govern record access, location, and safe maintenance.
(DOCUMENT)
Observation of record storage.
(ON-SITE)
Finally, rating indicators are given. For example:

Rating Indicators (D.2.06)

1. Policy exists and is explicit and detailed.

2. Policy is very general, but provides some guidance.

3. Policy has been violated in rare instances.

4. No policy and/or careless procedures exist. The potential exists for breach of confidentiality or actual breach.

---

*Child Welfare League of America. (1990). *Agency accreditation manual of the Council on Accreditation of Services for Families and Children, Inc.* Washington, DC: Author.

GUIDELINES FOR PREPARATION OF EARLY CHILDHOOD PROFESSIONALS*

Each of the six components (child development and learning, curriculum development and implementation, family and community relationships, assessment and evaluation, professionalism, and field experiences) are framed as outcomes of teacher preparation. Thus, at the end of preparation, teachers are to be prepared to demonstrate the "knowledge, performances, and dispositions," in keeping with their teaching specializations. For example, the outcomes for Component 3—"Family and Community Relationships" are:

Programs prepare early childhood professionals who:

3.1 Establish and maintain positive, collaborative relationships with families.

3.1.1 Respect parents' choices and goals for children and communicate effectively with parents about curriculum and children's progress.

3.1.2 Involve families in assessing and planning for individual children, including children with disabilities, developmental delays, or special abilities.

3.1.3 Support parents in making decisions related to their child's development and parenting.

3.2 Demonstrate sensitivity to differences in family structures and social and cultural backgrounds.

3.3 Apply family systems theory, knowledge of the dynamics, roles, and relationships within families and communities.

3.4 Link families with a range of family-oriented services based on identified resources, priorities, and concerns.

3.5 Communicate effectively with other professionals concerned with children and with agencies in the larger community to support children's development, learning, and well-being.

Source: *National Association for the Education of Young Children. (1995b). *Guidelines for preparation of early childhood professionals.* Washington, DC: Author.

Appendix 4

※ ※ ※ ※ ※

Professional Organizations
Concerned With Young Children

American Montessori Society (AMS)
150 Fifth Ave.
New York, NY 10011
Phone (212) 924-3209; Fax (212) 727-2254

History

The American Montessori Society (AMS) was founded in 1960. Although Montessori's ideas held great interest for the U.S. public between 1912 and 1918, no central organization supported them, and her psychological principles were dissonant with the times and were frowned on by leaders of the educational community. Not until 1958, when Nancy McCormick Rambusch opened a Montessori program at the Whitby School in Greenwich, Connecticut, and the first American Montessori teachers training course was offered in 1960, did the Montessori movement experience an American revival.

Purposes

The basic purposes of the society are to promote better education for all children through teaching strategies consistent with the Montessori system and to incorporate the Montessori approach into the framework of U.S. education. The purposes are implemented by:

1. Serving as a clearinghouse for information about Montessori methods, materials, teachers, and schools
2. Affiliating programs for the training of Montessori teachers in preprimary, primary, and secondary levels and issuing credentials to persons successfully completing accredited course requirements
3. Maintaining a consultation/resource service to assist member schools
4. Conducting one national seminar/conference and three regional seminars per year
5. Assisting research projects
6. Providing assistance to those interested in starting Montessori schools
7. Maintaining a materials/publications center with Montessori and Montessori-oriented teaching aids and literature
8. Maintaining communication with and assistance to state departments of education in relation to Montessori and early childhood education legislation

Publications

1. *Montessori Life* (journal published quarterly)
2. *Annual Report*
3. *Teaching Opportunities*, a list of staff openings in AMS affiliates (the list is reserved for school and teacher members)
4. *Directory of Affiliated Montessori Schools* (annually)
5. *Directory of AMS*, Affiliated Teachers Preparation Programs
6. Newsletter for Heads of Schools three times per year

※ ※ ※ ※ ※

Membership

The society is comprised of and supported by public, private, and parochial schools, Montessori teachers, and concerned individuals. Membership classes are:

1. Organizational Affiliates
   a. Schools: Furnish documentation of Montessori training of teachers, details of their organization, and evidence of compliance with state and local requirements. School affiliates are required to have a consultation the 1st or 2nd year of affiliation and every 4 years thereafter.
   b. Subscribers: An interim membership for schools working toward full or auxiliary status.
   c. Associates: Any group or individual interested in starting a Montessori school.
   d. Corresponding: Overseas Montessori schools meeting full requirements.

2. Individuals
   a. Teachers' Section: Open to teachers furnishing copies of a recognized Montessori credential and details of their academic background
   b. General: No restrictions
   c. Heads of Schools
   d. Lifetime

Association for Childhood Education International (ACEI)
11501 Georgia Ave., Suite 315
Wheaton, MD 20902
Phone (301) 942-2443; Fax (301) 942-3012

History

During the 1892 meeting of the National Education Association, the International Kindergarten Union (IKU) was founded. In 1915, 30 representative educators in the kindergarten and primary fields met in Cincinnati, Ohio, and formed another association, the National Council of Primary Education (NCPE). The IKU's official journal, *Childhood Education*, was launched in 1924. In 1930, the IKU and the NCPE united under the title the Association for Childhood Education. The word *International* was added to the name in 1946. Today, the association is a not-for-profit, professional organization supported by dues and income from the sale of publications. The national headquarters of the association is in Wheaton, Maryland.

Purposes

The ACEI's purposes are:

1. To promote desirable living conditions, programs, and practices for children from infancy through early adolescence
2. To support the raising of standards of professional preparation
3. To bring into active cooperation all organizations concerned with children in the home, the school, and the community
4. To inform the public of the needs of children and how the educational program must be organized and operated to meet those needs

Publications

1. *Childhood Education* (journal, published five times a year)
2. *ACEI Exchange* (newsletter, included in *Childhood Education*)
3. *Journal of Research in Childhood Education* (journal, published two times per year)
4. Other special publications

Membership

Membership is open to all concerned with the well-being and education of children. The three types of membership are (a) institution, (b) professional, and (c) student and retiree.

Association Montessori Internationale (AMI)
161 Koninginneweg
1075 CN Amsterdam
The Netherlands
Phone (31) (20) 6798932

History

In 1929, a Montessori Congress was held in Helsingor, Denmark. At the congress, the idea of the Association Montessori Internationale was born. From 1935, the organization has had its seat in Amsterdam, the Netherlands.

Purposes

The AMI's purposes are:

1. To further the study, application, and propagation of the Montessori ideas and principles for education and development

2. To propagate knowledge and understanding of the conditions necessary for full development from conception to maturity both at home and in society

3. To accredit centers where people may be trained according to the principles and practices of education as envisioned by Dr. Maria Montessori

4. To create a climate of opinion and opportunity for the full development of the potential of all young people so that humanity can work in harmony for a higher and more peaceful civilization

5. To promote general recognition of the child's fundamental rights as envisioned by Dr. Maria Montessori irrespective of racial, religious, political, or social environment

6. To cooperate with other bodies and organizations that promote the development of education, human rights, and peace

Publications

1. *Communications* (quarterly journal)

Membership

Membership includes (a) ordinary members, such as individuals or unincorporated groups, incorporated societies, or institutions; (b) legal persons; (c) life members; and (d) honorary members.

Child Welfare League of America, Inc. (CWLA)
440 First St., N.W., Suite 310
Washington, DC 20001
Phone (202) 638-2952; Fax (202) 638-4004

History

The CWLA, founded in 1920, is a nonsectarian federation of affiliated agencies in the United States and Canada. The league is financed from (a) dues paid by member agencies, (b) restricted grants, (c) foundations, (d) United Way allocations, (e) bequests and contributions, and (f) publication sales.

Purposes

The CWLA's purposes are:

1. To devote its efforts to improvement of child welfare services for deprived and neglected children

2. To develop standards for services

3. To conduct research and to publish professional materials

4. To provide consultation to agencies and communities and to maintain a literary information service

5. To cooperate with other organizations in an effort to improve child welfare services for deprived and neglected children

Publications

1. *Child Welfare* (journal, published bimonthly)

2. *Children's Voice* (magazine, published bimonthly)

3. Books and monographs

4. *Washington Social Legislation Bulletin* (bulletin, published semimonthly)

5. *Children's Monitor* (newsletter, published monthly)

Membership

Membership requirements are not applicable.

National Association for the Education of Young Children (NAEYC)
1509 16th St., N.W.
Washington, DC 20036-1426
Phone (800) 424-2460

History

The NAEYC began in 1926 as the National Committee on Nursery Schools. In 1931, it was organized under the title of the National Association for Nursery Education (NANE). The NANE became the National Association for the Education of Young Children in October 1966, with national headquarters in Washington, DC. The association has focused on enhancing the development and advancement of programs for children under 8 years of age and on facilitating the professional growth of people working for and with young children.

Purposes

The expressed purpose of the NAEYC is to serve and act on behalf of the needs and rights of young children, with primary focus on the provision of educational services and resources to adults who work for and with children. This purpose is accomplished through a variety of services—publications, training videos, and conferences—designed to expand the understandings and skills of adults working with and for children; sponsorship of the Week of the Young Child; dissemination of public policy information to assist members in speaking on behalf of the developmental needs of young children; and affiliate group activities that provide advocacy and growth opportunities in communities and states.

Publications

1. *Young Children* (journal, published bimonthly). The official journal changed its title from the *Journal of Nursery Education* (begun in 1945–46) to *Young Children* in 1964–65.
2. NAEYC books: The association offers more than 70 titles reflecting a broad base of information in the field of early childhood education.
3. National Academy of Early Programs: Administers a voluntary accreditation system that recognizes high quality in centers and schools.
4. Information Service distributes child care information to the public, media, and government.

Membership

Membership is open to persons engaged in work with or for young children. The two categories of membership are (a) independent—membership through the national headquarters and (b) affiliate—membership through one of the state or local affiliated groups.

National Association of Early Childhood Teacher Educators (NAECTE)
Dr. Doris Bergen
Miami University
Department of Educational Psychology
201 McGuffey Hall
Oxford, OH 45056
Phone (513) 529-6621; Fax (513) 529-7270

History

The NAECTE was started in 1977 by a group of early childhood professors from 4-year colleges under the leadership of Michael Davis. The first meeting was held in Chicago at the annual Fall NAEYC Conference.

A steering committee was formed, with Mary Elizabeth York serving as chairperson. In the 2nd year, the name Early Child Teacher Educators was selected, purposes formulated, and dues levied. In 1980, a steering committee was elected, and Marlis Mann served as chairperson. In 1980, the bylaws were adopted and *National* added to the title. Officers and a governing board of representatives took office in 1981.

Purposes

The purposes of the association are to promote the professional growth of its membership and to discuss the educational issues specific to members. To this end, it shall

1. Provide a forum for consideration of issues and concerns of special interest to educators of early childhood teacher institutions that grant bachelor's, master's, and doctoral degrees
2. Provide a communication network for early childhood teacher educators

Publications

1. *NAECTE Bulletin* published three times per year (fall, winter, and spring)

Membership

Membership is open to persons subscribing to the purposes of the organization. Regional early childhood teacher education groups and student memberships may form affiliate groups.

Society for Research in Child Development (SRCD)
5720 S. Woodlawn Ave.
Chicago, IL 60637
Phone (312) 702-7470

History

In 1922, a subcommittee on child development was appointed under the Division of Anthropology and Psychology of the National Research Council. The subcommittee became the Committee on Child Development in 1925. In 1933, the committee was dissolved and replaced by the Society for Research in Child Development. The headquarters of the society are located in Chicago at the University of Chicago Press.

Purposes

The SRCD's purposes are:

1. To advance research in child development
2. To encourage interdisciplinary consideration of problems in the field of child development
3. To encourage study of the implications of research findings
4. To enable specialists to share research tools and techniques
5. To sponsor national and regional conferences

Publications

1. *Child Development* (journal published bimonthly)
2. *Child Development Abstracts and Bibliography* (journal, published three times per year)
3. *Monographs of the Society for Research in Child Development* (journal, published two to four times per year)
4. Newsletter
5. A membership directory
6. *Social Policy Reports*

Membership

Membership application may be made by an individual who is engaged in research in child development or a related field, who teaches undergraduate and graduate courses in child development, and who has published in the field of child development; or by an individual who actively promotes the purposes of the society. All applications are considered by the governing board. The three types of memberships are (a) individual, (b) graduate or medical student, and (c) emeritus.

Southern Early Childhood Association (SECA)
P.O. Box 56130
Little Rock, AR 72215-6130
Phone (501) 663-0353; Fax (501) 663-2114

History

This organization began, in September 1948, as the Nashville Council for the Education of Children Under Six. During the third meeting of the group, the participants voted to become the Southern Regional Association on Children Under Six and adopted a constitution. At the 1954 conference, in Biloxi, Mississippi, the constitution was amended to delete *Regional,* and the official organization became the Southern Association on Children Under Six (SACUS). In 1992, the name of the association was changed to the Southern Early Childhood Association (SECA).

Purposes

The basic purposes of SECA are to work on behalf of young children and their families and to provide opportunities for the cooperation of individuals and groups concerned with the well-being of young children. Particular concerns are:

1. To further the development of knowledge and understanding of young children and the dissemination of such information
2. To contribute to the professional growth of persons working with and for young children
3. To encourage the provision of educational and developmental resources and services for young children
4. To improve the standards for group care and education of children and their quality of life
5. To provide support for state associations in their work for these objectives.

Publications

1. *Dimensions of Early Childhood,* the quarterly journal, began as a regular publication in 1973
2. *Proceedings,* the proceedings of the annual conference, published each year except 1966
3. Other special publications

Membership

Membership is open to all persons concerned with infants and young children. The two classes of membership are (a) affiliate (members of a state affiliate association) and (b) individual.

Appendix 5

꽃 꽃 꽃 꽃 꽃

Additional Organizations of Concern to Early Childhood Educators

AAUW Educational Foundation
1111 Sixteenth St., N.W.
Washington, DC 20036

Action for Children's Television
20 University Rd.
Cambridge, MA 02138

American Academy of Pediatrics
141 Northwest Point Blvd.
P.O. Box 927
Elk Grove Village, IL 60009–0927

American Bar Association
National Legal Resource Center for
    Child Advocacy and Protection
1800 M St., N.W., Suite 20005
Washington, DC 20036

American Dietetic Association
216 West Jackson Blvd.
Chicago, IL 60606

American Federation of State,
    County, and Municipal
    Employees, AFL-CIO
1626 L St., N.W.
Washington, DC 20036

American Home Economics
    Association
1555 King St.
Alexandria, VA 22314

American Library Association
50 E. Huron St.
Chicago, IL 60611

American Medical Association
515 N. Gate St.
Chicago, IL 60610

American Psychiatric Association
1400 K St., N.W.
Washington, DC 20005

American Speech-Language-
    Hearing Association
10801 Rockville Pike
Rockville, MD 20852

Association for Retarded Citizens
National Headquarters
500 E. Border St., Suite 300
Arlington, TX 76010

Association for Supervision and
    Curriculum Development
1250 Pitt St.
Alexandria, VA 22314

Association for the Care of Chil-
    dren's Health
7910 Woodmont Ave., Suite 300
Bethesda, MD 20814

Bananas
6510 Telegraph Ave.
Oakland, CA 94609

Cease
17 Gerry St.
Cambridge, MA 02138

Center for Law and Social Policy
1616 P St., N.W., Suite 150
Washington, DC 20036

Center for the Study of Evaluation
Graduate School of Education
145 Moore Hall
405 Hilgard Ave.
Los Angeles, CA 90024

Child Care Action Campaign
330 Seventh Ave., 17th Floor
New York, NY 10001

Children's Book Council, Inc.
568 Broadway, Suite 404
New York, NY 10012

Children's Defense Fund
25 E St., N.W.
Washington, DC 20001

Children's Foundation
725 Fifteenth St., N.W., Suite 505
Washington, DC 20005

Conference Board
845 Third Ave.
New York, NY 10022

Council for Early Childhood Pro-
    fessional Recognition
1341 G St., N.W.
Washington, DC 20005

Council for Exceptional Children
1920 Association Dr.
Reston, VA 22091-1598

꽃 꽃 꽃 꽃 꽃

Council of State Governments
P.O. Box 11910, Iron Works Pike
Lexington, KY 40578

Department of Health and Human
  Services
Public Health Service
Centers for Disease Control and
  Prevention
Atlanta, GA 30333

Early Childhood Directors
  Association
A National Organization for Early
  Childhood Administrators
450 N. Syndicate, Suite 5
St. Paul, MN 55104

Education Commission of the
  States
707 Seventeenth St., Suite 2700
Denver, CO 80202

ERIC Clearinghouse on Disabilities and Gifted Education
Council for Exceptional Children
1920 Association Dr.
Reston, VA 22091-1598

ERIC Clearinghouse on Elementary and Early Childhood
  Education
805 W. Pennsylvania Ave.
Urbana, IL 61801

Family Resource Coalition
200 S. Michigan Ave., 16th Floor
Chicago, IL 60604

Family Service America, Inc.
11700 W. Lake Park Dr.
Park Place
Milwaukee, WI 53224

High/Scope Educational Research
  Foundation
600 N. River St.
Lafayette, IN 48198

HIPPY USA (Home Instruction Program for Preschool Youngsters)
53 W. 23rd St.
New York, NY 10010

Institute for Women's Policy
  Research
1400 Twentieth St., N.W., Suite 104
Washington, DC 20036

Jean Piaget Society
Society for the Study of Knowledge
  and Development
University of Toledo
Toledo, OH 43606

John Tracy Clinic
806 W. Adams Blvd.
Los Angeles, CA 90007

Kempe National Center
1205 Oneida St.
Denver, CO 80220

Learning Disabilities Association
  of America
4156 Library Rd.
Pittsburgh, PA 15234

March of Dimes Birth Defects
  Foundation
1275 Mamaroneck Ave.
White Plains, NY 10605

National Association for Family
  Day Care
815 Fifteenth St., N.W., Suite 928
Washington, DC 20005

National Association of Child Care
  Resource and Referral Agencies
1319 F St., N.W.
Washington, DC 20004

National Association of Children's Hospitals and Related
  Institutions
401 Wythe St.
Alexandria, VA 22314

National Association of Elementary School Principals
1615 Duke St.
Alexandria, VA 22314

National Black Child Development
  Institute, Inc.
1023 Fifteenth St., N.W., Suite 600
Washington, DC 20005

National Center for Clinical Infant
  Programs
733 Fifteenth St., N.W., Suite 912
Washington, DC 20005

National Center for the Early
  Childhood Work Force
(formerly Child Care Employee
  Project)
733 Fifteenth St. N.W., Suite 3800
Washington, DC 20005

National Coalition for Campus
  Child Care, Inc.
Box 258
Cascade, WI 53011

National Coalition for Parent
  Involvement in Education
National Education Association
1201 Sixteenth St., N.W., Rm. 810
Washington, DC 20036

National Commission on Working
  Women for Wider Opportunities for Women
1325 G St., N.W., Lower Level
Washington, DC 20005

National Committee for Citizens in
  Education
10840 Little Patuxent Pkwy., #301
Columbus, MD 21044

National Committee to Prevent
  Child Abuse
332 S. Michigan Ave., Suite 1600
Chicago, IL 60604

National Conference of State
  Legislatures
1560 Broadway, Suite 700
Denver, CO 80202

National Congress of Parents and
  Teachers
700 N. Rush St.
Chicago, IL 60611

National Council of Jewish
  Women
53 W. 23rd St.
New York, NY 10010

National Council of the Churches
of Christ in the United States of
America
475 Riverside Dr.
New York, NY 10115

National Council on Family
Relations
3989 Central Ave. N.E., Suite 550
Minneapolis, MN 55421

National Easter Seal Society
230 W. Monroe St., Suite 1800
Chicago, IL 60606

National Governors' Association
Hall of the States
444 N. Capital St., Suite 267
Washington, DC 20001

National Head Start Association
1220 King St., Suite 200
Alexandria, VA 22314

National Institute of Health
Department of Health and Human
Services
Public Health Service
Bldg. 31, Rm. 2A32
Bethesda, MD 20892

National League of Cities Institute
Children and Families in Cities
Project
1301 Pennsylvania Ave., N.W.
Washington, DC 20004

National PTA
330 N. Wabash Ave., Suite 2100
Chicago, IL 60611

National School-Age Child Care
Alliance
1742 Norwood Blvd.
Zanesville, OH 43701

National Society to Prevent
Blindness
500 E. Remington Rd.
Schaumburg, IL 60173

Nine-to-Five, National Association
of Working Women
614 Superior Ave., N.W.
Cleveland, OH 44113

Office of Communication Services
John F. Kennedy Center for
Research on Human
Development
Vanderbilt University
Box 40, Peabody Station
Nashville, TN 37203

Parents Anonymous
National Office
6733 S. Sepulveda Blvd., Suite 270
Los Angeles, CA 90045

Project Home Start
AIS—Whirlpool Corp.
P.O. Box 405
St. Joseph, MI 49085

Resources for Child Caring
450 N. Syndicate, Suite 5
St. Paul, MN 55104

School-Age Child Care Project
Wellesley College
Center for Research on Women
Wellesley, MA 02181

Spina Bifida Association of America
1700 Rockville Pike, Suite 540
Rockville, MD 20852

United Cerebral Palsy Associations
of New York State, Inc.
330 W. 34th St.
New York, NY 10001

U.S. House of Representatives
Select Committee on Children,
Youth, and Families
H2—385 House Office Bldg.,
Annex 2
Washington, DC 20515

Work/Family Directions, Inc.
930 Commonwealth Ave., West
Boston, MA 02215

Appendix 6

※ ※ ※ ※ ※

Suppliers of Early Childhood Equipment, Books, and Materials

ABC School Supply, Inc.
3312 N. Berkeley Lake Rd.
Duluth, GA 30136

Addison-Wesley Publishing Co.
2725 Sand Hill Rd.
Menlo Park, CA 94025

American Playground Corp.
Box 2599
Anderson, IN 46018

Angeles Toys, Inc.
9 Capper Dr.
Dailey Industrial Park
Pacific, MO 63069

Beckley-Cardy
1 E. First St.
Duluth, MN 55802

Encyclopaedia Britannica Educational Corp.
310 S. Michigan Ave.
Chicago, IL 60604

Carlisle Tire & Rubber Co.
Subsidiary of Carlisle Corp.
P.O. Box 99
Carlisle, PA 17013

Channing L. Bete Co, Inc.
200 State Rd.
South Deerfield, MA 01373

Childcraft
20 Kilmer Rd.
P.O. Box 3081
Edison, NJ 08818-3081

Childlife Inc.
55 Whitney St.
Holliston, MA 01746

Children's Defense Fund
25 E. St., N.W.
Washington, DC 20001

Chime Time (a division of Select Service & Supply Co., Inc.)
2440-C Pleasantdale Rd.
Atlanta, GA 30340-1562

Classic School Products
174 Semoran Commerce Pl., A106
Apopka, FL 32703

Community Playthings
P.O. Box 901
Rifton, NY 12471-0901

Constructive Playthings
U.S. Toy Co., Inc.
1227 E. 119th St.
Grandview, MO 64030

Creative Educational Surplus
9801 James Circle, Suite C
Bloomington, MN 55431

Cuisenaire Company of America, Inc.
10 Bank St., P.O. Box 5026
White Plains, NY 10602-5026

Delmar Publishers, Inc.
P.O. Box 15015
Albany, NY 12212-5015

Delta Education, Inc.
P.O. Box 915
Hudson, NH 03051

Demco
500 E. North St.
Deforest, WI 53532

DLM (a division of Macmillan/ McGraw-Hill
P.O. Box 543
Blacklick, OH 43004-0543

Educational Activities, Inc.
P.O. Box 392
Freeport, NY 11520

Educational Development Corp.
10302 E. 55th Pl., Suite B
Tulsa, OK 74146-6505

Educational Insights
19560 S. Rancho Way
Dominquez Hills, CA 90220

Educational Productions, Inc.
7412 SW Beaverton Hillsdale Hwy., Suite 210
Portland, OR 97225

Educational Products Division
Binney & Smith, Inc.
1100 Church Ln., P.O. Box 431
Easton, PA 18044-0431

Education Center, Inc.
1607 Battleground Ave.
P.O. Box 9753
Greensboro, NC 27429

※ ※ ※ ※ ※

Educators Publishing Service. Inc.
75 Moulton St.
Cambridge, MA 02138-1104

Environments, Inc.
P.O. Box 1348
Beaufort Industrial Park
Beaufort, SC 29901-1348

Fibar Systems
141 Halstead Ave.
Mamaroneck, NY 10543-2650

Films for the Humanities & Sciences, Inc.
P.O. Box 2053
Princeton, NJ 08543-2053

Gleason Corp.
316 Milwaukee St.
Milwaukee, WI 53202

Gryphon House, Inc.
Early Childhood Teacher Books
P.O. Box 275
Mt. Rainer, MD 20712

J. L. Hammett Co.
P.O. Box 9057
Braintree, MA 02184-9057

Hand in Hand
Route 26, Box 1425
Oxford, ME 04270

HarperCollins Publishers
10 E. 53rd St.
New York, NY 10022-5299

Humanics Learning
P.O. Box 7400
Atlanta, GA 30357

Insight Media
121 W. 85th St.
New York, NY 10024

Kaplan School Supply Corp.
1310 Lewisville-Clemmons Rd.
Lewisville, NC 27023-0609

Kendall/Hunt Publishing Co.
4050 Westmark Dr.
P.O. Box 1840
Dubuque, IA 52004-1840

Kenner Parker Toys, Inc.
Hasbro, Inc.
200 Narragansett Park Dr.
P.O. Box 200
Pawtuckett, RI 02862-0200

Kids Rights
10100 Park Cedar Dr.
Charlotte, NC 28210

Kimbo Educational
P.O. Box 477
Long Branch, NJ 07740

Lakeshore Curriculum Materials
2695 E. Dominquez St.
P.O. Box 6261
Carson, CA 90749

Learning Products, Inc.
700 Fee Fee Rd.
St. Louis, MO 63043

Learning Seed
330 Telser Rd.
Lake Zurich, IL 60047

Learning Things, Inc.
68A Broadway
Arlington, MA 02174

Lego Dacta
555 Taylor Rd.
P.O. Box 1600
Enfield, CT 06083-1600

Love Publishing Co.
1777 S. Bellaire St.
Denver, CO 80222

Macmillan/McGraw-Hill
860 Taylor Station Rd.
Blacklick, OH 43004-9615

Mayfield Publishing Co.
1280 Villa St.
Mountain View, CA 94041

Melody House Publishing Co.
819 N.W. 92nd St.
Oklahoma City, OK 73114-2710

Meridian Education Corp.
236 E. Front St.
Bloomington, IL 61701

Mitchell Rubber Products
491 Wilson Way
City of Industry, CA 91744

Modern Curriculum Press
13900 Prospect Rd.
Cleveland, OH 44136

Morrison School Supplies, Inc.
304 Industrial Way
San Carlos, CA 94070

Nasco
901 Janesville Ave.
Fort Atkinson, WI 53538

National Geographic Society
1145 17th St., N.W.
Washington, DC 20036-4688

Nystrom Division of Herff Jones, Inc.
3333 Elston Ave.
Chicago, IL 60618-5898

PCA Industries Inc.
5642 Natural Bridge
St. Louis, MO 63120

Peninsula Publishing, Inc.
P.O. Box 412
Port Angeles, WA 98362

Perfection Learning Co.
1000 N. Second Ave.
Logan, IA 51546-1099

Play Designs
P.O. Box 427
New Berlin, PA 17855-0427

Playsafe Surfaces, Inc.
240 W. Bristol Ln.
Orange, CA 92665

Playskool, Inc
Hasbro, Inc.
200 Narragansett Park Dr.
P.O. Box 200
Pawtucket, RI 02862-0200

Power Up Software Corporation
2655 Campus Dr.
San Mateo, CA 94403-7600

J. A. Preston Corp.
P.O. Box 89
Jackson, MI 49204-0089

Redleaf Press
450 N. Syndicate, Suite S
St. Paul, MN 55104-4125

Rhythms Productions
Tom Thumb Records/Books
P.O. Box 34485
Los Angeles, CA 90034-0485

Riverside Publishing Co.
8420 Bryn Mawr Ave.
Chicago, IL 60631

Scholastic, Inc.
P.O. Box 7502
Jefferson City, MO 65102

School-Age Notes
P.O. Box 40205
Nashville, TN 37204

Science Research Associates
Macmillan/McGraw-Hill
P.O. Box 543
Blacklick, OH 43004-0543

Stoelting Co.
Oakwood Centre
620 Wheat Ln.
Wood Dale, IL 60191

Teachers College Press
Teachers College, Columbia
    University
New York, NY 10027

Thompson Recreation Products,
    Inc.
1315 Lakewood Circle
New Braunfels, TX 78130-2982

Trend Enterprises, Inc.
P.O. Box 64073
St. Paul, MN 55164

Troll Associates
100 Corporate Dr.
Mahwah, NJ 07430

United Learning, Inc.
6633 W. Howard St.
Niles, IL 60648-3389

Wadsworth Publishing Co.
Ten Davis Dr.
Belmont, CA 94002

Warren Publishing House, Inc.
P.O. Box 2250
Everett, WA 98203

Weekly Reader Corporation
3001 Cindel Dr.
P.O. Box 8996
Delran, NJ 08370-8996

Whitney Bros. Co.
P.O. Box 644
Keene, NH 03431

Wood Designs of Monroe, Inc.
P.O. Box 1308
Monroe, NC 28110

Zane-Bloser
2200 W. Fifth Ave.
P.O. Box 16764
Columbus, OH 43216-6764

CHILDREN'S BOOKS AND MAGAZINES

Early childhood educators may use several sources in finding titles of quality books:

Bulletin of the Center for Children's Books
University of Chicago
5750 Ellis Ave.
Chicago, IL 60637

Christian Science Monitor
One Norway St.
Boston, MA 02115 (spring and fall reviews)

Council on Interracial Books
1841 Broadway
New York, NY 10023

Horn Book (bimonthly magazine)
585 Boylston St.
Boston, MA 02166

New York Times
229 W. 43rd St.
New York, NY 10036 (spring and fall reviews)

Notable Children's Books
Children's Service Division of the American Library Association
50 E. Huron St.
Chicago, IL 60611

Saturday Review/World
Saturday Review Magazine Co.
214 Massachusetts Ave., N.E., No. 460
Washington, DC 20002 (spring and fall reviews)

To keep abreast of new publications of children's books, teachers may also note reviews in many professional journals.

In addition to books in early childhood education, some excellent magazines are also available:

Child Life
1100 Waterway Blvd.
Indianapolis, IN 46206

Children's Digest
1100 Waterway Blvd.
Indianapolis, IN 46206

Children's Playmate
1100 Waterway Blvd.
Indianapolis, IN 46206

Cricket
Carus Corp.
Box 300
Peru, IL 61354

Ebony, Jr.
820 S. Michigan Ave.
Chicago, IL 60605

Humpty Dumpty
1100 Waterway Blvd.
Indianapolis, IN 46206

Jack and Jill
1100 Waterway Blvd.
Indianapolis, IN 46206

Ranger Rick
National Wildlife Federation
1400 16th St., N.W.
Washington, DC 20006

Scienceland
Scienceland, Inc.
501 Fifth Ave.
New York, NY 10017

Your Big Back Yard
National Wildlife Federation
1400 16th St., N.W.
Washington, DC 20006

SOFTWARE

Publishers of Software

Accolade
5300 Stevens Creek Blvd., Suite 500
San Jose, CA 95129

Agency Systems
7645 Production Dr.
Cincinnati, OH 45237

American Guidance Service
4201 Woodland Rd., P.O. Box 99
Circle Pines, MN 55014-1796

Apple Computer
20525 Mariana Ave.
Cupertino, CA 59014

Aquarius Instructional
Phillip Roy
13064 Indian Rocks Rd.
Largo, FL 34644

Baudville
Desktop Publishing Solutions
5380 52nd St., SE
Grand Rapids, MI 49512

Broderbund Software
P.O. Box 6125
Novato, CA 94948-6121

Computer Curriculum Corp.
1287 Lawrence Station Rd.
Sunnyvale, CA 94089

R. J. Cooper & Associates
Adaptive Technology Specialists
24843 Del Prado, #283
Dana Point, CA 92629

Davidson and Associates, Inc.
19840 Pioneer Ave.
Torrance, CA 90503

DIL International
2115 Boivin
Ste-Foy, Quebec, CANADA G1V 1N6

Disney Software
500 S. Buena Vista St., 20th Floor
Burbank, CA 91521

Ebsco Curriculum Materials
P.O. Box 1943
Birmingham, AL 35201

Edmark Corp.
6727 185th Ave., N.E.
Redmond, WA 98073

Educational Activities, Inc.
1937 Grand Ave.
Baldwin, NY 11510

EduQuest
International Business Machines
    Corporation
P.O. Box 2150
Atlanta, GA 30301

Eureka!
Lawrence Hall of Science
University of California
Berkeley, CA 94720

Exceptional Children's Software
2215 Ohio
Lawrence, KS 66046

Gamco Education Materials
P.O. Box 1911
Big Spring, TX 79721-1911

Great Wave Software
5353 Scotts Valley Dr.
Scotts Valley, CA 95066

Heartsoft Software
P.O. Box 691381
Tulsa, OK 74169-1381

Humanities Software
408 Columbia St., Suite 222
Hood River, OR 97031

Intellimation
Library for the Macintosh
130 Cremona Dr.
Santa Barbara, CA 93117

Kidsview Software, Inc.
P.O. Box 98
Warner, NH .03278

Laureate Learning Systems, Inc.
110 E. Spring St.
Winooski, VT 05404

Lawrence Productions, Inc.
1800 S. 35th St.
Galesburg, MI 49053-9687

Learning Box
4508 Valleycrest Dr.
Arlington, TX 76013

Logo Computer Systems Inc.
P.O. Box 162
Highgate Springs, VT 05460

MicroEd
P.O. Box 24750
Edina, MN 55424

Micrograms, Inc.
1404 N. Main St.
Rockford, IL 61103

Micro Learning
Route 1, Box 162
Amboy, MN 56010

Micro Power & Light Company
8814 Sanshire Ave.
Dallas, TX 75231

Minnesota Ed. Computing Corp.
6160 Summit Dr.
Brooklyn Center, MN 55430-4003

Mobius Corp.
405 N. Henry St.
Alexandria, VA 22134

Nordic Software
6911 Van Dorn
Lincoln, NE 68506

Optimum Resource, Inc.
5 Hiltech
Hilton Head, SC 29926

Orange Cherry/New Media
    Software
A Division of Multi Dimensional
    Communications, Inc.
P.O. Box 390, 69 Westchester Ave.
Pound Ridge, NY 10576

Queue
338 Commerce Dr.
Fairfield, CT 06432

Scholastic Software Inc.
2931 E. McCarty St.
Jefferson City, MO 65101

Sierra On-Line
P.O. Box 485
Coarsegold, CA 93614

Society for Visual Education
6677 N. Northwest Hwy.
Chicago, IL 60631

SouthWest EdPsych Services
9 Barker Dr., P.O. Box 1510
Pine, AZ 85224

S.R.A. Order Services
P.O. Box 543
Blacklick, OH 43004

Teacher Support Software
Systems for Learning, Inc.

201 Evans Rd., Suite 113
Jefferson, LA 70123

Tom Snyder Productions, Inc.
80 Coolidge Hill Rd.
Watertown, MA 02172-2817

Troll Asociates, Inc.
100 Corporate Dr.
Mahwah, NJ 07430

UCLA Microcomputer Project
1000 Veteran Ave., Rm. 23-10
Los Angeles, CA 90095

Hardware and Software for Children With Special Needs

Closing the Gap
P.O. Box 68
Henderson, MN 56044

Special Education Technology Lab
University of Connecticut
249 Glenbrook Rd., U-64
Storrs, CT 06269-2064

Technology and Media
Council for Exceptional Children
(See Appendix 5)
Trace Research and Development
    Center
S-151 Waisman Center
1500 Highland Ave.
Madison, WI 53705

Software Evaluation Systems

Binghamton City School District*
Computer Services Dept.
Binghamton, NY 13902

Children's Software Revue**
ATTN: Warren Buckleitner
520 N. Adams St.
Ypsilanti, MI 48197-2482

Developmental Evaluations of
    Software for Young Children**
ATTN: Susan W. Haugland &
    Daniel D. Shade
The KIDS Project, Center for Child
    Studies
Southeast Missouri State University
Cape Girardeau, MO 63701

High/Scope Buyer's Guide to Chil-
    dren's Software**
600 N. River St.
Ypsilanti, MI 48198

Technology and Learning*
330 Progress Rd.
Dayton, OH 45449

---

*General evaluation
**Constructivist approach evaluation

Appendix 7

※ ※ ※ ※ ※

Grants and Other Assistance

FEDERAL ASSISTANCE

Department of Agriculture
Fourteenth St. & Independence Ave., S.W.
Washington, DC 20250
(202) 720-8732

Food and Nutrition Service (FNS). Administers programs to make food assistance available to people who need it. These programs are operated in cooperation with state and local governments.

10.553 SCHOOL BREAKFAST PROGRAM

AUTHORIZATION: Child Nutrition Act of 1966, as amended, Section 4 and 10, 42 U.S.C. 1773, 1779, 1779.

OBJECTIVES: To assist states in providing a nutritious nonprofit breakfast service for school students through cash grants and food donations.

TYPES OF ASSISTANCE: Formula Grants.

10.555 NATIONAL SCHOOL LUNCH PROGRAM
(School Lunch Program)

AUTHORIZATION: National School Lunch Act, as amended, 42 U.S.C. 1751-1769.

OBJECTIVES: To assist states, through cash grants and food donations, in making the school lunch program available to school students and to encourage the domestic consumption of nutritious agricultural commodities.

TYPES OF ASSISTANCE: Formula Grants.

10.556 SPECIAL MILK PROGRAM FOR CHILDREN

AUTHORIZATION: Child Nutrition Act of 1966, Sections 3 and 10, as amended, P.L. 89-642, 80 Stat. 885, 889, 42 U.S.C. 1772, and 1779.

OBJECTIVES: To provide subsidies to schools and institutions to encourage the consumption of fluid milk by children.

TYPES OF ASSISTANCE: Formula Grants.

10.557 SPECIAL SUPPLEMENTAL FOOD PROGRAM FOR WOMEN, INFANTS, AND CHILDREN (WIC Program)

AUTHORIZATION: Child Nutrition Act of 1966, as amended, Section 17, P.L. 92-433, 86 Stat. 729, 42 U.S.C. 1786.

OBJECTIVES: To provide, at no cost, supplemental nutritious foods, nutrition education, and referrals to health care to low-income pregnant, breast-feeding and postpartum women, infants, and children to age 5 determined to be at nutritional risk.

TYPES OF ASSISTANCE: Formula Grants.

10.558 CHILD AND ADULT CARE FOOD PROGRAM

AUTHORIZATION: National School Lunch Act, Sections 9, 11, 14, 16 and 17, as amended, 89 Stat. 522-525, 42 U.S.C. 1758, 1759a, 1762a, 1765 and 1766.

OBJECTIVES: To assist states, through grants-in-aid and other means, in maintaining nonprofit

※ ※ ※ ※ ※

food service programs for children and elderly or impaired adults in public and private nonprofit nonresidential institutions providing care; family day care homes for children; and private for-profit centers that receive compensation under Title XX for at least 25% of enrolled children or 25% of licensed capacity; and under Title XIX and/or Title XX for at least 25% of adults enrolled in nonresidential day care services.

TYPES OF ASSISTANCE: Formula Grants; Sale, Exchange, or Donation of Property and Goods.

10.559 SUMMER FOOD SERVICE PROGRAM FOR CHILDREN

AUTHORIZATION: National School Lunch Act, Sections 9, 13 and 14, as amended, 42 U.S.C. 1758, 1761 and 1762a.

OBJECTIVES: To assist states, through grants-in-aid and other means, in conducting nonprofit food service programs for needy children during the summer months and at other approved times when area schools are closed for vacation.

TYPES OF ASSISTANCE: Formula Grants.

10.560 STATE ADMINISTRATIVE EXPENSES FOR CHILD NUTRITION

AUTHORIZATION: Child Nutrition Act of 1966, as amended, Sections 7 and 10, 42 U.S.C. 1776, 1779.

OBJECTIVES: To provide each state agency with funds for its administrative expenses in supervising and giving technical assistance to local schools, school districts, and institutions in their conduct of child nutrition programs. State agencies that administer the distribution of USDA-donated commodities to schools or child or adult care institutions are also provided with state administrative expense funds (SAE).

TYPES OF ASSISTANCE: Formula Grants.

10.564 NUTRITION EDUCATION AND TRAINING PROGRAM (NET Program)

AUTHORIZATION: Child Nutrition Act of 1966, Section 19, as amended, 42 U.S.C. 1788.

OBJECTIVES: To help subsidize state and local programs that encourage the dissemination of nutrition information to children participating,

or eligible to participate, in the school lunch and related child nutrition programs.

TYPES OF ASSISTANCE: Formula Grants.

**Department of Education
400 Maryland Ave., S.W.
Washington, DC 20202
(202) 208-5366**

Office of the Secretary (ED).   The secretary of education advises the president on education plans, policies, and programs of the federal government. The secretary directs department staff in carrying out the approved programs and activities of the department and promotes general public understanding of the department's goals, programs, and objectives. The secretary also carries out certain federal responsibilities for four federally aided corporations: the American Printing House of the Blind, Gallaudet University, Howard University, and the National Technical Institute for the Deaf. The under secretary, the deputy under secretaries, the assistant secretaries, the inspector general, and the general counsel aid the secretary in the overall management of the department.

84.003 BILINGUAL EDUCATION

AUTHORIZATION: Bilingual Education Act; Elementary and Secondary Education Act of 1965, Title VII, Part A, as amended, P.L. 89-10, P.L. 100-297, 98 Stat. 2370-2387, 20 U.S.C. 3281-3341.

OBJECTIVES: To develop and carry out programs of bilingual education in elementary and secondary schools, including activities at the preschool level, that are designed to meet the educational needs of children of limited English proficiency; to demonstrate effective ways of providing such children with instruction designed to enable them, while using their native language, to achieve competence in English; or to develop alternative instruction programs that need not use the native language; to develop the human and material resources required for such programs; and to build the capacity of grantees to continue programs of bilingual education when assistance under this program is reduced or no longer available.

TYPES OF ASSISTANCE: Project Grants; Direct Payments for Specified Use.

84.010 CHAPTER 1 PROGRAMS—LOCAL EDUCATIONAL AGENCIES (Chapter 1 Basic and Concentration Grants)

AUTHORIZATION: Elementary and Secondary Education Act of 1965, Title I, Chapter 1, Part A, 20 U.S.C. 2701 *et seq.*

OBJECTIVES: To improve the educational opportunities of children who are educationally deprived by helping them succeed in the regular school program, attain grade-level proficiency, and improve achievement in basic and more advanced skills.

TYPES OF ASSISTANCE: Formula Grants.

84.011 MIGRANT EDUCATION—BASIC STATE FORMULA GRANT PROGRAM

AUTHORIZATION: Elementary and Secondary Education Act of 1965, Title I, Chapter 1, Part D, Subpart 1, 20 U.S.C. 2781 *et seq.*

OBJECTIVES: To establish or improve programs to meet the special educational needs of migratory children of migratory agricultural workers or migratory fishers.

TYPES OF ASSISTANCE: Formula Grants.

84.012 EDUCATIONALLY DEPRIVED CHILDREN— STATE ADMINISTRATION (Chapter 1, State Administration)

AUTHORIZATION: Elementary and Secondary Education Act of 1965, Title I, Chapter 1, Part E, Section 1404, 20 U.S.C. 2824, Part F, Subpart 2, 20 U.S.C. 2851 *et seq.*

OBJECTIVES: To help state educational agencies meet their administrative responsibilities under the Chapter 1 programs.

TYPES OF ASSISTANCE: Formula Grants.

84.014 FOLLOW THROUGH

AUTHORIZATION: Follow Through Act, Title II, as amended, P.L. 97-35; Augustus F. Hawkins Human Services Reauthorization Act of 1990, P.L. 101-501.

OBJECTIVES: To sustain and augment in primary grades the gains that children from low-income families make in Head Start and other quality preschool programs. Follow Through pro-

vides special programs of instruction, as well as health, nutrition, and other related services that will aid in the continued development of children to their full potential. Active participation of parents is stressed. Emphasis is placed on the demonstration and dissemination of effective approaches specifically designed to improve the school performance of children from low-income families and the provision of comprehensive services.

TYPES OF ASSISTANCE: Project Grants.

84.024 EARLY EDUCATION FOR CHILDREN WITH DISABILITIES (Early Education Program)

AUTHORIZATION: Individuals With Disabilities Education Act, Part C, Section 623, as amended, P.L. 91-230, 98-199, 99-457, 100-630, 101-476, and 102-119, 20 U.S.C. 1423.

OBJECTIVES: To support demonstration, dissemination, and implementation of effective approaches to preschool and early childhood education for children with disabilities.

TYPES OF ASSISTANCE: Project Grants; Project Grants (Cooperative Agreements); Project Grants (Contracts).

84.027 SPECIAL EDUCATION—STATE GRANTS (Part B, Individuals With Disabilities Education Act)

AUTHORIZATION: Individuals With Disabilities Education Act, Part B, Sections 611-620, as amended, P.L. 91-230, 93-380, 94-142, 98-199, 99-457, 100-630, and 101-476, 20 U.S.C. 1411-1420.

OBJECTIVES: To provide grants to states to assist them in providing a free appropriate public education to all children with disabilities.

TYPES OF ASSISTANCE: Formula Grants.

84.029 SPECIAL EDUCATION—PERSONNEL DEVELOPMENT AND PARENT TRAINING (Training Personnel for the Education of Individuals with Disabilities)

AUTHORIZATION: Individuals With Disabilities Education Act, Part D, Sections 631, 632, 634, and 635, as amended, P.L. 91-230, 98-199, 99-457, 100-630, and 101-476, 20 U.S.C. 1431, 1432, 1434, and 1435.

OBJECTIVES: (a) To address identified shortages of special education teachers and related service personnel; (b) to improve the quality and increase the supply of teachers, supervisors, administrators, researchers, teacher educators, speech pathologists, educational interpreters for the hearing impaired, and other special personnel such as specialists in physical education and recreation, paraprofessionals, vocational/career education, volunteers; and (c) to provide parent training and information services.

TYPES OF ASSISTANCE: Project Grants; Project Grants (Cooperative Agreements); Project Grants (Contracts).

84.151 FEDERAL, STATE, AND LOCAL PARTNERSHIPS FOR EDUCATIONAL IMPROVEMENT (Chapter 2, State Block Grants)

AUTHORIZATION: Elementary and Secondary Education Act of 1965, as amended, Title I, Chapter 2, Part A; Augustus F. Hawkins-Robert T. Stafford Elementary and Secondary School Improvement Amendments of 1988, P.L. 100-297, 20 U.S.C. 2911-2952, 2971-2976.

OBJECTIVES: To assist state and local educational agencies in improving elementary and secondary education.

TYPES OF ASSISTANCE: Formula Grants.

84.173 SPECIAL EDUCATION—PRESCHOOL GRANTS

AUTHORIZATION: Individuals With Disabilities Education Act, Part B, Section 619, as amended, P.L. 94-142, 99-457, 100-630, 101-497, 101-476, and 102-119.

OBJECTIVES: To provide grants to states to assist them in providing a free appropriate public education to preschool children with disabilities, ages 3 through 5 years.

TYPES OF ASSISTANCE: Formula Grants.

84.181 GRANTS FOR INFANTS AND FAMILIES WITH DISABILITIES (Early Intervention Grants)

AUTHORIZATION: Individuals With Disabilities Education Act, Part H, as amended, P.L. 91-230, 99-457, 100-630, 101-476, and 102-119, 20 U.S.C. 1471-1485.

OBJECTIVES: To assist each state in developing a statewide, comprehensive, coordinated, multidisciplinary, interagency system to provide early intervention services for infants and toddlers with disabilities and their families.

TYPES OF ASSISTANCE: Formula Grants.

84.206 JACOB K. JAVITS GIFTED AND TALENTED STUDENTS EDUCATION GRANT PROGRAM (Javits Gifted and Talented)

AUTHORIZATION: Jacob K. Javits Gifted and Talented Students Education Act of 1988; Elementary and Secondary Education Act of 1965, Title IV, Part B, Sections 4101-4108, 20 U.S.C. 3047, 3061-3068.

OBJECTIVES: To provide financial assistance to state and local educational agencies, institutions of higher education, and other public and private agencies and organizations, to stimulate research, development, training, and similar activities designed to build a nationwide capability in elementary and secondary schools to meet the special educational needs of gifted and talented students. To supplement the use of state, local, and Chapter 2 funds for the education of gifted and talented students.

TYPES OF ASSISTANCE: Project Grants.

84.213 EVEN START—STATE EDUCATIONAL AGENCIES

AUTHORIZATION: Elementary and Secondary Education Act of 1965; Even Start Literacy Act, Title I, Chapter 1, Part B, 20 U.S.C. 2741 *et seq.*

OBJECTIVES: To provide family-centered education projects to help parents become full partners in the education of their children, to assist children in reaching their full potential as learners, and to provide literacy training for their parents.

TYPES OF ASSISTANCE: Formula Grants.

84.214 EVEN START—MIGRANT EDUCATION

AUTHORIZATION: Elementary and Secondary Education Act of 1965, Title I, Chapter 1, Part B, 20 U.S.C. 2741 *et seq*; National Literacy Act of 1991, P.L. 102-73; Adult Education Act, 20 U.S.C. 1201.

OBJECTIVES: To provide family-centered education projects to help parents of migratory children become full partners in the education of their children, to assist migratory children in reaching their full potential as learners, and to provide literacy training for their parents.

TYPES OF ASSISTANCE: Project Grants (Discretionary).

84.266 TRAINING IN EARLY CHILDHOOD EDUCATION AND VIOLENCE COUNSELING

AUTHORIZATION: Higher Education Amendments of 1992, P.L. 102-325.

OBJECTIVES: To recruit and train students for careers in early childhood development, care and counseling of young children and their caregivers affected by community violence.

TYPES OF ASSISTANCE: Project Grants (Discretionary).

**Department of Health and Human Services
200 Independence Ave., S.W.
Washington, DC 20201
(202) 619-0257**

Public Health Service (PHS). Promotes and ensures the highest level of health attainable for every individual and family in the United States and develops cooperation in health projects with other nations. The major functions of PHS are to stimulate and assist states and communities with the development of local health resources and further the development of education for the health professions; to assist in the improvement of the delivery of health services to all Americans, with reinforced emphasis on assisting the health care needs of the nation's homeless population; to conduct and support research in medical and related sciences and disseminate scientific information; to protect the health of the nation against impure and unsafe foods, drugs, and cosmetics and other potential hazards; to provide national leadership for the prevention and control of communicable diseases, most especially the acquired immunodeficiency syndrome (AIDS); and other efforts to improve the quality of public health. PHS is comprised of nine major components structured to meet specialized public health needs: Substance Abuse and Mental Health Service Administration, Agency for Toxic Sub-

stances and Disease Registry, Centers for Disease Control and Prevention, Agency for Health Care Policy and Research, Food and Drug Administration, Health Resources and Services Administration, Office of the Assistant Secretary for Health, Indian Health Services, and the most expansive component, National Institutes of Health. Each has its own unique mission in the arena of public health.

93.110 MATERNAL AND CHILD HEALTH FEDERAL CONSOLIDATED PROGRAMS (Special Projects of Regional and National Significance [SPRANS])

AUTHORIZATION: Social Security Act, Title V, Section 502(a)(1), as amended; 42 U.S.C. 702

OBJECTIVES: To carry out special maternal and child health (MCH) projects of regional and national significance; to conduct training and research; to conduct genetic disease testing, counseling, and information development and dissemination programs; and to support comprehensive hemophilia diagnostic and treatment centers. These grants are funded with a set-aside from the MCH Block Grant program. SPRANS grants are funded with 15% of the Block Grant appropriation of up to $600 million, and when the appropriation exceeds $600 million, an additional 12.75% is set aside for the Community Integrated Service Systems grants.

TYPES OF ASSISTANCE: Project Grants.

93.268 CHILDHOOD IMMUNIZATION GRANTS (Section 301 and 317, Public Health Service Act; Immunization Program)

AUTHORIZATION: Public Health Service Act, Section 301, 42 U.S.C. 241, and Section 317, 42 U.S.C. 247b, as amended; Health Services and Centers Amendments of 1978, P.L. 95-626; Omnibus Budget Reconciliation Act of 1981, as amended, P.L. 97-35, Preventive Health Amendments of 1984, P.L. 98-555.

OBJECTIVES: To assist states and communities in establishing and maintaining preventive health service programs to immunize individuals against vaccine-preventable diseases (including measles, rubella, poliomyelitis, diphtheria, pertussis, tetanus, hepatitis b, mumps, hemophilus influenza type b and hepatitis b).

TYPES OF ASSISTANCE: Project Grants.

93.575 PAYMENTS TO STATES FOR CHILD CARE ASSISTANCE

AUTHORIZATION: Child Care and Development Block Grant Act of 1990; Omnibus Budget Reconciliation Act of 1990, Section 5082, P.L. 101-508, as amended, Sections 658J and 658S, P.L. 102-586.

OBJECTIVES: To make grants available to states, territories, and tribal governments to assist low-income families with child care services. The purpose of the program is to increase the availability, affordability, and quality of child care and to increase the availability of early childhood development and before- and after-school programs.

TYPES OF ASSISTANCE: Formula Grants.

93.600 HEAD START (Head Start)

AUTHORIZATION: Head Start Act; Omnibus Budget Reconciliation Act of 1981, Title VI, Subtitle A, Chapter 8, Subchapter B, P.L. 97-35, as amended; Human Services Reauthorization Act of 1990, Title I, P.L. 101-501; Omnibus Elementary and Secondary Human Education Act, Part E, P.L. 100-297, 42 U.S.C. 9801 *et seq.*

OBJECTIVES: To provide comprehensive health, educational, nutritional, social, and other services primarily to economically disadvantaged preschool children, including Indian children on federally recognized reservations, and children of migratory workers and their families; and to involve parents in activities with their children so that the children will attain overall social competence.

TYPES OF ASSISTANCE: Project Grants.

93.608 CHILD WELFARE RESEARCH AND DEMONSTRATION

AUTHORIZATION: Social Security Act, Title IV, Part B, Section 426, P.L. 86-778; Adoption Assistance and Child Welfare Act of 1980, Title I, Section 103, P.L. 96-272; Omnibus Budget Reconciliation Act 1987, P.L. 100-203, 42 U.S.C. 626.

OBJECTIVES: To provide financial support for research and demonstration projects and technical assistance in the area of child.

TYPES OF ASSISTANCE: Project Grants.

Department of the Interior
1800 C. St., N.W.
Washington, DC 20204
(202) 208-3100

Bureau of Indian Affairs (BIA). Encourages and trains Indian and Alaska Native people to manage their own affairs under the trust relationship to the federal government; to facilitate, with maximum involvement of Indian and Alaska Native people, full development of their human and natural resource potentials; to mobilize all public and private aids to the advancement of Indian and Alaska Native people for use by them; and to use the skill and capabilities of Indian and Alaska Native people in the direction and management of programs for their benefit.

15.103 INDIAN SOCIAL SERVICES—CHILD WELFARE ASSISTANCE

AUTHORIZATION: Snyder Act of 1921, P.L. 67-85, 42 Stat. 208, 25 U.S.C. 13.

OBJECTIVES: To provide foster home care and appropriate institutional (nonmedical) care for Indian children who are dependent, neglected, or have disabilities and who are in need of protection residing on or near reservations, including those children living in Bureau of Indian Affairs service area jurisdictions in Alaska and Oklahoma, when these services are not available from state or local public agencies.

TYPES OF ASSISTANCE: Direct Payments for Specified Use.

15.130 INDIAN EDUCATION—ASSISTANCE TO SCHOOLS (Education Contracts Under Johnson-O'Malley Act)

AUTHORIZATION: Johnson-O'Malley Act of April 16, 1934; as amended, 25 U.S.C. 452; P.L. 93-638; 25 U.S.C. 455-457.

OBJECTIVES: To provide supplemental education programs for eligible Indian students attending public schools.

TYPES OF ASSISTANCE: Direct Payments for Specified Use.

15.144 INDIAN CHILD WELFARE ACT—TITLE II GRANTS

AUTHORIZATION: Indian Child Welfare Act; P.L. 95-608, 92 Stat. 3075, 25 U.S.C. 1901.

OBJECTIVES: To promote the stability and security of Indian tribes and families by the establishment of minimum federal standards for the removal of Indian children from their families and the placement of such children in foster or adoptive homes and by providing assistance to Indian tribes in the operation of child and family service programs.

TYPES OF ASSISTANCE: Project Grants.

Department of the Treasury
1666 Connecticut Ave., N.W.
Washington, DC 20235
(202) 884-7750

Appalachian Regional Commission. The Appalachian Regional Commission is a federal-state governmental agency concerned with the economic, physical, and social development of the 13-state Appalachian region, which includes parts of Alabama, Georgia, Kentucky, Maryland, Mississippi, New York, North Carolina, Ohio, Pennsylvania, South Carolina, Tennessee, Virginia, and all of West Virginia. The comprehensive goals of the commission are to provide the people of Appalachia with the health and skills they need to compete for opportunities and to develop a self-sustaining economy and environment capable of supporting a population with rising incomes and standards of living and increasing employment opportunities. To accomplish this task, the commission has concentrated on areas of development in which great needs remain throughout the region: community development and housing, education, the environment, health and child development, industrial development and management, tourism, and transportation.

23.013 APPALACHIAN CHILD DEVELOPMENT

AUTHORIZATION: Appalachian Regional Development Act of 1965, Section 202, P.L. 89-4, as amended; 40 App. U.S.C. 202.

OBJECTIVES: To provide child care services throughout the region that meet the needs of industry and its employees.

TYPES OF ASSISTANCE: Project Grants.

Environmental Protection Agency
1100 Vermont Ave., N.W.
Washington, DC 20525
(202) 606-5135

Corporation for National Service. Administers and coordinates the domestic volunteer programs sponsored by the federal government that are linked by a commitment to a "bottom-up," locally initiated development process that fosters self-reliance and uses available human and economic resources to overcome conditions of poverty. Through special demonstration grants and programs, the Corporation for National Service also tests new ways of bringing volunteer resources to bear on human, social, and economic problems. It identifies and develops the widest possible range of volunteer service opportunities for Americans of all ages and ethnic backgrounds. The agency actively encourages private-sector involvement in support of its goals and programs. The Corporation for National Service includes Volunteers in Service to America (VISTA), the Foster Grandparent Program (FGP), the Retired Senior Volunteer Program (RSVP), the Senior Companion Program (SCP), the Demonstration Grant Program, the Mini-Grant Program, the Technical Assistance Program, and the State Offices of Voluntarism.

72.001 FOSTER GRANDPARENT PROGRAM (FGP)

AUTHORIZATION: Domestic Volunteer Service Act of 1973, as amended, Title II, Part B, Section 211, P.L. 93-113, 42 U.S.C. 5011, as amended; National and Community Service Transit Act of 1993, P.L. 103-82.

OBJECTIVES: Dual purposes of the program are (a) to provide part-time volunteer service opportunities for low-income persons age 60 and over and (b) to give supportive person-to-person service in health, education, welfare, and related settings to help alleviate the physical, mental, and emotional problems of infants, children, or youth having special or exceptional needs. In addition, eligible agencies or organizations may, under a Memorandum of Agreement with Corporation for National Service, receive technical assistance and materials to aid in establishing and operating a noncorporation for National Service funded Foster Grandparent Program project using local funds.

TYPES OF ASSISTANCE: Project Grants.

FOUNDATIONS

Various types of grants are offered by the following foundations:

Aetna Foundation, Inc.
Corporate Public Involvement, REIB
151 Farmington Ave.
Hartford, CT 06156-3180

American Express Company
American Express Tower, World Financial Center
New York, NY 10285-4710

Annie E. Casey Foundation
One Lafayette Pl.
Greenwich, CT 06830

Burton G. Bettinger Corp.
9777 Wilshire Blvd., Suite 611
Beverly Hills, CA 90212

Carnegie Corporation of New York
437 Madison Ave.
New York, NY 10022

Center for Research for Mothers and Children
National Institutes of Health
9000 Rockville Pike
Bethesda, MD 20892

Citibank, N.A.
850 Third Ave., 13th Floor
New York, NY 10043

DuPont
External Affairs Dept.
9541 Nemours Bldg.
Wilmington, DE 19898

Ellen Browning Scripps Foundation
Union Bank
P.O. Box 109
San Diego, CA 92112-4103

Foundation for Child Development
345 E. 46th St.
New York, NY 10017-3562

Hasbro Children's Foundation
32 W. 23rd St.
New York, NY 10010

J. C. Penney Co., Inc.
P.O. Box 10001
Dallas, TX 75301-1321

Johnson & Johnson Family of Companies
Contribution Fund
One Johnson & Johnson Plaza
New Brunswick, NJ 08933

KMART Corporation
Public Affairs Dept.
3100 W. Big Beaver Rd.
Troy, MI 48084-3163

Meyer Memorial Trust
1515 Southwest Fifth Ave., Suite 500
Portland, OR 97201

Ronald McDonald Children's Charities
One McDonald's Plaza
Oak Brook, IL 60521

Thrasher Research Fund
50 East North Temple St., 7th Floor
Salt Lake City, UT 84150

Wal-Mart Foundation
Wal-Mart Stores, Inc.
702 SW. Eighth St.
Bentonville, AR 72716-8071

Grants are in a constant state of flux. Check the most up-to-date edition of the following directories:

Annual Register of Grant Support

The Foundation Directory

The Foundation Grants Index

Appendix 8

※ ※ ※ ※ ※

Parent's Handbook

1. OUR SCHOOL

Dear Mom and Dad,

It's going to be 4 months before I can start kindergarten. I went to see my school today so that I can find out about kindergarten. That way, I'll be ready to go in September.

My school is in a big building. I've never seen so many toys, books, and records. And, some classes even have hamsters and lots of other animals—almost like a zoo!

My teacher's name is _____.
I asked her lots of questions and found out all about kindergarten. My school is a kindergarten-primary school. The children will be 5, 6, 7, and 8 years old. My teacher said there will be plenty of things for all of us to do. At first, I'll have easy things to do. Then, as I learn, I'll get harder things to do. My teacher said most children go to school here 4 years, but a few go 3 years and a few stay 5 years. It's called a "continuous progress" approach. I don't understand what that means, but you will hear about it in the Spring Orientation Meeting tomorrow.

2. ENTRANCE REQUIREMENTS

Age

Little children can't go to kindergarten. I'm big now. I'm 5! This was printed in our newspaper:

A child may attend kindergarten if he or she is 5 years old on or before November 1st.

※ ※ ※ ※ ※

Birth Certificate

Our state requires that children have a legal birth certificate to enter school. I have to bring it when I register. If you do not have it, you will have to write to:

Bureau of Vital Statistics
State Capitol Building

_____
(Capital City)

_____
(State)

_____
(ZIP Code)
The charge is $ _____ .

Emergency Information Form

You always give me lots of good food, put me to bed early, and let me play outdoors. I'm very careful because skinned knees hurt. My teacher will take care of me while I'm at school and will need an "emergency information form" in case I get sick or hurt. It's in the back of this book. I'll get your pen, and you can give my teacher the information.

Health History
Physical Examination
Immunizations
Dental Examination

My teacher says I must be healthy and strong in kindergarten. You will have to call my doctor and dentist soon because they're so busy. They have to write on all the other forms in the back of this handbook. Will I need to get a pen for the doctor and the dentist? I'll bring one, just in case.

3. REGISTRATION, SUPPLIES, AND CLOTHING

Registration

I am assigned to the school in the school attendance area in which I live. You found out where my class was by calling the Elementary School Director's Office. About 2 weeks before school starts, our town's newspaper will tell all about the school attendance areas and when to register.

The newspaper will also tell you about bus routes and the times the bus will pick me up and bring me back home if I am to ride the bus.

Supplies

My teacher gave me a list of supplies. Here is a copy.

One box of large washable crayons
One 20 in. × 48 in. plastic mat stitched crosswise in several sections
One terrycloth apron with Velcro fasteners
These supplies are sold in our two discount stores.

Clothing

With so many children and with so much for each of us to do in kindergarten, the teacher says these are good qualities for school clothes:

1. Labeled for identification
2. Easy to handle (large buttons and buttonholes; underwear convenient for toileting; boots the child can put on and remove; loops on coats and sweaters for hanging)
3. Washable
4. Sturdy
5. Not too tight
6. Shoes that are comfortable for play

4. ATTENDANCE, SESSION TIMES, AND EARLY DISMISSAL

Attendance

Our school has attendance regulations. My teacher says it is important that I go to school every day so that I'll get to do all the fun things with my friends.

Session Times

Our kindergarten starts at _____ and closes at _____ . I should arrive at school no more than 10 minutes before school starts. If you bring me to school in the car, we should drive in the circular driveway, and I should enter the school at the side door. I should never leave our car at the curb by the street. You can pick me up at the same place right after school.

Early Dismissal

My teacher says I'm not to leave early unless there is an emergency. These are the rules parents have to follow:

1. Only the principal can dismiss a student.
2. A student cannot be excused by a telephone call without verification of the telephone call.
3. A student can be dismissed only to a parent or a person properly identified.

5. LUNCH AND MILK

I want to eat lunch and drink milk with the other children. Here's a note that tells all about it.

> A hot lunch will be served in the cafeteria every day. It costs _____ a day, or you may pay $ _____ a week. Checks may be made payable to _____ . If your child wishes to bring his or her lunch, milk will cost _____ cents a day. Those who wish to inquire whether their children qualify for free or reduced-cost lunches may secure forms in the central office.
>
> When sending money to school, place it in an envelope and write the child's name and the teacher's name on the envelope.

6. A CHILD STAYS HOME

When Ill

I'm supposed to stay home if I'm sick. Here is a list of reasons.

Looks or acts too ill to participate

Oral temperature of 101°F or greater

Oozing lesions untreated or unable to be covered

Difficulty breathing

Bloody or black stool

No urine output in 8 hours

Vomiting more than twice in 24 hours

Uncontrolled diarrhea

Certain Diseases

Childhood diseases (chicken pox, measles, mumps, pertussis, rubella)

Haemophilus influenza, type b (HIb) infection

Hepatitis A

Impetigo

Meningitis

Ringworm

Scabies

Streptococcus

Scarlet Fever

During Family Emergency

I may stay home if there is a death or serious illness in our family.

During Extremely Inclement Weather

Mom and Dad, you must decide whether the weather is too bad for me to go to school. Sometimes, there will be no school during bad weather. Local radio and television stations that carry school closing announcements are WKID, WKDG-TV, and WBUG-TV.

Bring a Note

I'm supposed to bring a note when I come back to school, telling my teacher why I've been absent. If I've been to the doctor, I must get a signed note before I return to school.

7. EVERYDAY EXPERIENCES

When I visited the kindergarten at my school, I saw children doing many things in the building and outdoors. Some of the children were singing in the music room, some boys were feeding the hamsters, a girl was walking on a balance beam, and a big boy was reading a story to a little boy. My teacher said that, in the kindergarten-primary school, we do all those things and much more, like counting, painting, working with clay, reading books, learning about ourselves and people near and far, and visiting places in our town. We even eat together at lunch and have a snack in the morning and afternoon.

8. SPECIAL EXPERIENCES

Field Trips

When our class plans a field trip, the teacher asks our parents whether we can go. The teacher will send a note to you each time we go on such a trip, and you will have to sign it.

Parties and Treats

Birthdays are a lot of fun. When it is my birthday, I can share some treats with my class. My teacher will give you a list of all the rules about birthday treats. Even grown-ups have rules!

We will have five other celebrations. My teacher will send a note to you.

At our school, we do not exchange gifts on any holiday. We just say, "Happy Holidays!" We can make cards. My teacher will send you a list of names.

Bringing Things to School

Sometimes, I can share a book, game, picture, or an object from nature and souvenirs from trips.

You can help me choose what to bring so that I don't bring fragile, valuable (expensive or family treasure), or sharp-edged objects.

9. HOW PARENTS CAN HELP

Guess what? My teacher says all the children's parents are teachers too! There are lots of teachers. Here is a letter from my school teacher to my parent teacher.

Dear Parents,

As parents, you have been responsible for the early teaching of your child. Although he or she is now old enough for school, you will still be the most important teachers in your child's life. Here are some ways you can help your child in school.

1. Attend individual and group conferences as often as you can

2. Read and answer all notes from the school

3. Give special help to your kindergartner by:

   Promoting good health and safety habits

   Praising your child for things done well

   Talking about everyday experiences

   Planning family activities

   Reading stories

   Watching children's television shows with your child

   Providing materials for cutting, drawing, writing, and building

   Helping your child start a collection, such as leaves or rocks

   Teaching your child to take care of toileting needs, to dress (outdoor clothing), and to put away toys

10. YOUR CHILD'S PROGRESS

Our school doesn't send home report cards, but you can find out how I'm doing in school. My teacher will get together with you several times this year, and you will talk about how I'm doing and see my portfolio.

You can talk with my teacher any time, and you can see me in school too. My school will also have some special meetings for you. I've got a list of the meetings the teacher planned. There's a blank space by each one. You can record the time when you get a note or telephone call from my teacher.

Get-acquainted conference (approximately 2 weeks after the beginning of school)

_____

Fall individual conference (November)

_____

Spring individual conference (April)

_____

11. PARENT'S CHECKLIST

Here's a "Parent's Checklist" to make sure everything is done.

Have you read this handbook? _____

Does your child have a legal birth certificate? _____

Have you completed and signed the emergency information form? _____

Have you completed and signed the health history form? _____

Has your physician completed and signed the physical examination form? _____

Has your physician completed and signed the immunization record form? _____

Has your dentist signed the dental report?

_____

Do you know the date of registration?

_____

Have you obtained the school supplies?

_____

Are all outdoor clothes labeled? _____

Does your child have the right type of school clothes? _____

Are you following the suggestions given in section 9, "How Parents Can Help"?

_____

List any questions you would like to discuss with the staff. _____

_____

_____

12. FORMS

Remember those forms* that are part of the entrance requirements? Here they are, and you will have to take them when I go to school the first day.

_____

*Forms from the state should be used if provided.

EMERGENCY INFORMATION

Child's name _____

Home address _____ Phone number _____

Father's name _____

Place of business_____ Phone number _____

Mother's name _____

Place of business_____ Phone number _____

Give name of another person to be called in case of emergency, if parents cannot be reached:

Name_____ Phone number _____

Address_____ Relationship _____

Physician to be called in case of emergency:

1st choice: _____ Phone number _____

2nd choice:_____ Phone number _____

Name of hospital to be used in emergency:

1st choice: _____

2nd choice: _____

Other comments: _____

_____

_____

_____

Date_____ Signed _____

(Parent or guardian)

HEALTH HISTORY

Child's name _____

General evaluation of family's health: _____

_____

Family deaths (causes): _____

_____

Child's illnesses. If your child has had any of these diseases, please state the age at which he or she had them.

_____ measles   _____ smallpox
_____ mumps   _____ diabetes
_____ whooping cough   _____ heart disease
_____ poliomyelitis   _____ meningitis
_____ rheumatic fever   _____ epilepsy (seizures)
_____ scarlet fever   _____ chicken pox
_____ diphtheria   _____ pneumonia
_____ serious accident   _____ asthma, hay fever

Has your child ever had tests for tuberculosis? _____
Skin test? _____ Date _____   Chest X ray? _____ Date _____

Please check any of the following that you have noted in your child recently.

_____ frequent sore throat   _____ shortness of breath
_____ persistent cough   _____ frequent nosebleed
_____ frequent headaches   _____ allergy
_____ poor vision   _____ frequent urination
_____ dizziness   _____ fainting spells
_____ frequent sties   _____ abdominal pain
_____ dental defects   _____ loss of appetite
_____ speech difficulty   _____ hard of hearing
_____ tires easily   _____ 4 or more colds per year

Describe your child socially and emotionally. _____

_____

_____

Are there any matters that you would like to discuss with the school staff? _____

_____

Date _____   Signed _____
                                                        (Parent or guardian)

PHYSICAL EXAMINATION

Child's name _____

Comment on any significant findings:

Eyes: Right _____   Left _____   Squint _____

Ears: Right _____   Left _____   Discharge _____

Nose _____   Throat _____

Glands _____   Tonsils _____

Heart and circulation _____

Lungs _____

Abdomen _____

Bones and joints _____

Reflexes _____

Nutrition _____

Posture _____

Hernia _____   Neurological _____

Hemoglobin (if physician indicates) _____

Urinalysis (if physician indicates) _____

Does the school program need to be adjusted for this child? _____

_____

_____

Date_____   Signed _____

                                                                      (M.D. or D.O.)

IMMUNIZATION RECORD

Child's name _____

Diphtheria-Tetanus (since age 3)

_____

          (1st date)   (2nd date)   (Booster)

Poliomyelitis (since age 3)

_____

       (1st date)   (2nd date)   (3rd date)   (Booster)

Measles (Rubeola): Disease or immunization _____
                                                               (date)

T.B. Test

Tine _____   Reaction: _____   Pos. _____   Date: _____

Mantoux _____   Neg. _____   Date: _____

Chest X-ray _____   Results: _____   Date: _____

Date _____   Signed _____
                                                                              (M.D. or D.O.)

DENTAL REPORT

Child's name _____

Cavities _____   Gums _____

Malocclusion _____

Please explain any abnormal findings or deformities. _____

_____

_____

Please indicate care given:

Prophylaxis_____   Cavities filled _____

Extractions _____   Orthodontics _____

What additional care do you plan for this child? _____

_____

_____

_____

Date_____   Signed _____

(D.D.S.)

MEDICATION PERMISSION FORM

Medications for children can be administered only when requested by the prescribing physician. Each container shall be childproof and carry the name of the medication, the name of the person for whom it was prescribed, the name of the prescribing physician, and the physician's instructions. Each child's medication shall be stored in its original container. This is in compliance with state and federal laws.

Child's name _____

Prescription name and number _____

Pharmacy name _____

Physician's name _____   Phone # _____

Description of medication (e.g., white liquid, red capsules) _____

Illness/Condition _____

Dosage _____   Time(s) of day to be given _____

Precautions _____   Date prescribed _____

Date to be discontinued _____

_____   _____
          Signature of physician   Date

_____   _____
          Signature of parent   Date

_____

Note: Because of space limitations, sections of the Parent's Handbook are indicated by numbers and headings. In making your school's handbook, arrange materials attractively on each page; a short paragraph can be centered; drawings and so forth can be added.

References

Abbott, C. F., & Gold, S. (1991). Conferring with parents when you're concerned that their child needs special services. *Young Children, 46*(4), 10-14.

Abbott-Shim, M. S. (1990). In-service training: A means to quality care. *Young Children, 45*(2), 14-18.

Abt Associates, Inc. (1980). *Day-care centers in the U.S.: A national profile, 1966-77.* Washington, DC: U.S. Department of Health, Education & Welfare, Administration for Children, Youth, and Families.

Adams, G. S. (1965). *Measurement and evaluation in education, psychology, and guidance.* New York: Holt, Rinehart & Winston.

Adams, P. K., & Taylor, M. K. (1985). *A learning center approach to infant education.* Columbus, GA: Columbus College, School of Education. (ERIC Document Reproduction Service No. ED 253 315)

Advisory Committee on Head Start Quality and Expansion. (1994). Creating a 21st century Head Start: Executive summary of the final report of the Advisory Committee on Head Start Quality and Expansion. *Young Children, 49*(3), 65-67.

Allen, E. (1983). Children, the Congress, and you. *Young Children, 38*(2), 71-75.

Allen, J., & Catron, C. (1990). Researchers at the early childhood center: Guidelines for cooperation. *Young Children, 45*(4), 60-65.

Almy, M. (1975). *The early childhood educator at work.* New York: McGraw-Hill.

America 2000: An education strategy. (1991). Washington, DC: U.S. Department of Education.

American Educational Research Association, American Psychological Association, & National Council on Measurement in Education. (1985). *Standards for educational and psychological testing.* Washington, DC: American Psychological Association.

American Montessori Society. (1973). *Approved teacher training programs.* New York: Author.

American Public Health Association & American Academy of Pediatrics. (1992). *Caring for our children—National health and safety performance standards: Guidelines for out-of-home child care programs.* Washington, DC: Author.

Anderson, C., Nagle, R., Roberts, W., & Smith, J. (1981). Attachment to substitute caregivers as a function of center quality and caregiver involvement. *Child Development, 57*, 53-61.

Anderson, J. (1947). The theory of early childhood education. In N. B. Henry (Ed.), *The forty-sixth yearbook of the National Society for the Study of Education, Part II* (pp. 70-100). Chicago: University of Chicago Press.

Anderson, S. B., & Messick, S. (1974). Social competency in young children. *Developmental Psychology, 10*, 282-293.

Andrews, S. R., Blumenthal, J. B., Johnson, D. L., Kahn, A. J., Ferguson, C. J., Lasater, R. M., Malone, P. E., & Wallace, D. B. (1982). The skills of mothering: A study of Parent Child Development Centers. *Monographs of the Society for Research in Child Development, 47*(6, Serial No. 198).

Arin-Krump, J. (1981). *Adult development: Implications for staff development.* Manchester, MA: Adult Development and Learning.

Arizona Center for Educational Research and Development. (1983). *Tucson Early Education Model (TEEM).* Tucson, AZ: Author.

Arnett, J. (1989). Caregivers in day-care centers: Does training matter? *Journal of Applied Developmental Psychology, 10*, 541-552.

Aronson, S. S. (1991). *Health and safety in child care.* New York: HarperCollins.

Aronson, S. S. (1993). Tree climbing and care of sand play areas. *Child Care Information Exchange, 90*, 79-80.

Ashton-Warner, S. (1963). *Teacher.* New York: Simon & Schuster.

Association for Childhood Education International (ACEI). (1986). *When parents of kindergartners ask "why."* Wheaton, MD: Author.

Association for Supervision and Curriculum Development. (1988). *A resource guide to public school early childhood programs.* Alexandria, VA: Author.

Ayers, A. J. (1973). *Sensory integration and learning disorders.* Los Angeles: Western Psychological Services.

Ayers, W. (1992). Disturbances from the field: Recovering the voice of the early childhood teacher. In S. Kessler & B. B. Swadener (Eds.), *Reconceptualizing the early childhood curriculum: Beginning the dialogue* (pp. 256-266). New York: Teachers College Press.

Bailey, D. B., Jr., & Wolery, M. (1992). *Teaching infants and preschoolers with disabilities* (2nd ed.). New York: Merrill/Macmillan.

Baker, K. R. (1968). Extending the indoors outside. In S. Sunderlin & N. Gray (Eds.), *Housing for early childhood education* (pp. 59-70). Washington, DC: Association for Childhood Education International.

Balaban, N. (1992). The role of the child care professional in caring for infants, toddlers, and their families. *Young Children, 47*(5), 66-71.

Bandura, A. (1977). *Social learning theory.* Englewood Cliffs, NJ: Prentice Hall.

Barbour, N. H. (1990). Issues in the preparation of early childhood teachers. In C. Seefeldt (Ed.), *Continuing issues in early childhood education* (pp. 153-171). New York: Merrill/Macmillan.

Barbour, N. H., & Seefeldt, C. (1993). *Developmental continuity: Across preschool and primary grades.* Wheaton, MD: Association for Childhood Education International.

Barker, R. G. (1951). *One boy's day.* New York: Harper.

Barker, R. G. (1968). *Ecological psychology.* Palo Alto, CA: Stanford University Press.

Barnett v. Fairfax County School Board, 927 F. 2d 146 (4th Cir. 1991), *cert. denied,* 112 S. Ct., 175 (1991).

Barnett, S. W., & Escobar, C. M. (1990). Economic costs and benefits of early intervention. In S. J. Meisels & J. P. Shonkoff (Eds.), *Handbook of early childhood intervention* (pp. 560-582). New York: Cambridge University Press.

Baruch, D. (1939). *Parents and children go to school.* Chicago: Scott, Foresman.

Bavolek, S. J., & Bavolek, J. D. (1985). *Nurturing programs for parents of young children.* Eau Claire, WI: Family Development Resources.

Beaty, J. (1992). *Preschool appropriate practices.* Orlando, FL: Harcourt Brace Jovanovich.

Behrmann, M. M., & Lahm, E. A. (1994). Computer applications in early childhood special education. In J. L. Wright & D. D. Shade (Eds.), *Young children: Active learners in a technological age* (pp. 105-120). Washington, DC: National Association for the Education of Young Children.

Bender, J. (1971). Have you ever thought of a prop box? *Young Children, 26*(3), 164–169.

Benham, N., Miller, T., & Kontos, S. (1988). Pinpointing staff training needs in child care centers. *Young Children, 43*(4), 9-16.

Bereiter, C., & Englemann, S. (1966). *Teaching disadvantaged children in the preschool.* Englewood Cliffs, NJ: Prentice Hall.

Bergan, J. R., Feld, S. K., Reddy, L. A., Li, F. F., Schwarz, R. D., & Cheng, Y. H. (1992a). *MAPS Developmental Observation Guide: Level KL.* Tucson, AZ: Assessment Technology.

Bergan, J. R., Feld, S. K., Reddy, L. A., Li, F. F., Schwarz, R. D., & Cheng, Y. H. (1992b). *MAPS Developmental Observation Guide: Level PL.* Tucson, AZ: Assessment Technology.

Bergen, D. (1993/94). Authentic performance assessments. *Childhood Education, 70,* 99, 102.

Berk, L. E., & Winsler, A. (1995). *Scaffolding children's learning: Vygotsky and early childhood education.* Washington, DC: National Association for the Education of Young Children.

Berk, R. A. (Ed.). (1986). *Performance assessment.* Baltimore: Johns Hopkins University Press.

Berres, M., & Knoblock, P. (1987). *Program models for mainstreaming.* Rockville, MD: Aspen.

Berrueta-Clement, J., Schweinhart, L., Barnett, W., Epstein, A., & Weikart, D. (1984). Changed lives: The effects of the Perry Preschool Program on youths through age 19. *Monographs of the High/Scope Educational Research Foundation* (No. 8). Ypsilanti, MI: High/Scope Press.

Berson, M. P. (1959). *Kindergarten: Your child's first big step.* New York: E. P. Dutton.

Berson, M. P. (1968). The all-day kindergarten. *Today's Education, 57*(8), 27-30.

Bettelheim, B. (1987). *A good enough parent.* New York: Knopf.

Beyer, N. R., & Morris, P. M. (1974). Food attitudes and snacking patterns of young children. *Journal of Nutrition Education, 6*(4), 131-134.

Biber, B. (1970). Goals and methods in a preschool program for disadvantaged children. *Children, 17*(1), 15-20.

Biber, B. (1977). A developmental-interaction approach: Bank Street College of Education. In M. C. Day & R. K. Parker (Eds.), *The preschool in action* (2nd ed., pp. 423-460). Needham Heights, MA: Allyn & Bacon.

Biber, B. (1984). *Early education and psychological development*. New Haven, CT: Yale University Press.

Biber, B. (1988). The challenge of professionalism: Integrating theory and practice. In B. Spodek, O. Saracho, & D. Peters (Eds.), *Professionalism and the early childhood practitioner* (pp. 29-47). New York: Teachers College Press.

Bijou, S. W. (1976). *Child development: The basic stages of early childhood*. Englewood Cliffs, NJ: Prentice Hall.

Biklen, D. (1985). *Achieving the complete school: Strategies for effective mainstreaming*. New York: Teachers College Press.

Birch, L. L., Johnson, S. L., & Fisher, J. A. (1995). Children's eating: The development of food acceptance patterns. *Young Children, 50*(2), 71-78.

Birch, L. L., Marlow, D. W., & Rotter, J. (1984). Eating as the "means" activity in a contingency: Effects on young children's food preference. *Child Development, 55*, 431-439.

Bissell, J. S. (1973). The cognitive effects of preschool programs for disadvantaged children. In J. L. Frost (Ed.), *Revisiting early childhood education* (pp. 223-241). New York: Holt, Rinehart & Winston.

Black, S. (1993). Born at risk. *Executive Education, 20*(6), 30-32.

Bloch, M. N. (1991). Critical science and the history of child development's influence on early education research. *Early Education and Development, 2*, 95-108.

Bloom, A. (1987). *The closing of the American mind*. New York: Simon & Schuster.

Bloom, P. J. (1992). Staffing issues in child care. In B. Spodek & O. N. Saracho, *Yearbook in early childhood education: Vol. 3. Issues in child care* (pp. 143-168). New York: Teachers College Press.

Bluma, S., Shearer, M., Frohman, A., & Hilliard, J. (1976). *Portage guide to early education* (Rev. ed.). Portage, WI: Cooperative Educational Service Agency 5.

Bolster, A. S., Jr. (1983). Toward a more effective model of research on teaching. *Harvard Educational Review, 53*, 294-308.

Bontá, P., & Silverman, B. (1993). Making learning entertaining. In N. Estes & M. Thomas (Eds.), *Rethinking the roles of technology in education* (pp. 1150-1152). Cambridge: Massachusetts Institute of Technology.

Boutte, G. S., Keepler, D. L., Tyler, V. S., & Terry, B. Z. (1992). Effective techniques for involving "difficult" parents. *Young Children, 47*(3), 19-22.

Bowman, B. (1986). Birthday thoughts. *Young Children, 41*(2), 3-8.

Bowman, B. (1990). Child care: Challenges for the '90's. *Dimensions, 18*(4), 27, 29-31.

Bowman, B. (1992). Reaching potentials of minority children through developmentally and culturally appropriate programs. In S. Bredekamp & T. Rosegrant (Eds.), *Reaching potentials: Appropriate curriculum and assessment for young children* (Vol. 1, pp. 128-136). Washington, DC: National Association for the Education of Young Children.

Bowman, B., & Brady, E. H. (1982). Today's issues: Tomorrow's possibilities. In S. Hill & B. H. Barnes (Eds.), *Young children and their families; Needs of the nineties* (pp. 207-217). Lexington, MA: Lexington Books.

Boyd, R., Stauber, K., & Bluma, S. (1977). *Portage Parent Program*. Portage, WI: Portage Educational Agency 5.

Bradbard, M. R., Sinclair, L., & Endsley, R. C. (1987). Parent-caregiver involvement, family status characteristics, and parents' feelings about day care. *Family Perspective, 21*, 213-222.

Bradburn, E. (1989). *Margaret McMillan: Portrait of a pioneer*. London: Routledge.

Brady, J., & Goodman, I. F. (1991). *Lessons learned: Head Start's experience with state activities*. Boston: Educational Development Center.

Bredekamp, S. (Ed.). (1987). *Developmentally appropriate practice in early childhood programs serving children from birth through age 8* (Exp. ed.). Washington, DC: National Association for the Education of Young Children.

Bredekamp, S. (1990). *Regulating child care quality: Evidence from NAEYC's accreditation system*. Washington, DC: National Association for the Education of Young Children.

Bredekamp, S. (1992). The early childhood profession coming together. *Young Children, 47*(6), 36-39.

Bredekamp, S. (1993). The relationship between early childhood education and early education special education: Healthy marriage or family feud? *Topics in Early Childhood Special Education, 13*(1), 19-37.

Bredekamp, S., & Berby, J. (1987). Maintaining quality: Accredited programs one year later. *Young Children, 43*(1), 13-15.

Bredekamp, S., & Rosegrant, T. (Eds.). (1992). *Reaching potentials: Appropriate curriculum and assessment for young children* (Vol. 1). Washington, DC: National Association for the Education of Young Children.

Bredekamp, S., & Shepard, L. (1989). How best to protect children from inappropriate school expectations, practices, and policies. *Young Children, 44*(3), 14-24.

Bredekamp, S., & Willer, S. (1992). Of ladders and lattices, cores and cones: Conceptualizing an early childhood professional development system. *Young Children, 47*(3), 47-50.

Briggs v. Board of Education of Connecticut, 882 F. 2d 688 (2d Cir. 1989).

Brody, G. H., Stoneman, Z., & MacKinnon, C. E. (1982). Role asymmetries in interactions among school-age children, their younger siblings, and their friends. *Child Development, 53*, 1364-1370.

Bronfenbrenner, U. (1974). *Is early intervention effective? A report on longitudinal evaluations of preschool programs* (Vol. 2). Washington, DC: U.S. Department of Health, Education & Welfare, Office of Child Development.

Bronfenbrenner, U. (1979). *The ecology of human development: Experiments by nature and design.* Cambridge, MA: Harvard University Press.

Bronfenbrenner, U. (1986). Ecology of the family as a context for human development: Research perspectives. *Developmental Psychology, 22*, 723-742.

Brown v. Board of Education (Brown I), 347 U.S. 483 (1954); Brown v. Board of Education (Brown II), 349 US. 294 (1955).

Bruner, C. (1991). *Thinking collaboratively: Ten questions and answers to help policymakers improve children's services.* Washington, DC: Education & Human Services Consortium.

Bruner, J. (1980). *Under fives in Britain.* Ypsilanti, MI: High/Scope Press.

Bryant, D. M., Clifford, R. M., & Peisner, E. S. (1989). *Best practices for beginners: Quality programs for kindergartners.* Chapel Hill, NC: Frank Porter Graham Child Development Center.

Bryant, D. M., Clifford, R. M., & Peisner, E. S. (1991). Best practices for beginners: Developmental appropriateness in kindergarten. *American Educational Research Journal, 28*, 783-803.

Buck, L. (1987). Directors: How to sell accreditation to staff, board, and parents. *Young Children, 42*(2), 46-49.

Buckleitner, W. (1993). Kids and computers update. *Child Care Information Exchange, 93*, 75-78.

Bureau of Labor Statistics. (1987). *Current population survey: 1986 annual averages and occupational proportions and training data.* Washington, DC: Government Printing Office.

Burts, D. C., Hart, C. H., Charlesworth, R., Fleeze, P., Mosley, J., & Thomasson, R. H. (1992). Observed activities and stress behaviors of children in developmentally appropriate and inappropriate classrooms. *Early Childhood Research Quarterly, 7*, 297-318.

Bushell, D., Jr. (1973). The behavior analysis classroom. In B. Spodek (Ed.), *Early childhood education* (pp. 163-175). Englewood Cliffs, NJ: Prentice Hall.

Butterworth, J. E. (1928). *The Parent Teacher Association and its work.* New York: Macmillan.

Byrnes, D. A., & Yamamoto, K. (1985). An inside look at academic retention in the elementary school. *Education, 106*, 208-214.

Cadden, V. (1994, March). The state of the states. *Working Mother,* pp. 31-38.

Caldwell, B. M. (1968). The fourth dimension in early childhood education. In R. D. Hess & R. M. Baer (Eds.), *Early education: Current theory, research, and action* (pp. 71-81). Chicago: Aldine.

Caldwell, B. M. (1977). Child development and social policy. In M. Scott & S. Grimmett (Eds.), *Current issues in child development* (pp. 61-87). Washington, DC: National Association for the Education of Young Children.

Caldwell, B. M. (1985). What is quality child care? In B. M. Caldwell & A. Hillard (Eds.), *What is quality child care?* (pp. 1-16). Washington, DC: National Association for the Education of Young Children.

Caldwell, B. M. (1989). Achieving rights for children. *Childhood Education, 66*, 4-7.

Caldwell, B. M. (1990). "Educare": New professional identity. *Dimensions, 16*(4), 3-6.

Caldwell, B. M. (1991). Continuity in the early years: Transitions between grades and systems. In S. L. Kagan (Ed.), *The care and education of America's young children; Obstacles and opportunities* (pp. 69-90). Chicago: University of Chicago Press.

Caldwell, T. H., Sirvis, B., Todaro, A., & Accouloumre, D. S. (1991). *Special health care in the school.* Reston, VA: Council for Exceptional Children.

Carlsson-Paige, N., & Levin, D. E. (1985). *Helping young children understand peace, war, and the nuclear threat.* Washington, DC: National Association for the Education of Young Children.

Carnegie Corporation of New York. (1994). Starting points: Executive summary of the report of the Carnegie Corporation of New York Task Force on Meeting the Needs of Young Children. *Young Children, 49*(5), 58-61.

Carnegie Forum on Education and the Economy. (1986). *A nation prepared: Teachers for the 21st century.* New York: Carnegie Corporation of New York.

Carran, N. (1984). *National directory of early childhood special education services, 1984. Consortium of State Education Agency Early Childhood/Special Education Coordinators.* Des Moines, IA: Department of Public Instruction.

Carter, M. (1992). Honoring diversity: Problems and possibilities for staff and organization. In B. Neugebauer (Ed.), *Alike and different: Exploring our humanity with children* (Rev. ed., pp. 70-81). Washington, DC: National Association for the Education of Young Children.

Carter, M. (1993). Developing a cultural disposition in teachers. *Child Care Information Exchange, 90,* 52-55.

Caruso, J. J. (1991). Supervisors in early childhood programs: An emerging profile. *Young Children, 46*(6), 20-26.

Caruso, J. J., & Fawcett, M. T. (1986). *Supervision in early childhood education: A developmental approach.* New York: Teachers College Press.

Casey, M. B., & Lippman, M. (1991). Learning to plan through play. *Young Children, 46*(4), 52-58.

Casper, L. M., Hawkins, M., & O'Connell, M. (1991). *Who's minding the kids? Child care arrangements: Fall 1991.* Washington, DC: Bureau of the Census, Population Division.

Cassidy, D. J., & Lancaster, C. (1993). The grassroots curriculum: A dialogue between children and teachers. *Young Children, 48*(6), 47-51.

Cataldo, C. Z. (1982). Very early childhood education for infants and toddlers. *Childhood Education, 58,* 149-154.

Chafel, J. A. (1990). Children in poverty: Policy perspectives on a national crises. *Young Children, 45*(5), 31-37.

Char, C. (1989, March). *Computer graphic feltboards: New software approaches for young children's mathematical exploration.* Paper presented at the meeting of the American Educational Research Association, San Francisco.

Char, C. (1990). *Interactive technology and the young child: Insights from research and design* (Report 90-2, Reports and Papers in Progress). Newton, MA: Center for Learning, Teaching, and Technology, Education Development Center.

Char, C., & Forman, G. E. (1994). Interactive technology and the young child: A look to the future. In J. L. Wright & D. D. Shade (Eds.), *Young children: Active learners in a technological age* (pp. 167-177). Washington, DC: National Association for the Education of Young Children.

Charlesworth, R., Hart, C. H., Burts, D. C., & DeWolf, M. (1993). The LSU Studies: Building a research base for developmentally appropriate practices. In S. J. Kilmer (Ed.), *Advances in early education and day care* (Vol. 5, pp. 3-28). Greenwich, CT: JAI Press.

Charlesworth, R., Hart, C. H., Burts, D. C., Thomasson, R. H., Mosley, J., & Fleege, P. O. (1993). Measuring the developmental appropriateness of kindergarten teachers' beliefs and practices. *Early Childhood Research Quarterly, 8,* 255-276.

Chattin-McNichols, J., & Loeffler, M. H. (1989). Teachers as researchers: The first cycle of the teachers' research network. *Young Children, 44*(5), 20-27.

Chavkin, N. F. (1989). Debunking the myth about minority parents. *Educational Horizons, 67*(4), 119-123.

Cheever, D. S., Jr., & Ryder, A. E. (1986). Quality: The key to successful programs. *Principal, 64,* 18-23.

Child Care Action Campaign & Communications Consortium Media Center. (1994). *Polling analysis of child care issues, 1988-1993.* New York: Author.

Children's Bureau. (1966). *Spotlight on day-care.* Washington, DC: U.S. Department of Health, Education & Welfare.

Children's Defense Fund. (1994). *The state of America's children: Yearbook 1994.* Washington, DC: Author.

Child Welfare League of America. (1945). *Day-care: A partnership of three professions.* Washington, DC: Author.

Child Welfare League of America. (1960). *Standards for day-care service.* New York: Author.

Child Welfare League of America. (1984). *Child Welfare League of America standards for day care service* (Rev. ed.). Edison, NJ: Coordinated Systems & Services.

Child Welfare League of America. (1990). *Agency accreditation manual of the Council on Accreditation of Services for Families and Children, Inc.* Washington, DC: Author.

Cinnamond, J., & Zimpher, N. (1990). Reflectivity as a function of community. In R. Clift, W. Houston, & M. Pugach (Eds.), *Encouraging reflective practice in eduction* (pp. 57-72). New York: Teachers College Press.

Clark, C. M., & Peterson, P. L. (1986). Teachers' thought processes. In M. C. Wittrock (Ed.), *Handbook of research on teaching* (3rd ed., pp. 255-296). New York: Macmillan.

Clarke-Stewart, A. (1985). The day-care child. In J. S. McKee (Ed.), *Early childhood education 1985/86* (pp. 94-98). Guilford, CT: Dushkin.

Clarke-Stewart, A., & Gruber, C. (1984). Day care forms and features. In R. C. Ainslie (Ed.), *Quality variations in day care* (pp. 35-62). New York: Praeger.

Class, N. E. (1968). *Licensing of child care facilities by state welfare departments.* Washington, DC: U.S. Department of Health, Education & Welfare, Children's Bureau.

Class, N. E. (1972). *Basic issues in day care licensing.* Washington, DC: U.S. Department of Health, Education & Welfare, Office of Education.

Clements, D. H. (1991). Current technology and the early childhood curriculum. In B. Spodek & O. N. Saracho (Eds.), *Yearbook in early childhood education: Vol. 2. Issues in early childhood curriculum* (pp. 106-131). New York: Teachers College Press.

Clements, D. H. (1994). The uniqueness of the computer as a learning tool: Insights from research and practice. In J. L. Wright & D. D. Shade (Eds.), *Young children: Active learners in a technological age* (pp. 31-50). Washington, DC: National Association for the Education of Young Children.

Clements, D. H., & Nastasi, B. K. (1992). Computers and early childhood education. In M. Gettinger, S. N. Elliott, & T. R. Kratochwill (Eds.), *Preschool and early childhood treatment directions* (pp. 187-246). Hillsdale, NJ: Erlbaum.

Clements, D. H., & Nastasi, B. K. (1993). Electronic media and early childhood education. In B. Spodek (Ed.), *Handbook of research on the education of young children* (pp. 251-275). New York: Macmillan.

Clyde K. and Sheila K. v. Puyallup School District, No. 93-35572, F. 3d (9th Cir. 1994).

Coelen, C., Glantz, F., & Calore, D. (1979). *Day care centers in the U.S.* Cambridge, MA: Abt Associates.

Cohen, A. (1984). *School-age child care: A legal manual for public school administrators.* Wellesley, MA: School-Age Child-Care Project.

Cohen, A. M., & Brawer, F. B. (1969). *Measuring faculty performance.* Washington, DC: American Association of Junior Colleges.

Collins, R. C. (1993). Head Start: Steps toward a two-generation program strategy. *Young Children, 48*(2), 25-33, 72-73.

Comer, J. P. (1986). Parent participation in the schools. *Phi Delta Kappan, 67,* 442-446.

Comer, J. P. (1988). *Maggie's American dream: The life and times of a black family.* New York: Penguin.

Committee for Economic Development, Research, and Policy. (1987). *Children in need: Investment strategies for the educationally disadvantaged, Executive summary.* New York: Author.

Committee on Nutrition Education, American Academy of Pediatrics. (1986). Prudent lifestyle for children: Dietary fat and cholesterol. *Journal of Pediatrics, 12,* 521-525.

Committee on Preschool & Parental Education. (1929). Training for the field of parental education. In G. M. Whipple (Ed.), *Preschool and parental education, Twenty-eighth yearbook of the National Society for the Study of Education, Part I* (pp. 443-449). Bloomington, IL: Public School Publishing.

Congressional Caucus for Women's Issues. (1988). Results of the child care challenge on employer-sponsored child-care services. *Young Children, 43*(6), 60-62.

Consumer Product Safety Commission (CPSC). (December, 1989). *Playground equipment-related injuries involving falls to the surface.* Washington, DC: Directorate for Epidemiology, Division of Hazardous Analysis.

Cooley, W. W. (1975). *Evaluation of educational programs for young children: The Minnesota Round Table on Early Childhood Education II.* Washington, DC: Child Development Associate Consortium.

Cooper, J. M., & Eisenhart, C. E. (1990). The influence of recent educational reforms on early childhood teacher education programs. In B. Spodek & O. N. Saracho (Eds.), *Yearbook in early childhood education: Vol. 1. Early childhood teacher prepa-*

ration (pp. 176-191). New York: Teachers College Press.

Copple, C. E., Cline, M. G., & Smith, A. N. (1978, September). *Path to the future: Long-team effects of Head Start in the Philadelphia School District.* Washington, DC: U.S. Department of Health and Human Services, Head Start Bureau.

Corsini, D. A., Wisensale, S., & Caruso, G-A. (1988). Family day care: System issues and regulatory models. *Young Children, 43*(6), 17-23.

Cost, Quality, and Outcomes Study Team. (1995). Cost, quality, and child outcomes in child care centers: Key findings and recommendations. *Young Children, 50*(4), 40-44.

Council for Early Childhood Professional Recognition. (1993). Quality programs in child care link army child development services and CDA program. *Competence, 10*(1), 1.

Cumming, J., & Cumming, E. (1967). *Ego and milieu.* New York: Atherton.

Cummings, M., & Beagles-Ross, J. (1983). Toward a model of infant day care: Studies of factors influencing responding to separation in day care. In R. C. Ainslie (Ed.), *Quality variations in day care* (pp. 159-182). New York: Praeger.

Cushman, K. (1993). The Montessori story. *Parents Magazine, 68*(1), 80-84.

Davis, M. D. (1932). *Nursery schools: Their development and current practices in the United States* (Bulletin No. 9). Washington, DC: Office of Education.

Davis, M. D. (1964). How NANE began. *Young Children, 20,* 106-109.

Day, D. E. (1983). *Early childhood education: A human ecological approach.* Glenview, IL: Scott, Foresman.

Day, D. E., Phyfe-Perkins, E., & Weinhaler, J. A. (1979). Naturalistic evaluation for program improvement. *Young Children, 34*(4), 12-24.

Day, D. E., & Sheehan, R. (1974). Elements for a better school. *Young Children, 30*(1), 15-23.

Day, M. C. (1977). A comparative analysis of center-based preschool programs. In M. C. Day & R. K. Parker (Eds.), *The preschool in action* (2nd ed., pp. 461-487). Needham Heights, MA: Allyn & Bacon.

Day, M. C., & Parker, R. K. (1977). *The preschool in action* (2nd ed.). Needham Heights, MA: Allyn & Bacon.

Deasey, D. (1978). *Education under six.* New York: St. Martin's Press.

Decker, C. A. (1995). *Children: The early years.* South Holland, IL: Goodheart-Willcox.

Decker, C. A., & Decker, J. R. (1984). *Planning and administering early childhood programs* (3rd ed.). New York: Merrill/Macmillan.

Decker, C. A., & Decker, J. R. (1992). *Planning and administering early childhood programs* (5th ed.). New York: Merrill/Macmillan.

Delgado-Gaitin, C. (1991). Involving parents in the schools: A process of empowerment. *American Journal of Education, 100*(1), 20-46.

Dempsey, J. D., & Frost, J. L. (1993). Play environments in early childhood education. In B. Spodek (Ed.), *Handbook of research on the education of young children* (pp. 306-321). New York: Macmillan.

Dempsey, J. D., Strickland, E., & Frost, J. L. (1993). What's going on out here? An evaluation tool for your playground. *Child Care Information Exchange, 91,* 41-44.

Derman-Sparks, L. (1992). Reaching potentials through antibias, multicultural curriculum. In S. Bredekamp & T. Rosegrant (Eds.), *Reaching potentials: Appropriate curriculum and assessment for young children* (Vol. 1, pp. 114-127). Washington, DC: National Association for the Education of Young Children.

Derman-Sparks, L., & A.B.C. Task Force (1989). *Anti-Bias Curriculum: Tools for empowering young children.* Washington, DC: National Association for the Education of Young Children.

Derman-Sparks, L., & Ramsey, P. (1992). Multicultural education reaffirmed. *Young Children, 47*(2), 10-11.

DeVries, R., & Kohlberg, L. (1987). *Constructivist early education: Overview and comparison with other programs.* Washington, DC: National Association for the Education of Young Children.

Dewey, J. (1897). My pedagogic creed. *School Journal, 54,* 77-80.

Dewey, J. (1900). *The school and society.* Chicago: University of Chicago Press.

Dewey, J. (1916). *Democracy and education: An introduction to the philosophy of education.* New York: Macmillan.

Dewey, J. (1964). The relation of theory to practice in education. In R. Archambault (Ed.), *John Dewey on education: Selected writings* (pp. 313-338). New York: Random House.

Diamond, E. E., & Fremer, J. (1989). The Joint Committee on Testing Practices and the Code of Fair

Testing Practices in Education. *Educational Measurement: Issues and Practices, 8*(1), 23-24.

Dinkmeyer, D., & McKay, G. (1976). *Systematic training for effective parenting.* Circle Pines, MN: American Guidance Service.

Dixon, S. (1990). Talking to the child's physician: Thoughts for the child-care provider. *Young Children, 45*(3), 36-37.

Dodd, E. L., & Brock, D. R. (1994). Building partnerships with families through home-learning activities. *Dimensions of Early Childhood, 22*(2), 37-39, 46.

Dokecki, P., Hargrove, E., & Sandler, H. (1983). An overview of the Parent-Child Development Center social experiment. In R. Haskins & D. Adams (Eds.), *Parent education and public policy* (pp. 80-111). Norwood, NJ: Ablex.

Donovan, E. (1987). *Preschool to public school: A teacher's guide to successful transition for children with special needs.* Syracuse, NY: Jowonio School.

Dopyera, J. E., & Lay-Dopyera, M. (1990). Evaluation and science in early childhood education: Some critical issues. In C. Seefeldt (Ed.), *Continuing issues in early childhood education* (pp. 285-299). New York: Merrill/Macmillan.

Downs, R. B. (1978). *Friedrich Froebel.* Boston: Twayne.

Dresden, J., & Myers, B. K. (1989). Early childhood professionals: Toward self-definition. *Young Children, 44*(2), 62-66.

Duckworth, E. (1987). *The having of wonderful ideas.* New York: Teachers College Press.

Duff, R. E., & Stroman, S. H. (1979). Mobilizing community agencies in coalitions for child advocacy. *Childhood Education, 55,* 210-212.

Durkin, D. (1987). A classroom observation study of reading instruction in kindergarten. *Early Childhood Research Quarterly, 2,* 275-300.

Early Childhood Education Linkage System Staff. (1993). *Model child care health policies.* Washington, DC: National Association for the Education of Young Children.

Educational Facilities Laboratories. (1965). *SER 2 environmental evaluations.* Ann Arbor: University of Michigan, Architectural Research Laboratory.

Educational Products Information Exchange Institute. (1972). *Early childhood education: How to select and evaluate materials.* New York: Author.

Egan, K. (1983). *Education and psychology: Plato, Piaget, and scientific psychology.* New York: Teachers College Press.

Einbinder, S. D., & Bond, J. T. (1992). *Five million children: 1992 update.* New York: National Center for Children in Poverty.

Elardo, P. T., & Caldwell, B. M. (1974). The Kramer adventure: A school for the future. *Childhood Education, 50,* 143-152.

Elbaz, L. (1983). *Teacher thinking: A study of practical knowledge.* London: Croom Helm.

Elder, J. L., & Pederson, D. R. (1978). Preschool children's use of objects in symbolic play. *Child Development, 49,* 500-504.

Eliot, A. (1978). America's first nursery school. In J. Hymes (Ed.), *Living history interviews* (pp. 7-26). Carmel, CA: Hacienda.

Elkind, D. (1983). Montessori education: Abiding contributions and contemporary challenges. *Young Children, 38*(2), 3-10.

Elkind, D. (1986). Formal education and early childhood education: An essential difference. *Phi Delta Kappan, 67,* 631-636.

Elkind, D. (1987a). The child yesterday, today, and tomorrow. *Young Children, 42*(4), 6-11.

Elkind, D. (1987b). *Miseducation: Preschoolers at risk.* New York: Knopf.

Elkind, D. (1988). The resistance to developmentally appropriate practice with young children: The real issue. In C. Warger (Ed.), *A resource guide to public school early childhood programs* (pp. 53-62). Alexandria, VA: Association for Supervision and Curriculum Development.

Elkind, D. (1989). Developmentally appropriate practice. Philosophical and practical implications. *Phi Delta Kappan, 71,* 113-117.

Elkind, D. (1991). Developmentally appropriate practice: A case study of educational inertia. In S. L. Kagan (Ed.), *The care and education of America's young children; Obstacles and opportunities* (pp. 1-16). Chicago: University of Chicago Press.

Ellis, D. (1977, May). *Focus on philosophies for educating young children.* Paper presented at the 22nd Annual Convention of the International Reading Association, Miami. (ERIC Document Reproduction Service No. ED 142 283)

Ellis, M. J. (1973). *Why people play.* Englewood Cliffs, NJ: Prentice Hall.

Elmer, E., & Maloni, J. A. (1988). Parent support through telephone consultation. *Maternal-Child Nursing Journal, 17,* 13-23.

Elsbree, W. S., & Reutter, E. E., Jr. (1954). *Staff personnel in the public schools.* Englewood Cliffs, NJ: Prentice Hall.

Emihovich, C., & Miller, G. E. (1988). Effects of Logo and CAI on black first graders' achievement, reflectivity, and self-esteem. *Elementary School Journal, 88,* 473-487.

Endsley, R. C., & Minish, P. (1991). Parent-staff communication in day care centers during morning and afternoon transitions. *Early Childhood Research Quarterly, 6,* 119-135.

Environmental criteria: Mentally retarded preschool day-care facilities. (1971). College Station, TX: Texas A & M College of Architecture & Environmental Design.

Epstein, J. (1986). Parents' reactions to teachers practices of parent involvement. *Elementary School Journal, 86,* 277-294.

Erikson, E. H. (1950). *Childhood and society.* New York: Norton.

Erikson, E. H. (1951). *A healthy personality for every child: A digest of the fact-finding report to the Mid-Century White House Conference on Children and Youth.* Raleigh, NC: Health Publications Institute.

Esbenstein, S. (1987). *An outdoor classroom.* Ypsilanti, MI: High/Scope Press.

Evans, E. D. (1982). Curriculum models and early childhood education. In B. Spodek (Ed.), *Handbook of research on early childhood education* (pp. 107-134). New York: Free Press.

Fallon, B. J. (Ed.). (1973). *40 innovative programs in early childhood education.* Belmont, CA: Fearon.

Fantini, M. (1970). *Community control and the urban school.* New York: Praeger.

Fassnacht, G. (1982). *Theory and practice of observing behavior.* London: Academic Press.

Federal Register. (1979, May 18). 44, 28424-28426.

Federal Register. (1988, July 6). 53(129), 25309.

Fedor v. Mauwehu Council of Boy Scouts, 143 A.2d 466 (Conn. 1958).

Feeney, S. (1990). Update on the NAEYC Code of Ethical Conduct. *Young Children, 45*(4), 20-21.

Feeney, S., & Christensen, D. (1979). *Who am I in the lives of children?* New York: Merrill/Macmillan.

Feeney, S., & Kipnis, K. (1985). Public policy report: Professional ethics in early childhood education. *Young Children, 40*(3), 54-58.

Feeney, S., & Kipnis, K. (1989). The National Association for the Education of Young Children Code of Ethical Conduct and Statement of Commitment. *Young Children, 45*(1), 24-29.

Feeney, S., & Sysko, L. (1986). Professional ethics in early childhood education: Survey results. *Young Children, 42*(1), 15-20.

Fein, G. (1975). A transformational analysis of pretending. *Developmental Psychology, 11,* 291-296.

Fein, G., & Schwartz, P. M. (1982). Developmental theories in early education. In B. Spodek (Ed.), *Handbook of research in early childhood education* (pp. 82-104). New York: Free Press.

Feistritzer, E. C. (1986). *Teacher crisis: Myth or reality?* Washington, DC: National Center for Educational Information.

Feld, J. K., Salado, M. A., Bergan, J. R., & Schwarz, R. D. (1990). *MAPS-M Perceptual Motor Scale.* Tucson, AZ: Assessment Technology.

Feldman, D. H. (1980). *Beyond universals in cognitive development.* Norwood, NJ: Ablex.

Fewell, R. R., & Vadasky, P. F. (1987). Measurement issues in studies of efficacy. *Topics in Early Childhood Special Education, 7,* 885-896.

Field, T. M. (1980). Preschool play: Effects of teacher:child ratio and organization of classroom space. *Child Study Journal, 10,* 191-205.

Fields, C. (1988, November 2). Poor test scores bar many minority students from teacher training. *Chronicle of Higher Education,* A1.

Fiene, R. J. (1985). The Instrument-Based Program Monitoring Information System and the Indicator Checklist for Child Care. *Child Care Quarterly, 14,* 198-214.

Fiene, R. J. (1986a). *National child care regulatory, monitoring, and evaluation systems model.* Washington, DC: National Association for the Education of Young Children.

Fiene, R. J. (1986b). *State child care regulatory, monitoring, and evaluation systems as a means for ensuring quality child development programs, licensing of services for children and adults: A compendium of papers.* Richmond, VA: Virginia Commonwealth University, School of Social Work.

File, N., & Kontos, S. (1993). The relationship of program quality to children's play in integrated early intervention settings. *Topics in Early Childhood Special Education, 13*(1), 1-18.

Fink, D. B. (1988). *School-age children with special needs: What do they do when school is out?* Boston: Exceptional Parent Press.

Fink, J., & Sponseller, D. (1977). Practicing for child advocacy. *Young Children, 32*(3), 49-54.

Finkelstein, B. (1988). The revolt against selfishness: Women and the dilemmas of professionalism in early childhood education. In B. Spodek, O. N. Saracho, & D. Peters (Eds.), *Professionalism and the early childhood practitioner* (pp. 10-28). New York: Teachers College Press.

Finn-Stevenson, M., & Stevenson, J. J. (1990). Safe care/safe play: Child care as a site for injury prevention. *Children Today, 19*(2), 16-32.

First things first. (n.d.). New York: Upjohn Laboratories.

Fite, K. (1993, Spring/Summer). A report on computer use in early childhood education. *Ed Tech Review,* pp. 18-24.

Flaherty, E. W. (1980). The boundaries of government intervention in federally funded services. *Evaluation News, 17,* 22-27.

Flavell, J. H. (1977). *Cognitive development.* Englewood Cliffs, NJ: Prentice Hall.

Forest, I. (1927). *Preschool education: A historical and critical study.* New York: Macmillan.

Forman, G. E., & Fosnot, C. T. (1982). The use of Piaget's constructivism in early childhood education programs. In B. Spodek (Ed.), *Handbook of research in early childhood education* (pp. 185-211). New York: Free Press.

Forman, G. E., & Hill, F. (1980). *Constructive play: Applying Piaget in the preschool.* Menlo Park, CA: Addison-Wesley.

Forman, G. E., & Pufall, P. B. (Eds.). (1988). *Constructivism in the computer age.* Hillsdale, NJ: Erlbaum.

For your information. Public opinion on teacher education. (1993). *Young Children, 48*(6), 8.

Fosnot, C. T. (1989). *Inquiring teachers, inquiring learners: A constructivist approach for teaching.* New York: Teachers College Press.

Foster, J. R., & Rogers, L. R. (1970). *Housing early childhood education in Texas.* College Station, TX: Innovative Resources.

Fowell, N., & Lawton, J. (1992). An alternative view of appropriate practice in early childhood education. *Early Childhood Research Quarterly, 7,* 53-73.

Fox, R. A., Anderson, R. C., Fox, T. A., & Rodriguez, M. A. (1991). STAR parenting: A model for helping parents effectively deal with behavioral difficulties. *Young Children, 46*(6), 54-60.

Fox-Barnett, M., & Meyer, T. (1992). The teacher's playing at my house this week. *Young Children, 47*(2), 45-50.

Fraas, C. I. (1986). *Preschool programs for education of handicapped children* (Report No. 86-55 EPW). Washington, DC: Library of Congress.

Francis, P., & Self, P. (1982). Imitative responsiveness of young children in day care and home settings: The importance of the child to the caregiver ratio. *Child Study Journal, 12,* 119-126.

Frank, L. K. (1937). The fundamental needs of the child. *Mental Hygiene, 22,* 353-379.

Freedman, P. (1982). A comparison of multi-age and homogeneous grouping in early childhood centers. *Current Topics in Early Childhood Education, 4,* 193-209.

French, D. C. (1984). Children's knowledge of the social functions of younger, older, and same-age peers. *Child Development, 55,* 1429-1433.

Friedman, D. (1986, March/April). Child care for employees' kids. *Harvard Business Review,* pp. 28-34.

Friedman, D., Galinsky, E., & King, M. (1990). *Working and family life: A briefing kit.* Washington, DC: U.S. Department of Labor, Women's Bureau.

Froebel, F. (1895). *Pedagogics of the kindergarten* (J. Jarvis, Trans.). New York: Appleton.

Frost, J. L. (1992a). *Play and playscapes.* Albany, NY: Delmar.

Frost, J. L. (1992b). Reflections on research and practice in outdoor play environments. *Dimensions of Early Childhood, 20*(4), 6-10, 40.

Frost, J. L., & Klein, B. (1983). *Children's play and playgrounds.* Austin, TX: Playscapes International.

Frost, J. L., & Wortham, S. C. (1988). The evolution of American playgrounds. *Young Children, 43*(5), 19-28.

Furman, W., Rahe, D. F., & Hartup, W. W. (1979). Rehabilitation of socially withdrawn preschool children through mixed-age and same-age socialization. *Child Development 50,* 915-922.

Galen, H. (1991). Increasing parental involvement in elementary school: The nitty-gritty of one successful program. *Young Children, 46*(2), 18-22.

Galinsky, E. (1987). *The six stages of parenthood.* Reading, MA: Addison-Wesley.

Galinsky, E. (1988). Parents and teacher-caregivers: Sources of tension, sources of support. *Young Children, 43*(3), 4-12.

Galinsky, E. (1989a). The staffing crises. *Young Children, 44*(2), 2-4.

Galinsky, E. (1989b). Update on employer-supported child care. *Young Children, 44*(6), 2, 75-77.

Galinsky, E. (1990a). The cost of providing quality early childhood programs. In B. Willer (Ed.), *Reaching the full cost of quality in early childhood programs* (pp. 27-40). Washington, DC: National Association for the Education of Young Children.

Galinsky, E. (1990b). Government and child care. *Young Children, 45*(3), 2-3, 76-77.

Galinsky, E. (1990c). Why are some parent/teacher partnerships clouded with difficulties? *Young Children, 45*(5), 2-3, 38-39.

Galinsky, E. (1991). The private sector as a partner in early care and education. In S. L. Kagan (Ed.), *The care and education of America's young children: Obstacles and opportunities* (pp. 131-153). Chicago: University of Chicago Press.

Galinsky, E., & Hooks, W. (1977). *New extended family.* Boston: Houghton Mifflin.

Galinsky, E., Howes, C., Kontos, S., & Shinn, M. (1994). The study of children in family child care and relative care: Key findings and policy recommendations. *Young Children, 50*(1), 58-61.

Galinsky, E., Shubilla, L., Willer, B., Levine, J., & Daniel, J. (1994). State and community planning for early childhood systems. *Young Children, 49*(2), 54-57.

Galinsky, E., & Weissbourd, B. (1992). Family-centered child care. In B. Spodek & O. N. Saracho (Eds.), *Yearbook in early childhood education: Vol. 3. Issues in child care* (pp. 47–65). New York: Teachers College Press.

Gallagher, J. M., & Coche, J. (1987). Hothousing: The clinical and educational concerns over pressuring young children. *Early Childhood Research Quarterly, 2,* 203-210.

Gannett, E. (1990). *City initiatives in school-age child care* (Action Research Paper No. 1). Wellesley, MA: School-Age Child Care Project.

Gardner, D. E. (1968). An ideal environment for learning. In S. Sunderlin & N. Gray (Eds.), *Housing for early childhood education* (pp. 3-6). Washington, DC: Association for Childhood Education International.

Gardner, H. (1983). *Frames of mind: Theory of multiple intelligences.* New York: Basic Books.

Gargiulo, R. (1985). *Working with parents of exceptional children.* Boston: Houghton Mifflin.

Gesell, A. (1931). Maturation and patterning of behavior. In C. Murchinson (Ed.), *A handbook of child psychology* (pp. 209-235). Worchester, MA: Clark University Press.

Giangreco, M., Dennis, R., Coninger, C., Edelman, S., & Schattman, R. (1993). "I've counted Jon": Transformational experiences of teachers educating students with disabilities. *Exceptional Children, 59*(4), 359-372.

Glass, G. V., & Smith, M. L. (1979). Meta analysis of research on the class size and its relation to attitudes and instruction. *Educational Evaluation and Policy Analysis, 1,* 2-16.

Goal I Technical Planning Group. (1993, December). *Reconsidering children's early development and learning: Toward shared beliefs and vocabulary.* Washington, DC: National Education Goals Panel.

Good, L. A. (1993). Kindergarten report cards: The new look. *Principal, 72*(5), 22-24.

Goodlad, J., & Anderson, R. H. (1963). *The nongraded elementary school* (Rev. ed.). New York: Harcourt Brace Jovanovich.

Goodlad, J. I., Klein, M. F., & Novotney, J. M. (1973). *Early schooling in the United States.* New York: McGraw-Hill.

Goodman, I. F., & Brady, J. P. (1988). *The challenges of coordination: Head Start's relationship to state-funded preschool initiatives.* Newton, MA: Educational Development Center.

Goodman, P. W. (1982). *Are the long-term effects of early childhood education effective even though the short-term effects seem ineffective?* (ERIC Document Reproduction Service No. 251 170)

Gordon, I. J. (1969). *Early child stimulation through parent education* (Final report to the Children's Bureau, U.S. Department of Health, Education & Welfare). Gainesville, FL: Institute for Development of Human Resources.

Gordon, T. (1970). *Parent effectiveness training.* New York: Peter H. Wyden.

Gormley, W. T., Jr. (1992). Public policy report. Public hearings on child care. *Young Children, 48*(1), 40-42.

Grant, C., & Sleeter, C. (1989). *Turning on learning: Five approaches for multicultural teaching plans for race, class, gender, and disability.* New York: Merrill/Macmillan.

Gray, S. W., & Klaus, R. A. (1970). The early training project: A seventh-year report. *Child Development, 41,* 909-924.

Gray, S. W., Ramsey, B., & Klaus, R. (1982). *From 3 to 20: The Early Training Project.* Baltimore: University Park Press.

Grazinano, W. G., French, D., Brownell, C. A., & Hartup, W. W. (1976). Peer interactions in the same-age and mixed-age triads in relation to chronological age and incentive condition. *Child Development, 47,* 707-714.

Greathouse, B., Moyer, J. E., & Rhodes-Offutt, E. (1992). Increasing K-3 teachers' joy in teaching. *Young Children, 47*(3), 44-46.

Gredler, G. R. (1984). Transition classes: A viable alternative for the at-risk child? *Psychology in the Schools, 21,* 463-470.

Greenberg, P. (1975). *Day care do-it-yourself staff growth program.* Winston-Salem, NC: Kaplan.

Greenberg, P. (1987). Lucy Sprague Mitchell: A major missing link between early childhood education in the 1980s and progressive education in the 1890s-1930s. *Young Children, 42*(5), 70-84.

Greenberg, P. (1989). Parents as partners in young children's development and education: A new American fad? Why does it matter? *Young Children, 44*(4), 61-75.

Greenberg, P. (1990). Before the beginning: A participant's view. *Young Children, 45*(6), 41-52.

Greenberg, P. (1992). Why not academic preschool? (Part 2): Autocracy or democracy in the classroom? *Young Children, 47*(3), 54-64.

Greenman, J. T. (1988). *Caring spaces, learning places: Children's environments that work.* Redmond, WA: Exchange Press.

Greer v. Rome City School District, 950 F.2d 688 (11th Cir. 1991), *opinion withdrawn by,* 956 F.2d 1025 (11th Cir. 1992), *opinion reinstated in part by,* 967 F.2d 470 (11th Cir. 1992).

Grotberg, E., Chapman, J., & Lazar, J. (1971). *The present status and future needs in day care research.* Washington, DC: Office of Child Development.

Grubb, W. N. (1991). Choosing wisely for children: Policy options for children. In S. L. Kagan (Ed.), *The care and education of America's young children: Obstacles and opportunities* (pp. 214-236). Chicago: University of Chicago Press.

Gruenberg, S. M. (1959/60). Parent education in six White House Conferences. *Child Study, 37,* 9-15.

Guddemi, M., & Eriksen, H. (1992). Designing outdoor learning environments for and with children. *Dimensions of Early Childhood, 20*(4), 15-24, 40.

Guilford, J. P. (1967). *The nature of human intelligence.* New York: McGraw-Hill.

Guillean, T. (Ed.). (1991). *A world of difference: A prejudice reduction activity guide.* Los Angeles: Anti-Defamation League of B'nai B'rith.

Guralnick, M. J. (1988). Efficacy research in early childhood intervention programs. In S. L. Odom & M. B. Karnes (Eds.), *Early intervention for infants and children with handicaps: An empirical base* (pp. 75-88). Baltimore: Paul H. Brookes.

Guralnick, M. J. (1989). Recent developments in early intervention efficacy research: Implications for family involvement in P.L. 99-457. *Topics in Early Childhood Special Education, 9*(3), 1-17.

Guralnick, M. J. (1990). Social competence and early intervention. *Journal of Early Intervention, 14*(1), 3-14.

Hadler, S. C. (1982). Risk factors for hepatitis A in day-care centers. *Journal of Infectious Diseases, 145,* 255-261.

Hadley, N. (1987). Reaching migrant preschoolers. *Children's Advocate, 14,* 19-20.

Haith, M. M. (1972). *Day care and intervention programs for infants.* Atlanta, GA: Avatar Press.

Hale-Benson, J. (1982). *Black children: Their roots, culture, and learning styles.* Baltimore: Johns Hopkins University Press.

Hale-Benson, J. (1986). *Visions for children: African American Early Childhood Education Program.* (ERIC Document Reproduction Service No. ED 303 269)

Hall, E. T. (1976). *Beyond culture.* New York: Doubleday.

Hall, G. S. (1897). *The story of a sand-pile.* New York: E. L. Kellogg.

Hall, G. S. (1907). *Aspects of child life and education.* New York: Appleton.

Hanson, B. (1973). *Trends and problems in comparison studies of early childhood education models.* Washington, DC: U.S. Department of Health, Education & Welfare, National Institute of Education.

Hanson, M. J., & Lynch, E. W. (1989). *Early intervention: Implementing child and family services for infants and toddlers who are at risk or disabled.* Austin, TX: PRO-ED.

Harbin, G., & McNulty, B. (1990). Policy implementation: Perspectives on service coordination and interagency cooperation. In S. Meisels & J. Shonkoff (Eds.), *Handbook of early childhood intervention* (pp. 700-721). New York: Cambridge University Press.

Harkin, G. L., Gallagher, J. J., & Terry, D. V. (1991). Defining the eligible population: Policy issues and challenges. *Journal of Early Intervention, 15*(1), 13-20.

Harms, T. (1992). Designing settings to support high-quality care. In B. Spodek & O. N. Saracho (Eds.), *Yearbook in early childhood education: Vol. 3. Issues in child care* (pp. 169-186). New York: Teachers College Press.

Harms, T., & Clifford, R. (1980). *The Early Childhood Environment Rating Scale.* New York: Teachers College Press.

Harms, T., & Clifford, R. M. (1989). *The Family Day-Care Rating Scale.* New York: Teachers College Press.

Harms, T., Cryer, D., & Clifford, R. M. (1990). *Infant/Toddler Environment Rating Scale.* New York: Teachers College Press.

Harris, L., Kagaj, M., & Ross, J. (1987). *The American teacher 1987: Strengthening links between home and school.* New York: Louis Harris.

Hartle, L., & Johnson, J. E. (1993). Historical and contemporary influences of outdoor play environments. In C. H. Hart (Ed.), *Children on playgrounds* (pp. 14-42). Albany: State University of New York Press.

Hartley, R. E., Frank, L., & Goldenson, R. M. (1957). *The complete book of children's play.* New York: Crowell.

Hartman, K. (1977). How do I teach in a future-shocked world? *Young Children, 32*(3), 32-36.

Haskell, E. M. (Ed.). (1896). *Child observations: First series. Imitation and allied activities.* Boston: Heath.

Hatch, J. A., & Freeman, E. B. (1988a). Kindergarten philosophies and practices: Perspectives of teachers, principals, and supervisors. *Early Childhood Research Quarterly, 3,* 151-166.

Hatch, J. A., & Freeman, E. B. (1988b). Who's pushing whom: Stress and kindergarten. *Phi Delta Kappan, 70,* 145-147.

Haugland, S. W. (1992). Effects of computer software on preschool children's developmental gains. *Journal of Computing in Childhood Education, 3*(1), 15-30.

Haugland, S. W., & Shade, D. D. (1994). Early childhood computer software. *Journal of Computing in Childhood Education, 5*(1), 83-92.

Hauser-Cram, P. (1990). Designing meaningful evaluations of early childhood services. In S. Meisels & J. Shonkoff (Eds.), *Handbook of early childhood intervention* (pp. 583-602). New York: Cambridge University Press.

Hawks, R. (1993). Fetal alcohol syndrome: Implications for health education. *Journal of Health Education, 24*(1), 22-26.

Hayes, C. D., Palmer, J. L., & Zaslow, M. (1990). *Who cares for America's children: Child care policy for the 1990s.* Washington, DC: National Academy Press.

Head Start Bureau. (1986). *Head Start performance standards* (45-CFR, 304; DHHS Publications No. [OHDS] 84-31131). Washington, DC: Government Printing Office.

Head Start Bureau (Parent and Child Centers). (1991). *Parent and Child Center (PCC) program fact sheet.* Washington, DC: Author.

Headley, N. E. (1966). *Education in the kindergarten* (4th ed.). New York: American Book.

Heafford, A. (1967). *Pestalozzi: His thought and its relevance today.* London: Methune.

Heath, S. B., & McLaughlin, M. W. (1987). A child resource policy: Moving beyond dependence on school and family. *Phi Delta Kappan, 68,* 576-580.

Henderson, A. (1981). *The evidence grows.* Columbia, MD: National Committee for Citizens in Education.

Henderson, A. (1987). *The evidence continues to grow: Parent involvement improves student achievement.* Columbia, MD: National Committee for Citizens in Education.

Henderson, J. (1988). A curriculum response to the knowledge base reform movement. *Journal of Teacher Education, 39*(5), 13-17.

Hendrick, J. (1992). Where does it all begin? Teaching the principles of democracy in the early years. *Young Children, 47*(3), 51-53.

Hendricks, C. M. (1993). Safer playgrounds for young children. *ERIC Digest.* Washington, DC: U.S. Department of Education. (Contract #RI 8806 2015)

Henniger, M. L. (1985). Preschool children's play behaviors in an indoor and outdoor environment. In J. L. Frost & S. Sunderlin (Eds.), *When children play* (pp. 145-149). Wheaton, MD: Association for Childhood Education International.

Henniger, M. L. (1994). Planning for outdoor play. *Young Children, 49*(4), 10-15.

Hernandez, D. J. (1994). Children's changing access to resources: A historical survey. *Social Policy Report (Society for Research in Child Development), 8*(1), 1-23.

Herr, J., Johnson, R. D., & Zimmerman, K. (1993). Benefits of accreditation: A study of directors' perceptions. *Young Children, 48*(4), 32-38.

Herr, J., & Morse, W. (1982). Food for thought: Nutrition education for young children. *Young Children, 38*(1), 3-11.

Hess, R., & McGarvey, L. (1987). School-relevant effects of educational uses of microcomputers in kindergarten classrooms and homes. *Journal of Educational Computing Research, 3,* 269-287.

High/Scope Educational Research Foundation. (1992). *High/Scope Child Observation Record.* Ypsilanti, MI: High/Scope Press.

Hilliard, A. G., III. (1991). Equity, access, and segregation. In S. L. Kagan (Ed.), *The care and education of America's young children: Obstacles and opportunities* (pp. 199-213). Chicago: University of Chicago Press.

Hills, T. W. (1987). Children in the fast lane: Implications for early childhood policy and practice. *Early Childhood Research Quarterly, 2,* 265-273.

Hirsch, E. D., Jr. (1987). *Cultural literacy: What every American needs to know.* Boston: Houghton Mifflin.

Hitz, M. C., & Wright, D. (1988). Kindergarten issues: A practitioners' survey. *Principal, 67*(5), 28-30.

Hitz, R., & Richter, S. (1993). School readiness: A flawed concept. *Principal, 72*(5), 10-12.

Hofferth, S., & Phillips, D. (1987). Child care in the United States: 1970-1995. *Journal of Marriage and the Family, 47,* 93-116.

Holmes, M. C. (1937). The kindergarten in American pioneer period. *Childhood Education, 13,* 269-273.

Holmes Group. (1986). *Tomorrow's teachers: A report of the Holmes Group.* East Lansing: Michigan State University.

Holt, B. (1977). *The enabler model of early childhood training and program development.* Ames: Iowa State University, Child Development Training Program.

Honig, A. S. (1993). Mental health for babies: What do theory and research teach us? *Young Children, 48*(3), 69-76.

Honig, A. S., & Brill, S. (1970). *A comparative analysis of the Piagetian development of twelve-month-old disadvantaged infants in an enrichment center with others not in such a center.* Syracuse, NY: Syracuse University Children's Center.

Hopkins, D. (1985). *A teachers' guide to classroom research.* Philadelphia: Open University Press.

Hostetler, L., & Klugman, E. (1982). Early childhood job titles: One step toward professional status. *Young Children, 37*(6), 13-22.

Houle, C. O. (1981). *Continuing learning in the profession.* San Francisco: Jossey-Bass.

House, E. R., Glass, G. V., McLean, L. D., & Walker, D. F. (1978). No simple answer: Critique of the Follow Through evaluation. *Harvard Educational Review, 48,* 128-160.

Howard, A. E. (1975). *The integrated approach design for early childhood programs.* Nacogdoches, TX: Early Childhood Consultant Services.

Howell, M. (1985). Is day care hazardous to health? In J. S. McKee (Ed.), *Early childhood education 1985/86* (pp. 99-100). Guilford, CT: Dushkin.

Howells, R. F. (1993). A new approach to school-age child care. *Principal, 72,* 29.

Howes, C. (1983). Caregiver behavior in center and family day care. *Journal of Applied Developmental Psychology, 4,* 99-107.

Howes, C. (1992). Child outcomes of child care programs. In B. Spodek & O. N. Saracho (Eds.), *Yearbook in early childhood education: Vol. 3. Issues in child care* (pp. 31-46). New York: Teachers College Press.

Howes, C., & Farver, S. A. (1987). Social pretend play in two-year-olds: Effects of age of partner. *Early Childhood Research Quarterly, 2,* 305-314.

Howes, C., & Hamilton, C. E. (1992). Children's relationships with caregivers: Mothers and child care teachers. *Child Development, 63*(4), 867-878.

Howes, C., & Hamilton, C. E. (1993). Child care for young children. In B. Spodek (Ed.), *Handbook of research on the education of young children* (pp. 325-335). New York: Macmillan.

Howes, C., & Olenick, M. (1986). Family and child care influences on toddlers' compliance. *Child Development, 57,* 202-216.

Howes, C., Phillips, D., & Whitebook, M. (1992). Thresholds of quality: Implications for the social development of children in center-based child care. *Child Development, 63,* 449-460.

Howes, C., & Rubenstein, J. (1985). Determinants of toddlers' experience in day care: Age of entry and quality of setting. *Child Care Quarterly, 14,* 140-151.

Howes, C., & Stewart, P. (1987). Child's play with adults, toys, and peers: An examination of family and child care influences. *Developmental Psychology, 23,* 423-430.

Hughes, R. (1985). The informal help-giving of home and center child care providers. *Family Relations, 34,* 359-366.

Hughs, P. C. (1980). The use of light and color in health. In A. C. Hastings, J. Fadiman, & J. S. Gordon (Eds.), *Health for the whole person* (pp. 73-97). Boulder, CO: Westview Press.

Hunt, J. M. (1961). *Intelligence and experience.* New York: Ronald.

Hunt, J. M. (1968). Revisiting Montessori. In J. L. Frost (Ed.), *Early childhood education rediscovered: Readings* (pp. 102-127). New York: Holt, Rinehart & Winston.

Huston, A. C. (Ed.). (1991). *Children in poverty: Child development and public policy.* Cambridge, UK: Cambridge University Press.

Hymes, J. L., Jr. (1944). The Kaiser answer: Child service centers. *Progressive Education, 21,* 222-223, 245-246.

Hymes, J. L., Jr. (1955). *A child development point of view.* Englewood Cliffs, NJ: Prentice Hall.

Hymes, J. L., Jr. (1987). Public school for 4-year-olds. *Young Children, 42*(2), 51-52.

Innes, R., Woodman, J., Banspach, S., Thompson, L., & Inwald, C. (1982). A comparison of the environments of day care centers and group day care homes for 3-year-olds. *Journal of Applied Developmental Psychology, 3,* 41-56.

Interstate New Teacher Assessment and Support Consortium (INTASC). (1992). *The model standards for beginning teacher licensing and development.* Washington, DC: Council of Chief State School Officers.

Irvine, D. J. (1982, April). *Evaluation of the New York State Experimental Prekindergarten Program.* Paper presented at the annual meeting of the American Educational Research Association, New York.

Isaacs, S. (1930). *Intellectual growth in young children.* London: Routledge & Kegan Paul.

Isaacs, S. (1933). *Social development in young children.* London: Routledge & Kegan Paul.

Jacobs, N. L. (1992). Unhappy endings. *Young Children, 47*(3), 23-27.

Jalongo, M. R. (1986). What's happening to kindergarten? *Childhood Education, 62,* 154-160.

Jalongo, M. R., & McCracken, J. B. (1986). Writing for professional publication in early childhood education. *Young Children, 41*(2), 19-23.

Jefferson, R. E. (1968). Indoor facilities. In S. Sunderlin & N. Gray (Eds.), *Housing for early childhood education* (pp. 41-52). Washington, DC: Association for Childhood Education International.

Jenkins, L., Speltz, M., & Odom, S. (1985). Integrating normal and handicapped preschoolers: Effects on child development and social interaction. *Exceptional Children, 52,* 7-18.

Jersild, A. T. (1946). *Child development and the curriculum.* New York: Teachers College Press.

Jipson, J. (1991). Developmentally appropriate practice: Culture, curriculum, connections. *Early Education and Development, 2,* 120-136.

Joffe, C. E. (1977). *Friendly intruders.* Berkeley: University of California Press.

Johnson, H. M. (1924). *A nursery school experiment.* New York: Bureau of Educational Experiments.

Johnson, J., & McCracken, J. B. (Eds.). (1994). *The early childhood career lattice: Perspectives on professional development.* Washington, DC: National Association for the Education of Young Children.

Johnson, J. E., Christie, J. F., & Yawkey, T. D. (1987). *Play and early childhood development.* Glenview, IL: Scott, Foresman.

Johnson, L. C. (1987). The developmental implications of home environments. In C. S. Weinstein & T. G. David (Eds.), *Spaces for children: The built environment and child development* (pp. 139-173). New York: Plenum.

Johnston, J. (1988, September). A performance-based approach to staff evaluation. *Child Care Information Exchange, 62,* 10-13.

Johnston, L., & Mermin, J. (1994). Easing children's entry to school: Home visits help. *Young Children, 49*(5), 62-68.

Johnston, W. B. (1987). *Workforce 2000: Work and workers for the 21st century.* Indianapolis, IN: Hudson Institute.

Jones, E. (1970). Involving parents in children's learning. *Childhood Education, 47,* 126-130.

Jones, E., & Prescott, E. (1978). *Dimensions of teaching-learning environments II: Focus on day care.* Pasadena, CA: Pacific Oaks College.

Jordan, K. F., Lyons, T. S., & McDonough, J. T. (1992). *Funding and financing for programs to serve K-3 at-risk children: A research review.* Washington, DC: National Education Association.

Jorde-Bloom, P. (1988). *A great place to work: Improving conditions for staff in young children's pro-*

grams. Washington, DC: National Association for the Education of Young Children.

Jorde-Bloom, P. (1989). *The Illinois Directors' Study: A report to the Illinois Department of Children and Family Services.* Evanston, IL: National College of Education, Early Childhood Professional Development Project.

Jorde-Bloom, P. (1992a). Looking inside: Helping teachers assess their beliefs and values. *Child Care Information Exchange, 88,* 11-13.

Jorde-Bloom, P. (1992b). Staffing issues in child care. In B. Spodek & O. N. Saracho (Eds.), *Yearbook in early childhood education: Vol. 3. Issues in child care* (pp. 143-168). New York: Teachers College Press.

Jorde-Bloom, P. (1993). Effective communication: The mortar that holds the team together. *Child Care Information Exchange, 89,* 5-8.

Jorde-Bloom, P., & Sheerer, M. (1991, June). *The effect of Head Start leadership training on program quality.* Paper presented at the Society for Research in Child Development National Working Conference on Child and Family Research, Arlington, VA.

Kagan, S. L. (1988). Current reforms in early-childhood education: Are we addressing the issues? *Young Children, 43*(2), 27-32.

Kagan, S. L. (1989). Early care and education: Beyond the schoolhouse doors. *Phi Delta Kappan, 7,* 107-112.

Kagan, S. L. (1991a). Excellence in early childhood education: Defining characteristics and next decade strategies. In S. L. Kagan (Ed.), *The care and education of America's young children: Obstacles and opportunities* (pp. 237–258). Chicago: University of Chicago Press.

Kagan, S. L. (1991b). Policy changes and their implications for early childhood care and education. *Dimensions, 19*(3), 3-7, 40.

Kagan, S. L. (1991c). *United we stand: Collaboration in child care and early education services.* New York: Teachers College Press.

Kagan, S. L. (1992). Readiness past, present, and future: Shaping the agenda. *Young Children, 48*(1), 48-53.

Kagan, S. L. (1994). Leadership: Rethinking it—Making it happen. *Young Children, 49*(5), 50-54.

Kagan, S. L., Powell, D. R., Weissbourd, B., & Zigler, E. F. (Eds.). (1987). *America's family support programs.* New Haven, CT: Yale University Press.

Kagan, S. L., & Rivera, A. M. (1991). Collaboration in early care and education: What can and should we expect? *Young Children, 47*(1), 51-56.

Kahn, A., & Kamerman, S. (1987). *Child care: Facing the hard choices.* Dover, MA: Auburn House.

Kahn, E. D. (1989). *Past caring: A history of U.S. preschool care and education for the poor, 1820-1965.* New York: Columbia University, School of Public Health, National Center for Children in Poverty.

Kamii, C., & Peper, R. (1969). *A Piagetian method of evaluating preschool children's development in classification.* Washington, DC: U.S. Office of Education, Bureau of Elementary and Secondary Education. (ERIC Document Reproduction Service No. ED 039 013)

Karnes, M. B., Shwedel, A. M., & Williams, M. B. (1983). A comparison of five approaches for educating young children from low-income homes. In Consortium for Longitudinal Studies, *As the twig is bent: Lasting effects of preschool programs* (pp. 133-169). Hillsdale, NJ: Erlbaum.

Karweit, N. (1988). Quantity and quality of learning time in preprimary programs. *Elementary School Journal, 89,* 119-133.

Karweit, N. (1993). Effective preschool and kindergarten programs for children at risk. In B. Spodek (Ed.), *Handbook of research on the education of young children* (pp. 91-104). New York: Macmillan.

Katz, L. G. (1972). Developmental states of preschool teachers. *Elementary School Journal, 73,* 50-54.

Katz, L. G. (1977a). *Ethical issues in working with young children.* Washington, DC: U.S. Department of Health, Education & Welfare, National Institute of Education. (ERIC Document Reproduction Service No. ED 144 681)

Katz, L. G. (1977b). *Talks with teachers.* Washington, DC: National Association for the Education of Young Children.

Katz, L. G. (1980). Mothering and teaching: Some significant distinctions. In L. G. Katz (Ed.), *Current topics in early childhood education* (Vol. 4, pp. 47-63). Norwood, NJ: Ablex.

Katz, L. G. (1984). The professional preschool teacher. In L. G. Katz (Ed.), *More talks with teachers* (pp. 27-42). Urbana, IL: ERIC Clearinghouse on Elementary and Early Childhood Education.

Katz, L. G. (1991a). Pedagogical issues in early childhood education. In S. L. Kagan (Ed.), *The care and education of America's young children: Obstacles and opportunities* (pp. 50-68). Chicago: University of Chicago Press.

Katz, L. G. (1991b). *Readiness: Children and schools.* Urbana, IL: ERIC Clearinghouse on Elementary and Early Childhood Education. (ERIC Document Reproduction Service No. ED 330 495)

Katz, L. G. (1994). Perspectives on the quality of early childhood programs. *Phi Delta Kappan, 76,* 200-205.

Katz, L. G., & Chard, S. C. (1989). *Engaging children's minds: The project approach.* Norwood, NJ: Ablex.

Katz, L. G., Evangelou, D., & Hartman, J. A. (1990). *The case for mixed-age grouping in early education.* Washington, DC: National Association for the Education of Young Children.

Katz, L. G., & Raths, J. D. (1986). Dispositions as goals for teacher education. *Teaching and Teacher Education, 1,* 301-307.

Katz, L. G., Raths, J. D., & Torres, R. T. (1987). *A place called kindergarten.* Urbana, IL: ERIC Clearinghouse on Elementary and Early Childhood Education.

Keener, T., & Sebestyen, D. (1981). A cost-analysis of selected Dallas day-care centers. *Child Welfare, 60,* 87-88.

Keister, D. J. (1969). *Consultation in day care.* Chapel Hill: University of North Carolina, Institute of Government.

Kennedy, D. (1991). The young child's experience of space and child care center design: A practical meditation. *Children's Environments Quarterly, 8*(1), 37-48.

Kerr, V. (1973). One step forward—two steps back: Child care's long American history. In P. Roby (Ed.), *Child care: Who cares?* (pp. 157-171). New York: Basic Books.

Kessen, W., Fein, G., Clarke-Stewart, A., & Starr, S. (1975). *Variations in home-based infant education: Language, play, and social development* (Final report to the Office of Child Development, U.S. Department of Health, Education & Welfare). New Haven, CT: Yale University.

Kessler, S. A. (1991a). Alternative perspectives on early childhood education. *Early Childhood Research Quarterly, 6,* 183-197.

Kessler, S. A. (1991b). Early childhood education as development: Critique of the metaphor. *Early Education and Development, 2,* 137-152.

Kilpatrick, W. H. (1918). The project method. *Teachers College Record, 19,* 319-335.

Kirst, M. W. (1986). Sustaining the momentum of state education reform: The link between assessment and financial support. *Phi Delta Kappan, 67,* 341-345.

Kisker, E. E., Hofferth, S. L., Phillips, D. A., & Farquhar, E. (1991). *A profile of child care settings: Early education and child care in 1990.* Washington, DC: U.S. Department of Education.

Klimer, S. (1979). Infant-toddler group day care: A review of research. In L. G. Katz (Ed.), *Current topics in early childhood education* (Vol. 2, pp. 69-115). Norwood, NJ: Ablex.

Kocarnik, R. A., & Ponzetti, J. J., Jr. (1986). The influence of intergenerational contact on child care participants' attitudes toward the elderly. *Child Care Quarterly, 15,* 244-250.

Kohlberg, L., & Mayer, R. (1972). Development as the aim of education. *Harvard Educational Review, 42,* 449-496.

Kontos, S. (1984). Congruence of parenting and early childhood perceptions of parenting. *Parenting Studies, 1*(1), 5-10.

Kontos, S. (1987). The attitudinal context of family-day care relationships. In D. Peters & S. Kontos (Eds.), *Continuity and discontinuity in experience in child care: Vol. 2. Annual advances in applied developmental psychology* (pp. 91-113). Norwood, NJ: Ablex.

Kontos, S. (1988). Family day care as an integrated early intervention setting. *Topics in Early Childhood Special Education, 8*(2), 1-14.

Kontos, S., & Fiene, R. (1987). Child care quality, compliance with regulations, and children's development: The Pennsylvania study. In A. P. Phillips (Ed.), *Quality in child care: What does research tell us?* (pp. 57-59). Washington, DC: National Association for the Education of Young Children.

Kontos, S., & Stevens, R. (1985). High-quality child care: Does your center measure up? *Young Children, 40*(2), 5-9.

Kontos, S., & Stremmel, A. (1988). Caregivers' perceptions of working conditions in a child care environment. *Early Childhood Research Quarterly, 3*(1), 77-91.

Kontos, S., & Wells, W. (1986). Attitudes of caregivers and the day care experiences of families. *Early Childhood Research Quarterly, 1,* 47-67.

Koralek, D. G., Colker, L. J., & Dodge, D. T. (1993). *The what, why, and how of high-quality early childhood education: A guide for on-site supervision.* Washington, DC: National Association for the Education of Young Children.

Kostelnik, M. J. (1992). Myths associated with developmentally appropriate programs. *Young Children, 47*(4), 17-23.

Kotch, J. (1990). *Reduction in transmission of infectious disease in child care settings* (Grant #MCJ-37111. Final report submitted to the Maternal & Child Health Bureau, HRSA, PHS, USDHHS). Chapel Hill: University of North Carolina, Department of Maternal and Child Health.

Kotch, J., Loda, F., McMurray, M., Harms, T., & Clifford, R. (1991). *Parents' reports of injuries among children in day care centers.* Chapel Hill: University of North Carolina, School of Public Health and Medicine.

Kraft, S., & Snell, M. (1980). Parent-teacher conflict: Coping with parental stress. *Pointer, 24*, 29-37.

Kramer, R. (1988). *Maria Montessori: A biography.* Reading, MA: Addison-Wesley.

Krechevsky, M. (1991). Project Spectrum: An innovative assessment alternative. *Educational Leadership, 48*(5), 43-48.

Kritchevsky, S., & Prescott, E. (1969). *Planning environments for young children: Physical space.* Washington, DC: National Association for the Education of Young Children.

Kromhout, O. M., & Butzin, S. M. (1993). Integrating computers into the elementary school curriculum: An evaluation of nine Project CHILD model schools. *Journal of Research on Computing in Education, 26*(1), 55-69.

Kuhn, A. (1947). *The mother's role in childhood education: New England concepts, 1830-1860.* New Haven, CT: Yale University Press.

LaFleur, E. K., & Newsom, W. B. (1988, June). Opportunities for child care. *Personnel Administrator, 12*, 146-154.

Lally, J. R., Mangione, P. L., & Honig, A. S. (1987). *The Syracuse University Family Development Research Program: Long-range impact of early intervention on low-income children and their families.* San Francisco: Center for Child and Family Studies, Far West Laboratory for Educational Research and Development.

Lally, J. R., Provence, S., Szanton, E., & Weissbourd, B. (1986). Developmentally appropriate care for children from birth to age 3. In S. Bredekamp (Ed.), *Developmentally appropriate practice in early childhood programs serving children from birth through age 8* (Exp. ed., pp. 17-33). Washington, DC: National Association for the Education of Young Children.

Lamb, M., Sternberg, K., Hwang, C., & Broberg, A. (Eds.). (1992). *Child care in context.* Hillsdale, NJ: Erlbaum.

Lambert, D. J., Dellman-Jenkins, M., & Fruit, D. (1990). Planning for contact between the generations: An effective approach. *Gerontologist, 30*(4), 553-556.

Lambie, D. Z., Bond, J. T., & Weikart, D. P. (1974). *Home teaching with mothers and infants* (Monographs of the High/Scope Educational Research Foundation No. 2). Ypsilanti, MI: High/Scope Press.

Langhorst, B. H. (1989). *Assessment in early childhood: A consumer's guide.* Portland, OR: Northwest Regional Educational Laboratory.

LaRossa, R. (1986). *Becoming a parent.* Beverly Hills, CA: Sage.

Latimer, D. J. (1994). Involving grandparents and other older adults in the preschool classroom. *Dimensions of Early Childhood, 22*(2), 26-30.

Laufer, R. S., & Wolfe, M. (1977). Privacy as a concept and a social issue: A multidimensional developmental theory. *Journal of Social Issues, 33*(3), 22-42.

Lauritzen, P. (1988). Sample budget for a family child-care system. In A. Godwin & L. Schrag (Eds.), *Setting up for infant care: Guidelines for centers and family day-care homes* (pp. 69-71). Washington, DC: National Association for the Education of Young Children.

Lawler, E. E., Mohrman, S. A., & Ledford, G. E., Jr. (1992). *Employee involvement and total quality management.* San Francisco: Jossey-Bass.

Lazar, I., & Darlington, R. (1982). A report from the Consortium for Longitudinal Studies. *Monographs of the Society for Research in Child Development, 47*(2-3, Serial No. 195).

Lebow, M. D. (1984). *Childhood obesity.* New York: Springer.

Leeper, S. H., Dales, R. J., Skipper, D. S., & Witherspoon, R. L. (1974). *Good schools for young children* (3rd ed.). New York: Macmillan.

Leeper, S. H., Witherspoon, R. L., & Day, B. (1984). *Good schools for young children* (5th ed.). New York: Macmillan.

Lehr, C. A., Ysseldyke, J. E., & Thurlow, M. L. (1987). Assessment practices in model early childhood special education programs. *Psychology in the Schools, 24,* 390-399.

Leitner, D. W., & Tracy, S. M. (1984, September). *The meta analysis of the effect of class size on achievement: A secondary analysis.* Paper presented at the annual meeting of the Mid-Western Educational Research Association, Chicago.

Lemerise, T. (1993). Piaget, Vygotsky, and Logo. *Computing Teacher, 20*(4), 24-28.

Levenstein, P. (1970). Cognitive growth in preschoolers through verbal interaction with mothers. *American Journal of Orthopsychiatry, 40,* 426-432.

Levenstein, P. (1987). The mother-child program. In M. C. Day & R. K. Parker (Eds.), *The preschool in action* (pp. 27-49). Needham Heights, MA: Allyn & Bacon.

Levin, R. A. (1991). The debate over schooling: Influences of Dewey and Thorndike. *Childhood Education, 68,* 71-75.

Lindle, J. C. (1989). What do parents want from principals and teachers? *Educational Leadership, 47*(2), 12-14.

Litwak, E., & Meyer, H. (1974). *School, family, and neighborhood: The theory and practice of school-community relations.* New York: Teachers College Press.

Lochman, J. E., & Brown, M. V. (1980). Evaluation of dropout clients and perceived usefulness of a parent education program. *Journal of Community Psychology, 8,* 132-139.

Lodish, R. (1992). The pros and cons of mixed-age grouping. *Principal, 71*(6), 20-22.

Logue, M. E., Eheart, B. K., & Leavitt, R. L. (1986). Staff training: What difference does it make? *Young Children, 41*(5), 8-9.

Lombardi, J. (1986). Training for public policy and advocacy. *Young Children, 41*(4), 65-69.

Lombardi, J. (1990). Head Start: The nation's pride, a nation's challenge. *Young Children, 45*(6), 22-29.

Lombardi, J. (1992). Early childhood 2001: Advocating for comprehensive services. *Young Children, 47*(4), 24-25.

Long, C., & Stansbury, K. (1994). Performance assessments for beginning teachers: Options and lessons. *Phi Delta Kappan, 76,* 318-322.

Longstreet, W. S. (1978). *Aspects of ethnicity.* New York: Teachers College Press.

Louchs, S. F. (1983). At last some good news from a study of school improvement. *Educational Leadership, 41,* 4-5.

Lougee, M. D., Grueneich, R., & Hartup, W. W. (1977). Social interactions in same-age and mixed-age dyads of preschool children. *Child Development, 48,* 1353-1361.

Love, J. M., Logue, M. E., Trudeau, J. V., & Thayer, K. (1992). *Transitions to kindergarten in American schools: Final report of the National Transition Study.* Washington, DC: U.S. Department of Education, Office of Policy and Planning.

Maccoby, E. E., & Zellner, M. (1970). *Experiments in primary education: Aspects of Project Follow-Through.* New York: Harcourt Brace Jovanovich.

Madera v. Board of Education, City of New York, 386 F. 2d 778 (2d Cir. 1967).

Mallory, N. J., & Goldsmith, N. A. (1990). Head Start works! Two Head Start veterans share their views. *Young Children, 45*(6), 36-39.

Mancke, J. B. (1972). Liability of school districts for the negligent acts of their employees. *Journal of Law and Education, 1,* 109-127.

Mantzicopoulos, P., Morrison, D. C., Hinshaw, S. P., & Corte, E. T. (1989). Nonpromotion in kindergarten: The role of cognitive, perceptual, visual-motor, behavioral, achievement, socioeconomic, and demographic characteristics. *American Educational Research Journal, 25,* 107-121.

Marazon, R. A. (1994). Mister Rogers' Neighborhood—As affective staff development for teachers of young children: A story of conflict, conversion, conviction, and celebration. *Young Children, 49*(5), 34-37.

Marchand, N., & McDermott, R. (1986, December). Mouse calls: A storytelling approach to teaching first aid skills to young children. *Journal of School Health, 56*(10), 453-454.

Marcon, R. A. (1992). Differential effects of three preschool models on inner-city 4-year-olds. *Early Childhood Research Quarterly, 7,* 517-530.

Marked kindergarten progress in the Northwest. (1925). *Childhood Education, 1,* 303-305.

Marx, F. (1990). *School-age child care in America: Final report of a national provider survey* (Working Paper No. 204). Wellesley, MA: Wellesley College, Center for Research on Women.

Marx, F., & Francis, J. (1989). *Learning together: A national directory of teen parenting and child care programs.* Wellesley, MA: Wellesley College, Center for Research on Women.

Marx, F., & Seligson, M. (1987). *Draft notes on state findings from Public School Early Childhood Study.* Wellesley, MA: Wellesley College, Center for Research on Women.

Marx, F., & Seligson, M. (1988). *The public school early-childhood study: The state survey.* New York: Bank Street College.

May, D., & Vinovskis, M. (1977). A ray of millennial light: Early education and social reform in the infant school movement in Massachusetts. In T. Harevian (Ed.), *Family and kin in urban communities* (pp. 62-69). New York: New Viewpoints.

Mayer, R. S. (1971). A comparative analysis of preschool curriculum models. In R. H. Anderson & H. G. Shane (Eds.), *As the twig is bent* (pp. 286-314). New York: Houghton Mifflin.

Mayore, R. (1989). *Childcare needs options for low-income families.* Princeton, NJ: Mathematica Policy Research.

McBride, B. A., & McBride, R. J. (1993). Parent education and support programs for fathers. *Childhood Education, 70,* 4-9.

McCarthy, J. (1988). *State certification of early childhood teachers: An analysis of the 50 states and the District of Columbia.* Washington, DC: National Association for the Education of Young Children.

McCarthy, J. (1990). The content of early childhood teacher education programs. In B. Spodek & O. N. Saracho (Eds.), *Yearbook in early childhood education: Vol. 1. Early childhood teacher preparation* (pp. 82-101). New York: Teachers College Press.

McCarthy, J. (1994). Envision the day: Developing professional standards. In J. Johnson & J. B. McCracken (Eds.), *The early childhood career lattice: Perspectives on professional development* (pp. 47-56). Washington, DC: National Association for the Education of Young Children.

McCartney, K. (1984). Effect of quality day-care environment on children's language development. *Developmental Psychology, 20,* 244-260.

McCartney, K., & Phillips, D. (1988). Motherhood and child care. In B. Birns & H. Hay (Eds.), *Different faces of motherhood* (pp. 157-183). New York: Plenum.

McCartney, K., & Phillips, D. (Eds.). (1993). *An insider's guide to providing expert testimony before Con-*

gress. Chicago: Society for Research in Child Development.

McCartney, K., Scarr, S., Phillips, D. A., & Grajek, S. (1985). Day care as intervention: Comparisons of varying quality programs. *Journal of Applied Developmental Psychology, 6,* 247-260.

McCauley, M. A., & Natter, F. L. (1980). *Psychological type differences in education.* Gainesville, FL: Center for Application of Psychological Types.

McChesney, K. Y. (1992). Homeless families. Four patterns of poverty. In M. J. Robertson & M. Greenblatt (Eds.), *Homelessness: A national perspective* (pp. 245-256). New York: Plenum.

McCollum, J. A., & Maude, S. P. (1993). Portrait of a changing field: Policy and practice in early childhood special education. In B. Spodek (Ed.), *Handbook of research on the education of young children* (pp. 91-104). New York: Macmillan.

McCormick, L., & Feeney, S. (1995). Modifying and expanding activities for children with disabilities. *Young Children, 50*(4), 10-17.

McCuskey, D. (1940). *Bronson Alcott, teacher.* New York: Macmillan.

McKey, R., Condelli, L., Ganson, H., Barrett, B., McConkey, C., & Plantz, M. (1985). *The impact of Head Start on children, families, and communities* (DHHS Publication No. OHDS 85-31193). Washington, DC: Government Printing Office.

McKibben, M. D. (1988). Alternative teacher certification programs. *Educational Leadership, 46*(3), 32-35.

McLoyd, V. C. (1990). The impact of economic hardship on black families and children: Psychological distress, parenting, and socioemotional development. *Child Development, 61,* 311-346.

McMillan, M. (1919). *The nursery school.* London: J. M. Dent.

Meisels, S. J. (1985). The efficacy of early intervention: Why are we still asking these questions? *Topics in Early Childhood Special Education, 5,* 1-12.

Meisels, S. J. (1989a). *Developmental screening in early childhood: A guide* (3rd ed.). Washington, DC: National Association for the Education of Young Children.

Meisels, S. J. (1989b). Meeting the mandate of Public Law 99-457: Early childhood intervention in the nineties. *American Journal of Orthopsychiatry, 59,* 451-460.

Meisels, S. J. (1992). *The Work Sampling System: An overview.* Ann Arbor: University of Michigan.

Meisels, S. J., & Wasik, B. A. (1990). Who should be served? Identifying children in need of early intervention services. In S. J. Meisels & J. P. Shonkoff (Eds.), *Handbook of early childhood intervention* (pp. 605-632). New York: Cambridge University Press.

Meltz, B. F. (1990, December 4). A little privacy: Children need a space to call their own. *Tallahassee Democrat*, p. D1.

Mickalide, A. D. (1993). Parents' perceptions and practices concerning childhood injury: 1987 versus 1992. *Childhood Injury Prevention Quarterly, 4*(4), 29-32.

Millar, S. (1968). *The psychology of play*. Baltimore: Penguin.

Miller, L. B., & Dyer, J. L. (1975). Four preschool programs: Their dimensions and effects. *Monographs of the Society for Research in Child Development, 40*(5-6, Serial No. 162).

Mills v. Board of Education, 348 F. Supp. 866 (D. D. C. 1972).

Mintz, N. L. (1956). Effects of aesthetic surroundings. *Journal of Psychology, 41*, 459-466.

Minuchin, P. P., & Shapiro, E. K. (1983). The school as a context for social development. In E. M. Hetherington (Ed.) & P. H. Musen (Series Ed.), *Handbook of child psychology: Vol. 4. Socialization, personality, and social development* (pp. 197-274). New York: Wiley.

Minuchin, S. (1984). *Family kaleidoscope*. Cambridge, MA: Harvard University Press.

Mitchell, A. (1988). *The Public School Early Childhood Study: The district survey*. New York: Bank Street College Press.

Mitchell, A., Seligson, M., & Marx, F. (1989). *Early childhood programs and the public schools: Between promise and practice*. Dover, MA: Auburn House.

Mitchell, E., & Mason, B. S. (1948). *The theory of play* (Rev. ed.). Cranbury, NJ: A. S. Barnes.

Mobley, C. (1976). *A comparison of the effects of multiage grouping versus homogeneous age grouping in primary school classes of reading and mathematical achievement* (Practicum report submitted in partial fulfillment of the Ed.D. requirements, Nova University). (ERIC Document Reproduction Service No. Ed 128 102)

Molmar, J. M., Rath, W. R., & Klein, T. P. (1990). Constantly compromised: The impact of homelessness on children. *Journal of Social Issues, 46*(4), 109-124.

Montes, F., & Risley, T. R. (1975). Evaluating traditional day-care practice: An empirical approach. *Child Study Quarterly, 4*, 208-215.

Montessori, M. (1966). *The secret of childhood* (M. J. Costelloe, S.J., Trans.). New York: Ballantine. (Original work published 1936)

Moore, W. E. (1970). *The profession: Roles and rules*. New York: Russell Sage.

Moran, J. J. (1989). Professional standards for educators making retention decisions. *Education, 109*, 268-275.

Morgan, E. L. (1989). Talking with parents when concerns come up. *Young Children, 44*(2), 52-56.

Morgan, G. (1982). *Managing the day-care dollars: A financial handbook*. Cambridge, MA: Steam Press.

Morgan, G. (1985). Programs for young children in public schools? Only if . . . " *Young Children, 40*(4), 54.

Morgan, G. (1986). Gaps and excesses in the regulation of child care: Report of a panel. *Review of Infectious Diseases, 8*, 634–643.

Morgan, G. (1991). Regulating early childhood programs: Five policy issues. In S. L. Kagan (Ed.), *The care and education of America's young children: Obstacles and opportunities* (pp. 173-198). Chicago: University of Chicago Press.

Morgan, G. (1994). A new century/A new system for professional development. In J. Johnson & J. B. McCracken (Eds.), *The early childhood career lattice: Perspectives on professional development* (pp. 39-46). Washington, DC: National Association for the Education of Young Children.

Morgan, G., Azer, S. L., Costley, J. B., Genser, A., Goodman, I. F., Lombardi, J., & McGimsey, B. (1993). *Making a career of it: The state of states report on career development in early care and education*. Boston: Wheelock College, Center for Career Development in Early Care and Education.

Morgan, G., Curry, N., Endsley, R. C., Bradford, M. R., & Rashid, H. M. (1985). *Quality in early childhood programs: Four perspectives* (High/Scope Early Childhood Policy Papers, No. 3). Ypsilanti, MI: High/Scope Educational Research Foundation. (ERIC Document Reproduction Service No. ED 264 944)

Morris, S. (1990, August). Sand and water table buying guide. *Child Care Information Exchange, 74*, 58-60.

Mounts, N. S., & Roopnairne, J. L. (1987). Social-cognitive play patterns in same-age and mixed-age preschool classrooms. *American Educational Research Journal, 24*(3), 463-476.

Mulrooney, M. (1990). Reaccreditation: A snapshot of growth and change in high-quality early childhood programs. *Young Children, 45*(2), 58-61.

Nachbar, R. R. (1989). A K/1 class can work—Wonderfully! *Young Children, 44*(5), 67-71.

NAEYC Business. (1988). Antidiscrimination policy. *Young Children, 44*(1), 38.

NAEYC Information Service. (1989). *Facility design for early childhood programs.* Washington, DC: National Association for the Education of Young Children.

NAEYC position statement on guidelines for compensation of early childhood professionals. (1990). *Young Children, 46*(1), 30-32.

NAEYC position statement on nomenclature, salaries, benefits, and the status of the early childhood profession. (1984). *Young Children, 40*(1), 52-55.

NAEYC position statement on the liability insurance crises. (1986). *Young Children, 41*(5), 45-46.

NAEYC to launch new professional development initiative. (1991). *Young Children, 46*(6), 37-39.

Naisbitt, J., & Auberdine, P. (1990). *Megatrends 2000.* New York: William Morrison.

Nastasi, B. K., Clements, D. H., & Battista, M. T. (1990). Social-cognitive interactions, motivation, and cognitive growth in Logo programming and CAI problem-solving environments. *Journal of Educational Psychology, 82*, 150-158.

National Academy of Early Childhood Programs. (1991). *Accreditation criteria and procedures of the National Academy of Early Childhood Programs.* Washington, DC: National Association for the Education of Young Children.

National Academy of Sciences. (1990). *Who cares for America's children? Child care policy for the 1990s.* Washington, DC: Author.

National Association for Family Day Care. (1988). *Family Day Care Accreditation Profile.* Philadelphia: Author.

National Association for the Education of Young Children (NAEYC). (1982). *Early childhood teacher education guidelines for 4- and 5-year programs.* Washington, DC: Author.

National Association for the Education of Young Children (NAEYC). (1984). *Accreditation criteria and procedures for the National Academy of Early Childhood Programs.* Washington, DC: Author.

National Association for the Education of Young Children (NAEYC). (1987). NAEYC position statement on quality, compensation, and affordability in early childhood programs. *Young Children, 43*(1), 31.

National Association for the Education of Young Children (NAEYC). (1988). NAEYC position statement on standardized testing of young children 3 through 8 years of age. *Young Children, 43*(3), 42-47.

National Association for the Education of Young Children (NAEYC). (1990). NAEYC position statement on school readiness. *Young Children, 46*(1), 21-23.

National Association for the Education of Young Children (NAEYC). (1991a). *Accreditation criteria and procedures of the National Academy of Early Childhood Programs* (Rev. ed.). Washington, DC: Author.

National Association for the Education of Young Children (NAEYC). (1991b). *Early childhood teacher education guidelines.* Washington, DC: Author.

National Association for the Education of Young Children (NAEYC). (1993). Washington update. The United Nations Convention on the Rights of the Young Child. *Young Children, 48*(6), 65.

National Association for the Education of Young Children (NAEYC). (1994). NAEYC position statement: A conceptual framework for early childhood professional development. *Young Children, 49*(3), 68-77.

National Association for the Education of Young Children (NAEYC). (1995a). *Guidelines for early childhood professional development.* Washington, DC: Author.

National Association for the Education of Young Children. (1995b). *Guidelines for preparation of early childhood professionals.* Washington, DC: Author.

National Association for the Education of Young Children & the National Association of Early Childhood Specialists in State Departments of Education. (1991). Guidelines for appropriate curriculum content and assessment in programs serving children ages 3 through 8: A position statement. *Young Children, 46*(3), 21-38.

National Association of Early Childhood Specialists in State Departments of Education. (1987). *Unacceptable trends in kindergarten entry and placement: A position statement of the NAECS/SDE.* Lincoln, NE: Author.

National Association of State Boards of Education. (1988). *Right from the start: A report of the NASBE Task Force on Early Childhood Education.* Alexandria, VA: Author.

National Black Child Development Institute. (1987). *Safeguards: Guidelines for establishing programs for 4-year-olds in the public schools.* Washington, DC: Author.

National Center for Clinical Infant Programs. (1989). *The intent and spirit of PL 99-457: A source book.* Washington, DC: Author.

National Commission on Children. (1991). *Beyond rhetoric: A new American agenda for children and families* (Final report). Washington, DC: Government Printing Office.

National Commission on Excellence in Education. (1983). *A nation at risk: The imperative for educational reform.* Washington, DC: Government Printing Office.

National Commission on Excellence in Education. (1984). *Nation at risk: The full account.* Washington, DC: Author.

National Council of Teachers of English (NCTE). (1990). On testing young children. *Language Arts, 67,* 92-93.

National Education Association (NEA). (1992). A bill of rights for children. *Childhood Education, 68,* 218.

National Education Goals Panel. (1991). *Goal I: Technical Planning Subgroup report on school readiness.* Washington, DC: Author.

National Education Goals Panel. (1993). *Reconsidering children's early development and learning: Toward shared beliefs and vocabulary.* Washington, DC: Author.

National Institute of Medicine. (1988). *Homelessness, health, and human needs.* Washington, DC: National Academy Press.

National Society for the Study of Education. (1929). *Twenty-eighth yearbook of the National Society for the Study of Education: Preschool and parental education.* Bloomington, IL: Public School Publishing.

Needle, R. H. (1980). Teacher stress: Sources and consequences. *Journal of School Health, 50,* 96-99.

Neill, S. R. St. J. & Denham, E. J. M. (1982). The effects of preschool building design. *Educational Research, 24*(2), 107-111.

Nelson, M. (1990). Mothering others' children: The experiences of family day care providers. *Signs: The Journal of Women in Culture and Society, 15,* 586-605.

Neugebauer, R. (1989, February). Child care 1989: Status report on for-profit child care. *Child Care Information Exchange, 65,* 19-23.

Neugebauer, R. (1992a). Child care 2000. In B. Spodek & O. N. Saracho (Eds.), *Yearbook in early childhood education: Vol. 3. Issues in child care* (pp. 1-8). New York: Teachers College Press.

Neugebauer, R. (1992b, September/October). Employer interest in child care revives. *Child Care Information Exchange, 87,* 21-24.

Neugebauer, R. (1993a, November/December). Employer interest in child care growing and diversifying. *Child Care Information Exchange, 94,* 66-72.

Neugebauer, R. (1993b, November/December). State-of-the-art thinking on parent fee policies. *Child Care Information Exchange, 94,* 4-12.

Neugebauer, R. (1993c, January/February). Status report #1 on school-age child care. *Child Care Information Exchange, 89,* 11-15.

Neugebauer, R. (1993d, March/April). Status report on children's programs on campus. *Child Care Information Exchange, 90,* 70.

New, R. (1990). Excellent early education: A city in Italy has it. *Young Children, 45*(6), 4-10.

Newman, S., Vander Ven, K., & Ward, C. R. (1992). *Productive employment of older adults in child care.* Pittsburgh, PA: Generations Together.

Nieman, R. H., & Gastright, J. F. (1981). The long-term effects of Title I preschool and all-day kindergarten. *Phi Delta Kappan, 63,* 184-185.

Nilsen, A. P. (1977). Alternatives to sexist practices in the classroom. *Young Children, 32*(5), 53-58.

Nimnicht, G. P., & Brown, E. (1972). The toy library: Parents and teachers learning with toys. *Young Children, 28,* 110-117.

Nimnicht, G. P., McAfee, O., & Meier, J. (1969). *The new nursery school.* New York: General Learning.

Nober, L. W., & Nober, E. H. (1975). Auditory discrimination of learning-disabled children in quiet and classroom noise. *Journal of Learning Disabilities, 8,* 656-659.

Norwood, G. R. (1984, June). *The relationship of health and nutrition to the learning process.* Paper presented at the annual meeting of the Association for Childhood Education International, Vancouver, British Columbia, Canada. (ERIC Document Reproduction Service No. ED 248 955)

Nuttall, E. V., DeLeon, B., & Valle, M. (1990). Best practices in considering cultural factors. In A. Thomas & J. Grimes (Eds.), *Best practices in school psychology-II* (pp. 219-234). Washington, DC: National Association of School Psychologists.

Oakes, J., & Lipton, M. (1988). *Making the best of our schools.* San Francisco: Jossey-Bass.

Oakes, P. B., & Caruso, D. A. (1990). Kindergarten teachers' use of developmentally appropriate practices and attitudes about authority. *Early Education and Development, 1,* 445-457.

Oberti v. Board of Education of the Borough of Clementon School District, 995 F. 2d 1204 (3d Cir. 1993).

Odom, S. L., & McEvoy, M. A. (1988). Integration of young children with handicaps and normally developing children. In S. L. Odom & M. B. Karnes (Eds.), *Early intervention for infants and children with handicaps: Am empirical base* (pp. 241-267). Baltimore: Paul H. Brookes.

Oettinger, K. B. (1964). *It's your Children's Bureau* (Rev. ed.). (Children's Bureau Publication #357). Washington, DC: Children's Bureau.

Olds, A. R. (1987). Designing space for infants and toddlers. In C. S. Weinstein & T. G. Davids (Eds.), *Spaces for children: The built environment and child development* (pp. 117-138). New York: Plenum.

Olds, A. R. (1989). Psychological and physiological harmony in child care center design. *Children's Environments Quarterly, 6,* 8-16.

Olenick, M. (1986). *The relationship between day-care quality and selected social policy variables.* Unpublished doctoral dissertation, University of California, Los Angeles.

Olsen, G. (1993). The exit interview: A tool for program improvement. *Child Care Information Exchange, 92,* 71-75.

Osborne, D., & Gaebler, T. (1992). *Reinventing government: How the entrepreneurial spirit is transforming the public sector.* Reading, MA: Addison-Wesley.

Osmon, F. (1971). *Patterns for designing children's centers.* New York: Educational Facilities Laboratories.

Paget, K. D., & Bracken, B. A. (1983). *The psychoeducational assessment of preschool children.* New York: Grune & Stratton.

Pallas, A. M., Natriello, G., & McDill, E. L. (1989). The changing nature of the disadvantaged population: Current dimensions and future trends. *Educational Researcher, 18,* 16-22.

Palmer, L. A. (1916). *Play life in the first eight years.* New York: Guinn.

Parker, F. I., Piotrkowski, C. S., & Peay, L. (1987). Head Start as a social support for mothers: The psychological benefits of involvement. *American Journal of Orthopsychiatry, 57,* 220-233.

Parker, S., & Temple, A. (1925). *Unified kindergarten and first-grade teaching.* New York: Guinn.

Patton, C. (1993). What can we do to increase public knowledge about child development and quality child care? *Young Children, 49*(1), 30-31.

Payne, C. (1983). MELD (Minnesota Early Learning Design). In C. Payne (Ed.), *Programs to strengthen families* (pp. 94-95). Chicago: Yale University and the Family Resource Coalition.

Peabody, E. (1835). *Record of a school: Exemplifying the general principles of spiritual culture.* Boston: James Munroe.

Peck, C. A., Furman, G. C., & Helmstetter, E. (1993). Parent and teacher perceptions of outcomes for nonhandicapped children enrolled in integrated early childhood programs: A statewide study. *Journal of Early Intervention, 16,* 15-63.

Peck, J. T., McCaig, G., & Sapp, M. E. (1988). *Kindergarten policies: What is best for children?* Washington, DC: National Association for the Education of Young Children.

Pederson, J. (1985). The adventure playground of Denmark. In J. L. Frost & S. Sunderlin (Eds.), *When children play* (pp. 201-208). Wheaton, MD: Association for Childhood Education International.

Pence, A. R. (1986). Infant schools in North America, 1825-1840. In S. Kilmer (Ed.), *Advances in early education and day care* (Vol. 4, pp. 1-25). Greenwich, CT: JAI Press.

Pence, A. R., & Goelman, H. (1987). Silent partners: Parents of children in three types of day care. *Early Childhood Research Quarterly, 2,* 103-118.

Pennsylvania Association for Retarded Children (PARC) v. Commonwealth of Pennsylvania, 343F. Supp. 279 (E. D. Pa 1972).

Perreault, J. (1991). Society as extended family: Giving a childhood to every child. *Dimensions, 19*(4), 3-8, 31.

Perreault, J., & Neugebauer, R. (1988, January). An ounce of prevention: How to write an employee handbook. *Child Care Information Exchange, 59,* 21-24.

Perrone, V. (1990). How did we get here? In C. Kamii (Ed.), *Achievement testing in the early grades* (pp. 1-13). Washington, DC: National Association for the Education of Young Children.

Pertz, D. L., & Putman, L. R. (1982). *What is the relationship between nutrition and learning?* (ERIC Document Reproduction Service No. ED 220 797)

Peters, D. L. (1993). Trends in demographic and behavioral research on teaching in early childhood settings. In B. Spodek (Ed.), *Handbook of research on the education of young children* (pp. 493-505). New York: Macmillan.

Peters, T. J., & Waterman, R. H., Jr. (1982). *In search of excellence: Lessons from America's best-run companies.* New York: Harper & Row.

Phillips, C. B. (1994). The challenge of training and credentialing early childhood educators. *Phi Delta Kappan, 76*, 214-217.

Phillips, D. A. (Ed.). (1987). *Quality child care: What does research tell us?* Washington, DC: National Association for the Education of Young Children.

Phillips, D. A., Lande, J., & Goldberg, M. (1990). A state of child care regulation: A comparative analysis. *Early Childhood Research Quarterly, 5*, 151-179.

Phillips, D. A., McCartney, K., & Scarr, S. (1987). Child care quality and children's social development. *Developmental Psychology, 23*, 537-543.

Phillips, D. A., & Whitebook, M. (1986). Who are child care workers? *Young Children, 41*(4), 14-20.

Phillips, D. A., & Zigler, E. (1987). The checkered history of federal child care regulation. In E. Rothkopf (Ed.), *Review of research in education* (Vol. 14, pp. 3-41). Washington, DC: American Educational Research Association.

Piaget, J. (1952). *The origins of intelligence in children.* New York: Norton.

Piaget, J. (1962). *Play, dreams, and imitation in childhood.* New York: Norton.

Piaget, J. (1963). *The psychology of intelligence.* Patterson, NJ: Littlefield, Adams.

Pickering, L. K., & Woodward, W. E. (1982). Diarrhea in day-care centers. *Pediatric Infectious Diseases, 1*, 47-52.

Pines, A., & Maslach, C. (1980). Combating staff burnout in a day care center: A case study. *Child Care Quarterly, 9*, 6-9.

Pinsker, M., & Geoffrey, K. (1981). Comparison of parent effectiveness training and behavior modification parent training. *Family Relations, 30*, 61-68.

Pipes, P. L., & Glass, R. P. (1989). Nutrition and feeding of children with developmental delay and related problems. In P. L. Pipes (Ed.), *Nutrition in infancy and childhood* (4th ed., pp. 361-386). St. Louis, MO: C. V. Mosby.

Pluger, L. W., & Zola, J. M. (1969). A room planned by young children. *Young Children, 24*(6), 337-341.

Popkin, M. (1990). *The Active Parenting Discussion Program.* Marietta, GA: Active Parenting.

Powell, D. R. (1977, March). *The coordination of preschool socialization: Parent caregiver relationships in day-care settings.* Paper presented at the conference of the Society for Research in Child Development, New Orleans.

Powell, D. R. (1984). Enhancing the effectiveness of parent education: An analysis of program assumptions. In L. Katz (Ed.), *Current topics in early childhood education* (Vol. 5, pp. 121-139). Norwood, NJ: Ablex.

Powell, D. R. (1985). Stability and change in patterns of participation in a parent-child program. *Professional Psychology: Research and Practice, 16*, 172-180.

Powell, D. R. (1987). Day care as a family support system. In S. L. Kagan, D. R. Powell, B. Weissbourd, & E. Zigler (Eds.), *America's family support programs: Perspectives and prospects* (pp. 115-132). New Haven, CT: Yale University Press.

Powell, D. R. (1989). *Families and early childhood programs.* Washington, DC: National Association for the Education of Young Children.

Powell, D. R. (1990). Home visiting in the early years: Policy and program design decisions. *Young Children, 45*(6), 65-73.

Powell, D. R. (1991). Parents and programs: Early childhood as a pioneer in parent involvement and support. In S. L. Kagan (Ed.), *The care and education of America's young children: Obstacles and opportunities* (pp. 91-109). Chicago: University of Chicago Press.

Powell, D. R., & Sigal, I. E. (1991). Searches for validity in evaluating young children and early childhood programs. In B. Spodek & O. N. Saracho (Eds.), *Yearbook in early childhood education: Vol. 2. Issues in early childhood curriculum* (pp. 190-212). New York: Teachers College Press.

Pratt, C. (1948). *I learn from children.* New York: Simon & Schuster.

Pratt, D. (1983, April). *Age segregation in schools.* Paper presented at the annual meeting of the American Educational Research Association, Montreal, Canada. (ERIC Document Reproduction Service No. ED 346 082)

Preschool immunizations. (1991). *Young Children, 46*(5), 21.

Prescott, D. A. (1957). *The child in the educative progress.* New York: McGraw-Hill.

Prescott, E. (1975). *Assessment of child-rearing environments: An ecological approach.* Pasadena, CA: Pacific Oaks College Press.

Prescott, E. (1978). Is day care as good as a good home? *Young Children, 33*(2), 13-19.

Prescott, E. (1984). The physical setting of day-care. In J. T. Greenman & R. W. Fuqua (Eds.), *Making day care better* (pp. 44-65). New York: Teachers College Press.

Prescott, E. (1987). The environment as organizer of intent in child-care. In C. S. Weinstein & T. G. David (Eds.), *Spaces for children: The built environment and child development* (pp. 73-86). New York: Plenum.

Prescott, E., & David, T. G. (1977, April). *Effects of physical environments in child care systems.* Paper presented at the annual meeting of the American Educational Research Association, New York. (ERIC Document Reproductive Service No. 142 284)

Prescott, E., & Jones, E. (1972). *Day care as a child-rearing environment* (Vol. 1). Washington, DC: National Association for the Education of Young Children.

Prescott, E., Jones, E., & Kritchevsky, S. (1972). *Day care as a child-rearing environment* (Vol. 2). Washington, DC: National Association for the Education of Young Children.

Proctor, T. B., Black, K. N., & Feldhusen, J. F. (1986). Early admission of selected children to elementary school: A review of research literature. *Journal of Educational Research, 80,* 70-76.

Public policy report. NAEYC position statement on licensing and other forms of regulation of early childhood programs in centers and family day care homes. (1987). *Young Children, 42*(5), 64-68.

Radin, N. (1971). *Three degrees of parent involvement in a preschool program: Impact on mother and children.* Ann Arbor: University of Michigan, School of Social Work.

Radomski, M. A. (1986). Professionalization of early childhood educators. *Young Children, 41*(5), 20-23.

Rambusch, N. M. (1962). *Learning how to learn: An American approach to Montessori.* Baltimore: Helicon.

Ramey, C. T. (1977). An introduction to the Carolina Abecedarian Project. In B. M. Caldwell & D. J. Stedman (Eds.), *Infant education for handicapped children* (pp. 101-121). New York: Walker.

Ramey, S. L., & Ramey, C. T. (1994). The transition to school: Why the first few years matter for a lifetime. *Phi Delta Kappan, 76,* 194-198.

Ramsey, P. G. (1987). *Teaching and learning in a diverse world.* New York: Teachers College Press.

Raver, C. C., & Zigler, E. F. (1991). Three steps forward, two steps back: Head Start and the measurement of social competence. *Young Children, 46*(4), 3-8.

Raymont, T. (1937). *A history of education of young children.* New York: Longmans, Green.

Read, K. H. (1976). *The nursery school: Human relationships and learning* (6th ed.). Philadelphia: W. B. Saunders.

Read, K. H., & Patterson, J. (1980). *The nursery school and kindergarten* (7th ed.). New York: Holt, Rinehart & Winston.

Readdick, C. A., Golbeck, S. L., Klein, E. L., & Cartwright, C. A. (1984). The child-parent-teacher conference. *Young Children, 39*(5), 67-73.

Reisner, E. H. (1930). *The evolution of the common school.* New York: Macmillan.

Rekers, G. (1985). *Family building: Six qualities of a strong family.* Ventura, CA: Regal Books.

Reutzel, D. R. (1992). Breaking the letter-a-week tradition. *Childhood Education, 69,* 20-23.

Revara, F., DiGuiseppi, C., Thompson, R., & Calonge, N. (1989). Risk of injury to children less than 5 years of age in day care versus home care settings. *Pediatrics, 84*(6), 1011-1016.

Ripple, R. E., & Rockcastle, V. E. (Eds.). (1964). *Piaget rediscovered: A report of the Conference on Cognitive Studies and Curriculum Development.* Ithaca, NY: Cornell University, School of Education.

Robinson, B. E. (1981). Changing views on male early childhood teachers. *Young Children, 36*(5), 27-32.

Robinson, B. E. (1988). Vanishing breed: Men in early childhood programs. *Young Children, 43*(6), 54-58.

Robinson, J. (1988). *The baby boards: A parents' guide to preschool and primary school entrance tests.* New York: Arco.

Robinson, S. L. (1993/94). Out of the mouths of experts. *Childhood Education, 70,* 84-86.

Robinson, S. L., & Lyon, C. (1994). Early childhood offerings in 1992: Will we be ready for 2000? *Phi Delta Kappan, 75,* 775-778.

Roe, M. F. (1991, December). *Portfolios: From mandate to implementation.* Paper presented at the annual meeting of the National Reading Conference, Palm Springs, CA. (ERIC Document Reproduction Service No. ED 343 103)

Rogers, C. S., & Morris, S. S. (1986). Reducing sugar in children's diets. *Young Children, 41*(5), 11-16.

Rogers, D. L., Waller, C. B., & Perrin, M. S. (1987). Learning more about what makes a good teacher good through collaborative research in the classroom. *Young Children, 42*(4), 34-39.

Rose, D. F., & Smith, B. J. (1993). Preschool mainstreaming: Attitude barriers and strategies for addressing them. *Young Children, 48*(4), 59-62.

Rosen, J. L. (1975). *Perceptions of the childhood self and teacher-child relationships* (Final report of the National Institute of Education). New York: Bank Street College Research Station.

Rosenholtz, S. J., & Kyle, S. L. (1984). Teacher isolation: Barrier to professionalism. *American Educator, 8,* 10-15.

Ross, H. W. (1992). Integrating infants with disabilities? Can "ordinary" caregivers do it? *Young Children, 47*(3), 65–71.

Rowe, M. P., & Husby, R. D. (1973). Economics of child care: Costs, needs, and issues. In P. Roby (Ed.), *Child care: Who cares?* (pp. 98-122). New York: Basic Books.

Rubin, K. H., Maioni, T. L., & Hornung, H. (1976). Free play behaviors in middle and lower class preschoolers: Parten and Piaget revisited. *Child Development, 47*(2), 414-419.

Runyan, C., Gray, D., Kotch, J., & Kreuter, M. (1991). Analysis of U.S. child care safety regulations. *American Journal of Public Health, 81,* 981-985.

Ruopp, R., Travers, J., Glantz, F., & Coelen, C. (1979). *Children at the center: Final report of the National Day Care Study.* Cambridge, MA: Abt Associates.

Ryan, M. P. (1975). *Womanhood in America: From Colonial times to the present.* New York: New Viewpoints.

Sampson, F. K. (1970). *Contrast rendition in school lighting.* New York: Educational Facilities Laboratories.

Sanger, C. (1985). *Day care center licensing and religious exemptions: An overview for providers.* San Francisco: Child Care Law Center.

Santrock, J. W. (1976). Affect and facilitative self-control: Influence of ecological setting, cognition, and social agent. *Journal of Educational Psychology, 68,* 529-535.

Saracho, O. N. (1993). Preparing teachers for early childhood programs in the United States. In B. Spodek (Ed.), *Handbook of research on the education of young children* (pp. 412-426). New York: Macmillan.

Saracho, O. N., & Spodek, B. (1983). *Understanding the multicultural experience in childhood education.* Washington, DC: National Association for the Education of Young Children.

Sarason, S. B. (1966). *Psychology of community settings: Clinical, educational, vocational, social aspects.* New York: Wiley.

Scallan, P. (1988, December). Ask and ye shall receive: A primer for large-scale fund-raising. *Child Care Information Exchange, 64,* 19-21.

Schaefer, E. (1985). Parent and child correlates of parental modernity. In I. Sigel (Ed.), *Parental belief systems: The psychological consequences for children* (pp. 287-318). Hillsdale, NJ: Erlbaum.

Schlossman, S. L. (1976). Before Home Start: Notes toward a history of parent education in America. *Harvard Educational Review, 46*(3), 436-467.

Schrag, L., Khokha, F., & Weeks, E. (1988). Sample budget for an infant care center. In A. Godwin & L. Schrag (Eds.), *Setting up for infant care: Guidelines for centers and family day-care homes* (pp. 51-52). Washington, DC: National Association for the Education of Young Children.

Schulz, J. (1987). *Parents and professionals in special education.* Boston: Houghton Mifflin.

Schuster, C., Finn-Stevenson, M., & Ward, P. (1990). *The hard questions in family day care: National issues and exemplary programs.* New York: National Council of Jewish Women.

Schuyler, N. B., & Turner, B. O. (1986/87). *Retention or promotion: Have policies passed or failed?* (Report No. AISD-ORE-86-31). Austin, TX: Austin Independent School District, Office of Research and Evaluation. (ERIC Document Reproduction Service No. 288 904)

Schweinhart, L. (1993). Observing young children in action: The key to early childhood assessment. *Young Children, 48*(5), 29-33.

Schweinhart, L., Koshel, J. J., & Bridgmann, A. (1987). Policy options for preschool programs. *Phi Delta Kappan, 68,* 524-530.

Schweinhart, L., & Weikart, D. (1985). Evidence that good early childhood programs work. *Phi Delta Kappan, 66,* 545-555.

Schweinhart, L., Weikart, D., & Larner, M. (1986). Consequences of three preschool curriculum models through age fifteen. *Early Childhood Research Quarterly, 2*(3), 15-45.

Scott, L. C. (1983). Injury in the classroom: Are teachers liable? *Young Children, 38*(6), 10-18.

Sears, R. R. (1975). Your ancients revisited: A history on child development. In E. M. Hetherington (Ed.), *Review of child development research* (Vol. 5, pp. 1-75). Chicago: University of Chicago Press.

Seaver, J. W., & Cartwright, C. A. (1986). *Child-care administration.* Belmont, CA: Wadsworth.

Seefeldt, C. (1985). Parent involvement: Support or stress? *Childhood Education, 62,* 98-102.

Seefeldt, C., & Barbour, N. (1988). "They said I had to . . . " Working with mandates. *Young Children, 43*(4), 4-8.

Seifert, K. (1988). Men in early childhood education. In B. Spodek & O. N. Saracho (Eds.), *Professionalism and the early childhood practitioner* (pp. 105-116). New York: Teachers College Press.

Seitz, V., Apfel, N. H., & Efron, C. (1976, August). *Long-term effects of intervention: A longitudinal investigation.* Paper presented at the meeting of the American Psychological Association, Washington, DC.

Seligman, M. (1979). *Strategies for helping parents of exceptional children.* New York: Free Press.

Seligson, M. (1986). Child care for the school-age child. *Phi Delta Kappan, 67,* 637-640.

Seligson, M., & Fink, D. B. (1989). *No time to waste.* Wellesley, MA: School-Age Child Care Project.

Seligson, M., & Gannett, E. (with Cotlin, L.). (1992). Before- and after-school child care for elementary school children. In B. Spodek & O. N. Saracho (Eds.), *Yearbook in early childhood education: Vol. 3. Issues in child care* (pp. 125-142). New York: Teachers College Press.

Senn, M. J. E. (1975). Insights on the child development movement in the United States. *Monographs of the Society for Research in Child Development, 40* (3-4, Serial No. 161).

Shade, D. D. (1992). A developmental look at award-winning software. *Day Care and Early Education, 20*(1), 41-43.

Shade, D. D., & Haugland, S. W. (1993, November). *1993 developmentally appropriate software awards.* Paper presented at the annual confer-

ence of the National Association for the Education of Young Children, Anaheim, CA.

Shapiro, E., & Biber, B. (1972). The education of young children: A developmental interaction approach. *Teachers College Record, 74,* 55-79.

Shapiro, S. (1975). Preschool ecology: A study of three environmental variables. *Reading Improvement, 12,* 236-241.

Shearer, M., & Shearer, D. (1972). The Portage Project: A model for early childhood education. *Exceptional Children, 36,* 210-217.

Sheehan, A., & Abott, M. S. (1979). A descriptive study of day care characteristics. *Child Care Quarterly, 8*(3), 206-219.

Shepard, L. A. (1991). The influence of standardized tests on the early childhood curriculum, teachers, and children. In B. Spodek & O. N. Saracho (Eds.), *Yearbook in early childhood education: Vol. 2. Issues in early childhood curriculum* (pp. 166-169). New York: Teachers College Press.

Shepard, L. A. (1994). The challenges of assessing young children appropriately. *Phi Delta Kappan, 76,* 206-212.

Shepard, L. A., & Smith, M. L. (1986). Synthesis of research on school readiness and kindergarten retention. *Educational Leadership, 44,* 78-86.

Shepard, L. A., & Smith, M. L. (1987). Effects of kindergarten retention at the end of first grade. *Psychology in the Schools, 24,* 346-357.

Shepard, L. A., & Smith, M. L. (1988). Escalating academic demand in kindergarten: Counterproductive policies. *Elementary School Journal, 89,* 135-147.

Shepard, O. (1937). *Pedlar's progress: The life of Bronson Alcott.* Boston: Little, Brown.

Shirah, S., Hewitt, T. W., & McNair, R. H. (1993). Preservice training fosters retention: The case for vocational training. *Young Children, 48*(4), 27-31.

Shonkoff, J. P., & Meisels, S. J. (1990). Early childhood intervention: The evolution of a concept. In S. J. Meisels & J. P. Shonkoff (Eds.), *Handbook of early childhood intervention* (pp. 3-32). New York: Cambridge University Press.

Shulman, L. (1986). Those who understand: Knowledge growth in teaching. *Educational Researcher, 15*(2), 8-9.

Sigel, I. (Ed.). (1985). *Parental belief systems: The psychological consequences for children.* Hillsdale, NJ: Erlbaum.

Sigel, I., Secrist, A., & Forman, G. (1973). Psychoeducational intervention beginning at age two: Reflections and outcomes. In J. Stanley (Ed.), *Compensatory education for children, ages two to eight* (pp. 25-62). Baltimore: Johns Hopkins Press.

Simeonsson, R. J., & Bailey, D. B. (1990). Family dimensions in early intervention. In S. J. Meisels & J. P. Shonkoff (Eds.), *Handbook of early childhood intervention* (pp. 428-444). New York: Cambridge University Press.

Simmons, B., & Brewrer, J. (1988). When parents of kindergartners ask "Why?" *Childhood Education, 61,* 177-184.

Skeen, P., Garner, A. P., & Cartwright, S. (1984). *Woodworking for young children.* Washington, DC: National Association for the Education of Young Children.

Skinner, B. F. (1938). *The behavior of organisms: An experimental analysis.* Englewood Cliffs, NJ: Prentice Hall.

Skinner, B. F. (1953). *Science and human behavior.* New York: Macmillan.

Slaughter, D. T. (1983). Early intervention and its effects on maternal and child development. *Monographs of the Society for Research in Child Development, 48*(4, Serial No. 202).

Slavin, R. E. (1987). Developmental and motivational perspectives on cooperative learning: A reconciliation. *Child Development, 58,* 1161-1167.

Sleeter, C. E., & Grant, C. A. (1988). *Making choices for multicultural education: Five approaches to race, class, and gender.* New York: Merrill/Macmillan.

Smilansky, S. (1968). *The effects of sociodramatic play on disadvantaged preschool children.* New York: Wiley.

Smith, M. L., & Shepard, L. A. (1987). What doesn't work: Explaining policies of retention in the early grades. *Phi Delta Kappan, 69,* 129-134.

Smith, M. L., & Shepard, L. A. (1988). Kindergarten readiness and retention: A qualitative study of teachers' beliefs and practices. *American Educational Research Journal, 25,* 307-333.

Smith, M. S. (1975). Evaluation findings in Head Start planned variation. In A. Rivlin & P. M. Timpane (Eds.), *Planned variation in education* (pp. 101-112). Washington, DC: Brookings Institution.

Smith, P. K., & Connolly, K. J. (1980). *The ecology of preschool behavior.* Cambridge, UK: Cambridge University Press.

Smith, P. K., & Connolly, K. J. (1981). *The behavioral ecology of the preschool.* Cambridge, UK: Cambridge University Press.

Smith, T. B., & Newman, S. (1993). Older adults in early childhood programs: Why and how. *Young Children, 48*(3), 32-35.

Snyder, A. (1972). *Dauntless women in childhood education 1865-1931.* Wheaton, MD: Association for Childhood Education International.

Software Publishers Association. (1993). *U.S. K-12 schools spent $2.1 billion on educational technology in 1992-93; Spending expected to grow 13% in 1993/94* [News release]. Washington, DC: Author.

Solomon, G., & McDonald, F. J. (1970). Pretest and posttest reactions to self-viewing one's teaching performance on video tape. *Journal of Educational Psychology, 61,* 280-286.

Sommerville, C. J. (1982). *The rise and fall of childhood.* Beverly Hills, CA: Sage.

Sparrow, S. S., Balla, D. A., & Cicchetti, D. V. (1984). *Vineland Adaptive Behavior Scale* (A revision of the Vineland Social Maturity Scale, by Edgar A. Doll). Circle Pines, MN: American Guidance Service.

Spivack, G., & Cianci, N. (1987). High risk early behavior patterns and later delinquency. In J. Burchard & S. Burchard (Eds.), *Prevention of delinquent behaviors* (pp. 44-74). Newbury Park, CA: Sage.

Spodek, B. (1973a). Curriculum models in early childhood education. In B. Spodek (Ed.), *Early childhood education* (pp. 27-34). Englewood Cliffs, NJ: Prentice Hall.

Spodek, B. (1973b). *Early childhood education.* Englewood Cliffs, NJ: Prentice Hall.

Spodek, B. (1985). *Teaching in the early years* (3rd ed.). Englewood Cliffs, NJ: Prentice Hall.

Spodek, B. (1987). Thought processes underlying preschool teachers' classroom decisions. *Early Child Care and Development, 28,* 197-208.

Spodek, B. (1988). Implicit theories of early childhood teachers: Foundations for professional behavior. In B. Spodek, O. N. Saracho, & D. L. Peters (Eds.), *Professionalism and the early childhood practitioner* (pp. 161-172). New York: Teachers College Press.

Spodek, B. (1991a). Early childhood curriculum and cultural definitions of knowledge. In B. Spodek & O. N. Saracho (Eds.), *Yearbook in early childhood education: Vol. 2. Issues in early education* (pp. 1-20). New York: Teachers College Press.

Spodek, B. (1991b). Early childhood teacher training: Linking theory and practice. In S. L. Kagan (Ed.), *The care and education of America's young chil-*

dren: Obstacles and opportunities (pp. 110-130). Chicago: University of Chicago Press.

Spodek, B., & Brown, P. C. (1993). Curriculum alternatives in early childhood education: A historical analysis. In B. Spodek (Ed.), *Handbook of research on the education of young children* (pp. 91-104). New York: Macmillan.

Spodek, B., Davis, M. D., & Saracho, O. N. (1983). Early childhood teacher education and certification. *Journal of Teacher Education, 34*(5), 50–52.

Spodek, B., & Saracho, O. N. (1982). The preparation and credentialing of early childhood personnel. In B. Spodek (Ed.), *Handbook of research in early childhood education* (pp. 399-425). New York: Free Press.

Spodek, B., & Saracho, O. N. (1992). Child care: A look to the future. In B. Spodek & O. N. Saracho (Ed.), *Yearbook in early childhood education: Vol. 3. Issues in child care* (pp. 187-197). New York: Teachers College Press.

Staff self-evaluation form. (1992). *Child Care Information Exchange, 87*, 19-20.

Stamp, L. N., & Groves, M. M. (1994). Strengthening the ethic of care: Planning and supporting family involvement. *Dimensions of Early Childhood, 22*(2), 5-9.

Starks, E. B. (1960). *Blockbuilding*. Washington, DC: National Education Association, Department of Kindergarten-Primary Education.

Status report on childhood in America. (1992). *Child Care Information Exchange, 88*, 7-9.

Stayton, V. D., & Miller, P. S. (1993). Combining general and special early childhood education standards in personnel preparation programs: Experiences from two states. *Topics in Early Childhood Special Education, 13*(3), 372-387.

Steedman, C. (1990). *Childhood, culture, and class in Britain: Margaret McMillan, 1860-1931*. London: Virago Press.

Stein, C. (1975). School lighting re-evaluated. *American School and University, 48*, 70-78.

Stephen, M. (1973). *Policy issues in early childhood education*. Menlo Park, CA: Stanford Research Institute.

Stephens, K. (1991). *Confronting your bottom line: Financial guide for child care centers*. Redmond, WA: Exchange Press.

Stewart, I. S. (1982). The real world of teaching two-year-old children. *Young Children, 37*(5), 3-13.

Stiggins, R. (1991). *Facing the challenge of the new era of assessment*. Portland, OR: Northwest Evaluation Association.

Stipek, D., Rosenblatt, L., & DiRocco, L. (1994). Making parents your allies. *Young Children, 49*(3), 4-9.

Strain, P., Hoyson, M., & Jamieson, B. (1985). Normally developing preschoolers as intervention agents for autistic-like children: Effects on class deportment and social interaction. *Journal of the Division for Early Childhood, 9*, 105-115.

Strickland, C. E. (1969). Transcendentalist father: The child-rearing practices of Bronson Alcott. *Perspectives in American History, 3*, 5-73.

Strickland, C. E. (1982). Paths not taken: Seminal models of early childhood education in Jacksonian America. In B. Spodek (Ed.), *Handbook of research in early childhood education* (pp. 321-340). New York: Free Press.

Strother, D. B. (1987). Preschool children in public schools: Good investment? Or bad? *Phi Delta Kappan, 69*, 304-308.

Sturmey, P., & Crisp, A. G. (1986). Portage guide to early education: A review of research. *Education Psychology, 6*, 139-157.

Surr, J. (1992). Early childhood programs and the Americans With Disabilities Act (ADA). *Young Children, 47*(2), 18-21.

Swadener, B. B., & Kessler, S. (1991a). Introduction to the special issue. *Early Education and Development, 2*(2), 85-94.

Swadener, B. B., & Kessler, S. (Eds.). (1991). Reconceptualizing early childhood education. [Special issue]. *Early Education and Development, 2*(2).

Swick, K. (1987). Teacher reports on parental efficacy/involvement relationships. *Instructional Psychology, 14*, 125-132.

Taaffe, K. (1994, Spring). Our babies, our future. *Carnegie Quarterly*, pp. 1-15.

Takanishi, R. (1977). *Public policy for children and families: Who shall decide?* (Report No. 3). Rockville, MD: U.S. Department of Health, Education & Welfare, National Institute of Mental Health. (ERIC Document Reproduction Service No. ED 148 494)

Takanishi, R. (1981). Early childhood education and research: The changing relationship. *Theory Into Practice, 20*, 86-93.

Talbot, J., & Frost, J. L. (1989). Magical playscapes. *Childhood Education, 66*, 11-19.

Teal, W., Hiebart, E., & Chittenden, E. (1987). Assessing young children's literacy development. *Reading Teacher, 40,* 772-776.

Thompson, D. S. (1984). *The professionalism of early childhood educators and administrators: Problems and prospects* [Opinion paper]. (ERIC Document Reproduction Service No. ED 256 468)

Thompson, F. C., & Rittenhouse, A. M. (1974). Measuring the impact. *Parks and Recreation, 9,* 24-26, 62-63.

Thompson, P. W. (1992). Notations, conventions, and constraints: Contributions to effective use of concrete materials in elementary mathematics. *Journal of Research in Mathematics Education, 23,* 123-147.

Thorndike, E. L. (1906). *The principles of teaching.* New York: A. G. Seiler.

Tinsworth, D. K., & Kramer, J. T. (1989). *Playground equipment-related injuries involving falls to the surface.* Washington, DC: U.S. Product Safety Commission.

Title V. Section 522a, U.S. Code 1976 Edition: Containing the general and permanent laws of the U.S., in force on January 3, 1977 (Vol. 1). (1977). Washington, DC: Government Printing Office.

Todd, C. M., Albrecht, K. M., & Coleman, M. (1990). School-age child care: A continuum of options. *Journal of Home Economics, 82*(1), 46-52.

Townley, K., Thornburg, K., & Crompton, D. (1991). Burnout in teachers of young children. *Early Education and Development, 2,* 198-204.

Travers, J., Nauta, M. J., & Irwin, N. (1982). *The effects of a social program: Final report of the Child and Family Resource Program's infant-toddler component* (HHS-105-79-1301). Cambridge, MA: Abt Associates.

Trawick-Smith, J., & Lambert, L. (1995). The unique challenges of the family child care provider: Implications for professional development. *Young Children, 50*(3), 25-32.

Troen, S. K. (1975). *The public and the schools: Shaping the St. Louis system 1838-1920.* Columbia: University of Missouri Press.

Tubbs, E. V. (1946). More men in our schools. *Schools and Society, 63,* 394.

Turnbull, A., & Turnbull, H. (1986). *Families, professionals, and exceptionality: A special partnership.* New York: Merrill/Macmillan.

U.S. Bureau of the Census. (1987). Who's minding the kids? *Current Population Reports* (Series P-70, No. 9). Washington, DC: U.S. Department of Commerce.

U.S. Bureau of the Census. (1989). *Statistical abstract of the United States: 1989* (190th ed.). Washington, DC: Author.

U.S. Department of Health and Human Services. (1985). *Federal model child care standards: 1985.* Washington, DC: Author.

U.S. Department of Health, Education & Welfare. (1972). *Guides for day care licensing.* Washington, DC: Author.

U.S. Department of Labor, Bureau of Labor Statistics. (1988, January). *BLS reports on employer child-care practices* (News release USDL 88-7, 7). Washington, DC: Government Printing Office.

U.S. General Accounting Office (GAO). (1990). *Early childhood education: What are the costs of high-quality programs?* (GAO/HRD-90-43BR). Washington, DC: Author.

U.S. General Accounting Office (GAO). (1993). *Poor preschool-aged children* (GAO/HRD93-111BR). Washington, DC: Author.

Uphoff, J. K., & Gilmore, J. (1986). Pupil age at school entrance: How many are ready for success? *Young Children, 41*(2), 11-16.

Vandell, D. J., Henderson, V. K., & Wilson, K. S. (1989). A follow-up study of children in excellent, moderate, and poor-quality day care. *Child Development, 59,* 1286-1292.

Vander Ven, K. (1986). "And you have a way to go": The current status and emerging issues in training and education for child care practice. In K. Vander Ven & E. Tittnich (Eds.), *Competent caregivers—Competent children: Training and education for child care practice.* New York: Haworth Press.

Vandewalker, N. C. (1925). Facts of interest about kindergarten laws. *Childhood Education, 1,* 323-325.

Van Dyk, J. (1994, February). *Learning style models: Do we really need them?* Paper presented at the annual meeting of the Association of Teacher Educators, Atlanta, GA.

Vartuli, S., & Fyfe, B. (1993). Teachers need developmentally appropriate practices too. *Young Children, 48*(4), 36-42.

Vartuli, S., & Rogers, P. (1985). Parent-child learning centers. *Dimensions, 14*(1), 8-10.

Vaughn, E. (1990). Everything under the sun: Outside learning center activities. *Dimensions, 18*(4), 20-22.

Vergeront, J. (1987). *Places and spaces for preschool and primary: Indoors.* Washington, DC: National Association for the Education of Young Children.

Vergeront, J. (1988). *Places and spaces for preschool and primary: Outdoors.* Washington, DC: National Association for the Education of Young Children.

Verstegen, D. A. (1994). The new wave of school finance litigation. *Phi Delta Kappan, 76,* 243-250.

Vollmer, H. W., & Mills, D. L. (1966). *Professionalization.* Englewood Cliffs, NJ: Prentice Hall.

Voyanoff, P. (1987). *Work and family life.* Newbury Park, CA: Sage.

Vygotsky, L. S. (1978). *Mind in society* (M. Cole, S. Schribner, V. John-Steiner, & E. Souberman, Trans.). Cambridge, MA: Harvard University Press.

Wachs, T. D. (1979). Proximal experience and early cognitive-intellectual development: The physical environment. *Merrill-Palmer Quarterly, 25,* 3-41.

Wagenblast v. Odessa School Dist., 758 P. 2d 968 (Wash. 1988).

Wallach, F., & Afthinos, I. D. (1990). *An analysis of the state codes for licensed day care centers focused on playgrounds and supervision.* New York: Total Recreation Management Services.

Wallach, F., & Edelstein, S. (1991). *Analysis of state regulations for elementary schools focused on playgrounds and supervision.* New York: Total Recreation Management Services.

Walsh, D. J. (1991). Extending the discourse on developmental appropriateness: A developmental perspective. *Early Education and Development, 2,* 109-119.

Walter, K. D., & Goldsmith, E. B. (1990). Child care: Corporate responses to employees' needs. *Journal of Home Economics, 82*(1), 21-24, 61.

Wardle, F. (1990, August). Bunny ears and cupcakes for all: Are parties developmentally appropriate? *Child Care Information Exchange, 74,* 39-42.

Warger, C. (1988). *A resource guide to public school early childhood programs.* Alexandria, VA: Association for Supervision and Curriculum Development.

Wasserman, R., Dameron, D., Brozicevic, M., & Aronson, R. (1989). Injury hazards in home day care. *Journal of Pediatrics, 114,* 591-593.

Waxman, P. L. (1991). Children in the world of adults: On-site child care. *Young Children, 46*(5), 16-21.

Webb, T. B. (1992). Multi-age grouping in the early years: Building upon children's developmental strengths. *Kappa Delta Pi Record, 28,* 90-92.

Weber, E. (1969). *The kindergarten: Its encounter with educational thought in America.* New York: Teachers College Press.

Weber, E. (1970). *Early childhood education: Perspectives on change.* Worthington, OH: Charles A. Jones.

Weikart, D. P. (1972). Relationship of curriculum teaching and learning in preschool education. In J. C. Stanley (Ed.), *Preschool programs for the disadvantaged: Five experimental approaches to early childhood education* (pp. 22-66). Baltimore: Johns Hopkins Press.

Weikart, D. P. (1989). Hard choices in early childhood care and education: A view to the future. *Young Children, 44*(3), 25-30.

Weinstein, C. S., & Weinstein, N. D. (1979). Noise and reading performance in an open space school. *Journal of Educational Research, 72,* 210-213.

Weiss, H. (1983). Introduction. In C. Payne (Ed.), *Programs to strengthen families* (pp. 2-6). Chicago: Yale University and the Family Resource Coalition.

Weissbourd, B. (1983). The family support movement: Greater than the sum of its parts. *Zero to Three, 4,* 8-10.

West, J., Hausken, E., Chandler, K. A., & Collins, M. (1991). Experiences in child care and early childhood programs of first and second graders prior to entering first grade: Findings from the 1991 National Household Study. In *Statistics in brief.* Washington, DC: National Center for Education Statistics.

Westinghouse Learning Corporation. (1969). *The impact of Head Start: An evaluation of the effects of Head Start on children's cognitive and affective development.* Athens: Ohio University, Westinghouse Learning Corporation. (ERIC Document Reproduction Service No. ED 036 321)

White, B. (1988). *Educating infants and toddlers.* Lexington, MA: Lexington Books.

White, S., & Buka, S. (1987). Early education: Programs, traditions, and policies. In *Review of research in education* (Vol. 14, pp. 43-91). Washington, DC: American Educational Research Association.

Whitebook, M. (1981). Profiles in day care: An interview with Millie Almy. *Day Care and Early Education, 8,* 29-30.

Whitebook, M. (1986). The teacher shortage. *Young Children, 41*(3), 10-11.

Whitebook, M., & Granger, R. C. (1989). Assessing teacher turnover. *Young Children, 44*(4), 11-14.

Whitebook, M., Howes, C., Darrah, R., & Friedman, J. (1982). Caring for the caregivers: Staff burnout in child care. In L. G. Katz (Ed.), *Current topics in early childhood education* (Vol. 4, pp. 211-235). Norwood, NJ: Ablex.

Whitebook, M., Howes, C., & Phillips, D. A. (1990). *Who cares: Child care teachers and the quality of care in America* (Final Report of the National Child Care Staffing Study). Oakland, CA: Child Care Employee Project.

Whitebook, M., Howes, C., & Phillips, D., & Pemberton, C. (1991). Who cares? Child care teachers and the quality of child care in America. In K. M. Paciorek & J. H. Munro (Eds.), *Annual editions, Early childhood education 91/92* (pp. 20-24). Guilford, CT: Dushkin.

Whitebook, M., Phillips, D., & Howes, C. (1993). *The National Child Care Staffing Study revisited.* Oakland, CA: Child Care Employee Project.

Whitehurst, W., Witty, E., & Wiggin, S. (1988). Racial equality: Teaching excellence. In J. Sikula (Ed.), *Action in teacher education: 10th anniversary issue* (pp. 159-167). Reston, VA: Association of Teacher Education.

Wiggins, G. (1989). Teaching to the authentic test. *Educational Leadership, 46*(7), 41-47.

Willer, B. (1987). Quality or affordability: Trade-offs for early childhood programs? *Young Children, 42*(6), 41-43.

Willer, B. (1990). Estimating the full cost of quality. In B. Willer (Ed.), *Reaching the full cost of quality in early childhood programs* (pp. 1-8). Washington, DC: National Association for the Education of Young Children.

Willer, B. (1992). An overview of the demand and supply of child care in 1990. *Young Children, 47*(2), 19-22.

Willer, B., & Bredekamp, S. (1990). Public policy report. Redefining readiness: An essential requisite for educational reform. *Young Children, 45*(5), 22-24.

Willer, B., & Bredekamp, S. (1993). A "new" paradigm of early childhood professional development. *Young Children, 48*(4), 63-66.

Willer, B., Hofferth, S., Kisker, E., Divine-Hawkins, P., Farquhar, E., & Glantz, F. (1991). *The demand and supply of child care in 1990.* Washington, DC: National Association for the Education of Young Children.

Wills, C., & Lindberg, L. (1967). *Kindergarten for today's children.* Chicago: Follett.

Winer, L. R., & Trudel, H. (1991). Children in an educational robotics environment: Experiencing discovery. *Journal of Computing in Childhood Education, 2*(4), 41-64.

Wingfield, L. G. A. (1979). How to get involved. *Childhood Education, 55,* 205-207.

Winnick, M. (1976). *Malnutrition and brain development.* London: Oxford University.

Wipple, G. M. (Ed.). (1929). Preschool and parental education. In National Society for the Study of Education, *Twenty-eighth Yearbook: Part I. Organization and development* (pp. 1-463). Bloomington, IL: Public School Publishing.

Wolery, M., Strain, P. S., & Bailey, D. B., Jr. (1992). Reaching potentials of children with special needs. In S. Bredekamp & T. Rosegrant (Eds.), *Reaching potentials: Appropriate curriculum and assessment for young children* (Vol. 1, pp. 92-111). Washington, DC: National Association for the Education of Young Children.

Wolf, D., Bixby, J., Glenn, J., III., & Gardner, H. (1991). To use their minds well: Investigating new forms of student assessment. In G. Grant (Ed.), *Review of research in education* (Vol. 17, pp. 31-74). Washington, DC: American Educational Research Association.

Woodcock, L. P. (1941). *Life and ways of the two-year-old.* New York: E. P. Dutton.

Woody, T. (1934). Historical sketch of activism: Part II. In G. M. Whipple (Ed.), *The thirty-third yearbook of the National Society for the Study of Education* (pp. 9-44). Bloomington, IL: Public School Publishing.

Woody, T. (1966). *A history of women's education in the United States* (Vol. 1). New York: Octagon.

Wortham, S., & Wortham, M. R. (1992). Nurturing infant and toddler play outside: Three cells of possibility. *Dimensions of Early Childhood, 20*(4), 25-27.

Wright, H. A. (1960). Observational child study. In P. H. Mussen (Ed.), *Handbook of research methods in child development* (pp. 71-139). New York: Wiley.

Wurtman, R. J. (1982). The effects of light on the human body. *Scientific American, 1,* 68-77.

Wyman, A. (1995). The earliest early childhood teachers of America's dame schools. *Young Children, 50*(2), 29-32.

Yawkey, T. D. (1987). Project P.I.A.G.E.T.: A holistic approach to early childhood education. In J.

Roopnairne & J. Johnson (Eds.), *Approaches to early childhood education* (pp. 197-212). New York: Merrill/Macmillan.

Zeichner, K. M. (1983). Alternative paradigms of teacher education. *Journal of Teacher Education, 43*(3), 3-9.

Zeichner, K. M., & Tabachnick, B. (1982). The belief system of university supervisors in an elementary student teaching program. *Journal of Education for Teaching, 8*(1), 34-54.

Zigler, E. (1970). The environmental mystique: Training of the intellect versus development of the child. *Childhood Education, 46,* 402-412.

Zigler, E. (1988). *Schools of the twenty-first century.* New York: Yale University Bush Center.

Zigler, E. F., & Berman, W. (1983). Discerning the future of early childhood intervention. *American Psychologists, 38,* 894-906.

Zigler, E. F., & Lang, M. F. (1991). *Child care choices: Balancing the needs of children, families, and society.* New York: Free Press.

Zimiles, H. (1986). The social context of early childhood in an era of expanding preschool education. In B. Spodek (Ed.), *Today's kindergarten: Exploring the knowledge base, expanding the curriculum* (pp. 1-14). New York: Teachers College Press.

Index

About the Authors

Celia A. Decker has been actively involved in early childhood education for over 30 years. She is currently serving a dual appointment in the Departments of Education and Family and Consumer Sciences at Northwestern State University as professor of early childhood education. She is the program coordinator of graduate studies in early childhood education and teaches courses in early childhood education, child development, and dynamics of family relations.

In addition to co-authoring this text, she has published a secondary school/junior college text, *Children, The Early Years*, along with the teaching supplements. She has presented papers at national, regional, and state annual meetings of professional association such as the National Association for the Education of Young Children, Southern Early Childhood Association, and the Association for Childhood Education International. She does extensive consultant work for Head Start, Even Start, and local school systems.

During her years of teaching as a kindergarten teacher in an inner-city school system and as a college professor, she has received many honors. Dr. Decker has been named to the Who's Who in Child Development Professionals, Who's Who in Personalities of the South, Who's Who in American Women, and the World's Who's Who in Education. In 1994 she was selected as the Outstanding Professor at Northwestern State University. She and her husband are the parents of twin sons in college and a daughter who will enroll in college as a freshman in the fall semester of 1996.

After graduating from Hutchinson Junior College in Hutchinson, Kansas, John Decker graduated from Missouri Valley College in Marshall, Missouri, with a BS in Human Relations. Following two years of military service, he served as a District Scout Executive. He obtained a teaching certificate from the University of Kansas and taught in two inner-city elementary schools in a large midwestern city. While completing the requirements for his masters and doctoral degrees in Educational Administration, he continued his teaching career at the elementary and college levels respectively.

Since living in Louisiana, he has taught college classes as an assistant professor of education and has taught elementary school and high school classes in the public schools. He continues to take graduate courses and teaches college courses in the summer sessions as an adjunct professor as needed. He belongs to several organizations in which he gives workshops and speeches. Recently, Dr. Decker was recognized for his twenty-five-year membership in Phi Delta Kappa.